C000281880

THROUGH EYES OF BLUE

THROUGH EYES OF BLUE

Personal Memories of the RAF from 1918

Edited by Wing Commander
A.E. Ross DFC

Airlife

First published in the UK in 2002
by Airlife Publishing Ltd

British Library Cataloguing-in-Publication Data
A catalogue record for this book
is available from the British Library

ISBN 1 84037 345 8

Printed in England by Bath Press Ltd., Bath.

For a complete list of all Airlife titles please contact:

Airlife Publishing Ltd
101 Longden Road, Shrewsbury, SY3 9EB, England
E-mail: sales@airlifebooks.com
Website: www.airlifebooks.com

Foreword

Marshal of the Royal Air Force – Sir Michael Beetham GCB CBE DFC AFC

This book is a fitting sequel to the earlier *75 Eventful Years* produced in aid of the Cheshire Foundation.

It brings up-to-date the history of the Royal Air Force from its formation in 1918 and into the new Millennium. The wide spectrum of personal stories gives a real feel of what life was like at the time whilst giving a broad perspective of the comprehensive scale of Royal Air Force operations in various parts of the world during an eventful period of our nation's history.

It is certainly a most appropriate tribute to Leonard Cheshire, a quite remarkable man who did so much to enhance the reputation of the Royal Air Force and who subsequently gave such dedicated service to the disadvantaged in our society.

ACKNOWLEDGEMENTS

I would like to express my gratitude to all my contributors for their generous and wholehearted support; to Squadron and other associations who helped with research and to Air Historical Branch, RAF Museum Hendon and Imperial War Museum who supplied many of the photographs.

Last, and by no means least, my heartfelt thanks to my wife, Joan, who bore the considerable burden placed on her by my preoccupation during more than ten years of time-consuming research, and to my son, Christopher, without whose computing skills in management of a very large data base and help with the proof reading and layout, this book would never have been completed.

Contents

Introduction

Air Chief Marshal Sir Peter Squire GCB DFC AFC

The credentials of the authors whose articles appear in this book are impeccable and their range of experience makes them uniquely qualified to describe the many historic events and spirit of the Royal Air Force from its birth, through two World Wars, to more recent conflicts in the Gulf and the Balkans. Despite great changes to the structure and organisation of the Service there has been one consistent binding thread – the outstanding quality of our Servicemen and women. Their loyalty, professionalism and courage has sustained the Royal Air Force through the turbulent periods, and it is they who make the Service the first-rate organisation it is today. This book is a fitting tribute to the men and women of the Royal Air Force and in particular, to one of our finest airmen, Leonard Cheshire.

Leonard Cheshire was without doubt one of the most remarkable officers ever to serve in the Royal Air Force. His achievements outside the Service were, however, arguably more extraordinary than his achievements in it – which, given the magnitude of his military contribution, is truly astonishing. After his 100th operational sortie in July 1944 his Air Officer Commanding took him off operations and recommended him for the Victoria Cross; the award of which was cited in the London Gazette on 5 September 1944. In four years of fighting against the bitterest opposition, Leonard Cheshire maintained a record of outstanding personal achievement, placing himself invariably in the forefront of the battle. On numerous operational sorties he displayed careful planning, brilliant execution and contempt for danger which established a reputation second to none in Bomber Command. He left the Royal Air Force in 1946 and went on to establish the first Cheshire Home for the incurably sick in 1948. The phenomenal world-wide success of the Cheshire Foundation is a tribute to Cheshire's remarkable gifts of determination, intelligence and leadership.

Air power, as *Through Eyes of Blue: Personal Memories of the RAF from 1918* demonstrates, can be used in peacekeeping and in crisis; it can be used defensively and offensively; it can be employed directly in the security of the home base or concentrated speedily in distant parts of the world. The 1991 Gulf conflict was a classic example of the employment of air power in a wide variety of roles. Air power also played a significant part in Operation Deliberate Force over Bosnia in 1995 and in 1999 air power was the dominant military factor in Operation Allied Force in the skies above Kosovo. In the years to come, both in support of NATO and in the wider security interest, the Royal Air Force will provide balanced and cost-effective forces capable of rapid reaction and deployment as required by Her Majesty's Government.

Therefore, as we progress into the new millennium, whilst recalling with pride our past achievements – as the many varied experiences recounted in this book reveal – we look forward to a future in which air power will have an ever more prominent part to play in world security. I am confident that this challenge will be met by all members of the Royal Air Force, who continually display the same high standards of skill and bravery so successfully demonstrated over the last eight decades.

1918–1939
The Birth of British Air Power

In 1882 a small military balloon factory was established at Chatham. In 1890 this became a unit of the Royal Engineers and later moved to Farnborough. Changing titles over the years reflected its growing importance. 'The Balloon Factory', 'His Majesty's Balloon Factory', 'The Army Aircraft Factory', 'The Royal Aircraft Factory' and finally 'The Royal Aircraft Establishment'.

In 1911 the Air Battalion of the Royal Engineers was created to gather together the total air power of the British Army. This consisted of the Balloon Factory, a handful of men and perhaps a dozen aircraft. The Navy had already established direct contact with a few aircraft manufacturers.

Germany and France meantime had developed much more substantial air forces. To counter this imbalance the Government appointed a Committee which recommended the creation of a British aeronautical service to be designated 'The Flying Corps'. This was to have a Naval Wing, a Military Wing and a Central Flying School. The Royal Flying Corps was constituted on 13 April 1912.

In practice the Military wing became the Royal Flying Corps and the Naval wing became the Royal Naval Air Service. Each established its own Central Flying School and went its own way.

At the outbreak of the first World War in August 1914, the Royal Flying Corps went to France with 63 assorted aircraft, 105 officers and 755 other ranks.

The Royal Flying Corps grew rapidly and performed a wide range of services for the Army. These included long and short range reconnaissance, photographic reconnaissance, aerial mapping, artillery co-operation, strategic bombing and close tactical support. These operations were on a very elementary scale. They did, however, illustrate the potential of air power.

In May 1917 the German Air Force began a series of air attacks on British cities using Gotha and other large bombers. The climax was a daylight raid on London on 7 July 1917 when twenty-one Gothas dropped about three tons of bombs on London killing some fifty-seven people. Four days later the War Cabinet instructed the Prime Minister and General Smuts of South Africa to examine 'the air organisation generally and the direction of aerial operations'.

General Smuts worked fast. One month later on 17 August he presented his report. It recommended that an Air Ministry should be formed as soon as possible and plans worked out for the creation of a third fighting service into which the Royal Flying Corps and the Royal Naval Air Service would be absorbed. At a time when the best front line fighters could achieve a top speed of around 120 miles per hour, the General made a remarkable prophecy:

'*...and the day may not be far off when aerial operations with their devastation of enemy lands and destruction of industrial and populous centres on a vast scale may become the principal operations of war to which the older forms of military and naval operations may become secondary and subordinate.*'

By 1918 British production had reached 2000 aircraft per month and the Royal Air Force, which was established on 1 April 1918, was the most powerful in the world.

RAF F.E.26 armed with twin Lewis guns (AHB)

Flying Training in the Royal Flying Corps

Lieutenant James Cross RFC

I reached the age of eighteen in August 1916 and volunteered to join the Army. Four months later I was posted to the Cheshire Regiment and was rapidly made an acting, unpaid Lance Corporal. A little later I read in 'Orders' that candidates were required for flying duties and applied. After an interview I was posted to the Cadet School at Denham.

We arrived at Denham in time for tea and – one of the outstanding memories of my life – we sat down at small tables for four, each covered by a white cloth and tea was poured by young ladies from tea-pots into china cups – what bliss after drinking from basins for months, seated at bare tables.

At No. 5 School of Aeronautics, we began to learn the business of flying. One of the main duties of the Royal Flying Corps was to fly over the battlefield and pass messages back to the Artillery telling them where their shells were landing. To train us for this an elaborate set up was provided. Up in the roof of the lecture hut was a nacelle fitted with a Morse key and down at table level was a representation in colour of a French landscape containing the target to be shelled. As each shell exploded, there was a flash and a puff of smoke appeared where it was presumed to have landed. It was the duty of the occupant of the nacelle to signal its position on the grid. The instructor directing the exercise did so with the aid of an instrument with a clock face and the hand pointed at the direction in which the next flash would appear. I found that I had a view of the clock face with its pointer so all I had to do was to concentrate on the distance to the target. I was getting so accurate that the instructor rumbled me and called up 'Come down Cross – you'll do' and that was the end of art. obs. for me.

I was gazetted on 8 November 1917 and posted to 4 TS at Northolt. Now life began in earnest. I was instructed on the MF Shorthorn and went solo after two and a quarter hours, which in those days was quite normal. I still remember my first solo quite vividly. My instructor was a tall well-built fellow weighing probably twelve or thirteen stone and when he got down the balance of the machine was disturbed. When I got into the air I had difficulty in keeping an even keel. In fact my circuits were a series of switchbacks and my landing was hardly straight out of the book. I had quite a bounce which didn't do the undercarriage any good and this resulted in further landing practice. My training transfer card states that in all I had four hours solo and five and three-quarters dual.

It was in London that I saw my first US troops. When we landed, the nearest US mechanic called out to his mates to 'come and see the flying bird cage'. At this point I might mention that it was common belief that before the last wire was fixed between the wings a small bird was slipped in. If it flew out after the wire was in place there was something wrong!

I was posted on 2 January 1918 to 7 TDS at Northolt. Here we flew Avro 504s which were a delight and undoubtedly one of the finest flying training machines ever designed. I was told that if one got into difficulties with 2000 feet to spare, one should shut off the engine, let go the joy stick, take one's feet off the rudder bar and the machine would do the rest. I proved this for myself later, but allowed a little extra height just in case. The next step was the Sopwith Pup.

The Avros were fitted with 100 hp Monosoupape engines which were very reliable, quite different from the 50 hp Gnome engine fitted in most of the Pups. In spite of the vagaries of the Gnome engine, once in the air the Pup was a delight to fly, so delicate and responsive and aerobatic. The only difficulty was getting it into the air! Unless one got full revs and tail up immediately with rudder, there was a tendency to swing to the left which could have dire consequences for the undercarriage. Luckily it never happened to me.

However I did get into a stall too near the ground and wiped off a complete machine. I was doing a spot of diving practice close to the village when, zooming up from the dive, the engine failed and I stalled immediately over a small wood just by the repair shops. I knew a crash was inevitable because of my lack of height over the trees, so I put my arm across the gun mounting to protect my face and, at the last moment, pulled back on the stick. Luckily there was some response, for I struck the ground at a slight angle and then stood on my nose. I went through the drill of shutting off the petrol and switching off before climbing down feeling little the worse for wear, except for rather a sore nose. My troubles were not over. I hung about the Flight all day waiting for my instructor to send me up again and then, just before dusk, I went to him and asked if I was going to fly again. He said he had been waiting all day for me to ask, and instead of putting me into a safe old Avro, he sat me in a Pup fitted with a Clerget engine – something I had not seen before and with quite different engine controls. He showed me how the controls operated and I had a go with some apparent success. I taxied to a nearby take-off point and then my problems began. Almost immediately after opening up, I swung left and was almost into the hangars before I found my revs and was able to turn right into the wind. There was I trying to get flying speed with left wing up and right wing down, the one just missing the guy ropes and the other just missing the ground. I finally got off the ground and saw that I had only just about cleared the roof of the building under construction. I made a couple of circuits then landed, again thanking my lucky stars.

I graduated on 16 March 1918 and shortly afterwards, the first training Camel arrived at Feltwell. I enjoyed flying the Camel, but I could never handle it as well as I managed the Pup. For instance, I never mastered the art of looping. More often than not I would fall out at the top – out of the loop I mean, not the Camel.

My transfer training card says that I had forty minutes training on fighting in the air which was the only air fighting I experienced. My adversary was my instructor in a Pup, with me in a Camel. I was shot down at least ten times whilst I managed to get him in my sights once. I then went on to the School of Fighting at Ayr. After sitting about for several days because of machine shortage, I managed to get into the air late one afternoon for about half-an-hour in an aircraft that had known much better days. The course was to have lasted two weeks but the following day I was posted to the School of Aerial Gunnery at Turnberry – another fortnight's course. I was there for about 48 hours during which I had one short spell with a Lewis Gun on the ground. I sailed for France on the following day, 11 May. Having arrived in Boulogne I went to the Pilots' Pool at Etaples. Here I spent three or four days during which I had firing practice on the range shooting at a fixed target from a moving mounting, travelling at some speed on a circular track.

I was posted to No. 209 Sqn at Bertangles where I made the acquaintance of the Bentley Camel which was a real eye-opener. Its 150 hp engine did not have to be 'blipped', but could be run steadily on the controls. I spent the next day or two getting used to the feel of the machine, learning to recognise local landmarks, and doing a little target practice.

Before my first operational patrol, on coming in to land from a practice flight, I found that I was seeing double and put it down to a spot of tummy trouble. I asked to see the MO to get a dose of something to put things right. To my amazement after he had given me what I thought was a routine look over, in a couple of shakes he had me in the nearest Casualty Clearing Station. By the next day things were working again. I pleaded with him each day to take me back or I would be struck off the strength of 209, but he would not give clearance.

I have often wondered what caused this problem. During my practice flight the day before I thought I would have a trip towards the front lines to see what was going on. As I was on my own I went up to about 19,000 feet for safety. We had, of course, no oxygen. Arriving back near base I lost height very rapidly and found I was seeing double just as I was about to land. At that time no one had given any thought to the effects of high-altitude flying.

I was eventually sent to the American Base Hospital where I had an exhaustive examination and was informed that there was nothing wrong that a few months rest and good food would not put right. The next two months were spent in Hospital in England (where, incidentally, I had a bad attack of the influenza that played havoc that summer). After a couple of weeks leave, I was posted to Eastchurch to instruct on Avros.

There was one other type of aircraft that I flew occasionally on special missions or, very rarely, just for fun, the Sopwith 1½ Strutter, the only plane I flew fitted with a tailplane angle adjustment. It was a pleasant machine to fly, but according to my instructions not to be used for stunt flying.

If I were asked which, of all the planes I flew, gave me the greatest pleasure in the air, I would say without hesitation a Sopwith Pup fitted with the 80 hp Le Rhone engine.

Eventually the Armistice came and flying began to fall off. In the middle of March 1919 I was asked if I would like to go home for good. Needless to say I was out of the office like a shot to get the necessary clearances. That was the end of my brief and inglorious career in the Royal Flying Corps and Royal Air Force.

On the 16 November 1992 I paid my quinquennial nostalgic visit to RAF Northolt as the guest of the Station Commander. This marked the seventy-fifth anniversary of my first reporting there.

The Camel (Crown copyright)

A Rigger in the Royal Flying Corps

Gladys Collett RFC

I joined the Royal Flying Corps in 1917 with a Service Number which I still remember after more than three quarters of a century: '2277'.

I was very lucky. We lived at Market Drayton and I was able to bicycle every morning to my station at Ternhill, which was only about four miles away. We worked from 8.30 in the morning to 4.30 in the afternoon, and were given a meal in the camp at mid-day.

Although I was classed as a Rigger, I was never given any training. I had to learn as I went along from the airmen who worked with us. Our job was to repair the aeroplanes, Avro 504s and other types. We patched or replaced the fabric on the body, wings and ailerons and then painted everything with dope. The unmistakable smell always filled the hangar and hung in my clothes. We also had to repair the struts and tighten all the wires which held the wings firmly in place.

All the girls wore very long, thick, voluminous skirts and we had to hitch these up to climb into the cockpit. We would sit there and move each control in turn so that the airmen could check that everything was working properly.

I bought some leather gauntlets which were not official issue! I am wearing them in the photograph. We were all proud to have the new peaked cap and my two friends in the back row had already been issued with theirs.

Gladys Collett (centre front) and friends – 1918 (Gladys Collett)

I have kept a paper-knife made from an aeroplane strut. The base is the gadget we used to tighten the wire bracing.

I eventually left in 1922, after five interesting years. I still have the RFC Cap Badge which at over 100 years of age is one of my most treasured possessions.

A Troubled Start 1918–1926

The Air Force (Constitution) Bill establishing the new service became law on 29 November 1917. Lord Rothermere was appointed first Secretary of State for the Royal Air Force and Major General Sir Hugh Trenchard became Chief of the Air Staff.

The speed with which the new Ministry and Service had been created did nothing to ease political and military disagreements and tensions. Heavy pressures were exerted on the new Ministry from all sides. The Army and Navy in particular resented losing their air units. Morale in the Department was low. By March 1918, Trenchard and many senior colleagues had resigned. Rothermere himself resigned a month later. Five months after its birth the Air Ministry seemed doomed.

The new Secretary of State, Sir William Weir, guided his charge through troubled waters until the Armistice in November 1918. When Lloyd George formed his new Government at the end of the war Weir in turn resigned.

At the beginning of 1919, Winston Churchill was appointed to the twin offices of Secretary of State for War and Secretary of State for Air. 'You can take the Air with you', said Lloyd George. 'I am not going to keep it as a separate department'.

One of Churchill's first actions was to restore Trenchard to the post of Chief of Air Staff. In November 1919, Sir Hugh Trenchard, encouraged by Churchill, produced a far-reaching plan for development of the peace time Royal Air Force. Amongst other things, he proposed creation of Territorial Air Force units, each affiliated with an individual town or county. He emphasised the need for high standards throughout the Royal Air Force not only in training, but also in the technical development of aircraft, engines, navigation, armament and photography. As the accounts in this section show, for many years these high standards would remain merely aspirations.

The RAF was quickly reduced from its wartime strength of 280 squadrons to only one tenth of that size. Most units were based abroad in Iraq, Egypt, Palestine and India. Only three squadrons were retained for Home Defence. Thousands of aircraft became surplus.

Lloyd George would have been happy to see the RAF reabsorbed by the Army and the Navy. Fortunately, Churchill was preoccupied with Army dissatisfaction over demobilisation arrangements. He also noted the efficiency with which the RAF developed a system of air control in hostile territories with very poor communications. Air operations were more effective and cheaper than conventional military campaigns. Air successes were achieved in Somaliland in 1919, and by March 1921 the defence of the new Arab Kingdoms of Iraq and Jordan had been entrusted to the RAF.

Operations in Iraq are described in the next two accounts. Here the RAF Commander had at his disposal eight squadrons of aircraft, an Armoured Car Company, some 5000 locals who formed the Iraq Levies, together with nine battalions of British and Indian infantry. Their main task was to maintain order and also to drive the Turks out of the northern districts of Mesopotamia which they had improperly occupied. Operations went well and Churchill therefore placed no obstacles in the way of the troubled new service.

His successor as Secretary of State for Air on 5 April 1921 was Captain Frederick Guest who held office until the fall of Lloyd George's Government in October 1922.

The new Prime Minister, Bonar Law, was no more sympathetic than Lloyd George. 'Off with its head' was his comment when Sir Samuel Hoare took over the unfortunate Ministry in November 1922.

By 1923, the demands of the Navy for the return of the Fleet Air Arm had reached such a pitch that Beatty, the First Sea Lord, threatened to resign if they were not met. The Government therefore set up a Committee under Lord Salisbury to examine the different claims. Despite all pressures the Committee was sympathetic towards continued development of the RAF and decided to leave it in control of the Fleet Air Arm. Some of the tensions between the two services which extended all the way down to working level are described later by AVM Peter Craycroft.

On the basis of the Salisbury Committee's Report, the Prime Minister made the following statement to Parliament on 20 June 1923:

'The Home Defence Force should consist of 52 squadrons to be created with as little delay as possible, and the Secretary of State for Air has been instructed forthwith to take the preliminary steps for carrying this decision into effect.'

Despite these fine-sounding words, it was to be many years before their promise was fulfilled. The Cabinet decided to delay the plan for fifty-two squadrons by five years. Fortunately, the proposals for the Auxiliary Air Force and Air Force Reserve were retained.

Moving the second reading of the 'Auxiliary Air Force and Air Force Reserve Bill' in 1925, the Secretary of State for Air, Lord Thomson, announced that the Home Defence Force was to consist of a solid foundation of the best possible regular units, supported by a national force based on the great centres of industry on the lines of the Territorial Army. Six of the fifty-two squadrons would be Auxiliary Air Force and seven Special Reserve.

Group Captain 'Cocky' Dundas describes in a later section the unique spirit with which this new force was imbued.

Mesopotamia 1920–1922

Group Captain W. Bentley DFC

I joined 30 Squadron at Baghdad in March 1920, when it was equipped with DH 9A aircraft with the 400 hp Liberty engine.

There were two squadrons in Iraq at that time. 30 with 'A' Flight at Mosul, 'B' Flight in Persia at Sultanabad near Kasvin and 'C' Flight at Baghdad alongside 6 Squadron which was equipped with Bristol Fighters. The hangars were the old canvas Bessoneau type.

At that time RAF Iraq formed part of the RAF Middle East Command. In 1920 there was no oil pipeline across the desert from Iraq to Palestine, no motor road, and no flying between Cairo and Baghdad. When we joined the Squadron things were comparatively quiet and peaceful. I was posted to 'A' Flight at Mosul and after only a few days at Baghdad I flew off to Mosul in a brand new DH 9A.

The aerodrome at Mosul was extremely small. It was bounded on two sides by irrigation ditches, on the third side by a road with the inevitable ditch, whilst at the fourth end were hangars. These were canvas tent-like affairs into which one aircraft could be tightly packed. They were made to fit RE 8s which had only just been replaced by the DH 9As The 9A was not an easy aircraft to put down in a very small space and wheel brakes were undreamed of. So if you overshot in any direction you were unlucky. Remember that those were the days of wooden under carts and bungee shock absorbers – no Oleo legs.

When we first arrived, things were about as quiet and peaceful as they ever were. But even then we received quite frequent calls to search rivers round about for troublesome gentry reported to be sailing downstream on large rafts made from numerous inflated goats skins. There was seldom a week when we did not drop a few bombs on some village or other. The bombs were mostly the 20 lb Cooper.

During the summer of 1920 a serious Arab revolt broke out. They cut rail communication between Baghdad and Basra for a considerable time. The alternative communication, apart from the air, was by the Tigris River steamers, mostly of the stern paddle wheel type. But that was precarious and many of the steamers were heavily attacked from the riverbanks. From Baghdad 30 Squadron were kept very busy bombing and shooting up hostile forces as well as dropping supplies to parties of British troops who frequently became surrounded.

Most of the flying was done at low altitudes, generally at about 1000 feet above ground level. One surprising feature was the great success of hostile marksman in bringing down aircraft with rifle fire. Certainly in that climate it only needed one bullet in the radiator or water cooling system to necessitate an immediate forced landing. Quite a few aircraft from 30 Squadron were brought down in that way and several crews were captured by the enemy. I remember in particular the case of two who had a very unpleasant time. Among other things they were made to march long distances barefoot. They were however finally rescued.

During 1920 the supply of new aircraft and spares, particularly tyres, was very inadequate. I mention tyres because we had a lot of trouble with them. The formidable

Mesopotamia 1920–22. DH 9A of 45 Squadron (AHB)

prickles of the camel-thorn undergrowth caused everlasting punctures. So much so that we fitted a spare wheel beneath the fuselage of each aircraft.

Soon after Christmas I flew to join B Flight who were still in Persia. After the first 45 minutes or so the route lay entirely over mountainous country and we soon found ourselves over snow-covered ground. At Kasvin there was some three feet of snow, but to enable us to land a large number of camels had been employed to trample snow so as to make a comparatively hard track about fifty yards wide.

During 1920 B Flight was engaged in scrapping with Russian aircraft which flew over Persian territory from bases to the south of the Caspian Sea. At the very beginning of 1921, when I joined them, preparations were in hand for the final withdrawal from North-West Persia of the British Forces.

Whilst I was at Kasvin there was an attempt to fly some mail from Baghdad with the local British army commander, General Ironside, as a passenger. That flight however ended with a forced landing in the snow. The General suffered a broken leg and we had great difficulty in getting him back to civilisation over snowbound roads. Some days later I set out to fly to Baghdad. At the point where I left the mountains to cross the remaining flat country for Baghdad I must have been well off-track and too far south. I ran into a heavy sandstorm, so landed for a time until it had eased off. After taking off again I became completely lost and finally landed far to the south of Baghdad.

At that time navigation was a closed book to most of us. Blind flying instruments were unknown, and the Turn and Bank indicator had not yet been introduced. Night flying was done only by a few special night flying squadrons, and they, together with the flying-boat squadrons and others who flew over the sea, were about the only people who ever bothered about navigation. In any case our compasses were of a small globular pattern, there was no verge ring, and you were lucky if you could steer a course to within thirty degrees. Compass swinging may have been practised but during two years in Iraq I never recollect having seen it done on a squadron.

Early in 1921 the nature of our work changed. Orders had been received to survey the route and put into operation an Airmail service between Baghdad and Cairo. A ground party with motor vehicles set out from Egypt. A similar ground party set out from Baghdad led by an army officer of the Royal Engineers.

Both parties had been equipped with small W/T (wireless telegraphy) sets with which they could communicate respectively with Egypt and Baghdad. It was decided that sites at about every fifty miles should be marked as emergency landing grounds. The first idea was to use a baked slab about eighteen inches square and about two inches thick. Carriers were made to fit on the bomb racks under the aircraft wings, and experiments were made to fly these slabs out. The intention was to mark the boundaries of the landing grounds with them and periodically to whiten them with paint. They were heavy and bulky. A very large number would be needed and only a few could be carried by an aircraft at one time. It was then found that on the hard baked sandy earth the tracks of the motor vehicles remained clearly visible from the air for several months. The idea of slabs was abandoned and instead at each site motor vehicles were driven round to mark the boundary. Not that the mark was really necessary because it was possible to land almost anywhere, but the main purpose of these landing grounds was to provide the only landmarks along that route. It was found that from an aircraft car tracks could be clearly seen and followed practically the whole way from Ramadi to Amman.

The progress of the motor vehicles on that first survey was slow and occupied some weeks. During that time aircraft from each side flew out frequently to each fresh landing ground as it was marked, taking with them drinking water, fuel, and supplies. In these operations about five aircraft would be sent out in formation. We had by then just started to use W/T sets in the aircraft, and probably one aircraft in the formation would carry a set and an operator. The sets were however most unreliable and failures were very frequent both on transmission and reception.

Then came the day when the ground parties met at a point approximately midway between Amman and Ramadi. On that day five aircraft set out from Baghdad just after dawn. There was an order that if over the desert one aircraft developed engine trouble and had to fall out from the formation another must join and follow him in order to mark where he had landed and then go for help. Very soon one aircraft fell out with engine trouble and of course a second left the formation to escort him. That left three. Amman was a very bad aerodrome. It was small and if you overshot at one end you went over a small cliff. In landing at Amman the third aircraft crashed thus leaving just two. At Amman we had a meal and an hour or so rest, but my passenger was naturally anxious to get through to Cairo in a day if possible. So we took off again. Soon afterwards I noticed that my engine was developing an intermittent misfire which rapidly grew worse. We were then somewhere near Jerusalem. I decided that I must land near a village called Raffa. The other aircraft continued and reached Cairo without trouble.

That was the start of the airmail routes between Baghdad and Cairo. I think the mail on that occasion consisted of one small canvas bag of a size to fit into a pocket. But it meant that from then on letters could be sent from Baghdad to Cairo in one day and they would reach England in easily ten days or a fortnight, whereas before letters between England and Iraq, which all went by sea via Bombay, had taken anything from five to eight weeks.

One way and another this route required a lot of work. From time to time motor vehicles were sent across to freshen up the tracks as a guide for the aircraft. Then fairly frequently an aircraft would be stranded somewhere along the route with engine failure or would perhaps break an undercarriage on landing. Some quite surprising feats were performed in the way of taking a Liberty engine to pieces, packing the whole thing in parts distributed between several aircraft, flying it out to a disabled aircraft, getting shear legs there either by surface transport or by the Vimys or a Handley Page, then assembling the engine and doing an engine change somewhere out in the blue along the route.

For a DH 9A the flying time between Baghdad and Cairo would normally be something between nine and ten hours, so that in normal conditions during the summer we would go through in the day. In the shorter hours of daylight during the winter, or if there were headwinds we would have to spend a night *en route* at Amman. There was keen competition to get detailed for a flight to Cairo because it involved a fortnight's stay there before flying back with a return load of mail in the other direction.

Keepers of the King's Peace (King Faisal 1st)

Wing Commander C. M. G. Anderson

Sahib! Sahib! Five O'clock Sahib! Sahib! Tea, Sahib!

Breaking through the mists of sleep the endless low voiced repetition goes on and I emerge at last awake and with a disapproving grunt reach out for the pale yellow liquid, thick with condensed milk, which has been deposited on a chair by the bed. The Bearer who carefully vanished at the actual time of awakening, now comes into the room with a can of shaving water and fusses about, arranging shirt, shorts, stockings and woolly on the old bomb box which does duty for a chest of drawers cum dressing-table. It is cold in the early morning at this time of year in southern Kurdistan and he himself is muffled to the eyebrows.

I know I have been detailed for the morning 'show', that the CO will be leading the formation and that he will want to see all pilots in his office at 05.30 hours. I know that my aeroplane was serviceable at last night's 'Mayfly' and that my Fitter will fly with me as gunner and bomb aimer and that I will be carrying a war load of four 112 lb high-explosive bombs and two 100 lb cases of baby incendiary-bombs.

I know that in a short while I will be endeavouring to drop them on a collection of mud huts tucked away in the mountains somewhere not far from the Persian border. I'm not quite sure why I have to do this, but rather suspect that the inhabitants of these huts, which constitute a village with a name as long as itself, have probably been aiding and abetting a rather sporting old boy called Sheikh Mahmoud who has been defying King Faisal 1st of Iraq and the might of Great Britain for a year or so.

I also know that my Squadron, who act as aerial policemen over 17,000 square miles of rather impossible country, will go on doing this sort of thing until 'S.M', as he is called, either surrenders or is captured, or stands too close to one of its bombs. Even then some silly ass will go on the rampage and the Royal Air Force will have to teach them to behave. In the meantime all I have to do is to get to the CO's office on time and be told my position in the formation, height for bombing over the target, and any other items that the CO thinks fit to expound.

The CO's briefing is short. The target is shown on a map and operating heights given. Each pilot is detailed to his position in the formation. A few instructions regarding the conditions which will probably prevail over the target area and an admonition to watch for the leader's signals, and the pilots troop down to the tarmac.

One pilot, who has hurried ahead of the rest, takes off in a cloud of dust. He is the warning aircraft and his job is to fly over the target first and drop leaflets telling the inhabitants of the village to evacuate at once because their homes are going to be destroyed. The leaflets also tell them why this is going to be done. In this type of war the Royal Air Force is not trying to kill people but punish them, and it is pointless doing this unless they are told why they are being punished. Incidentally, this is about the only occasion when a lone aeroplane without WT is allowed to fly over enemy territory. There is always the danger of a forced landing and resultant capture by irate tribesmen who have never heard of the Hague Convention.

I settle myself in the cockpit, do up my safety belt and wait while the 'Hucks Starter' fusses up and engages its coupling with the claws on the propeller boss. The ground crew stand clear and as the propeller begins to turn I switch on and help the engine with a little throttle, easing it back again as the 'Hucks Starter' backs away and goes to the next aeroplane.

I am flying number three in the formation which is on the left-hand side of the leader. The Squadron has perfected its take off procedure so that as little time as possible is wasted. The airfield, a brown area of dusty earth, is too small for formation take offs and there is, too, the danger of the pilots in the rear being blinded by dust, so the Squadron takes off individually in reverse order of seniority.

The leader takes the formation in a wide left-hand circuit climbing steadily at about 1550 to 1570 revs. The airspeed shows about 75 mph. He is heading east towards the mountains. Having settled in my cruising position a little behind and above the leader and about five wing spans from him I am concerned about my water temperature. The atmosphere although it is chilly on the ground at this time of the morning, is extremely hot at 800 to 1000 ft and will continue in, as it were, a hot belt of air up to 2000 ft. Radiators are liable to boil even with the shutters wide open unless the revolutions can be reduced.

It is difficult to reduce revolutions and still keep to the steady climb as the air in this belt is rather thin and lacks lift, and the aeroplanes themselves, apart from their bomb load, normally carry a 200 lb overload of desert rations, five gallons of drinking water, ground strips, cockpit and wheel covers, a spare wheel, fitters tools and 1500 rounds of ammunition for the front and rear guns. Still the CO is leading the formation perfectly as usual and with revs reduced to 1550 rpm and the temperature gauge showing about 95°C, the aeroplanes come out into fresher air at 1500 ft and are able to reduce revolutions to about 1500 rpm and still continue to climb.

We are over the foothills now and about twenty miles ahead we see the first range of hills. Slightly to the left of the course is a V cut in the yellowish brown wall of hills. Near the foot of it is a camp of Assyrian Levy troops and an emergency landing ground. It is comforting to know the position of possible landing grounds in this mountainous country as engine trouble is not unknown and forced landings, though infrequent, do occur.

It is very bumpy near the mountains and I have my work cut out to keep formation. One moment I am dropping like a stone below the leader and the next I'm soaring above him and the aeroplane is seldom on an even keel. I have developed a technique of correcting lateral bumps with my rudder and sliding out of them. This is permissible in open formations and is less tiring than using the control column the whole time but it is uncomfortable for the passenger. However, the gunners of the Squadron are used to it and have developed stomachs of cast iron.

I load the gun. It is a Vickers firing through the propeller by means of a synchronising gear. I indicate to my gunner that I'm going to test my gun and tell him to do the same. I pull up the plunger of the gear mechanism and fire a couple of bursts of ten rounds by pressing the lever attached to the control column. The gunner, who has already fitted a drum of ammunition to his Lewis gun, swings the Scarfe ring around, and pointing the gun down and away from other aircraft in the formation fires a short burst. He is aiming towards a plume of smoke which has been visible for some minutes rising from the crest of the ridge of hills a mile or so to one side. This is a signal sent up by watching Kurds and will be repeated as the formation approaches each range of mountains. The gunner will not hit anyone or deter the use of smoke signals but whoever is there will hear the gunfire and know that the Squadron means business.

The Squadron is at 6000 ft now. The last range is passed and the formation begins to lose height slowly. All eyes are on the CO watching for his signals. There it goes, a red Very light, and the formation forms line astern still at fairly wide intervals. The CO alters course for the target. This is a cluster of half a dozen flat-roofed huts looking like dirty packing cases. The aeroplanes are at bombing height now. The CO does a right-angled turn to find the wind direction and gauge its strength by the drift of the aircraft. He does a wide turn once more and heads for the target into wind and drops a bomb. He's into wind all right, but short, and the gunners increase the wind setting on the sights, estimating the amounts by the smoke drift of the CO's bomb burst.

The formation follows the leader around and comes up to the target again. Bombing starts in earnest now and each aeroplane drops one bomb every circuit. My gunner and I are

'Hucks Starter' (Cambridge University Air Squadron)

reasonably old hands at the game and know each other. We have worked out a division of responsibility which obtains very good results. Roughly, if the bomb falls on either side of the target, it is my fault. If it falls short or over it is the gunner's fault.

I fly my aeroplane dead into wind at a constant height and speed, looking over and down the right side of the fuselage, keeping the aeroplane level and dead over the target. The gunner is standing up working the sight which is on a bracket on the right side of the fuselage with a row of bomb release toggles just behind it. As his sights come on he jerks a toggle and sees the bomb drop away. He taps me on the head and I immediately turn away following the aircraft in front of me so that the air over the target is clear for the aeroplane behind me. This goes on until all high-explosive bombs have gone. The bombing is good this day and the houses are looking very sorry for themselves. All eyes are now on the CO. Will he go down to drop his incendiaries or will he stay up at bombing height? It really depends on the accessibility of the target and the amount of the ground opposition in the shape of rifle fire.

Down goes the leader's nose. Good show, he's going down after all. The line of aircraft snakes down one after the other and drop their incendiaries on to the broken houses from about 200 to 300 feet. Round once more for the second canister. As I dive on the burning village I fire my gun, not that I have seen anything to fire at, but if there is any one intrepid enough to remain and shoot at the aeroplanes' radiators as they approach, a good burst of machine-gun fire acts as a deterrent. Not to be outdone the gunner strafes the place with his Lewis gun as the aeroplanes turn away.

The CO has finished now and is climbing up in wide spirals silhouetted against the sky, easy for the other aeroplanes to spot. Like a good leader, he's giving the formation plenty of time to catch him up and aeroplane after aeroplane rises out of the valley and joins the formation which passes over the ridge of mountains and heads for home. No plumes of smoke now. It is hot now, even at 5000 ft, and even bumpier than before, but the aircraft are lighter and nicer to handle. We have a sense of a job well done and the prospect of a good breakfast in the not too distant future.

The Challenge to Test Pilots in the 1920s

Harald Penrose OBE

Despite the enormous use of aeroplanes in World War I, there was very little understanding of their handling behaviour. By a process of trial and error many of the leading aircraft designers had stumbled on relationships between the centre of gravity and tail area. Though the main object of prototype flight trials was performance checking, step by step alterations were attempted to eliminate the many faults that initially snagged almost every new machine. This despite the availability of considerable technical information from the Royal Aircraft Factory at Farnborough on strength and stability. Successful Sopwith aeroplanes for instance, were often the result of an evolutionary sequence of alterations which might be as fundamental as a complete change of wing structure from single to multi-bay or vice versa.

The inadequate dashboard of aeroplanes before the days of blind flying instruments necessitated piloting only by 'feel'. Without a visual horizon it was all too easy to begin an accidental turn in a cloud, rapidly lose speed as the turn tightened, and flick into a spin. This was equally easy to do on making a slow gliding turn when approaching to land.

Throughout the 1920s and 30s stalling remained the prime cause of accidents, both in the RAF and civil aviation. Quite early this led to the development of the Handley Page Slot which delayed stalling at the wing tips. In a more complex direction there was the swept wing Westland Tailless Pterodactyl with independent controllers beyond the stalling area of the wing tip. The first demonstrations were made of the Cierva Autogiro, which had a freely spinning horizontal rotor as precursor to the helicopter. Each of these types opened a new vista of investigation.

Although the method of recovery from a spin had been discovered before World War I and was practised by many pilots during that war, it remained a peril of considerable magnitude. In order to reduce fatalities it was essential for Farnborough to establish the factors of design and piloting which induced spinning. That research was completed some years later and dealt with the mathematics of the motion and general principles of design which should be followed if stalling accidents were to be prevented.

Thereafter spin tests up to six turns became mandatory during development trials of prototypes except for big bombers and flying boats. It could be hazardous when exploring behaviour beyond the design operational limit. The risk was, however, lessened in later years when it became customary for Farnborough to examine and modify spinning characteristics in a vertical wind-tunnel, using a special inertia-corrected free-flying model of each new prototype, before full-scale trials were attempted.

One of the illusions of the early days of aeroplane development was that we often felt that a peak had been reached by current types in service – yet when a prototype was flown on initial trials it was immediately apparent to all concerned that new aeroplanes rarely conformed to pattern. Occasionally there was aberrant behaviour fantastically beyond the experience of any pilot, despite broad design agreement with predictions based on horizontal wind-tunnels.

I found controls so heavy that it was impossible to move them. Another aeroplane might take charge through over-balance. There were wings which twisted when aileron or elevon was moved; wings which came off; vital mechanisms which broke or burned through; main fittings which failed; fires in the air and engines which ceased to function. Minor difficulties with fuel systems, hydraulics, air systems and electrics were countless.

I flew aeroplanes in which I tried one particular manoeuvre and another resulted; spins which were impossibly erratic and gave inverted recovery; propellers which over-speeded so that it seemed the engine must burst; oil and cooling systems that failed; flaps which failed. Difficulties of this kind were the common experience of all test pilots. It was part of the challenge that a valuable prototype should be brought safely back to earth. This was reinforced by one's natural impulse to stay rather than attempt escape by parachute!

In the 1920s there was a growing tendency to use recording instruments, and although the simplest measuring methods were used wherever possible, a number of special devices became available for test and aerodynamic research. An air log suspended on a wire, well below the aeroplane's turbulence, was used to check the air speed of the machine. The attitude of control surfaces could be recorded continuously on a light-sensitive film by means of instruments attached to tail and wing, and simultaneous records were synchronised through clockwork controlling the lamp circuits. A recording control column was used to measure the hand force applied to the top of the column on operating aileron and elevators. Already there was an automatic observer comprising a small cinematographic camera which gave readings of a number of dials on a single film. Electric failures, vibration and low temperature caused occasional malfunctioning, and the pilot and his reactions remained the yardstick by which instrument readings were interpreted.

Knowledge steadily accumulated with which to co-ordinate full scale and wind-tunnel results, and by the end of the decade it was possible to give the test pilot accurate pre-flight guidance on tail trim setting and to warn of likely zones of difficulty.

A new phenomenon we occasionally experienced was flutter. What might have been accepted as a vibration of tolerable degree in early post-war aeroplanes could prove catastrophic at the faster speeds of new designs. There were fatal accidents. Extensive investigation was initiated with structural models, but although this enabled preventative proposals to be formulated there was no guarantee that these would prove an absolute insurance. Despite cautious step-by-step exploration when trying the higher speeds of a prototype I found it dramatically disturbing when the whole machine suddenly violently vibrated as a control or wing oscillation took charge.

Terminal dives, limited either by mounting drag of the aeroplane or the maximum safe engine revs, became the ultimate test of control, stability, and structural strength. Very occasionally we overshot the safety speed and found it impossible to pull out because of a nose-down change of trim which the elevators could not overcome and there was always the risk that the aeroplane might shed a wing or break up.

High altitude investigation, oxygen equipment, engine development and cooling, propellers, brakes, cockpit heating and many other facets became the subject of increasing test flying, coupled with allied development of instruments and associated techniques. When the manufacturer's test and design team had brought the prototype to as near perfection as practicable within a reasonable time scale (though possibly with residual defects for later attention) the machine was flown to the Aircraft and Armament Experimental Establishment at Martlesham Heath, Suffolk. Here RAF pilots would officially confirm its performance and suitability, followed by tests of guns, bomb dropping, and ease of maintenance.

The Pterodactyle IV being tested by Harald Penrose 1931 (Westlands)

By the mid 1920s most of the major aircraft manufacturers had an Air Ministry specified prototype in the offing for limited series production to replace the RAF's outdated wartime and immediate post-war aeroplanes. At the end of 1926 the reorganised RAF comprised 730 aircraft in sixty-one Squadrons of which twenty-five were for Home Defence. All the new aircraft were biplanes and still had open cockpits. Metal framed structures had been evolved though these were still externally surfaced with doped and painted fabric. Nevertheless they were regarded as perfection and comprised the Gloster Gamecock single-seat fighter replacing the early Grebe; Armstrong Whitworth two-seater Atlas for Army co-operation work; Westland Wapiti, a general purpose two-seater replacing the DH 9A; and many others. Already in service were the Hawker Woodcock single-seater fighter, the impressive Horsely two seat day bomber, and more recent fully metal-structured Bristol Bulldog single-seat day and night fighter.

Shattering current conceptions of a two-seat single-engined bomber was the aerodynamically clean Fox biplane introduced as a private venture by Fairey Aviation. Powered with an imported USA 480 hp Curtiss engine, it was as fast as the Gamecock, and Air Chief Marshal Sir Hugh Trenchard was sufficiently impressed to order eighteen. Fairey also made history with a long-range monoplane in the form of a huge 80 foot span cantilever shoulder-winger ordered by the Air Ministry for an attack on the world long distance record. Although attempts in 1928 and 1929 failed there was a determination to achieve success early in the next decade.

Indicative of the future, but of unrealised importance, was the work of Dr. Griffith at the renamed Royal Aircraft Establishment, who evolved a new theory of aerodynamic turbine design in 1926. Quite independently, in 1928 Flying Officer F. Whittle published proposals for a gas-turbine for jet propulsion. Significantly in September 1929 a rocket propelled aeroplane in Germany flew for one and a quarter miles, attaining a speed of 85 mph, but ending in a crash. What did the future hold?

The Avro 504K

Air Marshal Sir Hugh Walmsley KCB KCIE CBE MC DFC

Flying remained primitive in the 1920s. Aircraft were light. The Avro 504K weighed only 1231 lb empty. It had therefore to be kept in a hangar or tied down to prevent it overturning if there was any wind. Fuelling was initially from tins, although by 1928 some airfields had acquired bulk storage for both aviation and motor transport fuels. Aircraft could then be filled from drums on wheels using semi-rotary hand pumps.

The Avro 504K had open cockpits. Goggles and flying jackets were essential. The bottom of the cockpit tended to accumulate dust, mud and much more solid objects such as tools. In any violent manoeuvre, these were likely to be dislodged and fall out past the startled pilot. Worse still, they might jam the various control wires and linkages passing along the inside of the fuselage.

When the aircraft had been wheeled from the hangar and the pilot strapped in, a carefully laid down procedure was followed. The controls were moved in turn to check that they had been connected correctly and that no foreign bodies were obstructing their movement. Chocks were placed in front of the wheels and the mechanic stood well clear of the propeller. He then called 'Switch off' and the pilot, having confirmed that the ignition was in fact switched off, replied 'Switch is off'. Even this could confuse the novice. For reasons best known to itself, the RAF had early adopted the practice of having ignition switches 'Down' for 'Off' and 'Up' for 'On', thus completely reversing normal domestic practice. (Air Vice-Marshal Colbeck-Welch recalls that his first instructor, Sergeant Baretto, drummed into his head 'UP is ON because ON is UP' i.e. if you want to go UP you must put the switch UP!)

With the ignition confirmed 'Off' the mechanic turned the propeller several times by hand. He then stepped clear and called 'Contact'. The pilot put the ignition switch up and replied 'Contact'. Up to three mechanics then linked arms to provide enough force to swing the propeller to start up the engine. If, as so often happened, the engine failed to start, the whole process started again.

The procedure could be dangerous unless all safety precautions were followed. Each pilot was himself trained in propeller swinging to ensure that he fully understood the risks faced by mechanics. An entry was then made in his log book certifying that he had been instructed in propeller swinging in accordance with the standard procedure laid down in the Flying Training Manual.

Once the engine was running the mechanic lay across the tail plane to hold it down whilst the pilot ran the engine up to full speed. If everything was satisfactory, the mechanic pulled away the chocks and the aircraft taxied out. The pilot looked at the windsock and turned his machine into wind. Having checked the sky for other aircraft, he took hold of the stick lightly and opened the engine full out. As the machine gained speed, he pressed the stick forward to get the tail up and balance the aeroplane on its wheels in the flying position. At a little over 45 mph, an Avro was ready to fly and delicate easing back of the stick took her into the air. The rush of fresh air past the face could be exhilarating in fine weather, but an open cockpit had distinct disadvantages in rain or snow. After a winter flight of some duration, we often found it difficult to ease our stiff bodies out of the aeroplane.

Gun mounting on Avro 504 – 6 September1918 (RAF Museum Hendon)

Landing could also present problems. The Flying Instructor of one squadron noted in his log on 25/05/29 'Turns up to 45 degrees – very good. Little wind and in overshooting ran into the sheep, killed one, broke hind legs of another which had to be killed'.

The pilot in his open cockpit, exposed to all the elements, had little to help him. He knew how fast his aeroplane was flying and its approximate height above sea level. A gauge told him how much fuel was left. To find his way over unfamiliar territory he relied mainly on his Air Gunner's map reading ability and on directions shouted to him through the voice tube above the noise of the engine and slipstream. Railway lines were invaluable since they eventually led to large and hopefully recognisable towns. Some pilots were even known to fly low to read the names of stations!

The air gunner too had his problems. Once the required track had been drawn, the map had to be methodically folded so that it could be opened section by manageable section in flight. A fully opened map in a cramped cockpit exposed to a hundred mile per hour slipstream was something to be avoided.

True the pilot also had a compass but this was known to be an idiosyncratic instrument not wholly to be relied on. If by mischance he lost sight of the ground, there was nothing to help him. He must rely on his own senses to tell him if the aeroplane was straight and level. Not until 1933 did 'turn indicators' and 'fore and aft levels' become standard. Radio Direction Finding and Radar were many years in the future. The art of finding the way from one place to another was known in those days as 'Air Pilotage'.

A regular RAF Officer, Squadron Leader J.H. Dand MBE, attempted to explain the limitations of the aircraft compass. He began 'An aeroplane, a little common sense and a map are all that are really necessary for a pilot and air gunner to fly cross country, provided the visibility is good'. On the first page of the Manual of Air Pilotage, however, there is a definition of the subject which dismisses rather summarily any idea that the art of air pilotage consists only of flying from point to point by referring to a map. It ends with the words:

'It includes the ability to maintain a given direction in or above the clouds and mist and by night. Neither in Mr Bradshaw nor in the Ordnance Survey, then, must we unreservedly put our trust, but rather look with understanding and faith to the compass and turning indicator if we desire to fly cross country with certainty of arriving at the destination entered in the Authorisation of Flights book. Any other way leads invariably to a Court of Inquiry.'

Squadron Leader Dand pointed out that the aircraft compass behaved erratically when the aeroplane was turning and with changes in air speed. He advised the pilot to study its behaviour during such manoeuvres, preferably in calm weather, and stressed the difficulties of trying to steer accurate courses (especially northerly) in bumpy weather. He concluded 'Once its limitations are known, a pilot should soon appreciate the value of the compass which can be relied upon with every confidence so long as it is not expected to do what, from the nature of its design and physical characteristics, it cannot do.'

The Fleet Air Arm 1927

Air Vice-Marshal P. Craycroft CBE AFC

I commenced my flying training in 1927 at 5 OTU Sealand on the Avro 504 K. Like most early aircraft it was very good tempered although there was always the chance of something going wrong. One of the first lessons impressed on pupils was to keep a constant lookout for fields which might be useful for an emergency landing. Just as well. I was flying a Snipe one day when a cylinder broke off the rotary engine. The vibration was terrific and I had to get down at once. I saw a small field and managed to land safely. I telephoned one of my instructors and he flew over to pick me up. Unfortunately he found it impossible to land in the same field!

My first posting was to the Fleet Air Arm on HMS *Furious*. At that time the Fleet Air Arm was officially part of the RAF but it had a complicated dual operational control system. Over the sea operations were the responsibility of the Navy but over land the Air Ministry was in charge. Squadron Commanders were initially RAF but later many were naval officers. RAF officers in the Fleet Air arm were distinguished by a badge on their left sleeves in the form of an anchor within a wreath.

Before going to sea we had to undergo a wonderful course at Leuchars to teach us how to behave on board. Most RAF and RN pilots took to one another like brothers. We became WFP – We Fighter Pilots. Some senior naval officers however treated RAF pilots like mud and *Furious* was not a happy ship. We always had the poorest cabins. Mine was under the quarterdeck so that there was constant vibration from the screws when we were at sea. When we were in harbour a sentry was posted on the quarter deck, marching up and down all night over my head.

The senior naval officers were very strict on protocol but we soon found a way to get our own back. An RAF pilot would innocently say 'I'm going to bed' only to be sharply corrected 'bunk' not 'bed'. Someone else might say 'I left something in my room' only to be told 'cabin' not 'room'. It was like fly-fishing – they rose to the bait every time.

Furious had a flush flight deck with no island and all exhausts were expelled from gratings over the quarter deck. This could cause problems when we were coming into land. Just as we came over the end of the flight deck we would hit the heated air and the aircraft would be tossed upwards. There was a ramp about two-thirds of the way along the flight deck which was supposed to help aircraft slow down.

I was preparing for my first take off from a carrier when a Fly Catcher piloted by John Martin, a Royal Marine, came in, bounced in the centre of the deck and went straight over the side. Fortunately he was unhurt and was picked up by a boat from an attendant destroyer. The Wing Commander (Flying) was standing behind me and said 'I want to see a better turn from you, Craycroft'. My nervousness was compounded when just before I took off a seaman came running up with a piece of paper. I leaned out and found it was a form on which to record my next of kin!

In 1928 I was sent to Lee-on-Solent to convert to Fairey 3D seaplanes. Whilst on the course I was instructed to tow a drogue over Portland for an AA shoot by the *Tiger*. The Fairey climbed very slowly and it took me half an hour to get to height. I told the Observer to stream the drogue at the end of 2000 ft of wire.

I was steering a straight course when suddenly there was

Flycatcher taking off from lower deck – HMS Glorious *1930 (AVM Craycroft)*

an explosion in front of me. I completed the run, turned and there was another explosion ahead. When the third shell exploded, also in front of me, I had had enough. I told the Observer to cut the drogue loose and returned to Portland. I managed to land in the harbour which was crowded with ships and taxied to the boom. This was not easy with only the small rudders on the floats which were almost useless in any wind. I cut the engine, tied up and climbed a long rope ladder with some difficulty. I found the gunnery officer and protested that *Tiger* was supposed to shoot at the drogue, not the towing aircraft! He said 'Sorry old boy. Carry on with the final practice'. I said 'Aye-aye, Sir' went back to my Fairey and promptly returned to Lee-on-Solent!

Early in 1930 I was transferred to the newly recommissioned aircraft carrier *Glorious*. She was a very happy ship and both the Captain and Commander (Flying) were keen on the RAF.

Glorious had two flight decks, one above the other. The far end of the lower deck was also the hanger and the deck had doors at the front.

We were equipped with the Fly Catcher, a single-seat fighter which could be converted to a seaplane or amphibian. It had a 400 hp Armstrong Siddeley Jaguar 1V engine and could reach 133 mph at 5000 feet. This dropped to 110 mph at 17,000 ft and its ceiling was 19,000 ft. It climbed at 100 ft per minute and had less than two hours' endurance. The perpetual complaint of its pilots was that they did not get enough flying.

The Fly Catcher had no brakes and there were no arrester wires. To land safely you had to judge the wind speed! There was no means of communicating with the ground or with the ship. It was started by swinging its propeller. Six Fly Catchers would be started up on the lower deck. As the engines revved up, the air became blue and the noise was deafening. There were whirling propellers everywhere. The doors would be opened and one by one the Fly Catchers would take off. This could be tricky. You had to keep the aircraft firmly on the deck to avoid hitting the hangar roof.

Some pilots would risk a roll as they left the flight deck – confident that they were concealed from the bridge by the forward edge of the upper flight deck.

The atmosphere was light hearted. We would all be sitting in the wardroom when the word went round 'Alan is coming in to land'. We would all pile up on to the flight deck to watch. Something usually went wrong and it was a good turn to see!

Glorious sailed to join the Mediterranean Fleet at Malta arriving in July 1930. There was plenty of entertainment ashore. Many naval wives joined their husbands and often brought with them their younger sisters, cousins or nieces. There were plenty of young bachelor officers and many a shipboard romance. The hopeful girls were known as 'The Fishing Fleet', the Ladies' Lounge in the Union Club, Valetta was 'The Snake Pit' and the Ladies' Pool at the Sleima Club was the 'Pool of Disillusionment'.

The Fly Catchers were based at Hal Far and the pilots had to keep their hands in. One challenge was to land as close as possible to the wall at the end of the field. Connolly Abel-Smith, 408's Flight Commander, misjudged, hit the wall and turned his aircraft upside down. He claimed he was obviously nearest but was promptly disqualified. It did not spoil his career and he retired as a Vice Admiral.

On 1 April 1931 *Glorious* sailed North East along the Spanish coast. With her were four destroyers and three cruisers. Ten miles to port were four battleships which *Glorious*'s aircraft were to attack. Some six or seven miles away to port was the French liner SS *Florida*. Her course was slightly converging on *Glorious*.

At 15.55 hrs *Glorious* had twenty-two aircraft in the air and was steaming at 20 knots to allow them to land. Suddenly she ran into an absolute pea-souper fog. Normally the ship would have slowed down or stopped, but her aircraft would then have been endangered. She could either steam on and hope the fog would clear or turn to get out of the fog again. She chose the latter course and proceeded at nine knots sounding a fog siren. The whistle of another ship was then heard.

Glorious stopped her engines and signalled 'full astern' but she still had way on when the SS *Florida* came into view about 200 metres away. The two collided at 1630hrs.

Glorious's bow drove into the *Florida*'s port side killing twenty-two passengers. One of her own seamen also died.

From above I could follow all that was going on and realised that other ships were heading for the accident, unable to see through the dense fog at sea level. Waving and gesticulating had no effect so as a last resort I parked my Fly Catcher in the sea in front of the *Broke*, the leading destroyer. This had the desired effect! Whilst all this was going on the other aircraft flew ashore to Chiriana near Malaga. (*For this courageous action Flying Officer Craycroft was awarded the AFC. Ed.*)

Following a brief posting to *Eagle* I was sent to CFS (Central Flying School) in 1931. Later that same year I was posted to Leuchars as a Flying Instructor. My hopes of a quieter life did not last long.

Three of us were flying from Donibristle to Gosport. The formation was led by a Lieutenant-Commander and I was flying as his No. 2. We refuelled at Catterick and Wittering and later in the day set out on the last leg to Gosport. It grew darker and darker. We had no exhaust manifolds and the sheets of flame from the engine made it difficult to read maps or see the ground. I finally decided that we were not going to reach Gosport and was planning to fly out to sea and ditch as near to land as possible. Suddenly we saw Worthydown, a grass field laid out with goose neck flares. We did not wait for authorisation but promptly landed in the middle of a night exercise. We had no navigation lights but fortunately did not hit anyone.

Another flight from Catterick to Donibristle was equally eventful. Two of us were flying Fly Catchers when we ran into bad weather. I decided to fly around the coast and my companion Lieutenant Commander Grant chose to take the direct route. The Fly Catcher had two air intakes facing forward and his became blocked with snow. The engine stopped and in a forced landing he hit the side of a hill but managed to get away with it. He walked until he found what seemed to be an inn and asked for whisky. He was told it was unlicensed, whereupon he set out again and walked another mile before he found somewhere that could meet his requirements. Meanwhile I reached the Forth at 8000 ft and also ran into snow. My engine cut but I put the nose down and managed to land safely in a long field. I promptly found an inn. This time licensed.

My final assignment in the Fleet Air Arm in 1936 was to HMS *Courageous* – a sister ship of *Glorious*. Here I was appointed Adjutant, a non-flying post. There was constant friction and much paperwork and I had a miserable time.

In 1937 I was posted as Chief Flying Instructor to Oxford University Air Squadron. Here my pupils included Christopher Foxley-Norris (later to become an Air Chief Marshal) and Leonard Cheshire. Leonard was always looking for a challenge and made detailed plans to fly across the Atlantic in a single-engined aircraft. His mother was very worried and asked me to dissuade him, which I eventually managed to do!

My association with the Navy had been fascinating, eventful and generally very happy. It was an unusual introduction to an RAF career.

A Halton Apprentice 1932

Flight Lieutenant W. G. Rogers MBE

Aircraft servicing in the early days of powered flying revolved around stitching, sticking, doping and general patching of fabric surfaces, together with garage type servicing of simple engines.

Rotary engines posed particular problems. In these the crankshaft was fixed and the rest of the engine, with the propeller attached, rotated round it. The caster oil it used was flung into the cylinder heads and choked them up. The Gnome rotary engine developing 100 bhp was regarded as being so unreliable that after less than every twenty flying hours it had to be removed and completely overhauled, including renewal of fatigued components. Re-assembly and refitting to the airframe was followed by ground testing before it was certified serviceable for air testing. The complete procedure would be carried out by one man. Even in the early days it was appreciated that to allocate one engine fitter permanently to each aircraft was advantageous whenever practicable, and so it proved to be for many years.

Starting procedures were revised, ousting the hand swinging which in the past had proved effective but fraught with danger. With a requirement for mass starting of seven or eight aircraft the single Hucks Starter – a device mounted on a model T Ford chassis made take off a prolonged affair. Air bottle starting on the Bulldog proved immensely successful. An engine fitter on each aircraft would, on a signal from the watch tower, start up the engine – endeavouring to be first on the line to have power on. Ironically most aircraft deployed in tropical climates retained a hand winding inertia starting system which often left ground crews exhausted.

The practice of teaming a specific pilot and engine fitter to each aircraft was an admirable arrangement. As often as not the fitter flew with his aircraft on the assumption that a forced landing would require his attention, and so it often proved. It may be noted that it was considered an indignity to have one's aircraft grounded, be it due to damage, failure or lack of spares. It was a sad occasion when a crewman was posted to other duties or another unit, such was the comradeship developed.

Trenchard's inspiration was to institute a highly efficient technical engineering element to support envisaged air supremacy. The establishment of a School of Technical

Starting a Bulldog with an air bottle (W. G. Rogers)

Training enabled the expansion of the RAF throughout the 1930s to proceed unabated. He must have been justifiably proud of the results.

The scheme evolved around the acceptance of Grammar School educated boys from the age of fifteen and a half years to enlist as aircraft apprentices at No. 1 School of Technical Training, RAF Halton. Unfortunately Halton was not prepared for the magnitude of the task, so RAF Cranwell was selected to accommodate the surplus in selected trades. Examinations throughout the country were held to contest approximately 1000 vacancies annually.

With courses lasting three years this obviously resulted in a strength of approximately 3000 boys at anyone time. There was an embarrassing introduction – the Service medical examination –whereby a long line of recruits revealed their all. With an occasional probe from the MO's walking stick, Boy Service in the Royal Air Force began.

From a list of available trades, predominantly Metal Rigger and Aero Engine Fitters, we selected a trade which appealed to our inclination. Initial Workshop practice involved the use of general purpose hand tools followed by a course in Mechanical Transport, Metallurgy, Blacksmith procedures, Machine Shop, and a period on aerodrome duties. Engineering educational subjects accounted for two or three half days a week, with the remainder of the time devoted to Sport, Parades or General Duties.

Food was not good by any standards, and punishment was often unreasonable. Petty Offences (rightly) received infliction of petty restrictions, and no doubt instilled an appreciation of discipline. The punishment for more serious misdemeanours such as stealing has rarely been publicised and the public nowadays would be appalled. If the authorities found a boy guilty of a serious offence they would write to his parents requesting permission to deal with the matter as they saw fit. No particular punishment was specified and the parents invariably agreed. Saturday morning was a drill occasion, the parade would be suspended whilst a trestle table was erected in front of the assembled apprentices. The unfortunate culprit would then be marched on, stripped to the waist, and held across the table for a stipulated number of lashings, administered by a service policeman. The boy would then be put into a waiting ambulance to be taken to hospital. This happened perhaps six or seven times in the period 1931–33. Despite such treatment, one of Trenchard's aims, the fostering of a spirit of comradeship, was achieved quite overwhelmingly.

As the three year course progressed, more advanced training was given by staff, many of them civilian instructors. Such test jobs in the fitters shop included the making, from castings, of a bench vice; the manufacture of white metal bearings; and many metal interchanging test pieces calling for precise limit fitting. The stripping down of complete engines and their ancillary components prepared the apprentice for his future role, and it must be said that he reacted well to his responsibilities. Practical experience on aircraft was perhaps the highlight of the apprenticeship. To most a short flight in a Fairey IIIF or Siskin was an added bonus.

The meagre pay of three shillings (fifteen pence!) per week did little to supplement the dining room fixed diet, especially as it was also expected to finance the purchase of toothpaste, soap, stamps, shoe polish and other sundries. A parcel or postal order from home was greatly appreciated!

With satisfaction, some relief, and much enthusiastic anticipation of the future our training period terminated with the chance to express a preference of posting. Since most favoured certain prestigious squadrons, few of us were granted our choice.

The 'Passing Out Parade' completed the three year term of apprenticeship, producing the requisite skilled force so desperately needed in the '20s and '30s. Later entries into No. 1 School of Technical Training were to find continually improving conditions and revised syllabuses commensurate with development of new equipment.

One of the hazardous duties of the newly qualified airman was attending to one of several paraffin flares marking a runway for night landing. An aircraft side slipping or slightly off course when landing caused anxious moments as the airman disappeared at high speed into the darkness!

Some satisfaction was now expressed by the critics, as it became apparent that the Engineering Branch of the RAF had attained a creditable standing and should be able to meet any eventuality.

The North-West Frontier 1933

Air Chief Marshal Sir David Lee GBE CB

I graduated from Cranwell in July 1932 and spent a few months on Gordons with 35 (Bomber) Squadron.

In February 1933, along with eleven other pilot officers, I sailed from Liverpool on the SS *California*. It was a cold grey day and our last glimpse of England for nearly five years.

My new Squadron was equipped with Wapitis. This was a two seater biplane with an air-cooled 480 hp Bristol Jupiter engine with nine radial cylinders. This drove a very large 16 foot two bladed propeller. The propeller was much too large to be swung by hand except by a chain of at least three airman, the strongest of whom grasped the tip of the propeller. Other methods of starting were the 'bag and rope' which consisted of twenty feet of rope with a canvas bag at one end which fitted over the propeller tip. Two or more airman grasped at the rope and at a given signal rushed away, usually collapsing in a heap if the engine fired. Alternatively there were two low geared starting handles reached by perching precariously on the lower wing. If the engine was hot the pilot and his gunner could wear themselves out winding these handles until the engine condescended to fire. It was dangerous to use unskilled men to wind these handles. If the engine backfired, as it often did, the sweating terrified men could easily fall into the propeller.

One snag when flying was the oil which the radial engine threw on to the windscreen during a long trip. A clean piece of rag was kept in the map case so the pilot could reach round to the front and clean it.

The gunner stood in the rear cockpit in the middle of a rotatable Scarfe gun ring which formed the top of his cockpit. He was tethered to the floor by a thin wire cable. He had a small tip-up flap to sit on when he became tired after standing perhaps for hours in often bumpy conditions. There was no dual control but an emergency 'stick' was clipped onto the side which could be plugged into the controls where they passed through the rear cockpit. There was also an auxiliary throttle so that if the pilot was injured the gunner had at least a chance of getting back to base.

Because of its nose heaviness the Wapiti was seldom flown solo without lead and ballast weights. These were kept on a steel bar pushed through the rear of the fuselage to simulate the weight of a passenger.

Communications could justifiably be regarded as primitive. Within the aircraft the crew used Gosport tubing. This consisted of mouthpieces connected by rubber tubes to the earpieces of the other member of the crew. An air gunner, irritated with his pilot, could 'accidentally' put his mouthpiece into the slipstream and almost blow his pilot's

Swinging the propeller of an Avro 504 K (Cambridge University Air Squadron)

head off. The pilot could, of course, do the same so it was mutually understood that the tubing was kept firmly in the cockpits.

Between aircraft the only form of communication was 'Zogging'. This consisted of transmitting Morse code by arm signals over the side of the cockpit. A long downward sweep of the arm with fist clenched indicated a 'dash'; and a short downward sweep from the elbow a 'dot'. It was not difficult, but required both concentration and practice.

If a ground post wanted to pass a message to an aeroplane it used a 'Popham Panel'. This was a square patch of ground outlined by whitewashed stones. White canvas strips of various shapes and sizes were laid out in the square in accordance with a code contained in a handbook held by every post and carried by every pilot and air gunner. For example, two white strips, two circles and an arrow meant 'Being fired on from direction of arrow'.

Having read the message, the pilot would write an answer on his knee pad, enclose it in a message bag which was lead weighted and had a long, multi-coloured canvas streamer. His gunner would then drop this as close to the 'Popham Panel' as possible.

Wireless communication was possible between ground stations but was often blanketed by mountains. For this reason ground parties took with them baskets of carrier pigeons so that they could send urgent messages or appeals for help back to base.

Parachutes had only been brought into general use late in the Twenties and they were still regarded with suspicion. I had done a parachute packing course in the UK and this had included one jump. A Vickers Vimy bomber took off with me standing on a small platform far out on the lower wing. I was facing forward pressed against one of the struts. At 800 ft the pilot signalled that I should edge round the strut hanging on like grim death. As the slipstream tried to tear me off, I grasped the ripcord and awaited a second signal. This came and I tightened my grip with one hand and with the other pulled the ripcord. For a second nothing happened then I was torn from the platform as my parachute opened.

In India, all parachutes had to be drop tested from 1000 ft once a year. For this purpose two dummies had been made in the workshops. They were made of hard wood with truncated arms and legs which held the harness in place. Their weight was made up to 170 lb by lead sheeting. Face and hair had been painted on their heads by an unknown artist and they were known as 'Mutt' and 'Jeff' after a popular strip cartoon. 'Mutt' and 'Jeff' were dropped from the bomb racks and the 'chutes opened by means of static lines.

Second only to flying duties in India was the fulfilment of social duties. It was important for every newly arrived junior officer to call upon the married officers, certain civilians and the Officers of the local regiments. Each new officer brought with him some hundred expensively engraved visiting cards. Officers below the rank of flight lieutenant were identified as Mr —, Royal Air Force. The most important people to visit were clearly the Station Commander and Squadron and Flight Commanders with whom you would be working closely. Next came civil dignitaries such as the Chief of Police, magistrates etc. Lastly the Officers of the local British and Indian Army regiments. Even the most carefully selected list could involve up to 30 calls.

Timing was important. You must not arrive so early that recipients were still enjoying the afternoon siesta, nor so late that they were changing for cocktails or dinner. Correct dress was essential – a lounge suit, collar and tie and a Bombay Bowler. It was not wise to go on foot as you might have to walk two or three miles in the dust and heat. A bicycle was the usual means of transport. Each bungalow had a square box with a slot in the top for visiting cards and a notice 'Not At Home'. This was always used unless the resident appeared to intercept you. Two cards were left, one for the husband and the other for his wife. The next stage was completed when the husband returned your card. He did this by placing one of his cards in your letter rack in the mess. In addition he usually returned your two cards knowing how valuable they were to a young impecunious officer. The game finished when you returned the husband's card. A little work with India rubber and breadcrumbs made them fit to use again and a hundred cards could last a full five years' tour.

Young women in Britain still led rather sheltered lives in 1933 and did not have the career opportunities or the freedom to meet young men which they enjoy today. If a girl in her twenties had relatives or close friends serving in India, her parents would often send her out to stay with them during the winter. This extended holiday was intended to widen her education but if she was attracted to one of the thousands of young eligible bachelors on military service in India so much the better. The numerous young ladies, always carefully chaperoned, who regularly visited India were irreverently known as the 'Fishing Fleet'.

Early marriage in the services was however discouraged. In the RAF no marriage allowance was granted until an officer reached the age of thirty or became a Squadron Leader. Any young officer marrying thus suffered considerable hardship unless he had a large private income. The pay of a pilot officer in India was the equivalent of £400 per annum, slightly more than the home rate of pay. Single living in a Mess was cheap and it was possible to save about £100 per annum.

It was suspected that the financial difficulties faced by one young officer had a tragic outcome. On a routine firing exercise a young married officer aged twenty-three was making his second approach to the target at 200 ft when he suddenly shouted to his air gunner 'Bale out, bale out'. The gunner knew it would be dangerous but merely said 'Can you give me a bit more height?'. The pilot nodded and pulled up to 800 ft and the gunner jumped, breaking his ankle on landing. The plane, which seemed to be in perfect condition then crashed, killing the pilot. When his affairs were looked into it was found he was in deep financial trouble about which his young wife knew nothing. Nothing was ever proved but many felt he had taken this tragic way out of his difficulties.

Boxing night saw one of the grandest events in the social calendar – the 'PIFFER' Ball (Punjab Frontier Force Rifles). Our dress was blue and gold mess kit, boiled shirt and white gloves. We were however outshone by some of the famous Indian regiments. The prize was perhaps taken by Skinner's

Horse whose black uniform was so heavy and stiff with gold braid that it was said it could stand up by itself!

On arrival, an Indian orderly handed each of us a neat dance card with a pencil attached by a silken thread. There were twenty dances on the card and an interval in the middle. The problem was to complete the card in such a way as to fulfil one's duty to the hostess and senior wives, leave time for drinking at the bar with friends, and find an attractive companion for supper. The 'Fishing Fleet' was there in full force but still outnumbered by the young officers.

With the frontier and wild tribal territory just outside the door, all the magnificence might be compared with the Duchess of Richmond's Ball before Waterloo!

The frontier was controlled by a process known as peaceful penetration. This involved pushing roads into tribal territory followed by the guarantee of safety for travellers on those roads.

On my arrival in India I was mystified by the many tribesmen who insisted on walking in the middle of the road even when vehicles approached. I found that the reason was that the British Government guaranteed the safety of all travellers provided they were within three feet of the road. Those who strayed off the road were fair game in the continual blood feuding which was a feature of this troubled territory.

Rewards, often in the form of rifles and ammunition, were given to helpful and co-operative tribes whereas heavy fines were imposed on offenders. If, as often happened, fines were ignored, head men were warned that their villages, houses or crops would be destroyed by air action. If this warning was ignored leaflets were dropped informing villagers of the time of the attack and telling them to keep well clear. These final warnings were invariably heeded so that casualties from air attacks were negligible.

One of the few places where tribes and British mingled was the cinema. At the box-office were piled rifles, not Regulation but every one home made. Strange looking weapons tied together with wire, pieces of tin and even string.

The one rupee seats which we occupied were on a low balcony. Below us the first dozen rows of seats were separated from the rest of the auditorium by a barbed-wire entanglement. These were occupied by a noisy and extremely smelly collection of tribesmen many of whom had tramped miles to see the silent film. The rule was that all weapons had to be left at the door and as the cinema was a protected place they were happy to abide by this. The cheerful friendliness of the tribesmen was extraordinary. Far from being anti-British, hostility on the frontier was almost entirely inter-tribal and the main British role was protecting the weaker law-abiding majority against a minority of powerful lawless, tribal leaders.

One of our tasks was to help to keep the 'Tribal Directory' up to date. This listed the resources, population etc. of every known village in the frontier region. Many were virtually unapproachable by road either because they were inaccessible or because the inhabitants were hostile. These could only be surveyed or photographed from the air. One of my earliest surveys could well have been my last.

My passenger, Captain Kelly, wanted to survey six villages. Five were quite straightforward. The last was located in one of the narrow defiles leading into the mountains. I circled it at around 1000 ft but Kelly wanted me to go lower. I dropped to 500 feet and got into a position to allow him to take a photograph. I then turned my attention to what lay ahead for my next manoeuvre. My heart almost stopped as I realised that the defile was narrowing so rapidly that I could not turn round and I had not the power to climb. I shouted to Kelly to hold tight, pushed the throttle wide-open and dived to about 200 ft from the floor of the gorge. I kept as low to the left side as I dared. The Wapiti responded and I reached 120 mph before I pulled the nose up steeply, let the speed fall to 80 mph, put on full right rudder and brought her over in a semi-stalled turn. The nose dropped vertically and I let her fall like a stone until she had enough speed to pull out – now pointing down the gorge in a safe direction. The trick of the sunlight and deep shadow had misled me into thinking we had more room than was in fact the case.

In December 1935 when the Squadron had been re-equipped with Harts, we were told we were to fly to Singapore on the annual replacement exercise. This was a flight of 4000 miles and would take about six days with ten intermediate stops. There were no navigational aids and we would rely entirely on map reading. Maps of India were reasonably detailed but those of Burma, Siam and the Malay States very sketchy and far from accurate. The sheer quantity required posed enormous difficulties for the confined open cockpit of the Hart. We rejected the idea of quarter inch to the mile maps as this would have required some 30 yards of map. Even ten miles to one inch represented thirty-three feet. None of us was too happy about using this small scale. It was adequate for fine weather but not for finding an obscure landing ground in a monsoon! In the end we compromised. Each pilot had a set of the small-scale maps and each air gunner had large scale maps of the potentially difficult areas. Even the set of small-scale maps would be too much to handle in the open cockpit with an 80 mph slipstream tearing at them. We therefore made up books for each pilot. We marked the track as a black line on each map and cut some fifty miles on each side. The pieces were then pasted on to thin cards with eyelet holes at the top. Large rings through these made them into books of thirty-two pages. One simply map read each page in sequence, dropping the book between one's stomach and the control column. It seemed a hell of a long way to page 32 and around page 23 there was a page with nothing but sea across which I had to map read for about half-an-hour. However even I ought to be able to hit the coast of Burma! In the event everyone made it safely.

After three years and eight months I was accepted for training as a Flying Instructor. All movement of Service personnel before World War II was by sea and I returned on His Majesty's Transport *Somerset*. I shared a cabin 8 ft by 6 ft with three Hussar subalterns. Only one person could dress, undress or change at a time and we had to dine in mess kit every night. We worked out a complicated and exact roster which often necessitated one person starting to change for dinner at 5.30 p.m. Toilet facilities included a chamber pot stored in a cabinet!

The Officers' Mess Heliopolis 1934
Group Captain F. C. Richardson CBE

There were no married quarters on the camp, the few officers with wives and families in tow had to make do with somewhat indifferent furnished flats hired in near-by private apartment blocks. The families of the other ranks were conspicuously absent. Consequently social activities centred on the messes which all had well-tended gardens, wide verandahs and cool stone floors, easy to wash and sweep. The anterooms in the messes and in the NAAFI Institute had been built with coal fireplaces against the cold winter nights; but all other areas were left to freeze.

Life in the officers' mess was very tolerable. We each had a large cool room in one of the two-storey blocks flanking the mess proper, with its anteroom, dining room, ladies room, billiard room and library. The catering was first-class, our private rooms comfortable, the company amusing and friendly. As there was no escape till we were thirty and free to marry, or, even less likely, squadron leaders with marriage allowances, the Mess was our only haven and rest.

Over the door of our anteroom, displayed in a glass case, was a silver-gilt plaque which had been presented some years earlier to No. 216 Squadron by a grateful Spaniard to record the rescue of his son from the desert. On a long refectory dining table stood the two squadrons' sporting trophies together with 2 ft long solid silver replicas of a Victoria and, in 1936, a Valentia, presented by Vickers. Similar scale versions of an Armstrong Whitworth Atlas and a Hawker Audax in solid silver belonging to No. 208 Squadron completed the display.

If not detailed for flying, our days began at 05.30 hrs with a cuppa, a shave and shower, followed by a five minute walk across the sand to No. 216's flight offices. We studied manuals, practised Morse code and watched maintenance being done to our aircraft, thus getting to know the erks and especially our own crew.

It would soon be 08.00 hrs and time for a bite back in the Mess, where a substantial English breakfast awaited, served by self-effacing, bare-footed, white-uniformed native staff, the best of whom were Berberines from Upper Egypt.

The native servants contributed greatly to our personal contentment. Faithful, hard working, long-suffering and efficient, they were delightfully simple and easy to amuse. No account of mess life would be complete without paying them sincere compliments.

There was a harsh mess rule that if any servant smelled of garlic – a staple item of ethnic diet – he was in danger of dismissal. Abomination of that marvellous but highly pungent vegetable has softened with the passing years, but in 1934 it was a fiercely upheld British prejudice.

We lived under the benign discipline of 'Henry' Ford, the suave senior Flight Lieutenant PMC. Henry was a born master of ceremonies to whom one spoke at the breakfast table only at grave personal peril. Silence at such an unspeakable hour was his golden rule – and not a bad one either.

Much of our spare time was spent in Cairo. If, for lack of cash, we had not 'warned out', we had to rush back to camp for a rapid change into dinner jacket, in time to greet the senior officer present in the anteroom and to take a glass of sherry before dinner was announced. Smoking was not allowed before dinner so as to preserve our palates for food, really quite a good rule; but in the days when smoking was so much in vogue it seemed irksome.

Fairy 111Fs of 45 Squadron over the Pyramids (AHB)

Every fourth Friday, a guest night was held to return hospitality and to entertain Service and civilian contacts. They were all-male affairs and an excuse for high jinks after dinner wearing expensive, uncomfortable tropical mess kit, comprising half-wellingtons, close-fitting white 'overalls' (i.e. stirrup trousers), a white 'bum-freezer' jacket, blue silk cummerbund, dress shirt with starched front, starched wing collar, starched cuffs, gold studs, cuff links and silk bow tie.

The horseplay was good-humoured and usually physically demanding. 'High cockaloram' required an anchorman standing with his back to the wall, facing two others in line and who bent down from the waist, braced against the others hips. The opposing side had to jump one by one on top of the two bent backs, piling higher and higher until they all toppled over – the winning side made the highest heap before collapsing. A great trial of strength was to try to go round the anteroom hanging on by fingertips from the picture rail – very few could manage to turn the first corner.

In 'Are you there, Moriarty?' two blindfold opponents lay face down on the floor holding each other's left hand and taking turns to ask the question. Then, armed with a roll of newspaper in the free hand, the questioner tried to whack the place from whence the reply had come. Having shouted

'Yes!' the player replying twisted away from the oncoming blow. In one spirited encounter, someone's hand was accidentally cut on a broken tumbler. Help was instantly available in the shape of a rather inebriated MO and the patient was marched off to sick quarters to be stitched up. Weeks later, a sizeable of chunk of glass emerged from the scar.

Another rough house 'game' involved our cotton dress shirts being torn from our backs without their being unbuttoned. A certain Flight Lieutenant who had 'married money' was nearly strangled when his shirt refused to tear – it had been made of silk. When we were exhausted, those still in the mood gathered round a budding pianist of whom there always seemed to be plenty. Sometimes I dug out the old clarinet I had played in my youth. There followed a rollicking singsong of mostly bawdy but tuneful ditties, the folklore of generations of sex starved Anglo-Saxons, many from WWI and some attributable to the Royal Flying Corps.

We had easy access to alcohol, but there was an absolutely golden rule: NO DRINKING BEFORE FLYING. Despite popular belief, I never once saw this ukase deliberately transgressed.

Things were always lively if Adjutant Paddy, Flight Lieutenant the Earl of Bandon was around. Known as the 'Abandoned Earl', he was always up to mischief. In his early thirties, Paddy, then a round-faced, dark-haired, urbane, married Flight Lieutenant with twinkling brown eyes, eventually reached the dizzy rank of Air Chief Marshal. A more amusing comrade would be very hard to imagine and he was up to every prank.

One winter guest night, when a welcoming fire was burning in the anteroom grate and the jollity had reached its peak, Paddy climbed unseen to the flat roof and dropped a red smoke candle down the chimney. The effect was spectacular, taking several fire extinguishers to smother the choking fumes: nobody was hurt – we were only covered in soot!

While our CO was away on home leave for a month, Paddy had a fleeting offer of an empty seat in an Imperial Airways flying boat to Marseilles, from where he could catch a train and be in the RAF Club the next day. The journey normally took a week to ten days and for this reason home leave was rigidly rationed.

This was a chance in a million, to be seized with both hands. Quickly appointing a stand-in to 'hold the fort' for a few days, he was happily ensconced at the Long Bar on the following morning, busily planning details for his stolen long week-end, when in walked Wing Commander Bill Mackey who was amazed to see the adjutant he thought he had left behind on duty in Heliopolis. Paddy was aghast to see his CO and had to catch the next flight back to Cairo, setting himself back a pretty penny.

60 Squadron in India 1936–1938

Group Captain F. L. Newall

In 1936 Pilot Officer Newall went out to India to join 60 Squadron based at Kohat near the northern border of what is now Pakistan and close to the Afghan border. His parents kept all his letters and Group Captain Newall kindly gave permission for the following brief extracts to be included in this book.

60 Bomber Squadron
Royal Air Force
Kohat

April 1936—Arrived Bombay. Our Mess is almost palatial and has swimming bath and tennis and squash courts. Our rooms are very high and airy with dressing room and bathroom behind. We fly very antiquated machines but the work is more interesting than at home. Kohat is very attractive. There is an 18-hole golf course and everyone plays there as there isn't much else to do. The aerodrome is outside the cantonment. We go out at 8.30 and come back at 1.30 for lunch. The rest of the day is free. Tea is at 4.30 and dinner at 8.30 and supper anytime before 10. Yesterday I went on a picnic with my Flight Commander and other married families. It was great fun. Dance on Wednesday. I dined with my Flight Commander. I think there has been a party every day.

My bearer has gone to Karachi and has called in his brother to look after me. I pay him Rs 30 per month plus Rs 4½ for wood to heat water. I pay the 'dhobie' Rs 7 per month for as much laundry as I like. Messing is over 4 shillings and does not include tea. It isn't awfully good.

June 1936—Rather a dull week as I only flew on Friday and didn't really do anything except go to the cinema and a bathing party at the Club. I shall try to get more flying. Went to Club. They had the Piffers Band. Piffer means Punjabi Frontier Force Rifles. It's amazing how the Services carry on in any state of efficiency in India. We have five aircraft in the flight, only three are fully equipped.

Very sticky – hardly a breath of air – didn't sleep much. Won't fly again until August.

(The Squadron now went to the hills for the hot season.)

July 1936 Murree Hills—Rather like September in Scotland. Paths are rough and very hard walking. My legs are aching. There is no electric light. We have to double up in very small rooms. One has to have a pass to go out at night. They don't work us officers very hard. We had an earthquake here last Monday. Funny sort of feeling. Also had rain for 48 hours. Jackals come round at night and the doctor had one in his quarters. We only do about 2 hours' work here and a bit of drill. The laundry is most primitive. They swing the wet garment around their heads and down onto a concrete slab with sharp edges.

Wapiti of 60 Squadron in India (AHB)

August 1936—We shall be getting new aircraft instead of Wapitis as they can't get any more Wop spares -either Vickers Wellesley or Bristol Blenheim. (*When he left 2 years later the Squadron still had Wapitis!*) My troops have behaved very well but some have gone broke and come to me. I've had to lend about Rs 100. I believe they are practising bombing very hard at Kohat as they may have to bomb a village only 500 yards from the Afghan border.

September 1936 Kohat—I suppose you never got my last letter owing to the flying boat sinking. I did my first night flying. Next week I shall do dusk to dark. It was really rather nice and not very frightening. You have a flare path in the direction of the wind. The flares give no light really but as you approach, losing height, you see the distance between them decreasing and you can tell when you are near the ground. My room tonight is at 95 degrees. We slept on the verandah and got bitten by bed bugs.

We have rumours of war. Two Flights from here are doing a demonstration over an old brigand who has dug himself in 500 yards from the frontier. He was given 'til Tuesday to hand himself over. If he doesn't they will bomb him. Went over to Kohar Pass Rifle Factory in Tribal Territory. It is very primitive – trigger guards and breech blocks are forged from old railway rails. They cost about Rs 30 but if there is a war Rs 100.

Two men were shot last night just on the road so it comes under Government jurisdiction. The killers will be punished if they are found or the tribe will be fined about Rs 1000. The tribe concerned have agreed to keep the peace for 2½ months for a Rs 4000 security. Then I suppose the family of the dead will set out to get the killer's family. These blood feuds go on the whole time between villages only half a mile apart. They set no store on life at all. Their bullets are awful looking things. Dum Dums aren't in it. We met two killers on the road. This is neutral ground and they can walk on it without getting shot at. That brigand fellow did a bunk into Afghanistan at the last moment.

I did survey work – it was about a 20 mile run and meant keeping the aircraft absolutely straight and level. Actually we drifted off and ended about 2 miles south. As they are doing the whole area it didn't matter much. Pilot and Air Gunner killed on firing range, why no-one knows. Early Wednesday one of our Flight Lieutenants died. Went into hospital with what they said was sand-fly fever and he was becoming paralysed from the feet. No one has any confidence in these hospitals in India. Either you never come out or you get other things on top of what you already have.

January 1937—We did a search exercise which was a fiasco. We all got separated and didn't find the 'lost' aircraft although we did fly over it twice! Thank you for your airmail which arrived after crashing and killing the pilot. One letter arrived covered in blood!

April 1937—Trouble in Waziristan getting worse and worse. They are attacking outposts and stations. Two posts have to be supplied from the air by parachute. There's not much doing except the war still.

June 1937—The war is over for us though the army is still being sniped. A Flight Sergeant shot himself while I was away, otherwise nothing interesting.

July 1937—Friday they were bombing the village near Rajmah and I went over on Saturday. All our bombs were hits except one but we didn't do much damage. Its a complete waste of time and money. They would burn it themselves with pleasure if we paid them about 10 chips.

August 1937—3 pilots and aircraft are going down to Manzai unless some Hindus are released.

The Bhittanis have been raiding a lot lately. If operations start tomorrow my Flight and a Flight from 27 are going to crack in and give them hell. Of course they dropped messages a week ago telling them to return the hostages.

September 1937—They bombed for 3 days, then let up. Apparently the Bhittanis took very little notice of our leaflets. There's hardly anything in the Indian papers about the war.

October 1937—The Indian troops at Sarwekai were shot up badly by tribesmen as they were going out for drill.

(*The Squadron now left on detachment to Singapore*)

January 1938 Seletar, Singapore—Arrived in Squadron formation and landed one after the other. It's a huge aerodrome. We are the first Wapiti Squadron to land complete. This is a huge station and a Mess which reminds me of a Hotel Splendide. There's h and c in all rooms and all mod cons.

February 1938—Our Squadron Leader went back to India with the AOC. The aeroplane they were going in is the old Willingdon's machine 'Star of India'. Just before they started a crane collided with it and knocked part of the wing off. All the wood inside was eaten by bugs and there was dry rot.

Looked at big 15″ battery. Our troops go back tomorrow by the Iraq troop carrier squadron. One of their officers was found to have taken a lot of photos of secret things. Their intelligence must be pretty good as he had already taken the photos to a Jap for developing.

March 1938 Kohat—The war is on again. 10 aircraft from here and 10 from Risalpur are going to Miramshah tomorrow.

April 1938—Operations started again. It was all very sudden as the Scouts bumped into about 250 and lost a British Officer. 12 aircraft are up there blockading and bombing.

They averaged about 15 tons of bombs dropped per day and did a lot of damage.

A good time was had by all. Amusing party at the Club. Two of the married women went 'scats' and jumped in the bath in evening dress!

May 1938—Chaps are still at Miramshah – very little to do. They are not using bombs, only gun ammo and can only fire on people in the fields but not if they are walking along the roads. Pretty concentrated bombing this week on the largest village in Maddakhel – about the size of Presteigne. Cholera has broken out all over India.

June 1938—I've been dicing with death again but it was too dark and I hadn't much idea where I was so I may have dropped a bomb in Afghanistan thereby causing a situation! Some bright spark thought it would be a good idea to do night operations, not thinking that none of the chaps had had a good look at the area by day. It's right on the border and not too big. I went off with 12 20 lb bombs and two parachute flares. Tried to follow the Tochi River, rather lost myself, then crossed it at right angles. Got into some cloud. Dropped one parachute flare – none the wiser – so flew back and tried to pick up some landmark. Cloud came up, dropped another flare and came home. We used the new floodlights for landing for the first time in India instead of the paraffin flares.

July 1938—We shan't have much to do. The Mada Khel have come in and we've settled Sharni Pir's hash. 3 aircraft from 20 Squadron caught a very large number of his men and killed so many that they immediately dispersed and he gave himself up.

We had a terrific flap on Saturday – 1500 tribesmen marching to attack the Khot-Bann road. Would we please go and see if we could find them. I waffled around for 2 hours. All I saw were 3 old women cutting grass. Though it was difficult country 1500 men couldn't hide themselves!

The Army advanced to try to get to Ipi's 'Cathedral'. They were to support the Scouts. Obviously Ipi could be miles away by that time. They got nowhere near the objective and didn't all get back to camp. If it hadn't been for the Army Co-operation squadron who knocked hell out of the enemy they would have been in a worse mess. The Army is now retiring and we bomber boys take over the area from Monday. If the idea was to capture Ipi it's damn silly to advance with 5000 troops. I've still seen no-one in our area and have great difficulty in deciding where to drop my bombs. After 3 days' foul weather we managed to bomb the village and stopped yesterday. The blokes brought their hostages in and came to terms.

October 1938—You must have a hell of time at home. A huge crowd listens around the Club wireless literally with bated breath. Anyhow one good thing it's done is to make all the RAF officers in Kohat pay their bills!

November 1938...only four more days. Then home!

THE GOLDEN AGE OF FLYING 1930–1938

From 1919 to 1934 the quality of the RAF's fighting equipment steadily deteriorated. By the time Trenchard left in 1929 its aircraft were largely unchanged from those at the end of World War I. Fighters were slow; guns were of World War I design. Techniques such as navigation were completely ignored. There were few tactical lectures and no attempt at instrument flying. For the young, however, flying was the great new adventure.

The Royal Air Force of the early thirties has been described as agreeably amateur and the best flying club in the world. The brightly painted Gamecocks of Fighter Command were only a few miles per hour faster than the SE 5s some 15 years earlier. They were, however, beautiful to handle and, in the rare event of an engine failure, could safely land on a soccer pitch. Flying training consisted largely of pretty aerobatics and tight formation flying.

The Hendon Air Displays

Air Marshal Sir Frederick Sowrey KCB CBE AFC

The first Royal Air Force Aerial Pageant at Hendon in 1920 was certainly spectacular, and the public flocked to see the flying service which had fought so effectively in 1918. The air battles of the western front took place above the warring ground forces and the average civilian had only a hazy idea of their pattern. However, the Zeppelin and Gotha raids on this country had put ordinary citizens in the front line and many wanted to see their Air Force at close quarters.

Military Tattoos or demonstrations of martial skills are a way of showing a nation the calibre of its ground forces. Warships in Fleet Reviews, in harbour or alongside on Navy Days are impressive. The Royal Tournament started in the nineteenth century featuring the Army and Navy. It was an essential part of the London season, bringing both services into the heart of the capital with musical rides, massed bands, and the Naval field gun competition. It was important therefore for the two year old Royal Air Force, whose existence was increasingly under threat, to be seen to be an essential part of the defence of the Empire. The relief and celebration of the War's end spilled over into the social scene and the new Service was in vogue with its exciting and innovating command of the new medium – the air. Certainly the popular press saw it that way as 40,000 flocked to Hendon on a sunny summer's day in 1920. So great was the traffic jam that even Winston Churchill left his car and walked.

Hawker Fury IIs of 25 Squadron (AHB)

Things were easier by 1923 when the tube reached Hendon. A daily paper wrote: 'A brilliant pageant, the crowds, cars, chairs, white painted railings and marquees, flags, lovely women in frocks that would look theatrical in any other setting than Ascot, escorted by handsome sun-tanned officers in their blue uniforms.'

From the beginning, the importance to the Service of the Hendon Air Displays (as they became known) was recognised at every level. It was realised that this was the RAF's public showpiece and that it must portray a blend of showmanship, colour, spectacle and high professionalism.

From the start the Displays had a charitable aim and were in aid of the RAF Memorial Fund, which in 1933 became the RAF Benevolent Fund.

Pageants have traditionally told a story and this was an element in every annual display in the form of a 'set piece'. Air drill and formation flying showed the precision of the new Royal Air Force, and aerobatics the skill of its pilots. Some form of competitive event enabled spectators to pick the favourite and bands played the popular numbers of the day.

The 1920 pageant had many reminders of wartime and saw the first appearance of that annual favourite, the attack on the kite balloon by the current front-line squadron fighters. The dummy Observer – cheerfully known as Major Sandbags – would leave by parachute and the balloon would satisfactorily fall in flames.

A feature in 1922 was 'sky writing' and the use of coloured smoke to signal to other aircraft and aerodromes. The set piece that year featured the destruction of an armed merchant cruiser, involving reconnaissance, a fighter attack to silence the gun crew and torpedo bombers to administer the *coup de grace*.

In the 1924 set piece an aircraft landed near a hostile fort and was in danger of being destroyed. It was saved by a passing RAF armoured car. An aircraft landed with spares, the fort was attacked with bombs and guns and the repaired aircraft took off with all returning safely. Three bands played that year – the Central Band from Uxbridge, Cranwell, and the Central Flying School. A Dinner Dance that night at the London Country Club in aid of the RAF Memorial Fund cost one guinea (or £1.05), including transport, and specified 'evening dress only'.

The complicated 1930 set piece involved a steamer in foreign waters carrying civil aircraft and ammunition. This was seized by pirates who assembled the aircraft to fly their 'booty' to receivers around the world. The Royal Air Force shot down the aircraft and disabled the pirates on the ground, destroyed their bungalow and landed an organised force of local planters who took prisoners and recovered the loot.

Hendon set-piece 1930 (AHB)

A 'Tortoise' Race in 1932 must have made knowledgeable spectators hold their breath as four Tiger Moths flew as slowly as possible without losing height or dropping out of the sky.

Many spectators made the annual pilgrimage to Hendon year after year.

In 1933 a spectacular formation of Hawker Furies linked by cables carried out 'Tied Together Drill' which anticipated to-day's formation aerobatics. The Furies landed in threes still tied together.

At the 1934 display HRH the Prince of Wales arrived in a Vickers Viastra. Air-to-air refuelling, then in its infancy, was demonstrated by a Vickers Virginia tanker refuelling a Westland Wapiti. That year introduced a new item. The aerodrome became a skittle alley with Vickers Virginias dropping small bombs on monster skittles. Even as a schoolboy I was surprised by the length of time it took for a skittle to fall after the aircraft had bombed. Presumably teams of aircraftsmen were pulling hard on ropes out of sight!

In 1936 Central Flying School flew their Avro Tutors inverted with the top wings coloured red so that spectators could see which way up they were. The parade of aircraft included the historical and the curious. The past was portrayed by the Antoinette of 1909, a Wright biplane, Bleriot, Sopwith Camel and Triplane, SE 5a and Bristol Fighter. The curious was represented by the tailless Pterodactyl.

The pressures to rearm could be seen in the latest prototypes on show – the Hawker Hurricane and the Supermarine Spitfire, Fairey Battle, Bristol 142, Vickers Wellington, Westland Lysander and the Armstrong Whitworth Whitley.

The last display in 1937 showed the continuation of expansion with prototypes of the Airspeed Oxford, Hawker Henley and Blackburn divebomber (the Skua). The afternoon started with a massed flypast of 250 aircraft including Avro Ansons and Gloster Gladiators and must have been an impressive sight. In the dress rehearsal the previous day someone pressed the 'destruct' button for the kite balloon. This delighted the school children who normally had to imagine it descending in flames. The final set piece was an attack on a small port handling foodstuffs by bombers, dive bombers and torpedo bombers which destroyed the warehouses and shattered the lock gates, whilst defensive fighters scrambled to attack the fighter escort.

Informative and well illustrated programmes of the eighteen displays give an excellent insight into the development and attitudes of an Air Force, fairly static in the 1920s and then gradually accelerating towards the massive expansion and rearmament of the late 1930s.

The two Empire Air Days before the outbreak of war were held country wide on RAF stations and enabled a much wider cross section of the population to see their air force.

A Torpedo Squadron in 1935

Air Vice-Marshal E. L. Colbeck-Welch CB OBE DFC

After completing the 1933/34 one year course at No. 5 Flying Training School, four of us were posted to RAF Donibristle, to join No. 22 (Torpedo-Bomber) Squadron, the only shore-based squadron of its kind in the home RAF. There were two similar squadrons in Singapore – Nos 100 and 36. We had each completed some 130 hours flying.

Donibristle was sited in parkland on the north coast of the Firth of Forth between Aberdour and Inverkeithing with views of Edinburgh and the Forth Bridge. It had a very small grass airfield tilted from north-east to south-west. The operating strip ran east and west and had a wooded ridge at the west end. On arriving we thought that it was a delightful place but wondered where the air field was. Surely not that grass slope? But it was!

Ours was the only Squadron based there, though the station was regularly host to disembarked aircraft carrier squadrons. These were occasions for much jollification.

The Vickers Vildebeest biplane with which No. 22 Sqn was equipped was a large single-engined aircraft of somewhat daunting aspect to new boys who had been trained on much smaller Avro 540 Ns and Bristol Bulldogs. The wing span was just under 50 feet, length 37 feet and height 18 feet. Power was provided by a Bristol Pegasus of 660 hp driving a large wooden propeller, apparently very slowly. The pilot's open cockpit was just forward of the leading edge of the upper mainplane giving an uninterrupted view, ideal for the role. The after cockpit with its ring-mounted Lewis gun was about ten feet from the pilot's position but accessible to it through a corridor with a sliding hatch just behind the pilot. Beyond this standing place, and under the cockpit floor, was the bomb aiming platform with its bombsight, hatch and inverted folding windscreen. With the hatch open, engine fumes were a powerful emetic.

Bomb loads varied from a maximum of two 550 pounders to practice bombs of 20 lb. All were carried on racks beneath the lower mainplanes. Our main weapon, the Whitehead 18″ diameter torpedo, was carried on a crutch between the struts of the split undercarriage. Access for setting depth and range was through the floor of the corridor on to the top of the weapon using long keys. Apart from a short torpedo course at Portsmouth, courtesy of the Royal Navy, all this was new and unfamiliar. So far we had only been taught to fly. There had been no operational training as understood today. All this was to come in the squadron.

Getting to know the aircraft came first. This involved dual instruction given mainly by Flight Commanders who, sitting waist high in the after cockpit, looked as if they were sitting in a bath. This detracted a little from their dignity and certainly did not improve their temper .

When we were judged ready we assembled at Turnhouse, a larger and therefore safer airfield, to be sent off on our first solo followed by practice circuits and bumps. After that and back at base there were several hours of solo flying before we were allowed to carry a crew. These would normally be airmen, none higher than corporal, who were keen volunteers and who got a few pence per day extra for their skills in the air additional to those of their basic trades.

Incidentally, our pay as Pilot Officers was about £17 per month. This was later reduced, along with the pay of everyone else, in the recession of those times.

We found our Vildebeests to be most tractable and forgiving, well suited to cope with the limitations of the airfield and the shortcomings of inexperienced pilots. And so our training to the required operational standards began.

The flying, accompanied by lectures and written exams, included cross-country navigation, formation flying, night flying, aerial photography, air firing, bombing, instrument and cloud flying, and practice with our primitive crackling R/T. We also practised high altitude flying and with no oxygen this meant 15,000 feet! To reach this took twenty-two minutes without a torpedo and thirty-nine and a half minutes fully loaded.

In addition, and most importantly, was torpedo dropping. These weapons were out of their element in air and not adapted to being flung from high above the water and at excess speed. So we had to conform to strict limits. Speed was easy to adjust to eighty or so knots. We needed much practice however to achieve the required height of some thirty feet above the water. This required hours of low flying over the sea leading to drops with dummy torpedoes, each drop being photographed for analysis.

The next stage was drops with runner torpedoes, the real thing except that, out of consideration for the target ships, they had cork collision heads rather than H.E. Concurrently we were learning and practising torpedo attack tactics often against naval ships who obligingly acted as sitting ducks to begin with and later took evasive action.

Torpedoes, being exceedingly expensive, had to be recovered from the sea and returned to the torpedo workshops at Donibristle for servicing and re-use. Recovery was done by the NCOs and aircraftmen of a small marine craft section at Inverkeithing. Here there was a small self contained hutted camp, a jetty with a railway linking the camp and Donibristle. The torpedoes were hauled by a train of adapted flat trucks pulled – or pushed – by a charming 0–4–0 steam locomotive called primly 'RAF No.1'. The original 'Thomas', perhaps.

The sea-going establishment included four 'Power Boat' high speed launches, two splendid long-funnelled naval pinnaces converted to diesel, and a small trawler.

Vickers Vildebeest dropping torpedo (AHB)

Navigation over land had been nominally by compass although the railway lines were much more useful. There was no Air Traffic Control. Navigation over the sea was much more challenging and was a regular feature of our training. It involved, amongst other antique measures, finding the wind speed and direction by taking back bearings on yellow dye sea markers dropped from the aircraft. All seemed to work well; at any rate no one was lost at sea.

After many months we had worked ourselves up to operational standards and had proved this by results locally and on detachment for exercises with the Home Fleet. One such trial involved bombing the ancient warship HMS *Iron Duke* to test its vulnerability. As the attack was made with twenty lb practice bombs the effect was NIL. We hoped that no false conclusions were drawn from this.

In August 1935, the squadron was suddenly warned for imminent duty overseas. This turned out to be Malta and the cause of the general flap was Mussolini's invasion of Abyssinia. We flew our aircraft to the Packing Depot at Sealand where they were stripped down to fuselage and wheels and then, along with their wings and other parts, packed like giant toys into huge packing cases for shipment to Malta.

We, with personnel from other units, were transported out there in luxury in the 17,000 ton liner, RMS *Caledonia*, which had been taken over for the purpose.

Our aircraft arrived in Malta shortly after us and were landed in their boxes at the flying-boat base at Kalafrana. Here they were unpacked and towed, wingless and tail first, up the hill to our new base at Hal Far. Soon the squadron was once more in full flying trim ready for whatever might come. In the event, the year we spent in Malta was pretty much the same so far as training was concerned, although the superb weather and the presence in great strength of the Royal Navy gave us more opportunities.

We shared the station at Hal Far with No. 74 Fighter Squadron which was equipped with Hawker Demon two-seater biplanes. This collection was referred to by Mussolini in one of his bombastic speeches as 'those flying bird-cages'. There were a lot of belligerent words from the Italian radio but no belligerent action against us. Pity really, as it might have stopped the much worse events that were to come.

No need to digress upon the social life in Malta. It was superb as were all the facilities for sport and entertainment. All was highly enjoyable – and memorable.

After about a year and no war, but with a great deal of experience, we returned to our comfortable home at Donibristle. There we formed, amoeba-like, a second unit, No. 42 (T-B) Squadron. This was equipped with the Mk IV Vildebeest which had the Perseus sleeve-valve engine giving a better performance. Despite this unfair advantage over us, the parent, the two squadrons got on very well together and benefited from the rivalry.

The original four in this account had now been about three years with No. 22 Squadron and it was time for postings. By now we had logged nearly 600 hours. Two went to the Central Flying School to train as flying instructors, one went to the Long Range Development Flight and was killed. The fourth went to the Engineering College at Henlow to become a specialist engineer officer.

The two squadrons soldiered on with Vildebeests well into the first year of the war but eventually were re-equipped with twin-engined Beaufort torpedo-bombers, a derivative of the Blenheim. Thus they left the biplane age, albeit a little late, but soon enough to earn fame in their slogging role in Coastal Command, sinking many enemy ships, bombing U boat pens and other maritime targets. It was a hard war for them, and bravely fought.

For the Squadrons in the Far East it was an even more daunting war. Vildebeests flying at 80 knots bravely attacked the Japanese invasion fleets off Singapore. Casualties were heavy in such an unequal contest.

(*An account of this campaign is given in* The Endau Raid 1942 *Ed.*)

LAST MINUTE PREPARATIONS 1935–1939

In 1934 Prime Minister Baldwin had stated that the British Government was determined 'in no conditions to accept any position of inferiority with regard to what Air Force may be raised in Germany in the future'.

The plan of air rearmament adopted was however little more than a facade. When war broke out in 1939 the Home Defence Air Force was still far inferior in size to the Luftwaffe. Some steps were nevertheless taken which slowly began to redress the balance.

Two monoplane fighter prototypes first flew in 1935 and 1936. These were the Hurricane and the Spitfire, the test flights of which are graphically described by Group Captain Wroath. The Air Ministry issued production orders straight from these prototypes.

An Air Staff specification in 1936 sought to create the first true strategic bombers with adequate range and bomb load and good defence capability.

Development of radar began in 1935.

Group Captain Richardson explains the belated attempts to introduce pilots to elementary navigation and Richard Gething describes the problems which faced the handful of more experienced crews.

The Volunteer Reserve was formed in 1936 and Air Commodore Berry's account highlights the importance of the contribution it made.

From 1938, aircraft production increased and by 1939 the rate of production of combat aircraft nearly equalled that of Germany. Numerically, of course, the RAF remained much weaker than the *Luftwaffe*.

Spinning at Martlesham in the 1930s

Group Captain S. Wroath CBE AFC

I joined as an aircraft apprentice at Halton and on completing my course was posted to 58 Squadron at Worthy Down. Accepted for training as an NCO pilot, I passed out from 3 FTS at Grantham and was sent to 1 Squadron, flying the Hawker Fury Mk. 1. Whilst there I was selected for the synchronised aerobatic team and this led to a posting to Martlesham where I joined 'A' Flight as one of their three test pilots. Our task was to test fighters and training aircraft.

Martlesham Heath test pilots were selected from the RAF. They received no special training for their role. However, they flew many different types of aeroplane. They built up their technical knowledge by 'On-the-job-learning', and flying many different types of monoplane broadened their outlook and developed their judgement. Whilst no less skilled, and benefiting from flying a wide range of aeroplanes from all the firms, most were, however, less experienced as test pilots than their civilian counterparts whose permanent job it was to carry out experimental and development testing on their firms' aeroplanes.

Most of the aeroplanes they tested were prototypes, some owned by the Air Ministry and others by contractors. Martlesham pilots were well aware of the crucial value of a prototype. Their task was essentially to verify what the contractor's test pilot had reported. A prototype was brought to Martlesham with a flight test report. These were of variable quality and, depending on past experience, many were read with some scepticism. Martlesham pilots never knowingly exceeded limits declared by the contractor's test pilots who had done the development flying. Much was left to the individual test pilot. As with any test pilot, he felt obliged to do his utmost to bring the evidence back – preferably to Martlesham, and without damage.

I regard myself as having been exceptionally fortunate to have been a test pilot at Martlesham in those years. I was eager to take on any task and this quickly built up my experience. In the spring of 1936 I was heavily involved in the acceptance testing on both the Hurricane prototype and on the Spitfire prototype at Martlesham after, of course, the Hawker and Supermarine test pilots respectively had completed the early development flying.

Hurricane Mk 1 (AHB)

My first flight in the Hurricane was cut short after twenty minutes by an engine failure and resulted in a 'Dead Stick' landing on the aerodrome – the first of several, for the early Merlin engines were extremely unreliable. I recall that both prototypes – with stub exhausts – were noisy. The early Merlin engine had a maximum boost pressure of only +6 lb, and with the wide blade, coarse pitch wooden 'Watts' propeller it was only possible to get 1900 out of the permitted maximum of 3000 rpm on take off. Consequently both that and the initial climb were leisurely. Only when the speed was much higher could the maximum 3000 rpm, and consequently full power, be obtained.

The Martlesham pilots had to work out their own techniques for flying the Hurricane and Spitfire. Flaps were fitted because without them the landing approach would have been flat and fast. With them down it was little faster and much steeper than on biplanes. Out went the virtually obligatory glide approach, when the ethos was that use of engine to 'stretch a glide' was an admission of lack of skill and judgement; one 'motored' the monoplane in with its flaps fully down. Aerobatics had to be done at faster speeds. Monoplanes tended to drop a wing at the stall and so aerobatics, where low airspeeds were likely (on top of a loop for instance), were best completed without allowing the aeroplane to stall. Entry speeds used were considerably faster.

The Hurricane's stability on all axes was more or less neutral. For a fighter that was no bad thing, even though it did need flying all the time. The Hurricane's flight envelope was significantly larger than that of its predecessors, and control forces and effectiveness at indicated airspeeds well over 300 mph had to be assessed. On the prototype the ailerons and much of the wings were fabric covered, and at high speeds they ballooned out. Whilst the aileron controls became progressively heavier above 300 mph, it was not necessary to modify them – in those days ailerons were expected to get heavy at high speeds. Indeed at that time the Martlesham pilots had no yardstick against which to assess the handling qualities of the Hurricane and Spitfire other than by comparison with their biplane predecessors. We quickly appreciated that the transition to flying (the then) sophisticated monoplanes should not present a problem to the service.

Some of the monoplane fighter prototypes produced to a specification before that for the Hurricane had serious difficulties in spin recovery, and some contractors' test pilots thought that such aeroplanes should not be spun deliberately. However Air Ministry insisted, and after George Bulman had spun it, a vestigial ventral fin was fitted underneath the Hurricane's rear fuselage and the tailwheel, which had been retractable, was fixed. In 'A' Flight the task fell to me because I had already spun the Spitfire. I found the Hurricane's spin was smooth but that after about three turns the engine stopped – the great wooden propeller just became stationary! On diving after the spin rotation had stopped, the propeller turned again and the engine fired, so up I climbed to continue the programme. I did spins starting with three turns, and progressed to twenty-four turns – all satisfactorily.

The first night flying sorties with the stub exhausts were unforgettable. When the big Merlin engine was opened up it was like a flaming torch. I had not realised the extent to which the exhaust flames streamed past the cockpit: never again did I put my head outside! Once airborne – with the speed up and the power reduced, the flames shortened and it was not so bad. On landing one hoped that it would not be necessary to overshoot. This was cured by fitting ejector exhausts – which also increased maximum speed by some ten mph.

The Supermarine test pilots had done the early development work on the Spitfire before taking it to Martlesham: it had both similarities and differences to the Hurricane. On the Spitfire the flaps were either 'up' or 'down': initially 'down' was somewhere between 45 degrees and 60 degrees; the approach was flat, with the Spitfire's long nose rather high in the air. Modifying them to go down to 90 degrees made a great difference. As expected, the Spitfire was faster than the Hurricane, and higher speeds were reached in the dive. At first the Spitfire had fabric covered ailerons. Faster than 300 mph indicated airspeed they became almost immovable, and the aeroplane tended to yaw strongly to the right.

The directive from Air Ministry that the Spitfire and the Hurricane were to be spun was closely followed by a letter from the RAF at Farnborough saying that the wind tunnel tests showed that the Spitfire might have problems, and it would have to be done 'at pilot's risk'. The Supermarine test pilots spun it first, of course, and at Martlesham it was handed to me. I was surprised when the nose rose up on the first turn of the spin, as it had done on a civil aerobatic monoplane I had tested earlier. The Spitfire had what later became known as an oscillatory spin: the nose would pitch up and down, and the rate of rotation would also vary.

A persistent problem with the Spitfire was its marginal longitudinal stability. Whilst quick response to the elevator with light stick forces was desirable in a fighter, I found that the Spitfire could become quite difficult. With the centre of gravity at its rearward limit you might have to push sharply on the stick when recovering from a dive. Some of the Martlesham pilots were not quick enough, and bent the wings. Later there were some structural failures in service. Supermarine did much work developing the Spitfire's stability and control. The ailerons and elevators, which were initially fabric covered, were later metal covered, and different profiles were tried. The principal solution developed and eventually installed in operational Spitfires was the 'inertia bob-weight' mounted in the elevator control circuit, and I was involved in the clearance of this work. In normal flight this had almost no effect, but when the aeroplane was under increased positive'G' as whilst pulling out of a dive, the extra 'G' pulling on the bob weight produced a forward force on the stick.

Although alleviating that problem, in doing so it did increase the pull force needed during a tight turn or pull-out from a dive, and it was unpopular with some fighter pilots. Rightly or wrongly, at first Fighter Command resisted it strongly.

Before the establishment left Martlesham Heath for Boscombe Down on the outbreak of war, they had two-pitch (fine and coarse) propellers, and finally a constant speed propeller on the Hurricane, which made a dramatic improvement.

The constant speed propeller permitted the full 3000 rpm to be obtained whenever needed. For the first time pilots experienced a great shove in the back on take off and more importantly, with greater power thus available at lower airspeeds, the rate of climb was similarly increased.

The Spitfire had great potential for development. I tested all of the many Marks of Spitfire at Boscombe Down up to the end of the War. I saw the engine boost develop from the initial +6 lb on the Merlin up to +32 lb in the more powerful Griffon engine; and the ailerons develop from the initial fabric covered ones to metal ones and finally to the highly effective spring tabs ones on the Mark 21. The torque from those very powerful engines was such that the challenge was to see how much boost you could apply on take-off before becoming airborne; it was seldom possible to get more than +18 of the possible +32 lb.

In the midst of the work on the Hurricane and Spitfire, another monoplane I had to test was the prototype of a version of the Miles Hawk Trainer which was to become the RAF's Magister primary trainer. On the first spinning sortie it was loaded to the maximum all up weight with the centre of gravity aft of basic.

At 8000 feet I put it into a left hand spin and recovered after the three turns usual for the initial test. From a right hand spin the aeroplane jibbed a bit before recovering, so I climbed up and repeated it, this time being meticulous to apply full right rudder and to get the stick right back. After three turns recovery action produced no effect. After more turns I was getting nowhere – the spin just went on and on. In the end, the green fields started to look awfully large! It is necessary to bale out on the inside of a spin. I undid my straps and got my right hand over the high cockpit side. However the rather bulky Spin Recorder strapped onto my left leg got caught beneath the dashboard. So I had to get back into the cockpit, slide the spin recorder down my left leg and climb out again. I did not have long in my parachute – time to avoid landing in the river Deben, and barely time to avoid a substantial wood before landing very heavily on my back, fortunately in a ploughed field. It was just as well it was a Saturday, because the empty aeroplane spun into a school playground.

At the 'wash-up' in Air Ministry I felt lonely at the end of the table. Miles reported that they had carried out many spins without difficulty. It was decided that another prototype was to be prepared and flown to Martlesham. One of the other two 'A' Flight test pilots repeated the right hand spin. He too had to bale out, but sadly he landed in the sea and was drowned.

The second inquiry revealed doubts about the exact centre of gravity at which the Miles' spinning tests had been carried out, and they were directed to prepare another aeroplane and demonstrate the spin at Martlesham. It arrived complete with a primitive spin-recovery parachute. The demonstration was before a keenly watching audience. The luckless Miles pilot put the aeroplane into a right hand spin.

After a couple of turns, the spin recovery parachute was seen to deploy and the aeroplane stopped spinning. After landing he emerged with his hands in the air – at least he still had a sense of humour! Subsequently the Magister's rear fuselage was fattened, strakes were added and a redesigned rudder was fitted.

Looking back I realise how primitive flight testing then was, and not just in this country. There were few written criteria for handling qualities, nor on the formal methods of testing. However, be he a Squadron Leader or a Sergeant, the onus was largely on the Martlesham test pilot to run the tests – and above all not to bend a contractor's unique prototype!

The Pre-war Auxiliaries

Group Captain Sir Hugh Dundas CBE DSC DFC

In all the history of arms there can seldom have been a body of men more outwardly confident and pleased with themselves than the pilots of the Auxiliary Air Force. We wore big brass 'A's on the lapels of our tunics and no amount of official pressure would persuade us to remove them. The regulars insisted that those 'A's stood for 'Amateur airmen', or even 'Argue and Answer back'. To us they were the symbols of our membership of a very special club. The pilots of the Auxiliary Air Force were lawyers and farmers, stockbrokers and journalists; they were landowners and artisans, serious-minded accountants and unrepentant playboys. They had two things in common – a passion for flying and a fierce determination that anything the regulars could do, the Auxiliaries could do better. In order to implement this determination a very high standard of flying had to be achieved, as every auxiliary pilot secretly appreciated, in spite of the assumed contempt for regulars and all their ways.

In every auxiliary squadron I ever knew there was an exceptional spirit of enthusiasm and *joie de vivre*. This auxiliary spirit had been born, curiously enough, in White's Club, during the twenties. It was fathered by a large and (judging from the pictures I have seen of him) somewhat florid aristocrat, Lord Edward Grosvenor, the third son of the first Duke of Westminster. This extraordinary man put his stamp on the auxiliaries and his influence lasted long after his death in 1929. The flame which he lit was still burning strongly when the Auxiliaries rose up to do battle in 1939. He had been one of the first Englishmen to own a plane – a Bleriot with which he offered himself to the Royal Naval Air Service in 1914. He had flown throughout the first world war and in peacetime his voice had been persistently raised to demand a Territorial Air Force to match the Territorial Army. So when the first auxiliary squadrons were formed in October 1925, Lord Edward raised and commanded the celebrated 601 County of London Squadron. He recruited his pilots in part from his old wartime acquaintances, in part from his friends at White's.

Wapiti formation 603 (City of Edinburgh) Squadron Auxiliary Air Force (A. E. Ross)

Simultaneously, No. 600 City of London was formed. Its commanding officer, the Right Honourable Edward Guest, was quite unlike Grosvenor in character and habit. He was a most serious-minded man, who had given all his life to public service. Already fifty-one years old when he formed 600 Squadron, he had first fought for his country on the White Nile and in South Africa at the turn the century.

After the first world war he turned to politics. The personalities of Guest and Grosvenor shaped their squadrons, which shared the same airfield at Hendon and set the pattern for the whole Auxiliary Air Force. Guest looked for solid, worthy and conventional qualities in his officers. Grosvenor wanted mercurial men around him and he did not care in the least whether they were conventional.

Thus, in an atmosphere combining light-heartedness and an underlying determination to excel at operational flying, the 'auxiliary spirit' was born and developed. It flourished strongly as new units were formed up and down the country between that first beginning and the outbreak of war fourteen years later.

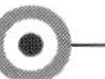

A Pre-war Auxiliary Air Gunner/Bomb Aimer

A. S. Liddle AE

When I joined an Auxiliary Squadron in 1931, any ground tradesman could apply for training as an Air Gunner provided he was passed fit for flying duties. The brass winged bullet insignia of the qualified Air Gunner was a most coveted one.

My training started in a dummy cockpit on the ground.

This had a Scarfe ring, with a 360 degree swing, on which a camera gun was mounted. The Instructor had a long pole with a model aircraft suspended from one end. He moved this around to simulate the approach of an enemy aircraft from different angles. When the film was developed the trainee gunner could quickly see how accurate his aim had been. When he had achieved a reasonable level the trainee carried out camera gun exercises in the air.

Every year Regular RAF fighter squadrons visited the station and their attacks were much more realistic. The Air Gunner was a jack of all trades. He was also responsible for bombing and for photography.

In bombing it was essential to find the wind speed and direction. We used three methods. The first was flying three courses in succession to form a triangle. This was known as 'the cocked hat' and it gave accurate results. The next method was to fly reciprocal courses, and the last was 'time and bead' in which sightings were made as the aircraft flew along.

Two methods of bombing instruction were used. In the first, the bomb aimer was seated on a high platform in the drill hall. A moving picture of the ground as seen from the air was projected on to the floor beneath him. This picture could be made to move at any required speed and in any direction. The picture stopped when the bomb release was pressed and the Instructor then calculated the probable point of impact. This method was useful when the weather was too bad for flying.

Sometimes the weather was not good enough to use the bombing range but local flying was possible. In this case we used the 'Camera Obscura', recently installed at Turnhouse. This consisted of a lens set in the roof of a small darkened building near one of the hangars. When an aeroplane flew high over the aerodrome its image was projected by the lens on to a chart of the area. The bomb aimer used the Camera Obscura building as his target. When he thought he was in the correct position to make a direct hit he pressed the release button. There was a flash and the exact position of the aeroplane was noted on the chart. The probable point of impact of the bomb was calculated by the Instructor.

Much better was the real thing – bombing on the range. The Air Gunner aimed at his target using smoke bombs. The most proficient could often achieve a seventy-five yard grouping.

During the fourteen days' annual camp at a regular RAF station things were completely realistic. We dropped live bombs and fired at towed and ground targets using the well trusted Lewis gun.

After qualifying the proud gunner sewed on his new insignia. He received one shilling and sixpence (seven and a half new pence) per day when he was actually flying over and above his normal rate of ground pay!

The RAFVR in 1937

Air Commodore R. Berry CBE DSO DFC

The RAFVR started in Hull and the East Riding in March 1937. I was one of the first ten successful applicants. Our average age was around twenty. The interview for selection was by a very good looking Squadron Leader, scar down one cheek, wearing his best blue uniform and the ribbon of the Air Force Cross. He was very switched on and inspired us to fly!

Flying started in April 1937 at Brough Flying School, the home of the Blackburn Aircraft Company. They built the B2, a very robust little biplane with a side-by-side cockpit. I recall that we all went solo after eight to ten hours' dual instruction. The weekends couldn't come round quickly enough for us to get into the air again. The flying spirit at Brough was superb.

The next four months, including annual holidays, provided great opportunities to improve our flying standards. We were rewarded by the introduction of the Hawker Hart to the School. Aerobatics in this aircraft were very exciting and the trips were longer. Cross country flights were more interesting and we flew higher and higher. My total flying in the first year was 120 hours.

Hawker Hart formation (AHB)

In 1938 flying continued unabated. Many more pilots were selected and the category of Air Observer was revived. The Air Observers had to be given air experience and this meant more flying for the experienced VR pilots at Brough.

Lectures were now organised to enable us to qualify for our 'Wings'. A town centre was set up in Hull. The building was appropriately named 'Churchill House'. This developed into a Headquarters with lecture rooms, administrative offices and a room for social events. A President, Treasurer and other officials were appointed, all from the VR. Finally a retired Admiral was appointed to oversee these activities. He was a splendid fellow and helped us all tremendously. I felt at the time that a retired Air Marshal would have been a better choice but the RAF, being the youngest Service, probably didn't have enough retired Air Marshals to go around!

A lot of our spare time was devoted to the lectures and these culminated in the exams for our 'Wings'. The first ten reservists were all successful.

In early 1939 we had the opportunity to be attached to regular front line fighter squadrons. I was sent to 66 Squadron at Duxford in February. They had the very latest fighter – the Spitfire!

After a checkout in the Squadron Magister I had my first flight in a Spitfire. I recall the words of the Flight Commander before take-off. With a tap on my helmet he advised 'Don't break it'. I quickly ran out of grass and by the time I had pumped up the undercarriage – something quite new to me – the airfield had disappeared. I took part in squadron flying activities for three weeks – an invaluable experience.

Back to the Hawker Hart at Brough. The VR were very honoured to be asked to take part in an RAF Empire Air Day flying display at Leconfield. I led a formation of five Harts in various formations.

The Air Ministry now arranged another element in our training. This was a scheme under which we could qualify for a civilian 'A' licence at the local Flying Club. This provided another twenty-five hours flying in a Tiger Moth and a BA Swallow – very different from the Spitfire but very enjoyable.

A Fairey Battle arrived at Brough to give a glimpse of another aspect of RAF activities. I was fortunate to have two flights in it before being called up.

I had been granted a five year commission in July 1939 and had flown a total of 350 hours, all in my spare time. I was posted to a Spitfire Squadron in October 1939 and had my first air combat on 7 December 1939.

As far as I was concerned the RAFVR was an outstanding success.

The Beaufighter

Sir Archibald Russell CBE

The great change in aeroplane design from biplanes to monoplanes came about in the middle 1930s. This was made possible when the boffins at Farnborough produced a complete analysis of monoplane wing flutter together with rules for its avoidance. With monoplanes, total strength and aero-elastic requirements are provided by the light alloy shell, suitably reinforced, conforming externally with the aerodynamic shape required. Obviously the design aim is to provide the necessary strength and stiffness for the least possible structure weight. This involves specialised techniques, experimental testing and complicated mathematics. Unfortunately this great change, with increased technical demands, coincided in 1935 with the urgent need to re-equip the Royal Air Force with battle-worthy aircraft. Inevitably some new designs would be less than the best.

In one notable case, a failure was turned into the very successful Lancaster. This was achieved by increasing the wing span and adding two engines.

The total failure of the Westland Whirlwind is more obscure. The Whirlwind had been designed to a 1935 specification for a twin-engined cannon-armed fighter. In mid 1938, problems found on flight trials were reported by the aerodynamic experts at Farnborough and found to be incurable without a total redesign. The prospect of the Royal Air Force having no twin-engined fighters for a very long time was indeed very serious.

Leslie Frise, the Bristol Chief Engineer, a man of great ingenuity with whom I worked at the time, had the idea of using Beaufort wings (that aircraft was behaving well on type test at the time) with its tail unit and undercarriage on a completely new fuselage. The military equipment installation would be as called for in the Whirlwind specification. The whole assembly seemed to have no problems except that the estimated maximum speed with higher powered engines was only 335 mph against the Whirlwind's supposed 360 mph.

By prior appointment, a general arrangement drawing together with weight estimates and performance calculations were taken to Air Staff. After a general discussion of the proposal with two officers, whom we thought to be the Director of Operations and his Deputy (judging by the number and width of rings carried, one was only a Wing Commander and the other a Squadron Leader) the proposal was obviously received with considerable interest. This we judged to be so by animated whispering with much finger pointing at the fuselage drawing. After half an hour or so, suddenly and without consulting higher authority, we were told to build four prototypes as soon as possible. Also a mock-up fuselage was required for equipment trial installations! This meeting was in November 1938.

The first prototype made its first flight in July 1939 only eight months later. A contract for 300 Beaufighters followed immediately.

The first 'Beau' night fighter Squadron was formed in September 1940. There were five Squadrons in service by Christmas 1940. Over this period, the Ground Control System failed to direct the fighters near enough for their own radars to pick up their chosen target. In the first four months of operation, the total number of Beaufighter kills was only three. Early in the New Year, a new Ground Control System was introduced and the number of kills increased rapidly. In May 1941 in a single raid on London, twenty-two raiders were shot down by night fighters against two by anti-aircraft fire.

The first major change from the night fighter role was seen in Coastal Command. After a successful demonstration of torpedo dropping, the Command decided to replace its Beauforts by Beaufighters. Apart from the North Sea and the English Channel, there were increasing demands from the Mediterranean. With large differences in equipment

Bristol Beaufighter of 236 Squadron (AHB)

installations and with more aircraft required, it was decided to build all Coastal Beaufighters in two shadow factories while night fighters were concentrated wholly at Filton, Bristol. The decision was taken that all development work for the aircraft, engine, equipment and weapon installations would be based at Filton. The number of aircraft so used varied from ten to twenty. Filton was also responsible for the development of all design changes.

One of the operational changes that excites the imagination was the installation of rockets designed in 1939 as anti-aircraft weapons. These were very effective against tanks and shipping. Their new intended use was in support of torpedo dropping. There could have been few less attractive assignments than an airborne torpedo attack against defended ships. The torpedo had to be dropped at low speed, low altitude and short range. The new tactic was for a first wave of Beaufighters to sweep the gun decks with rockets and a second wave closely following the first would drop their torpedoes.

Through the very large number of design changes, including new equipment, the empty weight increased from 13,800 lb to 15,600 lb with the maximum weight staying at 21,000 lb. The horse power from the air-cooled radial Hercules increased from 1400 to 1600.

In 1940 instructions came to fit 450 new Beaufighters with Rolls Royce 1250 hp watercooled Merlins. These engines had been intended for the Lancaster but that programme was evidently running late. The last time Bristol aircraft were powered by Rolls-Royce engines was in World War I with the Bristol Fighter. It was thought that, with this long break in association, Rolls should be made wholly responsible for the installation of Merlins in the Beaufighter. The comparison as regards performance was much as expected: in level flight, the water cooled engines gave the same speed with 10% less power. The night fighter pilots preferred the extra power giving a shorter take off on a dark night.

The Beaufighter must be close to the record for the number of equipment changes and armament variations. In total the number of Beaufighters built was just under six thousand. The 'Beau' was also used by the Royal Australian Air Force, with 365 aircraft being built with locally made supplies, apart from the engines.

If You Want to Know the Way
Group Captain F. C. Richardson CBE

During 1935 No. 216 Squadron was tasked to operate as easily by night as by day and was more or less on 24-hour call, if not on active stand-by. Sorties were mostly scheduled days ahead, but sometimes blew up without any warning, requiring a flight to anywhere in our extensive 'parish', more or less at the drop of a hat.

Like almost everywhere else in the Service overseas, the vital importance of air navigation failed to be appreciated owing to the prevailing normal excellent visibility. The one serious navigator, Squadron Leader Philip Mackworth DFC was generally dubbed a 'bit of an old woman' because he tried hard to improve the squadron's primitive navigation practices.

About this time we underwent some 'spit and polish' for an inspection by Sir Phillip Sassoon, Air Under Secretary of State, who was on a grand tour of the Middle East.

In Baghdad, Sir Philip found himself in the thick of a costly search for a certain Wing Commander Peter Warburton, lost in the Syrian desert. Warburton was eventually found, partly with the help of Sir Philip's own aircraft which had been commandeered for the crisis. In due course, Warburton was asked by the Air Council to state his reasons in writing for getting lost. He replied that it was really quite simple – he hadn't the foggiest idea about navigation. The fault lay with the Central Flying School where pilot instructors learnt to fly upside down and many other aerobatics, but never how to go from A to B.

Their 'Airships' promptly despatched Air Marshal Sir

Edward 'Chillie' Chilton, then a lowly Flight Lieutenant navigation specialist for the flying boat squadrons at Mount Batten, to RAF Wittering, to give the Group Captain and the instructional staff of CFS a three-month indoctrination course in air navigation. Thereafter, every qualified flying instructor was able to carry out simple cross-country flights in fair weather and in foul, and an important step was at last taken towards the general education of RAF pilots in air navigation.

In 1936 the School of Air Navigation was moved from the flying-boat base at Calshot, where the cost of meeting its flying programme by using flying-boats was really prohibitive, to Manston, on the Isle of Thanet. Here No. 48 Squadron combined the training of its own pilots for maritime reconnaissance with the provision of taxi-drivers in Avro Ansons Mk I for the flying exercises needed by the School. In 1938 enough Ansons and pilots became available to give the School its own fleet.

Although the Anson Mk I was largely made of wood and canvas, it was a monoplane with two engines and retractable undercart – a great step forward! Easy to handle, it cruised at 120 knots and had good all-round view from its glass-house cabin and bomb-aimer's window, from where the drift was measured. The navigation station behind the pilot on the port side had an airspeed indicator, altimeter and a magnetic compass for monitoring the course flown. A W/T operator sat behind. Its ability to fly at 19,000 ft was invaluable when a view of the stars was needed on cloudy nights, but the lack of oxygen and the cold were both limiting human factors. Its Mk II successor was metal-bodied and, being heavier, had a lower ceiling. There was of course still no oxygen or cabin heating and the crew wrapped up well. As a weapon of the maritime war, the Anson Mk II was just as bad a joke as the Mk I.

Pupils were detailed to fly in pairs, alternating duties as first and second navigator, the latter's first job on take off being to wind up the wheels – 150 turns of a crank-handle meant five minutes of very hard puffing. The long trailing aerial had also to be wound out (and hopefully wound in again) before landing! But comparisons with the dear old Valentia were also breath-taking!

For me the biggest changes concerned the weather and the air traffic. Unlike the normally very clear, empty skies of Africa, here was a land of clouds, rain and fog, with plenty of aircraft flying around. Aeroplanes had only rarely been seen in African skies and although we had had plenty of sandstorms, smog had been quite unknown. This horror was very common in industrial Europe and with south easterly winds it drifted across from industrial Northern France, Belgium and the Ruhr.

One summer day, flying over Sheffield in yellow sulphurous fumes at 5000 ft, I could only just make out the chimney stacks of John Brown's steel mills spewing filth into the air: the town itself was invisible. To make matters worse, weather is notoriously variable from one place to another in the British Isles.

When a drop in air temperature of a mere ½°F. often made the difference between possible and impossible visibility for landing, such finesse remained for years beyond the forecasting skills of the duty 'Met' officers on our flying stations.

Despite the urgent promptings of obviously dire necessity to deal with weather limitations, their 'Airships' lacked both the resolve and the funds to sponsor adequate national research and simply relied on the meagre resources of the RAE at Farnborough.

In 1937 a squadron of Heyford 'heavy' bombers, flying from Aldergrove in Northern Ireland to their base in England, ran into icing conditions and all but one crashed. Incredibly, our masters did nothing more than wring their hands for over a year, leaving it to C-in-C Bomber Command to put together a national network of available radio aids, which was really making the best of a bad job and only a makeshift solution.

'Blind approach' for the RAF was still a long way off and our acquisition of the ability to fly in all weather had to wait for the arrival of foreign radio aids in the late Thirties and for refinements of British radar in the War.

So with a dozen pilots, I now embarked on a three month navigation course followed by six months on the advanced course at Manston to qualify myself for a career commission.

Like all RAF stations in the Thirties, Manston possessed very few officers' married quarters. Most of the married staff and all the married students had to find their own digs off the camp.

Heyford bomber (RAF Museum Hendon)

When at last a timid step of expansion of the RAF was actually authorised, a shortage of pilots was foreseen. So the extinct air observer was revived in late 1937 though it took another year to recruit and train these new aircrew before they began to appear in squadrons.

For lack of its own air navigation instructors, retired mercantile marine officers were recruited by the RAF for the task, though some had never flown, let alone ever navigated an aeroplane. Nor were there enough really suitable aircraft for the programmes of practical flying training. It was therefore no surprise that the first trickles of air observers were poorly received when they arrived for duty in the Front Line.

These problems were unknown to us students in 1937 when we assembled to begin our own laborious climb through the higher mathematics and sciences that underpin the many mysteries of air navigation.

Some of the Course had been pilots in flying-boat squadrons and were well versed in coping with such simple navigation exercises as long flights over the sea to find distant lightships in the North Sea and the Channel. We must have been very welcome diversions for those lonely keepers.

Our web-footed comrades had another advantage, having already encountered the marine sextant as a tool of their trade! In acknowledging their privileged membership of the 'Flying-boat Union', we also gradually came to believe in ourselves as being members of an equally elite 'Navigation Union' which, after much discussion and combined effort in the coming years, was destined to influence and ultimately to transform the future RAF.

Our six-month course started in January 1938 and we had to make great efforts to keep up with our tutorials while coping with the intensive flying schedule in fair weather and foul.

At Manston we had some extremely 'hairy' night flights, navigating through continuous cloud and the threat of fog back at base with only poor radio aids on call. Manston had no homing device except for a coded flashing beacon sitting near the airfield which might or might not be visible.

Our short navigation course was followed by the 'long' N course. We travelled to Greenwich to meet the astronomers of the Royal Observatory; we drove to the Admiralty Compass Observatory at Slough; we visited the National Physical Laboratory at Teddington. At the Barking factory of Henry Hughes, who were making the newfangled Mk I bubble sextants, we were shown round by their technical 'rep' who, in 1941, was to share my office in the Air Ministry. He became a highly esteemed colleague and eventually my much-lamented friend, being none other than the one-and-only Francis Chichester.

As a result of the months of cramming that climaxed in July 1938, we were annotated 'N' in the Air Force List and were chuffed to be posted as new instructors to the expanding School.

In air navigation we were carrying a heavy handicap of lost time and nursing a bagful of false hopes pinned on improved astro. Unfortunately there was simply nothing better to offer and although exciting strides were being taken to simplify its use, seen from to-day astro was almost a non-starter. If only we had seriously considered the practical effects on a bubble sextant of weaving about trying not to be shot down, our first years of night bombing failures could have been anticipated and alternative electronic devices developed much more quickly.

We each went 'solo' on Ansons and, in addition to running our Courses and flying our students on exercises, we participated in air trials of a new drift sight and an air log to evaluate their suitability for the Service and their general performance.

Sir Edgar Ludlow-Hewitt, AOC in C Bomber Command, now thought it propitious for as many of his squadron and flight commanders as possible to be indoctrinated into the latest processes of air navigation. A series of highly concentrated astro courses were at once organised at Manston for dozens of navigationally illiterate wing commanders and squadron leaders.

To get clear night skies often meant flying Ansons at 19,000 ft in the perishing cold without oxygen. This feat was repeated over and over by Flt Lt Jenkins, their instructor, until the task was accomplished. It was better than doing nothing, but it was really only clutching at straws.

Per Ardua Ad *Australia 1938*

Air Commodore R. T. Gething CB OBE AFC

At dawn on 5 November 1938 three modified Vickers Wellesley single-engined light bombers of the Royal Air Force took off from Ismailia Egypt. Almost exactly forty-eight hours later two of them landed at Darwin having established a new world record for distance in a straight line. The third aircraft landed in Timor having also beaten the record which the Russians had set up a year or so earlier. The flight of the three Wellesleys was the culmination of the work of the Long Range Development Unit which had been formed on 1 January 1938 to study the problem of long distance flying with the ultimate object of breaking the long-distance record.

The unit was equipped with five specially modified Wellesleys. There were four crews consisting of chief pilot, navigator, and a wireless operator. Three of the wireless operators were NCO pilots and the Signals Officer was a recently commissioned NCO pilot. The navigators were pilots who had completed the specialist navigation course at Manston.

The route for the record attempt was to be a modified great circle track from Ismailia to Darwin. The direct great circle track involved long sea crossings of over 1000 miles across the Arabian Sea and of over 1300 miles across the Bay of Bengal. By splitting the track into three great circle tracks – Ismailia to Jask on the Iranian coast, Jask to Port Blair in the Andaman Islands and Port Blair to Darwin, the sea

Vickers Wellesley of Long Range Development Unit (AHB)

crossings were reduced to two of 800 miles and one of 450 miles. The increase in distance, which would not count towards the record, was only approximately three miles. Even on this modified route 60% or 4000 miles was over the sea.

As a safety precaution, the Air Ministry and the Admiralty made arrangements to provide a Persian Gulf sloop in the Arabian Sea, a Royal Indian Navy sloop in the Bay of Bengal, a Royal Australian Navy sloop in the Timor Sea and the RAF Auxiliary *Aquarius* in the South China Sea. Flying boats from Singapore would be based in the Andaman Islands and at Kuching in Sarawak.

Maps of the International 1/1-million series were obtained to cover the whole route as far as land was concerned and Admiralty charts of scales ranging from about fifteen to forty miles to the inch were used to cover the areas over the sea. These were joined together in strips, linen backed and made into four rolls.

All four crews carried out twelve-hour flights around the British Isles. The object was to become accustomed to the Wellesleys and acclimatised to flying for extended periods at 10,000 ft or more. On these flights the navigator and wireless operator relieved the captain at the controls for an hour or so.

Seat changing was quite a simple operation even in the standard Wellesleys which were not fitted with 'George'. When the pilot wished to be relieved at the controls he undid his parachute harness and raised himself from his seat. In this position he still had control of the aircraft. The relief then undid a catch at the back of the seat and the seat could then be folded down backwards. The pilot then backed out and pushed his way past the relief who then climbed into the seat which was pushed up and locked in position.

Tankage was increased from 485 gallons to 1290 gallons by the fitting of twelve extra tanks. All petrol with the exception of the 16-gallon gravity tank in the nose was carried in the wings. The petrol cocks and an emergency hand pump were in the fuselage. The outer front and rear tanks were fitted with jettison valves so that the greater proportion of the overload could be got rid of in an emergency. With blown tanks it was calculated that the aircraft would float indefinitely in a level attitude, provided of course she did not break up. Fortunately this wasn't put to the test.

The maximum all-up weight was increased from 12,500 to 18,400 lb. The empty weight of the standard Wellesleys was 6253 lb so the modified aircraft was carrying nearly three times its own weight. The undercarriage was strengthened and heavier tyres were fitted .

The engine was a Bristol Pegasus with a slightly raised compression ratio running on lead free 100 octane petrol specially developed by Shell. A Rotol constant speed airscrew, not then in general use, was fitted in place of the de Havilland two-pitch type. A long chord NACA engine cowling replaced the Townend ring and the shape of the fuselage was altered by fitting bulges to conform with the engine cowling. Important additions were a Bowser flow meter registering gallons used and a Mk IV automatic pilot. Flotation jackets were provided but parachutes were only carried in the training flights. Neither dinghies nor oxygen were carried. Stowage had to be arranged for food, water and navigation equipment.

The Wellesley in standard form had a claimed range of 2270 miles, yet there was no provision for a navigator, the normal crew being a pilot and a wireless operator/air gunner. In the long-range aircraft a position for the navigator was arranged, sitting facing aft, on a canvas sling seat with a canvas sling back rest.

A folding chart table with brackets for the roller strip maps took up the full width of the narrow fuselage. Mounted on either side were an airspeed indicator, altimeter, outside air temperature gauge and a clock. Other instruments included an 02- Bearing Compass, two Mk VIII Bubble Sextants, two Navy Deck Watches in anti-vibration mountings, a Smith Floor Drift Sight and a Mk VI Tail Drift Sight. Books included the Air Almanac, Dreisonstock Tables, Inmans Tables and a Star Atlas. The long duration sealed Barographs were also the responsibility of the navigator.

After an extended trial flight, the work of overhauling the Wellesleys and fitting new engines began. Fairings were made to fit neatly, all unnecessary excrescences were removed, the remainder carefully faired over and all holes and gaps filled. This probably resulted in an increase of two or three mph. All the aircraft were fitted with a separate electrical intercom unit instead of the long Gosport tubes which had been used previously.

On 5 November at 03.56 LR 1 took off, quickly followed by LR 2 and LR 3. All three were off the ground in 1200 yards. At 500 feet. we turned slowly on to a course for Jask, 1590 miles away. In thirty-two minutes we had reached our cruising height of 10,000 feet.

When the auto pilot was engaged it was clearly unserviceable. Fortunately the Corporal Instrument Maker had taught us to make simple adjustments. After a minute or two the fault was traced to a sticking valve and rectified. From then on it behaved perfectly. During the early flying tests the auto-pilot had tended to hunt. This was cured by fitting adjustable friction clamps to the elevator and aileron control wires in the fuselage. We found these clamps were also a great help when flying manually, except of course during take offs and landings.

Drifts were measured at intervals and course was altered accordingly. The compasses were checked by taking a bearing of the Sun and comparing it with its calculated azimuth. Five Sun sights were taken before the Persian Gulf was reached. The first two when the Sun was roughly ahead to check the ground speed and the second two when the Sun was roughly abeam to check the track. The fifth was just before we crossed the coast. With the aid of the position line it was possible to recognise ground features. Surprise, surprise! We were on track after the first 1020 miles in six hours.

Over Arabia unusually cloudy conditions were met and the bumps experienced were unpleasant in our heavily loaded condition and we climbed to 11,500 feet. We put the wind on the wrong way over the sea but quickly realised this and corrected the mistake.

Down the Persian Gulf the weather conditions were good with a clear sky and excellent visibility. There were plenty of checking points and navigation was no problem. Jask was reached just after dusk when the navigator was at the controls. When the coast of India was reached we descended to 10,000 feet.

Since the start LR 2 had been in company with us but lost touch at dusk and we didn't see them again. After take-off LR 3 had been delayed as the port leg of the undercarriage would not retract properly. This was overcome by the navigator and wireless operator cutting into the wheel well, putting a rope round the stubborn wheel and heaving while the captain all but stalled the aircraft. They had not caught up with us.

Two hours after leaving Jask a star fix was obtained. This took a little time to work out but was very satisfactory. Two more fixes were obtained before the Indian coast was reached at the mouth of the Gulf of Kutch – a distance of 2350 miles in a little over fourteen hours.

We fixed our position after crossing the Gulf of Cambay and then saw nothing of India until the East coast was reached. It was a lovely night in the moonlight above the cloud. The navigation was carried out entirely by star sights. Since the Persian Gulf we had encountered headwinds but in India they increased to 5–10 mph. The east coast of India was reached at 24.00 GMT, one hour and ten minutes after Moon set and just before dawn. A star fix just before reaching the coast put us 100 miles north of track. Some doubt was felt about this, as what could be seen of the ground below looked very much like the Delta of the river which put us more or less on track. We pushed on to the Andaman Islands, nearly 100 miles away, hoping to confirm our track later by further Sun sights. Unfortunately the Sun was obscured by high cloud and when visible it was too bumpy. Constant drifts were taken but I found taking drifts over the sea from 10,000 feet even more difficult than it had been over the desert. To make matters worse the weather began to deteriorate with stronger headwinds and thunderstorms. Our landfall in the Andamans was Little Andaman, fifty miles south-west of track.

From Little Andaman we set course for the southern coast of Siam and the north of Malaya. Headwinds continued in spite of Westerlies being forecast. Again track was maintained by taking drifts and on crossing the coast we had no difficulty in maintaining our correct track by a visual reference. The winds now turned favourable as forecast, but only for about two-and-a-half hours as we left the North East coast of Malaya at dusk and headed out into the South China Sea. From this point onwards headwinds of ten to twenty mph were experienced all way to Darwin. As we looked back towards the coast of Malaya there was a beautiful line of towering thunderclouds all flashing pink in the moonlight.

We crossed the coast of Borneo at 11,000 feet. two hours and forty minutes after leaving the coast of Malaya, having checked our position on the Anamba Islands and other islands in the South China Sea. Very soon no stars were visible and we were flying blind in almost continuous thunderclouds and heavy rain for about three hours. It was extremely rough and unpleasant.

During this time two DF bearings were received from Singapore. The first was obviously way out but the second appeared reasonable.

Before dawn the sky cleared and I was able to take two star sights, but before these had been worked out we were able to pinpoint a position on Laut island on the south-east corner of Borneo. The star sights confirmed the visual sighting. The result was very encouraging as during the previous three hours only one small change of course had been made.

The sky clouded over again and there were vivid displays of lightning. Dawn came at the end of the second night in the vicinity of Macassar and we passed the Russian record shortly after. I think the captain was a little tired after the rough night. It took him quite a time to digest the news. Five minutes later he suggested a celebratory tot of the medicinal brandy.

The evening before, a rendezvous had been arranged north-west of Timor. We appeared to be upwards of one hour ahead of LR 2 and 3. This was the reverse of the situation during the training flight to the Middle East when LR 1 was the runt of the litter. We in LR1 must have had the luck of the draw when new engines were fitted.

A check of fuel states revealed that LR 3 had adequate fuel but that LR 2 might be unable to reach Darwin. They therefore landed at Timor. This was hard luck on the crew but they had the satisfaction of holding the world record until we landed at Darwin. To their surprise the special Shell 100 octane petrol was available and they were able to refuel and fly on to Darwin within a few hours.

We arrived at the rendezvous forty-five minutes before LR 3's ETA. We circled waiting for them. When there was no sign of them we set course at a reduced speed, arranging another rendezvous at Bathurst Island, some seventy miles from Darwin. However three hours and 35 minutes later LR 3 suddenly appeared, formating closely, and we proceeded to Darwin together.

During the crossing of the Timor Sea we managed to have a shave and wash and brush up.

We were overhead Darwin at 03.50 and landed at 04.00 GMT to be greeted by the Port Doctor: 'Any sickness on board?'.

Fuel left in LR 1's tank was 44 gallons and LR 3's a mere 17 gallons.

ABYSSINIA

Abyssinia had been an independent kingdom for centuries. In 1896 it had defeated an invading Italian army at Adowa. In 1930 Haile Selassie became Emperor and introduced a number of reforms.

There were frontier disputes between Abyssinia and the neighbouring Italian colonies of Eritrea and Somaliland. These were referred to the League of Nations but Mussolini continued to reinforce his East African colonies.

On 3 October, 1935 Italian troops from Eritrea entered Abyssinia and captured Adowa. The League of Nations introduced ineffective sanctions but the Italian advance continued. Addis Ababa was captured on Fifth May 1936 and the Emperor fled. He returned in 1941 when the British drove the Italians out once more.

Background to a Forgotten Campaign

Air Vice-Marshal G. B.'Digger' Magill CBE DFC

A thousand miles to the south of the HQ in Cairo, similarly remote from their service colleagues in Kenya, with their nearest neighbours to the east in Aden and with the expanse of Central Africa to the west, No. 47 (B) Sqn at Khartoum was the Royal Air Force in the Sudan.

Commanded by a Squadron Leader with about twenty officers and around 250 other ranks, the Squadron's responsibilities extended over the whole of Anglo-Egyptian Sudan, from the desert tracts of the north to the equatorial south, an area roughly the size of the whole of Western Europe. Quite a parish!

Royal Air Force Khartoum and No. 47 Squadron were literally one entity on the outskirts of town. An RAF Wing Commander was located alongside the GOC Land Forces to advise him and the Governor on air matters, and that was it.

The squadron had been in the Sudan from the late '20s. At first it was equipped with Fairey IIIFs and Gordons. In due course Vickers Vincents arrived. The Squadron was then organised into three Vincent flights and one of Gordons. The Gordon flight was unique in that for half the year the aircraft had wheels and for the other half floats so that visits could be made to places on the Nile when the rains denied the use of landplanes. Who would have thought of gaining floatplane experience in that part of Africa!

Designated a bomber squadron, we were very much multi-purpose. Tasks included reconnaissance, direct support of the army, photography, communications, some meteorological flights, calibration of early radio D/F stations in support of the developing Empire air route to the Cape, search and rescue and any odd jobs that arose out of aid to the civil power.

With these sorts of duties and some 120 so-called landing grounds and floatplane reaches to be visited from time to time, operational life on the squadron was full indeed and the source of splendid experience. Of particular interest were the opportunities to visit the Sudan Defence Force outstations and to see the District Commissioners at work alone, administering areas about the size of England.

Naturally, the squadron had its formal functions to fulfil in the official life of the Condominium as well as taking part in the more social activities of the 'colonial' society of the British abroad with its strict pecking order of social status. Although below the equivalent income level, we officers were treated as 'honorary grade three' by virtue of holding the Monarch's commission!

Gordon float plane 47 Squadron, Sudan (AHB)

In off-duty hours there was enough for us to do, with sporting activities, sailing on the Nile, some shooting and the facilities of the exclusive Sudan Club, to say nothing of the somewhat dubious attractions of the Gordon Cabaret, the only such establishment 'in bounds'. The airmen were less well served but seemed to manage well enough. In this it should be remembered that in those days Khartoum was a three-year, unaccompanied by family, posting without 'home' leave!

The full life went on. There was little talk of war. However, during one of the several crises the sight of a Vincent loaded with WWI type 112 lb bombs and some ancient 20 lb Coopers and allocation of a target on the Red Sea coast of Eritrea, gave rise to some thought. That the attack was to be after dark meant to one young pilot at least that he would double his night flying experience in the process, even if he found the target, let alone got back!

A major event in July '39 was re-equipment with Vickers Wellesley aircraft. They were obsolete by UK standards but a very real advance on the old and trusted Vincents. They were monoplanes with retractable undercarriages, wing flaps, more power driving a variable pitch airscrew, faster (160 mph cruising speed!), much greater range and a useful payload. Thus the elderly Gordons were pensioned off and the squadron reorganised into three Wellesley flights with one retaining Vincents.

With war now much more of a probability, training was concentrated on the basic bomber role and night flying intensified. There seemed little doubt but that Mussolini would side with Hitler. It was interesting indeed to stand aside and watch Italian Air Force tri-motor bombers staging through the civil side of the airfield to reinforce Eritrea in the knowledge that we would probably soon see them again in rather different circumstances.

Declaration of War with Germany brought the squadron immediately to a war footing, but with no immediate enemy in sight. Things soon began to happen in earnest. War stations were prepared in the desert in the north-east of the country nearer the Eritrean border. The Wing Commander left the GOC's staff to form a small headquarters to command what was initially to be a Wellesley Wing. Number 14 Squadron arrived at Port Sudan with their Wellesleys from Amman in Jordan. Number 223 Squadron came up from the attractions of life in Kenya to move via Khartoum to an isolated spot to the west of the Red Sea Hills. Number 47 Squadron was redeployed to a similarly desolate spot beside an unmade road.

In the afternoon of 10 June 1940, aircraft were bombed-up and crews briefed for operations very early the following morning. Tension rose. At about eleven o'clock news came through that the raid was off. An hour later crews were awakened again to be told that the show was on after all. This was it.

Group Captain 'Black Mac' MacDonald at Wing HQ was not one to hang around. A three-pronged early morning pre-emptive attack was laid on against the air forces in Eritrea. Number 14 Squadron attacked the force protecting the port of Massawa. Number 47 Squadron went for the main base at Asmara. Number 223 Squadron attacked the fighter base at Gura. Surprise was complete. The British were up and about too early! Targets were hit: enemy reaction was slow and ineffective. One aircraft of No. 47 Sqn went down on the way to the target but news that the crew was safe came through quite soon. The telephone line between Khartoum and enemy Asmara was not cut for a day or so!

As the air war went on by day and by night, targets were struck throughout Eritrea. Number 14 Squadron also kept watch over the Red Sea shipping lanes and had some spectacular successes against enemy naval units that ventured from port. Opposition varied considerably and losses were sustained. Enemy fighter attacks could sometimes be less than heroic but there was one leader who earned considerable respect. Nicknamed 'Pedro', when he was about the unescorted bombers were in for real trouble.

In all this it is well to recall that the Wellesleys were operating from strictly limited base facilities bedevilled by heat, sand and dust. The terrain was inhospitable in the extreme, meteorological assistance was meagre to non-existent. There were no aids to navigation and maps could be unreliable. Even target material could be faulty. The altitude of one main target was found to be 2000 feet higher than shown!

Though strong in structure, the aircraft were relatively slow and had neither self-sealing tanks nor any armoured protection. But the squadrons quickly absorbed the lessons of war and morale was high.

A few special events occurred. A detachment from No. 223 Sqn sent to Aden for the purpose attacked Addis Ababa in daylight thoroughly upsetting the Italians' belief in security through isolation! Number 47 Squadron using one of their old Vincents flew the then Major Orde Wingate to a specially prepared strip well inside enemy territory to join the British-led locally raised forces harassing the enemy from within their own lines.

A major reverse was suffered when No. 47 Sqn deployed eight Wellesleys and four Vincents temporarily to Gedaref for tactical reasons. But the enemy got to hear about it and a day or so later a bomber appeared overhead in the early morning with the local commanding general on board and leading Fiat CR 42 fighters. Down came a few bombs followed by the fighters and in no time at all the aircraft on the ground were ablaze. A detachment of SAAF fighters positioned on a nearby strip could not be raised. The telephone line, which was the only link, had been cut overnight by a collaborator. There was nothing for the squadron to do but return to Khartoum by train and the ignominy of this was not lost on the other squadrons!

One day when we were bombing enemy troop positions in a raging battle we were surprised to see an enemy bomber formation appear quite close by, obviously doing similar things to our side. Some long range fire was exchanged as the formations turned for home but this was not the time or the place for a bomber 'shoot out'.

Then there was the venerable Caproni bomber/transport which surrendered and landed intact. Repainted white with large red crosses and with its Italian volunteer pilot aboard as part of the crew, it served well for a while on casualty evacuation duties.

Early on we aircrew were given 'blood chits' in bold Amharric to proffer to possibly uncooperative tribesmen should we be shot down. Shown to a loyal and trusted mess steward who spoke the language, he grinned from ear to ear. The phrase intended to introduce the bearer as 'a good friend' freely translated into 'a great lover'. Not an ideal approach to locals inclined to be jealous of their wives, particularly if Europeans were about. A much simpler version was rapidly produced, emblazoned with the emblem of the Lion of Judah – Emperor Haile Selassi.

Crews returning to Khartoum on occasional trips for urgent spares or whatever found the general tenor of civilian life little changed. The war was a long way away. Nevertheless a great deal was happening.

Control of the air forces was now vested in No. 203 Group commanded by Air Commodore (later ACM) L H Slatter, of Schneider Cup fame.

Number 1 Squadron, SAAF, was re-equipped with Hurricanes enabling them to further reduce the fighter opposition. A squadron of Gladiators had arrived for the protection of the Port Sudan area. The fourth flight of No. 47 Sqn was given some old but welcome Gauntlets to help in their support role. A small force of Free French Blenheims were grafted on to No. 47 Sqn's base facilities at Khartoum. They had problems and did not achieve a lot. But Wellesley crews were most envious of their aircraft.

Meanwhile, the position on the ground was changing dramatically. Considerably reinforced with British and Indian troops the Army was on the offensive to drive the Italians from temporarily occupied Sudanese territory and to pursue them into Eritrea. Naturally, the air forces were heavily engaged in direct and indirect support and co-operation between the services was very good.

Kassala was retaken and the advance towards Asmara begun. Ahead lay the major obstacle of the only pass through the most formidable mountainous territory before Keren. In this truly precipitous country the enemy held all the vantage points overlooking the only line of advance. Fighting was bitter and prolonged with many casualties. Number 47 Squadron was particularly closely involved even to the extent of 'dive bombing' temporarily isolated British troops with food and light ammunition whilst under direct fire from the hills above.

Outstanding heroism and determination finally carried the day. The pass was cleared and access to Eritrea proper achieved. The Italians quickly declared Asmara an open city. The port of Massawa was cleared and opened for much needed supplies. The enemy was chased southwards.

At the same time the advance up the coast from Kenya into Abyssinia was squeezing the enemy from the south. The end was near.

Squadrons began to be withdrawn to join the hard pressed forces in Egypt. But No. 47 Sqn remained to continue in support of the army in some of the most formidably mountainous areas encountered so far.

Commanded by the Duke of Aosta the remaining Italian forces eventually capitulated in their beleaguered mountain stronghold and the campaign was over.

By now RAF Khartoum was a much changed place and developed almost beyond recognition. It was about to become a major link in the West African air reinforcement route from Takoradi along which a multitude of aircraft were later to be delivered to the Middle East theatre and beyond.

By then No. 47 (B) Sqn was gone and its splendid isolation in the Sudan a distant memory.

Defensive Posture

Group Captain F. C. Richardson CBE

Mussolini had long nursed designs to increase 'his share' of Africa by grabbing undeveloped but fertile Abyssinia – the uplands of Ethiopia – by war if need be, thereby consolidating his strategic hold on the Horn of Africa, where he already ruled over Eritrea through Asmara and its port Massawa and over most of Somalia with its coastal capital of Mogadishu.

By 1934 his plans were well ahead for a campaign, using poison gas as one of his weapons and making a pincer thrust against Addis Ababa.

Number 216 Squadron was now re-equipped with Victoria Vs. Compared with a single-engined aircraft, an empty Victoria weighed a ponderous 11,942 lb and fully loaded was 18,000 lb It rode more like a shire horse than a bucking pony.

Depending on air temperature and altitude, it came

Victoria (AHB)

unstuck at 65, climbed slowly at 75, cruised at 100, reached 105 flat out, glided at 70 and stalled at 45 mph.

It was so badly under-powered I once took half an hour to climb 1000 feet after leaving Atbara at midday, struggling in the very bumpy hot air with a load of passengers bound for Khartoum.

On landing, a foot-wide cast-iron tail-skid tore up the ground, acting as an anchor. But the leaky water-cooled Napier Lions refused to re-start when hot, despite endless hand-cranking, so in 1934 Victoria VIs, with four-bladed propellers and air-cooled Bristol Pegasus engines were gladly welcomed.

In 1935 Valentias began to appear and, wonder of wonders, they had a tail wheel and differential brakes for steering from the cockpit! No more jumping out to hang on to wingtips for a turn, these brakes were invaluable for making the most of small clearings bordered by scrub, typical of many tropical African airfields.

Cruising at 110 mph, their reliable air-cooled radials gave a reassuring throaty roar as we flew across the wilder parts of our 'parish'. At night our exhaust manifolds glowed red-hot, showering carbon sparks like tiny shooting stars into the dark slipstream. Effective inertia engine-starters saved us time at every stop for fuel, sparing our erks an awful lot of sweaty labour.

Italian ambitions were so half-heartedly resisted by the League of Nations that *Il Duce* blatantly cocked a snook at every protest emanating from Geneva, aided and abetted by Adolf Hitler. The paper-thin Hoare-Laval Agreement was contemptuously ignored.

We watched the Italians preparing for the fray from our grandstand seats in Egypt. Early in 1935 more than the occasional troopship began to pass through the Suez Canal bound for Massawa or Mogadishu. Increasing numbers of fast, sleek Caproni metal-bodied (!) monoplane (!!) transports staged through Almaza, the Royal Egyptian Air Force airfield adjacent to Heliopolis, all heading for East Africa, making even our latest and most admired Mk. VI Victorias look like dodos.

Sabres started to be rattled on Libya's southern borders, where Egypt and the Sudan also converge in the mountainous region of Gebel Ouweinat. Evidently the Italians were up to something and, seen in the light of other suspicious moves, their unwelcome activities in that remote frontier area had to be investigated without delay.

First on the scene were four Victorias from No. 216 Sqn whose crews humped their own fuel in the ubiquitous four-gallon petrol cans together with all spares, water and rations, leap-frogging in short hops across 700 miles of desert south west from Cairo. This took two days.

Sure enough, when seen from the air, there was much hustle and bustle on the far side of the unmarked frontier, though it was unclear exactly what was afoot. So, after observing the scene for a couple of days, the Victorias returned to Heliopolis, having at least demonstrated their ability to find and occupy a remote desert region should any future need arise. In the light of their subsequent 1935 hostilities, it is possible Gebel Ouweinat was used by Italy as an air staging post for flying reinforcements to Eritrea, crossing the deserts of the Sudan clandestinely, without opposition and unobserved.

Hardly had we drawn breath from the Gebel Ouweinat flap than it was decided to see if No. 208 Sqn Atlases could reinforce the very thin ground defences that the Sudan was able to muster on her eastern borders with Abyssinia. For 208 Sqn to reach those tropical regions, 1500 miles from Heliopolis, they needed 216 Sqn to carry their ground crews and spares. The short-ranged Atlas two-seaters of 208 Sqn, ill equipped to navigate seriously on their own, needed to be convoyed in two-hour hops across desert, tropical savannah and finally thick bush to reach remote destinations in southern Sudan.

We seldom saw anything suspicious going on but were ourselves sometimes shadowed by a gleaming, part metal-bodied Caproni 133 monoplane of the Regia Aeronautica, keeping an eye on us! Its sleek modern lines put our bumbling old Victorias to shame and when the Italian pilot became tired of trying to formate on us, hanging on his three variable-pitch propellers at our paltry 105 mph, he would open his throttles and speed happily away at 140 mph.

We were later transferred to Nairobi to support the Army in Kenya. However the war moved steadily north away from the borders of Kenya and our flying support became less needed. At the same time, it became obvious that the probable success of the Italians in seizing Abyssinia would leave them in a strong strategic position on the eastern flanks of the Sudan, Uganda and Kenya, not to mention a potential stranglehold on the Red Sea, a vital artery of the British Empire.

So, although life on Nairobi airfield had grown very quiet, the Air Ministry, with a view to possible future requirements, decided to make the RAF presence in Kenya permanent.

1939–1945
THE OUTBREAK OF WAR

Following the outbreak of war on 3 September 1939 events for a time moved relatively slowly.

Hitler had invaded Poland on 1 September 1939 and by the end of the month the country had fallen.

Two RAF formations were dispatched to France in September 1939. The first was the Air Component of the British Expeditionary Force which included Lysanders, Blenheims and Hurricanes. This force was to operate only on that part of the front occupied by the BEF.

The second was the Advanced Air Striking Force. This consisted of ten squadrons of Battles and Blenheims which were to attack the advancing German divisions. With them were four squadrons of Hurricanes for air defence.

Limited fighting took place along the French/German border throughout the rest of 1939 and the first few months of 1940. There was considerable activity at sea with losses on both sides. The RAF carried out reconnaissance and raids on shipping.

Over the British mainland there was air activity along the Scottish coast. Heinkel 111s and Junkers 88s from the island of Sylt, just south of the Danish/German border, carried out reconnaissance and raids on Scottish ports. On 16 October 1939 the two Scottish Auxiliary Squadrons – 602 (City of Glasgow) and 603 (City of Edinburgh) – shot down two Ju 88s, the first enemy aircraft destroyed in World War II.

King George VI inspects 611 Squadron, Digby, 2 November 1939 (Crown copyright)

First Victory of World War II
Group Captain H. M. Pinfold

Number 603 (City of Edinburgh) Auxiliary Squadron was embodied into the RAF on 23 August, 1939. By 18.00 hrs nearly all serving personnel had assembled at Turnhouse, fully kitted and prepared for war. I also sent out an urgent recall notice to men who had left the Squadron but were still on the Reserve. I formed an Operations Room at Turnhouse and began to instruct pilots on elementary R/T Procedure. The Squadron was then flying the biplane Gloster Gladiator.

On 14 September, eleven days after the declaration of war, our first Spitfire arrived. We were to be one of only eleven squadrons in the RAF to be equipped with the very latest single-seater fighter. By 20 September we had received our 17th and last Spitfire.

I now had to undertake the third conversion of 603 Sqn's pilots within eighteen months. In February 1938 the Squadron had been flying Harts. In March 1938 it converted to Hinds and exactly one year later to Gladiators.

After only a few weeks, 603 Sqn was regarded as being operational on Spitfires and on 11 October we began to transfer our Gladiators to 152 Sqn. Less than one week later the Squadron's effectiveness was to be put to the test.

On 16 October the Observer Corps Centre reported several high-level reconnaissance aircraft during the morning. These were aircraft of *Kampfgeschwader* 30 operating from Westerland on the island of Sylt, just south of the Danish/German border. The round trip of almost 1000 miles called for considerable skill. The aircraft used were He 111s, primarily for reconnaissance, and Ju 88s. Numbers 602 and 603 Sqns had earlier been on patrol but no interceptions had been made.

Just before 1430 the alarm suddenly went off whilst we were standing at dispersal. Galashiels had reported that hostile planes had been seen near Berwick-on-Tweed. There were nine and their objective appeared to be warships at anchor East of the Forth Bridge. Red Section of 'A' Flight were at readiness but this was the first chance to put their training to the test. One young pilot was rather confused and I had to encourage him to get into his aircraft. I felt like grabbing his parachute and helmet and going myself! Led by Flight Lieutenant Patsy Gifford, a solicitor in civil life, 'A' Flight reached 3000 ft over East Lothian. Visibility was not good due to a combination of bright sunshine and autumn haze. There were numerous patches of heavy cumulus cloud.

Flying Officer MacDonald suddenly saw a twin-engined aircraft above and to starboard heading in his direction. Red Section went into a steep climbing turn, the enemy aircraft broke away into cloud and its rear gunner opened fire. Having gained height, Patsy Gifford identified the aircraft as a Heinkel 111. He led his section into a dive coming up again under the bomber's tail. Each of 603 Sqn's pilots fired in turn and hits were observed. After a second engagement the enemy broke away over the coast. The rear gunner was now silent and at 1415 Gifford closed in for the final attack. The enemy aircraft ditched and its crew abandoned it. Three of the four member crew were rescued by fishermen. It was in fact a Ju 88. (Aircraft recognition was a young science!). The wreckage was later recovered.

At 1500 Flight Lieutenant Pinkerton of 602 Sqn shot down an enemy aircraft off Crail. He also identified it as a Heinkel 111 and once more it turned out to be a Ju 88.

In view of the short time between the two engagements there was much argument between the two squadrons as to which had destroyed the first enemy victim of the RAF in World War II.

According to Pinkerton's Combat Report he claimed his victim at 1500. This was confirmed by Dunfermline Observer Corps which noted in its log '1455 Enemy aircraft down in sea three miles east of Crail.' (P. 1731.)

However by 1455 Gifford had already landed back at Turnhouse. His Combat report gave the time of attack as 1445.

Air Intelligence was asked to adjudicate and eventually on 20 December 1941, replied
'*... From this record you will see that the first aircraft to be destroyed was by 603 Squadron at 1445 hours on 16th October, 1939 and the second by 602 Squadron at 1500 hours on October 16th 1939. As these two aircraft were the first enemy aircraft destroyed by Fighter Command during the present war it clearly gives the honour of the first blood to 603 Squadron.*'

Gloster Gladiator formation (AHB)

Still the argument continued and it was next referred to Headquarters Fighter Command. This drew the following reply:

'*From Headquarters Fighter Command to Headquarters Number 11 Group (for the attention of Squadron Leader Milner). Ref . FC/s 18162/int date 24th January, 1942.*

Claims of 602 and 603 Squadrons Re: destruction of first enemy aircraft.

1. With reference to the above subject, it has now been established that the first enemy aircraft to be destroyed by Fighter Command was shot down by 603 Squadron at 1445 hours on the 16th October, 1939. 602 Squadron destroyed an enemy aircraft at 1500 hours on the same day.

2. 603 Squadron therefore has the honour of destroying the first enemy aircraft during the war. Copies of the Combat Reports are enclosed.

Signed: E C de Rougement for Air Vice-Marshal
Senior Air Staff Officer, Fighter Command'

It was very clear that the first two victims of World War II had gone to the Auxiliaries – but the argument continues to this day!

Early War-time Days on Flying Boats

Air Chief Marshal Sir John Barraclough KCB CBE DFC AFC

In the sixty-three years since I joined No. 269 Squadron on Avro Ansons in Coastal Command the advances in aviation have been so astonishing that readers today may find it difficult to credit the primitive facilities and equipment with which we entered the '39–'45 War. But that was the state of the art at the time: a mere twenty-three years since the great sea battle of Jutland and little more distant in time than the Falklands conflict is from us at the time of writing this memoir. Also, it should be remembered that for much of that period there had been a Government embargo on any war planning so, quite understandably, that inconclusive battle between British and German Naval might provided a reference point and background colour to our maritime strategy in the approach to the World War II. Interestingly, in view of what was to happen later, the small force of German U-Boats, only half of which were ocean-going, was seen as a minor threat to be dealt with as need arose by the very effective sonic ASDIC system in our destroyers.

We did not have separately trained navigators in Coastal in those days and second pilots were trained in navigation at the School of General Reconnaissance where we were groomed to be the long range 'eyes of the fleet'. We were schooled in naval tactics and codes, and such matters as crossing the enemy's 'T' and the positioning of destroyer and cruiser screen around the capital ships were part of our stock in trade as was, very essentially if less intellectually, a facility of eight words a minute in Morse code on the Aldis lamp. These marine skills were to be followed later, when on flying boats, with tests on knots and splices and semaphore as part of the promotion examination to Flying Officer.

In the hasty expansion of the Command in 1938, a decision out of the blue that twelve of us from the GR course were to be transferred to boats was greeted with excitement, tinged, personally, with some sadness at leaving friends in 269 Squadron which went on to chalk up a distinguished war record as it had in 1914–18. But the web-footed world was something apart and we had dreams of patrolling the seas and subduing the King's enemies in the majestic new Sunderland with its long range and seven guns. But in my case that was not to be, for I was posted to the newly forming 240 Squadron equipped with the SARO London – a charming machine for peacetime swanning – with a performance just about akin to the best of the RFC aircraft at the end of the Great War except that its two Bristol Pegasus engines were very reliable and we could stay in the air for nine hours, ten at a pinch, if only at about 80 knots. The armament of three Lewis Guns, which hated the salty atmosphere, mounted in open cockpits, had a quadrant of oiled hide as a windbreak for the gunners. All of this was quite familiar to those who had seen the film 'Hell's Angels' while on holiday from school in the mid thirties, as most of us had.

Being the eyes of the Fleet we did not at first have an offensive anti-submarine or anti-shipping role nor the armament to match, but we were soon to carry four 250 lb A/S bombs with a dubious delayed-action fuse. The officially recommended process was to release them by eye in a shallow dive with a chinagraph mark on the windscreen serving as a sighting aid of the Captain's choosing. They were viewed with not a little suspicion after two naval Swordfish had their tails blown off in an attack on a surfaced U-Boat in the early days of the war. We had little or no training in the use of these unfriendly weapons although I do recall simple dive-bombing exercises on a target off Calshot Spit with our rigger throwing 20 lb practice bombs out of the ward room window when given a prod with a boat hook from the second pilot, prompted in turn by a nod from the Captain. This practice was suspended after we put one through the roof of the NAAFI following some confusion in that chain of command.

Our maritime strategy in the early days took up very largely where it left off in 1918, namely blockading Germany by intercepting her merchant ships on the high seas and containing her warships in the Baltic or, if unsuccessful in the latter case, pursuing them and bringing them to battle. In this strategy Coastal had a clear role of flying a network of patrols across the North Sea from the first day of the War. This was aimed at monitoring all shipping of any flag not under Royal Naval protection and detecting any attempts by the German Navy to break out from the Baltic into the Atlantic either through the Channel, or more probably northabout through the Iceland/Faeroes or Shetland/Faeroes gaps and later of course, as in the *Bismarck* action, through the Denmark Straits between Iceland and Greenland. I should add that this high strategic thinking was not shared with the likes of us at squadron level – our job was to do as we were told and that kept us fully occupied.

Through the timidity of the British and French Governments the German Navy, with a relatively low priority for its U-boat programme, had been allowed to build a truly formidable fleet of fast powerful ships headed by the battleships *Bismarck* and *Tirpitz* and the battlecruisers *Scharnhorst* and *Gneisenau* with pocket-battleships, cruisers

Early wartime days in flying boats (Sir John Barraclough)

and destroyers to match. The ship recognition problems from a distance – a vital part of our reconnaissance skills – were compounded by the way these formidable ships of such different size and capabilities all had remarkably similar silhouettes. The prospect of any of them breaking out into the Atlantic, as they were soon to do, and getting loose among our merchant convoys made naval blood run cold. Paradoxically this was the period of the so-called 'phoney war' at home, with the citizens still spending comfortably undisturbed nights in their beds, while to the north every nerve and sinew was being strained at sea with the Home Fleet's essential base at Scapa Flow being ruled untenable after Lt Prien in his U-boat so skilfully penetrated the nets and blockships to sink our battleship *Royal Oak* in the first five weeks of the war.

The Anson, though faster than our Londons, did not have the range to span the wider reaches of the North Sea and it was with our 900 mile Londons that the gap was to be closed, at least theoretically, but – and it was a very big 'but' – we lacked a northern operating base. So, in early 1938 the Air Ministry chartered the British India Steam Navigation (BISN) company's old cargo/passenger ship SS *Manela* (9000 tons) as a depot ship. That was the start of her remarkable after-life in support to the Royal Air Force throughout the war. In her younger days she had sailed on the pilgrim runs from the Gulf and other Muslim centres to the Red Sea during the Haj until even the devout pilgrims felt that her deck conditions were too primitive and she was left to rust in Falmouth Roads until, in the words of the old mess ballad '...when the Air Force saw her'. In the summer of 1939 she was cranked up and creaked her way to Sullom Voe in the North of the Shetlands where she was to be the depot ship for 240 and 201 Squadrons for well over a year.

At that time there was no landing stage nor even the smallest of jetties from which to land on the romantic shores of Yell Sound so pervaded with Norse legend. To do that, on a rare fine day, called for rolled-up trousers and jumping ashore from one of the skimming dinghies by which we went to and from our aircraft at their moorings. This was a welcome change from the confines of our ship after a month or so, and a far cry now from one of the largest and most important oil terminals in the world. But we lived comfortably enough aboard the old *Manela*, with a large saloon but cramped 'over-and-under' bunks in two-berth cabins for the officers and mess-deck hammocks for the airmen. Among our attentive and obliging Lascar crew (we soon adjusted to being addressed as Sahib up near the Arctic circle) was one with the engaging soubriquet of 'Can-Do' who took up a self-appointed stewardship in the operations room providing hot drinks and biscuits at any hour of the day and night. Sadly that happy arrangement came unstuck when Can-Do having learnt how to read a chart in the ops room discovered that Sullom Voe was above latitude 60 N which was the limit for employment in their contract with the BISN. A complete change of crew ensued under cover of canvas screens to ensure that the outgoing crew did not impart this vital intelligence to the incoming one. But life on the *Manela* was never quite the same without Can-Do.

Our bulk fuel was held in lighters replenished by small oilers from Lerwick and bombs (later depth charges) and ammunition were similarly held at a safe distance from the main ship. Our smaller marine craft mostly lay alongside to take aircrew and servicing crews out to the aircraft as part of the daily routine. In that first winter the weather was particularly fierce and the limiting factor on flying was usually the sea state. In gales this could prevent us getting aboard our aircraft in the great seas rolling down Yell Sound as the winds swept those treeless islands. The loss of aircraft at their moorings was not uncommon with our old biplanes which tended to lift at their moorings in gusts above fifty or sixty knots and crash back on the sea as the gust passed. Storm crews were sometimes put aboard, and by running the engines it was thought that snatch on the mooring pennant plates, a frequent cause of foundering, could be eased. It was not a popular duty and sometimes forty-eight hours would pass before they could be relieved. We carried pigeons for emergency communications in those days, lent by proud fanciers, and my crew came under suspicion after one of these stints when two of them were found missing.

As a general rule if we could board and get the engine covers off then we were expected to fly and without any external navigation aids we flew routinely in some awful weather. Frequently with an open side-window for a better view, and often at 100 feet or so above the sea under low cloud, or in the snow, sleet and rain that blanketed the North Sea, especially in that unkind first winter. But we flew slowly and were quite manoeuvrable and, looking back on it, dead reckoning was the state of our art: we had, and knew, nothing else.

The nearer we flew to the water the more accurately we navigated because we quickly became very skilled in assessing wind speed and direction at the surface from the white caps and wind lanes. On approaching the Norwegian coast we also grew canny lest Stadtlandet, our most frequent and forbidding landfall, should loom out of the mists and leave us insufficient air space to manoeuvre. In that event we knew that the escape route had to be hard to port where the headland fell away to the North East. Also for early warning of approaching land we learnt to read the habits of the seagulls and cormorants whether flying or taking it easy on the sea, and of course a small open fishing boat was a clear warning of a coast ahead. It was this combination of airmanship and seamanship which often saved us from navigational dangers in the air far greater than the risk of an occasional encounter with a superior enemy aircraft, or perhaps an unfriendly greeting from our own merchant ships who could be free with their machine guns despite our good intentions.

A standard patrol was from Muckle Flugga (the northernmost point of the United Kingdom) to fifty miles north or south of Stadtlandet. We then flew up or down Norwegian territorial waters to monitor the shipping in both directions, much of it bringing the neutral Swedish iron ore from Narvik safely through territorial waters back into the Baltic, or less safely across the North Sea to feed the respective enemy war-machines. Also German merchant ships from distant ports were coming back around the North to take shelter in that long corridor of immunity which Churchill called the 'covered way'. At that stage our Government had declared internationally that it would meticulously observe the rules on territorial waters in our blockade. Nevertheless we would sometimes 'inadvertently' infringe those rules by flying low past interesting ships to note their names, ports of registration, estimated tonnage, course and speed and whether in ballast or with deck cargo. One hoped that the picture built up in the Admiralty was of some use. Clearly it was in the case of the *Altmark*, the *Graf Spee*'s supply ship spotted creeping back around the north after the scuttling of her parent in the River Plate, which resulted in the happy release from her hold of our merchant seaman prisoners of war into the arms of the Royal Navy.

We were kept together as a crew for as long as possible and this was particularly important on the London and the Stranraer where we had no intercommunication system. In the air, a small tear-off pad was the medium for messages between the front-end crew while electric bells bought from local shops gave us a system of coded rings with meanings varying from 'action stations' to 'another cup of tea for the captain'. My first crew was a particularly happy one with our Captain Flight Lieutenant Vincent Pam, myself as second pilot and Roger Hunter who was a legendary figure in the Services boxing field: just on 6 ft 8 in in height. With me at 6 ft 3 in and Vincent topping 6 ft. 1 in the total length of the piloting and navigating cast if laid end to end came to exactly 19 feet. Tiny Hunter was well known, apart from being one of the nicest of men and a Heavyweight Boxing Champion, for having done his *ab initio* training on flying boats. He could not be loaded into the Tiger Moth like others of his entry so he was put on the much more exciting Hawker Hart. But that did not last long – his instructor was showing off in an early flight with swishtailing sideslips on the final approach to land when the stick in the pupil's cockpit disappeared beneath Tiny's knee and could not be retrieved before the Hart slipped into the ground. Neither was seriously hurt but it was decided that he should be taught to fly on a more commodious aircraft and hence we came together for a very happy association and long friendship.

Vincent, alas, was killed by an unlucky burst from a Heinkel 111 off Norway. It was our first battle casualty and the reality of war came home to us as we laid him to rest in the hillside cemetery at Lerwick. Although in a selfish way it was probably a lucky escape for me – I was the Orderly Officer on the ship that day and Vincent was sitting in my accustomed seat in K5286. Air engagements with the enemy were fortunately rare as we had little to give in return. From time to time we saw Dornier 18 Flying Boats on parallel tracks in the opposite direction but as their performance was almost exactly the same as ours, give or take a knot or two, there was no question of an engagement unless both parties were of the same mind. However the 111's did pay us attention in Sullom Voe with occasional exciting but unsuccessful passes at the *Manela* and the strafing of our moorings where another member of our crew met his end. As a result we were given an old C Class Anti-Aircraft Cruiser, HMS *Coventry*, as a guard ship. She could put up a truly magnificent barrage which though never lethal to my knowledge was extremely good for morale. We also had the first Coastal fighters (three Gloster Gladiators) operating from a short strip near Lerwick. They were called out by land-line from the ship so they could not be expected until after the event but, as with the *Coventry*, they made us feel important and appreciated.

The middle and rear end crews – who shared the cooking – usually a fitter, one or two riggers and two wireless operators, were ground tradesmen responsible for servicing the aircraft on the water who then, for an extra two shillings a day (10 p.), flew with us in their own trades and as air-gunners. When we got safely back on the water it was their duty, while the captain and his navigator were ferried to the ship for debriefing, to put the aircraft safely to bed with properly moused copper wire locks on all mooring lines, and engine covers, on a pitching upper wing, securely lashed against the disputing claims of the wind. They were marvellous men and touchingly confident that the skills and wisdom of the 22-year old grey beards at the front end would get them safely home, or at least back to their hammocks, with never a thought of complaint about a hard life or being soaking wet from dawn to dusk. In so many ways these two-bob a day aircrew and the coxwains and crews of our marine craft, on whom all depended, were among the unsung heroes of flying boat operations throughout the war, and especially so at remote and sparse bases.

In the weeks before Germany invaded Poland the Reserve Fleet had been mobilised and a few days before war was declared an exercise was mounted from Invergordon with the Home and Reserve fleets manoeuvring off the middle Norwegian coast trying to evade on the one hand and to bring to battle on the other. This really was Jutland re-visited. We were on patrol with the Home Fleet and it was a privileged historical insight to have seen these great but aged fleets at sea. We now know that, ironically, while the muscles of this great panoply of naval power were being flexed, the pocket battleships *Graf Spee* and *Deutschland* slipped out from the Baltic and went northabout to the Atlantic to take up their commerce raiding stations. It was still peace-time of course but it would have been interesting, to say the least, if they had turned up in the middle of that great exercise.

Despite the maximum efforts that our limited Coastal Command resources could sustain across this North Sea grid, it was patchy at best through lack of range and endurance and, more decisively, because of the very bad weather over the area during that autumn and winter. During the long nights and bad weather that marked the start of the war, the battlecruisers *Scharnhorst* and *Gneisenau* got out in the first six weeks, sailing northabout the Shetlands to sink our Armed Merchant Cruiser *Rawalpindi* in the Faeroes/Iceland gap. My log book shows that we were patrolling across their track just 24 hours too late!

While still at Sullom Voe in the spring of 1940 we were intensively tasked to escort our expeditionary force to Norway – that ill-starred and ill-prepared but heroic British effort by the Green Howards among others. We flew some sorties as long as ten hours which was pushing our luck to nearly dry tanks. Huddled against the sea and weather on the foredecks of their transports they presented a valiant but improbable motley of soldiery setting off at great odds to an unknown war.

But in 1940 the gathering U-boat campaign in the Western Approaches prompted a change of emphasis away from the North Sea to the North Atlantic and the squadron moved over to Stranraer on the West Coast from where we could reach out to about fourteen degrees west for A/S sweeps and convoy escort, now with depth charges, for the east and west bound convoys from the Clyde and Liverpool. If by 1941, we had not sunk a single U-boat and a few oil slicks had been depth-charged more out of frustration than hope, it must be said that we had never had a ship sunk while under our escort and although an enemy warship sighting was not to come our way our recce role had been pursued assiduously and professionally. That the U-boats were there was never in doubt because of the daily reminder as one rejoined a convoy at dawn to find it depleted from the night before and to be tasked by Aldis lamp from the Senior Escort to search for survivors and home an escort to the lifeboats and Carley floats that littered a melancholy sea with stoical merchant seamen raising a weary arm in relieved recognition and hope, as we played our retrieving role.

At about this time, and now living ashore in a small hotel in Stranraer, we swapped our Londons for Supermarine Stranraers a slightly later bi-plane boat from the drawing board of no less a genius than Mitchell, the designer of the Spitfire. It was a pleasure to fly – a little faster but alas no greater range and no intercom or R/T. We still had to shout or write to one another in the air to keep the crew in line. This was not what we wanted and we just could not understand why we could not be given the Sunderlands for which we yearned. But help was on the way and shortly we were to get the PBY Catalina, an aircraft of astonishing range and endurance – up to 3000 miles and twenty-four hours, that was to bring great distinction to our maritime airmen in the U-boat battle and the finding, in 1941, by Denis Briggs of 209 Squadron of the *Bismarck* after she had sunk the *Hood* and in another theatre the shadowing of the Japanese Fleet.

Around this period I remember that my boat was put in the hands of some 'boffins' for the installation of secret equipment and later in bad weather, by consulting this device, they conned us accurately through the channel south of the Mull and got some echoes from various ships. They went away delighted with their boxes under their arms but we were not unduly impressed: after all we could find our way between Rathlin Island and the Mull with our eyes shut. But little did we know what lay ahead, for this was the first practicable model of ASV to be succeeded by the centimetric Mk III version that was in due course to play such a decisive part in the battle against the U-boats.

But my time was up – I had done 1200 hours flying in 15 months and was sent for a spell as an instructor at the OCU at Invergordon, where we at least had some modern aircraft in the Sunderland and Catalina and were occasionally thrown an interesting operational task from the East Coast. Amongst them I remember being sent, with a Sunderland and three Cats, to rescue the crew of the renowned Free French submarine *Rubis*, on a gin-clear day with an escort of Beaufighters and Blenheims, led by Barry Heath, later chairman of Guest Keen and Nettlefolds. The *Rubis* was thought to be in dire trouble on the surface close in to the Norwegian coast under the nose of the *Luftwaffe* near Bergen. In fact her crew (68 men and a dog) were having a jolly time in Queensferry celebrating their return from another successful patrol. Such were communications in those days!

My next posting was as flight commander of 209 Sqn of *Bismarck* fame, re-equipping with the latest mark of Catalina for an urgent deployment to the East with Japan now in the war. That is a very different chapter of the maritime air story, but securing threatened sea lanes around the Cape to the Middle East and India against German and Japanese submarines from bare bases and a background of mangrove swamps and malaria, called for exactly those qualities of resourcefulness, flexibility and youthful optimism, in making do with little or nothing, that had been inculcated in us from earlier days in the outposts of Scotland and the Shetlands.

By 1944, when the U-boat threat had been largely subdued around the Cape, by Catalinas from Madagascar finding, and arranging the demise, of the German supply ship *Elizabeth Schliemann* down towards the Roaring Forties, an old hand from Shetland days on convoy escort in the Mozambique Channel wiped his eyes in disbelief as a straggling six knotter of about 9000 tons with 'salt-caked smoke stack' hove into view ploughing up to the North East. He was not to know that she was heading towards Penang and Singapore for another stint of familiar duty with the flying boat squadrons which were by then engaged from India across the Bay of Bengal. This was the final chapter of her loyal and unsung support of the Royal Air Force and its maritime air operations.

Yes – it was the SS *Manela*.

THE FALL OF EUROPE

In April 1940 everything changed as Hitler launched his massive European *Blitzkrieg*. On 9 April he invaded Denmark and Norway. Denmark offered no resistance and Norway finally fell on 10 June.

On 10 May Hitler began his assault on the Low Countries. Belgium held out for eighteen days, Holland for fourteen days and Luxembourg offered no resistance. His main thrust was however, to the south. Forty-four German divisions swept through the Ardennes in the Sedan area and reached the Channel at Abbeville some ten days later. This broke the French Army into two and left the British Expeditionary Force cut off from its supply lines. It was then fifty miles from the sea with a continuous line of Germany armour to the south and the disintegrating Franco-Belgian front to the north. Against all odds Lord Gort managed to withdraw his forces to the coast at Dunkirk where he established a bridgehead.

Completely surrounded, out-numbered and out-gunned the British and French armies fought bravely to defend their positions on and around the beaches. Evacuation began on 26 May and Navy and civilian ships worked tirelessly under constant attack to evacuate as many troops as possible.

The full force of the *Luftwaffe* was now committed to the

crushing of the evacuation. To counter this the Chief of Air Staff, Sir Cyril Newall, ordered a supreme effort by 11 Group of Fighter Command. Over 2700 fighter sorties were launched across the Channel and the *Luftwaffe* could seriously hamper operations on only two of the nine days the British Army were penned in.

At the time many asked the question 'Where is the Air Force?' Most operations were, of course, directed at keeping enemy aircraft away from the bridgehead and actions took place out of sight of the troops. There was another point. In his history of World War II Sir Maurice Dean comments, *'Neither the Royal Navy nor the Army were reliable judges of what Royal Air Force aircraft looked like. As a result, when the Royal Air Force appeared at reasonable distances they were invariably fired at enthusiastically by the Army or the Navy, or more usually by both. Safety first no doubt, but it seems that more friendly aircraft were around than some people supposed.'*

This is borne out by the accounts of Aubrey Lancaster and Eric Barwell which follow.

A third of a million men escaped the trap.

Italy took advantage of the situation to declare war on France and Britain on 11 June.

The massive military power of France surrendered after thirty-seven days. Marshal Petain agreed an Armistice with Germany and Italy on 25 June 1940.

In less than eleven weeks Hitler had overrun most of Western Europe.

The Maastricht and Meuse Bridges

L. R. Clarke

In May 1940 I was a Wireless Operator/Air Gunner in 12 (Bomber) Squadron based at Amifontaine, near Reims in France. We were equipped with Fairey Battles, a monoplane with a crew of three.

On 12 May the Squadron had attacked the bridges at Maastricht. Five aircraft had taken part. Four were shot down and the fifth was badly damaged. The first Air VCs of the War were awarded posthumously to the Flight Leader, Flying Officer Garland, and his Observer, Sergeant Gray. The Air Gunner, LAC L. R. Reynolds received no award.

A new threat was developing against the Allied Front in France. After four days the main thrust of the German offensive had moved from Holland and Belgium further south towards Sedan on the River Meuse. An operation was planned in response to an appeal by the French for a maximum counter-effort by the Advanced Air Striking Force. It was designed to stop the German breakthrough by destroying their pontoon bridges across the River Meuse. The briefing emphasised the serious military situation and the importance of the operation. The attack was to be made by approaching at 6000 ft and dive-bombing the target. The four 250 lb bombs fitted with instantaneous fuses would be released at 2000 ft and we were to return at low level.

The Squadron's contribution was five aircraft, the maximum available after the earlier heavy losses. The targets were a pontoon bridge west of Sedan and another south of the city.

The two aircraft of B Flight were intercepted by Bf 109s and both were shot down. We were second of the three aircraft of A Flight. We climbed steadily to 6000 ft, the signs of war beneath us, much of it due to *Luftwaffe* bombing – bombed trains, burning buildings, halted road convoys and streams of refugees.

Approaching Sedan we ran into concentrated flak just as Bf 109s were coming up behind. Hit by flak L5538 was last seen, after jettisoning its bomb load, going down trailing smoke. However, it managed to reach base, the only aircraft to return to Amifontaine. The lead aircraft was also hit and only the Wireless Operator survived. We dived at the target and at 2000 ft were fatally hit and my pilot gave the order to

Fairey Battles in France (L.R. Clarke)

bale out. By this time he was forced to stand in the cockpit. I went out first and experienced that unique sensation of falling into a bottomless pit before being jerked into silent downward flight. Looking across I could see the smoke trail left by our aircraft and two parachutes close to the ground in the distance. Shortly afterwards I almost dropped into the canal leading from the River Meuse, all my weight going on my right leg as I hit the canal towpath, my left leg sinking deeply into soft ground. As I gathered myself together a dozen Bf 109s flew overhead. It was about 1600 hours.

A German motorcycle combination was fast approaching and, feeling rather ludicrous, I put up my hands as directed by the two Germans holding Tommy guns. They searched me, removing my belongings and expressing surprise that I had no pistol. To me the whole situation seemed unreal, I felt detached from the scene as an onlooker watching a drama played out – I couldn't really believe that I was involved. I was put in the sidecar and we drove for about half a mile to a cafe filled with German troops. All along the road tanks were sheltering under the trees.

I was the first British airman the Germans had encountered and naturally they regarded me with some curiosity, their attitude in the main being friendly and surprisingly sympathetic. I had a cut on the back of my head which they bandaged and I was plied with cigarettes, fruit and some coffee. The English speakers introduced me to that familiar phrase of later days 'for you the war is over'. Many laughed, exclaiming that I would not be a prisoner for long because the war would soon be over – how nearly right they were.

During this time a Hurricane flew over and the Germans let rip with their rifles. The pilot, recklessly I thought, did a few aerobatics, at low level, for which the Germans cheered, then flew off. Soon after a Fairey Battle of 218 Squadron – who lost ten of the eleven aircraft despatched that afternoon – came streaking past at ground level on full boost, smoke pouring from its exhausts. The aircraft showed signs of damage and the rear position was unmanned. The tanks and other guns opened up but it disappeared over a ridge. A column of smoke shot into the air and the sound of an explosion followed a few seconds later. The Germans shrugged and exclaimed '*es its Krieg*'.

Eventually my personal belongings were returned to me and a 21-year old Unteroffizier introduced himself, said he was my escort and that he had orders to shoot should I attempt to escape. My right leg was by this time very painful. We started walking along the road, the troops having said goodbye, wishing me luck. We walked for probably thirty minutes, the exercise easing the pain in the leg, until we came to a small village. At the end of the street we saw a dying French soldier, a cigarette in his mouth. He had been manning an anti-tank gun which received a direct hit. Another Frenchman was holding him in a sitting position while a German medical orderly attended to his terrible injuries.

We were about half way through the village when shells started falling. The troops dropped into the wayside ditches and my escort suggested that we shelter in the front entrance of one of the houses. The house opposite us received a direct hit and a shell splinter spun across the road and hit my flying boot. I picked it up – it was very hot – and put it in the pocket of my sidcot. My escort decided it would be safer to join the troops in the ditches. This we did, and then followed an incident which often comes to my mind. I got down and lay alongside a German soldier who turned to me and said in perfect English 'Haven't you got a helmet?', I said 'No I haven't'. He replied 'Get underneath me' and moved over. I did so and lay with this soldier sheltering me. The shelling ceased about five minutes later and the troops started getting out of the ditches. I got up and thanked the German. He said it was nothing, that I was lucky, I would survive the war, but for him and his comrades, no one knew what the future held. He wished me luck and a safe return to my home. And so we parted... I have often wondered about this German – who was he?, what was his motivation?, did he survive?

After some time we came to a local HQ and my escort, after wishing me well, handed me over. I was taken to an armoured vehicle in which sat a senior officer studying maps at a table. The officer, who spoke perfect English, asked me about the wound on my head, congratulated me on surviving my action and asked where I had come from, to which I replied – England. He asked if I had any complaints about the treatment given me and said that if any of my personal property had been taken he would take steps to get it back. He mentioned that in peacetime he was a regular visitor to England. He said goodbye and suggested I should have a meal in the house, but I was not hungry. My escorts said we should move on. We walked for a little way and came to the river where a number of rubber boats were being used to ferry troops across. We were standing by the bank when tracer was seen a few hundred yards up the river. A mobile searchlight switched on illuminating a Blenheim. A two-man operated machine gun opened up and tracer criss-crossed the aircraft but it flew on.

We got into one of the boats which was paddled to the other bank. We then walked for some time along a road jammed with stationary vehicles until we came to a farm. I was handed over and taken to a building full of French soldiers. By this time it was midnight. I sat on the straw, my head swimming with exhaustion, sundry aches, cuts and bruises forgotten and went to sleep. It had been a long day.

And so ended an operation which resulted in the RAF suffering its heaviest loss ever in the war for an operation of comparative size: forty of the seventy-one bombers despatched being shot down. And what was achieved? Sadly, very little.

Two pontoon bridges destroyed and two damaged with very little effect on the German advance. Of the forty crews lost, seventeen members made their way back from enemy-held territory, the other 103 were mostly dead or prisoners of war.

I met up with the other members of my crew next morning at the farm. We journeyed by lorry through the Ardennes with a stay overnight in a church and a few days in a warehouse in Belgium. We encountered rougher treatment as we got further away from the front. A two-day coal truck journey to Stalag IV B followed, then Muhlesburg, and eventually *Dulag Luft*, Limburg, Lamsdorf, Barth, Sagan, Hydekrug, Thorn, Fallingbostal and the March. The escape from the March and arrival in Blighty on 23 April 1945 is another story!

Expedition to France

Michael J. Pitt

Towards the end of my apprenticeship at Halton in July 1939, I selected RAF Bicester as one of my three options for posting. I was fortunate and obtained my first choice. The food was much better, one had twenty-eight shillings per week to spend, civvies to wear off-duty and adult company – at least a year or two older – to listen to.

As the influx of recruits straight from civilian life grew, the gradations of rank grew less severe, less formal. In peacetime, one step in rank, say from LAC to Corporal, or from Pilot Officer to Flying Officer, represented quite a large gap, but as war progressed it took two or three elevations before friendships became difficult to maintain. Contact between Officers and men was, however, very limited in the early days. Officers had little interest in the welfare of personnel under their command. Ground crew got to know their aircraft's pilot to a very limited extent. Smiles, words of encouragement, or enquiries about your welfare were unknown. In ten months my Commanding Officer never spoke to me and I am quite sure he did not know my name. At no time did he address the Squadron, even when we were suffering tremendous losses.

On Saturday, 2 September, airliners from Imperial Airways arrived at Bicester to transport ground crew and essential stores and equipment to France. Twelve of the Squadron's Battles and its Magister took off *en route* to Berry-au-Bac, approximately 20 km north of Reims.

Over the next few days the civil aircraft, now with camouflage paint roughly daubed all over their original shining silver surfaces, continued to ferry men and equipment to Berry. The men were living in very Spartan conditions, feeding on a diet of horsemeat stew provided by the French, supplemented by apple turnovers, baguettes, butter and honey bought, with their own money, from the village bakery; in the evenings the local cafes did a roaring trade.

The Battles were bombed up and operationally ready within three hours of the declaration of War. Two days later, armour plating for pilots and observers was received and fitted. The next day the Vickers K-guns were loaded with ammunition which included armour-piercing and incendiary rounds.

The rest of the ground crew arrived at Berry-au-Bac on 18 September, after a most exhausting overland and sea journey. We crossed in a ferry from Southampton to Cherbourg. The train journey (about 300 miles) to Guignicourt near Berry-au-Bac, took more than twenty-four hours. Our travelling accommodation was little better than the renowned '*40 hommes – 8 chevaux*' standard. Slatted wooden seats for that length of time became torture. All stops were unpredictable, and none of them were at stations where one could alight and stretch legs. The appearance of unshaven, bleary-eyed officers and men in crumpled uniforms when we eventually arrived at Guignicourt would be duplicated only a few months later when many were prisoners-of-war.

That night we joined with our Squadron mates in the billets they had been occupying for the past couple of weeks. Mine was in the hayloft of a barn above the stalls of twenty oxen. There was no chance of a long sleep. We were awakened at 5 a.m. by the shouts of the farmer driving his beasts out to work. By seven a.m. we were on our way to the cookhouse for a delicious breakfast and an even more welcome mug of hot, sweet, thick tea. A new life was beginning, and I was totally enthralled by everything.

My recollections of our ten days at Souge tend to concentrate on the beautiful June weather and the fact that we could, at times of idleness – and there were many of these – swim in the River Loir, which flowed, bordered by shady trees, alongside the airfield. As usual, our accommodation in the village was in a loft, but by now we had become well accustomed to this style of life. With the weather so favourable, it was a great joy to have all our meals in the open, on trestle tables set out in the main street. The war seemed quite remote from us and there was plenty to eat and drink in the local cafe.

This enjoyable existence came to an end on 14 June. I had been detailed with two others to accompany a driver with lorry to fetch petrol from a dump some miles on the other side of Vendôme. I got this 'cushy' job, because it was thought necessary to have someone with at least a smattering of French. Refugees had not been passing through Souge in any numbers, but our route now took us on to the main Paris–Bordeaux road, and there was a constant stream of them, but this time quite different from what we had encountered when leaving Amifontaine: no more pathetic horse-drawn carts or laden walkers, but cars, vans and trucks.

The petrol dump was concealed in a forest, and we loaded the lorry with boxes, each containing two 4-gallon cans. The thought of what would have happened had a German fighter shot us up did not occur to me. I cannot remember that we had to sign for the amount we had loaded: it all seems quite haphazard in retrospect. Perhaps things had become so chaotic with frequent moves and poor communications that no-one cared any more about such formalities as would have been strictly observed only a month earlier. At one small town through which we passed, we stopped for refreshment at a cafe and found that the whole population appeared to be selling up and getting out. Presumably the locals, seeing the refugees pouring through, thought that it was the sensible thing for them to do. Rumour was rife. In fact, it would be some time before the enemy, busy with affairs along the Channel coast, would consider their town worthy of any attention.

We had many stops on our return journey to help stranded motorists who had run out of petrol, a problem we were only too happy to solve. The rewards for dispensing our 4-gallon cans could have been tremendous, but were happily declined. The relief shown by these unfortunate people, uprooted from their homes would have melted any heart. In retrospect, I fail to understand why we seemed quite careless about any danger the Germans posed to us. We were quite ignorant of the war situation; certainly we were not aware that within three days we would be in Plymouth.

We stopped in Vendôme in the evening for a meal, and the town was bombed by a solitary aircraft. On return to Souge, however, we learnt that aircraft had attacked the airfield at about 5 p.m. destroying several aircraft and causing casualties. It must have been about 10 p.m. when we got back to the village, to find that our lorries had been loaded for an immediate move further west. How grateful I was to friends who had kindly packed up my kit in my absence.

The convoy of about twenty vehicles set off at about midnight. Rumour had it that we were on our way to a new airfield close to Rennes. A beautiful morning dawned, and we soon rolled back the tarpaulin covering the rear of our lorry; we lay comfortably on our baggage, enjoying the scenery, while at the same time keeping a careful lookout for any Jerry planes. Breakfast, cooked in the mobile kitchen, was the one we never tired of, bacon, eggs, baked beans and fried bread, hot mug of tea, thickened by condensed milk, all tasting so much better alfresco, and – for me – because I had not had a lot to eat the previous day. More than once the convoy was stopped and we lay in ditches at the side of the road, but nothing untoward happened.

The Fairey Battle (AHB)

About midday, when we must have been approaching Rennes, a dispatch rider raced past us and the convoy was halted. We could see the CO reading whatever message the dispatch rider had brought. We passed through Rennes and left it further and further behind, so it became obvious that new instructions had been received. Every signpost we passed was now pointing to Brest, and the thought began that perhaps we were on our way back to UK. Even so, we felt this would only be for us to re-equip, perhaps with Blenheims, and that we should soon be returning to France. It needs to be said here that our only sources of information were the BBC Radio broadcasts, and there was still the naive thought that everything emanating therefrom was genuine truth, and only the enemy resorted to propaganda. So, we must be forgiven for our blissful ignorance. (The notion that, whatever happened, we would never lose the War persisted for the duration.) Whereas we could not be expected to know how bad things were, it is now quite evident that the High Command knew little more.

On our way to Brest, we met a huge Army convoy, later identified as the Canadian First Division, which had just disembarked and was on its way to the Front. There was a lively interchange of views as to who was going in the right direction. Little did we know that within a short time they would be turned back, and all their equipment would be driven over the cliffs at Brest, just as our vehicles were. High Command considered there was not time, nor the facilities, to load them for return to UK.

We halted just outside Brest for the night, taking as much rest as possible on our lorries, looking and feeling quite wretched after forty-eight hours without wash and shave, or any change of clothing. We were probably purposely not told that we would be leaving all our kit – except for rifle and water-bottle – otherwise we would no doubt have been spending the night secreting what valuables we had about our persons.

We marched through the city to the docks, joining hundreds of others on board a cross-Channel passenger ship. Soon after embarking there was an air-raid. A single Heinkel 111 flew over and dropped mines in the entrance to the harbour. It soon dawned on us that we were trapped and that we would be at the mercy of the bombers that would inevitably follow. The sole consolation was that, with many ships of the French Navy also trapped in the huge harbour, including the battleship *Richelieu*, we might be overlooked.

We had nothing to do until the mines were cleared, hoping that this might be in time for us to catch the next tide. Military commanders are often blamed in retrospect for obvious blunders; on this occasion we all had reason to thank some German commander for not dispatching those bombers. As it was, steam was raised before 1800 hours, and before the sun set we were well clear of Brest, and heading northwards through open sea.

It was a long time since we had eaten: we were quite exhausted, we were in danger of being torpedoed at any moment, but we were not despondent – we were on our way home, realising at last that a return to France in the near future was out of the question. We entered Plymouth Sound at about 1000 hours, were marched to the Citadel near the Hoe and supplied with tea and the inevitable hard biscuits. The tea was nectar after so many dry hours made worse by chain-smoking.

We completed our journey to Finningley, and were granted a short home leave, with special passes to explain to Service Police the state of our uniforms and lack of parts of it. On the journey to my home at Hampstead I had to show mine several times to Police who would not believe that there could be any excuse for appearing in public in gym shoes and minus headgear!

Hurricanes in France

Group Captain W. D. David CBE DFC AFC

The Royal Air Force in France in 1940 was hopelessly outnumbered compared to the *Luftwaffe*. We had insufficient up-to-date aircraft and we had little idea how to deal with the enemy. We had to learn our fighter tactics from the enemy. They were the experts and veterans who had already fought in Spain, Poland, Belgium and France. The veterans were called 'The Spaniards' in their own air force, (the *Luftwaffe*). We quickly learned these new tactics as we were being shot down relatively easily whilst we were busy flying in tight formation in preparation for our out-dated Fighter Command Attacks. It was an easy task initially for the *Luftwaffe* to pick us off while we formatted closely. Later we learned to weave and to get really close to make a kill, and above all to look behind us all the time. We quickly adopted the smaller formation of the finger-four variety. We learned never to fly in tight collars which prevented us from turning our necks – these also had a nasty habit of tightening up if one landed in water. We passed on these new ideas to the RAF at home, and they were introduced into the operational training syllabus at the Fighter OTUs (Operational Training Units).

As always, our ground crews were first class. They gave us serviceable aircraft to fly. We were in the open with no hangars but somehow they managed – it was the coldest winter for many years (1939–40) and this did not help.

We were part of the Air Force Component of the British Expeditionary Force which was sent to France on the outbreak of war in September 1939. This consisted of four Hurricane Squadrons, four Lysander Squadrons for Army Co-op and four Blenheim Squadrons for Bomber/Recce. All these aircraft were to work with the BEF which was digging in along the France/Belgium frontier. In addition, the four Hurricane Squadrons had to give close support to the Army as well as providing air defence for over 200 miles of Frontier!

War was declared on the 3rd and we flew to France a few days later. We went to Boos just outside Rouen first, and we had to refuel our Hurricanes by hand, using Chamois Leathers as filters. We used hand pumps and it all took a long time. I remember seeing a French mechanic cleaning a carburettor by throwing petrol over it and setting it alight. I will never forget our Flight Sergeant's face when he saw this. Our ground crews never relaxed their high standards.

The Advanced Air Striking Force in France was composed of ten Fairey Battle Squadrons. These were no match for the Me 109s, and the Battles were to have had help from the French Air Force. Alas, the strength and quality of the German Air Force surprised all. The Fairey Battles were shot down in large numbers, and it was no surprise that the *Luftwaffe* thought they could control the air in France. Gradually, but very gradually, we fighters in our Hurricanes got the measure of the German Air Force and we began to destroy them. I have met many *Luftwaffe* Aces since the war and one said to me, 'Dennis, you Brits were different, you started to shoot us down'. (Ulrich Steinhilper)

The French Air Force fought well, but they were outnumbered, and the German fighters, (the Me 109), were superior to anything the French had to fight with. Their Moranes were good but too slow for the 109s. The fact that the French and British fighters did destroy many hundreds of enemy aircraft in France is often forgotten. These very aircraft would have made the eventual Battle of Britain (which took place a few weeks later) an even harder tussle for the RAF.

We seldom met the Germans in France on equal terms – often the odds were ten to one. In those days the *Luftwaffe* did not believe they could be beaten. My own score of enemy mounted because the German bombers were sometimes unescorted by 109s, and in France they were relatively easy to destroy. It was a different task in the Battle of Britain when the German Air Fleets were given escorts of Me 109s when they attacked the UK.

We all knew Dowding was our overall Commander, but we really listened to Keith Park, who was the tactical genius. He was, after all, an 'Ace' from WW I and he had really studied the German mentality. He told us always to go for the Leaders in an enemy formation, and he was adamant that we should attack the enemy as soon as possible, i.e. on way to target. We did just that. On different talks with these German 'Aces' I asked them why they had stopped coming over the UK at the time they decided to end the Battle of Britain. They answered 'Dennis, you and your friends had destroyed too many of our Leaders.' (Dr. Heinz Lange)

Here we have the **truth**. It is a great pity that Sir Keith Park could not have heard these words before he died. His policy of attrition paid off in the end. The Germans are just as brave as us but they do have to be led. They instinctively obey – even unto death. Sir Keith knew this – anyway I always think it was his policy for dealing with the enemy which won the Battle of Britain.

We attacked the enemy whenever and wherever possible – individual 'scores' mounted but our system of claims differed from that of the Germans. Perhaps it was this policy which caused them to over-claim, since they got higher decorations as their number of claims increased. We just kept on going, and for us to make a claim, we had to see the enemy catch fire or prepare for a crash when not in control of the aircraft. This was not always possible as the *Luftwaffe* seemed always to be on our tails, and to wait around was inadvisable.

I remember an incident in France. Whilst flying back to our base by Lille I saw an Me 109 lining up to shoot down an unaware Hurricane. I was out of ammunition, having been involved in a scrap earlier over Belgium. I remember being scared but I dived down in front of the 109 to show my presence. The enemy aircraft sheered off. Luckily he did not know he flew away from two Hurricanes with empty guns. We were not dismayed by them, just outnumbered.

Another memory. It was difficult to make out combat reports as we were busy flying, sighting guns etc., and we tended to postpone this chore. I only went to see one of my victims – a Heinkel 111 which I shot down over Lille. In the attack my windshield had suddenly been covered with oil. As my engine kept going I followed the German down to his forced landing at Herlies. His wheels had come down and he was smoking and in a bad way.

Hurricanes in France (Dennis David's Hurricane painted by Geoff Nutkins)

I only left the airfield as I thought my own Hurricane was unserviceable. I borrowed the flight truck and drove to the German's crash and was met there by a French Officer who was busy destroying enemy bombs. He had seen me flying over the German and confirmed my story that the 111 had blown up after crash-landing. The pilot had managed to get out of the bomber, and had waved to me, but just then a bomb went off and he was no more. I felt sad.

We cheered up when I arrived back at flight to be told my Hurricane was serviceable. The ground crew had checked all oil pipes and they had confirmed that the oil on my windscreen was German oil. A close attack!

I remember the French officer kissing me on both cheeks and saying '*Vous êtes un as*!' The Ace sounded like posterior. I knew my fellow pilots thought of me as an ass, but this was my first confirmation that I had joined the ranks of 'Aces'. The French Officer's action was prompted on hearing this was my fifth victory.

Number 87 Squadron gave a good account of itself, but we lost many experienced fighter pilots who were irreplaceable. This was Dowding's greatest worry. Whereas his personal feelings were to give more fighters to France to relieve our hard pressed forces there, he knew he had to preserve his few fighter pilots for the forthcoming Battle of Britain which was to come a few weeks later. He made enemies during this period even Churchill was not on his side, but the Prime Minister later acknowledged that Dowding had been correct in his judgement of the situation. The Squadron did destroy over seventy enemy aircraft in France but we lost fourteen experienced fighter pilots. Even with these figures we were on a losing ratio. It was a sobering thought.

We had few facilities and our ground crews achieved the near impossible: somehow they gave us serviceable aircraft in which to fly and fight. These same wonderful men re-armed and refuelled us sometimes under fire from enemy aircraft. What more can one say except 'Thank you'. This seems very inadequate.

The next morning I carried out a recce and ran into some enemy. I managed to make it back but crashed on landing. I was then bundled into an Imperial Airways airliner. We flew back to UK at low level and eventually touched down at RAF Hendon. Of course all this meant that I had to leave my dear old Hurricane at Merville in Northern France. I had shot down six enemy aircraft in L1630, and it was an old two-blader. Before setting fire to the remains my ground crew took off the cockpit door. He carried this door all through Dunkirk and after return to UK he surrendered it to the military police. Apparently it then resided in Whitehall where I eventually tracked it down. It is now in a Museum, in Shoreham, where it is earning money for RAF Charities.

Upon arrival at Hendon I was informed 87 Sqn was re-forming at Church Fenton. I was given forty-eight hours leave. I remember sleeping for twenty-four hours – my Mother thought I was dead!

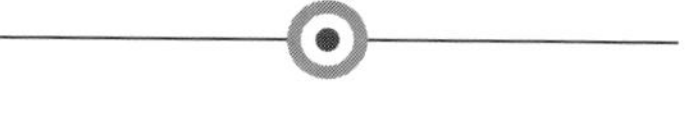

The Lysander

Air Chief Marshal Sir Peter Le Cheminant GBE KCB DFC

After seventeen hours on Lysanders and eleven hours on Hectors (another Hart variant with a potent Napier Dagger engine), I was posted to France to an Army Co-operation Lysander Squadron, No. 4, at Monchy Lagache near Peronne. Its duties included tactical reconnaissance, reporting fall of shot and artillery reconnaissance. I had a total of 163 flying hours, of which all but seventeen were on totally outmoded biplanes. None of my contemporaries were any better placed: we were all effectively untrained, the 1940 equivalents of the RFC pilots who were posted to the Western Front with as little as eight hours total flying. We were mercifully unaware of this at the time, filled as we were with totally unjustified pride and self-confidence.

The Lysander met its specification perfectly: the problem was that this had been drawn up by the Army to meet the needs of static warfare on the 1914–18 model. It would have been fine anywhere where there was no serious opposition, but it was totally unsuitable in the France of 1940. It was quite massive for a single-engined aircraft, with a heavy fixed undercarriage and strong struts supporting its high wing. This was fitted with slots and flaps, which gave it its remarkable short field performance. It was slow and extremely stable so that you could easily fly it with your knees, which was just as well as there was plenty to keep you busy. You sat high up in a large Perspex canopy and had an excellent field of vision, except to the rear where there was an air gunner with a single .303 calibre Vickers K gun. You had a message pad strapped to your right knee on which you wrote the details of what you saw. There was a Morse key on the starboard side of the cockpit for you to transmit this information by W/T, as the only effective R/T sets were all needed for fighters. Left-handed pilots must have managed with considerable difficulty and it was not all that easy for right-handed pilots either, as one was supposed to be able to send and receive at fifteen words a minute: a feat I was unable to achieve even on the ground. You had also to be proficient in aerial photography, as the Lysander could be fitted with cameras for either oblique or vertical photography. All of this was fine in peacetime conditions but, predictably, was not viable in the face of fighters and anti-aircraft fire.

I remember little of that time in France when the so-called Phoney War was about to come to an abrupt end. It was a somewhat unreal atmosphere, living as we did surrounded by the battlefields and graves of the 1914–18 war whilst waiting for our war to start in earnest. We trained as we would have done in England, rehearsing our outmoded tactics as we became familiar with that rather featureless part of north-east France. Everything seemed in the grip of lethargy, almost paralysis.

Lysander formation (AHB)

I was billeted on an elderly couple in the little village of Estrees. Their house had been occupied by the Germans in the Great War and they were apprehensive that history might repeat itself – as indeed it was about to. I did my best to reassure them. After all, we had beaten the Germans in 1918 and Hitler was only a jumped-up corporal. Their attitude and their doubts were typical of the older generation: they had seen it all before, and they were fearful.

A few days before the German offensive began I was ordered back to England for an operation which would have involved flying off an aircraft carrier to operate in either Norway or Finland. In the event this was overtaken by the German *Blitzkrieg*.

A Devastating Attack

Eric Clayton

On 19 May 1940, 56 Squadron's five remaining Hurricanes were made ready for action on what was to be our final but fateful day at Vitry. Two early morning patrols were carried out without result. As pilots and ground crew were standing by, there was talk of escorting an RAF bomber force to attack targets at the battle front later in the morning. Suddenly, the telephone rang shrilly. One of the pilots raced to take the call and bellowed 'scramble'. Everyone ran to the aircraft, pilots clambered on to the wing and into the cockpit, engines started up with a deep roar and belch of smoke and flame, and aircraft taxied hurriedly upwind to the take-off point.

The order to scramble had presumably been received simultaneously by the flights on the other side of the airfield, because aircraft there also began taxiing out for take off. The first section of B Flight opened throttles and took off, wheels up and clear of the airfield. The second formation quickly followed, racing across the field: it had just cleared the boundary, wheels going up at about 200 ft. when, it seemed out of nowhere, thirty Bf 109s followed by twelve Bf 110s dived down on to the airfield and formed up into a circle around the field at about 300 ft above our heads. From there they attacked our Hurricanes as they were taking off, picking them off at will. From above our heads, as we stood at dispersal point, the dry chatter of machine guns, the dull thump of the 109s' cannons sounded loud in our ears. We were dumbstruck and not a little afraid as spent cartridge cases showered down on to our heads.

Though the first section of three had got clear and been able to climb to an attacking position, the second section had no chance at all. It had struggled to perhaps 200 ft or more when the encircling 109s pounced on them: a 109 would drop down out of the circle and direct a devastating burst of fire towards the stricken Hurricanes. It would then return to the circle and its place be taken by another Me 109. The

Hurricane scramble, France 1940 (AHB)

leader of the second section had retracted his undercarriage and turned to come over the airfield, presumably to bring his guns to bear on the attacking 109s. But, at this point, he was attacked from behind. There was an enormous roar from his Merlin engine and the aircraft went into a dive with flames coming from it like a torch. Horrified, we watched it crash, with an enormous explosion, between the airfield and the adjacent village of Vitry. The burst of cannon fire had probably killed the pilot instantly (protective armour plating had not yet been fitted to Hurricanes), causing him to slump forward and push the throttle wide open – hence the sudden roar and fatal dive into the ground.

It was horrifying and unusual for ground crew to witness, at such close quarters, aerial combat and one of their own squadron pilots shot down in flames. While watching him go down, I did not notice what happened to the rest of his section, though all were shot down. As the slaughter continued, I was aware of several Hurricanes from the other squadrons making crash landings on different parts of the airfield. Suddenly, after perhaps five or seven minutes (it was impossible even then to estimate exactly how long, such was the intensity of the experience), the attacking 109s broke off and quickly the sky was empty and strangely quiet after the noisy pandemonium of the aerial onslaught.

Some minutes later, we heard the unmistakable roar of Merlin engines: two Hurricanes were returning in formation at about 200 ft, making for the middle of the airfield, doubtless wondering what had happened below during the attack. When they were just above our heads, out of the blue a Me 109 appeared and formated on the two Hurricanes making a perfect vic formation; he obviously thought they were part of his own squadron! For a split second we watched this astonishing sight. The pilots must have looked at each other with absolute horror; the 109 pilot was the first to recognise his predicament, for he slammed open his throttle and roared off at great speed and rapidly disappeared. Our pilots seemed too dumbstruck at what had happened, or perhaps they were too unnerved by their recent narrow escape: either way, they gave no chase which would anyway have been fruitless against the faster enemy. The surviving pilots landed at intervals and taxied towards the waiting ground crews.

Given the complete surprise and the ferocity of the *Luftwaffe* attack on virtually defenceless aircraft, it was amazing that three of our pilots and their three Hurricanes had survived, though two of them were damaged. The ground crew immediately started to patch them up, with the minimum of resources, to get them operational again. We had no idea what casualties the squadrons on the other side of the airfield had suffered. Indeed, although we shared the same field and later the same escape route, we were never able to make physical contact with each other. In any case, the attacking Bf 109s missed a rare opportunity to eliminate, with minimal risk, all the aircraft at Vitry – an opportunity given to them by an effective, collaborating 'fifth column', which was to dog our every movement from the time we set foot in France to the time we left.

Later, when we were able to review what had happened, we thought it likely that the person at the other end of the field telephone had been a French collaborator – a fifth columnist. On that bright and sunny but fateful morning, the Bf 109 squadron had been above the airfield, at great height, invisible to us but watching our every move. When in position, the agent had telephoned the order to 'scramble': the unsuspecting pilot who answered the phone had no means of verifying the authenticity of the order and simply ran out of the hut yelling 'scramble'. From that moment, what followed was inevitable; the Bf 109s witnessed the process of 'scrambling', chose their moment to dive on to the airfield, and put into action their prepared plan of attack. It was clearly not a chance happening that they had come across some RAF Hurricanes that happened to be taking off. We were under close surveillance and could do nothing about it.

In the afternoon, the *Luftwaffe* delivered the *coup de grace*. At around 4 p.m., a squadron of twelve Bf 110s appeared over Douai, near enough to be potentially dangerous. The remaining section took off to intercept the potential raiders. Soon all was quiet; the afternoon sun shone down with a golden light on the airfield. Water was being boiled on an open fire to make tea. We were standing around in anticipation, for we had only a meagre breakfast that day. The quiet was broken suddenly with the shout 'Here they come'. We looked up, and low over the horizon, about half a mile away in the direction of Vitry, a squadron of enemy bombers was approaching the airfield at about fifty feet. At the perimeter, the force split in two to cover each side of the field where the remaining Hurricanes were parked. They flew at low speed over the aircraft, with bomb doors open, and proceeded to drop their bombs – clearly visible to us as shiny black objects – among the Hurricanes. To our intense relief, they did not explode on impact with inevitable casualties: they were clearly delayed action bombs which, on reflection, they had to be with such a low level attack. We raced away from our aircraft and flung ourselves down about 100 ft away from them. The Dorniers resumed formation and climbed away rapidly disappearing from sight. Within minutes the first bombs began to explode near the remaining aircraft; they were small, of a low explosive/high shrapnel content, presumably to create maximum damage in open space. It meant that their explosive force was quite modest, but immediately they set fire to the aircraft. Some of the bombs were set to explode later making it dangerous to approach in an attempt to put out the fires – though we had no means of doing this.

Whilst this was happening, with Hurricanes blazing on both sides of the airfield, two of the section which had taken off earlier to intercept enemy aircraft over Douai landed and taxied towards the burning aircraft. By now the intense heat of the burning planes had set off their ammunition, accompanied by staccato-like cracks with bullets flying in all directions. The fighting capacity of B Flight, 56 Squadron had been reduced to two aircraft.

The Boulton Paul Defiant

Wing Commander Eric Barwell DFC

When I joined 264 Squadron at Martlesham Heath in February 1940 it was being re-equipped with the new Boulton Paul Defiant. This was roughly the same size as a Hurricane but a little longer. It was unique among British fighters in that it had no forward firing guns. Instead it had a hydraulically operated gun turret behind the pilot with four Browning .303 machine-guns.

This clearly demanded new fighter tactics which our CO – Squadron Leader Phil Hunter – quickly developed. If an enemy formation was low-flying we would cross in front of it giving the gunner the chance to rake the oncoming planes. For higher flying formations we would attack from behind and to one side.

Early in May the Low Countries were invaded and, on 12 May, 264 went into action. On the 13th, six aircraft escorted Fairey Battles to bomb bridges across the Albert Canal. Four Defiants were shot down, one crashed more or less intact in Belgium and the last returned shot up. Fortunately German intelligence were slow in examining the wreck and assessing the problem posed by the Defiant.

It seemed at first that the Defiant was outclassed but seven days later the Squadron shot down seventeen Me109s without loss. Later the same day 11 Ju 87s and 88s were destroyed. It seems that the 109 mistook the Defiants for Hurricanes. Attacking from the rear they presented ideal targets for the gunner's rear firing turret. The Defiant had another advantage: it could turn more tightly than the 109.

The Squadron was also successful later that month in shooting down a large number of enemy aircraft over Dunkirk.

A second Defiant Squadron – 141 – was formed, but in daylight combat on 19 July it lost six aircraft out of nine and in addition one was badly damaged.

On 24 August, 264 lost five aircraft and two were damaged. Amongst those killed was our CO – Phil Hunter. Four days later we lost three aircraft and three more were damaged.

It was clear that the Germans had now assessed the vulnerability of the Defiant in daylight operations and we were withdrawn to Kirton Lindsey to retrain as a night-fighter squadron.

264 Squadron Defiant (Author back row 4th from right) (Eric Barwell)

Dunkirk

Aubrey Lancaster

Number 235 Squadron was equipped with the Blenheim Mk 1 in fighter configuration. This had 4 .303 machine guns in its belly and another in the wing. Bomb racks etc. had been stripped off.

Although we were aware that the evacuation was taking place from Dunkirk, we had not been involved. However, on the afternoon of 28 May we were told to grab our razors and tooth brushes and report to flights. We, as observers, were asked to report to the operations room where we were told that we were to fly to Detling, an aerodrome in Kent near Maidstone. Nine aircraft took part in the operation.

When we got there the station was in a state of chaos – the only accommodation being tents, but with nothing to sleep on except soaking wet grass, this we refused to do and we finished up sleeping on chairs in the mess.

The morning of the 29 May dawned bright and sunny which was more than could be said of our personal viewpoint. However after a cup of tea and some breakfast we tried to find out what was happening. We were told that we were to fly a protective role, from Calais to Dunkirk for the full duration of our fuel, say four hours, and attempt to protect our troops from dive bombing Ju 87s.

One flight was already on station over the beaches, with the next ready to go, then we were to follow. It was not long before the first crews landed and reported that the trip was 'a piece of cake' and that there was no air activity at all. This of course helped to lift our spirits in spite of the continuous roar of artillery and bombs which could clearly be heard.

Eventually our time came and off we went to Calais where we turned north along the coast to Dunkirk. As soon as we turned we could see the columns of smoke from the burning oil tanks at Dunkirk. We seemed to be there in minutes and soon we spotted lots of aircraft circling, silhouetted against the black background of the smoke. We had been warned that we might come across some Spitfires and that is what I hoped these were. Almost as soon as we saw them they must have seen us because they came screaming towards us and turned behind on our tails. I was trying to see where they were, when out of the corner of my eye I saw an aircraft sweeping across our bows with the obvious Jerry black cross markings – a Messerschmitt!

Almost immediately I glanced across to our number one and he had a Messerschmitt on his tail. As I looked, what seemed to be a solid sheet of flame shot from the nose of the Me and hit his aircraft. John Cronan, our pilot swept across and just poured everything we had into the attacker's fuselage but at that moment we also had an Me on our tail. John went into a tight turn to Starboard and whilst we were in that steep bank I looked down at the sea and saw what I am certain were **two** splashes – one of ours and one of theirs.

I had little time to bother about that as we still had one on our tail. John went into a steep dive (with the +9 Boost in operation) but we were sitting ducks at that speed and soon we were being riddled. I remember seeing one of my instruments floating in mid-air a couple of yards in front of me when it suddenly disappeared, having been hit by a bullet which must have just gone past my ear. We were now heading for the water at a faster speed than I had ever done in a Blenheim when John started to try and pull out. In the end he had both feet on the instrument panel to try and get some leverage. My head was getting heavier and heavier with the pull of gravity. At last his efforts bore some result and we started to level out and finished up only a few metres off the water.

Our Port engine now stopped and we started going round in circles. John tried to adjust but found that all the trimmers on the tail section had been shot away. His only resort was to put both feet on the port rudder to try and force the aircraft on to a straight course. In the end I sat on the floor and got hold of the starboard rudder pedal and pulled with all my strength to try and help. I gave John a course to steer which would bring us somewhere near home. A quick mental calculation to hit England – anywhere.

It was about this time that we both realised that we were still losing height and John told me that we would not be able to make it. He shouted to the gunner to get the dinghy ready as we were almost certainly going to ditch.

From my position, where I sat on the floor, I could see the water getting closer and closer. I was not worried unduly, since I thought we were on a nice shallow approach and visualised a condition similar to throwing a flat stone and getting it to bounce. However it was nothing like that. Instead, as we hit the sea, the large flat windows in the nose suddenly burst and flew back into my face. I shot forward into the nose and was immediately under water. I can't swim!

I thought, well I have only been shot forward and all I have to do is to take a few steps backwards and stand up. This I tried to do but couldn't move backwards. Alright I thought, go forwards – but I couldn't do that either. By this time I was short of breath and breathed in with dire results. Eventually my hands found a hole which I later realised were the holes

Blenheim Mk 1, Dunkirk (AHB)

where the front windows had been. I pulled myself through, but came up by the guns which were of course on the belly. By this time I was almost bursting for fresh air. I did a couple of swimming strokes or dog-paddles and this time got entangled in the undercarriage which had dropped down on impact. One last despairing paddle and I was under the smooth wing and with a final desperate swirl came up about five metres from the aircraft which was still afloat but nose down with its tail in the air.

John and Phil were in the dinghy wondering what had happened to me and John was just preparing to get back on to the aircraft and look for me. Again using my newly found ability to swim, I got to the dinghy and got in with their help. The dinghy was still fastened to the aircraft by parachute cord but luckily I had a penknife in my pocket and we cut ourselves free only seconds before the plane went down.

We could see a cross-channel ferry which was on its way to take the men off the beach. John asked me if I knew how to use the distress rocket, which I did. At this point I remembered quite clearly our instructor at the Bombing and Gunnery School whose task it was to instruct in the use of these signals. He told us that the operation was quite a simple one. You simply pulled a ring and the thing was self-igniting. To demonstrate the method we were taken down to an open space at the back of the hangars where the instructor proceeded to fasten the rocket casing to a post set in the ground. He then attached a piece of string to the ring of the detonator and stood back. We asked him why he did that and were told that his pal, giving the same instruction at some other gunnery school, blew his bloody hand off!

This was all in my mind when I was pleased to be able to point out that they had spotted us and it wasn't long before they took us aboard. They must have radioed Ramsgate for it didn't seem long before a motor launch came alongside and took us off and back to Ramsgate and a heroes' welcome from the crowds lining the dock side. My only injuries – apart from being waterlogged – were very badly bruised stomach and shoulder muscles.

The Death of a Squadron – Norway

Air Chief Marshal Sir Kenneth Cross KCB CBE DSO DFC

On 25 April 1940, I was told that 46 Squadron, which I commanded, was to go to Norway to replace 263 Squadron whose Gladiators had been almost completely destroyed by German bombing. They had been using a frozen lake as an airfield but this was now considered unsuitable. There was an open space nearby and I was instructed to see if it was suitable for our Hurricanes. It turned out to be a grass platform so soft that even the Gladiators had left deep ruts. It would be no good for our heavier Hurricanes. On my return I reported this and was told that it was irrelevant because the Government had decided to evacuate central Norway.

Nevertheless, ten days later we received instructions to proceed to northern Norway. We flew to Abbotsinch and taxied our Hurricanes across a field to a wharf where they were hoisted on to barges. These sailed to Greenock where *Glorious* was anchored. It would have been far simpler to fly on to the flight deck but Air Ministry had decreed it was too short for Hurricanes.

The plan was to recapture Narvik, which the Germans had now occupied. The attack would be launched as soon as our Hurricanes were available to provide fighter cover. When Narvik's facilities had been destroyed the assault force would withdraw.

I decided to fly off in three separate formations of six aircraft. I would lead the first, land, refuel quickly and come to 'readiness'. Meantime the second formation would patrol overhead to guard us. They would then land and be replaced by the third formation. This would be the first time high performance monoplane fighters had taken off from a British carrier.

There was a major snag. The front two thirds of *Glorious* deck was about one foot higher than the rear and the two sections were joined by a ramp up which our aircraft would have to ride. Our Hurricanes had heavy three-bladed variable pitch metal propellers. Their length would allow little clearance over this ramp if our tails were in the take-off position. If we kept our tails down to increase clearance the aircraft would not accelerate so quickly and we felt we would need all the speed we could get to take off in 100 feet instead of our normal 800 yards. We decided to raise the tail a little, get over the ramp, then put the stick hard forward with full throttle and hope for the best.

Our plan worked and most aircraft were airborne with a third of the deck still to go. Our maps were very poor but the shape of the fjords was accurate enough for us to locate the new airfield.

As I came in to land I saw that the surface was Summerfield Track – wire-mesh over coconut matting. As weight came on to the wheels I felt them dragging. The end of the runway was too close for me to give a burst to keep the tail down. I had almost stopped when the wheels dragged again and I tipped gently forward with the propeller touching the track. Two inches of propeller tip were bent on each of the three blades. The next two landed safely but the fourth was flung on its back. Clearly the airfield was not suitable and we would have to go to Bardufoss where the Gladiators were based. I told the other two sections over the R/T to divert, hoping they would find the place even with inadequate maps.

Our task was to keep a standing patrol over Narvik from 1930 that evening when the bombardment by cruisers would start. This was to be maintained until further notice and would be strenuous for my twenty-one pilots, none of whom had had much sleep for thirty-six hours.

We had thirty-odd fighters at Bardufoss against a *Luftwaffe* strength of approximately 300. Our main aim was to prevent the bombing of Allied forces, and by spreading the resources of the two squadrons we achieved a fair degree of success. Narvik was captured on 27 May and its facilities destroyed. Evacuation of allied forces began on 3 June.

On 4 June it was decided that 263 Squadron's Gladiators would fly on to *Glorious*. For us there were two choices. We could fly to the north of Norway where it was hoped our Hurricanes could be dismantled and loaded on to a steamer. Alternatively we could burn them. Neither course appealed to me. We had no maps of northern Norway and the dismantling of aircraft without cranes etc. was not practical. I suggested landing on *Glorious*, although Air Ministry had said this was impossible. Taking off had been much simpler than forecast. Perhaps landing would be the same.

The 7 of June started early for me. I took off hurriedly at about 03.00 to intercept four Heinkel 111s. I selected the starboard aircraft and fired. My target's undercarriage dropped and his starboard engine started smoking. At the same time the Perspex on the port side of my windscreen disintegrated and the cockpit filled with smoke. I had been hit by one of the Heinkel's rear gunners. I landed safely and found that the bullet had gone through the armour plate where my head would normally have been. Luckily I had scrambled in a great hurry and had not had time to fasten my straps. I had therefore been crouching forward over the column to steady myself and the bullet had missed.

Glorious was happy to co-operate and promised to work up to full speed for the occasion. *Ark Royal*'s flight deck was some hundred feet longer than that of *Glorious*. Her lifts were, however, smaller and the Hurricanes' wings would have to be sawn off before they could be taken down to the hangar. We therefore decided to try to land on *Glorious*. If this failed we would go to *Ark Royal*.

We were navigated out to sea by a Swordfish. It wasn't a nice feeling knowing that if we couldn't get on to the deck there was no other way out. We began to land at 01:15 , all perfectly. We'd been flying continually for practically twenty-four hours, and went to bed absolutely flat out. Glorious, with her escorts *Acasta* and *Ardent* then detached from the fleet to proceed independently to Scapa Flow.

I felt I could relax. We had saved ten experienced operational pilots and ten invaluable Hurricanes. We had shown that high-performance fighters could take off from, and land back on, carriers. I was convinced that the Hurricane was a practical proposition as a Fleet fighter.

I woke up later that morning, puzzled by the lack of activity. On our voyage out there had been constant air patrols but now the flight deck was deserted. One Swordfish and three Sea Gladiators were at ten minutes' notice but they were not on deck. We were about 200 miles off the Norwegian coast, exactly right for the *Luftwaffe*. I said 'Have we got a search out?' and was told we were travelling too fast for a U-boat to torpedo us. With that I had to be satisfied.

We were having tea when *Glorious* turned hard to starboard and we heard the sharp crack of explosions. We had been located by the German battle cruisers *Scharnhorst* and *Gneisenau*. These had opened fire at a range of some fourteen nautical miles. The first salvo was short, the second a straddle and the third, at 16:38, a hit.

I went to my cabin, put on my flying jacket and Mae West, collected the Squadron funds and records and my logbook. I thought I would go up to the bridge. As I stepped on to the flight-deck a salvo wrote off the ladder I had just climbed. I went back by another route to the quarter deck just as 'Abandon ship' was passed by word of mouth.

Although many of the ship's company were injured and burned, the ship was abandoned in an orderly manner and several hundred men got away. Jamie, my Flight Commander, later wrote 'I shall always remember the calm businesslike way in which the officers and men of the Royal Navy set about their task. The discipline was superb and there was not the slightest sign of panic. They could have been getting ready for a picnic or boat race'.

I asked one of the Fleet Air Arm pilots 'What's the form on this?' We were still doing a fair speed and there was a stream of Carley floats going by. He said 'Wait until they drop one of those and then go. Otherwise you'll have a long way to swim'. So that's what I did! The coldness of the sea took my breath away. I hardly went under, so effective was the Mae West. In a few strokes I reached a float and climbed aboard.

The Carley floats were ovals of canvas stuffed with cork. Inside the oval was a latticed wooden deck, laced with rope. Another rope ran round the outside rim for men to cling to. There was no right or wrong way up. The wooden deck would settle in the water whichever way the float fell. As the floats were free flooding, survivors' feet and legs were in the sea water. There was no food or drinking water and few floats had paddles. They were designed to hold twenty-five men.

One by one other survivors reached the float and, to my great joy, one of them was Jamie. We eventually finished with thirty-seven, the rest being sailors and Marines.

The *Scharnhorst* and *Gneisenau* came quite close to us and I was sure they would pick us up. I therefore threw away the Squadron records and my logbook. However, they did not stop and were soon out of sight.

All that was left were floats, rafts and pieces of wreckage with men clinging to them. The sea was rough and very cold – we were a hundred miles inside the Arctic Circle.

I was appalled to see how quickly the survivors began to die. Men would settle into the well of the float. We checked to see if they were still alive and, if not, pushed them over the side. This happened again and again. We were constantly wet and very cold. Later the wind dropped and the sea became calm but by then only seven were left.

I knew it was essential to keep morale up. It would help if we could keep our legs out of the water. I got everyone working on cutting the ropes which held the wooden trellis to the float. They were thick and there were about a hundred of them. With only one small penknife this took several hours but it helped to keep our minds off our plight. We eventually got the trellis sideways across the float. This gave us a platform on which some could doze off whilst others maintained watch. Someone produced a small Oxo tin full of brown sugar which he passed round and each of us took a pinch.

Thirst was my main problem. One sailor tried sea water, which didn't help. I had a bone collar stud which I sucked to keep my mouth moist. During one watch I carelessly let it fall out of my mouth and watched hopelessly as it descended through the clear cold water. I cursed and woke up the entire float. A Warrant Officer consoled me 'I shouldn't worry, Sir, they don't bother much how you're dressed in these circumstances'.

On 11 June we saw a distant ship. Its masts were in line with us most of the time but we couldn't be sure if she was approaching or sailing away. Gradually she got larger and we shouted and waved, forgetting our thirst and the pain in our feet. Soon we were all aboard and being treated by our rescuers with the utmost kindness. The ship was the 350 ton Norwegian *Borgund*.

Glorious and *Acasta* had a combined complement of 1550 men. Only thirty-nine survived, including the seven on our float, two of whom died later in hospital. Barely seventy hours had passed since *Glorious* sank.

The Norwegian engineer understood our needs perfectly. It was water and more water. He held a little metal cup to our lips and let us take a sip or two. When we indicated 'more' he shook his head and rationed us to sips every half hour or so. Others drank too much and made themselves quite ill. We were taken to the Faroes suffering from a mixture of frostbite and trench feet. We were treated royally by the Danish nurses. Eventually we were taken aboard HMS *Veteran* and brought back to Rosythe.

Of the ten experienced, combat-tested pilots of 46 Squadron who had landed on *Glorious*, only 'Jamie' Jamieson and myself remained.

Prelude to the Battle

Aubrey Lancaster

Little the worse from having been shot down over Dunkirk on 29 May we rejoined 235 Squadron at Bircham Newton. For the next three weeks we were fully occupied covering the evacuation from France and the Channel Islands.

We provided air cover to the 51st Highland Division who were attempting an evacuation from St Valery. We were hit by flak which punctured our pressure tank. As a result we had no guns, no brakes, no flaps and the undercart had to be wound down by hand. A bit of a hairy landing.

We gave air support to the Royal Navy who had the job of sinking an old WW I destroyer across the mouth of the harbour at S. Malo.

We covered ships evacuating people from the Channel Islands.

Then came 27 June 1940 – a beautiful day with hardly a cloud in the sky and very warm.

My flight came on to Stand-by at approximately 1100. and we were allowed to leave off our uniform jackets, it was so warm. Everything was quiet, we were told at midday to go and have our lunch and so, taking off our parachute harness and replacing our jackets, off we went. I remember borrowing a pen to drop a line to my girl friend Dorothy, later my wife until she died.

Half way through our meal the alarm went and all air crew of 235 Squadron were asked to report immediately to the Flight offices (Observers to the Operations Room for briefing).

Our dismay can be imagined when we were told that the object of our mission was a reconnaissance of Amsterdam and the southern end of the Zuider Zee looking for invasion barges. The dismay – because the day before we had been told to keep away from Amsterdam as Jerry had his fighter concentration in that area.

This trip from the outset had a no-return feeling. However the North Sea crossing was uneventful and we finally crossed the Dutch Coast just north of the Maas and Scheldte estuaries and turned north towards Amsterdam. We continued on this course for a few minutes when suddenly we were beset with Messerschmitts and all hell was let loose. We were the object of a burst of machine gun fire which ripped through the length of the aircraft, killing the gunner and hitting the pilot in the shoulder. I got a slight crease on my left leg but I was OK.

The pilot slumped over the 'stick' and I leaned over to try and help him out of his seat so that I could take over (I had learned to fly for just such an occasion). However my efforts to move brought him round and he sat back to try and fly the aircraft. As soon as he moved the 'stick' he realised that the controls had been shot away. He yelled at me to get out (note we were told that you should never go out of the top hatch of a Blenheim because you would almost certainly be hit by the tail, and that the escape should be from the forward downward hatch in the nose). I went immediately to the hatch and pulled the opening mechanism, but apart from showing daylight round the edges it refused to budge. I banged it, jumped on it, cursed it, but it remained closed. We were now at about 2000 feet and seemed to be heading for a herd of cattle. I thought what a mess there would be when we hit.

Realising that there was no future in the forward hatch I turned to the main top hatch (noticing as I turned that the gunner's body was riddled with bullets). The pilot must have seen what was happening to me and got out through the top hatch so that I could get out by standing on his seat. This I set out to do but suddenly remembered about the tail. I deliberated for a second or so to see if there was any way in which I could get on to the wing and drop off that way.

Whilst I was pondering, there was a sudden lurch and I was thrown clear. Something hit me on the temple and I was knocked out. Although I can't have been unconscious very long, when I came to I was tumbling through the air with a kaleidoscope of land, sky, land, sky passing before my eyes. I suddenly realised where I was and went to pull my ripcord but my parachute was not there. I knew that I put it on when we took off so where the hell was it? I looked up and there it was floating about some six feet above my head – unopened. I pulled it towards me and pulled the release and it opened with a bang. I remember thinking what a big thing it was. I reckon that I was only twenty to thirty feet above the ground when it opened. I had a bit of a bump when I landed but soon was wrestling with the canopy which was trying to pull me into a canal. I suddenly remembered about the quick release button, hit it, and I was free and safe. Later, Jan van der Maas, a Dutch researcher, discovered eye witnesses to my landing who confirmed that my chute opened some twenty-five metres off the ground.

I was near a small farm-house where I met a farmer and his wife who beckoned me inside, but it wasn't long before a Dutch doctor and nurse came along and bandaged my various bits of wounds. Later still a Dutch policeman arrived, who indicated that he must take me prisoner.

The doctor had a car and we went to where my pilot's body lay. He had hit the tail and one side of his face was battered to a piece of steak.

I was feeling all alone and sorry for myself when a German motor-cycle came roaring up, a German officer jumped off, gave me a smart salute and told me that I was his prisoner and would I get into the side-car.

Off we went up the road towards Schiphol airport where the Jerries had a temporary HQ on a house-boat moored opposite the entrance to the aerodrome. After lengthy discussion as to what to do with me it was discovered that all RAF prisoners were passed through an interrogation camp, a *Durchgangslager* (*Dulag*) at Frankfurt am Main. It appeared that there was a Major in the area who was going that way.

In the meantime it was decided to parade me before some big-wigs in Amsterdam in the Hotel Bristol (I think that was the name). They didn't get much joy out of me and so I was sent back to Schiphol.

By the time I got back the Major had arrived to take me to Frankfurt and off we went via Arnhem on to an *Autobahn* which took us the length of the Ruhr valley. We arrived at Frankfurt about 0800. the next morning and I was official Prisoner Of War No. 81.

There were six 235 Squadron aircraft on the reconnaissance of the Zuider Zee. Four were shot down and I was the only survivor of the four crews.

Pioneer Pathfinders

Group Captain Hamish Mahaddie DSO DFC AFC

The first experiment in target marking was after a briefing in June 1940. At that time most Whitley crews in 4 Bomber Group were averaging twenty-five sorties per month after the German breakthrough in the Low Countries.

Flying Officer Jimmy Marks of 77 Squadron (later Wing Commander H. J. Marks DSO DFC, killed in action whilst CO of 35 (PFF) Squadron), got a few of us together and suggested that we made a time and distance run from the seemingly everlasting fires of Rotterdam to the target – a large troop concentration some thirty-fives miles away.

It was relatively easy to navigate from Spurn Head to the Dutch coast, since the glow of Rotterdam could be seen over 100 miles away. Marks suggested that after a careful time and distance run from the centre of Rotterdam we should all drop a flare and at the same time fire a red Very Light. The interesting thing about this (in my experience the first ever co-ordinated attempt to find a target) was that, despite the assurance of all the enthusiasts, one Flying Officer Leonard Cheshire included, and bearing in mind that the run was made with great care, not one of the dozen or more taking part in this quite unofficial effort claimed to have even seen one of the other flares or Very Lights. This attempt was made under ideal conditions, from an easily defined starting point and with no opposition.

Marks was not deterred by this initial failure and he then selected crews for another sortie the following night and reduced the number to the four best navigators. The navigator at that time was also the second pilot. I considered mine as good as any on the Squadron and he was included. On this occasion the timed run was made with a stop watch, all compasses had been re-swung and the air speed indicators re-calibrated. At the end of the run from Rotterdam, and within three or four seconds, four flares and four Very Lights were visible in a radius of approximately three miles and one

Armstrong Whitworth Whitley (AHB)

flare had pinpointed the target, a large distinctly shaped wood concealing troops and armour. More flares were at once dropped to identify the aiming point and a fair concentration of bombs was directed on to the target. Its accuracy was confirmed by the immediate reaction from the ground. This, it should be recalled, was in June 1940.

However little was learned at higher levels, and at best Bomber Command was only able to leave an estimated three per cent of its lifted weight within five miles of any target. Despite the gallantry and 'press on' spirit, the early bomber offensive was a dismal failure.

Bomber Command – the Early Days

Frank Metcalfe CBE AE

In 1938, when it became clear to many that Hitler was bent on war and we were thinking about volunteering to be ready, the newspapers were full of the slogan 'the bomber will always get through'. It was in 1940, after a long period of 'phoney war' during which nothing much happened, the real war started and everything was to be learned. The enemy certainly 'got through', when their Stuka dive-bombers blasted their way through France and Holland to knock them out of the war and our forces were temporarily withdrawn from the battlefield with heavy losses.

It was at this point that I and my crew (George Martin, navigator and Sid Merritt, wireless operator – gunner) arrived from Operations Training Unit to 82 Squadron based at Watton in Norfolk to fly Blenheim bombers on operations. We were welcomed by the adjutant, who told us:'The squadron is out on a show. Twelve Blenheims attacking a fighter base at Alburg in Denmark. They'll be back about three. Meet me back on the tarmac after finding yourself a room and I'll introduce you to your new CO.' In the event, 3 o'clock became 4 o'clock and then 5 o'clock; and finally none came back. All had been shot down by fighters, including the CO. It was a sober crew that returned to their newly acquired rooms to begin their war.

What had gone wrong? Clearly these bombers had not 'got through'. The painful fact was that the Blenheims, our principal light bombers, were not up to the job. At a speed of about 200 mph and a single defensive rear-turret of one Vickers K machine gun the Blenheims were clearly outclassed by a Messerschmitt 109 fighter at 350 mph with eight machine guns or equivalent cannon. Comparisons were not much better for our other bombers flying by day, unless they could be escorted by our own fighters, but these could not be spared from the Battle of Britain.

There was no alternative but to carry on as we were, putting up our best fight in daylight by attacking single targets at low level or by taking advantage of the rather scarce cloud-cover when we could. This was usually against enemy airfields or shipping, or harassing the accumulating barges assembling in the Channel ports in preparation for the planned German invasion of England (code-named Sea Lion). It was tough and dangerous work. I recall weaving through a barrage at Dunkirk harbour, where we had some success against barges at the cost of a fuel tank penetrated by a shell on one side and a dead engine on the other. Eventually, however, the losses were too great, and it was decided that Blenheims were to convert mainly to night operations. Few of the air crew had much experience of night-flying, but the reduction in casualties was immediate and tension quickly declined.

At that early time in the war, specialist night-flying aircraft and techniques had not been developed but flak was neither intense nor particularly accurate – all that was to come later. New problems, however, arose from our limited experience in navigation in the dark winter conditions. The peacetime RAF had been largely trained to fly by day, certainly in the Volunteer Reserve, using the pencil-paper

German invasion barges at Dunkirk, 1940 (Crown copyright)

techniques of dead-reckoning. I, for example, had made only one night landing before I made my first night operation and I doubt if my navigator had experienced many more. As the winter of 1940 advanced, the lack of cockpit heating and the unavailability of specialist clothing made night-flying more demanding and perhaps less accurate. (An RAF Air Historical Branch Narrative on the bombing offensive of June and July, 1941, showed that only one in five of the aircraft despatched arrived within five miles of the target.)

We were allotted fairly easy night targets to start with, having regard to our lack of experience, such as Gris Nez, the docks at Dunkirk, Calais and Ostend with targets of barges, searchlights and dock concentrations, but gradually they were extended to more distant and more heavily defended targets at Krefeld, Gelsenkirchen, Schwerte and Cologne.

On the 11 November 1940 (Armistice day) we were briefed to make a night raid (our 19th) on the railway marshalling yards at Hamm, which we were told were packed with German traffic of tanks and other armaments. It was a grim and stormy day and at take-off we were soon plunged into heavy rain and cloud, although with promises of better weather later. As we climbed, conditions got steadily worse with ice cracking off the props, flashes of lightning and all the indications of being gripped by a severe weather front. Alarmingly, we were quite unable to calculate a wind so as to determine our position. As time went by and our repeated attempts to climb above the cloud were unsuccessful, we had to acknowledge we were thoroughly lost. The radio, never particularly reliable, was unresponsive to the efforts of our wireless operator – gunner Sid – to obtain bearings and I started to be concerned about fuel consumption.

No doubt we'd spent too much time trying to locate Hamm or obtain a fix that would help us to track our way to the target. I expressed my unwillingness to risk getting down too low because of uncertainty of our position. Why should the fuel consumption be excessive? At one point we were fired on by flak but I hadn't heard any strikes on the fuselage. Perhaps I was uneasy that I'd delayed too much on starting home because of a reluctance to admit a failure to find the target. I really couldn't think of anything to justify my suspicion of loss of fuel but it was clearly time to abandon the mission.

The weather was still foul, but George made his best estimate of a course home to Watton (Bodney), still not having been able to find a secure position. After a long haul we broke cloud at the islands to the north of Holland (Texel?) and, with a sigh of relief and for the first time in several hours, were able to set course for the lighthouse at Southwold from which we'd first started from England.

But the dangers were not over, yet. My original suspicion proved only too real. We ran out of fuel a few miles from the English coast and were forced to ditch in a huge swell. Sid was killed. I was knocked unconscious with severe head injuries. George was slashed across the face and head, but bravely managed to pull me out on to the wing. Eventually, after much bravery from George, we were picked up by a destroyer, HMS *Vega*. But the day was still not finished. In pulling away after getting us aboard the destroyer was hit by a mine. She was listing badly, but slowly and painfully made it to Harwich harbour, from where George and I were transferred to hospital. (It emerged later that another Blenheim from 82 Squadron, targeted for Hamm that same night, also ditched on return, some 300 miles to the north, off Flamborough head.)

This was hardly what was meant by 'the bomber will always get through'. It is evident that the slogan was woefully optimistic from Bomber Command's point of view at this stage of the war (towards the end of 1940). New strategies and techniques, as well as new equipment, were essential and were already being fashioned.

For myself, I spent six months in hospital undergoing plastic surgery. After a spell instructing, I became a Flying Controller, ultimately using Oboe, one of the new techniques which would help us achieve that accuracy which had so eluded us at the beginning of the war.

The Battle of Britain

Spitfires of 611 Squadron (AHB)

The entire might of the *Luftwaffe* was now directed against Britain. Analysis of German records after the war showed that the *Luftwaffe* had committed 1480 bombers, 989 fighters and 140 reconnaissance aircraft to the attack. Against this massive Armada Fighter Command could deploy only 666 combat ready fighters, backed by 513 in various states of repair at Maintenance Units. Failure would be swiftly followed by invasion.

The Battle of Britain can be divided into several phases.

The first phase began on 10 July with German attacks on Channel convoys and South coast ports.

The 24 August saw the beginning of heavy attacks on fighter airfields near London. This seriously drained the strength of Fighter Command but the *Luftwaffe* also suffered heavy losses.

Goering now switched the main attack from airfields to daylight raids on London and this gave Fighter Command some breathing space. The German bombers again lost heavily and Goering now believed that Fighter Command could seriously cripple any daylight attacks.

In the final phase the *Luftwaffe* switched to fighters and fighter bombers for daylight raids whilst using bombers for raids at night. By late autumn Hitler had concluded that early invasion of Britain was not practical and was beginning to turn his attention eastwards towards Russia which he was to invade on 22 June 1941.

The Battle of Britain

Air Vice-Marshal Sandy Johnstone CBE DFC AE

610 Squadron Spitfires (AHB)

It is doubtful if the outcome of any battle in modern times had a more significant effect on world events than the Battle of Britain. Granted it has been acknowledged as the victory which gave Britain time to regroup its military strength after the debacle of Dunkirk, but it can also be argued that, but for Air Marshal Dowding's superb handling of his meagre fighter resources during that fateful summer of 1940, the United States would not have come to the aid of beleaguered Europe when it did and the subsequent battles which took place in the Western Desert, Italy and later on the Continent of Europe, would never have taken place. Indeed the outcome of this battle, the only major conflict ever to have been fought and won entirely in the air, can be claimed as the key which opened the door to the Allied Forces ultimate victory in Europe.

Speaking as one involved, it is fair to say that few were aware of the true significance of the battle in its early stages. The two Scottish Auxiliary squadrons, 602 (Glasgow) and 603 (Edinburgh), for instance, had been in continual action against aircraft of the *Luftwaffe* from as far back as October 1939, when we had jointly accounted for the first enemy aircraft brought down over British soil during that historic raid on Naval units moored off Rosyth. From then on both squadrons were to be in regular contact with the enemy and, by the time we moved to the South Coast in early August 1940, we had already accounted for a sizeable bag of downed enemy aircraft. To us then, operating from our new bases on the South Coast, it seemed little different from what we had already become accustomed to up North – except that we were being asked to operate at much greater intensity.

However, as the battle progressed through August and into September one became ever more mindful of Mr Churchill's earlier warning of what was at stake: 'Upon this battle depends the survival of Christian civilisation. Upon it depends our own British life, the long continuity of our institutions and our Empire...

Let us therefore brace ourselves to our duties, and so bear ourselves that, if the British Empire and its Commonwealth last for a thousand years, men will say: "This was their finest hour".'

It was a sobering thought.

We soon adapted to the ever increasing pressures of being in action three, four and sometimes five times a day, occasionally losing one's closest colleagues in the process and never able to relax for a moment. However fatigue soon took its toll and it was not uncommon for the lads to fall asleep as soon as they returned to dispersals, only to be rudely awakened by their Intelligence Officers demanding details of the actions for their Combat Reports or to be ordered into the air again to meet a fresh attack. On one occasion a Hurricane landed back at base and stopped at the end of its run, whereupon the Rescue services assumed its pilot had been wounded in combat and rushed to his aid, only to discover him fast asleep in the cockpit.

But each day gained was of inestimable value. By now Dowding had at his disposal fifty-seven squadrons of Hurricanes and Spitfires to match the four-fold strength of the *Luftwaffe*. Under Lord Beaverbrook, the output of replacement aircraft rose steadily. In fact the shortage of trained aircrew became a much more telling factor than a shortage of aircraft and numbers could only be made good by disbanding a number of Army Co-operation squadrons and posting pilots with no previous experience of flying high-speed aircraft to the beleaguered Spitfire and Hurricane squadrons. Obviously no front line aeroplanes could be spared for training these unfortunates and they often had to 'learn on the job', frequently finding themselves in action before becoming fully competent on the types. That they succeeded so well speaks volumes for their bravery, and I for one have only the highest regard for their achievements.

Few will ever forget those warm summer months of 1940 when the sun shone brightly day after day with hardly a cloud in sight. Our German adversaries must have thought the Gods were on their side and took full advantage of the fine conditions to set up attack plans almost at will. At the receiving end, however, we cursed this fine weather which was allowing the enemy such freedom to operate continually at strength, particularly when he was concentrating much of his effort against our fighter airfields in a series of accurate and well executed pin-point attacks. Never were periods of rain and low clouds more welcome, for they gave at least a little temporary relief from the seemingly endless onslaught on our slender resources.

Few fighter airfields were spared, yet, in spite of the chaos and destruction all around, the system went on working and the enemy continued to be given a bloody nose. Staff and ground crews worked themselves to the bone to keep their airfields serviceable and aircraft flying – nothing else mattered. Inessential routine was cheerfully ignored, yet morale and discipline were never higher. But one wondered for how long one could go on taking such a regular hammering.

Then, on Saturday 7 September, Goering decided to change tactics and switched his attack from the fighter installations to mount a massive bombing attack on London itself. It is said the *Reichsmarschal* was angered that a small force of Wellington bombers had succeeded in dropping a few bombs on Berlin and was bent on revenge. History now shows that it was probably his biggest mistake for, frightful as it was for those having to endure the bombing of their city, it allowed the fighter defences that vital breathing space to recover their full potential. From then on, the writing was on the wall insofar as the *Luftwaffe* was concerned.

Much has been written about the exploits of 'The Few' during this fateful period in the Nation's history, but their contribution, great as it was, must be viewed in proper perspective. Granted we were ever in the limelight, watched by countless spectators on the ground whilst fighting it out with the enemy in cloudless skies high above their heads, but spare a thought, too, for the ground crews who, working under most uncomfortable makeshift conditions, and often under fire, never failed to have the machines ready and armed whenever they were needed. Without their sterling help on the ground, nothing could have been achieved in the air. They gave us the tools: we merely finished the job.

Nor should one overlook the part played by the average men and women of this realm. On a personal level I shall never forget the unstinting support of those civilians who lived near our airfield and mucked in to a man to support us in whatever way they could. Hospitality was unstinting and homes were thrown open to all ranks. Items of furniture were gladly handed over to help ease the discomforts of our living conditions. The Battle of Britain was indeed a team effort, with everyone pulling his weight, and the country as a whole was never in a more healthy state.

It is fair to say, too, that the Royal Air Force came of age as a result of this battle. Before 1940 the RAF had been striving hard to convince The Powers that Be of its worth as an independent Service, but there had been many who continued to maintain that it was an unnecessary extravagance and that military air matters could better be handled by the military. But the public had now been able to see for itself how much it owed to inspired planning and execution by men able to devote their whole time to the air defences of their country. It also established once and for all that members of the Auxiliary and Reserve forces were more than able to play their full part alongside the Regular squadrons. After all, more than a third of all aircrew taking part in the battle had been 'part-time aviators' before the outbreak of the war.

The Operations Room at Biggin Hill

Elspeth Green MM

How lucky I was to have joined up at the beginning of 1940, a volunteer who did not have to go through the 'square-bashing' that came later when WAAF numbers were increased. I had only two weeks' sketchy training before I was posted to Biggin Hill. I remember thinking 'What an odd name and where on earth is it?' When someone said that it was near London, I thought that wouldn't be too bad – little did I know!

At first we did not have uniforms, just shirts with any skirt we happened to have. When our uniforms arrived some weeks later, we were very proud of them and protested against wearing them for jobs like washing the Operations Room floor!

On our first morning we reported to the Operations Room and the RAF looked us over thinking, I am sure, 'I wonder what we've got here'. They soon discovered that we were quite able to take over from the airmen who had been acting as plotters and were later to go to France to continue working there. The squadrons were not at Biggin Hill at this time as the runways were being lengthened so it was a good opportunity for Flight Lieutenant Russell to introduce me to the then secret Radar, Observation Posts, Fighter Command and No. 11 Group. There were always one or two Controllers on duty who directed the planes according to the enemy raids plotted on the table.

The Operations Room, more often called the Ops. Room, was a somewhat ramshackle building which we shared with the Signals Section. On duty at night we slept under the table. Someone had a kind idea and provided straw palliasses for us to lie on with the result that we coughed and sneezed all night. We went back to sleeping on the hard floor, sleeping bags not having been invented, until a rest room and shelter were built near the Ops Room later in the summer – and what a glorious summer it was!

It was April before the squadrons came back and they were continually in action over France. We would count the planes returning to Biggin Hill and sigh with relief if they all came safely home. As the time of the evacuation of Dunkirk approached, we would hear the gunfire from France. One day in June I was watching tennis when word went round that France had fallen. I thought sadly of French friends and the lovely countryside I had known.

Before long invasion rumours were widespread and our Commanding Officer, Group Captain Grice was told to issue the plotters with truncheons! He decided that that was nonsense and instead we learnt how to use rifles on the range. If I remember right, we were quite good shots but I had a highly coloured bruised shoulder! Luckily we were never to use them as we would probably have shot the wrong person!

We were paid seven shillings a week (thirty-five p), later increased to fourteen shillings, and when we were off duty we went to the 'Sally Am' for suppers of eggs, peas and chips or whatever was available. There were occasional trips to local pubs or on forty-eight hour passes to friends in London or elsewhere. As the glorious summer advanced to July and August, we always had a stand-by watch to take over if the Operations Room was destroyed and a butcher's shop in Biggin village was converted into a temporary operations room. Two watches were always on duty or stand-by.

It was in August that Hitler launched his attack on British airfields. First it was Croydon, then Kenley and we awaited Biggin Hill's turn, which began on 15 August.

An operations room, 1940 (Crown copyright)

The tension in the Ops. Room was unbearable as enormous enemy raids were plotted on the table heading for South East England and we speculated on whose turn it would be next. Steel helmets were always worn. Naturally ours were worn at what we considered to be the most becoming angle, regardless of complaints by the Army!

The bombs on the 15th were directed at the runways on the airfield and, when it was over, all hands available were directed to fill in the craters. That day, a WAAF Sergeant, Elizabeth Mortimer, earned the Military Medal for going out on to the airfield with a bunch of flags to mark unexploded bombs, so preventing more casualties. For the remaining days of August, the raids were usually at midday and late afternoon. Buildings were flattened, a bus somehow landed on the roof of the camp cafe and a plane landed on the roof of the Officer's Mess.

In spite of difficulties in getting meals and coping in our houses, which had been badly shaken, the Ops Room watches were maintained. We all preferred to be on duty. Working, you did not have time to think and worry, in the shelter you did. We had a majority of blondes and redheads in our watch and it was suggested that we wore camouflage nets – but we didn't!

It was on the 31st that the Op. Room was destroyed. I was on duty and I remember how I felt as we dived under tables and desks for cover. It was a kind of detached curiosity – 'this is me and this is happening to me' – somewhat selfish thoughts. Work and actual danger were never the worst, the worst was the anticipation with butterflies in the tummy and time to worry about families at home. When we were getting out of Ops, our runner, an airman called Townsend, encouraged us all by calling 'Come on, Miss, you can make it!' I remember that one or two of us threw ourselves down on a grassy piece of ground, coughing from the plaster which had fallen in the Operations Room. We became aware of a Warrant Officer trying to attract our attention by calling repeatedly. We finally made out what he was saying – 'Move gently away, you are leaning against an unexploded bomb!' – and having learnt that Warrant Officers should be obeyed, we did! In the meantime, Flight Lieutenant Osmond and the Signals team were working miracles in repairing the communications on which we depended and in getting the temporary Operations Room ready for use.

It was impossible to carry on living on the Station as most buildings had been destroyed with the exception of one large hangar and one day the CO's voice was heard over the Tannoy saying 'All personnel not on essential duty go to the shelters – This is not an enemy action!'. The resulting explosion destroyed the hangar in the hope that the enemy would leave us in peace and lives would be saved. We highly approved of this wise move but Group Captain Grice was not the Air Ministry's blue-eyed boy!

About this time the air raid siren went out of use and the CO asked for a bugler as a substitute. When the bugler was found and went into action, his repertoire was limited to 'Come to the Cookhouse door, boys!', hardly suitable for getting everybody into the shelters! We were dispersed to Keston village, first sleeping in the air raid shelters of kind local residents and then in a large house. I can't remember much about meals except that there was always corned beef. To find accommodation and organise meals must have meant a lot of hard work on the part of Section Officer Hanbury (as she was then) and the other officers.

The temporary operations room, now at Biggin Hill, was quite a distance and to get there we made a detour as the camp was pitted with craters. On the night of 7 September we were going on duty in an RAF truck when we saw a red glow over London and realised that London was on fire. It was an unforgettable, dramatic and terrifying sight when we thought of what the people of London were enduring.

The attacks on Biggin Hill were reduced which gave time for the airfield to be repaired as the squadrons were still in action daily.

At the beginning of October, it was decided that the plotters who had been there since the spring should be posted elsewhere, and some of us, like me, were commissioned. It was with sadness that I left Biggin Hill where I had known the extremes of fear, of friendship and of fun in spite of the distress, the anxiety and the horrible discomfort. But above all there was the privilege of knowing these young men who faced enormous odds in the air, regardless of their own lives, to protect others.

The future was to take me to a Bomber station, Dishforth in Yorkshire, where I met Leonard Cheshire when, as a shy newly commissioned officer, very embarrassed by the glances at my very clean new medal ribbon, I was in a Ripon hotel with a group of friends. Leonard Cheshire was then attracting praise and admiration for his skill as a pilot and, on this occasion, he left his party at some distance from where we were and came over to congratulate me and say how pleased he was that a woman had been decorated with the Military Medal. A typically kind gesture that I shall never forget.

A Busy Day

Air Commodore R. Berry CBE DSO DFC

The batman's knock on the door before dawn signalled the beginning of another day. The date was 31 August 1940 and we were required to report almost immediately for dawn to breakfast standby. This day began like most others – a quick cup of tea in the Mess, a few quips from the chaps, then out to the three-ton truck which took the pilots to Squadron dispersal – a hut on the far side of the airfield.

Wearing my Mae West, and after a briefing by the CO, I went to meet my ground crew, two devoted airmen who treated and cared for my Spitfire like the thoroughbred she was. After that, back to the dispersal to report aircraft OK. The Squadron came to readiness. It was still dark.

It was too early to play the usual Mah Jong or shove ha'penny. The pilots sat, or lay around, waiting to 'scramble' or to be relieved by another squadron for breakfast.

As the sun mounted, it revealed a familiar pattern of weather – blue sky with high thin white wisps of cloud, a clear indication of a fine day ahead. Then came the order 'Squadron scramble, patrol Thames Estuary 30,000 ft. Many bandits'.

In seconds we were airborne and climbing eastwards, stringing out to take positions which would leave us enough room to manoeuvre and to keep a good lookout. We were soon on patrol at 30,000 ft across the Estuary. The French coast looked near.

On this occasion my section was not in action. The other section encountered twelve Me109s and destroyed two.

Twelve of us were scrambled again at 1240 to help break up a raid heading for North East London. We reached 28,000 ft. when we were ordered to return as Hornchurch was being bombed. We found fourteen Do17s at 17,000 ft, protected by Me109s.

Vehicles modified for airfield defence, 1940 (AHB)

We were soon in the thick of a mass of wheeling, milling Me109s which were covering their big brothers which, we saw, also included Heinkel bombers. We split up and in seconds I was in a dogfight with an Me109.

The turn got tighter. The question was, which of us would straighten up? Would the 109 roll over and disappear or stay long enough for me to get a bead on him?

He left it too late, I got in a long burst, then another, and he burst into flames.

Another quick turn to check that no one was on my tail. I could see several dogfights going on around me and hear quick high-pitched calls 'Look out behind you – so and so'.

Another 109 crossed below and in front. I waited a second or so and then rolled over and followed him. He never saw me. I gave him a long burst as I closed rapidly on his tail. There was a long trail of smoke and flame and he went straight into the ground. The next thing I knew was that the German attack was withdrawing, badly mauled.

I returned to Hornchurch, my aircraft unscathed to give my combat reports to the 'Spy' (Squadron Intelligence Officer). Unfortunately the airfield had been badly bombed – and we landed at the reserve field to learn that three of our groundstaff had been killed and five injured.

Two more raids on the airfield followed in the afternoon and I was airborne again at 1751 with twelve other squadron aircraft. I climbed to a high altitude but found my oxygen was low and had to descend again.

I reached the Hornchurch area at about 10,000 ft having run out of oxygen completely. I could see a large beehive of fighters around a straggling cluster of enemy bombers and some flashes on the ground where bombs were falling. Then in my rear mirror I saw the flash of a 109 streaking across Hornchurch heading East. I did a half roll, called on my Spitfire for all she could give and chased after him. I was mad after seeing all those bombs fall.

Soon we were both at treetop height over the fields and villages of southern Essex. I crept nearer and nearer until over the houses of Southend I was in range. I held my fire until I crossed the coast at Shoeburyness and was almost on the 109 when a film of oil hampered my vision, so I kept giving short sharp bursts and peering out to see the effect. Bits were falling off the 109 and without any warning it made a long turn and finally crash-landed on the mudflats of Shoeburyness.

I circled for a moment and saw the enemy pilot standing beside his wrecked aircraft shaking his fist at me. The pilot, *Oblt* Rau was later captured.

Three enemy raids on Hornchurch, three sorties, three victories. A very eventful day.

A Colourful Encounter

Air Vice-Marshal David Scott-Malden CB DSO DFC

On 23 November 1940 we were patrolling over Rochford when we were diverted to a raid against coastal shipping ten miles south-west of Dover.

We saw twenty CR 42s at 20,000 ft, flying west, parallel to the English coast. There were two separate groups flying line astern. In the first group were four aircraft flying wing-tip to wing-tip. There was a single aircraft to Starboard and several to Port. The second formation consisted of Vics and pairs in no particular order. Behind, and about 300 ft above, were two aircraft flying straight with no weaving.

Rearming Spitfire of Flt Lt F.D. Scott-Malden DFC, Hornchurch, September 1941 (AVM Scott-Malden)

The Fiat CR 42 bis was slow with a maximum speed of 267 mph. It was, however, a highly manoeuvrable biplane, single-seat fighter. They belonged to the *Corpo Areo Italiano* operating from Belgium. They had white spinners, yellow engine cowling and green and black camouflage resembling a mackerel. Someone remarked they were so pretty it was a shame to shoot them down!

The Italians were flying at about 200 mph and we dived through the misty cloud from 28,000 ft to 20,000 ft to engage the rear formation. It was to be no easy encounter. Although our Spitfires were much faster and better armed, the CR 42s were more manoeuvrable.

Any Italian aircraft actually under attack took violent evasive action, but the rest of them flew straight ahead maintaining formation. The CR 42s who were engaged in dogfights were very willing to fight it out and we were impressed by their morale which seemed much higher than that of the German 109 pilots we had encountered.

None of the enemy pilots baled out. Generally each combat ended with the pilot being killed.

Even one very experienced pilot had his problems. In the course of a fight with two CR 42s he found that they turned inside him each time. Even when on three or four occasions he tried to break away by spinning he found an enemy fighter waiting for him when he came out of the spin. He commented later 'I was sick of spinning'.

The end was inevitable. Seven of the CR 42s were destroyed and the rest fled back to Belgium.

Even Our Hospitals Were Not Safe

Iris Bower MBE ARRC

During my nursing service I served in two RAF Hospitals that suffered bombing raids. By some sort of fate, I had been on duty on both occasions. The first of these was at St Athan, a typical hutted hospital on the airfield. I was a junior Sister at the time, but it so happened that on this particular night I had been detailed to be in charge in the absence of the Senior Sister. I was making one of my routine rounds of the hospital with an experienced VAD (Voluntary Aid Detachment). She was one of those wonderful Red Cross nurses who contributed so much during the war years.

Suddenly we heard bombs dropping with no warning at all, they had beaten the siren to it. It seemed an eternity before the siren started wailing in the darkness.

In a few seconds I had reached a ward full of patients and found the entrance had vanished. It was pitch black. Shouting, moaning, and rushing water could be heard. Suddenly I seemed to be falling into a deep hole and realised it was a bomb crater. I climbed out pretty fast, and the first patient I came to was still sitting on a lavatory seat; all the walls had disappeared. I could see by the light of my torch that blood was streaming down his face. He was shocked but by some miracle was not badly hurt. In no time at all, we could see the funny side to the situation that he was still sitting on the 'loo'. We groped our way in the darkness and seemed to be wading through water before reaching some of the other patients who were injured and in obvious pain. Fortunately most had minor injuries, only due to the fact that the wards were wooden huts and there was no heavy masonry.

The most menacing sound in the darkness was that of rushing water, as all the pipes had been fractured. In no time at all help was on hand. Doctors, nurses and Medical Orderlies descended upon us and the task of moving patients began. Some were moved temporarily to an underground shelter and others evacuated immediately to the then Royal Infirmary in Cardiff. The ghostly figures running about and the ambulances coming and going made it a hectic night, still vivid in my mind. The medical staff worked tirelessly with great efficiency and there was a great deal of courage amongst the patients. We were all glad to see the dawn.

There was a common saying in the Services in those days, 'Right place at the right time'. It turned out that I was to receive the Royal Red Cross Medal, or to be more precise,

Associate of The Royal Red Cross. I received the honour from His Majesty King George VI at an investiture at Buckingham Palace in February 1941. I don't think I deserved it more than anyone else, but I just happened to be the Sister-in-Charge. It took me hours to come down to earth after leaving Buckingham Palace. Later that evening I saw myself walking out of the Palace on the Pathe Gazette News in one of the London Cinemas. However my moment of glory didn't last long. I was soon back on routine duty and had to be very much my old self.

I remember too the horror of one Sunday, when the RAF Officers' Hospital was bombed. The Palace Hotel Torquay had been taken over by the RAF for use as a Hospital. About this time, Lord Haw Haw in one of his propaganda broadcasts had threatened that there would be a reprisal. He claimed that the RAF had bombed some hospital or convalescent home in Germany. On this Sunday morning I was walking along the first floor of the hotel where the operating theatre was, and all the surgical cases. With me was a very young, delightful and very pretty Australian VAD. She was affectionately known, to all the staff and patients, as 'Tinkle Bell'. At that moment, a Medical Officer asked me to accompany him to see four patients in a nearby room. I told the VAD that I would join her as soon as I could.

The MO and I walked into the room and at that moment we both saw, through the large windows, German planes with their Swastikas clearly visible. There was no time to be brave or heroic, we dived under the bed and heard the unforgettable sound of bombs dropping. They had come without warning from the clear skies.

Although there had been several explosions which missed the hotel, one was a direct hit. The four patients, the Doctor and myself were in one piece, but the door and windows of the room were out. An Australian pilot in the bed by the window, who had his leg in traction, was covered in broken glass, but mercifully was not badly injured. We hurried out of the room to find just dust and rubble everywhere and, where there had been a further room, just one big gaping hole. We looked to the right, where I was originally heading, and were filled with horror. The first body we came to was that of 'Tinkle Bell'. I saw her hand and arm with its frilled cuff sticking out beneath the heavy masonry. I also saw the incredible sight of two bodies which seemed to be hanging from the girder. The bomb had gone through all the floors down to the basement. The whole wing had collapsed. Many patients and staff were killed. Some had miraculous escapes, like myself, and some ended in tragedy. One young pilot, who had gone to a waiting taxi just before the bombing, returned to his room to collect something and was killed.

We were all rushing about and I remember nuns appearing from somewhere assisting with the casualties, one in particular comforting a Group Captain who was one of my surgical patients, but as the result of the bombing had additional serious injuries. All the injured were soon evacuated to other hospitals. Like many of the nursing staff, I accepted the hospitality of a Torquay family and slept the night in their home.

The following morning we were on our way by coach to RAF Hospital, Wroughton, in Wiltshire. I think it took us several days to feel normal. I had the strange unnerving experience of feeling the closeness of the little VAD 'Tinkle Bell'. Her presence was with me everywhere I went for about three days, then it seemed to leave me suddenly. I have never in my life experienced such a feeling. It was almost frightening.

Bomb Disposal

Wing Commander John MacBean MBE

Quite rightly, much publicity was given to the fliers of Fighter Command during the Battle of Britain, but, for security reasons, little or no public attention was focused on the Bomb Disposal organisation which worked hard and incessantly on airfields across the south of England.

In pre-war days little was known about German bombs and their complex fusing systems and consequently, the British authorities paid little attention to them. This was hastily altered when a number of bombs were dropped near the village of Sullom in the Shetlands in November, 1939. Some failed to explode and such bombs were ever after that known as UXBs. On 6 December, 1939 they were recovered by the RAF and closely examined. It was clear that the Rhein metal fuzes remained dangerous, and it was realised that possibly in the near future there might be raids by aircraft carrying similar bombs fitted with timed fuzes and booby-traps. This possibility highlighted the rapid need to institute suitable precautions to confront the problem.

Various Government directorates were hastily deputed to research and see what should be done to confront the threat. It was agreed that the three Services, Royal Navy, Army and Royal Air Force should be responsible for dealing with UXBs within their own precincts and that the RAF would be responsible for unexploded bombs on both crashed enemy aircraft and our own.

Responsibility for the RAF Bomb Disposal organisation, training, and UXB operations was vested in two successive Air Ministry directorates. Far from being desk-bound warriors many of their staff undertook dangerous tasks and gained important awards.

In the early war years (1940–42), before fully trained Bomb Disposal Wings, Squadrons, and flights were established throughout the UK and overseas, the UXB task was handled by established senior Armament Warrant Officers, senior NCOs and their junior staffs at prominent RAF bases known as X Stations – some eighty in number. At the same time a number of Mobile Demolition Squads (as those on Stations were also known), were formed to support

Defusing a German bomb (Wg Cdr J. McBean)

X Stations in distress. I, as a Sergeant, led one of these.

The contribution made by the Demolition Squads and their supporting staff was never fully appreciated or recorded in detail. Nevertheless, but for their substantial effort there is little doubt that flying at a number of important and vital airfields would have been seriously curtailed if not brought to a standstill. Among these were Biggin Hill, Manston, Debden, Detling and Eastchurch. I helped at the last three during August and September 1940.

Undoubtedly, owing to repetitive enemy attacks, Manston and Detling were most vulnerable and were seriously damaged. However, to 'The Few' certain members of the Bomb Disposal Squads stood out and they were heard to remark 'Better you than me' – and mean it too. It must also be said that many of the individuals who had to deal with the bomb fuzes, a most stressful and hazardous task at all times, did not envy the erks (junior airmen) who received little glory, but who had to dig for UXB's for hours at a time knowing that perhaps they could be blown to oblivion at any time.

Generally all those involved in Bomb Disposal accepted the challenge under severe stress and sweated it out knowing that other bombs awaited their attention. Some would have liked to quit, but, like aircrew, would not wish their name to be saddled with the stigma of LMF (Lack of Moral Fibre).

Bombs handled during the Battle of Britain ranged from 50 to 1800 kg (110–3960 lb) – some with one fuze and others with two. A goodly number were fitted with direct impact systems and many with time-clocks and others with booby-traps which caused detonation if attempts were made to withdraw them from the bomb casing even if the operator had managed to stop a clock ticking.

No-one who has not confronted a bomb with a fuze ticking can ever appreciate the courage and dedication displayed by the Demolition Squads who, with little experience and primitive tools, made a very significant contribution to the victory achieved by the RAF during the Battle of Britain. Perhaps this will be better understood by pointing out that in the last weeks of August 1940 the number of UXBs not yet dealt with included fifteen at Detling, sixteen at St Athan, eighteen at Thorney Island, eighteen at Debden, twenty at Wattisham, twenty-one at South Cerney, twenty-six at Kenley, twenty-seven at Manson, thirty at St Eval and sixty-two at Biggin Hill. By October 1940 the RAF BD Squads had dealt with 977, whilst the Air Ministry officers neutralised a further 114. These figures do not include bombs recovered from crashed aircraft.

On 2 September 1940 a 250 kg German Bomb penetrated some twenty-three feet into the ground adjacent to the Sheppey Island Light Railway on the RAF Eastchurch airfield boundary. In conjunction with a team of Royal Engineer diggers supervised by F/Sgt Bishop, Station Armoury, it was agreed that once the bomb was exposed, I would be called in to neutralise the fuze. Armed only with a 'Crabtree' two-pin discharger, I reached the Eastchurch Guardroom just as there was a very loud explosion which killed F/Sgt Bishop and three Royal Engineers. Another was seriously injured. Fortunately, Sgt Blackwood (Station Armoury) had just left the scene when the bomb was exposed. It could only be assumed that the sleeping fuze clockwork was disturbed by a movement of some kind. Stethoscopes to detect ticking clocks were not available at this time. Had I arrived a few minutes earlier I would almost certainly have been killed.

Many RAF Bomb Disposal operators were killed or seriously injured in the UK and on the Continent during bomb recovery and the German Weapon Disarmament Programme between 1944 and 1947.

This band of poorly equipped but enthusiastic pioneers was to develop into a highly skilled organisation, which during the rest of the war and the early post-war days dealt with 83,700 weapons in the UK and over 92,000 in the European and other theatres of operations. Quite rightly many Decorations and Medals were awarded.

The George Cross was created by Royal Warrant on 24 September 1940 for acts of the greatest heroism or most conspicuous courage in circumstances of extreme danger. Six Bomb Disposal Officers were awarded this highest honour:

Flight Lieutenant J. Dowland
Mr L. Harrison (later Wing Commander)
Squadron Leader E. L. Moxey (Posthumous)
Flight Lieutenant W. H. Charlton
Wing Commander J. S. Rowlands MBE
Squadron Leader H. Dinwoodie OBE MC

Decoy and Deception

In 1939 Colonel Sir John Turner was put in charge of British decoy and deception schemes. His headquarters was Sound City Film Studios at Shepperton.

Heavy German bombing raids were expected on towns, airfields and other military installations. The idea was to establish dummy sites which bombers would hopefully mistake for their intended targets.

The first decoys were 'K' type airfields. From the air they looked like operational aerodromes with dummy aircraft, bomb dumps, building sites etc. Night time decoy airfields were known as 'Q' sites. The early ones had paraffin gooseneck flares which were later converted to electric lighting.

To draw the bombers from towns and cities, dummy sites known as 'Starfish' were set up on open ground between one and eight miles from potential targets. These were most elaborate and were intended to deceive night bombers. Fires could be set off to look like bomb explosions, incendiaries burning and buildings on fire. Finishing touches included simulated railway signals, tram flashes and lights from apparently incompletely screened windows.

By the end of World War II there was a chain of 500 decoy sites. Dummy airfields were bombed 443 times and decoy towns 100 times. Many casualties and much damage were avoided.

Life on a 'Q' site in 1940
James Cant

After initial training at Blackpool, I was posted to RAF St. Eval in Cornwall. My Post Office savings book was empty and my pay was two shillings per day (10 p). Out of this I made an allowance of seven shillings per week to my mother (35 p)!

Saint Eval was obviously a new station, lacking a lot of equipment – including beds – so myself and a number of 'erks' were allocated a hut, an empty palliasse and instructions on where to fill it with straw. I shall never forget that first night as the airman sleeping next to me was a very nice, somewhat reserved schoolteacher. When he awoke in the morning he was covered from head to toe with flea bites. He needed treatment from the MO, he looked terrible. He obviously chose the wrong straw! But soon after we got beds and biscuit mattresses, and life was much more comfortable.

I was ordered to report to the Station Warrant Officer to find out what my duties were. There was another sprog airman waiting, a Welshman ('Taffy' for ever afterwards) and we were to serve the next three years together. The SWO offered us the duty of operating a 'Q' site, and went on to explain that this was a night time decoy airfield, the purpose of which was to attract enemy bombers away from the parent station. We both accepted the job eagerly, and became firm friends from then on. We were ordered to complete secrecy and warned not to talk about our duties to anyone, friends or family – 'our lips were sealed'!

We had to report to Flying Control to get a bit of experience of flare paths and general duties. I discovered that the flare path was made up of gooseneck flares and it was the duty of the flare path party of about ten men to dash out and light the flares when needed, and douse them when 'Jerry' had gone. Night flying was very much a hit and miss affair in those days. It was here that I had my first experience of what a real war was all about. The mortuary was fairly near to the flying control building and one of our aircraft returning from operations had taxied around the perimeter to get as near as possible to the mortuary. It was then I saw that the rear turret had been shot to pieces along with the gunner's head: it was a sight that shocked me and I have never forgotten it.

The time came to report for 'Q' site duties. The drill was to meet at the MT section for transport to be taken about four miles to the site.

There was an underground bunker with an escape hatch.

A worried James Cant inspects an unexploded bomb (James Cant)

This had two rooms, one the living room, with two beds and a coal-burning stove in one corner for heat and cooking. The other room was the engine room, but there was no engine as at that time the flare path was made up of gooseneck flares which contained paraffin oil. We lit the flares before dark and they stayed alight until we were ordered by Ops room to douse them. This was a very unsatisfactory arrangement and within a few months a generator and Glim lamps were installed. At one end of the flare path was a huge pile of timber and burnable rubbish like a very large Guy Fawkes bonfire. In the middle was a large drum of inflammable liquid to which a cable was attached that went back about 80 yards to the bunker. There was, I think, a 12 volt car battery in the operations room of the bunker and the idea was that if the Q-site was attacked the drums of oil would be fired by connecting the cable to the battery terminals, hopefully indicating to the enemy aircraft that they had hit something important.

The only weapon for our protection at the site was an old World War I Canadian Ross Rifle and a bandolier of about twenty ·303 shells. France had fallen, but optimism was high, and I remember our feelings were 'Let 'em all come!' Years afterwards, thinking about it, I was glad that they didn't all come. But at the time, Winston was behind us!

Most of the enemy attacks at St Eval in 1940 were in daylight and I remember on one occasion being off-duty and relaxing on my bed reading when there was the roar of approaching aircraft and suddenly bullet-holes appeared in the painted asbestos ceiling of the hut. There was a bit of panic with airmen trying to reach the shelters outside. I remember the billet corporal's admonition 'The RAF's Eleventh Commandment is – don't panic!'

Night raids started and one of the first was taken up by the Q-site. The bonfire went up in flames and the raid lasted a considerable time. The Downs were pockmarked with craters.

One night I recall a low level attack on St Eval, the enemy were flying at less than 1000 ft. and were silhouetted against wispy cloud and a bright moon. They passed over our Q-site and dropped a few bombs, and I lay on my back with the old Ross rifle to my shoulder optimistically shooting at them.

Soon afterwards a new and much more sophisticated Q-site was opened about two miles north west from the old one.

I went on a course to Sound City Studios at Shepperton and received training on the proper use of the 'Q' site. It was called 'Colonel Turner's Department' and dealt with all kinds of decoys. There were daylight and night time sites. The daylight sites used dummy aircraft etc. and they were being constructed at the film studios. There were 'Starfish' sites which were decoy towns etc., and 'QL' sites which were decoy marshalling yards, and many more. It was quite amazing, the efforts that were being made to confuse the enemy.

Back at my own Q site I was now Corporal in charge and there were several incidents, but as time went on less and less enemy activity in the West Country as the war was being taken more and more to the Nazis.

I had quite a few flights from St Eval to view the Q-site when operating, sometimes in a Whitley or an Anson, sometimes as the crew were practising circuits and bumps.

Time passed and the huge build up for D-Day was beginning, and Falmouth, approximately twenty miles south of my Q-site, was one of the major ports for the embarkation of invasion troops, mainly American. The surrounding country lanes were a mass of men and transport.

This was to be the last significant action at my Q-site. I was on duty late that night and we were warned that hostile aircraft were approaching. However I was told by Ops not to operate the Q-site. It wasn't long before I heard an obviously single enemy aircraft approaching from the South and passing quickly over the Q-site at a height I would guess at about 5000 ft, going north. It was soon out of earshot. Five minutes later it returned going North to South over the Q-site and once again going out of earshot, only to return again exactly as before. I got on to the direct line to Ops suggesting that I should do something about it. I was told to remain inoperative. The aircraft returned once again on the same line, and I was getting annoyed so I made a decision. When it was within hearing distance again, I had the flare path switched-on and after about ten seconds switched off. Sure enough there was a change in the sound of the engine as the aircraft made for our flare path and dropped four bombs. I made a dive for the bunker and the enemy bomber made his way to the east. At first light we made an inspection of the flare path and found four neat craters. I had informed Ops in the night and they told me to make my report to Flying Control in person. The Duty Officer was puzzled as to why we had been bombed when we weren't operating. He said we would hear more about it.

I reported this to my crew and we all had a good laugh. Two of us were off duty and went to Newquay that evening to have a celebratory drink. What pleased us most was the thought that we had beaten the Establishment. I never heard any more about it. There may have been a strategic reason for not wanting my Q-site operating, but I always felt justified for what I did, for I am sure the enemy aircraft would have dropped its bombs somewhere else and might have caused a lot more damage.

From D-Day most of the action moved away from the West Country. Enemy activity was practically nil and our Q-site became obsolete and was closed down.

THE BATTLE OF THE ATLANTIC

Even before the war began, U-boats were at sea and German warships were in the Atlantic. The liner *Athenia* was sunk on the day war was declared. She was sailing from Glasgow to Canada with 1418 people on board. She was torpedoed and the U-boat surfaced to shoot away her radio mast. Her SOS had however already been heard and rescue ships were soon on the scene. One thousand three hundred and six people were saved. By the end of September 1939, 150,000 tons of Allied shipping had been sunk. German ships and aircraft laid magnetic mines in the approaches to British ports and naval bases.

217 Squadron Anson Mk1 with turret, 1938/40 (Air Cdr Gresswell)

The Challenge to Coastal Command

Air Vice-Marshal W. E. Oulton CB CBE DSO DFC

When World War II broke out in September 1939, Coastal Command could muster only 160 front line aircraft. These comprised four squadrons of flying boats (Sunderlands, Londons and Stranraers), eight of GR landplanes, (Ansons and Hudsons) and one of the elderly torpedo bombers. Most of these were deployed facing the North Sea or the English Channel to meet the Navy's need for location of German naval units. The Air Officer-Commanding-in-Chief of Coastal Command, 'Ginger' Bowhill, with vivid memories of 1917–18, was sceptical about the Admiralty's estimate of the U-boat threat, and kept part of his organisation and strength facing westward – to the Atlantic shipping routes. Within days he was proved right and there began the Battle of the Atlantic, the U-boat v. our supply lifeline, which came perilously close to defeating us.

From the start, we in Coastal Command had no suitable aircraft, no suitable weapons, we were not trained in anti-submarine warfare and did not even have a tactical doctrine on how to go about the job. Even worse, there was very little co-operation between Coastal and the Navy and most of such air effort as was available was wasted. No requirement for such endeavour had been foreseen and we had no means of attacking a U-boat, even had we seen one, until months later by local initiative, the naval depth charge was adapted for this purpose.

Shipping losses were severe, even when the forgotten convoy system was belatedly introduced and aircraft, within their very limited range from their shore bases, could provide 'scarecrow escort'. Unhappily the navigation of both ships and aircraft was often very poor and aircraft sometimes failed to meet the convoy which they had been sent to escort. All this from a handful of U-boats operating with difficulty at a great distance from their Baltic bases.

When France was over-run in 1940 the U-boats began to operate in larger numbers from French bases and were free to attack our ocean shipping routes well beyond the reach of our scanty air cover. At the same time the *Luftwaffe* long-range reconnaissance aircraft began to operate from French airfields to locate and give early advice on convoys, enabling U-boat 'wolf-packs' to be positioned to make devastating attacks. Fortunately for us, co-operation between *Luftwaffe* and *Kriegsmarine* was appalling: even so, our shipping losses became absolutely disastrous, particularly in the vast mid-Atlantic gap between the air cover available from Canada in the west or from UK, in the east.

There was just one small but vital saving grace. A small number of American 'Lease-Lend' B24's – Very Long Range Liberators – was allotted to Coastal and sent to Iceland to operate as 120 Squadron. The convoy tracks were a thousand miles away and the air cover which could be provided at such a range was scanty. But it made a vast difference. One typical escort group commander, whose convoy was being assaulted by a pack of six U-boats which might have sunk many ships despite his vigorous defence, was mightily relieved when one of 120's Liberators turned up in the nick of time. The aircraft was sent off in all directions to investigate contacts and attack – or at least force the enemy to dive. The 120 pilot – Jimmy Proctor – made his classic remark over the radio – 'As Mae West said, one at a time, "gentlemen, one at a time, please!" The convoy passed safely. One U-boat sunk.

Urgent requests for more Liberators were disregarded for the time being and 120's vital efforts gradually wasted away. So shipping losses in mid-Atlantic continued to mount.

An important, if novel, contribution was also made by the Merchant Ship Fighter Unit, so vividly described by Air Vice Marshal Michael Lyne.

Meanwhile, Coastal Command, with a much lower political priority, flew a variety of aircraft – notably Wellingtons and Whitleys snatched from a reluctant Bomber Command – as well as Sunderland, American Catalina and other flying boats. But, except for the few Catalinas, they were all of medium range and the 'Gap' persisted – and shipping losses increased. Much of the air effort was therefore switched to offensive operations in the Bay of Biscay to attack the U-boats as they transited between their bases and their operational areas. At first this had no success; but here began the great technical battle between the opposing operational research scientists. To get through the Bay, the U-boats had to surface for some of the time to charge their batteries. At first they did this at night, remaining submerged by day. Although they could be detected by the early ASV radar, this was useless for carrying out a blind attack at night. Also the U-boats were then fitted with the Metox receiver which gave warning of detection by radar, enabling the U-boat to dive safely. The RAF responded by fitting aircraft with the Leigh Light, a searchlight which brightly illuminated the U-boat in the final approach to attack. This was immediately very successful, as Jeff Greswell describes.

Early in 1943, under an instruction by Churchill himself, four squadrons of somewhat longer range aircraft, Halifaxes and Fortresses, together with fifty sets of the new centrimetic radar, were transferred to Coastal Command: the Halifaxes to operate in the Biscay offensive, the Fortresses for escort and anti-shipping.

The U-boats were then fitted with heavy defensive armament and changed their tactics to submerging by night and proceeding on the surface at high speed by day, hoping to shoot down any attacking aircraft. Also, as by now the aircraft had much more effective 10 centimetre radar, the U-boats responded with the Naxos receiver to give warning of attack. So the battle became a slugging match between aircraft and U-boat, the overall trade-off being about one for one. To reduce crippling losses, the Germans introduced Ju 88 long range fighters to the scene, and the RAF responded with Mosquito fighters – a fine example of the flexibility of air power and of the value of Coastal Command being part of the RAF.

Finally the U-boat losses were too great to bear and they were withdrawn from the Atlantic, just barely in time to allow the passage of sufficient resources for Operation 'Overlord' – the re-entry to Europe. The climax came in June 1944 when our maritime air forces laid on Operation 'Cork'

Sunderland iced-in on Lough Lone northern Iceland (CAVM Oulton)

to exclude all U-boats from the English Channel while the invasion of Normandy took place. Not one of the many hundreds of ships taking part was sunk by U-boat, and young Flying Officer Moore, flying a Liberator that night, created some kind of a record by sinking two U-boats in twenty minutes.

Development of the Leigh Light Wellington

Air Commodore J. H. Greswell CB CBE DSO FFC

The Spitfire and Hurricane Squadrons of Fighter Command are famous for winning the Battle of Britain. The Lancasters of Bomber Command are best remembered for the low level night attack over water by the Dam-buster Squadron. However, very little has been written about the Leigh Light Wellington Squadrons of Coastal Command and the vital part they played during the Battle of the Atlantic.

These Squadrons had no publicity during the war because of the secrecy of their operations and the equipment they carried. The Leigh Light Wellingtons also carried out low level attacks at night over water, often in the face of heavy gunfire from the U-boats they hunted. Between June 1942, when they started operations, and May 1945, they suffered very heavy operational losses: these were higher than any other type of anti-submarine Squadron in Coastal Command.

'Coastal Command War Statistics' record that 144 Wellingtons were lost on Coastal Command operations. Of these 111 were Leigh Light Wellingtons lost between 3 June 1942 and the end of the war.

I was involved in the development trials of the Leigh Light aircraft, and served in both No. 172 and No. 179 Wellington Squadrons. This is a tribute to the inventor of the Leigh Light, and to the gallant crews who flew the Leigh Light equipped aircraft on operations.

After the outbreak of war, the numbers of German U-boats at sea increased rapidly. During the first months of 1942, our losses of merchant ships reached alarming numbers. Between June 1941 and June 1942 these amounted to an average of half a million tonnes per month. During the same period the Germans lost 55 U-boats sunk, considered by Doenitz to be a small price to pay for such exceptional results. Naval surface escort vessels, operating beyond the range of aircraft patrols, were responsible for these U-boat kills.

During 1941 Coastal Command provided aircraft for offensive patrols over the Bay of Biscay, aimed at sinking U-boats in transit before they could reach the North Atlantic. Between June 1941 and May 1942 however, only two U-boats had been sunk by Coastal Command aircraft. Coastal Command thus had two vital operational requirements. These were: first the very long range aircraft to provide air cover for convoys in the Atlantic Gap where the U-boat packs were most effective (the VLR Liberators of 120 Squadron); secondly the ability to kill U-boats on offensive patrols at night.

In December 1940 I was posted to the newly formed Coastal Command Development Unit (CCDU) as a Flight Commander. I was involved in numerous flight trials with flares, trying to find a solution to the problem of attacking U-boats at night. These included the 4 in delayed action parachute flare, released from 4000 ft, followed by a rapid descent to low level to pick up the target in the reflected beam on the water when the flare lit and to attack within 30 seconds – a most uncomfortable and hairy manoeuvre in heavy aircraft like a Whitley in the dark! Then there was the towed reconnaissance flare, like a bunch of bananas on the end of a wire: jerk the wire for the next flare to ignite. This was resurrected from pre-war. I had already done trials on these in Ansons as a means of locating surface ships at night – obviously useless against U-boats. Finally there was the parachute flare in the head of a rocket projectile (an early Gloworm): cock the nose of the aircraft up on the low level approach to an ASV Contact to propel the flare to the other

Leigh Light Wellington with searchlight extended (H. de V. Leigh)

side of it, and attack along the reflected beam. All of these failed to measure up to the all-weather requirement to attack a U-boat at night before it could crash dive within 30 seconds.

Wing Commander H. de V. Leigh flew anti-U-boat patrols during World War I. He returned to the RAF in 1939 and was posted to Headquarters Coastal Command. In September 1940, the C-in-C asked for 'bright ideas' to enable aircraft to kill U-boats at night. Mk. II ASV being installed in Coastal Command aircraft, could detect surfaced U-boats at ranges of about seven miles, but the radar was 'blind' to objects closer than about one mile when the target 'blip' was blotted out by the clutter on the screen. U-boats charging their batteries on the surface were therefore immune from air attack at night.

In October 1940, Leigh suggested the installation of a searchlight in the mid-under turret of a Wellington for identification and attack of ASV contacts at night. In December 1940, Vickers finalised details of the modifications of a DWI Wellington to carry this light. By March 1941, the searchlight installation in Wellington P.9223 proved satisfactory and ASV Mk. II was then fitted to the aircraft. Full scale night tests of Leigh's invention began at Limavady and these culminated on 4 May when, with Leigh himself operating the searchlight, the aircraft successfully homed on to, and illuminated, the British submarine H-31, holding it in the beam as it passed below the aircraft. The aircraft was then sent to CCDU for tactical trials.

Two pilots were detailed to fly the aircraft, overseen by Sammy Leigh during his frequent visits to check on progress. The first Leigh Light Wellington VIIIs carried a 22 in Naval carbon arc searchlight with a four degree diverging beam in the mid-under turret. This was lowered by gravity by the Navigator, and was retracted by a hand operated hydraulic pump. The second Pilot operated the light from a seat in the plastic nose (which replaced the front gun turret), using standard gun turret hand grip controls to move the beam in azimuth, and up and down. Two large dials indicating the direction of the beam to port, starboard and depression enabled the beam to be pre-set before the light was switched on. The batteries to power the light were carried in the centre bomb bay, resulting in there being room for only four depth charges instead of the standard stick of six. Each outer bomb bay carried a 140 gallon overload tank.

The aircraft was a converted Wellington Ic. At full war load it was very tail heavy, having no front turret, and the Leigh Light turret being aft of the centre of gravity. The aircraft was under-powered, the general rule being to pull the stick back for take off at 100 knots or the end of the runway whichever came first – it was normally the latter! The two Pegasus engines did not have feathering propellers and the aircraft could not maintain height if one engine failed.

There was a crew of six: two pilots, a navigator and three WOP/AGs who took it in turn to man the ASV, radio, and tail turret. In the patrol area, the WOP/AG's changed places every twenty minutes to ensure that the night 'eyes' of the aircraft, the ASV watch, was as alert as possible.

Although the Naval 22 in carbon arc searchlight, with its four degree diverging beam, was capable of illuminating a U-boat at a range of 2 miles from 2000 feet on a clear night, an accurate attack could only be carried out from low level.

The standard attack procedure eventually devised by CCDU was that on calling 'action stations', the navigator lowered the turret and the second pilot manned the searchlight controls. The ASV operator homed the pilot onto the target, calling out reductions in range every half mile. The pilot gradually reduced height, compensating for drift, and judging the descent so as to arrive at exactly 250 feet at one mile from the target, having already opened the bomb doors.

The searchlight operator, listening to the ASV homing instructions to the pilot, was able to judge the drift of the aircraft caused by wind speed and direction, and also the target speed, and set this on the azimuth dial. He also set the other dial to a fifteen degree undershoot. At between one mile and three-quarter mile range the light was switched on, the beam then being gently raised until the U-boat was illuminated. Advised of this by the searchlight operator, the pilot reverted from instrument control of the aircraft to carry out a visual attack from fifty feet, releasing the stick of depth charges himself.

This attack procedure was dangerous. When the Leigh Light had illuminated the U-boat, the visual descent for a low level attack was as clear as daylight. If, however, the pilot looked out whilst the beam was still moving in search of the target, he could very quickly become disorientated and hit the sea in a matter of seconds. It was therefore a golden rule to fly by instruments, and not be tempted to fly visually until told by the searchlight operator that the U-boat was in sight.

By early July 1941, Leigh was satisfied that the attack procedure was right for the job, and took action to get the production line of Wellington VIIIs started. And so it was that, when the first of these aircraft was due for delivery in January 1942, No. 1417 Flight was formed at Chivenor and I was posted from the Development Unit to command it.

The Extreme Solution

Air Vice-Marshal M. Lyne CB AFC

A year after the Battle of Britain, my diary has entries bracketing the memorable 15th:

10 Sep. 41 – Empire Hudson torpedoed.
19 Sep. 41 – Empire Burton torpedoed 600 m. SW of Iceland.

These sinkings resulted in the first battle casualties suffered by a new Fighter Command unit – The Merchant Ship Fighter Unit (MSFU) which had been formed in April 1941. The involvement of Fighter Command with the Battle of the Atlantic flowed out of the Battle of Britain itself. Volunteer naval pilots replaced casualties, so that several famous squadrons rejoiced in their gallant 'admiral'. Alas many of them were lost in battle and this aggravated the shortage of pilots in the expanding Fleet Air Arm at the very time that long range German bombers were rivalling the U-boats in their sinking of allied ships. Shore based fighters were powerless and under a plan of Churchillian boldness the authorities set about mounting expendable Hurricane fighters on merchant ships. Although the technique of catapult off and parachute back was developed at Farnborough and proved by Lieutenant Everett of the Royal Navy when he destroyed a Focke Wulf bomber in August 1941, the provision of fifty fighter pilots could only be carried out by a bewildered Fighter Command. Thus on 1 July 1941 the *Empire Ocean* set out in convoy from Gourock with a Hurricane and a light blue pilot on board. Two months later a fighter pilot and his supporting airmen were in an open boat wallowing in the Atlantic swell 600 miles from Iceland.

But to make this unpleasant result possible much work had to be done ashore. The Hurricane was too heavy and required too great a take off speed for the existing catapult. In a brilliant feat the scientists and engineers (looking at the result one is tempted to add 'and blacksmiths') made a practical catapult in twenty-five days 'designed, constructed and tested'. Propulsion was by surplus anti-aircraft rockets so arranged that some 130 pounds of cordite could be fired to accelerate the Hurricane from 0 to 70 mph in one second (Porsche owners please note). This was the important part for fighter pilots, but they got the impression that although they themselves lost no sleep over protocol and maritime law their seniors certainly did. Hundreds of years of touchy relations between the Royal and Merchant Navies seemed to us to have thrust the catapults and German bombers firmly to the back of the queue for attention. Later we were to realise that we were fighting the same war, that the bravery of seamen who had been torpedoed several times was worthy of high respect, and that most problems could be solved by common sense personal dealings without the confusion induced by lawyers.

It was easy to accept that the Captain had the right to command. For his part he had already come more than half-way by accepting the loss of 500 tons of cargo in exchange for becoming a special target with that catapult and aircraft high above the bows. We were content with the logic that the Chief Engineer should have oversight of the girderwork and trolley. Our RNVR colleague had full control of his radar, radio and the men who serviced them and the catapult. It was only when the operation of the firing switch became the task of the First Mate that we blanched. He would never have fired anything bigger than a shotgun. On the other hand one had to accept that a carelessly thrown switch could not only smash the aircraft but also blow in the glass on the bridge and toast its occupants.

Hurricane being launched from Camship (AVM Lyne)

The drill for firing was elaborate. First the ground crew replaced the safety breaks in the electrical circuit and removed the heavy locks which stopped the trolley from breaking loose in a storm. Then only a thin metal strip held things in place until snapped by the power of the rockets. The water cylinders which would bring the trolley to a halt had already been checked – extra carefully since the news got round that empty buffers had smashed on impact, allowing the rocket propelled trolley to over-take the aircraft after take off. Another practical lesson from earlier tests was absorbed and special attention was given by the pilot to the rudder trim. A take off had been marred by the Hurricane swinging under airscrew torque as soon as released from the trolley and bouncing off the sea. The throttle friction nut was tightly screwed up so that the 3¼ G acceleration would not close the throttle. At this stage a white flag was shown (very appropriate for most of us by now), the engine was given full boost and the poor Hurricane threatened to shake itself to pieces.

The coming shock of the launch had to be foreseen, head braced back on the rest, right elbow braced against the leg to hold the stick steady, rudder bar firmly held. Then the pilot raised his arm to show that in three seconds the Mate could throw the switch. To be fair on only one occasion did an over anxious Mate fire before the drills were complete, though he did so even before the pilot had full power. Fortunately there was a quick thinker in the cockpit and he got power on as he charged down the catapult. Most newcomers could not have done so well. Many said they did not take over until 100 yards off the end, when they came to and found themselves flying. Experience of several launches speeded people up. Before long they would be in command halfway along the catapult.

Shipping losses from air attack dropped sharply away as increasing numbers of Hurricanes put to sea and pilots got frustrated at being just an insurance policy. They'd gone to sea to fight and without this satisfaction would blow off steam at the end of a voyage. A letter from Canadian authorities speaks of the 'attempt to stop their practice of low flying along the streets of Halifax'. However when Camships (catapult armed merchant ships) were included in convoys to Russia, action was guaranteed.

On 25 May 1942 Flying Officer John Kendal, controlled by Lieutenant Peter Mallett, fought the first successful action inside the Arctic Circle. He destroyed a Junkers 88, but tragically became the only MSFU pilot to die in air action, when his parachute failed in a difficult abandon aircraft in cloud. As a witness wrote 'it was a very sad ending to a brilliant display of flying skill and courage'.

On the same day that Kendal died the Unit scored its second success when Flying Officer Alastair Hay was launched in defence of a convoy outward bound to Russia. Alone against many German aircraft and wounded by return fire he destroyed one Heinkel 111 and damaged another. When he baled out Hay found that his troubles were not over. A bullet had punctured his dinghy. In spite of violent attacks by German aircraft, HMS *Volunteer* rescued him almost at once, establishing the tradition followed always afterwards by the Royal Navy of sparing neither effort nor risk to honour their part of the MSFU contract.

Six further combats were fought by MSFU pilots, mostly with complete success, on the Russian voyages or on the Gibraltar route. The most economical was that of Flight Lieutenant Jack Burr whose attack in Arctic waters caused two Heinkel 111s to collide. He then flew over a desolate and foggy area of North Russia to land at Archangel with almost empty tanks.

Jack Burr's attack on fifteen Heinkel 111 torpedo launchers at fifty feet above the sea was one of the more bold and dramatic incidents in the unit's history. He was greeted by considerable fire and had the prospect of a swim in Arctic waters for his pains. It is no denigration of his courage and effectiveness to compare his perils with those of a pilot engaging the Focke Wolf Kondor, which had been the reason for the formation of MSFU. Yet in retrospect it is clear that against the well trained and heavily gunned Kondor the Hurricane was in at least as much danger from concentrated return fire as those facing formations in the North. And of course the single aircraft enjoyed the advantage of full freedom of manoeuvre to frustrate attack and present opportunities to the gunners.

Perhaps a look at the last combat of them all, our pilot never having been in combat, the Kondor crew experienced and desperate, will bring out this difference. Flynn's first attack was 200 feet above the sea. As he opened fire he received heavy calibre returns from three positions. Breaking away he resumed attacks from the beam and quarter. When aiming at the Kondor's cockpit he received many strikes on his Hurricane and part of his hood was shot away close behind his head. The Kondor's last blow at him came from the explosion of the jettisoned bomb load. Flynn was out of ammunition. He was far from the convoy in a damaged Hurricane. His target was also heavily hit, but still flying. For ten minutes Flynn flew on his estimate of the convoy's position, unable to make radio contact. He heaved a sigh of relief on sighting the ships and prepared to bale out, but on seeing another Kondor at medium level he climbed to chase it off, finally returning to abandon aircraft and await collection. Later it was confirmed that his target had failed to reach home.

If air battles and the retrieval of pilots went off surprisingly well, conditions on the surface of the sea were hazardous. In one autumn month of 1941 four Camships were lost. Five more were lost by submarine or air attack between February and July 1942. In the end twelve of the thirty-five Camships had been sunk. Winter sinkings were not humorous: on average one third of the crew would be lost. Miraculous escapes like that of the engineer who saw a torpedo enter the engine room but was protected from the explosion by heavy machinery were balanced by bad luck. An RAF corporal tried, at night, to take a short cut across a battened down hatch. The explosion had blown off the hatch planks and he had a long, fatal fall into the hold.

The arrival of the Royal Naval 'Woolworth' aircraft carriers reduced the need for the one-shot Camships. Salty fighter pilots, proud of their corroded green cap badges, strangely short of flying hours but with a number of DFCs among them, were released for more conventional service. It was characteristic of MSFU, which was seldom wholly subordinate to authority, that its last two triumphantly successful encounters with the enemy took place after the unit had been formally closed down. The polite obituary notices exchanged between the Admiralty and the Air Ministry proved premature. On 28 July 1943 *Empire Darwin* and *Empire Tide* homeward bound from Gibraltar launched two Hurricanes. Sub-Lieutenants Pickwell and Ward directed Flying Officers Stewart and Flynn against three Focke Wulf four-engined long range bombers of the type that had caused such havoc in 1941. Two of them were destroyed and, although their return fire damaged both the British aircraft, our pilots survived.

Thus ended the fighting history of one of the Royal Air Force's strangest units.

The Anti-Submarine Campaign

Air Commodore J. H. Greswell CB CBE DSO DFC

After two months of intensive training, the C-in-C, Air Marshal Joubert de la Ferte, decided that the ultimate test of the Leigh Light could wait no longer and ordered the first operational patrols to be carried out.

On 3 June 1942, four aircraft took off from Chivenor for Bishop Rock, off the Scillies, and set course on fan-shaped patrols across the U-boat transit area of the Bay of Biscay towards the north coast of Spain. It was a dark night with no moon. Shortly after 0200 hrs, seventy miles north of Gijon off the Spanish coast, my radar operator using the forward aerials reported a contact five and a half miles to port. Using the standard attack procedure, the Leigh Light was lit at three-quarter mile range at 250 feet, but failed to pick up the target dead ahead in the beam as we had hoped. However I sighted a large U-boat disappearing under the port wing, impossible to attack. I quickly realised what had happened. The barometric pressure set on the altimeter some 400 miles away at Chivenor was such that, when indicating 250 feet, we were actually flying nearer 400 feet when the light was switched on – the beam had overshot the target.

Cursing our misfortune, I reset the altimeter reading by visual reference to the fleeting glimpse of the U-boat and climbed away, turning to port thinking that the U-boat would have crash dived before I could line up for a second attempt. We had reached a height of about 500 feet still turning, when I was amazed to see the U-boat start firing coloured flares into the sky, giving me a perfect reference point towards which to start homing for a second approach. It seemed that the flares must be recognition signals, but friend or foe? A hurried discussion with the crew ended when I recalled that British submarines burned coloured candles on the sea surface. So this was clearly not one of ours, and I pressed on with the attack.

This time, the homing procedure worked perfectly. I opened the bomb doors, the Leigh Light illuminated the U-boat, and I attacked from the starboard beam, dropping a stick of four depth charges. The tail gunner saw the depth charge plumes saying they had straddled the U-boat, and he opened fire on the conning tower as we flew over. The U-boat turned out to be the Italian submarine *Luigi Torelli*, which was severely damaged .

On the return leg of our patrol, I successfully carried out a perfect homing and Leigh Light attack on an east bound U-boat (with rear turret machine gun fire, having no depth charges left). The other three aircraft did not share in our good fortune, but the primary aim of these first Leigh Light sorties had been achieved.

I recall that special efforts had been made to provide the new Torpex 250 lb depth charges with fuses designed to explode at twenty-five feet for use on our three June patrols. This was done, and my attack was made with them. Why, therefore, was the *Torelli* not sunk when a straddle was achieved? The fact is that the fuses were defective, the explosions occurring well below twenty-five feet. It was not until early 1943 that the 'serious fault' was remedied. It seems certain that this was the reason why 172 Squadron damaged, instead of killed, so many U-boats between June 1942 and May 1943 – eight out of a total of ten.

During one of Sammy Leigh's visits we suggested that, if the batteries for the light could be housed in the nose of the aircraft, a full stick of six depth charges could be carried. Pilot Officer Blackmore had worked out how this could be done. Remove the searchlight operator's seat and replace it with a mattress on top of the batteries on which he could lie face down to control the light. The aircraft would be slightly less tail heavy, and a 'scare' gun, filled with tracers, could be installed in the Perspex nose, operated by the Navigator, standing astride the searchlight operator. Leigh approved the idea.

Since it was now clear that there was no requirement for the light to be used at distances in excess of one mile, Leigh installed a lens in the searchlight to spread the beam into a 12° x 4° fan, which would make it easier to gain initial contact with a target. The replacement of ASV II with centimetric radar greatly improved the search efficiency and made homing easier. The crews welcomed the arrival of the Leigh Light Wellingtons powered by Bristol Hercules engines, which had feathering propellers and would stay airborne if one engine failed.

Because of the secret nature of the Light and ASV, we were told we were **not** to bale out over Spain in emergency, but instead to ditch in deep water. My crew and I decided not to carry parachutes, and to rely on our Mae Wests and the aircraft dinghy for survival. Ten hours wearing parachute harness was very uncomfortable.

During a patrol in late 1943, I lit up a contact near Cape St Vincent which turned out to be a Royal Naval A/S frigate, fortunately early enough to avoid over-flying it. Next day the Station Commander invited me to drinks to meet his Naval brother, who said to me 'Whilst rounding Cape St Vincent, my ship was lit by a searchlight. I didn't have time to order open fire'. Needless to say, we left the party to introduce him to a Wellington!

In the autumn of 1943, Doenitz ordered seven U-boats to sail through the Straits of Gibraltar to reinforce the U-boat flotilla at Toulon. One was severely damaged by 179 Squadron aircraft off Cape St Vincent and returned to St Nazaire. A second was sunk by Cornish, and the third by Sgt

Wellington VIII ASVII (searchlight retracted) 1942 (Air Cdr Greswell)

A. N. Ellis. The Navy sank the fourth, and two U-boats got through the Strait. Squadron Leader D. B. Hodgkinson attacked and damaged one of these at about midnight. The U-boat was beached and abandoned and later destroyed by Naval gunfire. This outstanding RN/RAF success was known as the 'Battle of the Straits'.

On 8 January 1944, I was on patrol in the Mediterranean east of Gibraltar when I sighted U-343 off Cape De Gata in moonlight. Because of the heavy gunfire, I approached relatively high and attacked in a shallow dive. My rear gunner believed that the depth charges had straddled the U-boat, which remained on the surface and appeared to be damaged. Whilst I was shadowing the U-boat, F/O W. F. Davidson attacked it from astern in the moonlight, not using Leigh Light, and was shot down by the heavy gunfire. Davidson, the sole survivor, was thrown clear and climbed into the aircraft dinghy he found nearby. He was rescued by the Navy and told me that the U-boat passed so close to his dinghy he pretended to be dead to avoid capture by the Germans.

One of 179's non-operational losses was very distressing. We had a Wellington at Gibraltar being repaired. I asked Ferry Command to fly it back. Two Army Officers, one a Chaplain, had just arrived in Gibraltar having escaped from a POW camp in Germany. Hearing of the flight they asked if they could go home in it. I recall how thin and exhausted they looked, and their joyful expressions when I said 'yes'. The aircraft took off for UK and disappeared without trace.

Doenitz had been much alarmed by the operation of our Leigh Light aircraft. He issued an order to his forces in the Bay of Biscay that they were never to surface by night. For ventilating their hulls and charging batteries, they were to surface by day. If attacked, they were to fight it out with additional armament with which they had been fitted. Further they were to proceed in small convoys of two or three boats. The results of this order were disastrous. So many U-boats were sunk in the Bay that they had to revert to the old procedure of surfacing by night and proceeding submerged by day.

U-boat Commanders' fear of surprise attack by Leigh Light aircraft severely restricted the U-boats use of the surface at night. This applied not only to the Bay of Biscay, but also to any other areas patrolled by Coastal Command aircraft whether they carried Leigh Light or not. In the North Atlantic this imposed severe restrictions on U-boats using high speed on the surface when ordered to converge on a convoy for a wolf pack attack. This, coupled with the availability of our VLR Liberators and escort carriers, resulted in Admiral Doenitz stating in early 1943 that the Battle of the Atlantic could not be won. The climax of the Battle was reached in May 1943 when Doenitz ordered the temporary withdrawal of U-boats from the North Atlantic because of his heavy losses.

The Very Long Range Liberators

Squadron Leader T. M. Bullock DSO DFC

After a tour flying Ansons and Hudsons over the North Sea and Western European harbours and airfields, I was given my first rest period. This came to an end when I was detailed to fly the RAF's first Boeing B17C (Flying Fortress) from Seattle via Montreal and Gander to Ayr in Scotland in April 1941.

I was then posted to 120 Squadron at RAF Nutts Corner, Northern Ireland. This unit had just been reactivated, having been disbanded in 1919, and was awaiting delivery of a batch of Liberator Mk I aircraft.

120 Squadron was the first and, for more than a year the only operational unit in Coastal Command equipped with the Liberator and capable of providing vital air support for convoys in mid-Atlantic.

Only the Liberator Mk I had sufficient range and endurance for this task. It carried 2500 gallons of fuel and could fly up to eighteen hours at 150 knots, with six or eight 270 lb Torpex filled depth charges.

My detachment of Liberators was in Reykjavik, Iceland from October to December 1942. It was capable of flying as far as forty degrees west, some 700–800 miles from base, into the North Atlantic Gap south-west of Greenland. Here U-boat packs congregated, awaiting the HX and SC convoys from Halifax, Nova Scotia and New York en route to the UK. The normal Liberator sortie out of Reykjavik lasted sixteen to seventeen hours. It is recorded that the U-boat crews were extremely surprised and worried to be attacked by aircraft so

Back row: L to R. Sgt McColl, Sgt Hollier, Sgt Turner, Sgt Millar. Front row: L to R. Mitchell (Nav), Terry Bullock, Mike Dear. October 1941 (Terry Bullock)

far from land bases.

Our crew consisted of two pilots, one navigator, one flight engineer and four W/Op. AGs. No crew rest facilities existed – an Elsan toilet was located in the rear of the fuselage. Cooking was carried out on a strange, small methylated crystal heater! The heating of the aircraft was practically non existent – it depended on some sort of petrol device. The crew had to wear their flying jackets and flying boots to keep any semblance of warmth!!

The W/Op. AGs took turns to man the radio operator's position and the Mk II ASV radar equipment. When the convoy was located, all W/Op. AGs manned their stations, and kept a visual lookout for enemy U-boats in the vicinity. We patrolled ten to fifteen miles astern of the convoy just below the cloud base. These tactics invariably resulted in a radar or visual contact of a U-boat.

Bomb doors would then be opened, and an attack manoeuvre commenced without delay. Diving down, the pilot would release six depth charges at a height of fifty to eighty feet at an angle of twenty to twenty-five degrees to the U-boat's track. Photographs of the explosions around the submerging U-boat would be taken automatically by a camera with a mirror attachment located below the rear fuselage.

I will never forget 8 December 1942, when we were escorting convoy HX217 south-east of Greenland. Flying some eleven miles astern of it, I attacked U-611 with six DCs from fifty feet. It sank with all forty-eight crew. This was confirmed by the Naval escorts.

Some two hours later two U-boats were sighted, one of which was attacked with the remaining two DCs sixteen seconds after submerging. Inconclusive, apart from a long streak of oil behind the swirl. No more DC's remaining!! However, during the rest of the time left with the convoy before returning to base in Iceland, five more U-boats were sighted, and attacked with four 20 mm cannons located in a blister below the flight deck, forcing them to submerge and hopefully losing contact with the convoy, which altered course accordingly.

The aircraft was airborne for sixteen hours twenty-five minutes. During this sortie, the flight engineer, besides his normal duties, was busy below the flight deck changing the sixty-round canisters, unloading and reloading the four 20 mm cannons. We had, unfortunately, no armour-piercing shells. These were all being shipped out to North Africa. We had a low priority.

The Liberator was the first aircraft I ever saw and flew equipped with a nose wheel assembly. It also had a new type of wing – the Davis wing – long and thin with a high aspect ratio, and an extremely high wing loading for that era. It required runways longer than those at standard RAF airfields – 1600 yards plus were desirable, especially for night take-offs!

The technique required was very different from what I was familiar with: rotate speeds at maximum gross take-off weight and landing speeds were considerably in excess of other aircraft I'd flown. Take off was followed by a shallow initial climb out. Needless to say, the Davis wing was designed to be efficient at high altitudes which we never attained!! We only operated from zero feet rising to a maximum of about 8000 feet when in transit to a convoy and later returning to base. However, the aircraft was equipped with, in my estimation, the most reliable and forgiving engines ever devised – four Pratt & Whitney Twin Wasp radials with two rows of seven cylinders. Each engine developed 1200 hp.

The main problem was the lack of self-sealing fuel tanks – there were only two large tanks in the centre section of the wing, with U-tube type gauges just at the rear of the flight deck, giving off a strong smell of high octane petrol which permeated everything! I imagine that was the reason Bomber Command rejected them. Our Liberators were always being overloaded beyond the manufacturers specification – from forty-seven tons to over fifty-six tons all-up weight.

The biggest hazard for crew survival, with any mark of Liberator, was the problem of ditching in the sea – calm or rough it became a veritable death trap. The bomb bay doors would collapse on impact, the aircraft break in two and flood, allowing very little chance of safe evacuation.

Of the twenty-eight U-boats I sighted, I attacked nineteen and sank four. All bar one attack was carried out flying the Liberator Mk I. It was a magnificent anti U-boat machine, and the various Marks of Liberator have been claimed by the RAF and the USN to have been the most successful U boat killers during World War II.

During World War II 245 U-boats were sunk by aircraft, and Coastal Command crews accounted for 200 of these.

The Hudson that Captured a U-Boat

Group Captain Hugh Eccles

In the autumn of 1941 I was flying Hudsons with 269 Squadron from Kaloadarnes in Iceland. The end of August and beginning of September proved to be an eventful period for the Squadron.

On 27 August at 0640 hrs Captain Rahmlow of the U-570 submerged to give his sea-sick crew a rest. He surfaced again to reconnoitre at 0730 hrs. Flight Sergeant Mitchell sighted the U-boat and attacked, but his depth charges hung up. The stand-by strike aircraft piloted by Sqn Ldr J. H. Thompson was therefore despatched.

Squadron Leader Thompson located the U-boat whilst it was resurfacing. He successfully attacked it as it crash-dived and it was forced to resurface. A subsequent machine gun attack resulted in its surrender. A Catalina took off from Reykjavik at 1100 hrs and sighted the U-boat at 1344 hrs. Its Captain was instructed to stand by pending arrival of surface

Lockheed Hudson III of 269 Sqn (RAF Museum Hendon)

forces. A Trawler was sighted at 2145 hrs and given the U-570's position. The entire crew of the U-boat was observed in the conning tower, approximately eight in the forward section and thirty in the rear. The weather at this time was poor, there were rain showers, visibility was eight to ten miles, falling in the rain. The cloud base was 800 feet and the sea rough. A second Catalina was on an anti-submarine sweep in the area and sighted U-570 at 1745 hrs – '10 men on deck waving a white flag'.

Next day the Royal Navy took U-570 in tow and she was beached at Hafnarskeio on 29 August. She was later taken in to Hvalfjord Naval Base and her Flag was presented to No. 269 Squadron. On 29 September U-570 sailed for the UK under RN command and in due course entered service flying the White Ensign as HMS *Graph*.

On 4 September 1941 a Hudson sighted U-652 on the surface and it crash-dived. A flash report was sent at 0921 hrs stating that a US destroyer was in the vicinity. Since the US destroyer (later reported to be USS *Greer*) was at that date a non-belligerent, the Navy decided to send the destroyer HMS *Watchman* from Iceland to carry out the kill.

I took the strike aircraft, was briefed on the situation and told that a second U-boat had been reported at 0715 hrs in the general area. We arrived on the scene at 1245 hrs, radio silence was broken and voice communication established (contrary to standard operating procedure). 'Ship' and 'airplane' were used as call signs to maintain security. At 1306 hrs USS *Greer* reported 'submarine bears dead ahead range 720 yards' and we circled the spot, with bomb doors open and gun turret manned in case the U-boat began to surface. Similar bearings followed at intervals.

At 1400 hrs we left the area to locate HMS *Watchman* and pass a bearing of the US destroyer. At about 1415 hrs, as we were rejoining USS *Greer*, she was seen to increase speed, drop a pattern of depth charges, carry out a sharp 360° turn to starboard and stop dead. On being asked what had happened, the ship replied 'Have lost contact'. We marked the position of the depth charges with a smoke float and aluminium sea-marker. HMS *Watchman* then arrived on the scene and we returned to base, where we learnt that USS *Greer* had retaliated to a torpedo attack by the U-boat.

HMS *Watchman* asked *Greer* to join the hunt but she declined for neutrality reasons and left for Iceland. At 1620 USS *Greer* informed HMS *Watchman* that she had another contact and had dropped three depth charges. At 1700 hrs USS *Greer* was still in the vicinity when HMS *Watchman* commenced another search which proved negative.

This incident was very significant for Britain. Churchill had been seeking vital support from President Roosevelt who was under strong isolationist pressure and needed some means to alter public opinion. The *Greer* incident gave him his opportunity. He made one of his 'Fireside Chats' on 11 September, described the attack on *Greer* and announced a 'shoot first' policy. In consequence Congress modified its isolationist attitude. Everything changed, of course, with Pearl Harbor a few months later.

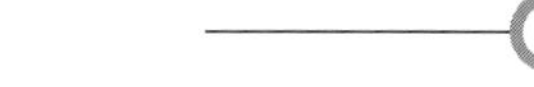

The Mediterranean Theatre

In no other theatre did the tides of war flow so rapidly to-and-fro as in the Mediterranean and North Africa.

Activities began with Italy's declaration of war on France and Britain on 10 June 1940. Air Commodore Raymond Collishaw, a Canadian commanding RAF units in Western Egypt, heard the broadcast from Rome announcing that from midnight a state of war would exist. Early next morning he launched an attack on a *Regia Aeronautica* base and caused the Italian Air Force both damage and embarrassment. He was rebuked by his C-in-C for 'excessive zeal'!

On 11 June Italy made its first bombing attack on Malta. For Italy, Malta was a natural and vital target. It was only some sixty miles away from the large Italian airbases in Italy and at that time was virtually undefended. It dominated the key strategic supply route from Italy to the Italian armies in North Africa. While the British held Malta the Royal Navy could fight its way through the Mediterranean to Egypt, saving fifteen thousand miles and forty five days on the journey round the Cape.

The Italians invaded Greece on 28 October 1940, and the next day 30 Squadron was ordered to move to Eluesis near Athens, the very first British fighting unit to arrive in Greece.

Seeing the Italian invasion of Greece failing, and wishing to secure his southern flank before invading Russia, Hitler declared war on Greece on 6 April. Immediately the British sent troops and more aircraft to Greece – the Greek Government having previously refused British troops lest it provoked Hitler. To deny Britain any foothold on mainland Europe, Hitler resolved to drive them out, and deployed veteran forces in great strength. In good spring weather they swept all before them. Most of the RAF's eighty-odd combat aircraft were quickly overwhelmed and destroyed, mostly on the ground, by 900 *Luftwaffe* aircraft. Within two weeks the British faced a second Dunkirk-like evacuation.

On 17 April 1941, 30 Squadron was ordered to Maleme in Crete. Hitler considered it essential to deny Crete to the British as an air base. The Germans tried invading by sea, but paid a very heavy price as the Royal Navy had undisputed control of the sea in the Eastern Mediterranean. Without control of the sea, the only way the Germans could successfully invade Crete was to use Airborne Forces. No more British resources could be spared to reinforce Crete. By 14 May the situation had become so bad that 30 Squadron was ordered to fly their remaining Blenheims back to Egypt.

Being the nearest airfield, and on the coast, Maleme was the key to Crete: with it the Germans would have a foothold and be able to fly in reinforcements. With adequate force and complete control of the air they would inevitably conquer Crete. Against a massive airborne assault Maleme was defended by some troops of 22nd Battalion of the New Zealand Regiment, and by those remaining from 30 Squadron (some four Officers and 114 men), and 33 Squadron. The RAF men were neither trained for this task, nor even armed with one rifle per man, and were woefully short of ammunition. The end was sudden and violent: in bitter fighting, sometimes hand-to-hand, against superior numbers and weapons, twenty men of 30 Squadron were killed: many acts of great bravery are told, not all of them officially recognised. In the ensuing chaos some men reached RAF HQ at Chania; thence Sphakia on the south coast, whence they were saved in another evacuation by sea.

Meantime in North Africa the Italian armies under Marshal Graziani had been driven west from Egypt and the British Army, with close support from the RAF, had reached Benghazi in Tripolitania.

In January 1941 Hitler sent German forces to North Africa to assist the Italians and within a very short time Rommel had advanced to the Egyptian border.

By 18 November 1941 the British had counter-attacked in North Africa and were again back in Benghazi. Their success was however short lived and early in 1942 Rommel counter-attacked.

Hitler now decided to invade Malta and in the first four months of 1942 11,000 tons of bombs rained down on the island. The scale of this assault can be judged when compared with the total of 19,000 tons of bombs which fell on the much larger area of London during the whole of World War II. There was, however, stout resistance.

Against the advice of Field Marshal Kesselring, Hitler, on 24 June 1942, instructed Rommel to press forward to Egypt and Cairo rather than risk the more difficult invasion of Malta.

Malta was for the moment neutralised and ample supplies reached the German armies in North Africa. This facilitated their advance to El Alamein. Fortunately the Allied Air Forces, including South African, Australian, American, Greek and Yugoslav squadrons, as well as the RAF, were able to minimise damaging attacks on Malta by *Luftwaffe* dive bombers.

During these months Malta was reinforced and a heavy toll was once more exacted on Rommel's supply line. Soon he was short of petrol.

Tedder had also acquired air superiority. When the last battle of El Alamein began he had around 1200 aircraft at his disposal whilst the *Luftwaffe* was about one third this strength in the theatre. By November 1942 Rommel had been driven back to Benghazi.

On 8 November 1942 the Allies landed in NW Africa and all German forces in North Africa surrendered on 13 May 1943. This was followed by the invasion of Sicily on 10 July 1943 and the surrender of Italy on 8 September 1943.

As Sir Fred Rosier's account recalls, it was in North Africa that the techniques of inter-service co-operation were perfected.

Sir Arthur Tedder, one of the outstanding airmen of World War II summed up the need in a letter to Admiral Cunningham in 1941.

'*In my opinion, sea, land and air operations in the Middle East Theatre are now so closely inter-related that effective co-ordination will only be possible if the campaign is considered and controlled as a combined operation in the full sense of that term.*'

He re-emphasised this in 1944 when he wrote:

'*I do not myself believe that any modern war can be won either at sea or in the land alone or in the air alone. War has changed to three-dimensional and very few people realise that.*'

Sunderlands at Malta

Wing Commander Dundas Bednall

Little has been written about the important role played by flying boats in the Eastern and Central Mediterranean in the early part of the war.

The Mk I Sunderland had been designed as a long range patrol flying boat. It had four Bristol Pegasus engines of 1010 horsepower each. Its wing span was some 113 feet and its length over eighty-five feet. Known as the 'Flying Porcupine', it had a four-gun rear turret; a single gun front turret and opening hatches for guns on either side amid-ships. In the air it handled much like any other aircraft. It could be side slipped and, with practice, good 'engines off' glide landings could be made.

The Sunderland was, however, not only a complete fighting aeroplane but also a seaworthy craft. It did not have a water rudder but relied instead on the differential operation of the outboard engines and the aerodynamic effect of its ailerons and tail fin and rudder. There were mooring techniques to be learned. The front turret could be moved aft on runners revealing an open cockpit and the 'sea equipment'. This included bollards, a winch and an anchor with lots of chains, cables and a fog bell. Even the brass and copper work was highly polished.

The faithful maintenance crew always flew with their Sunderland. When flying, the fitters and riggers became air gunners. After landing they were seamen for the mooring operations. Engine inspections were facilitated by small platforms which were actually the leading edge of the wing, folding down to give access to the engine. In a rough sea with the wind blowing their problems and dangers can be imagined. A spanner dropped was a spanner lost!

Number 230 Squadron with Sunderlands, based in Alexandria Harbour, was regarded by Admiral Cunningham as an important ancillary to his Mediterranean Fleet. Our principal role was to scout the area east of Malta, including the Ionian Sea, to keep track of the potentially threatening Italian Navy. However boring it seemed, a patrol of twelve hours with negative results provided vital information for Admiral Cunningham. He could then be sure that the Italians were not in the area. We flew, however, many more positive operations.

Within a month of Italy entering the war in June 1940 we flew to Kalafrana, Malta. Apart from the legendary Gladiators – Faith, Hope and Charity – we were the only RAF aircraft on the island. Soon afterwards we were on a twelve-hour patrol of the Ionian Sea when we spotted an Italian convoy of three small freighters accompanied by a destroyer just off the Calabrian coast. On our approach the destroyer made a feeble attempt to produce smoke and then turned away towards nearby Taranto. We made two runs over the freighters and dropped six rather ineffective twenty-five lb anti-submarine bombs, meanwhile spraying the freighters' decks with machine gun fire. This was the first attack on enemy Italian shipping of the war. When we returned to Alexandria, instead of the expected congratulations we were castigated for aggression which might 'provoke the enemy'!

Later we came across a small craft laden with shipwrecked Italian sailors. An Italian Hospital Ship had been spotted nearby and we successfully directed it towards the survivors. These, we later discovered, were from the Italian Cruiser *Bartolomeo Colleoni* which had been sunk off Crete by HMAS *Sydney*. Occasionally the Italian Fleet was seen, invariably only a short distance from their home port of Taranto and usually returning there at high speed!

Sunderland mooring. Front turret retracted (Shorts)

An odd naval order at this time sent us or our colleagues from 228 Squadron over the well defended Augusta harbour in Sicily at 1000 hrs each day to see what was there. Considering the fact that we went in at between 500 and 1000 feet, the vast bulk of the Sunderland could hardly be missed by the most short sighted Italian! The inevitable happened and several of us were shot up by Italian CR 42 fighters. One Sunderland was lost and several damaged.

We patrolled daily throughout the autumn and winter of 1940 and 1941. With no reliable radar we relied entirely on visual reconnaissance. The two pilots were always in the cockpit and, contrary to some reports, did not retire occasionally to the wardroom below for a siesta! The eye strain was considerable. This and tiredness eventually seriously affected the health and efficiency of the crew. To give some idea of the effort, I logged 167 operational flying hours in the month of March 1941 alone: moreover, we had had no leave since the Italians entered the war in June 1940.

Advanced bases were opened at Suda Bay in Crete and Scaramanga not far from Athens in Greece. Early on 28 March 1941 we set off on what we thought was to be a routine patrol of the eastern part of the Ionian Sea. On nearing the starting point of our search off Cape Matapan we saw a squadron of Italian cruisers making their way towards Taranto. We shadowed them for many hours and found yet another squadron of cruisers nearby. These were apparently some distance north west of the position calculated by Admiral Cunningham. This unexpected sighting enabled the Mediterranean Fleet to head towards the enemy in the belief that one of Italy's newest battleships the *Vittoria Veneto* was with them. Although the battleship escaped, the Royal Navy's night action off Matapan resulted in the destruction of three eight-inch cruisers.

The German advance in Greece continued and in April 1941 my aircraft was the first to begin evacuating British personnel from Greece, first to Crete and then to Alexandria. Each available aircraft carried out many missions daily and the evacuation placed heavy strain upon the already overworked Squadron. Valuable assistance was given us by the Sunderlands of 228 Squadron and many heroic rescues were undertaken. Among those saved were members of the royal families of Greece, Albania and Yugoslavia.

Our Sunderlands took off with gross overloads and little attention was paid to the niceties of stowage and calculations of centres of gravity. Several retreating senior officers were deprived of their golf clubs and other weighty items of 'excessive' baggage which were dumped overboard. After all our job was to rescue people, not their luggage – particularly if the latter was in the 'luxury' category .

At least two BOAC Empire passenger flying boats also helped. We were responsible for defending these unarmed aircraft in the event of an enemy fighter attack. Perhaps luckily for all concerned, such an attack never developed!

After the German invasion, squadron aircraft carried out several brave rescue attempts at night by alighting near the now enemy-held coast; some of these were successful. The evacuation could never have been carried out by land-based aircraft: it was an excellent example of the operational flexibility of the much-loved Sunderland flying boat.

Escape From Crete 1941

Jack Baker

In those days before the German invasion of Crete, we survivors of 30 Squadron lived in a sort of vacuum. No one told us what was going on: there were no plans that we were aware of, no exercises and no training. There were plenty of rumours.

Just after the last of our Blenheims had departed for Egypt, a Captain of the New Zealand Company responsible for the defence of Maleme airfield, gathered us together and explained that we were going to have to man the trenches. For those without firearms the only weapons he could offer were a few dozen bayonets. This was not very reassuring. By coincidence I was due on guard duty, so I had been issued with a rifle and ammunition, which made me feel a little more confident.

About 0700 hrs on 20 May 1941, when the bombing started and the strafing became much more intensive we ducked down into the deeper trench nearby. This attack went on for hours and then there was a lull. Looking up through the heavy dust pall and the surrounding olive trees, I saw the gliders drifting down to what was obviously their landing ground in the dried up river bed.

We dashed down to the trenches dug along the riverbank. The nearest already had five men in it, one badly wounded and two dead had already been put outside. We could see some enemy movement but there did not seem to be a determined advance.

As the day progressed the shell and mortar fire became more intense. Fortunately most was going overhead towards the top of Hill 107 where most of our defensive fire was coming from. For the many hours we were in that trench we had no orders, information or visits.

Towards the end of the day a sergeant New Zealander, quietly crouching low, ordered my friend and me to follow him in the direction of Hill 107.

As we passed our tent I nipped in, threw my respirator out of the bag and stuffed in half a loaf and a tin of pilchards. As our normal rations were somewhat meagre it was not unusual to add a few supplements of your own. I regret that we had to abandon everything else, personal and service kit. But I did, of course, keep my Lee Enfield and just a few rounds of ammo.

We carried on in the direction that the sergeant had taken but lost sight of him. Eventually we came to some sort of outpost with a field telephone. It seemed like a good idea to try to contact someone and so I rang it repeatedly, but there was no reply. In a nearby hole there were some juicy oranges and a wallet with lots of Greek money. The money was not going to be a lot of use, but the oranges were worth their weight in gold. I lost sight of my friend and later found that he had been captured.

I was beginning to wonder how much longer my own luck would hold out. I had not been wounded during all the bombing and strafing on the riverbank nor again at the last position. I decided by now that the only thing to do was to make my way to the only other known control position at RAF Headquarters in Chania. I spent that night on a hilltop

A Bombay that transited through Maleme, Crete, from Greece. 20 April 1941(Jack Baker)

just lying on the ground using my respirator, now tuckerbag, as a pillow.

Next morning I pressed on and under the olive trees saw two figures, one sitting down and the other standing. I could see that he was wearing khaki and so I made my way towards them. The one sitting down had a wide white bandage around his head. The New Zealander told me that he had been left to look after this young German paratrooper who, despite his injuries. was quite cocky and confident.

He said that his comrades wouldn't be long winning the battle and he would soon be released. The New Zealander asked me to take over his prisoner and take him to a first aid post just a couple of miles down the road. In fact the road was no more than a cart track but as it seemed to lead generally in the direction of Chania it suited me. The Kiwi gave me his Bren gun with a half empty pan, and a breast pouch with six hand grenades already primed and ready to throw. 'Just pull the pin' he said! So I set off with the German in front of me with his arms tied. I wasn't taking any chances.

As we came nearer the first aid post more people started to appear. It was a great relief to see some friendly faces. I was not enjoying the experience of marching a prisoner ahead of me like some sort of prize, so I was relieved to pass him over to the army at the field dressing station. I tried to find out from the others who were drifting in what was going on, but everyone just seemed stunned, lost, and no one had any sense of what to do.

I decided to press on to Chania and set off with a Maori, whose appearance was to say the least unconventional. He was wearing kid gloves, two pistols in his belt, a Tommy gun and a nasty Commando knife. What most appealed was a tin of plums he was carrying. We swapped a bit of my bread and a pilchard for a plum!

As more stragglers formed up we became a target for the ever present Stukas. This sort of ducking and diving for cover went on the whole time during our trek towards Chania. We went from one hilltop to the next, getting some sleep whenever we could.

On one occasion I met a large group and we were

crossing some open ground when all hell broke loose. Machine gun fire was coming from all directions. Again I was lucky not to get wounded.

There were some New Zealand officers there who were ignoring the bullets flying about and trying to get people moving. But no orders were given to return the Germans' fire nor to avoid further ambush, although from their static position they must have seen what was happening. No doubt we were all suffering from the lack of communication and clear orders. I gave my Bren gun, ammo and grenades to one of the officers, telling him how I had come by them, but kept my Lee Enfield: after all, I had signed for it!

Although large numbers of men were arriving at the post there was no proper organisation and so I decided to continue heading for the coast road. I came out onto the road opposite Theodora Island and was surprised to find it quiet. But not for long, as I heard an aircraft coming and just had time to get behind a wall.

Somewhere about 25 May I made it to RAF HQ at Chania. We were fed and then taken to a transit camp further east and then on to an evacuation point on the south coast. It was sad to see large quantities of stores and equipment being burned to prevent them being taken by the Germans.

On 27 May we were piled into lorries. We left the transit camp and headed over the mountains on a moonless night without lights. It was a nerve-racking journey but we arrived at Sphakia in the early morning at the end of the track.

The lorries stopped at the top of the cliff, short of the village itself. I suspect this was deliberate as the lorries could not turn around and so were simply pushed over the cliff.

We were told to go down towards the beach but to keep away from the shoreline and to make ourselves scarce. Again, it was reassuring to find that control and order had returned. Clearly, the beach control party did not want to make the evacuation obvious to the enemy, but nevertheless troop movement and transport being pushed over the side attracted the attention of the ever present German aircraft.

About 0300 hrs on the morning of 29 May we were ordered down the beach, walking wounded first. Longboats from a destroyer came ashore and we loaded stores and ammunition. We were then rowed out and taken aboard HMS *Napier*. Although we were initially left on deck, as it got light we were attacked by bombers, and then we were told to go below. I was immediately below the foredeck AA gun and the noise was deafening. Aboard *Napier* we were told that two aircraft had been shot down; we were not hit.

The remainder of the crossing was glorious: a flat sea, blue sky and a warm welcome in Alex. Ladies were there handing out tea and cigarettes. Finally we were posted to our various units.

The Desert Air Force 1941

Air Chief Marshal Sir Fred Rosier GCB CBE DSO

I arrived with most of my 229 Squadron pilots at Abu Soeur, an RAF base in the Canal zone of Egypt, on 7 June 1941.

The first few weeks in Egypt were disheartening as my squadron pilots had left on attachment to other squadrons, the ground crews had still not arrived and I was left with nothing to do. Then I received orders to go to a Landing Ground (LG) at Sidi Haneish. It was the start of eighteen months in the desert.

Life in the desert was tough and demanding. Apart from the ever present operational stress, we had to put up with extremes of heat and cold, the discomforts of sandstorms, the shortage of water, and the monotony of the daily diet of hard biscuits, bully beef and jam, enlivened sometimes by tins of Maconochies 'M & V' – Meat and Vegetables.

There were compensations: the vastness and the beauty of the desert, the night sky, the sunrises, the silence. During the first few months, until it was lost, I had a violin and in the late evenings I would scrape away under the night sky and the sound would come back to me, transformed. Then there was the uplift that came from the arrival of the beer ration. Above all was the camaraderie, the tremendous spirit that prevailed amongst the squadrons – RAF, Australian, South African and later American – and the strong friendships that were struck up, though far too many came to an early end.

At Sidi Haneish I was given command of No. 73 Squadron which had not long come out of Tobruk and to which my pilots had been attached.

After initial outstanding successes against the Italians the situation in the desert had undergone a dramatic change with the arrival of the Germans. Rommel's offensive in April had resulted in our withdrawal to the Egypt/Libya border, and in Tobruk becoming a besieged fortress. Efforts to push back his forces and to relieve Tobruk in mid June had failed and the situation was stalemate.

During the next five months, whilst preparations went ahead for the next offensive, we were engaged in training, air defence, including night patrols over Mersa Matruh, offensive sweeps and much disliked patrolling over shipping going to Tobruk. The task of defending slow moving ships, particularly in the late afternoons when they were close to the main German LGs at Gambut and with the prospect that Stukas with fighter cover would appear without warning out of that huge red ball of a setting sun, was not one we relished.

On one patrol I was rapidly overhauling a Stuka flying low when my Hurricane went into a roll and for a moment I thought we would crash into the sea but I was lucky: by using harsh rudder and aileron control I was able to stop the roll and to get back to Sidi Barrani, a forward LG. A large piece of metal skin had come adrift from a wing.

I left the squadron in October, having been posted to Air HQ Western Desert. I was sorry to leave for, apart from spending a few months in hospital and in convalescence, I had been in the squadron as Flight Commander and then CO from October 1939, when it was formed.

Gladiators being refuelled in Western Desert (AHB)

One evening in the Air HQ Mess Wg Cdr Bowman and I discussed the possibility of finding and flying back a Stuka dive bomber, a few of which had forced landed or crashed in the forward area. We put our proposal to the Air Officer Commanding (AOC), Air Vice-Marshal 'Mary' Coningham. To our delight he agreed. Thanks to the help of an enthusiastic contingent from the 11th Hussars we found a Stuka late one afternoon in 'no-mans-land'. Having jettisoned its bombs (by mistake) and put in some petrol we eventually got the engine started and took off. After some twenty minutes came disappointment. We had to land because of a systems failure and in the process damaged the undercarriage. The next morning, with almost no water and with the prospect of at least a forty mile walk, we spelled out a message with stones and then set off going north. Fortunately we were picked up that afternoon by a South African patrol.

Before the end of October I was delighted to be told by the AOC that a second Wing was to be formed (No. 262) and that I was to be promoted and take it over. We were to be responsible, in conjunction with 258 Wing, for the detailed operations and control of the Desert Fighter Force. Both Wings, which in many respects corresponded to the Group Control Centres later in the war, were fully mobile and self-contained.

By the time of Operation Crusader on 18 November (the offensive aimed at pushing back the Axis forces and relieving Tobruk), we were operational and located close to the new fighter LGs at Maddalena on the Egypt/Libya border.

One afternoon, some days later, and with an escort of two Tomahawk squadrons, I set off in my Hurricane for Tobruk where I was to organise a forward operating base. We were intercepted by Me 109's. During the fight I dived down after a Tomahawk which was streaming white smoke. It landed only a few miles away from an enemy column. I landed my Hurricane alongside and the pilot, an Australian, ran across and got in my cockpit: I sat on top of him and started to take off – and then disaster. A tyre burst, the wheel dug into the sand and we came to a dead stop. Friendly territory was a long, long way away!

I quickly removed all my possessions from the Hurricane, including a silver tankard, and hid them under some nearby brushwood. We ran to a nearby Wadi. Soon trucks arrived and soldiers began to search for us. They found all my possessions but although they came close to where we were hiding behind rocks they did not see us. Three days later, after walking mostly at night with the aid of the Pole star and having had another narrow escape from capture, we got back to Maddalena.

A strange sequel to this story is that my silver tankard inscribed 'in memory of 73/229' was returned to me several months later. It had been found when a South African armoured car unit shot up an enemy convoy. The unit CO, a major, had eventually traced me.

In November 1941 we were based at El Adem. After very heavy rain our airfields were a sea of mud and our aircraft were bogged down. The Italians to the west were still able to operate, and we learned that they were planning a raid on Tobruk. I knew that they had radio monitoring and decided to try to hoodwink them by scrambling imaginary fighters and instructing them to intercept the raid. To add realism, I told Controller at Gazala to respond to any instructions by the simple word 'Roger' which was too short for the Germans to locate the source.

As the Italian Stukas, escorted by German 109s neared Tobruk, I scrambled the imaginary fighters and vectored them to the raid. Enemy Control warned the Stukas that Allied fighters were about to intercept. Suddenly the Stukas jettisoned their bombs and turned tail whilst the angry leader of the 109s told them what he thought of them!

After initial setbacks in which we lost great numbers of tanks, Operation Crusader began to succeed and by 7 December Rommel's forces began to withdraw. The positive effect of air action during that time cannot be over-estimated. Offensive fighter action had limited enemy air attacks on our Army; attacks against enemy supply columns and dumps had inflicted much damage, and when circumstances were right the light bombers had been most effective. We had also found out that we often knew more about the position of our army units than did Army HQ's; and that from our armed reconnaissance sorties, we were finding and attacking many more targets than we received from army calls for support.

Group Captain Cross and I were at Antellat, our most forward base, on 20 January 1942 when heavy and continuous rain made the LGs unusable. The situation was serious, for had the enemy air force found out they could have destroyed six squadrons of grounded aircraft. Our only defence was a Bofors gun unit.

The following morning we decided that every effort must be made to get the aircraft away. All personnel, perhaps 2000 altogether, were used to fill in all the holes in the only possible take-off strip and by early afternoon the work was completed. Aircraft were manhandled to the take-off point and before nightfall three squadrons got away. The remaining squadrons left the next morning. It was only then that we heard that Rommel had started an offensive the previous day. Nine days later he reached the Gazala line. As we withdrew, our fighters continued to attack his forces wherever they could be found by our reconnaissance aircraft. My Wing acted as a forward information post.

There followed a difficult four months trying to maintain air superiority by offensive action and defending our LGs and Tobruk with a depleted force, as many of the squadrons had been withdrawn for rest and re-equipment.

It was also a time of change. Number 211 Group, of which I became second in command, assumed the responsibilities of the Wings previously commanded by Group Captain Cross and myself, whilst the squadrons were placed by type into mobile wings with a consequent alleviation of the non-operational demands on squadron commanders. I, with an element of the Group, was based at El Adem where I was responsible for the forward control of the fighter force. The main Group HQ and all the fighter Wings were at Gambut.

The enemy air force did not remain inactive during this time, carrying out frequent escorted bombing raids against Tobruk and straffing attacks by fighters, which now included the superior 109F, against the Gambut LGs. With good tactical information from the Y Service and a radar unit at Gazala, we were able to intercept many raids, but the strafing attacks were difficult to counter.

One day, to my delight, part of a detachment I had sent to Benghazi many weeks before for fighter control duties and whom I thought had been captured, turned up. With the exception of a very brave RAF Chaplain who was wounded and captured, they had managed to evade the enemy patrols and under the most stressful conditions had walked over 200 miles from Benghazi to Gazala. It was a tremendous feat.

Rommel's offensive started on 26 May 1942 and by the end of June he had reached El Alamein. During his 400 mile advance his columns came under frequent air attacks whilst our army units, often moving bumper to bumper along the coastal road, saw little of the enemy air force. There is no doubt that action by the Desert Air Force, the night bombers, the Malta based squadrons and the Royal Navy had so weakened Rommel's forces that he was unable to penetrate the Alamein defences and to advance further. Again there was stalemate.

It had been an exhausting move backwards with the Wings and Squadrons moving by night and operating by day. There had been no panic. Unserviceable aircraft which could be moved were towed behind three-ton trucks. Serviceability rates were surprisingly high: ground and air crews deserved the highest praise; and then came respite.

The Group and its Fighter Wings settled at Amariya, a two hour drive from Alexandria with its hotels, restaurants, bars and night clubs. To spend an evening there after the rigours of the desert was like entering another world.

Both sides were now intent on building up their forces. We began to receive more Kittihawks and, thankfully, Spitfires and were reinforced by a Kittihawk equipped American Pursuit Group. The 8th Army too was reinforced. General Montgomery arrived on the scene. As the new commander of the 8th Army he was able to instil fresh heart into his men and a confidence which had been lacking. He also made it clear that he and the Air Force would work closely together. He was putting into action what had long been advocated by our brilliant AOC, Air Vice-Marshal Coningham.

The results of subsequent joint planning and joint action were seen clearly during Rommel's unsuccessful final attempt to break through at the Battle of Alam Halfa. No longer was the ground situation allowed to become so confused that it restricted the air support we could provide. By day and night the Axis forces were attacked continuously from the air.

The pattern was repeated at the Battle of Alamein and although it took a long time to achieve the breakthrough, the end result was never in doubt. Then came the long pursuit and the last time I would pass those never to be forgotten places, Mersa Matruh, El Adem, Gazala, Msus and Antellat, before striking fresh ground on the way to Tripoli.

It was the end of a fascinating part of my life. At the age of twenty-six I had been given a position of high responsibility in a force which had been successful: a force which had provided the blueprint for future Army Air support and co-operation; and a force composed of some of the finest men with whom I have been privileged to serve.

Defence of Malta 1942

Flight Lieutenant Tony Holland DFC

Spring and summer 1942 were certainly rough on the Island of Malta. When recalling and recounting events and actions experienced by groundcrew and operational aircrew at that time, there are some ghosts which are probably best left lying.

However, leaving them out completely might amount to distortion of the truth. I have often been asked 'Were you afraid?' The answer is 'yes', but fear is an elastic emotion, intermingled with rage, which stretches between mild anxiety and stark terror, depending on what is going on.

As a Flight Commander at a flying school, I had been happy to drop rank when the opportunity came my way to join a famous auxiliary fighter squadron (No. 603 City of Edinburgh), commanded by Lord David Douglas-Hamilton. I had been posted direct to the Squadron from the flying school without attending a fighter OTU course, and found myself pitched in at the deep end, along with several other pilots who, like myself, had little or no operational experience.

When in April 1942 we stepped aboard USS *Wasp*, an American aircraft carrier bound for Malta, we little realised that we would be required to fly our Spitfires off the carrier, something none of us had ever done or even contemplated! This was at a time, when to quote Winston Churchill 'The Island was being pressed – to the last gasp'.

When we arrived, with No. 601 (County of London) Auxiliary Squadron (forty-six Spitfires Mk Vc, in all), there were approximately eight serviceable Hurricanes and

Spitfires to cover our arrival. Thirty-seven aircraft landed at Takali but within a week our numbers were reduced to six, such was the ferocity of the sustained onslaught by 600 German and Italian front line bombers and fighters based sixty miles away in Sicily.

One of many incidents sticks clearly in my mind. In between devastating raids on our airfield, Takali armourers were still rearming the last of our Spitfires which had just returned from a scramble. The sirens wailed yet again and anti-aircraft bursts appeared in the sky over St Paul's Bay. One of the armourers started to slide off the wing and a few of us pilots made a move in the direction of the dispersal point slit trenches. We halted in our tracks when the Sergeant in charge let the armourers know in no uncertain terms that they must finish the rearming. Shamefaced, we waited alongside as the Ju 88s put their noses down, fortunately for us, at Luqa rather than Takali on that occasion. This was typical of the quality of our groundcrew NCOs to whom we owed the means to hit back.

Slit trenches were certainly effective. Ordered to return from a late evening scramble, we were followed in by enemy aircraft. We had barely landed and climbed out of our cockpits, excitedly discussing the scraps in which we had just been involved, when an airman gave a warning shout. Eight diving Ju 88s were releasing their loads directly at our dispersal point, the bombs consequently appearing round in shape. Pilots and ground crew together leapt for a slit trench, as a 500 kg bomb landed about twenty feet away. The explosion created a vacuum which prevented any intake of breath for a few very uncomfortable seconds before the dust laden air could be breathed in. Two of our precious Spitfires, still outside their blast-proof pens, and a steamroller were riddled with shrapnel. Miraculously there were no human casualties.

When we had arrived at Takali on 20 April, our reception had been somewhat loose and slightly casual. Our AOC, a most excellent Commander but perhaps more orientated to the manner of Coastal than Fighter Command, told us he planned to hold half of our newly arrived Spitfires on the ground in reserve, and put half into the line.

Our assailants had other ideas, and it was with dismay that we watched Ju 87s dive on Takali, bombing with great accuracy so that before nightfall on that first day plumes of black smoke arose from many of the sand-bagged or stone walled pens in which the reserve, and front line Spitfires, had been parked.

This was catastrophic and before the USS *Wasp* was due to bring in sixty-four new Spitfires in the second instalment of reinforcements, our Junior Commanders, including Wing Commanders 'Jumbo' Gracie and Stan Grant, had persuaded the AOC to let them handle arrival arrangements. Every pen was allocated a crew of airmen, soldiers or sailors to guide each new arrival into the pen allocated and immediately recover the 90 gallon slipper drop tank and any kit the incoming pilot had brought with him. They would then refuel, rearm and make the aircraft ready for immediate use by a Malta experienced pilot who was standing by with the crew. As most of our petrol bowsers had been 'spitchered' (destroyed), slit trenches alongside were loaded with sufficient stores of petrol in four gallon cans. They also held canisters of 20 mm shells, and belts of .303 ammunition.

Tony Holland taking off from USS Wasp (Tony Holland)

The day before the arrival, Jumbo Gracie assembled all Takali personnel on the airfield. We formed up two or three deep around his car in the manner of a Waterloo Square, while Jumbo mounted the bonnet and briefed everybody on the morrow's events starting at first light. All would stay on the airfield all day, come what may. Rations, such as they were, would be brought to pens by whatever means were available. This indeed would be our Waterloo. The island's six remaining Spitfires were allocated to 'B' Flight 603 Squadron and in company with very few Hurricanes from Halfar, would cover the arrival in the air.

I flew in 'B' Flight and we were scrambled about 1030 hrs. Several engagements took place in which a number of Bf 109s were destroyed or damaged, and sadly we lost John Buckstone, our flight commander. As we returned to land, twelve new Spitfires were climbing away from Takali, and others followed intermittently in pairs or fours. Some had been 'turned round' within eight minutes of landing from the carrier. Before the day was over, all new arrivals would fly and fight.

Ferocious engagements continued all through the 9th and 10th of May during which time sixty-three enemy aircraft were destroyed or damaged over Malta, either in combat or by the Ack-Ack guns. There were nine further trips by carriers bearing reinforcements up to 29 October 1942. The state of serviceable Spitfires never again shrank to the piteous levels pre 9 May, and the great air battles of 9 and 10 May are regarded as the turning point. They led eventually to Operation Husky, the Allied invasion of Sicily, launched from Malta in July 1943.

The Bisley

Air Chief Marshal Sir Peter Le Cheminant GBE KCB DFC

Blenheim V (Philip Jarrett)

On 3 December 1942 614 Squadron was converted to Bisleys. This successor to the Blenheim IV was a cobbled-up disgrace to Bristols, not fit to operate in the air in 1942. We did what we could to correct its worst fault, which was excessive weight. It had a great deal of additional armour plating, and a large, heavy Heath Robinson system of mirrors which enabled the navigator to fire two .303 guns rearward from the nose. We got rid of these additions but kept the power-operated mid turret which was the only real improvement.

In November 1942 we flew out to Blida SW of Algiers. None of our ground crew had arrived, nor our equipment and transport. The First Army advanced more rapidly than expected and we spent less than three weeks at Blida.

The 3rd of December was the last raid I carried out from Blida – and very nearly my last raid of any sort. I had bombed Bizerta docks and had been briefed to follow this up by strafing Sidi Ahmed airfield from low level. It was a beautiful moonlit night and I naively steamed straight up the runway at 300 ft, no doubt presenting a good silhouette to the German LAA batteries sited to either side. All might possibly have been well, except that Ginger had neglected to change to night tracer, so that when I ordered him to open fire we presumably became a dream target with our day tracer illuminating our exact position most effectively. At all events, no sooner had he opened fire than both batteries opened up simultaneously and we were suddenly caught in a cone of 40 mm fire: most of it passing just above the canopy, although the guns on the port side scored at least one hit in my engine and managed to make great holes in my wing and to shoot away most of my aileron on that side. Until that moment I would not have contemplated a near vertical dive at night from 300 ft, but it seemed preferable to the alternative of being shot out of the sky. I recovered very low indeed and, having got clear, faced some two and a half hours back to Blida with a barely controllable aircraft. I soon realised that I would not have the strength to keep up the necessary downward force to starboard with my arms alone, and passed most of that seemingly endless flight back to base with my right knee crooked over the control column.

Next day, 18 Squadron, who also had Bisleys, were ordered to carry out a raid with eleven aircraft on a landing ground – Chouigui. Two aircraft crashed on or shortly after take-off. The remaining nine were shot down by Me 109s and Fw 190s.The leader, Hugh Malcolm, was awarded a posthumous VC.

That afternoon the whole Wing moved to the west of Constantine.

It had been a disastrous nineteen days from our shambolic arrival without even our aircraft records (Form 700). Everything had to be improvised. The Wing had lost thirty aircraft to the beginning of December and a further twenty-five were lost in December. We had sixteen remaining out of the original seventy-two!

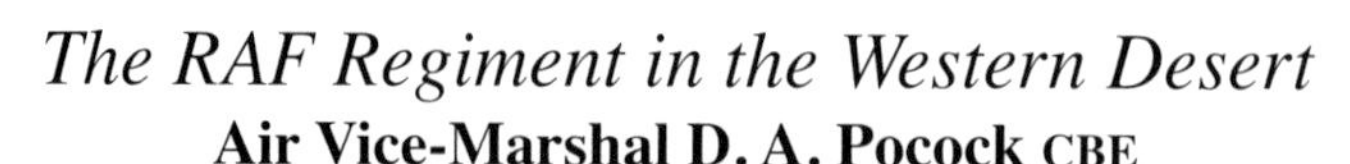

The RAF Regiment in the Western Desert

Air Vice-Marshal D. A. Pocock CBE

The first four operational squadrons of the RAF Regiment overseas were part of the Desert Air Force during the final advance from Alamein in 1942.

The loss of Maleme airfield in Crete, and the subsequent withdrawal of Commonwealth forces from the island, caused the Air Council to give a high priority to the adequate defence of airfields and installations in all areas where a likely threat of air or ground attack existed. Starting in mid-1941 large drafts of airmen with the trade of ground gunner were despatched from the United Kingdom on the lengthy sea journey via South Africa to Egypt.

On arrival, the ground gunners were deployed throughout the Middle East Command which then extended from West Africa to the Sudan, Aden, Syria, Iraq, Palestine, Egypt and the Western Desert. The initial deployment of ground gunners assumed that air or ground threats existed throughout the Command and that there were insufficient men and weapons for effective defence. Defences were therefore adjusted to provide effective cover where it was most needed.

In the Desert Air Force, flights of between twenty and thirty ground gunners were established on each operational flying squadron and at some important installations. During Rommel's advance towards Libya these ground gunners had some successes against the German and Italian air forces, but they were limited by the relatively short range of their anti-aircraft weaponry.

In September 1940 the RAF Armoured Car Companies had moved to the Western Desert from their bases in Iraq and Transjordan and had been particularly effective in providing protective screens in defence of our forward landing grounds.

Before pushing forward on the great advance from Alamein which started in October 1942 the Eighth Army emphasised the importance of airfield defence with a directive:

> '...Our aim must be to ensure that the fighter force is never left unprotected – a properly constituted defence force would achieve this aim, but so long as we rely upon the present haphazard arrangement for the protection of valuable and vulnerable targets, we shall continue to risk losing aircraft on the ground on a scale which is alarming to think of. We must have security on the ground if we are to operate efficiently in the air'.

By September 1942 all ground gunners in the Middle East had been embodied in the RAF Regiment and formed into independent flights commanded by officers commissioned in the Administration and Special Duties Branch (Ground Defence). A training school was established at Amman to provide weapon and tactical training. The new RAF Regiment was taking shape.

In the Desert Air Force the framework for ground defence continued to be based on an RAF Regiment flight of about thirty men to each operational flying squadron. Subsequently, when two or more flying squadrons were operating from the same landing ground, an RAF Regiment officer was provided at the associated flying wing headquarters to co-ordinate the defence. The RAF Regiment flights were primarily equipped for the light anti-aircraft defence role.

Earlier in the campaign and prior to Rommel's advance towards Libya, Operation 'Crusader', which led to an enemy retreat, had been a victory for air support to the Army and highlighted the importance of mobility. Thus, on the final advance from Alamein the flying squadrons along with their controlling wing headquarters were divided into self-contained 'A' and 'B' Parties which leap-frogged from landing ground to landing ground, with the RAF Regiment flights moving in advance to secure each new landing ground.

A rather amusing incident occurred during one of these deployments, when importance was attached to securing a landing ground which the enemy might attempt to deny to us. RAF Regiment flights from the forward Spitfire Wing were formed into an ad hoc squadron to go forward and secure the landing ground prior to the arrival of the aircraft. En route the RAF Regiment unit found itself on the main axis of the 51st (Highland) Division whose GOC was not amused to find the RAF Regiment integrated into his column. However, on arrival at the landing ground at dusk the RAF Regiment deployed standing patrols and covered the approaches. At dawn the rumbling of diesel engines was heard, and the defenders with some alarm assumed that Rommel's Panzer units were about to arrive on the landing ground. However, the vehicle noises turned out to be from South African airfield construction engineers who were grading the runway. They told the RAF Regiment commander that they had been working there for two days and hadn't seen any enemy!

Much of the motor transport in the Desert Air Force had been supplied 'off the shelf' from America under the lease-lend agreement. The three-ton personnel and load-carriers had rather narrow rear wheels which were not wholly suitable in soft sand, but we found them and the fifteen cwt trucks which were also supplied generally reliable despite the extreme conditions. Other items of lease-lend included large motor-cycles and Thompson Machine-Guns ('Tommy' guns).

RAF armoured cars – North African desert 1942 (RAF Regiment)

Subsequently, the ubiquitous Jeep was provided, which considerably enhanced mobility.

The moment of the advance from Alamein by the Eighth Army and the early achievement of air superiority minimised direct attack against our landing grounds and installations. In terms of clandestine operations the Germans failed to carry out raids on our parked aircraft, whilst our Long Range Desert Group with their deep penetration 'hit and run' tactics inflicted much damage on the German air effort.

An aspect of light anti-aircraft gunnery which came to light during the campaign was that the German gunnery tended to put up a dense curtain of fire against attacking aircraft whereas British gunnery practice was to employ deliberate aimed fire. The Germans appeared to have greater success with their method of fire than the British.

We quickly adjusted to the rigours and demands of the desert. Despite rugged living conditions with heat by day, long cold nights (with no commercial radio), and biting sandstorms, morale was high. The overseas tour for a married man was three years and for a single man four years. Away from home – except for protracted postal services, the man was cut off from the family circle and divorced from the normal amenities of life in surroundings which lacked any of the usual landmarks – no houses, no trees, no hills and no roads. The length of the overseas tour meant that within units there was a good measure of continuity and units tended to be closely knit with few diversions. Consequently, a high degree of character and self-sufficiency developed.

The ration scale seldom varied from bully-beef – which was cooked in a variety of ways deserving its own recipe book – tinned 'M & V' and sausages made from soya beans. There was no bread and porridge was made out of hard tack biscuits reinforced by a few raisins and, fortunately, an almost unlimited quantity of 'Carnation' milk. Water was restricted to half-a-gallon a man per day for all purposes. The quality of water varied and was frequently brackish, which curdled the milk in tea. Some of the wells had been contaminated by the Germans on their retreat. On the move units became very adept at improvisation and during a ten minute halt it was possible for us to have a mug of 'char' which had been quickly brewed by a small amount of petrol, some readily available sand and an empty seven lb jam tin.

A weekly ration of half a pint of beer from a variety of brewers was mostly appreciated although some felt that the taste of such a small amount would arouse too many memories of British pub life. Also a weekly issue of cigarettes made in India were smoked, not so much for enjoyment but because they were free.

After the desert our arrival at Castel Benito in Tripolitania was overwhelming. The airfield was set in Mussolini's shining example of colonisation. Houses were covered in bougainvillaea, farms were supported by an excellent irrigation system, there were large vats of wine adjacent to the vineyards, bars were open and there were attractive girls. Instead of several weeks' wait, mail from home was arriving within a few days and concert parties arrived to entertain the troops.

At this stage in the advance the first overseas operational squadrons of the RAF Regiment were formed by concentrating the first independent flights established on each of the flying squadrons. This arrangement clearly created better combat effective units although many of the airmen who had served for several months with their associated flying squadron were disappointed with the move.

These first squadrons were equipped for the dual role of light anti-aircraft and ground defence and were organised into six flights with a total establishment of 200. A period of reorganisation to shake down the new organisation and training was facilitated by the excellent conditions available in Tripolitania. Time was available for us to visit the city of Tripoli which offered a variety of attractions unavailable in the desert. The port of Tripoli was full of shipping bringing fresh supplies for the Army and the Air Force, and against these targets the Germans mounted a number of night bombing attacks.

Shortly after moving forward into Tunisia, the combined successes of the Eighth Army and Desert Air Force and the forces which had earlier landed in Algiers Bay as Operation 'Torch' led to the early defeat of the Axis forces in North Africa.

The practical experience in the Western Desert campaign and of the force which landed in Algiers confirmed the importance of integrating the RAF Regiment units with the flying squadrons they were required to support. The experience thus gained also proved invaluable to the RAF Regiment in other theatres of war.

Following the victory in North Africa most of the RAF Regiment units which had sailed from the United Kingdom as part of Operation 'Torch' were committed to subsequent operations in the Mediterranean – notably Sicily, mainland Italy and the Balkans. Those squadrons which had arrived in Egypt and joined the Desert Air Force mostly redeployed to Egypt, Libya, Palestine and operations in the Aegean.

An example of the experience in mobility and flexibility learned in the desert can best be illustrated by one of the newly formed RAF Regiment squadrons whose independent flights had been part of the forward Spitfire wing. On approaching Tunisia it was ordered to do a sharp 'about turn'. The squadron motored back along the route which the Desert Air Force had taken since Alamein. *En route* to Egypt the squadron received a signal from Cairo to proceed to the RAF Maintenance Unit located between Alexandria and Cairo where all the command stocks of engine oil were held. The vast area covered by these stocks had encouraged thieving on a large scale as the thieves rolled the forty-gallon drums down to a tributary of the Nile to be floated away down stream. With the ingenious but wholly unorthodox use of No. 36 hand grenades, the squadron quickly halted the losses and the Egyptian Police were grateful.

The squadron was then tasked with duties on the outskirts of Cairo, at Cairo West airfield and at the Mena House hotel where a 'Big Four' conference was being held. The squadron's duties included a Guard of Honour for the British Prime Minister Mr Winston Churchill.

The squadron then moved on by road to Palestine for re-equipping prior to moving on to the Turkish/Syrian frontier to participate in Operation 'Turpitude', which was a diversionary operation and required the squadron to deploy with a force of South African Air Force aircraft at Minnick airfield close to Aleppo. This was the first occasion when an

RAF Regiment squadron in the Middle East had deployed operationally with the Bofors 40 mm gun.

From Syria the squadron moved back to Egypt and embarked for Italy where it provided light anti-aircraft defence on the Foggia Plain and on the Adriatic Coast.

Subsequently, the squadron embarked for the Dalmatian island of Vis where until the end of the European war it supported Balkan Air Force operations in Yugoslavia.

Military matters have a habit of going full circle, and today more than fifty years later RAF Regiment officers are back in what used to be called Yugoslavia as part of the United Nations Protection Forces.

IRAQ

A Short War in Iraq 1941

Air Vice-Marshal A. G. Dudgeon CBE DFC

The spring of 1941 brought one of the crucial turning points in the war. A failure at that time and place could have resulted in losing the war. The first turning point was the Battle of Britain. The second, largely unrecognised even to the present day, was a vital and bloody battle fought in Iraq by a Flying Training School against the Iraqi armed forces. The third was the Battle of Alamein.

The Iraqi battle was assuredly vital: the Air Commander-in-Chief Lord Tedder said in hindsight: 'If the School had not prevailed, the whole course of the War would have been changed – if we had not lost it altogether'. It was bloody because the School, with no modern operational aircraft and cut off from reinforcements, lost a third of its effectives from enemy action in the first fourteen hours.

Iraq was a British creation after the First World War. It was of great strategic importance in the Middle East and to retain control was vital. There were, however, two problems. Army High Command in Cairo gave it less priority than the other serious events that were then pressing on Britain. The Germans had occupied Yugoslavia and Greece and General Rommel's Afrikakorps had appeared in Libya. How and where to find extra forces to defend Iraq?

The Army High Command in Egypt decided that as Iraq was politically an ally, it should be left to diplomats to find the solution to any unrest.

Early in 1941 General Rommel began his drive towards Egypt. There was not one member of his *Afrikakorps* who did not believe their ultimate objective was Iraq, cutting us off from our oil. At the same time an Egyptian army hot-head, Colonel Gamel Abd el Nasser was plotting to stage an Army coup and drive the British from Egypt. Turkey was teetering about which side to back and in neighbouring Syria it was plain that the Axis collaborator Marshal Pétain was in favour, not General de Gaulle.

In Iraq, Raschid Ali, a rabidly anti-British ex-lawyer, had seized total power. He was a great admirer of Nazi Germany and of Germany's military successes. By contrast Britain, which had been driven back from all mainland Europe and as far south as Crete, looked a poor bet. He was preparing a coup to be staged in conjunction with Germany and in tandem with Nasser's coup in Egypt. The avowed objective was to drive Allied forces out of the entire Middle East. Raschid Ali had the support of the Iraqi armed forces. Perhaps more significant were the links he had established with the Foreign Ministry in Berlin using the Italian Legation which we had failed to close in Baghdad.

The first part of his coup came on 3 April. Ribbentrop sent a letter offering Germany's unconditional military and financial aid in support of an Arab war of liberation against Britain. During April, influenced by violent pro-Axis propaganda, even the Arabs in the streets were convinced that the British were done for.

Thus encouraged, Raschid Ali quoted limitations on the British under the Anglo-Iraq treaty. In April he took a strong

Audax at Habbaniya (AHB)

line with the British Ambassador and accused him of introducing new troops into Iraq, contrary to the Treaty terms.

When a small number of troops landed, he informed the Axis powers that he regarded this as an Act of War! – and asked for implementation of Ribbentrop's earlier promises of aid. In return he said the Axis could have the use of all Iraqi airfields and facilities. Fortunately for us he took action which jumped the gun as far as practical Axis assistance was concerned. Towards the end of April, without confirmation of Axis support, he insisted to the British Ambassador that his actions had been an Act of War and on 28 April he ordered the Iraqi army to lay siege to Habbaniya.

The Iraqis surrounded Habbaniya and prepared for a serious attack. The build-up took two days. Their land force was about 7500 infantry with light tanks, field-guns and anti-aircraft weapons. They had on call an Iraqi Air Force of seventy operational aircraft which fortunately for us played only a minor part in the battle. They dug gun and howitzer emplacements with trenches on a plateau actually overlooking the camp and airfield. Their commander sent in an envoy demanding that all flying should cease, adding that any aircraft taking off would be fired on. This demand for virtual surrender was rejected.

RAF Station Habbaniya was an obvious and tempting target. It was only ninety kilometres from Baghdad and astride the only road by which any land forces could come from the Middle East; it had an excellent airfield and supplies of high-octane fuel for the promised German aircraft. Its defences on the ground amounted roughly to 400 British riflemen with half-a-dozen RAF armoured cars of 1917 vintage, plus 1000 Iraqi-Assyrian levies, employed by the RAF primarily as guards and who, being Iraqi nationals, were of unproven value and loyalty. Not a great defensive force.

In the air things were similarly slender. Habbaniya was not an operational base and had no operational aircraft. It was simply the home of the RAF's No. 4 Flying Training School. None of our training aircraft were capable of carrying more than a few light bombs. But the School was ingenious and productive. This was thanks largely to the efforts of a young, strong-minded Squadron Leader with plenty of initiative. He contravened the categorical orders of his rule-bound WW I superiors, who threatened to have him arrested for flagrant disobedience.

We made DIY modifications to Oxford trainers, obsolescent biplane Audaxes and Gladiator fighters. This produced sixty aircraft capable of some warlike action – and nineteen of them could now carry much bigger 250 lb bombs. We could not increase the meagre total of only thirty-nine pilots, mostly flying instructors who had never flown a live sortie.

For the RAF it was a clear case of attack being the best form of defence. The School opened the battle at dawn on 2 May with our thirty-nine qualified pilots, supported by sixty part-trained pupils as aircrew. For maximum effect on this first day of operations, a squadron of ten Wellington bombers from Basra added extra force. Our plan was to harry the besiegers with continuous bombing and machine-gunning, trying to keep them pinned down. Survival depended on hitting the guns, readily identifiable from their flashes, and hitting every heavy offensive vehicle before it could rush the camp. We had no force capable of stopping a ground attack.

One pilot who took part compared the airspace above the plateau to the front end of a wasps' nest. The Iraqis must have thought much the same. Take offs and landings under continuous shellfire were, to say the least, hair-raising. Some pilots flying off a makeshift airstrip on the golf-course in the middle of the camp made over forty sorties in the one day. No one stopped their engines while loading bombs, only when refuelling or for incapacitating wounds and damage.

By the end of the day the enemy had failed to make any land attack, though their shellfire was causing a lot of harm. But for us the balance on the day was deadly serious. A third of our aircraft and a quarter of the irreplaceable pilots had been put out of action. Night-time allowed some limited recuperation of manpower and repair to aircraft but it also allowed the Iraqis to increase their shelling with impunity.

We would have to mount a similar effort at dawn – there was no alternative. During the night the Air Officer Commanding suffered a nervous breakdown. In the morning he was flown to Basrah and never returned.

So it went on with varying tactics. To keep up twenty-four-hour pressure the fatigued pilots even flew at night both by moonlight and after moonset in the pitch dark even though no flarepath could be used under the enemy guns. Only three pilots were judged to have the skills to attempt the pitch-black flying. Even so, on that first night one lost his nerve and another crashed and was killed – leaving only the highly nervous young Squadron Leader. He carried on with two extra sorties each night. But it did reduce the Iraqi night-shelling.

After five days and four nights success was achieved on 6 May. The siege was lifted because the Iraqi Army ran away. They fled towards Baghdad, heavily bombed and strafed by the remnants of the School. British assessment put the Iraqi casualties on that last day alone at over 1000. They left behind in working order substantial quantities of guns, pom-poms, shells, machine-guns, rifles, half-a-million rounds of ammunition and even ten armoured cars and a tank. On the RAF side no precise casualty figures were kept (no one had time) but the loss of pilots from all causes – nerves, wounds and death – was certainly not less than 50%.

On the day after the Iraqis had fled, the British Army relief column left Palestine on its long drive across the desert. It achieved a stunning administrative task, being put together and doing 400 to 500 miles to reach Habbaniya on the 18th. It had luck too! – for it met no Iraqi ground or air opposition and it arrived to find Habbaniya in a relaxed mood! No Iraqis and an empty Plateau.

Meanwhile, having cleared away the crashed aircraft and filled in the bomb-craters, the School swung into offensive action. They could use some of the part-trained pupils as pilots and they could accept some longed-for aircraft reinforcements from Egypt and Palestine. They had become so efficient that they destroyed virtually all the Iraqi Air Force operational aircraft on the ground at their own bases within six days.

By 12 May those young Habbaniya tigers reckoned they had made it possible for a disciplined troop of boy-scouts to march into Baghdad and accept a surrender. Why not send our 400 British riflemen to complete the job?

In Germany, on 3 May, Ribbentrop put a proposal to Hitler for helping Raschid Ali. The *Führer*'s only practical decision was for the *Luftwaffe* to organise a small force to fly out to Iraq. Berlin by its dilatoriness had passed up a golden opportunity to do untold damage to the British in the Middle East. But the *Führer* was primarily concerned with preparations for 'Barbarossa', his summer attack on the Soviet Union. In retrospect it all looks like the familiar 'too little and too late'. For him action in Iraq would have raised tiresome politico-military problems with Turkey, with the French in Syria, and even with Mussolini .

So only a small effort was made. On Goering's instructions a *Luftwaffe* Colonel was summoned from France and ordered to lead a force to Iraq. He was told 'The *Führer* wishes a heroic gesture'. The forces he was allotted were disappointingly small: a handful of He 111 bombers and Me 110 twin-engined fighters, with a few Ju 52 transports in support. His brief? 'To try and prevent the British relief column reaching Habbaniya! – and to 'stiffen the spines' of the Iraqi army for the capture of that base.' He would be working from the Iraqi Air Force station at Mosul.

On 15 May five He 111s were in position and ready for action. With French co-operation his force crossed from Athens via Rhodes, French-Syrian bases at Damascus, Palmyra and Aleppo. By that date however – 15 May – horrific tales of our air-bombing, rumoured and wonderfully magnified, had been spread throughout the Iraqi forces by the survivors. Indeed, the Iraqi army flatly declined to co-operate. They never reappeared in strength.

For all its size and lack of support the *Luftwaffe* commando did a fair amount of damage, although in return we caused them many operational losses and their aircraft engines were damaged due to lack of high-octane fuel. Its remnants were withdrawn to Greece by 26 May.

Arriving at the comparative peace and quiet of Habbaniya, the 'rescue' column from Egypt held back. They spent no less than ten days regrouping and cleaning up before starting an advance to Baghadad on the 27th. On the 28th they had some sporadic skirmishes but no significant opposition. On the 29th they entered Baghdad and the Iraqi Government surrendered on the 31st. Raschid Ali, in flight to Iran, was temporarily held at the frontier town of Ba'Quba and in his luggage were found 17,000 Dinars, reported to be the pay of his own troops.

On 1 June Iraq was once again a British ally and its Royal Family returned to the palace. The Foreign Office wished to reinstate the pro-British Royal Iraqi family, so all publicity at that time was suppressed. It was deemed to be potentially bad propaganda for us to have given an Ally a bloody nose! So the whole matter was shuffled under the carpet and slipped into oblivion until the true facts began to reappear in the official histories twenty to thirty years later. By then it was all of little interest.

No other case exists of a well-armed land-force with air support being beaten by air-attack alone. Later that year Syria was occupied. In 1942 Egypt and the Suez Canal were secured through victory at Alamein – which in turn made possible the Allied landings in Algeria and the opening of a Southern Front in Italy – coinciding with D-Day in France. None of these, probably, could have been successful without that victory at Habbaniya.

The Battle of Habbaniya can be judged in retrospect as critical for the retention of British prestige and power in the Middle East. It was won decisively by a minuscule force of instructors and students in spite of swingeing casualties and the most desperate fatigue. It was deservedly described by Marshal of the Royal Air Force Lord Tedder as 'an RAF epic'.

It had been a short war in Iraq but by no means an insignificant one.

The RAF Armoured Car Companies

E. Melluish

It was May 1941 and I had been selected for guard duties at the power house at RAF Habbaniya. This was a new duty which was deemed necessary owing to the presence of the Iraqi army surrounding the camp and the threat of an imminent attack.

Let me explain the significance of this power house. Inside a massive building were three very large generators which provided the power for the whole of the camp including the civil cantonment of some 5000 civilians who were engaged in various types of work – NAAFI, staff billet orderlies and cleaners etc. – in fact any job that relieved airmen for their normal duties.

It was also the main power source for drawing drinking and washing water from the river Tigris which formed part of the camp border. These generators, which were diesel driven, were supplied by a 50,000 gallon fuel tank alongside the main building. Towering some sixty feet above the site was a 250,000 gallon assembly of tanks to store the purified water.

The rota for twenty-four hours was the standard guard duty of two hours on and four off. The airmen were drawn from different units each of which issued their own men with .303 Enfield rifles. My trade was armourer and my unit was No. 1 Armoured Car Company who, when on reconnaissance out on the blue, wore side arms consisting of a .45 Webley revolver, webbing holster and a pouch for ammunition. Instead of drawing rifles from the armoury for this duty we were given permission to use our revolvers. We were instructed to go on duty with empty guns. The orderly officer would give permission to load and fire if the occasion required. When we queried this instruction, pointing out that the orderly officer would most probably be in the mess, we were informed that this was King's Rules and Regulations.

I was given the 2200 hours to 2400 hours shift and when the time arrived I was marched to my post in the power

HRH the Duke of Kent inspects RAF armoured cars, Habbaniya 1942 (Crown copyright)

house enclosure, all alone, not another human being in sight. It was a very long two hours. Whilst on my rounds I did peer into the power house itself and saw one of the engineers but the noise was so terrific he never heard me and it was too much for my ears, so I moved on. It was a great relief when my time was up, even if it was only for that shift.

My next tour of duty was from 0400 until 0600 then the third shift from 1000 to 1200. At least it was now daylight and I only had one more shift to do. About 1030 the air-raid warning sounded and, not having being given instructions as to this eventuality, I was puzzled as to what to do. Did I jump into the slit-trench which had been dug without any thought for the personnel who would use it? It ran alongside the diesel storage tank, and in my estimation this would be the main target for the bombers. Crippling the power house would cause chaos on the camp.

I decided to stick it out on the surface, telling myself with false bravado that I could not repel intruders whilst lying in the bottom of a slit trench. This was all very well but I had not counted on the flying bullets. I saw holes appearing in the blast walls of sandbags and this altered my interpretation of my duty. I jumped into the trench and lay as close to the ground as was humanly possible.

I glanced furtively skywards and could see three Heinkel 111s flying serenely above the camp, uninterrupted. A lone Gladiator was fighting hard to reach the altitude required to attempt an attack. Although the enemy aircraft were not long over the camp, to me it seemed a lifetime. As the Gladiator neared the enemy planes I could hear the sound of gunfire and kept my head as close to the ground as possible. And as I lay there I heard this slight moaning sound and then felt this terrific blow in the small of my back. Oh my goodness I've been hit! I shouted for help, but the engineer in the power house was oblivious and most probably didn't even know there was an air-raid on. All manner of things popped into my head, and I thought, well you just can't stay here, you must do something. I made an effort to move so that I could ascertain the damage and in doing so I felt something drop off my back into the bottom of the trench. I looked around carefully and saw an empty cartridge case lying there. I realised that this is what had hit me and on further examination I found that, apart from a tender spot on my back, I was unhurt. I picked up the empty cartridge case and noticed from the markings that it was German. Feeling very sheepish at my panic I put the case in my pocket and decided not to say anything about the incident. I was afraid that I might be subject to ridicule.

It is surprising what goes through your head in incidents like this. After feeling the blow I could have sworn that I could feel blood trickling down my back, but I guess it was the sweat, as the temperature that day was 118 degrees in the shade. The temperature in the trench, which was in full sun, must have been considerably higher.

A few days later, after the Iraqis had been driven from the vicinity, I was told that I was to accompany a half-section of armoured cars to clear up any pockets of resistance. We had orders to rendezvous with a part of Habcol which had been formed specifically to relieve the besieged camp at Habbaniya. This force was to proceed up the Euphrates to Abu-Karnal and thence on to Deir-Ez-Zor which was in Syria. This would coincide with the entrance into Syria of the main party of Habcol which was standing ready at Rutbah.

My party consisted of six RAF armoured cars, three Australian Army twenty-five lb guns and a company of the 10th Indian Army Division. We were to proceed up the eastern bank of the river whilst the rest went up the west side. All went well and on approaching Abu-Karnal the men of the Indian Division cautiously advanced on the town. No opposition was encountered. We then made our way towards Deir-ez-Zor while the other half of the force continued up the west bank.

We came across a fort occupied by some 200 members of the French Foreign Legion. They were signalled to surrender but their Commanding Officer refused. Our Commanding Officer was with the Australian twenty-five pounders and ordered the gunners to fire three shots: one to the left of the fort, one to the right, and one just beyond the rear. Again the offer of surrender was signalled and again refused. The Aussie then ordered one gun to fire a shot as near to the front gate as possible without causing damage. This was done and another signal was sent stating that, unless the fort surrendered, the next shells would be directed at its interior. A figure bearing a white flag then galloped out to meet us. He was a typical French officer, small and dapper with a goatee beard and moustache, wearing a monocle. He appeared to be protesting vehemently and making threatening gestures. I don't think that the Aussie officer understood what he was saying and as the fort commander refused to be quiet the Aussie beckoned to my car commander and said 'Throw him in the back of that armoured car and get him out of my sight'. We did so with gusto and this put a stop to his protesting.

As we slowly approached the fort we could see some of the native population leading away horses loaded with booty and others laden with what they could carry. By the time we entered the fort the Arabs had almost stripped the place: guns, food and clothing had all gone.

The main part of the Habcol force which had progressed from Rutbah was making some headway and two of their patrols made contact with Glubb Pasha and his Arab Legion about twenty miles outside Deir-ez-Zor. Glubb had a brush with an Arab insurgent named Fawzi who had been a thorn in the side of the British in Palestine for a number of years pre-war. Glubb Pasha had captured seventeen armoured fighting vehicles and had no intention of handing these over to anyone.

Meanwhile after finding Deir-ez-Zor quiet, The No. 1 Armoured Car detachment was ordered to proceed to Mosul (Iraq) and assume policing duties. On arrival we were housed in the old WW I Turkish barracks, a high domed building with scorpions running around and rather large centipedes scurrying across the ceiling. This was now to be my home. However, after eight weeks of inactivity, I was sent back to Habbaniya.

I often wondered what happened to the magnificent horse of the French fort commander!!

North West Europe

In the dark days of 1940/41 Britain was alone, facing a hostile Continent. The whole European coast line from the Arctic Circle to the south of the Bay of Biscay was in enemy hands.

Action by the RAF was generally limited to bombing with twin engined aircraft with inadequate navigational facilities; countering attacks on shipping by U-boats and the long-range German Kondors; ground attacks on targets in north-west Europe, and special operations.

Three events in 1941 changed the world picture. Germany invaded Russia on 26 June; the Japanese attacked the US fleet at Pearl Harbor on 7 December, and four days later the USA entered the war.

Aerial Reconnaissance

Air Chief Marshal Sir Neil Wheeler GCB CBE DSO DFC AFC

An important milestone in the development of photographic reconnaissance was the coming together in the 1930s of Wg Cdr F. S. Cotton, a buccaneering entrepreneur, and Maurice Longbottom. Cotton had gone to Malta to photograph Italian targets and met Longbottom, an enthusiast about aerial photography. Cotton enlisted him as an assistant. Longbottom produced a memorandum entitled 'Photographic Reconnaissance of Enemy Territory in War' and submitted it to the Air Ministry in August 1939. It divided reconnaissance into two categories: tactical work in the immediate vicinity of the front line, and strategic reconnaissance of enemy territory behind the area of conflict. The memorandum was remarkable in that Longbottom foresaw the problems of reconnaissance and suggested the solution. In his words: 'This type of reconnaissance (strategic) must be done in such a manner as to avoid the enemy fighter and aerial defences as completely as possible. The best method of doing this appears to be the use of a single small machine relying solely on its speed, climb and ceiling to avoid detection.' To my mind, this was a most profound statement and it's worth remembering it was not made in the Air Ministry. It was made by a Flying Officer. He was saying, in effect, do not try to outfight the enemy but use stealth. It took a long time for that to sink in and for everyone to accept reliance on altitude and speed.

Cotton had the problem of getting the right aircraft. He wanted Spitfires, but in 1939 they were like gold dust. Fortunately, the Special Reconnaissance Unit at Heston (which eventually became the PRU) came under Fighter Command and Dowding had been impressed by Cotton's work. It is recorded that Dowding – perhaps rashly – asked if there was anything he could do for the Heston Flight, and the persuasive Cotton immediately said: 'Lend me two Spitfires'. And he got them! They landed at Heston the next day in October 1939.

Longbottom had always felt that the Spitfire was robust enough to carry a large load and it certainly had the power. Without its service load as a fighter it could carry a considerable amount of extra fuel, oil, oxygen and cameras. The Spitfires were prepared by removing all armament, radio and surplus weight such as the heavy bullet-proof windscreen. Gun holes were filled by metal plates and all cracks were blocked with plaster of Paris, as well as polishing all the external surfaces into a hard, sleek gloss. All of this raised the top speed of about three hundred and sixty miles per hour to three hundred and ninety.

Camouflage was obviously important and duck-egg blue (Camotint) became the initial PR colour. It did not last long and, quite early in 1940, sky-blue was introduced. Camotint was retained for low-level sorties.

But the important thing was range. All major modifications had to be approved by the Royal Aircraft Establishment at Farnborough and the RAE were only willing initially to allow an extra twenty-nine gallon tank

Supermarine Spitfire PR III (Philip Jarrett)

behind the pilot. This was obviously going to be a great help. It took the fuel to one hundred and fourteen gallons and was known as the PR IB. The first was collected from RAE on 16 January 1940. It had a range of about seven hundred and fifty miles. Pressure for distant areas to be covered, particularly by naval intelligence, gradually led to the fuel being increased by thirty-gallon stages. This led to the F-type with twenty-nine gallons behind the pilot. Finally in October 1940 we received the PR III, designed as a Spitfire for PR. It had sixty-five gallons in each wing leading edge. It was in other words a wet-wing aircraft, an unusual thing in those days. The fuel load went up to two hundred and fifteen gallons and the range to about one thousand seven hundred and fifty miles.

Naturally this great extension of the range of the Spitfire and the Merlin engine brought other requirements. We had to have considerably more oil and a tank was designed to fit like a large chin under the nose just behind the propeller. But most of our early problems came from the altitude at which we were flying. Before the war there was not much flying over twenty thousand feet. Most of our Spitfire PR sorties took place between 25,000 and 35,000 feet where temperatures were around minus fifty degrees centigrade. In the early days we had problems with, for example, the vent of the oil tank, and some form of heating was required. The same was true of the cameras.

Cockpit heating was an obvious necessity. Because we were not experienced in flying in low temperatures nobody thought of harnessing the hot air from the coolant radiator until 1942 when, at long last, cockpit heating was provided. Frankly, I found the extreme cold most uncomfortable. On my feet I wore a pair of ladies' silk stockings, a pair of football stockings, a pair of oiled Scandinavian ski socks and RAF fur-lined boots. On my hands I wore two pairs of RAF silk gloves and some special fur-backed and lined gauntlets which I had to buy for myself. It was essential to retain some fingertip control, particularly for the camera control box. Otherwise, I wore normal uniform, with a thick vest, roll neck sweater and a thing called a Tropallining which was stuffed with a form of kapok

But to me the most serious shortcomings that the lack of high-altitude flying experience brought, were the use of oxygen and the almost total ignorance about condensation trails. Before the war it was mandatory to turn on oxygen above ten thousand feet on the rare occasions that you went to that great height, but the supply system was primitive. We had a crude, very leaky cloth mask and a form of continuous supply. In other words, once you turned it on, you got it whether you were breathing in or out. To say the least, it was most wasteful, and oxygen cylinders are heavy. We had to change things since we were using oxygen for about four or even more hours. We had our own doctor and, with RAE's help and the use of other masks including a captured German one, we designed a good rubber mask. In November 1940 the oxygen economiser was introduced which worked with a form of bellows and only gave you oxygen when you inhaled. Inevitably we called it 'Puffing Billy'. Even here we had low temperature problems with the fabric used in the construction of the early economisers. Nonetheless, all these things greatly helped our operations.

Most people commenting on unarmed photographic 'recce' concentrate on the fear of deep penetration of enemy territory in an unarmed aircraft. Frankly, I do not recall that it loomed large in our minds. One simply could not fight it out once intercepted. The only thing to do was to go flat out for home ... and pray ... and forward firing guns certainly would not have helped.

Fortunately, for most of the war, we did out-perform the enemy, although there were periods when the reverse was true. Our greatest problem as regards the enemy was the condensation trails. Radar was still in its infancy and, on the whole, there was a reasonable chance that a lone Spitfire, operating at around 30,000 feet, could penetrate deep into enemy territory without detection. Indeed, the deeper you penetrated, the less likely the detection.

My own experience in summer 1941 proves my point. When flying over north Germany I suffered trouble with my oxygen supply. At about 28,000 ft. I passed out and did not recover until about 1,500 ft over the entrance to Kiel Harbour. It was about 1100 hrs on a brilliantly clear morning and nobody seemed to take the slightest notice. The comment of a *Luftwaffe* general after the war was that nobody would have expected a lone enemy aircraft in daylight a few miles from Kiel at a few thousand feet! It would, however, have been a different story had I, before my oxygen troubles started, been leaving a condensation trail or even operating above the level where trails had been created. Until the Battle of Britain I have to admit I had never heard of a condensation trail.

In PRU we removed the bullet-proof windscreen plus the rear-view mirror on the top. We fashioned teardrops in the side of the canopy, principally to get a better downward view and in them we fitted small rear-view mirrors. The mirrors were less to see approaching fighters than to prevent one producing a condensation trail over enemy territory – signing one's name in the sky was a certain route to disaster!

From Heston we carried out a great deal of research into the formation of condensation trails aided by Oxford University, before we established that it was the exhaust and not the propeller that produced the tell-tale trail. Normally one endeavoured to keep just below condensation height, but, on rare occasions, one could pass through a layer and fly above with the advantage that one could see enemy fighters climbing up.

Needless to say we faced great problems with weather forecasting and navigation. I have always maintained that a high proportion of our casualties were due to what I would call 'natural causes', and not the enemy. When one returned from a four-hour flight, say to Kiel, the weather could have changed remarkably and one had to let down through the cloud with no radio and no clear idea of one's exact position. Moreover, there was only one engine – a matter of some importance when operating from Scotland over Norway. That was the area when navigation produced many anxious moments. On a flight from Wick in January 1941 I aimed at Peterhead from Stavanger for my return, but made a landfall in the Firth of Forth and was intercepted! It is also as well to remember that, returning from Trondheim to Wick, one only had to have a twelve degree error, either side of track, to run out of fuel before seeing land.

I would like to end with a few words about low level operations. But, before dealing with Spitfires, I should add that, from the outset in 1939, we had used Hudsons, Blenheims and Marylands for low-level operations when cloud cover was available. They did not become a regular activity, but low-level sorties by Spitfires did.

After the evacuation of Dunkirk, it became essential to get photographic cover of the ports from Flushing to Cherbourg on at least a daily basis to monitor enemy preparations for invasion. If because of weather we could not get high level photographs we went at low level and took obliques. The aircraft generally had an extra thirty gallons behind the pilot, the standard armoured windscreen and the full armament of the fighter version. As I said earlier, they were camouflaged duck-egg blue, although we did experiment with off-pink

When the threat of invasion decreased towards the autumn of 1940, low-level sorties continued in order to meet the other requirements of intelligence.

Throughout the war, the work of PRU was a most valuable source of intelligence. Spitfires continued to do the job and were gradually improved, including the reinstallation of radio and, of course, the introduction of cockpit heating and even some pressurised cabins. The great step forward in 1942 was the arrival of the Mosquito. It was a complete natural for the job and I am happy to say that the first aircraft came to PRU. The Mosquito not only had outstanding speed and range but also the great advantage of a navigator. As well as better aircraft, there were considerable improvements in cameras and the science of photography. Cotton's and Longbottom's concepts of strategic reconnaissance by unarmed stealth had come to stay.

The Formative Years of the WAAF

Air Commodore Dame Felicity Peake DBE

In ten years' service with the WAAF and WRAF I experienced, and played my part in, the most profound changes in the role of women in the Armed Services. During those years I saw the recreated Women's Auxiliary Air Force make its contribution to the role of the Royal Air Force in the Second World War and in 1949 become the Women's Royal Air Force. Most of us who 'joined up' did so in a very lowly capacity, not having the slightest idea of what was in store for us. I enlisted in April 1939 as a Volunteer Storewoman in the 9th Royal Air Force (County of London) Company of the ATS – which was how the 1939–45 WAAF began, with forty-eight such Companies throughout the UK, and I remember how proud we were when we took part in a National Defence Rally in Hyde Park on 28 June, wearing Women's Auxiliary Air Force uniform for the first time.

In those early days, we trained to help the RAF with various duties. The Companies were attached to the Auxiliary Air Force squadrons – in my own case, to No. 601 (County of London) Squadron. Thus the foundations of the WAAF were laid, its early members all being potential officers or NCOs (I was commissioned in August 1939).

When war came, there was a rush of recruits, and by October 1939 the strength of the WAAF was over 8000. In that month I felt the impact of war sharply when my first husband, Jock Hanbury, was killed in a night flying accident when serving with No. 615 (County of Surrey) Squadron.

It was perhaps fortunate that there was a period of 'phoney war' in 1939–40, because as far as the WAAF were concerned there was initially a great deal of disorganisation, particularly in the matters of discipline, training and postings. But these problems gradually got sorted out. The real test came when the Battle of Britain began. How would these young women behave under fire? The answer proved to be – magnificently.

I was posted to Biggin Hill in mid-May 1940 – altogether there were 250 WAAFs there. It was not only a fighter station, with a prominent geographical location, but also a Sector Headquarters – and therefore a prime target for the *Luftwaffe*.

Of course we were scared when the attacks began, but

there was a great bond of friendship and admiration between us and the fighter pilots, who daily had to fight terrifying life-and-death battles. The WAAF behaved magnificently when the airfield was attacked with bombs and machine-gun fire, sticking to their duties with the utmost courage, and three of them were awarded the Military Medal.

When the Battle was over and I got my next posting – early in 1941 – I went first to the Inspectorate of Recruiting and then, more interestingly, to the Directorate of Public Relations. There, my job was to publicise the WAAF, and while doing that I had the unique opportunity of meeting the Chief of the Air Staff, Sir Charles Portal, and his Vice-Chief, Sir Wilfrid Freeman. They were both anxious to know – in the midst of all their other preoccupations – how things were going in the WAAF, and how it was regarded in comparison with the other Women's Services. I realise now that they looked on me as a sort of sounding-board because of my involvement in recruiting and publicity. The RAF was extremely fortunate to have had two men of such strong and perceptive character in command during the war years.

I encountered also another outstanding commander, Sir Arthur Harris, when I was posted to Bomber Command Headquarters in February 1943, but the real test for me – and for the WAAF – came when I was appointed to command the WAAF Officer's School at Windermere in August of that year. I was, by that time, an Acting Wing Officer. With hindsight – although I did not realise it then – I can say that this was a crisis time for the WAAF.

Not long after I had arrived at Windermere, and when I had already encountered opposition to the changes I wished to introduce there, I was summoned – at very short notice – to see the CAS. I travelled to London overnight, and when I saw Sir Charles Portal in the morning he questioned me keenly about the WAAF and about my ideas and hopes for it. I was unaware at the time that he was interviewing me as a possible future Director. When I left he asked me to keep him informed as to how things were going at Windermere: he had heard that I had encountered trouble there. Unfortunately, the fact that I had been to see him – although I myself told nobody about my visit – only made my situation worse, for the jealousy of some senior officers was increased: they were hostile to every effort I made to improve training at the School – an improvement I felt was necessary if the WAAF was to have better leadership – and I felt that I was banging my head against a brick wall.

The Chief of the Air Staff and Sir Wilfrid Freeman – who by now was at the Ministry of Aircraft Production, although he still kept a close eye on RAF affairs – knew about the situation at Windermere. They felt that the WAAF had fallen behind the other Women's Services in public esteem, and that it needed new and imaginative leadership: there had been too much promotion on the basis of length of service – which, as we had all started together in early 1939, was in some cases only a matter of weeks or months.

I had a short spell at 60 Group which controlled the radar stations after I left the Officers' School (which moved to Stratford-upon-Avon in July 1944). One of my jobs at No. 60 Group – one that moved me deeply and still affects me even to this day – was to interview girls who were to be landed in France and work with Resistance groups as wireless operators. If captured, they were tortured by the Gestapo and sent to concentration camps: many were never seen again. How can anyone say that women are not as brave as men in war?

I was lucky enough to be posted to Headquarters Middle East in Cairo in July 1945 as a Group Officer, responsible for the welfare of all the WAAFs in that vast Command: visiting all the units in which they were serving involved thousands of miles flying, over areas of the world I had only heard of before in legends and history books.

When I had been in Cairo about a year I was summoned to Athens to meet Sir John Slessor, the Air Member for Personnel, another formidable senior officer who was later to become Chief of the Air Staff. In a private talk, he asked me if I would be willing to accept the appointment of Director of the WAAF. After some consideration – for this offer came as a complete surprise to me – I decided that I would, although I realised that holding that post would mean the end of my Service career.

I became Director in October 1946, and I was fortunate enough to see the Service which I loved so much become – in February 1949 – the Women's Royal Air Force, of which I became the first Director. All my hopes and ambitions had been realised: the WRAF was to serve side by side with, and on equal terms with, the RAF. I felt that a long-fought, and often difficult battle had been won.

But there was a long way to go before this victory was finally achieved and I had many skirmishes, particularly with the Air Council, on which I needed allies who would support my ideas for a permanent Service.

Like the RAF, the WAAF had to be drastically reduced in size after the war. When I took over as Director (at the age of thirty-three) its total strength – officers and airwomen – was 97,744. During the next fifteen months it had to readjust to a reduction of 71,916 personnel, and by the time I retired in 1950 its strength had been reduced to 11,545 officers and airwomen.

The then Prime Minister, Clement Attlee, had announced in the House of Commons in June 1946 that the Women's

WAAFS in the Middle East (RAF Museum Hendon)

Services would be retained on a regular voluntary basis. Then in November of that year the Air Council announced an Extended Service Scheme for women – which enabled many WAAF personnel to postpone their release from the Service until conditions for a regular peacetime force had been worked out. But the delays in forming this were such that, in addition to the Extended Service Scheme, a Special Short Service Scheme also had to be introduced.

One major problem which had to be solved in the creation of a new Service was that of pay, and it was one which caused me great anxiety, much hard work and many sleepless nights. What I greatly feared was that the Treasury would approve a separate pay scale for Servicewomen – which would mean that, every time the men's rates were increased, there would be arguments about increasing women's rates. I was determined to prevent this at all costs and sought the help of Dame Caroline Haslett (an outstanding administrator and a good friend of the WAAF) in persuading the Chancellor of the Exchequer, Sir Stafford Cripps, to change his mind after he had endorsed the principle of a separate pay scale for women. She was successful in this – I remember dancing round the office when the news came through – and in 1947 the Air Council decided that two-thirds of men's pay rates should be paid to women, plus the full rates of allowances. This, with 'in kind' benefits, would give women four-fifths overall of the rates of pay for single men.

This battle for a better pay rate for women continued throughout my time as Director and long afterwards: by 1971 basic pay became equal, and by 1984 women became equal with the men in all grades. They now, I am happy to say, can be trained as aircrew.

It was a proud moment for me when, on 31 January 1949, an Inauguration Ceremony marking the formation of the Women's Royal Air Force was held in the Air Council Room at the Air Ministry, and on the following day the terms of service in the WRAF became public knowledge. All I had struggled for and worked for had been accomplished, and now it is taken for granted that RAF and WRAF personnel work side by side – including pilots – without discrimination of sex.

I would not like to suggest that my time in the WRAF – which ended when I retired in July 1950 – was all work and worry over the formation of the new Service: there were many compensations and excitements. During my four years as Director of the WAAF/WRAF (I had been invited to stay on for an extra year) I visited personnel in the United Kingdom and in Germany, and had an extraordinarily interesting visit in 1949 to the United States.

This occurred when the Berlin Airlift – the Anglo-American operation to supply the city during the Soviet blockade – was still going on, and I was asked many questions about it, particularly about what part WRAF personnel were playing.

I was able to tell my hosts about the role of airwomen at Gatow, the very busy 'receiving end' for aircraft from the UK. Impressed as I was by the WAF (Women in the Air Force) – especially their smartness and discipline, and their selection and training procedures – I was not dismayed by any comparison with our own Service, and my visit to the United States, during which we enjoyed wonderful hospitality, gave me renewed inspiration and zest for my own work as Director of the WRAF .

Looking back now on my years in the Service, I can only feel deep gratitude for having come through the war unscathed and having made many wonderful friends, without whom I could have done nothing. I know from my own experiences that women have done all that was asked of them in the RAF – in Bomber and Fighter Commands, on radar sites, as radio operators with the French Resistance, in code and cypher duties, on air traffic control: in fact in every field.

What I have also learned about is the splendid camaraderie of Service life – that 'mutual trust and sociability' found in the Royal Air Force, both in war and in peace.

Gunnery Leader

Squadron Leader Mike Henry DFC

The category of air gunner in the Royal Air Force lasted for less than fifty years. World War I saw the first aerial gunners who also acted as Observers. Now, post World War II, they are as outdated as the archers of Crécy.

On heavy bomber squadrons in World War II, air gunners were the largest category of aircrew and the wireless operator was also a qualified air gunner. The heavy losses of bomber aircrew during the war included more air gunners than any other category. Sometimes a pilot managed to bring his crippled aircraft back but with the vulnerable rear or mid-upper gunners dead.

An air gunner was an other-ranker until June 1940 when his 'trade' was recognised and he was automatically promoted to Sergeant. His brass-winged bullet insignia was then replaced by a brevet.

In June 1941, having completed twenty-six sorties on medium bombers (Blenheims), I was posted to the Central Gunnery School on a 'gunnery leader's course'. We were given many hours instruction on all facets of our trade – theory and practice. One new and important subject added to the syllabus was 'Fighting Control'. This gave the Gunnery Leader, who was in the leading aircraft, virtual control of his formation in daylight raids.

When his formation was about to be attacked by enemy fighters, the Gunnery Leader was responsible for warning the pilot and preparing him for the manoeuvres necessary to prevent his formation from being enfiladed. The formation had to be moved into a position enabling all or most gunners to bring their guns to bear on the enemy fighters. Quite often the gunner sat in his turret behind his twin or four Browning machine guns hoping not to have to blast away – even though his secret ambition was to shoot enemy fighters out

Blenheim IVs (AHB)

of the sky. Those of us who did survive have a vast accumulation of differing experiences. Some brought down enemy aircraft with their guns. Others didn't get the opportunity and were lucky not to be attacked.

No air gunner however, could ever relax. His eyes were always searching the skies around him to protect his crew and aircraft from surprise attack. He often endured freezing conditions in the confined 'office' of his turret. He was blinded by millions of candlepower from a cone of searchlights, and all felt helpless against heavy and light flak against which the turrets were useless.

Between us we flew by night and day. Some trips were long and wearisome: others comparatively short but just as 'dicey'. Some of the low-level daylight attacks on enemy shipping were both short and nerve-shattering. These usually suffered the heaviest losses as we, flying in 2 Group Blenheims, were well aware.

On return to base after a gruelling flight the air gunner shared with his crew the exhilaration of being back in one piece and after enjoying the privileged egg and bacon breakfast, entered another 'op' in his logbook. Then, maybe twenty-four or forty-eight hours later, he would go to the armoury to clean the recoiling portions of his guns before taking them back to the aircraft to complete a comprehensive list of checks before the next briefing. He was then ready to face another take-off on what could be his very last flight.

Despite heavy losses, surviving air gunners still cling to the sacred memories of their wartime service. Though there aren't many of us left, surprisingly the number of members of the Air Gunner's Association remains pretty high.

Hunters in the Night

Wing Commander Eric Barwell DFC

After 264 Squadron Defiants had suffered heavy losses during the Battle of Britain we were withdrawn to Kirton Lindsey to retrain as a night-fighter squadron.

One Flight was stationed at Northolt. This presented a number of difficulties. The airfield was almost surrounded by the balloon barrage and we soon moved to Luton. We were still controlled by Northolt but found that we lost radio contact below 2000 ft over Luton. We therefore rigged up some local radio equipment which enabled Luton to speak to the aircraft. We had no homing device but instead posted someone outside the hut to listen for returning aircraft. As soon as he heard the sound of the engine he would shout up to the radio operator in the hut 'north', 'south', 'east' or 'west', depending on his assessment of the aircraft's bearing. This information was relayed to the pilot who, with continued comment from the ground, could then locate the Glim lights of the runway. Despite its Heath Robinson nature we had no casualties!

During an operation, the Controller at Northolt would give us vectors and tell us when the target should be in range. Error could be up to 4000 or 5000 ft in altitude and several miles in distance. This made contact with the enemy very chancy if the night was dark. In my case it was six months before I saw a target well enough to attack. On that night I found a Heinkel 111 and my gunner shot it down. We were credited with a second 'probable' Heinkel which dived and disappeared from the radar screen. The .303 machine-guns were not always effective against enemy bombers. Our tactics were those we had evolved for daylight operations – we attacked from below and to one side.

During this period we operated from a number of different fields:– Debden, Rochford, Biggin Hill and West Malling. Sector control varied from Northolt to Debden and Biggin Hill. Flying two nights on and two nights off this could be very disorienting.

There were heavy raids on London during this period and we could see bombs bursting underneath and the flames spreading. Even so it was difficult to locate the enemy bombers. We flew high up, hoping to see them against the flames – or on clear nights lower so that they would be silhouetted against the sky. It was depressing not finding them though we often flew through slipstreams. I was fortunate on 10 October 1941, when we shot one bomber down near Eastbourne and I chased another to sea in the moonlight and eventually saw him crash in the water. We were lucky that no one was hit by our own AA or brought down by barrage balloons. We were however sometimes caught in the searchlights.

In July 1941 I was posted as Flight Commander to a new Defiant Squadron – 125 (Newfoundland) – to train new pilots, including Newfoundlanders. We were based at Fairwood Common at Swansea. We flew a lot with no success and suffered one casualty. An aircraft flying through the balloon barrage hit the last cable. Both crew baled out but the pilot broke his neck.

In December I was promoted Squadron Leader and

appointed CO of 125. This appointment only lasted two months, since in February 1942 the Squadron was re-equipped with Beaufighters. Commanding Officer of twin engined aircraft squadrons was a Wing Commander post and I reverted to being a Flight Commander again.

We now had the Beaufighter Mk II with Merlin engines. This was under-powered and swung on take-off and landing. It was however heavily armed with four 20 mm forward firing cannon in the nose and six .303 machine-guns in the wings. It also had its own AI Radar. Instead of the Defiant's gunner, the Beaufighter required a navigator who also operated the AI. He was seated behind the pilot and could reload the canon with spare magazines.

During operations the aircraft was initially under Sector control until the local Ground Control Interception Station identified both the blips of the Beaufighter and the enemy aircraft on its radar screen. The Controller would direct the aircraft until the enemy came within range of the Beaufighter's own radar. The navigator would pick up the trace and guide the pilot towards the enemy aircraft. This could be quite tricky if the enemy was crossing the Beaufighter's track. Hopefully the pilot would eventually see the enemy and identify before attacking.

My only combat in the Beaufighter was against a Dornier 17. I identified it in reasonable moonlight and decided to use cannon since the source of cannon fire was less easy to see than the continuous fire of the machine-guns. The cannon were fired by a brass trigger on the control column and the machine-guns by a button above it. Unfortunately the cannon would not fire and I used the machine-guns. I saw hits on the Dornier and it dived out of sight. The cannon then went off and the vibration upset the AI so I had to return to base. It was subsequently confirmed that the Dornier had been damaged. It jettisoned its incendiaries near the WAAF quarters at St Athan and bullet-holes were found in the incendiary canisters.

After a six month rest period I was posted back to 125 Squadron. By now this had been re-equipped with Beaufighter Mk VI with Hercules XVI radial engines. There was however little enemy activity.

In February 1944 we were again re-equipped, this time with Mosquitos Mk XVII with four 20 mm cannon in an elongated nose. It was very pleasant to fly and had the much more accurate and longer-range 10 cm AI. The navigator sat beside the pilot and this was also an improvement.

My first combat in a Mosquito was on 24 April 1944, when a number of raiders attacked Bristol. I identified a Ju 88 which caught fire and crashed near Warminster.

In preparation for the Normandy Invasion the Squadron was now posted to Hurn. I was granted short leave but whilst away heard that the invasion had started. I hurried back to take part in patrols over the beachheads.

We were controlled from a ship stationed in the Bay of the Seine which had very efficient equipment and excellent controllers. They played an important role in my shooting down a Ju 88.

A squadron of American Black Widows now arrived and we were told to give them every opportunity to engage the enemy so that they could gain experience. Although the pilots were good they had not flown with their navigators before and missed many easy victims. Partly as a result of this our GCI ship was sunk.

The Squadron was now diverted to countering the raids by the V1 unmanned flying bomb. I was warned by people with experience that two things were important when attacking these bombs at night. I must close one eye when firing so that the resulting explosion would not completely blind me and, second, break away as soon as anything started flying off the bomb.

I made several interceptions but only managed to hit one or two. The difficulty was that the V1 was faster than the Mosquito flying straight and level. I realised that I must gain considerable height advantage and attack with the greater speed achieved in a dive. On one occasion I saw the flames of the ram jet, dived and fired, closing in to around 100 ft. Suddenly the bomb exploded and I was completely blinded. When my night-vision returned I was struggling with the aircraft buffeted by the explosion. We later found a couple of pieces of shrapnel in the Mosquito.

In August 1944 I was posted to Ford where an experimental squadron was being formed to develop improved tactics against the flying bomb. This was equipped with Tempests and Mustangs. By the time we were operational the V1 launching sites had been overrun and my operational activities were over.

Bristol Beaufighter MkII (Philip Jarrett)

The RAF Eagle Squadrons

Colonel James A. Goodson

(One of the leading fighter pilots of WW II, Colonel Goodson was credited with thirty-two enemy aircraft destroyed. He won many US decorations – Presidential Citation, Distinguished Service Cross, Distinguished Flying Cross, Silver Star, Air Medal, Purple Heart, etc. as well as many European ones.)

Many think that the American contribution to the Allied air offensive came after Pearl Harbor, when the United States entered the war against the Axis powers, and American airmen started flooding into England. For some Americans the war started before their country was involved. They joined the RAF.

They risked losing their US citizenship by volunteering their services and falling foul of the US Neutrality Act, so they did not advertise their nationality. They were there from the beginning and flew in the Battle of Britain after flying in the Battle of France.

One of the first to volunteer was Billy Fiske: he was also one of the first to be killed, bringing his badly shot-up plane back to Tangmere, where it caught fire on landing. The British showed their respect by placing a plaque to his memory in St Paul's Cathedral. Had he lived a little longer, he would probably have been the first CO of the Eagle Squadrons.

I lived to join the Eagles by surviving the sinking of the SS *Athenia*, the first ship to be torpedoed on the first day of the war whilst I was on my way back to the States. I returned to Britain and joined the RAF.

After training in Canada, I was posted to 43 Squadron at Tangmere in the Wing led by Douglas Bader. The Americans kept coming. Some crossed the border and joined the RCAF and some joined the RAF directly, as did many Canadians.

The Powers-That-Be decided to tidy things up a little and, with some other Americans, I was sent to 416 Squadron RCAF.

In 1914–18, American volunteers had been formed into Escadrille No. 124, the Lafayette Squadron. Prominent amongst their number was Colonel Charles Sweeny. In WW II his nephew, also Charles Sweeny, was an American businessman living in London. He was convinced that America would eventually come into the war, but in the meantime there were far more young men with flying experience in the States than there were in England, and England badly needed pilots.

After a little arguing with the Air Ministry, Sweeny was able to form the RAF Eagle Squadrons from Americans flying with the RAF. The first squadron, No. 71, was formed in September 1940 at Church Fenton. It was followed in due course by 121 and 133 Squadrons. It was with the latter that I eventually found myself flying.

It is interesting that, after all the effort that went into the formation of the Eagles, for a while 71 Squadron couldn't get into combat. It was felt that severe American losses might prejudice the Americans against coming into the war. It was Sholto Douglas who decided to get the Squadron to 11 Group and the action, followed by 121 and 133. It was also Sholto Douglas who got me into the Eagle Squadrons. Many of us were enjoying our time with our regular RAF squadrons and we didn't want to leave our friends. I had refused all suggestions that I transfer to the Eagles. But one night I got a call from Sholto Douglas: 'I've asked you before to transfer to the Eagles – now I'm ordering you to. Get down to 133 Eagle Squadron at Great Sampford NOW!'

It was 26 September 1942. Escorting bombers over Morlaix, 133 Squadron had been given incorrect weather reports and when the wind changed they were above cloud and got totally lost. When Ray Fusch and I arrived at Great Sampford (a satellite of Debden) there was no-one to be seen. Every room was empty but for the half-finished letters, the hair cream and shaving soap on the lockers. In the last room, we found one man, Don Gentile. 'Take any room you like', he said. 'None of them have come back.'

It would have been disastrous for morale and public relations if it had got back to the States that a whole squadron of American volunteers had been lost, so our task was to re-form 133 Squadron as quickly as possible. They couldn't have given it to a better man than Don Blakeslee. He was a brilliant pilot and a great man.

There were many great men among the 288 who joined the Eagle Squadrons, over a third of whom were killed in action. It was only three days after Morlaix that all three Eagle Squadrons transferred to the US 8th Air Force to form the 4th Fighter Group. The fact that the 4th became the highest-scoring fighter unit of the Allied Air Forces was due

Spitfires of 121 Eagle Squadron (RAF Museum Hendon)

in no small way to the nucleus of pilots who had been trained by and flew with the RAF. We had been given a grounding in tactics, discipline and skills such as only the RAF could provide. That saved the lives of many of us.

We were proud of it. We only agreed to transfer to the US Air Force on condition that we could continue to wear our RAF wings and British decorations.

I am still immensely proud to have flown with the RAF and to wear my British decorations and to have been an Eagle. So are all the others, who still turn up for annual re-unions. There are damn few of us left.

I sometimes remember the words of Thomas More:

'I feel like one
Who treads alone
Some banquet-hall deserted
Whose lights are fled,
Whose garlands dead,
And all but he departed.'

Most of them died young, which is sad, but at least our memories of them are of handsome, fun-loving, carefree boys, the way they were when they joined the RAF.

Turning a Blind Eye

Jack Batchelor DFC

I remember flying a Spitfire at the age of nineteen (a member of 54 Fighter Squadron, at Hornchurch). I was twenty years old when I was shot up by an Me 109 and had to crash land with cannon shell fragments in my eyes.

The magnificent skills of the civilian eye surgeons and Wing Commander Keith Lyle, Consultant Eye Surgeon at RAF Hospital Halton, brought me back from blindness, removing the fragments from my eyes. After a number of operations the sight in my right eye recovered. The lens in the left eye was dissolved and a large glass contact lens was fitted. This in 1941 was something of a miracle.

I had been hospitalised for eight months but was passed fit by the RAF Central Medical Board in May 1942. I was fortunate to be attached to Station Headquarters Hornchurch where the Station Commander was Group Captain George Lott DFC, who had lost an eye in action against an Me 110 in the Battle of Britain. To me he was a kindred spirit who asked me if I would like to fly his personal Spitfire. I took advantage of his offer and climbed into the cockpit to fly for the first time since the crash, and also since being fitted with the contact lens. It felt as though I had a glass jug under my eye lid. It was a nervous thirty-minute flight in the Spitfire but George Lott's confidence was a great encouragement and I was passed to 64 Squadron to get flying experience before being posted to them to fly on operations from June 1942.

To the end of the war I was conscious of trying to avoid other pilots seeing me fit the lens in my eye before take off. The lens made my eye irritable and my eyeball extremely red if it was in position for periods exceeding ninety minutes. The glare of the sun at high altitudes was tiring, but I still had good vision. To combat the glare I wore dark-lensed, steel-framed sunglasses which almost gave the impression of a blind man flying a Spitfire. I often wondered what the other pilots thought about the situation but at all times I was treated as one of them.

I subsequently flew Spitfires on operations with 1, 64, 81, 229, and 603 Squadrons. As my experience grew, so other pilots had to follow me into action and never at any time did they express any lack of confidence. It was this trust which so affected me when I left the service in 1946. The sense of comradeship has stayed with me ever since.

Oxford University Air Squadron

His Honour Judge C. R. Dean

I went up to Queen's College, Oxford in the Autumn of 1941 at the age of 18. My Grammar School in West Yorkshire had no cadet force and my only 'military' experience was as a motorcycle despatch rider in the Local Defence Volunteers (LDV), forerunners of the Home Guard. This occupied two evenings per week and provided my only chance to ride a motorcycle! Like everyone else I had been thrilled by the exploits of the RAF fighter pilots in the Battle of Britain. I had developed a consuming ambition to become an RAF pilot myself.

So it was that after arriving at Oxford I joined the University Air Squadron.

One great bonus was that it was possible to get a pint of very good beer at a very competitive price. The members of the Squadron were divided into two groups, each with its own training programme. It has to be borne in mind that our Air Squadron activities had to be carried out as one facet of our lives to be fitted in along with academic lectures, tutorials, sporting activities and College Clubs. We represented a good cross-section of Oxford Colleges and of society in general, but all of one mind so far as our future in the Service was concerned.

We had instruction in drill and in some of the subjects which we would be required to study in greater depth when we went into full-time service, including navigation, aircraft recognition and armaments. I remember in particular that on the subject of armaments we were taught about the .303 Lee Enfield rifle and the Vickers gas-operated machine-gun! The

Oxford University Air Squadron Tiger Moth (AHB)

latter was still in use in some operational aircraft although by that time it was obsolescent. We became very proficient at stripping down the Vickers machine gun and reassembling it. Some of the components had names which, even after more than fifty years can never be forgotten! An example was the rear sear spring retainer keeper!

In addition to lectures we visited nearby RAF Operational stations and had our first glimpses of the aircraft then in the front line such as the Whitley bomber with its characteristic 'nose-down' flying attitude, the Hampden (known as the 'flying coffin'), and the Wellington. We also got the occasional treat by way of a flight in a Tiger Moth – as passengers, of course, since the University Air Squadrons ceased to give flying instruction at the outbreak of war.

One of my happiest recollections is of a week's camp at Middle Wallop in Hampshire. Here we lived as ordinary airmen (AC2s) and tasted every day life on an operational station. Middle Wallop was a Beaufighter night-fighter station. The leading figure was the great 'Cats eye' Cunningham. Each aircraft had to be flight-tested before an operation and I was fortunate enough to be given a ride by 'Cats eye' himself. I stood behind the pilot's seat as there was nowhere for me to sit down. This camp whetted my appetite still further in my quest to become an RAF pilot.

The young man who joined the RAF in the ordinary way as a trainee pilot had, of course, to pass the appropriate medical board and intelligence tests – as we had – and the first step in his career was then to go to an Initial Training Wing (ITW) where he was given basic training in relevant subjects before moving on to more advanced training. Those of us who had been members of University Air Squadrons avoided this stage when we entered the RAF proper at the conclusion of our first academic year in 1942. We entered as Leading Aircraftsmen (LACs) and were proud to wear the coveted white flash of the trainee pilot in our forage caps. So our time in the University Air Squadron was well spent. It was the best possible introduction to Service life and I, for one, will be eternally grateful for it. I made many friends in the Air Squadron some of whom remained with me up to the time of getting my 'Wings'. This flying training was at No. 1 British Flying Training School in Texas and in that respect, too, I deem myself to have been very fortunate.

Russian Interlude 1941

F. J. Crewe

On 30 July 1941 I was posted to 81 Squadron at Leaconfield for overseas duties. No one seemed to know where we were going but we were assured it was to be soon. I eventually found that I was in B Flight and that we were part of No. 151 Wing which also included 134 Squadron.

The next couple of days saw us getting inoculated against everything. Tropical kit was issued and then, to confuse the situation, warm winter clothing.

We were sent on forty-eight hour overseas leave, and on return found that twenty-four experienced pilots had been nominated to take off from an aircraft carrier, whilst the rest of us, which included the CO and an equal number of very experienced and not so experienced pilots were to go (wherever we were to be going) by convoy.

Little did any of us know that we were to participate in a unique part of Royal Air Force history.

The whole wing (with the exception of the twenty-four pilots who were to fly off the carrier), totalling just under 550 personnel, boarded the SS Llanstephan Castle at Birkenhead. We joined a convoy, and together with our escorts sailed northwards for a while, calling briefly at Iceland and then eastwards and north of Bear Island. We learned that our destination was to be the Soviet Union.

Initially it was planned to go to Murmansk but the convoy was diverted to Archangel. Our time on board was spent attending lectures on the Soviet Union, covering politics and the language. After some eighteen days of sailing through the clear arctic waters we turned southwards and entered the White Sea: an olive green misnomer! On the 31st of August we tied up alongside a dock at Archangel. A rather flat featureless sight greeted us: the docks were wooden, the roads were mostly wooden, most of the buildings were wooden; but everyone was bustling about.

The priority now was to get an advance party up to Murmansk to provide a reception party at the airfield (named Vyanga) where the twenty-four Hurricanes from the carrier were due to land. Simultaneously the main body of personnel had to be transported round the White Sea by train up to Vyanga Airfield in order to become operational as quickly as possible. An engineering party would have to remain at Archangel to assemble the crated Hurricanes in preparation for the flight across the White Sea to Vyanga via Kandalaksha.

The Hurricanes were the Mk. IIB, equipped with twelve .303 Machine Guns. Work commenced on the assembly very quickly and went very well, apart from the fact that not all the tools that should have been in the crates were present. This did cause a few problems, but we had the greatest co-operation from our Soviet colleagues who produced locally made tools overnight to eliminate the deficit.

Things were moving quite fast at Vyanga – the advance and main parties were virtually complete at the airfield in readiness to receive the aircraft from the carrier, HMS *Argus*, on 7 September.

Meanwhile at Archangel the remaining aircraft were assembled and test flown and the first batch of nine aircraft were despatched to Vyanga on 12 September. That day several reconnaissance flights were carried out both by the *Luftwaffe* and the RAF. The Germans lost two Me 109s and an HS 126. We unfortunately suffered our only combat loss when Sgt Smith was shot down and killed. He was buried with full military honours in the Military cemetery on the outskirts of Murmansk.

On 16 September the remaining Hurricanes were flown up to Murmansk from Archangel. Because we were unable to effectively swing our compasses we asked the Soviets to provide an aircraft to lead us across the White Sea; with a little bit of 'bull' we tactfully asked for something fast. They provided an aircraft which looked very much like the Me 110: it was quite fast, we had the whips out to keep up with it.

We were greeted by the local Commissar who took us to lunch. After some very tasty soup, a man came round and filled our glasses with a copious supply of water. The Commissar stood up and proposed a toast to Churchill, Roosevelt and Stalin; he raised his glass to his lips and knocked the drink straight back. (Up to this time in my life, I had only drunk warm weak English wartime beer.) I did the same: the explosion that hit me was out of this world, I felt a large hole appearing in my head, my eyes watered and my ears could hear the three national anthems. Thinking that that was the end of it I sat down. Along came the same man with the 'water bottle' and refilled our glasses for more toasts! After about a hour or so we were taken back to our Hurricanes and carefully took off for Vyanga.

A few words about Vyanga: the airfield was situated just north east of Murmansk. It should be noted that we were just thirty-two km (or twenty miles) east of the German lines, and that when taking off to the west we hardly had time to clean the Hurricane up before we were over enemy held territory. It is also worth remembering that during our time in Russia the German advance had got as far as the 'gates of Moscow'. The Soviets were fighting for their very survival.

Leningrad was under siege, and yet anything that was needed by us to fulfil our support to them was always given willingly and without argument or hesitation.

During the next few weeks, the squadrons escorted Soviet bombers on missions to attack targets near and often well beyond the front line. We managed to carry out over forty missions without losing a single Soviet bomber due to enemy aircraft action. We adopted close escort and top cover tactics. Sometimes this would require most of the wing, on other occasions it would only require a flight to carry each function.

The other main operational task was the defence of Murmansk and of course our airfield. The Germans knew we were there. In most cases we had enough warning to get airborne and repulse much of the raid; inevitably some got through and dropped bombs whilst we were taking off. We depended upon the Soviet warning system to alert us when enemy aircraft were approaching. This was a visual system and the enemy front line was only thirty-two km away.

The approach of winter was changeable, with quite variable temperatures: never warm but never yet down to the arctic temperatures we were to experience later. The airfield was in a pretty sorry state, particularly after the first snow falls melted. There was plenty of slush and mud which made taxiing difficult. Any movement of the Hurricane under these conditions needed two lads on the tail to prevent the aircraft from tipping up on its nose. Even for a scramble we sat two lads on the tail plane, dashed out to take-off point, stopped, waved them off, and opened the throttle and got airborne. Regrettably, on one occasion, someone tried to take off with the two lads on the tail plane. The aircraft staggered into the air, stalled, and went in. Unfortunately the two lads on the tail were killed instantly, and the pilot severely injured.

However, once the really cold weather set in, the Soviets rolled the snow with very large heavy rollers, and this provided an acceptable operating surface. It was pretty level, and it provided reasonable braking action. Initially, we had a little difficulty in judging our height when landing due to the lack of ground definition, but provided one felt for the ground with the wheels, it became fairly easy. We certainly had no accidents due to that problem.

As the winter approached, the question of the Hurricanes being placed in revetments for servicing and camouflage was raised by General Khutsnetsov (General Commanding the Air Fleets Murmansk area). The General said that it would be necessary for all the Hurricanes to be placed in these revetments. There were some forty or more of these on the airfield which had been used for the previous occupants: a little biplane fighter with a wingspan of only twenty-eight feet. The Wing Commander pointed out that the Hurricane had a wingspan of forty feet, and that it could not use these partially underground revetments. The General agreed, and said that they would be enlarged so that all the Hurricanes could be put away. To do this meant taking off the roof and digging out the sides. The Wing Commander asked the General when he would be able to arrange for this task to be carried out. The General replied that it would be completed by noon the following day. The time was about 1530 hrs and, as this was obviously going to be quite a large task, we had our doubts.

Next morning as we were driving down to dispersals for early morning readiness, we passed literally thousands of Mongolian labourers, marching and singing away, waving cheerfully to us, each carrying a pick or shovel or a spade. On arrival, they attacked the revetments, un-roofed them, dug out the sides, re-roofed, built up the sides, turfed over each new roof; and at 1200 hrs they finished the last Hurricane revetment. They then shouldered spades, shovels and picks, and marched off the airfield still singing.

Winter set in shortly after this, and the days when the weather was fit for flying were becoming fewer and fewer. The Hurricane engines had to be kept warm, and were run up every forty minutes day and night in order to keep them serviceable. We also blanked off half the oil radiators. This kept the oil temperature within limits when flying in the very cold conditions.

Operations continued as required, and Soviet pilots and ground crews received training in flying and maintaining the Hurricane. Most of this training was carried out by No. 134 Squadron. They sent the General off on his first solo very successfully.

The Wing was now winding down and the Soviet Air Regiment took over. The first plan was for the Wing to move south and then to the Middle or Far East. This was dropped as the movement would have cut across the Soviet's supply lines.

Eventually we received the news that we were going home. Without any fuss we marched down to the docks and most of us boarded HMS Kenya. A smaller number were put aboard two destroyers. The commander of the squadron told us that we would putting to sea that night and would be sailing up to the north of the Norwegian coast to look for some E Boats which were known to be operating in that area. If we failed to find any E Boats we would then attack the installations at Petsamo and then return to Murmansk. We did not find the E Boats so the secondary target was attacked, and after quite a heavy bombardment we returned to Murmansk. From there we sailed home and passed under the Forth Bridge about 1600 hrs on 7 December.

Some four hours later we trained over the Bridge and arrived at RAF Turnhouse where some kind souls had kept the bar open and lined up a welcoming pint for each of us. We were sent on leave the next day but we were not allowed to say that the Wing had returned home. It was not until April 1942 that it was tacitly accepted that the Wing was back, when the Soviet Ambassador presented our Wing Commander, the two Squadron Commanders and Flight Sergeant Charlton Haw with the Order of Lenin.

In summary, the Wing made a significant contribution to Anglo/Soviet relations, although it was not until some of us returned to Russia in 1994 that it was publicly recognised there that the Wing came to Russia and fought alongside them in their darkest hours. They publicly stated that the Wing was the first of all the allies to go into action with them and thanks to 'Glasnos' this could now be unreservedly stated.

During operations in the Soviet Union, the Wing destroyed fifteen German aircraft for the loss of one Hurricane and its pilot. It escorted Soviet bombers on over forty missions without the loss of any Soviet bomber due to enemy aircraft action.

Special Duties Operations

Group Captain Hugh Verity DSO DFC

West European countries overrun by the enemy in 1940 soon needed links with London. They needed contacts with their governments or potential governments in exile. They needed moral and material support for infant resistance movements.

Great Britain needed links with occupied countries, initially for intelligence and later for the exploitation of potential guerrilla forces and sabotage. In Churchill's phrase this was to 'set Europe ablaze'.

These links could be arranged by air and sea. The first clandestine operations by the Royal Air Force, parachuting agents into France and Holland, were as early as August 1940. The first secret agent picked up (in October 1940) was a junior RAF officer, Philip Schneidau. His pilot, Flt Lt Farley, was the CO of No. 419 SD (Special Duties) Flight. This had a few twin-engined Whitley bombers adapted for parachuting people and supplies, and single-engined Lysanders for landings on meadows in enemy-held territory.

In 1941 the Flight grew into No. 138 SD Squadron. Its customers, SIS (the Secret Intelligence Service), were joined by SOE (the Special Operations Executive).

Operations were extended as far as Poland and Czechoslovakia, where Ron Hockey dropped the Czechs who killed Heydrich. In 1942 No. 161 SD Squadron was formed on the nucleus of the King's Flight. It took over the Lysanders and their pick-up role from 138. RAF Tempsford, near Sandy on the great North Road, became the main base for these squadrons for the rest of the war.

In 1943 Halifax four-engined bombers took over the parachuting role and a few Hudsons, including the King's personal aircraft, joined the Lysanders in pick-ups. Dropping

Hugh Verity's Lysander IIIA modified for special duties (Hugh Verity)

zones and landing strips were proposed by agents in coded W/T messages. If these were approved by Air Ministry Intelligence, operations on them were laid on by SIS or SOE direct with Tempsford. Almost all our sorties were flown within one week of full moon. When weather forecasts and priorities allowed an operation to be planned for the night, a pre-arranged personal message after a foreign language news bulletin from the BBC alerted the 'reception committee'.

If, in spite of enemy action and unreliable weather forecasting, both the ground party and the aircraft succeeded in reaching the agreed field – as they generally did – we checked each other's identities by flashing Morse letters. The standard pattern of torches would then be switched on as a target for parachutes or a 'flarepath' for pick-ups. For our Lysanders this was an inverted 'L' of three torches, 150 yards long.

In England in 1944 plans for the landings in France made it urgent to arm and train the thousands of young volunteers in the maquis camps in the mountains. The specialist SD squadrons were heavily reinforced by Stirling bombers from 3 Group and Albermarles from 38 Group. The American 'Carpetbagger' Liberators and Dakotas also played their part. To give an idea of the scale of these operations over the European and Balkan countries occupied by the enemy, the official history *Royal Air Force 1939–45* (HMSO 1954) says: 'Between 1942 and 1945, in round figures, 6,700 persons of 18 nationalities were dropped or landed in Europe and 42,800 tons of supplies conveyed to their correct destinations in 22,000 sorties, many by American pilots and crews'.

The passengers carried – in both directions – included: agents of British and Allied intelligence, action and escape services, maquis leaders, politicians, generals, and escaping aircrew. Wing Commander L. McD. Hodges, who commanded No. 161 SD Squadron in 1943–44, picked up in his Hudson two future Presidents of France: Vincent Auriol and François Mitterrand.

Many aircraft were lost because of bad weather. So the Royal Air Force had to develop skills to find inconspicuous pinpoint targets by moonlight in enemy occupied territory. The following episode illustrates the sort of airmanship required.

There were times when things did not go according to plan. An example of this was the long-range sortie flown by John Bridger, which nearly ended in disaster during the landing. This was on the night of 16 April 1943 and his target was a small plateau west of Issoire in the hilly area south of Clermont-Ferrand.

The weather on parts of the route was bad, with a lot of cloud making the navigation difficult. Even so he had had enough nerve – and enough confidence in his navigation – to let down through cloud on his dead reckoning ETA (Estimated Time of Arrival). But the main hazard was the landing strip which was on a plateau on a mountain, between two valleys. There was quite a wind that night and this created a down-draught over the escarpment on the approach to the plateau. To avoid over-shooting, he had to give a burst of throttle during the last part of his approach to land.

He slightly overdid this and touched down well past the first light, rather fast, and on a downward slope. He realised that he was rapidly rolling towards the valley on the far side of the little plateau and would probably not be able to stop in time. So he opened up the engine to go round again, but failed to build up flying speed before his Lysander rolled off the end of the plateau and virtually fell over the edge. He put the nose down to build up flying speed as quickly as possible, diving into the valley. When he had done this, at maximum power, he climbed as steeply as possible towards the other side of the valley. Above him in the moonlight he could see the crest. He very nearly cleared it, but not quite: in fact he bounced twice. His first bounce took him just over some buildings; his second was even more alarming, taking him through high tension cables between pylons. There was a dazzling flash which temporarily blinded him. But he had not crashed: he was now really airborne. He flew round quietly while his night vision repaired itself. Then he shone a pocket torch on to his undercarriage on both sides. All seemed to be reasonably well, though one tyre had been torn in one of the bounces. He returned to the plateau and lined himself up for another approach. This time he made allowances for the down-draught and motored carefully down to make a short landing precisely by lamp. Expecting the torn tyre to cause a swing to port, he was ready to correct it with the rudder and starboard brake. He taxied round, drew up by the agent in charge, Michel Thoraval, and the highly excited reception committee and climbed out of the cockpit to inspect the damage.

While the passengers were changing over the loads, he decided to flatten the good tyre, believing that the take off would be easier to control on the rims of two wheels rather than on one good tyre and one flat one. Having failed with his Commando knife, he used a Smith and Wesson .38 service revolver to puncture it. It was not until he had fired five bullets into it that it finally subsided. It went down with a very slow hiss. The ground was dry and hard: the wheels did not dig in, and he took off with very little difficulty. He is reported to have flown through the HT wires again! I remember the metre and a half of thick copper wire that we found coiled round the boss of his propeller and the seven metres of it that his Lysander trailed behind it as he landed at Tangmere. Looking back on it, that landing of John Bridger's must have been about as near cinematic stunt-riding as any of us ever got.

The Staff College in Wartime

Air Chief Marshal Sir David Lee GBE CB

Like the Royal Air Force College, Cranwell, the Staff College was one of the projects initiated by Lord Trenchard as soon as the Royal Air Force was formed on 1 of April 1918. Training in command and staff responsibilities was sadly lacking among officers in the middle ranks of Squadron Leader and Wing Commander within a new Service emerging from a long and crippling war. There had been little time to devote to studying the potential of air power in future military operations, and the remarkable growth of aviation during the previous few years needed to be studied and appreciated by the new breed of RAF officers who had mainly come from the Royal Navy and the Army.

Under its first Commandant, Air Commodore H. R. M. Brooke-Popham, the College opened on 4 April 1922, in a collection of huts on the airfield at Andover. A challenging syllabus was introduced for the carefully selected young officers, many of whom rose to high rank subsequently – e.g. Portal, Baldwin, Sholto-Douglas and Park, to name but four. The College expanded and prospered throughout the 1920s and 30s until the outbreak of World War II in 1939.

It was soon realised that the RAF needed well-trained staff officers in war as much as in peace, and a short, intensive course of only three months' duration was started at Bulstrode Park near Gerards Cross. Lectures and syndicates were held in the large, rambling house but the students were accommodated in Nissen huts in the grounds.

I completed this course myself in 1942 and, like most students, resented this distraction from the war at a time when, although we had triumphed in the Battle of Britain, things were not going too well for Britain elsewhere. However, I well remember the Chief of the Air Staff, Sir Charles Portal at that time, giving us a final address and saying that, although we were not endangering our lives for the moment, he would see that any officer posted to his staff would be worked so hard that his life could well be in danger. After this cheerful promise, I was posted to his staff!

One of my course, a Wing Commander Anderson, managed to retain command of a Mustang fighter squadron throughout, and went off each weekend to fly on operations with his squadron.

On a cold November night when my hut mates and I were working and shivering at our desks in the Nissen hut, there was a rattle of what sounded like machine-gun fire on the roof and side of the hut. We dived for cover under the beds only to find later that a cow had rubbed its horns along the corrugated iron with which the hut was clad!

The war came to an end and, after a brief interregnum, the College was set up at Bracknell, again in hutted accommodation, which had been the wartime Headquarters of the Second Tactical Air Force.

Memories of Barrage Balloons

Jean Shepherd

A Balloon Operator's (Bal/Op) life was rough, tough and at times dangerous. The fact that we were stationed in small units usually meant there was a close-knit, almost family, atmosphere. I say usually because that was typical of our site.

Balloon sites varied in size depending on their positions, but all had the standard 'ninety-feet circle'. This was the wire rope to which the 'tail guy' was attached when the balloon was bedded: it was held in place by wire strops embedded in concrete. The 'bed' itself was a gravel circle with a shallow pit in the centre in which wire stays were attached to anchor the balloon when it was close-hauled or bedded down. It was also anchored by several one-hundredweight concrete blocks which had to be shifted around as the wind changed. The two nose-blocks were only half a hundredweight!

There was a static winch with a Ford V8 engine to raise and lower the balloon. I learned a great deal about V8 engines! There was also the balloon transmission which actually raised and lowered the balloon, turning the cable drum: the last few feet – it could have been a couple of hundred – were painted red. Woe betide any winch operator who let the cable run red as that could mean the cable would come off the drum and the balloon would be loose and a danger, especially to any balloon operator on the bed who might well be decapitated. The maximum flying height was 4500–5000 feet but the normal height at which most people remember seeing the silver-grey 'elephants' floating in the sky was only 500 feet. By the time I was on site nearly all the winches were static ones under cover, and we were supposed to take a flying leap into them from ground level to avoid static electricity. Not that I can ever remember even the most athletic doing so.

When the balloon was close-hauled it was attached by its rigging and also a tail guy which was anchored to the ninety-feet circle by a free-running flywheel; as the wind changed that had to be changed, altering it by means of a strop. This meant a great deal of hard work in a gale and the normal two-girl duty guards had to call out other members of the crew. I can well remember being called out in the middle of the night in howling gales and pouring rain, and not just once either. In fact, I remember one night we had no dry clothes amongst us.

We wore battledress with men's overalls over it – they never fitted – and boots. We had wellies and sea-boot stockings and black waterproofs, again man-size, for bad weather which seemed to be most of the time. Also sou'westers, I think.

Guards were armed with truncheons and torches. We did two hours on and four off through the night. Just what we were supposed to do in case of invaders we never really found out! More to be dreaded was the occasional visit of the duty officer who could well find us sheltering in doorways or even making cocoa in the kitchen.

In theory I think we were supposed to have a crew of fourteen, plus two NCOs, a Sergeant and a Corporal, but we were lucky to have ten – often reduced by leave, forty-eight-hour or twenty-four-hour passes. Our particular Flight was a small one: seven sites – 1 to 6 plus 13 which was closed later as being too exposed for girls, I believe. Site 2, on which I started, was also closed after the balloon cable wrapped itself round the chimney of the farmhouse in which we were billeted and pulled it through the roof where most of it landed on my bed. Site 2 was in the village of Pill at the bottom of a cabbage field: we could smell our way home in the blackout.

We were moved to Site 6, an exposed site more or less opposite Avonmouth Docks. The site was near an old WW I Prisoner of War Camp. This time we were near the piggeries so could smell our way home as before. Our accommodation consisted of a kitchen which was part of a POW hut: this led into a wooden hut divided into a recreation room and the NCO's bedroom and then into the telephone room which we manned in turn at night. Our main accommodation was a

Smart parade of balloon operators Cardington (Vera Hoare)

Nissen hut in which we crew slept. This was heated by a round coke stove which did not always draw as well as we would want: lighting was Aladdin and Tilley lamps BUT we did have flush lavatories! Our 'ablutions' were a breeze-block hut with a coke-fired boiler to heat the water and, as I said, we had the luxury of two flush lavatories. It seemed that sites had either that or electricity!

The balloons were filled with hydrogen, except the fins and tail which were inflated by the wind. Balloons were topped up at intervals from a gas trailer driven by the Heavy Gang. These were mostly local (Bristol) men who had originally manned the balloons and who came to help in emergencies. The gas bottles had to be handled with heavy gloves as the hydrogen could freeze-burn.

We lived a very healthy outdoor life, I suppose – at any rate it cured my chilblains for all time – but it was hard. The girls came from every kind of background. Another girl and I were transferred to Site 2 as some of the girls there had to be parted for fighting! We were terrified as Site 2 had a bad reputation. However, I found the crew were so kind and very protective of the middle-class innocent as I then was. In fact, I went through the war without learning to swear or what the words meant – the girls said it didn't suit me!

On our posting to Site 6 we became a tight-knit group and there are still five of us who keep in touch, as well as about half a dozen from other sites on our Flight. Site 6 was very isolated – there was a farm nearby where Henry and his sister lived: they had a milk round. There was an orchard from which we scrumped apples and there were bramble bushes everywhere, especially on the river bank and round the ruined docks which yielded the biggest, juiciest berries I have ever tasted. There were also lots of mushrooms – mostly large horse-mushrooms – all of which were added to our diet.

When we were on evening pass we would go to Pill to the pub, usually the Duke of Cornwall, or to a dance at Pill Hut or to the canteen. Sometimes we would take the ferry to Shirehampton to the pictures, or the dance. Many's the time we had to run for the last ferry.

We had two bicycles on the site and I brought my own old bike so we had three, which meant that six of us could ride! Once down from the POW camp it was a straight road to Easton-in-Gordano with lines on one side but when there was a gale it was hard work going home. I have known it so bad that one made no progress at all.

In the summer we would often walk to Pill along the river bank, on dykes. If we had a twenty-four-hour pass we might go to Bristol and stay in the Sally Army hostel, and go to the cinemas there. There was a good bus service from Portishead to Bristol and a better one from Shirehampton. In those days there was a train service on each side of the Avon, and the one on the south side from Portishead went along the Gorge and was most delightful.

When we went to Site 6 we inherited a large ginger cat from the men. We were told he did not like women, but in three weeks he had taken to us and not only slept on my bed but in it. He would come in (often soaking wet) from hunting and insinuate himself into my bed, and when I was called either for guard duty or in the morning the girls would find me under the bedclothes and Sandy with his head on the pillow.

We had to do our own cooking on a range-type coke-burning stove, but were not very good at it until Vi was posted to our site. A big, buxom girl from Brixham, I think, who was a born cook and did it magnificently. Her father was a fisherman and once sent a box of fish which we all enjoyed. Sadly, she decided to remuster as a cook and we were back to our own efforts. It was on site that I became addicted to cheese and marmalade sandwiches, also cheese and onion, often made with shallots 'liberated' from the HQ garden adjacent to our site, and drinking gallons of cocoa as I did not like tea.

A last few words about balloon maintenance, carried out daily. Checking and replacing any rope or wire rigging in need of it, daily checking the rip link (the armament situated at the base of the balloon rigging where the cable joined it). The idea was that when a plane flew into it the cartridge would fire and part the balloon from the cable, pulling the ripcord as it fired. This was attached to a panel on the balloon which would pull away, allowing the balloon to deflate eventually, while the cable fell to earth attached to a parachute.

It was every balloon operator's fervent wish to pull the ripcord! It happened to us once, in Plymouth in a terrific storm when the balloon was tearing itself to pieces and Jessie (our sergeant) had the honour.

This was just before they disbanded the balloon sites in the West of England in about October or November 1944, after which we were posted to other trades and stations. A very sad day for us all.

Routine on a Balloon Site

Vera Hoare

The day started with the cook getting up at about 6.30 a.m., just before the girls. Breakfast would be between 7 and 8 a.m. Next would come the stacking of the beds and polishing the bed space. This would have to be spotless!!

Buttons, cap badges and boots would be polished, berets on and out on parade for 9 a.m. in battle-dress ready for the day's work.

The WAAF Officer would often come to see that the girls were smartly turned out and that all was well. An RAF Flight Sergeant or an Officer would inspect the technical side of the site. The crew would be detailed for their duties: these would be given through a megaphone by the site NCO.

We were told that leave was a privilege, not an entitlement! On home leave I was given two shillings (10p) a day for my Mother. My own pay was three shillings (15p) per day until I was promoted.

During our leisure hours we would write home, read, knit or embroider. I cannot ever remember being bored.

We were out in all weathers. Bringing the balloon down in a gale force wind required skill. The more one put one's foot down on the accelerator the smoother the balloon would come down. Otherwise it might take a dive or shoot back up again.

Welfare in the WAAF was great! It was hard, but a good life.

Ground Control Interception (GCI)

Wing Commander Clare Quill

I think before I tell my tale that I should explain 'Control with Radar'. Ground Control during the daytime Battle of Britain type raids is well known. The range and bearing techniques of the 'floodlight' radar beam gave reasonably accurate positions of the contestants. The Controller gave a course to steer and the estimated height of the enemy. Sighting, using the term 'tally-ho', was possible from some miles distant.

At night the requirements changed. The Combat Rules stated that positive visual identification was necessary prior to opening fire. This meant that the attacking aircraft had to get very close to the target in the dark. A more sophisticated ground radar was developed (GCI), and a small radar (AI – Airborne Intercept) – was fitted in the nose of the night fighter. The Controller on the ground was required to direct the fighter to within five to eight miles of the target – the pick up range of the aircraft's radar.

All being well, the fighter would locate and turn in behind the enemy, identify and shoot it down. Many interceptions were carried out but so many things went wrong that the proportion of 'kills' was not great.

The following events occurred in 1943/44 not long after I had completed training as a Controller. I had under my control Flying Officer Hedgecoe. The interception had run according to plan. He had reported contact on his radar pick up and transmitted 'Judy', which meant that he wanted no further help from me. There were two blips about four miles apart on the radar screen. In those days the aerial revolved slowly which meant a delay before positions were updated. Suddenly the pilot said 'I've lost contact. He's gone'. The screen in front of me still had two blips – though a little displaced and further apart. Could they have changed places? There had been rumours of such happenings. Another aerial turn – two blips but closing. I said 'There are still two of you – Dive!'. In our conversation afterwards we agreed that somehow the German had managed to change places.

About a week later we were summoned to a small conference with engineers at Ford. We were told there was now enough evidence to indicate that the Germans had installed a radar in the rear of some bombers. Nothing was known of this device but we were warned of the danger.

I went on duty that evening and was given control of the early patrol – Flight Lieutenant Steve Hodsman. Before long the early 'Hun' appeared. I say 'the' because quite often a single aircraft would come in advance of the main raid. The interception went well and Steve shot at the aircraft in the region of Brighton. The enemy aircraft turned west losing height, but did not fall out of the sky. It eventually left our radar cover and the tracking was taken over by the next station. The main raid was on its way: there was no time for further inquiries.

I went off duty and in the middle of a late supper back at the Mess, I was called to the telephone. It was the intelligence officer at Ford. 'Are you the popular girl tonight!' he said. It appeared that Steve had killed the pilot of the Ju 88 and the navigator had taken over. He had managed to crash land west of Bournemouth – and there in the back of the aircraft intact was a backward looking radar!

Strangely, I do not remember any other interception being interfered with by this backward looking radar. If the Germans continued to use it, evasive action must have been the main advantage. They did of course try other means to make life difficult for us. Not least of these was the expert use of 'Window' – that little piece of metal fabric which on the radar resembled an aircraft.

One moonlit night about five aircraft trailing 'Window' appeared at the edge of the screen. 'How easy' we said to ourselves, as we sent the Mosquitos southwards. But it was not to be. The leading aircraft turned back on themselves thus hiding those following behind. The 'Window' spread until at least ninety-five per cent of the radar was obliterated.

Everywhere that is except for a clear space south of Beachy Head about the size of my thumbnail. I had under control a seconded Fleet Air Arm pilot. The best I could do was – with the aid of dead reckoning – to patrol him back and forth across the clear space. To our astonishment, as he was flying on one leg west to east, he appeared in the space at the same time as a 'Hun' coming north. Luckily they were about the same height. There was a quick 'Contact' and 'Judy', with a successful result.

It seems strange now, so many years later, to be recalling these incidents that we looked upon as being such triumphs. Closely connected as I was with the Germans on the Tornado production programme, I have many friends in Germany who have remained so to this day.

Pathfinding Comes of Age

Group Captain Hamish Mahaddie DSO DFC AFC

Seen through the eyes of a bomber captain, 1942 saw the awakening of the 'sleeping giant'. The most pertinent thing was the advent of Arthur Harris as the new C-in-C. His arrival at the 'Petrified Forest' (Bomber Command HQ) coincided with the publication of the Butt Report – one of the most deadly denunciations of the only serious offensive we were able to mount against the enemy.

Whilst the Report had a devastating effect on Bomber Command, the Directorate of Bomber Operations at Air Ministry were under no false illusions as to how able the Command was in striking its targets. A few experienced bomber squadron commanders, 'bomber barons', who had endured nearly three years of bombing, but now occupied an office in Air Ministry were all agreed that the basic cause of our dismal failure was NAVIGATION.

Discounting the gallantry and the will to 'press-on' in the face of all the efforts of the enemy – his flak defences, searchlights, decoy targets and the lethal, ever-increasing fighter 'boxes', we simply could not find and destroy our targets. This 'think tank' at Air Ministry therefore started talking about a Target Finding Element which evolved into a Target Marking Force and ultimately, a Pathfinder Force (PFF).

Long before the actual birth of PFF in August 1942, the concept of the Target/Finding/Marking Force was well received by the hard-pressed bomber crews, but, oddly enough, not by the staff at Bomber Command. It took many months to get them to evaluate the possibilities of such a scheme.

It should be remembered that Harris inherited a virtually bankrupt concern, achieving little and suffering appalling casualties. The incredible thing at this 'halfway' stage was that crew morale was as high as it was. This was due in my view, mainly to the excellent field rank officers, the Flight and Squadron Commanders – and in no small degree to the basic training of aircrews, and the support of the Empire Air Training Schools in Canada and Rhodesia.

The sadly-lacking mainspring of the entire offensive was the slow build-up of planned routing and the lack of any electronic devices to assist navigators and bomb aimers. It is odd to reflect that whilst the 'boffins' managed to save the country in 1940 with radar in the Battle of Britain, no parallel devices were obviously being developed to help Bomber Command. There was a scientific hiatus and it took the Butt Report and the prodding of the Air Ministry to mount an effort in this direction. *(See R V Jones' account which follows – Ed.)*

GEE was an excellent start, but soon negated by jamming. It did, however, assist in the concentration of bombers *en route* to the target and was invaluable in getting aircraft back to the UK in conditions of bad weather.

It is difficult to understand why Bomber staff were so reluctant to accept Ministerial direction. We are told they feared the weakening of squadrons by withdrawing the best crews. Nevertheless a Pathfinder Force was formed on 15 of August 1942 and its first commander was Group Captain D. C. T. Bennett, DSO (later Air Vice-Marshal, CB CBE DSO) who was officially appointed on 5 July 1942.

Once the formation of PFF was a fait accompli, and apparently against the personal wishes of the Bomber C-in-C and most of his Group commanders, the bomber Groups were instructed to send selected Volunteer crews to a squadron recruited by each Group.

By the end of the war, PFF comprised eight Lancaster squadrons and twelve Mosquito units, plus the Met. Flight Mosquitos and the PFF (Navigation) Training Unit.

The early problems of the PFF gave its critics much to enjoy since the force was Pathfinder in name only. The four original squadrons, each with a different type of aircraft, had essentially different operational capabilities. The one redeeming feature was that Groups initially did select good crews, many of them second-tour types. All the original crews were expected to volunteer for forty-five sorties. By and large, this meant in effect that each PFF crew would start with about a full Bomber Command tour of thirty sorties. Very few, in fact, claimed the 'let-out', and sixty sorties was nearer the average. This incredible sense of duty should be considered against the average sortie life of aircrew in the main Command force which was never higher than nine at the best of times and as low as seven sorties per crew in the worst period of casualties. Whilst 100 bomber sorties was quite normal in PFF Mosquitos, particularly in the OBOE squadrons, several 'heavy bomber barons' did achieve over 100 sorties, and all in Western Europe.

One of the most fascinating aspects of the Pathfinders was its attraction for 'characters'. The nature of the force seemed to beckon to the most unusual types. The very mandate of PFF was that crews had to volunteer. Which meant in effect that they were volunteering twice – first as aircrew and then, if selected, again to do an extended tour as Pathfinders. Although originally we demanded experienced crews, many actually started their operations with PFF. These

Lancaster Bomber (AHB)

I personally selected at training schools, generally those with 'Distinguished' passes.

After the initial flush of good intentions by Groups, within three months there began a steady deterioration in the standard of crew replacements. In many cases they were not even volunteers. After a further period of three months or so, Don Bennett appointed me Group Training Inspector – and I became virtually a 'horse thief'.

My function was to tour the squadrons daily, using the previous evening's raid as my theme, to explain the difficulties and, in general, to make contact with the Main Force. And I suppose to make a plea on the spot for greater support in the shape of the best crews, because the best was only just good enough ...

Another source of crews was the instructional staff at flying and navigation training schools. In my endless lectures to the Training Groups, I charged a 'fee' – two tour-expired instructors. Many of the OBOE pilots were in fact Blind Approach Training (BAT) instructors. *(See Ron Curtis' account 'The Ultimate Pathfinders 1944' – Ed.)*

Possibly the main strength of the PFF lay in the hotch-potch of nationalities. Approximately half the force were from the Commonwealth – Aussies, Canadians, New Zealanders, South Africans, Rhodesians; and even from as far afield as Hong Kong, Fiji and the West Indies. This all made for healthy competition. I have in recent years got into a deal of trouble in certain Commonwealth countries by claiming that any All-Canadian or Australian squadron was not as good as a mixed squadron. In fact I have gone further and said a 'mixed' crew was, in my view, infinitely better than any 'national' crew.

One of the reasons, possibly, for the high proportion of Commonwealth crews was my established policy of spreading my selection 'net' as widely as I could in view of the poor co-operation of the Groups. Because I literally plagued the various HQs in London – the Aussies at Kodak House etc. – I was able to have the pick of excellent crews practically on the dock side as they arrived in the UK.

An excellent seam of Dutchmen was worked. These were all Dutch naval aircrew, not particularly experienced, but their lack of hours was more than compensated by their zest for flying. Amongst the first of these was Erik Hazelhoff, at one time Naval aide to Queen Wilhelmia, who held the Dutch VC. He was the 'bait' that brought many Dutch pilots and navigators to our Mosquito squadrons. Amongst other nationals was an outstanding Norwegian, Major Christie – later a General in Norway's air force. A host of Americans served, but were thinly disguised in RCAF uniforms. These were first-rate 'press-on' types. One, a Texan, would never wear the issue flying boots but preferred the cowboy type with high heels! It took the whole of his crew to hold him on a table whilst I got a hacksaw and cut at least two inches off his fancy boots – though, somehow, he managed to get them restored. My objection to his high heels was that he would do himself a mischief if he had to bale out!

After a short while Groups sent crews who had not volunteered to join the PFF and, in many cases, had made a nuisance of themselves. By mid-1943 it was made very clear to the Main Force Groups that their 'selection' was not acceptable as we were sending more crews back than we were keeping. About this time I noticed that those crews who consistently got aiming point pictures on the bomb plots after each raid were never selected for PFF. I sought these crews out and, almost without exception, found they had in fact volunteered for PFF but had their applications rejected. It was a very simple matter to reverse this procedure, generally after some unpleasantness with the appropriate Squadron Commander.

When we had a regular flow of sound, keen material and the PFF Navigation Training Unit was in full swing, we saw the steady development of tactics geared to the constant production of new and better target indicators, hooded flares and many other innovations. All of which was more than matched by the improvement in navigational techniques.

Whilst all this was going on, the enemy night defences were of course more than keeping pace with our ever-changing tactics. It is true to say that the German night fighter dictated the tactics we were forced to adopt. It was a critical struggle – a battle of wits between ourselves and the *Luftwaffe* night defences, with the edge always in favour of the Germans. We were never given any long period free from a fight from the coast to a target and back to the coast. Happily, there were few disasters like the Nuremburg raid of 30/31 March 1944. Of 795 aircraft which set out, we lost ninety-three which failed to return, some seventy-four badly damaged which reached England – twenty-two of these being write-offs after crash-landing and burning out. The total loss of these aircraft and crews was the bitterest blow Bomber Command had to suffer in the entire war, and it is difficult to understand why it happened.

Normally, the PFF planned the route which took account of many factors such as the avoidance of heavily-defended areas, the upper winds, etc. The usual dog-legs associated with a bomber raid were inserted into the route to give a false impression of the final destination. The Mosquito Light

Night-Striking Force carried out spoof attacks on either side of the main track, with 'window' attacks and actually dropping TIs on probable targets along the route.

In the case of Nuremburg however, the PFF planned route was rejected by the Group Commanders and one single leg inserted of some 260 miles. Willi Herget, a *Luftwaffe* nightfighter ace with seventy-four confirmed kills, told me later that halfway along this track it was easy to guess at the target, because a line of burning British bombers pointed the way to Nuremburg ...! This disaster was written-off as an 'accident', 'one-of-those-things' – but Nuremburg was no 'accident'. It was caused. To the best of my belief, the PFF routing was never challenged thereafter.

The chief architect of this incredible advance in bombing efficiency was unquestionably Don Bennett. His single-minded pursuit of operational perfection had to be witnessed to be appreciated. He was the only Commander in the field who was able to change the entire concept of Strategic Bombing; moreover he was the only Group Commander with any worthwhile operational background. My personal researches accredit him with more than a full Bomber tour of operations, and that includes his escape from Sweden – and yet Bennett was the only wartime Group Commander who was never knighted.

It's ironic to reflect that had he served the *Luftwaffe* in a similar role to that he graced in the Royal Air Force, there can be little doubt that he would have been invested with the Highest Order of the Iron Cross – with Diamonds.

Number 61008 Secret IC/Foreign Air Forces West Evaluation Great Britain/British Pathfinder Operations as at March '44 Issued by *Luftwaffenfuhrungsstag IC/Fremde Luftwaffen West* starts off: 'The success of the large scale night raids by the RAF is in increasing measure dependent on the conscientious flying of the Pathfinder crews ...'

Service and Science

Professor R. V. Jones CH CB CBE

The rise of the Nazis, with the prospective bombing threat to our cities, brought scientists and the serving officers in Fighter Command closely together, especially under the aegis of Henry Tizzard, who in 1935 chaired a new Committee for the Scientific Survey of Air Defence. Existing methods for intercepting incoming bombers were clearly inadequate, even in daylight, and a basic invention was required before satisfactory techniques could be developed. Fortunately, through the advances in radio technology, the time was ripe for the invention of radar. This was demonstrated in February 1935, and the following five years saw efforts of the utmost urgency to develop it into an effective defence system. Time was very short.

Some serving officers inclined to caution. But the German air threat after 1933 was so imminent that in the general pressure to get a working system as quickly as possible, scientists and engineers worked closely with serving officers, some of the former flying with their devices in airborne trials, while some of the latter joined the scientists in their laboratories. The scientists therefore sharpened their ideas about what was needed, and the serving officers gained a better grasp of how the devices worked and how they might best be applied. The result was that, although radar had been invented in Germany rather earlier than it had been in Britain, we not only had a practical, and indeed superior, system of defence by 1939 but also a cadre of serving officers who knew how to get the best out of it.

A typical pattern of development was for serving officers to say what they would like. The scientists might then say that they could not provide exactly what was wanted, and then go on to say what was the nearest they could do. 'If we could produce that, could you use it?' And useful equipment might thus spring from such an informal exchange which would never have been born had relations between serving officers and scientists been exclusively formal.

The result of that collaboration was indeed to turn the balance in the Battle of Britain, and looking back on the period in 1946, Tizard observed that:

> 'The first time, I believe, that scientists were ever called in to study the needs of the Services as distinct from their wants, was in 1935, and then only as a last resort. The Air Staff were convinced of the inadequacy of existing methods and equipment to defeat air attack on Great Britain, and a Committee was established for the scientific survey of air defence. I want to emphasise that this committee, although it consisted on paper only of scientists, was in fact from the first a committee of scientists and serving officers, working together.'

Lest we become carried away by this happy example, though, there was a sobering corollary to Tizard's memorable comment. So successful was his Committee for Air Defence that a similar Committee was set up for Offence, and Tizard himself was again made Chairman. This Committee, however, was not nearly so successful and Tizard afterwards wrote 'It did not meet with such enthusiastic welcome from the Royal Air Force. As a result its influence before the war started was only small'.

Those of us who had to work with both Fighter and Bomber Commands in the early years of the war were struck by their difference in attitudes. At Fighter Command, even the C-in-C would readily see us, whereas – although we were hospitably entertained at Bomber Command, it lacked the keenness of Fighter Command in trying to develop new methods. The doctrine that 'the bomber will always get through' complacently prevailed, and it was only after two years of war, when we showed that Bomber Command was not hitting its targets and when losses were beginning to mount, that the Command became as keen on the development of new scientific devices as Fighter Command had been.

Sidewinder missiles (AHB)

Following Tizard, we therefore learnt the further lesson that help to any organisation can only be truly effective when that organisation realises that it needs help.

The support that science could provide to the RAF fell broadly into three categories: new devices and technical improvements, operational research, and intelligence about new enemy weapons and techniques. Let us look at each of these in turn.

We have already noted what a vital contribution was made by radar and air defence in 1940, first with ground-bases and then with airborne equipment, where performance was much enhanced by the invention of the cavity magnetron. The magnetron also became the vital component that made H2S possible, and a much improved ASV. Inventions have continued to be made in electronics, for example with the exploitation of the Doppler Effect in AWACS and JOINT-STARS for battlefield surveillance, as well as air defence. Infra-red, too, has become a powerful technique, particularly for night vision and for homing missiles where, for example, twenty-seven out of twenty-nine Argentinian aircraft shot down in the Falklands campaign were credited to the IR homing missile Sidewinder AIM-9L, and where eleven out of thirteen US naval aircraft shot down in the Gulf War of 1991 were thought to have been victims of IR missiles, mainly hand-launched, in Iraqi hands.

Another vital device, the radio proximity-fuse, was a joint contribution by scientists and engineers, as have since been the precise time-keeping devices such as quartz and atomic clocks in providing greatly improved bases for precise navigation; and while these devices might be vulnerable to electronic counter-measures, the parallel development of inertial navigation has resulted in electronic immunity.

The jet engine, of course, was the invention of Frank Whittle, a serving officer, but scientific support has continuously improved the engine through the mastery of gas dynamics and through the development of single-crystal turbine blades. Other improved materials, too, have come from scientific research, such as titanium and carbon fibres.

While science and technology have placed some superb instruments and devices in the hands of airmen, though, it may be one thing to possess a Stradivarius and it may be quite another to be able so to play it as to get the best out of it. And if it was one thing in 1939 to have a radar system, it was another to use it to the best effect in operations. Fortunately for us, the urgency of the defence situation in 1939 was so great that both our scientists and engineers who were developing radar, and our serving officers who would have to use it, were drawn closely together. And one further development in their collaboration, springing mainly from the scientists, was operational research. This was started under Tizard's sponsorship in an effort to see how the prospective plots to be expected from a successful radar system might best be used to direct fighters to intercept incoming bombers. It was at this stage, in 1937, that the idea of 'operational research' developed. The success of the operational research at Fighter Command led to operational research officers being attached to the other Commands in September 1939; these were shortly withdrawn because these Commands saw no need for them. The rising threat from U-boats, however, led to Professor P M S Blackett being transferred in 1941 to Coastal Command to form an Operational Research Section, which quickly showed that impressive results could follow the scientific analysis of operations.

Previously the depth charges dropped by an aircraft when a U-boat had been spotted had been set to explode at a depth of 100 feet, on the argument that, having detected the U-boat, the aircraft would on average take two minutes to reach its position, and in this time the U-boat would probably have submerged to about 100 feet depth. But in this same time the U-boat would have moved some distance from its last position on the surface, and would therefore probably be too far away for a depth charge dropped on that position to be effective. Moreover, if nevertheless the aircraft had been able to surprise the U-boat enough to catch it near the surface, the depth charge, if set at 100 feet, would again be relatively ineffective. The Operational Research Section, therefore recommended that charges should be set at twenty-five feet, where their explosions would more seriously damage a submerging U-boat. The shallower setting thus introduced was the main factor in improving the chance of an aircraft sinking a sighted U-boat from two to three per cent in 1941 to about forty per cent in 1944. The improvement was so marked that the German Navy concluded that a more powerful explosive was being used in the depth charges.

Another contribution from Operational Research was the introduction of 'planned maintenance' of aircraft. This had been started by a serving officer in Flying Training Command, but it was taken up and enthusiastically pursued by the Operational Research Section in Coastal Command. Hitherto, as in the Battle of Britain, each pilot had his own aircraft with its own ground crew to service the aircraft. This resulted in a marvellous 'team spirit' between pilot and the ground crew, who felt they shared the success of the pilot in every kill, but it was expensive in personnel. The Operational Research Section in Coastal Command showed that a given number of ground crew could maintain a greater number of aircraft if maintenance were centralised so that, having completed a sortie an air crew would return its aircraft to a central servicing unit, and on starting a new sortie the air crew would take out whatever aircraft had been made ready by the servicing unit.

Under routine conditions, the central servicing plan was indisputably more efficient. Trials with No. 502 Squadron (Whitleys) showed that the number of flying hours per unit of maintenance manpower was doubled. In emergency though, as in the Battle of Britain or the anti-V1 campaign, the older system could produce better results because ground crews naturally worked with greater enthusiasm when they could identify themselves with a particular air crew and aircraft, and where pilots would be readier to accept an aircraft whose faults and idiosyncrasies they already knew than a strange one coming from an impersonal servicing unit. So the cold conclusions of scientific analysis may need to be warmed by an allowance for human nature and relationships.

In 1944 a special experimental unit, the Fighter Interception Unit, was given the task of increasing the speed of fighters so that they could catch the V1s when the German retaliation campaign started. The Unit had not completed its development work when the first V1s arrived, and so its Commander, Christopher Hartley (later Air Marshal Sir Christopher Hartley) had to take it into action alongside the regular squadrons at, I think, Tangmere. After some days of operations, the Station Commander sent for Hartley and asked him what his secret was, because the Commander had observed that Hartley's Unit produced about twice as much effort as did the other two squadrons. 'It's simple, Sir, I've got the last squadron in the Air Force.' Hartley proceeded to explain that while the regular squadrons in Fighter Command had been moved over to the planned maintenance system, this instruction had not applied to his Unit, because it was an experimental one, and so it still operated on the old system.

One unforeseen advantage of the Harrier, incidentally, has been that to gain maximum benefit from its ability to operate from dispersed positions, it needs a ground crew to be based with it, remote from a planned maintenance centre, as I found when visiting No. 1 Squadron in Belize during the Guatemalan Emergency in the '70s. Even though the ground crews were suffering from heat, humidity, snakes, sandflies and other discomforts of the tropical swamp, the old *esprit de corps* of the Battle of Britain flourished with hearty enthusiasm.

Having remarked the importance of human relationships in keeping up morale, though, I must also record that operational research sometimes discovered situations where too ready a concern for these relationships could produce a false conclusion. In Bomber Command, for example, there were some losses due to aircraft 'icing up'. Would it not therefore be better to fit de-icing equipment to bombers? At first sight this must save both the aircraft and aircrew lives. But the weight of the de-icing system meant that bomb loads would have to be lightened; and an analysis involving the expected losses due to enemy action, the likelihood of icing conditions, and the extra weight of the bombs, showed that in terms of 'bombs on target' per aircraft lost, it was better not to fit de-icing equipment because more aircraft would now be lost to enemy action against the extra number of aircraft required than would be lost to icing by a force without de-icing equipment.

Besides contributing basic techniques and devices for improving the military performance of the Royal Air Force, and the methods of operational research, science also aided the Air Force in anticipating the weapons and techniques it would have to counter in the *Luftwaffe*. The fact that we had developed radar led the Tizard Committee in 1939 to ask whether the Germans had done so, too. It transpired that our pre-war intelligence services knew very little about any German technical developments largely because secret intelligence, MI6, was run by the Foreign Office, which concentrated on political and military intelligence, and was almost entirely insensitive to technical developments. The revelation of this vital gap led to the start of scientific intelligence, whose first success was to establish that the Germans had developed a system of radio beams by which their bombers could hit a target at night and through cloud. This discovery made a double contribution to British air power. In the first place, it provided almost the only defence against the bombing of our cities in the Blitz, where jamming could spoil the accuracy of the German bombing. Moreover, it also showed that while some senior officers in the RAF had dismissed such radio means of bombing as 'adventitious aids', which it did not need because it could find its targets in Germany by astro-navigation and dead reckoning, these techniques were far from satisfactory in operations, and Bomber Command had to learn from the German example in using Pathfinders which would guide the main force by accurate bombing based on radio aids such as Oboe and H2S.

These successes in the defence field led to Scientific Intelligence being charged with responsibility for discovering the scientific basis and technical details of the German air defence system, and from 1941 onwards its work in support of Bomber Command became the major objective of scientific intelligence.

Among the results were the development and employment of 'Window' and other electronic countermeasures, and even the directing of our long-range night fighters to harass the German night fighters as they orbited their assembly beacons before our raids.

Scientific Intelligence had also established the locations of almost all the German radar stations on the coast of Europe between the north of Denmark and the south of France; and this led to the virtual elimination of the German radar defences for D-Day in Normandy, where complete surprise was achieved by the Allied landing forces.

Defence, of course, could not be neglected: and here again, Scientific Intelligence was able to provide detailed warning of the V1 and V2 threats, including the improving performance of the V1 missiles as they were fired in trials at Peenemunde, so that our defences knew six months ahead what they would need in order to parry the threat. Negative Intelligence could be useful, too, particularly in the case of the atomic bomb, where we were able to establish that the Germans were never near to producing one.

In retrospect, the idea of serving officers and scientists working together on the closest possible terms seems so obvious that it would have been expected to happen everywhere. Fortunately for us, though, it did not – and particularly in Germany, where after the war General Kammhuber, commanding night fighters, and General Martini, commanding Signals and Radar, were astonished to find that our own collaboration between science and the services was so close that I, a civilian, occupied a regular position on the Air Staff, responsible to the Chief of Air Staff and with a mixed team of serving officers and scientists responsible to me. Out of our mutual collaboration came inventions such as the cavity magnetron, Operations Research, and Scientific Intelligence. None of these might have happened if we had not been in such a tight corner in 1939 and 1940.

Let me therefore recall a further comment by Tizard which points the moral:

> 'When I went to Washington in 1940, I found that radar been invented in America about the same time as it had been invented in England. We were, however, a very long way ahead in its practical applications to war. The reason for this was that scientists and serving officers had combined before the war to study its tactical uses. This is the great lesson of the last war.'

May it never be forgotten.

THE DOCTOR PILOTS

Throughout the history of the RAF Medical Services many doctors have behaved with great gallantry during flying operations, as the following examples show:

> Air Marshal Sir Geoffrey Dhenin, a pilot as well as a doctor, was awarded the George Medal in 1943 and was mentioned in Despatches in 1945. After the war he won two Air Force Crosses.
>
> Wing Commander John MacGown DFC MD ChB was Group Medical Officer for the Pathfinder Force. He flew on fifty-two bombing missions to study at first hand the effects of combat operations amongaircrews. He flew withmany different crews, often those on the last two or three operations of their tour. He knew that having survived so long they would inevitably be worried about the possibility of their luck running out at the last minute. He was awarded the Distinguished Flying Cross and his Pathfinder badge.

'Doc Corner'
(Wing Commander H W Corner AFC MD CHB MRCP)

Group Captain Duncan Smith DSO DFC

A frequent visitor to Hornchurch was 'Doc' Corner, the Command expert on aviation medicine. He usually arrived in a trim looking Gladiator biplane and used to let some of us fly it for the sheer joy of flying. Aged about fifty, it was quite extraordinary how competent he was at flying Spitfires, and how keen he was to get first hand information on the flying equipment we used and the effects of high altitude and combat strains on pilots.

He flew as my number two on a number of occasions, carrying out exacting missions with skill and verve. We tried out better designed equipment that he brought with him. Oxygen masks and regulators, a Mae West, flying boots, gloves, overalls and helmets were all produced in turn and left for us to test thoroughly.

His formation keeping was superb and he stuck to me like a leech. Several times I put him in a good attacking position on Me 109s, but I never saw him fire his guns. Eventually I got the message. He had no intention of shooting anything down. Although he took frightful risks and understood the dangers he faced, he concerned himself only with the medical aspects. He regulated his life by the code of the medical profession and the deliberate taking of life was outside the limits he had set for himself.

'Doc' Corner did not confine his flying to the Hornchurch Wing, but flew also with other Wings. In the middle of 1942 he was shot down by an Fw 190 off Folkestone and killed.

The Far East

After the fall of France in 1940, Japan threw in her lot with the Axis powers through the Tripartite Pact of September 1940. This was followed by a non-aggression pact with Russia in April 1941.

In July 1941 Japan occupied French bases in southern Indo-China with the full agreement of France's Vichy Government. This reduced the distance between Japanese bases and Singapore to 600 miles.

Japan began her unprovoked assault on 8 December 1941 with air attacks on targets in Hawaii, Manila, Shanghai, Malaya, Thailand, Hong Kong and Singapore.

Seventy days later all resistance in Malaya and Singapore was at an end. The Japanese held vast quantities of British equipment, oil, air bases and a large number of prisoners – British, Australian, Indian and Malayan.

In January 1942 Java and Sumatra also fell and there were heavy naval losses. Rangoon and Mandalay were captured and Japan was poised for an attack on India. Here the line was drawn.

Allied strength began to grow at sea and in the air during 1942 and 1943. In February 1943 the first Chindit operation was launched. Army columns disappeared into the Burmese jungle without any lines of surface communication. They were to be supplied entirely from the air. Success depended on two factors – air superiority over the Japanese and a large enough Air Transport Force. When these had been achieved they transformed operations throughout the rest of the Burma campaign.

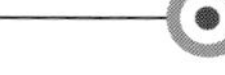

The Endau Raid

Squadron Leader R. J. Allanson DFC

I was posted to Singapore in June 1939, and on arrival joined 36 Squadron equipped with the Vickers Vildebeest III biplane, affectionately nicknamed 'The Flying Brick'! It could be armed with either torpedo or bombs and had a maximum speed of 140 miles per hour.

1940 and 1941 passed quietly with routine patrols and intensive training. All this changed in December 1941 with the Japanese attack on Pearl Harbor.

I was in the north of Malaya at the time and insisted that my wife and three young children booked the first available flight to India. It was a wise decision, for the assault on Malaya began almost immediately. The airfields in Thailand and Northern Malaya quickly fell to the Japanese. All RAF fighters were withdrawn to Singapore to protect the naval base. Hudsons and Vildebeests attacked troop ships with slight success.

As the number of captured airfields grew the Japanese were able to deploy their formidable Zero single-engined fighters. These were more manoeuvrable but less heavily armed than the RAF's Hurricanes.

On 26 January 1942 a concentration of Japanese troop ships was reported at Endau on the east coast of Malaya some 100 miles north of Singapore. The incredible decision was now taken to launch two Vildebeest daylight bombing attacks against this well defended fleet. The water was too shallow for torpedoes.

The first wave of twelve Vildebeests went in the afternoon with some advantage of surprise, even though there was a standing patrol of two Japanese fighter squadrons. Five Vildebeests were shot down by fighters. The second wave of twelve Vildebeests was timed to arrive over the target at 1730 – about one and a half hours before dark. I saw seven of my friends go down in flames, including the Commanding Officer.

I was slightly wounded and decided to give the appearance of crashing out of control, changing at the last minute to a diving attack on the hordes of Japanese on the beach.

Vildebeests at Singapore (AHB)

On breaking away, my crew became very excited about the approach of three Navy Zeros on our port beam. I, too, had been watching them and it seemed to me that they were taking too long to close. I forced myself round in my Sutton harness and saw that the Zeros were attempting to distract us from a rear attack by Army 97s which were closing in on my tail. The leader was just within range and I immediately used brute force on the rudder, putting us into a very sharp skidding turn. At the same time bullets ripped through the port side of my cockpit, spraying me with metal.

I realised we had a good chance, since any capably driven biplane can run rings round a monoplane fighter provided that there is a capable observer in the rear cockpit to give a running commentary on the enemy fighters' movements. In Pilot Officer Glowery, RAAF, I had just such an observer. We successfully avoided some five or six attacks.

So I became one of the few survivors of a criminally stupid operation. I went to a friend's bungalow and got very drunk on his whisky. Perhaps this helped me cope with the shock.

A few hours later, and a series of night attacks could have been launched almost without risk, for the Japanese fighters did not operate in the dark, and their ack ack was ineffective. We did in fact, carry out night attacks on Japanese shipping at Rembang a few days later with remarkable success.

Air Vice-Marshal Brooke-Popham, the AOC, sent a congratulatory signal and added that Vildebeests would not, repeat not, be used again on daylight operations.

Despite this, one week later I was ordered to arrange a daylight op! I cited the AOC's order but was told that the long anti-submarine search was essential. I refused to ask anyone else to do it and flew myself.

On returning I was told to report immediately to the Station Commander. He instructed me to have what was left of my squadron take off for Java via Sumatra at 0240 next morning. I had no time to rest, for long range tanks had to be removed, torpedoes loaded and the aircraft refuelled. We eventually reached Kemajoran on the south coast of Java.

Early in March we heard that the Dutch had agreed to surrender to the Japanese at midnight on 7 March. Our total strength was now two technically unserviceable aircraft – but both could be flown. I decided that rather than be taken prisoner I would try to escape to Ceylon or India.

My idea was to get as far as possible up the west coast of Sumatra and ditch in the sea in the hope of being able to get to the north of the island and thence cross to India – some 1200 miles to the north – or to Ceylon, perhaps 1000 miles to the west. It was a hare-brained scheme but better than folding one's arms and waiting for captivity.

Meantime, although I did not know it, I had been posted 'missing, believed killed'!

Take off at night would be difficult. There was no moon and the Dutch refused to let us use any runway lighting as we would be leaving a few hours after they had officially surrendered.

The runway was pitted with small craters made by the anti-personnel bombs which the Japanese always used when bombing airfields. In addition the Dutch had parked a bulldozer in the middle of the runway as an obstacle to Japanese aircraft attempting to land.

I walked down the runway with Warrant Officer Peck who had begged me to let him fly the other plane. I paced out the distance and decided we could miss the bulldozer if we were to take off with our port wings over the edge of the runway. The cockpit of the Vildebeest was high up and it should be possible even in the dark to distinguish between the concrete runway and the grass.

We took off successfully and headed along the coast. For some reason Peck decided to fly quite a long way out to sea. I had just calculated that I had enough petrol to fly another 20 minutes when my crew told me that they had seen a Very light further out to sea. I was sad to lose men who had been friends and comrades for more than three years. I was now the sole survivor of the original eighteen pilots. I ditched in an area of sea sheltered by a headland.

We got ashore but unfortunately were betrayed within hours by natives who sent a cyclist to telephone the Japanese. We were soon surrounded by a dozen soldiers with sub-machine guns.

By the greatest ill luck we had ditched less than ten miles from Bencoolen, which the Japanese had occupied only twenty-four hours earlier. I had hoped to reach Padang which I was sure would still be in Dutch hands.

I was brutally interrogated for about ten days. One result: concussion and a perforated eardrum by a well-aimed kick on my right ear. They used a Hong Kong Chinese as interpreter and this helped me since his English was not particularly accurate and I could claim misunderstanding. I soon realised that my questioners were ignorant peasants. They had heard about the second aircraft and by 'power-assisted' questioning tried to find out more about it. In the end I had a brain wave and told the interpreter to ask my tormentors if it was the custom in the Japanese army for senior officers to betray those under their command. The situation was then transformed as a result of their obsession with the honour of all those serving 'The Son of Heaven'!

I was returned to my comrades in a filthy cell in the prison for Indonesian criminals and later sent to the concentration camp at Palembang. Here for a short time conditions were almost tolerable but they soon deteriorated and our rations were reduced. We reached a stage when we relied on 'rice substitute'. This was old tapioca roots which were yellow and bitter due to the ravages of maggots. We learnt from fellow Dutch prisoners that they were pre-war stocks which were normally shipped to Europe for the production of size. Other 'delicacies' included water weeds from the River Moesie and the leaves of manioc plants. These, our RNR Medical Officer insisted, must be boiled three times and the first two lots of water thrown away. If I remember rightly he believed that the leaves contained a mild solution of prussic acid but hoped that they would be safe after this lengthy treatment.

I was a big man in those days – 6 feet tall and well proportioned. My weight at the end was only 6 stone!

There were always plenty of rats and I recalled that the inhabitants of Paris had eaten them during the siege of Paris in the Franco-Prussian War. Our naval MO Lt Cdr Reed confirmed that their flesh was about 40 per cent protein and that there should be no danger in eating properly butchered rats. I asked if he would share a meal with me when I caught my first rat and after a moment's hesitation he replied 'Yes, by God. I will, just invite me!'

I manufactured two traps out of a short length of bamboo, odds and ends of packing cases, paraffin tins and scraps of galvanised wire. It was a bit of a task since gravity was the only source of power. This was the protein which kept me alive despite the brutal and sadistic treatment which continued to the end.

A flight of RAF fighter bombers on their way back from an attack flew over the camp and waggled their wings to encourage us that release was near at hand.

Whilst this was happening, one of the guards happened to see me trying to light a cigarette with a magnifying glass and smashed me to the ground with the butt of his rifle. The last six months of the war I spent in the so-called 'hospital' hut, more dead than alive.

With the surrender of the Japanese a US Dakota came in to check on the situation and Lt Cdr Reed decided I should be flown out to Singapore on the first evacuation plane.

Everything was chaotic and at Singapore I was left in the aircraft for two hours in the hot sun. Eventually I got out and tottered over to the hangar. There I found a reporter who turned out to be the *Times* correspondent. I asked if he could get my name and initials into the paper next day if I gave him my story and he readily agreed. My family thus learned that I was still alive much more quickly than through official channels.

So I survived a suicidal shipping attack, an unsuccessful escape and three and a half years' brutal captivity. More than fifty years later my memories of those dreadful days remain bitter and undimmed.

Singapore Disaster

Terence O'Brien

When Japan entered the war I had just been promoted to Flying Officer, was on my second tour of operations, and then the squadron – recently switched from Blenheims to Hudsons – was ordered to send a detachment to Singapore. I led out the first contingent and, to give you an idea of our impressions on arrival in January 1942, I'd like you to read a piece cut from a book of mine.

'An air of defeat hangs over the island' Stanley quoted. This was a few days after our arrival. We were sitting on the terrace outside the Officers' Mess at Tengah, looking across the airfield, When he read out that sentence, just written in his letter, I wondered just what it was that made the atmosphere of Tengah so perceptibly different to that of our previous station in Cornwall, and then we ALL began to search for particulars. Here's our list – I still have it today:

ST EVAL	TENGAH
Bomb damage quickly repaired.	Bomb damage scarcely touched.
Ground crews swarm over returning aircraft.	Ground crews widely dispersed never waiting for aircraft on return.
Civilians at work on roads, drains, water, electricity, etc.	Local labour run away, no work being done on airfield services.
Signature required for drinks to go on month's mess bill.	You help yourself to drinks, no talk about end of month.
Cars are valuable, you keep your's for your own use.	Cars of little value, three of them abandoned outside the Mess.
Bomb attacks rouse anger, calls for reprisal ...some fear, too.	Bomb attacks rouse fear only. No anger. No thought of reprisal.
Flare path ready every night, you accept risk of being bombed.	Night flying not permitted – flare path might bring bombers.
Station and squadron records kept proudly up to date.	Station and squadron records have been abandoned.
There are more machines than crews to fly them...	There are far more crews than machines for them to fly.

There were many more items, but that's enough to give you the picture.

The ways of local command were incomprehensible to us newcomers. For example, every morning eighty-one Japanese aircraft would arrive in formation, then separate off-shore into groups – twenty-seven, usually – for targets chosen from the four airfields, town docks, the city, naval dockyard, and the oil tanks.

We heard of this on arrival – the oil tanks were still burning then from the previous day's bombing – and saw it happen next morning when Tengah was not on the list. Naturally, therefore, our group – five more Hudsons arrived that afternoon – decided we'd miss out bomb time next day. We'd fly away south over the Java Sea, then came back when the bombing was finished.

The station commander refused permission. 'Fuselage tanks must first be removed', he declared, quoting this local regulation for refusal. And he wouldn't query it with Command, despite our protests.

So we stayed on the ground. Two formations of twenty-seven bombed Tengah. They knew that Hudsons were there, of course – they'd done their usual PRU run the previous afternoon. Two Hudsons were completely destroyed, two damaged. Just flown out eight thousand miles, and not even one sortie from them.

Another peacetime order: 'Fighter gun panels must be locked away every night'.

We took off on an attack: no one could find the locker key, so we had no fighter escort. A single Japanese Zero shot down two more aircraft. That evening the station commander at Tengah put a pistol to his head and pulled the trigger. I know of two other suicides about that time.

The rapidity of the Japanese advance, the sheer ease of it, had shattered morale. With so many aircraft lost on the ground up country Tengah was crowded with surplus air and ground crews – just waiting, apprehensively, for the next setback. We, fresh from a fighting England – and the Middle East Blenheim crews too – naturally had a different ethos, and this division in spirit lasted right through to the end.

After only four days in Singapore we had pulled back to Sumatra. We then had twenty-four Hudsons left out of the English arrivals, about the same number of Blenheims from the Middle East; and, of the original bomber force, two biplane squadrons and two Australian Hudson squadrons still survived. But then – at the height of the full moon – we lost a third of our total force in a daylight attack against a Japanese landing at Endau. Our fighter escort never arrived, of course. The two biplane squadrons were wiped out – both commanding officers were among the dead – and we lost three more Hudsons.

By then, no more reinforcement flights could get through. And of those that had arrived, a further fifteen were shot down in the next fortnight in Sumatra – all in daylight sorties, all crews killed.

And here is a note I made about our final day at Sumatra.

> '14 Feb:
> 1000. G'Cpt calls meeting. Jap ground forces approaching. Instructions about action to be taken when shooting starts. Burn unserviceable aircraft, burn all spares and documents. Wait in planes with engines running till told take-off. If no such orders in reasonable time (???) take off for Java. Meanwhile stand-by.
> 1100. I am to lead a 3-aircraft attack on off-shore naval force.
> 1145. Wimpy takes my place. I am to take the second trio at 1230.'

Instead, at about midday, came an urgent message to dispersal: the field was being abandoned, with trucks standing by to take everyone down to the coast where a ship was waiting. I was to lead our last six aircraft off to Java at once, and hunt down the AOC for instructions. On that job I did, finally, get airborne. The trio who had taken our place never returned. The chaos in Java lasted only eight more days. Three aircraft were shot down – then the Zeros found our strip and finished off the last three.

We got out on a freighter – crammed on the deck and filling the holds. Some 2000 out of the 8000 original RAF strength. Two other boats got clear with us that night, en route to Australia, but then our captain decided to strike out alone for Ceylon. We made it – the other two ships did not.

A Futile Interlude in India 1942

J. F. P. Archbold

Towards the end of March 1942 a new squadron, No. 215, was formed at El Fayid and ordered to take some fairly clapped-out Wellington Ics to India. We were to fly in four batches of three aircraft, the first leaving on 30 March: we followed in the second batch on 1 April. A skeleton ground crew was carried in each aircraft with some tools and spares. We went via Habbaniya, Sharjah and Karachi to our new base at Asansol in West Bengal, arriving there on 6 April.

Asansol was some 130 miles north west of Calcutta and had two tarmac runways, the longest of which was about 1500 yards. This was unsuitable for our under-powered Wimpys, which needed at least 2000 yards to take off with a full fuel and war load in the very hot conditions. We stayed here for a few days.

Living conditions were fairly primitive at the airfield and there was no room for us there: a convent school for girls was requisitioned in the town of Asansol as a temporary measure and we were billeted there for a few days. This may well be one of the sources of the well-known story about the electric bell in one of the dormitories labelled 'In case of need, ring for Mistress'! We tried, but without success! Food was in general uninspiring to awful. At Asansol we made up for this by going to the local railway station restaurant, where an excellent curry could be had for two rupees – about fifteen p!

A new natural surface strip was being completed at a place called Pandaveswar, about twenty miles away: it was 2500 yards long and would serve well until the monsoon began. We moved there on 17 April. There was a tented camp, and here the main party of our ground crew caught up with us, having left the UK in February by sea.

Number 215 Squadron was the first RAF 'heavy' bomber squadron to arrive in India: it was closely followed by 99 Squadron with its Mk III Wellingtons at Allahabad.

In November some Liberators arrived, but they were badly affected by lack of spares and were grounded for long periods. Between March and June 1942 the air force in India increased from five squadrons to twenty-six, aided by a small but growing contribution from the Indian Air Force.

The RAF in India in early 1942 was just emerging from the Wapiti/Hart era, with operational emphasis on the North West Frontier: the possibility of an attack from the east was thought remote and unlikely. There was a limited number of airfields in Eastern India, not all with all-weather runways. New construction was going ahead but was hindered by materiel shortages and by the passive rebellion of the Indian Congress Party in April.

There was little or no infrastructure for a modern air force in eastern India. There were no navigational aids: no D/F stations, no M/F beacons. The only radio source was the Calcutta station of All India Radio, and this shut down at 2230 hrs. There was almost no Met. information. There were no Mercator plotting charts for the Burma area; the only maps were 1:1,000,000 topographicals, not very accurate over Burma, and with dangerously wrong spot heights shown for the Burmese hills. Our astro tables were out of date and the Astrograph sight plotting device could not be used because of the lack of charts. Navigation was thus by dead reckoning, backed up where possible by visual pinpoints – not easy to find on a dark night, and a small scale map. In those conditions one river bend looks much like another.

When we arrived at Asansol the retreat from Burma was almost at an end. There was a tremendous flap going on, and rumours were rife. The Japanese Fleet had just attacked Ceylon and had sunk the carrier *Hermes*, two cruisers and a destroyer. Carrier-based bombers had attacked the small ports of Vizagapatam and Coconada on 6 April, and Japanese cruisers were supposed to be approaching the Hooghly River, the main port for Calcutta, and full of vulnerable merchant ships; the Jap bombers were expected any minute.

In this heated atmosphere the newly-arrived Wellingtons must have seemed the answer to a prayer. Because of the shortcomings at Asansol it was decided to detach six aircraft to Calcutta/Dum Dum airport, refuel them there and load two extra 250 lb bombs aboard. They would then take off and scour the Bay of Bengal for these Jap cruisers and/or the main Fleet and attack them at all costs.

The operation was a total shambles. Refuelling was delayed by a shortage of bowsers, unfamiliarity with the aircraft caused further delays, and bombing up was not completed until after dark. Eventually the sortie was scrubbed, much to the relief of the crews, who found the bar of the Grand Hotel more congenial than the waters of the Bay of Bengal!

Another briefing at Asansol a few days later proposed an attack on Rangoon/Mingaladon aerodrome, allegedly stuffed full of Japanese aircraft. This target was well beyond the range of our Wellingtons, which would have run out of fuel soon after coasting out on the return flight, assuming any of us would have made it after a daylight attack on the target. 'Not to worry', said the briefing officer, a Wing Commander, 'Get back as far as you can, ditch the aircraft, and the Navy will pick you up'! I was there and can vouch for this; he wasn't joking ... Needless to say, the operation was cancelled. Rangoon was then beyond the range of the USAAC B17s. Some of these bombed the Andaman Islands from Asansol on one occasion.

Soon after these episodes it was established that the Japanese fleet had left the Bay of Bengal and plans began to be made to begin operations over Burma. It had been feared that the Japanese Army would follow our retreating troops into India: air attacks on their lines of communication might hinder this process. It was hoped to add some extra range to the Wellingtons by operating from a forward base on the island of Akyab. It was not known whether this place had fallen to the Japs. Akyab was some 150 miles south of Chittagong and had a hard surface runway. The CO went off in a Lysander to see if Akyab was suitable and available. When he approached the airfield he was fired upon, and that was the end of that idea.

An operation was laid on for the night of 30 April/1 May 1942, with six aircraft being tasked to bomb the airfield at Magwe, in Burma. Take-off was at 2230 hrs. We were the third aircraft off, carrying a load of 250 lb bombs and some incendiaries, and enough fuel for about nine hours. Over the Bay of Bengal we flew through a tropical storm which bumped us about a little but we passed it fairly soon and continued on our way. Four of the other aircraft turned back in this storm, and one other had engine trouble and force-landed out in the country near base.

My crew pressed on to the target. We bombed what we thought was Magwe – it was fairly dark when we arrived in spite of a moon – dropped our bombs and turned for home. The aircraft was using a lot of fuel, possibly because of a leak, and the captain decided to divert to one of our briefed diversions, Chittagong. We called them continuously on R/T with no reply. For some reason they could not, or would not, light their flarepath. Our fuel ran out after only six and a half hours, and the skipper had to ditch the aircraft at night, with no power. Somehow he got her down but she broke in half just aft of the bomb bay and sank almost at once. Both pilots were killed or drowned, as was the front gunner. The wireless operator and rear gunner were only slightly hurt. I broke my leg rather badly. My watch stopped at 0510 hrs. We were about a mile off shore. We could see people walking about but could not attract any attention. After four or five hours in the water we were spotted by two local fishermen in a canoe and taken ashore to their village: this was some ten miles from Chittagong, so we must have drifted there on the fairly strong current setting up the coast.

That was the end of my operational experience in India in 1942: it lasted all of three weeks, but was enough to impress all I saw and heard on my mind. I spent the next fourteen months in hospital where I was able to write down my experiences and these notes have survived. Memory can play strange tricks, but I think that what I have recorded above comes close to what really happened to me. It is a matter of regret that the history of the first Wellington squadron to go to India has become garbled and does not mention our somewhat futile efforts to attack the Japs. I have a photograph taken in May 1942 of an attack by 215 Squadron on the airfield at Akyab: the official histories give the first attacks on Burma as being in 1943. It is part of the tragedy of Burma that my captain and fellow crew members gave their lives without any record of their efforts, to say nothing of the waste of a perfectly good aeroplane. But that is part of the futility of war.

Air Battle over Colombo

P. M. Hamilton

Early in 1942, 30 Squadron was transferred from the Western Desert to the Far East. We were taken out to the Indian Ocean on the aircraft carrier *Indomitable* and flew off it to Ratmalana in Ceylon on 23 March.

Ratmalana at that time was a civilian airfield with one concrete runway. Our Hurricanes were parked around the perimeter – there were no blast bays. The ack-ack units arrived but were not dug in – just sandbagged and located in the open.

Communications were primitive. The signal to scramble was a Very light from the control tower. The radar shut down regularly on Sunday mornings for maintenance.

An inter-service dance was being held in Colombo on Saturday evening, 4 April, when all personnel were ordered to return to their units. A Japanese carrier fleet had been sighted by Catalinas of 403 Squadron, and 30 Squadron went on to full readiness.

We went down to dispersal on Sunday morning and after an hour or so were sent off to breakfast as 'B' Flight returned from theirs. It was an overcast day with broken rain cloud and an average ceiling of some 1000 feet.

At about 0730 we were standing outside the Officers' Mess waiting for the remaining pilots to come out. Suddenly we heard the sound of many aircraft. We looked up and there, in the open sky between great banks of cloud, were two 'Vics' of nine aircraft passing over at about 3000 feet in the most perfect formation. We looked at them with interest. Suddenly someone shouted 'Japs!' They were Japanese Type 99 with elliptical wings similar to those of a Spitfire, but with a radial engine.

Then followed a mad rush to get into the *gharri* and a high speed dash down to the dispersal. There was no Very light and no instructions or orders were given: it was quite clear what we had to do and that was to get airborne as quickly as possible. I must have been one of the last to reach the grassed area. Halfway towards the runway a 'Val' passed above my head at about 500 feet. I watched fascinated as a bomb slowly toppled from the rack towards me. However by the time it landed I was out of harm's way. Other bombs were falling across the field and in the direction of the railway workshops and Blind School.

As I took off I saw a Hurricane just clearing the far end of the runway. Once airborne I looked around: there was not a single aircraft to be seen. Admittedly there was an unusual amount of heavy cloud about and I suppose many of the Japs would already be on their way back to their carriers.

I headed for the harbour. I was flying at about 1000 feet round a large black cloud when a 'Val' suddenly appeared near me. I wrenched round in a steep turn and got on its tail immediately and very close behind. I fired a long burst as we both plunged into the cloud. Eventually I came out of the cloud at about 700 feet over the harbour. There was no sign of the 'Val'. I flew around the cloud base for some time but it never reappeared.

I started to fly south and climb to a better height. As I approached Ratmalana I noticed a 'Vic' of three aircraft at about 8000 feet several miles away, heading south. I decided to chase them. Just then I watched a Hurricane going down vertically from about 10,000 feet at a fantastic speed. It went in about two miles east of Ratmalana.

I kept on after the three aircraft. I was overtaking them painfully slowly because I had 7000 feet to climb and several miles to catch up on. They were flying down the coast and then they began to head out over the sea. I stepped up the power, but I did not go 'Through the Gate' because I felt that I might need all the endurance that I could muster. I was well aware that at any time I could find myself heading south in amongst a stream of Jap aircraft.

After what seemed an age I began to close on them. I would have liked to get above and ahead of them in order to deliver a proper quarter attack, but I felt that I could not spare the time. I decided to attack from below so that their tails would hinder their rear gunners. As I got within range I put my finger on the button, but at that same instant the three 'Vals' began to jink about madly. I got underneath them and waited until they settled down. I pulled up again and got a bead on the left-hand aircraft. Tracer was now coming back from all three in that typical lazy, undulating manner. I fired a long burst with no obvious result. I dived under them again and came up for another go. I pressed the button, but was absolutely shocked to discover that I had no ammunition left. There was no point in hanging about so I turned for home. As I did so I looked back and was gratified to see that the left hand aircraft had left the formation, lost height and was emitting grey smoke.

I landed back at Ratmalana and I could see that the ground crew were pleased and excited when they saw that the gun-port patches had been blasted away. Later the rigger showed me a bullet he had found lodged in the tail and told me that there were some bullet holes in the tail fin.

We found later that no one told Radar there was an emergency – it was shut down, and so we had no early warning. The signaller in the tower was so excited by the raid that he forgot he was under the roof when he fired the Very pistol. Apparently it was pretty exciting for people in the tower dodging the flare!

The raid we learned was by Admiral Nagumo's Air Striking Force which had earlier attacked Pearl Harbor. It had consisted of some 125 'Val' dive bombers escorted by Zero fighters. Twenty-one of 30 Squadron's Hurricanes took off despite the heavy bombing. Eight were shot down and a further eight damaged. The Squadron destroyed fourteen Japanese aircraft, claimed six 'possible' and another five 'damaged'.

Dive Bombing in a Catalina

Air Vice-Marshal J. N. Stacey CBE DSO DFC

In October 1941 I was posted to 202 Squadron in Gibraltar, flying Catalinas. I was promoted to Squadron Leader and became the flight commander there in February 1942. In April that year I took a flight of four Catalinas to Ceylon, following the Easter raid on that island by aircraft from a Japanese fleet.

By April 1942, the Far East was in a sorry state: Singapore had fallen, Malaya, Thailand and much of Burma were over-run, India was threatened and the armed forces were woefully short of men and equipment. For example, the total Maritime Forces to cover the entire Indian Ocean and Arabian Sea (!) – were the four Cats I took out, the remnants of No. 205 Sqn from Singapore and 413, a Canadian Cat Sqn, all at Koggala in south Ceylon; another Cat Sqn in Madras and a fourth near Karachi, and that was the lot. I became Flight Commander of 205.

A system of advanced bases had been introduced to enable this small force to operate as widely as possible. These were set up in such places as the Seychelles, Mauritius, Addu Atoll (now Gan in the Maldives, some 600

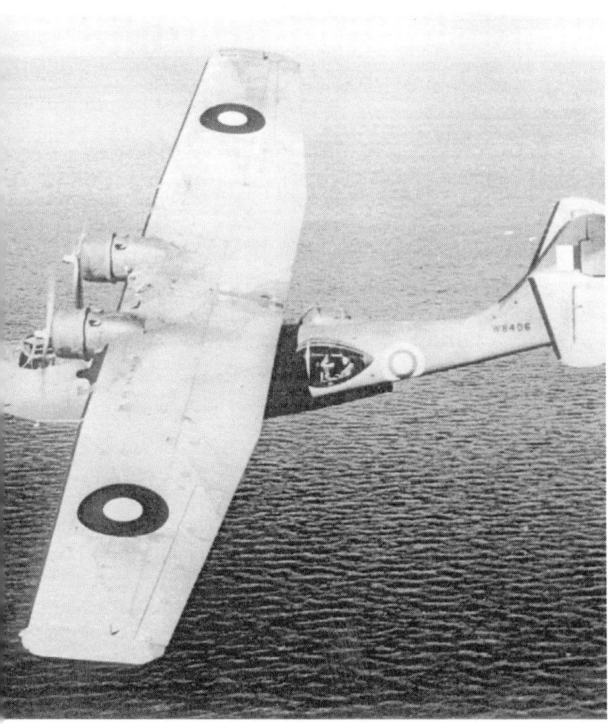

Air Vice-Marshal Stacey's Catalina (AVM Stacey)

miles south of Ceylon) and the Cocos islands. Each base had about twenty men for radio communications, refuelling and marine craft, two officers to administer the base and to brief and debrief aircrews, and mooring buoys for flying boats.

Things generally were very primitive. 'Refuelling' usually consisted of four-gallon cans of petrol being ferried out in local fishing boats and humped and poured through filters into the Cat's tanks by its crew – an exhausting process, rewarded at the end by swimming in the incomparably blue sea of the equator. Radio aids did not exist and a good navigator was essential to find a tiny island over these vast distances. Most of these advanced bases were in sparsely populated areas with no spare buildings. Huts were built for housing and feeding the visiting crews and the ground crew they took with them. The number of ground crew to service the boats, and the spares carried, depended upon the number of boats in the detachment and how long the detachment was expected to last. For a two week detachment for three boats, some twelve ground crew representing all trades with a Flight Sergeant in charge would be the norm. We never got the spares dead right and considerable ingenuity was needed to overcome problems because the right part was not available. Sometimes we flew boats which normally would be considered unserviceable but there was no alternative and no serious mishap.

Great care was taken to generate good relations with the local population and maximum use was made of local labour for cooking, cleaning, crewing marine craft, and so on. Detachment personnel led the life of Riley and, not surprisingly, were changed frequently.

On arrival in Ceylon, however, our main task was searching the Indian Ocean for a return of the Jap fleet which, fortunately did not materialise because whoever found it would have left for the great beyond after, hopefully, sending a first sighting report! Another role was to look for submarines, but we had an unusual diversion in December 1942.

Our Headquarters in Colombo wanted to know what was happening at an airfield and in the harbour of an island, Sabang, off the northern tip of Sumatra; also at an airfield on Sumatra itself. Three Catalinas were detailed for this, one for Sumatra and two for Sabang. Our masters also wished to demonstrate some aggression by dropping some bombs. A Cat from the Canadian squadron, No. 413, was to go to Sumatra, and two from ours to Sabang.

We were briefed to go in some ten minutes apart and to make a first low level run over the airfield via the harbour to assess activity and then to drop bombs on the harbour on a second run. We set off early afternoon of 20 December to be at Sabang about midnight. The transit time of some ten hours gave plenty of time to contemplate tactics. The more I thought about it, the less I liked it: the first run would alert defences who would then have an odds on chance of hitting us on the second run – we should be at low level in full moon at our max. level speed of about 100 knots! I decided dive bombing offered a better chance!

We completed the first run in total peace and saw practically nothing. We climbed to about 4000 feet and started our dive attack about eight minutes after our first run. Dive bombing is not a normal role for a flying boat and I had no experience of the technique although I had read about it. My impression was of about a 60 degree dive but it was probably nearer about half that. I started with closed throttles but progressively opened them to keep ahead of quite a lot of light flak which started astern but seemed to be catching up. Throttles were fully open when we dropped bombs at about 800 feet, at what speed I have no idea, but controls were stiff and structural damage was evident later. I'm sure we exceeded max permitted but the good old Cat's pedigree coped, as usual.

The second Cat obeyed orders, was hit by flak and had difficulty in returning but, again, the Cat and the captain, Tom Maxwell-Hudson, and crew did their job. With hindsight, we should have gone in together and combined the look-see and bombing on the one run.

An advantage of the advanced base system was the opportunity it offered to see wonderful places like Mauritius and the Seychelles which then still reflected the charm of half a century or more earlier and before modern 'civilisation' had caught up with them. It also had its disadvantages. I left Ceylon with another detachment for Mombasa in 1942, but was immediately sent on to Cape Town which was much colder than the tropics: I was not only very uncomfortable but felt a clown and attracted many curious looks walking down the main street in tropical clothes, shorts and a topee!

North West Europe

Planning for the invasion of Europe commenced in May 1943. Improved navigation facilities: the advent of the four-engined heavy bombers and the daylight operations of the big American bombers now began to tilt the scales in the allies' favour.

The Halifax (AHB)

The Bay of Biscay

Group Captain the Rt Hon. the Earl of Selkirk KT GCMG GBE AFC AE

Following appointments in Fighter Command, the Air Ministry, and as Station Commander Andover, I was posted to East Africa Command.

I rang Transport Command and offered to fly an aircraft out to Cairo. They had no Beaufighter available but offered me a Wellington X with the powerful new Bristol engines.

I flew down to Portreath in Cornwall and at briefing was told I need only fill one tank and fly straight to Finisterre. I knew, however, that German fighters tended to patrol far out into the Bay of Biscay and, being fairly senior, was allowed to make my own arrangements. I therefore filled both tanks and set course to a point about fifteen degrees west – some 1,000 miles into the Atlantic.

Soon after passing the Scilly Isles I saw five aircraft in formation to starboard. Although I tried to persuade myself that they were Beaufighters, I knew they were Ju 88s. I had more petrol that they did so I turned west, put revs and boost to maximum and dropped down to sea level. They made a good formation attack, two from the front and two behind. I took standard evasive tactics, pulling the throttles back and turning in to the attacking aircraft. The engagement lasted less than ten minutes but it seemed much longer. The rear gunner hit one 88 which we saw descending, smoking badly. A cannon shell came through the windscreen and tore the sleeve of my jacket and a few bullets went through the fuselage. I was glad to be able to get into cloud when the attack broke off.

Mk X Wellington (Crown copyright)

With the windscreen gone the force of the air blew away my coffee each time I tried to drink it: I was cold and this was most irritating. I gradually veered south, found the Portuguese coast and then Gibraltar. We landed in Morocco at Raz-el-Mar without much difficulty. I spent the night in a local hotel, full of French, all beautifully dressed, sipping expensive cocktails. I greatly enjoyed the first atmosphere of peace for many years.

My nephew, Lord James Douglas Hamilton, kindly researched German records after the war. He discovered that four of the Ju 88 A4s were from K626 of Group J based at Montpellier in France. None ever returned to base. Whether they were damaged or ran out of fuel is not known.

Peenemunde – August 1943

Professor David Balme CMG DSO DFC

One memorable effort in 1943 was Peenemunde on 17 August.

'Cocky' Cochrane (Air Vice-Marshal The Hon. Ralph A Cochrane), AOC No. 5 Group, laid on a special practice for it – what he called indirect bombing. We had to do a timed run south from Mablethorpe pier, find the wind, and then use it for a new course from a further point to Wainfleet, where we were to bomb on time alone without looking through the bombsight (except that if Lincoln Cathedral should appear in front we were to go round again). Cocky made it into an inter-squadron competition. The winning error turned out to be over 300 yards, but this did not perturb us since we assumed it was to be a method of attacking some large target like Berlin through cloud. But Cocky blew his top. He visited each squadron in turn, called a mass meeting, and told them that they would be the laughing stock of the Air Force. He reached 207 at the end of a morning, and having torn us apart announced that he would stay for lunch and then take up a Lancaster himself and have a go.

Lunch was not pleasant: everyone within earshot was mercilessly quizzed on the latest operational bumf from Group. Meanwhile, with Chiefy's connivance, we arranged for a suitable aircraft for Cocky, the one that was usually kept for the squadron commander because no one else would fly it: it was one of those that went better sideways than forwards. With it we detailed a crew not famous for subservience. When they got back, Cocky emerged poker-faced, reeled off a list of unserviceabilities, and drove away to harass the next squadron. Wainfleet rang through his result: he had made three runs, with an average error of thirty-eight yards. After that Cocky could do no wrong in our eyes.

When the actual operation was put on, we were amazed to find that the target was not the big city, but this tiny research station on the Baltic. Its importance was not explained but since the bombing height was to be 5000 feet in full moon, and since we were kindly told that if we missed it tonight we would go again every subsequent night regardless of casualties, we got the message.

Other groups were to go in first on separate aiming points while 5 Group had the place of honour – last – and our target was the workshops.

To overcome the Peenemunde smoke-screen, we were to make a timed run down a north-south coast surprisingly like Mablethorpe–Wainfleet, and then the run-in from a second pinpoint after finding the wind. Z hour was soon after midnight, so take-off was about 2000 hrs, still daylight.

There was radio silence as usual, and a green Very summoned us to trundle along the peri-track like dinosaurs and queue up until a green Aldis invited us on to the flare path as the previous aircraft began to move: when his tail came up we opened full throttles on the brakes, then gently let her go.

As always, a little group stands there to see us off: the station commander salutes (the only occasion when a Group Captain salutes a Sergeant first), the WAAFs wave, and off we go with that never forgotten roar. The engineer's left hand supports the pilot's right hand on the throttles; keep her straight, ease her off, wheels up as soon as you think you won't bounce back, flaps in bit by bit, gain speed before height, and now there is half an hour to fly around making as much height as possible before setting course. From the ground they seem like angry wasps circling aimlessly, until suddenly they all vanish in the same direction; then an anxious wait begins down there, with wondering whether all the equipment was checked, and what the weather will do at the target, and how soon will the German fighters cotton on to our route (there is a diversion on Berlin, hoping to cause them to refuel).

Over the North Sea we waddle along under full bomb and fuel load, with luck making 20,000 feet at 160 knots indicated. The light fades, but up comes that unloved moon. Near the Danish coast we start letting down, then turn north to find our first pinpoint. A sea mist makes it difficult, and as we fly around we stir up the shore batteries. At 5000 feet now, the light flak seems to spiral lazily towards you and then whizzes past: we tend to prefer the heavy, which can be outwitted, whereas this stuff is hosed up all over the place.

At last we are ready for the timed run-in, the navigator has made his wizard-like calculations, and we suddenly hear the 'Master of Ceremonies' telling us to avoid certain target indicators which are falling towards the sea. Some crew is bombing too early, and he is peeved: 'Please remember that I'm down here you stupid prune'.

Our run is nearly finished, and in a moment we must decide whether to bomb on markers or on time; but now we are in luck, for the bomb-aimer says 'Target sighted dead ahead'. So both Cocky and our navigator are vindicated, and finally everything is up to the bomb-aimer and gunners: if they can't get us accurately and safely to the target, the whole enterprise will go up in smoke only too literally. So here we come, full boost and revs: 'Steady, steady – right a bit – steady – bombs going – steady'. Bombing runs are our least favourite moment and last forever. This time the bomb-aimer is moved to uncharacteristic eloquence: 'Cor, look at that' he says. Then 'Bombs all away, flash gone off' and a climbing turn west to get the hell out of here. As the bombs left, the aeroplane lifted like a young horse and is now beautifully responsive. A quick glance shows roofless burning buildings below and a runway to the right, but this is no time for sight-seeing: all eyes are watching for fighters, of which there is no shortage. But nothing hits us, though we see other aircraft burning on the ground and one poor devil blows up in the air over there. We climb away to max. height, maybe even 30,000 feet, and as we get clear out to sea we reach what really is the favourite moment. Everything has gone quiet: I look out along the wing where the two port engines crouch like tigers, purring now under reduced boost and revs but nursing their power if it should be needed; soon the W/Op will bring that disgusting coffee which is pure nectar. But not before he performs one vital task: having had to listen out in silence all night, he is now permitted one call to base. He comes up with information about the airfield state and the barometric pressure there. We set the altimeter for home.

There comes the English coast – dark, dangerous, precious, containing everything that this whole exercise is about. Two searchlights stand like crossed swords, marking an emergency landing strip for those in trouble; but we are not in trouble tonight, touch wood.

At base the flare path is already lit up (Hello Squirrel) and aircraft are plentiful, so that we deem it prudent to put on nav lights though we dislike them, having regard to intruders. Flying control even want to stack us up to 11,000 feet if you please: what an absurd notion. We all go round the circuit together, and since the people in front look a bit close we make a tight orbit in the funnel, a manoeuvre which displeases the Station Commander, as we later discover. All safely down, quick chat with the ground crew to tell them how marvellously their aircraft performed, debriefing and pint of alleged cocoa (containing, so it is said, bromide for the protection of WAAFs), our operational eggs, bacon, sausages, beans and fried bread, without which we should unquestionably mutiny, and then to get our heads down.

Presently a WAAF orderly comes quietly round the quarters and pulls down the sheet from each sleeping face.

Somebody wakes and asks what she is doing. 'Just checking that my family are all back' she says.

Though 5 Group's total losses are heavy, the nine 207 crews are all back without casualties, and every one of their photographs that can be plotted is on the aiming point – there are so many altogether that Group, penny-wise as ever, stops handing out those Lanc pictures to crews that get aiming-points: pity, for it would have been a good souvenir.

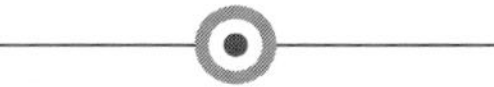

The Hawker Typhoon

Squadron Leader L. W. F. Stark DFC AFC

The Typhoon, successor to the Hurricane, was bigger and heavier than both the Spitfire and the Hurricane by some 2000/3000 lb empty weight. The armament consisted of four 20 mm cannon as standard (early versions had twelve .303 machine guns) plus, in the fighter-bomber role, eight or twelve 60 lb HE Rocket Projectiles (RPs) or two 500 lb bombs or two 1000 lb bombs. The power plant was the Napier Sabre twenty-four cylinder horizontal H type sleeve valve piston engine of 2180 hp.

The first squadrons to be equipped with the Typhoon were 56, 266 and 609, with deliveries starting in September 1941, but the early days were plagued by structural failures (at the fuselage/tail assembly joint) and engine failures due mostly to seizure of the sleeve valves. While these problems were being resolved (although the structural one was never fully solved) the first squadrons became operational and in August 1942 came the first successful combats with the enemy.

My own introduction to this big, heavy fighter came in January 1943 when I had the good fortune to be posted to 609 Squadron at Manston in Kent. The main task was defensive patrols and cockpit readiness against attacks by so called 'hit and run' raiders, mostly Fw 190s and Me 109s, whose targets were mainly the coastal towns of Kent and Sussex.

Within two months of my arrival the Squadron, led at this period by R. P. Beamont, had destroyed sixteen enemy aircraft plus three probables for the loss of four pilots, the last of which was as a result of the aforementioned structural failure.

Our defensive role was interspersed with the occasional offensive sortie such as attacks against coastal shipping and railway trains and these offensive sorties became more frequent and more successful as the year progressed. Especially helpful was the acquisition of long range drop tanks (two forty-five gallon), and with these we were able to penetrate to Paris and beyond and into Belgium and Holland.

Consequently, from September onwards the squadron score was mounting steadily. In October I had the luck to be 'in the right place at the right time' and destroyed the squadron's 200th enemy aircraft, a Ju 88. In February 1944, having been with 609 for fourteen months I was posted to 263 Squadron as a Flight Commander. During those fourteen months 609 had shot down sixty-one enemy aircraft (of which my share was six and a half – including one on the ground) and this using an aircraft which in 1942 had been on the verge of being cancelled as not being suitable for Fighter Command.

From November 1943 Typhoon Squadrons were being gradually equipped for the carrying of bombs and RPs, and eventually were transferring from Fighter Command to 2nd Tactical Air Force, the former being renamed Air Defence of Great Britain (ADGB).

A few squadrons remained in ADGB for the time being, one of these being 263 which I had just joined, so we happily continued in the fighter role with some success on 'Rangers' over NW France; but eventually the 'Ground Attack' business caught up with us and by the end of April we were in the dive-bombing and RP modes operating from Barrowbeer and later from Bolt Head in Devon. Our targets were mainly shipping off the coast of the Brest Peninsula and as far east as the Channel Islands.

We eventually had half our aircraft carrying bombs and the other half RPs thus enabling us to ring the changes depending on the type of target. I first used bombs (two 500 lb) on 29 April and continued dive bombing throughout May (thirteen sorties in all). I first fired RPs on D Day, and between that day and the end of June I took part in seventeen rocket attacks and three dive bombing attacks.

However, on 3 July, during a rocket attack on a transformer station in the middle of the Brest Peninsula, I was hit in the engine by flak and eventually was forced to bale out due to overheating around the feet. I managed to evade capture with help from the locals and the Maquis and arrived back in Devon in ten days courtesy of the Royal Navy.

After debriefing in London and some leave I asked if I could rejoin the Squadron but Air Ministry said 'No', and after some discussion I was lucky enough to be seconded to the Gloster Aircraft Co. for Production Testing duties on Typhoons for six months. As a result I missed Falaise, Mortain and the advance up to the Netherlands, but having heard first hand from colleagues with whom I kept in touch, this period of the war was without doubt the most hectic as far as the Typhoon squadrons were concerned. With rockets, bombs and cannon, in support of the ground forces, they harassed the enemy on every day that the weather permitted and in so doing suffered many casualties. Between D Day and VE Day some 350+ Typhoon pilots were lost at a rate of thirty-two per month. Many others evaded capture or became POWs.

Having flown a further 125 hours over the lovely Gloucestershire countryside I was posted at the beginning of March 1945 to 123 Wing, 84 Group, 2nd TAF based at Gilze Rijen in Holland. On arrival I was further posted to 164 Squadron as a Flight Commander. The day before my arrival the CO of 609 Squadron, my old friend and colleague back in 1943, E. R. A. Roberts, had been shot down by flak and taken POW.

Three days later the Wing CO informed me that I had been appointed as CO of 609. I was surprised, delighted and

The Hawker Typhoon (AHB)

proud to be appointed to command the Squadron with which I had started my operations some two years earlier as a Flight Sergeant.

So it was back to firing RPs in close support of the Army. The Wing moved on 21 March to a new strip (B.91) Kluis, just south of Nijmegen and quite close to the front line: so close in fact that the odd shell arrived on occasions at night. On the 24th the Allied Armies crossed the Rhine and the largest air armada of all time appeared from the West – paratroop aircraft, gliders of all shapes and sizes with a variety of tugs in a steady stream that continued for hours, or so it seemed. It was a most impressive sight.

Our task was to provide anti-flak patrols to protect these airborne forces. It was all very exciting if somewhat dangerous: the main danger seemed to be that of collision with other aircraft.

The Allied advance continued at an ever increasing pace over the Rhine, north towards the Baltic and east across the north German plain, and we followed in support. Another thirty-nine rocket attacks on a variety of targets and someone said 'STOP'. I fired my last load of rockets on 4 May and it was all over!

But it wasn't! The shooting having ceased, we were sent to Fairwood Common, Armament Practice Camp, near Swansea, by someone in a very high place, to be taught to shoot and fire RPs! At least it gave everyone a three week break in the UK and I had the pleasure of introducing my wife of some fourteen months to the Squadron.

Back to Germany and lots of formation flying – both Squadron and Wing, fly-pasts and displays in Holland and Belgium. The Squadron personnel changed almost daily with our Belgians returning to their own Air Force and the Canadians, New Zealanders, Australians etc. going home. New pilots arrived and were keen to complete their training and conversion on to the Typhoon and so we were kept busy. We were frequently required for demonstrations and fly-pasts for VIPs, the press and local communities. There were more 'flag waving' formations and demonstrations over various towns and cities in Belgium and Holland, so we were not allowed to become bored with peacetime flying.

On 20 September 1945, 609 Squadron, accompanied by our sister Squadron of many months 198, flew from Wunstorf (via Manston) to Lasham to disband and leave our Typhoons sadly on a scrap heap.

During my service on Typhoons I had flown 578 hours behind the Napier Sabre engine with never a failure; I had survived 255 operational sorties and only failed to return from one: perhaps more importantly I had served with pilots from sixteen countries not counting the UK – and what a marvellous team they made. I still see some of them from time to time and we talk about old chums and the thing that bound us all together – the aircraft.

In my opinion the Typhoon was a most splendid operational aeroplane and an excellent weapons platform. I last flew one on 4 November 1945, borrowed from my old Wing Commander Flying. I would dearly like to fly one again!

Doctor in Distress

Wing Commander R. H. Winfield DFC AFC

In June 1942 I was a doctor at the Physiological Laboratory based at the Royal Aeronautical Establishment at Farnborough. I was also a pilot and had completed the parachute jumping course at Ringway. We were responsible for solving medical problems not reproducible on the ground.

A flight was planned to see if it was possible for a tug to tow a glider which was using automatic pilot. This would reduce the hours needed to train a glider pilot. I was interested to learn if airsickness was likely to be greater under such conditions and if so, what could be done to reduce it. It was essential to land an airborne force ready to fight, without a trace of airsickness. I knew a lot about airsickness, partly because I myself was a victim when being flown in rough weather. I was trying out some tablets of my own formulation.

Unhappily I had a monumental hangover, but there were two good reasons I couldn't turn down this flight. First, the cumulus clouds were beginning to form and this flight would have more than its fair share of sick-making bumps. Secondly, I knew that to fly – particularly in rough weather – with a hangover, was one of the most likely ways to court a bout of airsickness. Therefore I reasoned that if my tablets stopped me from airsickness, I should have valuable evidence that my pills were on the right lines.

The previous night had been quite an occasion. The staff and pilots at the RAE had invited me to a party to celebrate the fact that I had been awarded the Air Force Cross. So I hastily swallowed four of my pills and went back to my room as fast as my fragile condition would allow to collect my parachute.

The fact that I kept my parachute in my room has a direct bearing on what was to happen. I was the only pilot on the station who kept his own parachute. This was because I had my own aircraft and a lot of my flying was done from airfields far from Farnborough. I only returned the parachute to the parachute section when it was due for repacking. Because I didn't have to go to the parachute section, I forgot to tell the Duty Pilot that I was going on this flight as second pilot. It was therefore assumed that only four people instead of the actual five were the crew of the glider.

I happened to meet Flight Lieutenant Kronfeld as I went towards the aircrew bus, and told him about the flight I was about to make. Thus it was that he alone knew that I was flying.

The Tug and Tow, the Whitley and the Hotspur glider connected by the tow rope, were in position on the far side of the airfield. I was the last to arrive, and the crew of the Whitley were already inside the aircraft waiting to start up. The crew of the glider were just climbing on board. Flight Lieutenant Davie was captain. I was the second pilot. There were two technical observers from Aero Flight and also Squadron Leader Macpherson who was interested in the much wider implications that would arise from the successful use of the automatic pilot.

I found it oppressively hot sitting in the glider in the blazing sun, and before I put on my parachute harness, I took off my battle dress jacket.

Soon we were set for take off. Davie gave the signal. The Whitley's engines roared into life and the take off began.

Our flight plan was to climb up to 6000 feet, circling in a series of spiral circuits. Then at 6000 feet, the tug would fly straight and level. This was to be the signal for Davie to engage the automatic pilot fitted to the glider and each member of the crew would make the observations required.

After the smooth take off, it soon became obvious that we were in for a rough ride. As we climbed, the air steadily became more bumpy. Davie took over and even he, with all his experience, had great difficulty. Each time we hit a patch of turbulent air the glider seemed to come to a sudden sickening stop that jolted us against our restraining harnesses. We sometimes soared vertically upwards with the vivacity of a lark or dropped vertically down in the manner

Dr Winfield in his physiological laboratory (Air Commodore Mike Gibson)

of a hawk descending upon its prey. The movements were totally unpredictable and equally unpleasant. Davie had all his work cut out to keep the tow rope that joined us to the tug at even tension. Unless you know exactly what you're about, it's the easiest thing in the world to let the rope slacken in bumpy air. Then the danger lies when the tug pulls the slack rope taut.

The moment that Davie switched on the automatic pilot, I became aware of two things. First, what a superb pilot Davie was to fly the glider up to this height keeping the tow rope firm and steady. Secondly I became aware that the rope must surely break in a matter of seconds – or at any rate long before he could possibly release us from the tug. I was right. The rope broke almost immediately. It snapped about halfway between the glider and the tug. The hum of the Whitley's engines was drowned by the rending crack made by the tow rope as it broke.

The glider shook and shuddered as if it were going to fall apart. The broken end of the rope attached to the glider slashed back towards us. It sliced off the upper part of the nose and the top of the cockpit hood. There was a grating sound as the broken end wrapped itself around our tailplane, trailing away beyond it in festoons of frayed rope and broken wire.

Then there was silence. For an instant the glider remained poised in the sky. Nobody spoke. Davie had been stunned for a moment and was bleeding from cuts about the face from the shower of shattered Perspex. What worried us was that the glider was already losing height in a steady dive which could not be corrected by use of the controls which were locked solid and immovable by the broken tow rope.

Certainly the glider had stopped shaking, but it was losing height in a steady dive that Davie was powerless to prevent. The rope had snapped at 6000 feet and now the altimeter continued to unwind. The needle had passed the 4000 feet mark when Davie gave us the order to bale out. The instant before I launched myself into space I noticed Macpherson leave. I watched his canopy develop and open and also saw that he had taken with him a tangle of wire cable and rope. He had fouled the broken tow rope and carried with him the cause of the controls becoming immovable. As soon as he jumped the controls were freed. However, by then four of the five occupants were skimming earthward and Davie alone remained in the Hotspur.

From the tarmac in front of the Watch Office men observed the glider wrench herself free from the tug. There was a pause and then in quick succession four specks detached themselves. Three soon swelled out. The fourth speck however still refused to swell into a white ball.

By now it was common knowledge that the four members of the glider crew, in fact its entire alleged complement, had bailed out and the glider was deserted. The watchers were astounded to see the glider make a leisurely circuit of the airfield, choose the runway in use and come in to land of its own accord. This was uncanny and when it came to rest at the end of the runway there was no ugly rush of enquiring humanity to approach this *Marie Celeste* of the skies.

When Davie told us to jump, I glanced at the altimeter which read 3800 feet, took a good look at the ground below and thought smugly to myself 'What a piece of cake – never have I had so much sky to jump into'. All jumps I had done at Ringway had been made from 1000 feet or less. I stepped smartly over the side of the glider and relaxed completely in the approved Ringway style. Instead of thinking of the differences between a training jump and an emergency one, I slid into the sky without a care in the world.

The vital difference between the Training and Emergency jumps is that a Training jump is made with a statischute which is so designed that when you drop through the exit hole of the aircraft, the weight of your body automatically pulls the ripcord and opens the canopy for you. By contrast, when you make an Emergency jump, the canopy will not open unless you pull the ripcord for yourself. Incredible though it seems, I forgot this elementary but vital fact.

I had fallen the best part of 2000 feet before I felt that my parachute was taking a long time to open; then, like a flash, I remembered that this was no training jump and that if I continued to do nothing about it, the parachute would never open. I began to panic. The first mistake I made was to fumble for the rip cord on the wrong side because I am left handed. At last, having found and pulled the rip cord, I made my second mistake. I tried to speed up the opening canopy by putting my fingers into the pack: this upset the natural development of the canopy and I began to fall though the forty-eight rigging lines. Already I had fallen another 1000 feet and was fighting to free myself from the lines. I knew that if I couldn't do this, the canopy would never open sufficiently to save me.

At about 600 feet from the ground the lines began to free themselves. Suddenly the canopy billowed out and I knew I was safe. I judged I had only about 200 feet to spare. I was drifting slowly towards a small wood and soon spotted a sandpit within it. There was practically no wind and the weather was ideal for parachuting. The hot summer sun was shining and warm air was rising from the ground to slow up my descent. A gentle pull on my right hand lift web and I side slipped towards the sandpit. Then I hung completely limp in my harness waiting to use the quick-release button for the landing. The warm up-currents of air were sufficiently strong that for the second time only in the whole of my parachuting career I landed upright without having to do either a forward or backward tumble.

I was pleased with this and began to roll up my parachute. Life was good again. My hangover was gone and in spite of forgetting to pull the ripcord, I was still alive. However, my peace of mind and the quiet of the sand pit were rudely shattered. Two men, who had been working on the land nearby, clattered into the sand pit. These were the days of the Home Guard, when many civilians over the age for joining the armed forces were banded together for useful purposes, such as aircraft spotting and spy hunting.

These two farm workers had been in a position to see the Whitley and the glider come in and land at Farnborough, but had missed the sight of the other members of the crew parachuting to safety. Suddenly I found myself facing the business end of a very unpleasant pitchfork and looking up the wrong end of the two barrels of an ancient, but obviously dangerous duck gun.

The conversation that followed went as follows:

'Reckon he's a bleeding spy, trying the burying of his parachute. Shall we finish him off, or shall we hand him over to authority?'

'Let's hear what's he's saying for his self first. That's if he speaks in English'.

Me: 'Don't be so bloody silly. I've just bailed out of a glider. The tow rope broke – wound itself round the tail plane of the glider – and the crew of the glider had to jump. Because it's so hot, I left my battle dress jacket and my cap in the glider.'

'Ho – a likely story, that. We spotted the glider going in to land at Farnborough, and we ain't seen others of the crew bail out.'

Of course they hadn't: the rest of the crew had landed out of sight and I didn't know what had happened to the glider. I could only suggest 'Take me in charge and let's go to the nearest pub. Then you can notify the local police by telephone and I can speak to the Chief Test Pilot at Farnborough. And what's more, I pay for all you can drink while we're waiting.'

The last sentence was an inspiration, but it turned the scales. Both were swayed by the thought of free liquor. You see, it was very, very, hot in that sandpit and the average English farmworker likes to be absolutely sure of his ground before he indulges in cold-blooded murder. As soon as I had made the offer, one said 'Let's see the colour of your money'. And, of course, my battle dress jacket pocket was still safely stowed in the glider with my Identity Card in it, and my trouser pockets were empty.

When they discovered this, Duck Gun said to Pitch Fork 'Blooming funny German spy, landing by parachute with only shirt, trousers, socks and shoes'. Pitch Fork pondered long before he pronounced 'Well, there might be something in that too. Curiouser things have happened. Couldn't do him no harm taking him to the four ale bar and see if he is as he says.' Duck Gun clinched the matter by adding 'Powerful hot sun this, and I'm mortal dry'. So off we went.

After about half a mile we came to a public house and after Duck Gun and Pitch Fork had explained their difficulty to the landlord, he telephoned for the police. Then I was allowed to make a call – charges reversed – to Willy Wilson, the Chief Test Pilot, while Pitch Fork and Duck Gun stood guard.

Wing Commander Wilson had just come from a meeting with the Director and had not yet heard what had been going on. It was not surprising, therefore, that we talked at cross purposes. I assumed he knew that I had bailed out and so I started 'I'm quite all right – but I've landed up at the pub in Hook – would you please send transport for me as soon as possible'. Willy, who had been at my party the night before, instantly jumped to the conclusion that I'd been drinking ever since. He obviously thought I was plastered. 'So you're really quite all right are you. But you've got the infernal gall to telephone me from a public house, where you've not yet stopped boozing and ask me for transport to bring you back. Well, just this once, I'll do it. After all, you don't win a decoration every day of the week. But never again.'

Willy Wilson never did things by halves. I suppose it must have been seconds after my telephone call to him that he learned the true state of affairs. He jumped into his staff car and must have broken the speed record between his office and that public house. He took charge of the situation. He first of all apologised to me, then gave the necessary explanations and reassurances, and finally paid the landlord after we had all had another round.

Later that evening I could have earned myself the reputation as 'Winfield, the Ace Delayed Drop Parachutist'. But as they say 'Murder will out', and I could not resist telling the truth about the matter. But I had not been sick!!

Dieppe

Air Chief Marshal Sir Peter Le Cheminant GBE KCB DFC

In July 1941 614 Squadron converted from Lysanders to Blenheim IVs, the long-nosed version. We were operating from Tranent, a small grass field east of Edinburgh. There was room but only just! Nothing much but near misses or accidents broke the monotony.

Some months later on 10 January 1942, I lost control in a snowstorm and very nearly killed myself and my crew. Flying out of Benson, near Henley, I ran into heavy snow near York and, with the cloud base down to 300 ft, resolved to turn back. I made the mistake of taking my eyes off the instruments and looking out of the bubble canopy to make sure that all was clear as I turned to port. When I looked back at my instruments my gyro-horizon had toppled, my altitude was about 1000 ft and my airspeed was down to 100 mph. As I had gone into the turn at 250 ft and 150 mph, it was quite evident that I had established a gentle climbing turn and gone on to my back in the process. Whether I was still on my back or had rolled through into the upright, or was betwixt and between, I had no immediate means of knowing. There have been a number of times in my flying life when I knew I had little chance of surviving, but on this occasion I thought I had none whatsoever. I remember a stillness as the aircraft hung there and a feeling of calm and resignation. I thought I was about to die and had no feeling of panic or even fear. I suppose that, although my reason told me that we had no chance of survival, my subconscious was determined to fight on.

I just centralised the controls and waited to see what would happen. The airspeed started to build up, slowly and then quite rapidly as the altimeter unwound. It was evident that we were in a dive so I cut the throttles and started to pull back on the control column. We broke cloud at 300 ft, heading straight for the top of a haystack. It looked huge and vertically below us but I think our angle must have been less,

Bostons (AHB)

possibly somewhere between 60° and 45°, otherwise I could never have pulled her through. Heaven knows what G she withstood but my navigator's metal seat in the nose just buckled under him.

I managed to land in a field so small that the aircraft had to be dismantled and recovered by road. Instead of a well-deserved reprimand from Command Headquarters I was awarded what was known as a 'Green Endorsement' and my Log Book was annotated 'a difficult precautionary landing carried out skilfully and successfully'. Seldom was any laudatory endorsement less well deserved.

In August 1942 we took part in the raid on Dieppe. It is hard to think of any incident or action in the war, with the exception of Arnhem, that caused more excitement at the time. Some 6000 troops were landed: 5000 of them Canadian, the remainder British Commandos and a small force of American Rangers. The Canadians in particular suffered very severe casualties but lessons were learned, albeit costly ones, that proved invaluable in the mounting of subsequent invasions – and in particular the D-Day landings. Perhaps the most important of these was that it would not be possible to capture a French port without a degree of destruction which would render it useless to the Allies. From this realisation the Mulberry Harbours were conceived. But the real excitement was engendered by the size of the air battle. On the Allied side, seventy-three squadrons were employed, made up of forty-seven Spitfire squadrons, eight Hurricane, three Typhoon, four Boston, two Blenheim, one Beaufighter, four Mustang and four B-17. Losses were high on both sides: the RAF losing seventy aircraft. Overall it was felt to be a success and was hailed by the Press as a glorious victory.

During our third sortie we laid a smoke-screen over the beach, We came over the beach low in close line astern and received intense light AA fire from the cliff top. I was directly behind Harry Sutton and could see his aircraft being hit repeatedly in and just forward of the tail section. I in turn took most of my five major hits in that same area, as did the following aircraft. I think we were saved from taking major damage in the cockpit area by the fact that we had been preceded over the target area by Bostons of 225 Squadron dropping at 300 mph whilst we dropped at 180 mph. This would almost certainly have caused the Germans to allow too much deflection, with the result that we were probably being hit by fire intended for the aircraft immediately astern of us. Either way it was a brisk and energising few moments. We split up and came home individually at low level, initially in +9 override boost which just about gave us 200 mph.

Five Blenheim aircrew were killed and one seriously wounded.

The Air Transport Auxiliary

Freydis Sharland

This is a brief and somewhat scrappy account of life as a ferry pilot in the Air Transport Auxiliary.

I started my flying in the Civil Air Guard before the War and paid two shillings and sixpence for each hour's flight in a Gypsy Moth. The cost was subsidised to keep the clubs flying in anticipation of imminent hostilities.

My first wartime experiences were as a VAD, and later as a worker in an aircraft factory.

Then with four hours forty minutes solo in my prewar logbook, I was finally asked to report to White Waltham on 2 August 1942 for a flight test and interview for the Air Transport Auxiliary. I went up with Cdr Macmillan in an Avro Tutor. It was great to be airborne again. I managed to keep my wits about me so that when told to return to the airfield and land, I was able to do so.

In February '43 I was interviewed at Luton by Flt Captain E. C. Mogridge, an avuncular type, who had been a fighter pilot in the First World War. He had volunteered for flying in the ATA and was soon ferrying four engined bombers. He told me to remember that all aircraft flew in a similar way regardless of size. Also, never to memorise numbers but always to fly with the relevant page of Ferry Pilots' notes open on one's knee to check before take off or landing. Finally not to listen to the horrendous stories of other pilots when about to ferry a new type. How right he was!

That first cold winter the Initial Flying Training School was at Barton-in-the-Clay, Beds. A French girl and I were the only women among a group of about twenty pilots seconded to the ATA from the RAF or Fleet Air Arm. They were there because they had been wounded or were surplus to requirements for some other reason.

When the weather was bad we would sit round a coke stove in a Nissen hut and I would listen to the stories they had to tell. It must have been therapeutic for them to get it off their chests. I sat quiet and listened because I had not been shot down or crash landed. The French girl disappeared soon after and I now suspect she was recruited by SOE to be dropped in France.

We had the great good fortune to fly many diverse and interesting aircraft. How did we do it? Well, largely through the foresight and skill of Commander A. R. O. Macmillan. He came from British Airways to be Chief Instructor of the Air Transport Auxiliary. He tested and selected the pilots. He also devised a training scheme for pilots to fly classes of aircraft rather than individual types. In 1943 he started a School at Thame for basic training and a school for ground engineers at White Waltham. In March 1943 he was recalled to British Overseas Airways to prepare its postwar training organisation.

The training at ATA was then changed so that each school had its own Chief Flying Instructor. The conversion courses for moving pilots from one class to the next were held mainly at White Waltham. However Joan Hughes, one of the most experienced (and youngest) instructors in the ATA, converted many pilots, both men and women, to four-engined Stirling bombers at Marston Moor.

The flying was sometimes gruelling. Ten days on and two days off. Our chief enemy was the weather. No satellites or weatherships – forecasting was entirely due to the genius of the Met. officers. Their tickertape brought news of the movements of fronts and what was actually happening at various aerodromes. Having no radio we relied on seeing the ground, and gradually learnt the lie of the land and the danger areas. Visiting Met. maps and signals was a must as soon as the mornings chits were received. Sometimes there would be only one or two, sometimes as many as five different aircraft to deliver. We each collected a two ounce bar of chocolate – there was rarely time for lunch.

We tried very hard to fly safely and to keep our aircraft at the correct speed so as not to strain an engine needed for combat. Thus on some aircraft the throttle was only opened enough to get airborne and then brought back to ATA Cruise. If a new type was to be flown, special Handling Notes

Joan Hughes of the ATA with Stirling bomber (RAF Museum Hendon)

needed to be studied. We all carried a complete set of maps for the British Isles plus a pair of pyjamas and toothbrush in case we were stuck somewhere. I soon discovered it was essential to learn some instrument flying. Thus whenever I was held up at an RAF station I would go to the Link Instructor and have an hour's tuition. After a while I felt confident of being able to fly through a snow shower or do a 180-degree turn to get out of cloud. One early morning I had to fly a Barracuda from Hamble to Lee-on-Solent. Halfway there I realised sea fog was rolling in. Everything vanished but the control tower stood out and the controller flashed me a green light, so I lined up where I imagined the field was and sank gently through the fog, landing in a whiteout.

Towards the end of the war the ATA had become very well organised. The Training Pool had started to train a few pilots ab initio, and even sick bays had been established. I remember that at Hamble a Matron was appointed to look after our health. She intended to write a novel about ATA pilots. She called it 'Paid to be safe'. The name stuck in my mind as being very apt. On joining at the start of 1943 I was paid two thirds of the pay of comparable men pilots. Later Sir Stafford Cripps, Minister for Aircraft Production, came to see how the ATA were coping with clearing the ever-increasing production of aircraft. He noted that men and women were doing the same work with the same risks. He had lunch with Pauline Gower, Head of the Women's section, and shortly afterwards equal pay was introduced. It was good to be able to put by something for the future.

I progressed from class to class and became a First Officer, qualified to fly any single or twin aircraft. With laundry and billeting allowances my pay was about £700 p.a. Riches indeed.

There were sixteen nationalities flying with the ATA, and the six hundred men and one hundred women all had special characteristics. Jung would have found them fascinating personalities. Their use of English was sometimes interesting too. Anna the Pole, taking over the taxi Anson from Margo Du Halde of Chile might say 'Chile, how many petrols did you got?' And Chile might reply 'Anna, it is not' 'how many petrols did you got?' 'but ''how many petrols have you get?''

Veronica Volkersz is another of the pilots who spring to mind. She learnt with me at Marshall's Flying School, Cambridge. She joined the ATA in March 1941 and left in November 1945. She became a Flight Captain and flew about seventy-five different types of single- and twin-engined aircraft including Meteors. After the war she flew Spitfires and Mosquitos, target-towing for Army Co-op Territorials. She and I also ferried Tempest Mk 2s to Karachi for the Pakistan Air Force in 1948.

Monique Agazarian Rendall learnt to fly *ab initio* in the ATA joining in October 1943 and leaving in 1945 as a Third Officer. Her brothers, the Agazarians, were famous fighter pilots in the Battle of Britain. Monique's energy, verve and kindness were recognised throughout the ATA and as long as she lived. After the War she started a charter firm, and got the concession for joy-riding at London Airport. Her two Dominies could be seen lined up to take off across the runway as soon as an airliner had taken off. Then a quick circuit and down again as soon as Air Traffic allowed. When Air Movements increased enormously she moved her operations to Croydon, and there I would often meet her trotting off to her aircraft with a French bulldog following close behind. Later she taught many to fly or take their Instrument training in her Link Trainer. Her book on Instrument Flying is a classic.

Mary Guthrie was another bright spark who learnt *ab initio* at the same time as Monique. One day she was flying northwards to White Waltham in the taxi Fairchild Argus. A doodle bug overtook her 100 ft above on its way to London. It was a very shaken Mary who landed.

One pilot had the misfortune to have a throttle stick wide open on take off in a Typhoon. She roared around a while then cut the engine and ploughed through a tree before landing wheels up in a small field. She was afraid to get out because of the cows who came to gaze at her!

Many of the stories were funny. Looking back I remember laughing more in the ATA and earlier as a VAD, or working in an aircraft factory, than at any time before or since. Was it just youth or did the concentration required make things seem funnier or more awful?

Tony had a tin leg as a result of a Fleet Air Arm accident. He would dance on a table swinging his tin leg round his head. Another time he got out of the taxi Anson and left his leg behind. Yet another time, taking off down the lane between the balloon barrage at Langley in a Hurricane, his tin foot got stuck under the rudder pedal. The aircraft slewed sideways and a balloon cable sliced a foot off the wingtip. He managed to free his foot, fly round the balloons and land back at Langley without further damage. A remarkable feat and the cause of much merriment.

But ATA was like that. If you could fly they would take you on even if you had shrapnel in your chest or one eye or one arm. I guess that too was thanks to the vision of Cdr. Macmillan and Commodore D'Erlanger and their medical team. Some of the pilots seemed rather old, but experience is worth a lot in flying, and flying experience keeps eyes, mind, hands and feet coordinating. Even old birds fly!

We have remained in touch, and expect to as long as life lasts. During the war about 10% of the pilots – men and women – lost their lives, mainly through being caught out by the weather. There were also deaths among the flight engineers and nursing staff, and one ATC cadet was killed. Now we are a crew dwindling through natural wastage but the spirit that kept us together on the ground and in the air will still be valued as long as the Air Transport Auxiliary is remembered.

The Secret War of the Autogyros

Squadron Leader Basil Arkill

So shrouded in secrecy were the operations of the Cierva autogyros during the 1939–45 war that few people, even within the RAF itself, were aware of what they were and what they were doing. Yet without their vital contribution, the crucial Battle of Britain might never have been won.

Only those directly involved were in the know.

My own involvement with these rotary wing aircraft came about in a somewhat roundabout way. With a background of Coastal Command training in the year before the war and a short spell with Bomber Command, all my flying experience was with conventional fixed wing aircraft.

Whilst flying with 500 Squadron I had a slight argument with a tree on a dawn take-off in patchy fog conditions and I finished up in hospital. It took nearly a year to patch me up and I came out with the ignominious medical category of A4h Bh, which meant fit for ground duties at home (UK) only. I was posted to the School of GR as a ground instructor but, though still partly disabled, I managed to scrounge a bit of flying when I wasn't lecturing.

I was able to get the CO to give me a letter confirming that I was capable of flying certain aircraft in spite of the disability. Eventually, I managed to persuade the medics to upgrade my category to A2 B1 but they limited it to single-engined aircraft as they maintained my injured leg would not be able to hold a multi-engined aircraft in the event of partial engine failure. So I had to remain instructing at the School of GR as there were no single-engined aircraft in Coastal Command.

After about a year, I heard that I was down for a posting to the flying boat operational training unit as chief ground instructor (CGI). The idea of being permanently grounded was anathema to me so I had a rapid look around for some alternative, and as it happened I was lucky. A propaganda rumour had appeared in the press that a marvellous new aircraft, called a helicopter, had been invented to fly from the deck of independently routed merchant ships to give them their own individual anti-submarine patrol. It was to be the key to winning the Battle of the Atlantic, so I quickly slapped in an application to be posted to these novel aircraft.

I heard afterwards that when my application was passed up to Coastal Command, they, not having any helicopters on their strength, asked Fighter Command whether they had any. Fighter Command, apparently not knowing the difference – as few did – between a helicopter and an autogyro, said they had – in No. 529 squadron, so there I was posted.

When I first saw the Cierva autogyros on the small grass airfield at Halton, I was inspecting them intently to see how depth charges could be fitted for the anti-submarine role. But after the ribald laughter had died down I had the real nature of the machines and their use explained to me. One demonstration flight in a dual control machine and I was completely hooked by this novel form of flying, so that thoughts of anti-submarine operations were relegated to some possible time in the future.

The secrecy surrounding these unusual aircraft was part and parcel of the secrecy surrounding that now famous British invention, radar: the radio detection and ranging of distant airborne targets.

By the beginning of 1939, a chain of radar stations had been set up, under No. 60 Group, Fighter Command, at intervals along the east and south coasts of England amid conditions of utmost secrecy. At first it was by no means as accurate and reliable as its inventors had predicted. Whilst its technological concept was brilliant, in practice its accuracy depended on the precise calibration of its highly sensitive aerials, which emitted a signal to detect the range, elevation and azimuth of an approaching aircraft.

During the summer of 1939 persistent efforts were made to find a reliable means of calibrating the aerials. Fixed-wing aircraft and even unmanned balloons were tried but with little success, and it was not until the war had actually started that the solution came. As in so many other things, it came from an unexpected source.

One of the Cierva company's flying instructors in its pre-war autogyro flying school had been an observer in the Royal Flying Corps during the 1914–18 war. He was still in the Reserve of Air Force Officers, volunteered for service when war was declared and was promptly accepted by Air Ministry for intelligence duties. There he came to hear of the radar calibration problem and suggested that possibly the Cierva autogyros could be used. As a result, in November 1939 the Cierva company were awarded a six-month trial contract, with one C.30, one pilot, and supporting crew. The autogyro was fitted with a special electronic device which responded to the radar beam and the trial was conducted by the company's chief pilot 'Reggie' Brie.

The results were immediate and eminently successful. Air Ministry extended the contract to six autogyros initially and this in due course led to the establishment of No. 1448 Flight based at RAF Duxford. Like the coastal radar stations, it was administered by No. 60 Group to ensure close co-ordination between the two. From then onward, intense pressure for the autogyros built up. All the radar controllers around the coasts wanted their aerial systems calibrated as a matter of greatest urgency. Everyone expected aerial attack but no one knew exactly where it would come from. There were no RAF pilots with any experience of rotating wings so Reggie Brie made contact with as many of the civilian pilots who had learned to fly the autogyros in peacetime before the war at Cierva's Hanworth flying school. To a man they dropped everything and worked like Trojans, flying up and down the country to get the radar stations calibrated. For some time they flew as civilian pilots, but eventually they were commissioned into the RAF.

Cierva Autogyro (Westlands)

Cierva's chief test pilot, Alan Marsh, was promoted to Squadron Leader as the unit's Commanding Officer. As the requirement grew, more regular RAF pilots were posted in and were trained in the autogyro techniques. Quite a number of them were partly disabled, like myself, from various operational injuries.

On the maintenance side, Cierva's chief maintenance engineer was appointed the unit's engineer officer and he brought a number of his prewar staff to service the autogyros. Maintenance personnel were not so much of a problem as the C.30's construction was based on the Avro Cadet two-seater trainer.

When the Cierva company finalised the C.30 design in 1934, they licensed the Avro company to put it into production because the fuselage of their Cadet biplane was perfectly suited to the rotating wing design and its use saved time and expense. As modified for the autogyro, the rotor pylon was fitted in place of the main-plane centre section. Just one control was needed – a hanging stick connected to the fully articulated rotor head, which allowed the rotor to be tilted in any direction. This replaced the conventional ailerons and rudder on fixed wing aircraft. The engine and other design modifications followed standard engineering practice and could easily be learned by conventional RAF fitters and riggers.

Reggie Brie, meanwhile, was scouring the country for additional C.30s and spare parts that had been sold by the Cierva company to its prewar customers since 1934. Many had gone overseas, but he managed to locate sixteen in reasonably airworthy condition. These were all requisitioned by Air Ministry to be added to the complement of 1448 Flight.

Later, the Flight was accorded squadron status and became No. 529 Squadron. It was moved from Duxford to RAF Halton with Sqn Ldr Marsh still remaining CO Reggie Brie himself, by then promoted to Wing Commander, was sent on a special mission attached to the British Air Commission in Washington DC, to investigate the prospect of either of the American helicopter developments by Sikorsky or Bell being sufficiently advanced to replace the autogyros in due course for radar calibration. For radar calibration, the helicopter would have been ideal but they were not fully developed at that time.

The fundamental requirement was for a vehicle able to maintain a stationary position in the air at various heights and distances from the radar station to enable the radar controller to beam on to the electronic response device with which it was fitted. Thus he could check the angles of elevation and azimuth of his aerials and calibrate his detecting instrumentation accordingly.

The autogyro could not maintain stationary hovering flight because its rotor was not powerdriven like the helicopter. It could fly very slowly under complete control, though, down to about 25 mph, and the autogyro pilots devised a special flying technique to enable the machine to come very near to the hovering capability.

The procedure was to slow down to minimum airspeed which put the machine into a slightly nose-up attitude with the stick held back, then apply left stick to initiate a left turn: as the turn steepened the stick was moved back a little more and to the right to hold off bank. The effect was as if the machine was side-slipping into a steep turn, but without losing height, while it gyrated around a tight axis, balanced between hanging on the propeller and rotor.

We used to call this manoeuvre 'orbiting', and it could be held for several minutes with constant juggling between engine throttle and rotor tilt to maintain the required height. In high winds or gusty conditions it became more difficult to hold a constant position but we could operate satisfactorily on the calibration in winds up to around 15–20 mph.

The call for a radar station to be serviced always came through Group HQ, and the C.30 would be dispatched promptly to the nearest RAF airfield to the radar station. Sometimes a machine might be sent direct from completing another calibration in the area to save the autogyros having to fly back to base between jobs. Normal cruising speed was only about 60-65 mph so positioning would otherwise have absorbed too many valuable flying hours. One fitter and one rigger would be sent overnight by road to the airfield selected, with the tools needed to set up their maintenance facility. There was usually some hangar space available.

When the pilot arrived he and the radar controller would check over any local variations to the standard calibration pattern. This comprised plotting a semi-circular track of ten miles radius to seaward of the radar station and marking off some ten to twelve positions along it at fifteen degree intervals. His job was to start at one end orbiting the first position and switch on the electronic responder which we called the 'squegg'. The radar controller and pilot were in constant touch over the R/T, so he would confirm when he had completed any adjustment to his aerials. The pilot would then move off to the second position around the track and the aerial adjustments began again and so on. As we moved out to positions over the sea, we would mark the new position to be orbited by throwing out an aluminium sea marker. These would last long enough before disintegrating to let the radar technicians make their adjustments.

Depending on wind speed and direction, the time taken to fly from one position to the next would be about six or seven minutes. Adding a few more minutes for each orbit, it was never possible to get right round the track in one sortie. About half-way round would be average with the amount of fuel carried. Maximum endurance of the C.30 was in the order of two hours, so that at least one refuelling trip back to the airfield would be usual. In reasonable weather, though, and if the radar technicians' adjustments went smoothly, a day's flying could complete a calibration at one particular height.

The somewhat elderly Genet Major engines, which powered the C.30s, used to give us some food for thought as we moved out towards the seaward positions around the track. We used to check the magnetos very carefully before leaving the comparative safety of the beach. A forced landing through engine failure over land presented few problems. The C.30 could be set down on almost any small patch of ground.

Over water, though, it was a different matter. We were never out of sight of land but for most of the time we were out of reach of land, as the C.30's gliding angle was steep without power so ditching would be inevitable. With the fuselage alone having the buoyancy of a brick, it was reckoned that the machine would sink quickly enough for the rotor to give the pilot a resounding crack on the head as he tried to get out. The rotor brake was not effective enough to stop the rotor when it was turning at flying revolutions, so the ditching drill we planned had to allow for this. The idea was to bring the autogyro down straight and level until the undercarriage was about to touch the water surface at zero airspeed, then apply full right stick quickly to tilt the rotor into the sea first to break the blades and hope to get out on the left side before the machine rolled right over. We thanked our lucky stars, and our engine fitters, that none of us ever had to put it to the test throughout the war years.

We orbited mostly at between 500 and 1000 feet. Sometimes the radar controller would ask for different heights at one position. At other times we would go right round the track at one height then repeat the performance at different heights as required. To complete a full calibration of a radar station could take anything from two or three days to more than a week or two.

The requirement continued throughout the war, as regular calibration checks had to be made every few months. Squadron personnel remained virtually unchanged throughout the war years, but in 1944 a few of us were detached to a US Coast Guard unit to convert to the early helicopters which were then coming into service.

We returned in 1945 with a number of Sikorsky R.4 helicopters, but it was then too late for these to be considered as replacements for No. 529 Squadron's C.30s. So it was to the Cierva C.30s that the credit goes for their crucial contribution to providing Fighter Command operation room controllers with the accurate information about incoming enemy bombers they needed to get their fighter squadrons up into the most advantageous position to intercept. The radar controllers had to get the elevation accuracy of their aerials precisely correct, or otherwise the intercepting fighters might be directed to heights below the incoming bombers.

In all, the autogyros flew just over 9000 hours in this calibration role during the five years of war. Not a bad effort for a bunch of second-hand aircraft operated by a bunch of 'amateur' and partly disabled pilots.

Prisoner of War

F. J. Crewe

On the 3 August 1943, 610 Squadron was briefed to attack Guipavas airfield and destroy the aircraft prior to a raid of Typhoon Bombers (Bomphoons), which were scheduled to attack airfield installations.

We took off around 1800 hrs GMT, crossed the Channel below 50 ft and started climbing at the French coast some twenty-three or twenty-four minutes later. Halfway up the climb to 6500 ft, some enemy aircraft could be seen already airborne and others were taking off. The Squadron dived and attacked those airborne, and I was hit by an explosive cannon in my engine. By this time I was very low, but had plenty of speed (415 mph). Pulling back the control column, undoing my safety harness straps, I called my CO on the radio and said I was hit and wouldn't be home tonight. He wished me luck. I expected to get high enough to bale out. However, by this time, my speed had decayed with little gain in height. Speed was about 120 mph and height just under 400 ft, much too low to jump out of the Spitfire. My windscreen was covered with oil and I could see nothing ahead. I opened the hood and saw that my engine cowlings had been blown out to about forty degrees; I saw a field to the left and headed for it. It meant coming over or through some trees; so I let the machine stall into the field: in so doing I was flung violently against the right hand side of the cockpit, from which I received a hard blow on my head. I regained my senses and found I was about twenty-five yards from the aircraft. The time being about 1835 hrs GMT.

On recovering consciousness I released my parachute harness and staggered to the corner of the field. I rested for a few moments and walked along a hedge-bounded track. At a junction, a figure appeared and enjoined me to follow him. He led me to a point where, with the help of a woman, he obtained a towel and water to bathe my head. We continued and later he obtained some food and drink before proceeding further away from the crash site. Eventually he found a cornfield where he advised me to rest. He also indicated that the Germans were present in a village, whose church spire could be clearly seen in the full moonlight. After resting for a few minutes, I passed out, and recovered about thirty minutes later.

I then started to walk around the field for about an hour, after which I lay down again to rest. Same result: passed out and recovered about twenty-five to thirty minutes later. On coming round I decided to try and reach the church despite the fact that there were Germans in the village. I found a road so I kept to the hedgerows until I came to another road. Taking off my shoes I walked along this road until I came to the gates of the churchyard. I quietly opened the gates and came face to face with two German soldiers having a quiet smoke. They asked if I was a friend, but I quickly I disillusioned them and was promptly marched off to their guardroom.

My wound was dressed, and apart from a short interrogation by the Detachment Commander, a German Lieutenant, who recorded my number, rank and name, I was left to sleep. I slept for about four hours and was woken and told that I was to be taken to the place where my aircraft had crashed. After a small fiasco with a motor cycle which would not start, I was taken by car to the crash site. There I was handed over to the *Luftwaffe*. A Feisler Storch landed in the field whilst I was there. I was then taken to Guipavas airfield where I spent the rest of that day, Thursday, Friday, Saturday and part of Sunday in the Sick Quarters. On the Sunday, another pilot and myself were taken by train from Brest to Frankfurt am Maine where I was escorted into the interrogation centre sited on the outskirts – *Dulag Luft*.

Whilst in the sick quarters where the interrogation was quite casual and not intensive, a German pilot visited me: he was the leader of one of the Fw-190 Squadrons and claimed he was the man who shot me down. His name was Lieutenant Joseph (Sepp) Wurmheller. I discovered many years later that he was killed during the early days of the 'Invasion'.

On arrival at *Dulag Luft*, I was placed in solitary confinement. The cell was about eight foot by five foot. There were no facilities in the cell and the food was totally inadequate. The weather was quite hot, but the heating was kept turned on. Rather uncomfortable.

The *Luftwaffe* was aware that the aircraft in which I had been flying was a modified type of Spitfire. As far as I know, it was the first of its kind to fall into German hands, albeit in a pretty sorry state. Their interrogation was persistent and was totally aimed at trying to get information concerning this particular type of Spitfire. I was equally determined that all they were going to get out of me was my number, rank and name. My stubbornness caused at least two confrontations with officers senior to myself. One threatened to hand me over to the Gestapo to be shot. With all the arrogance of 'youth' I told him that they couldn't shoot me as I was a British Officer. This resulted in two days without food – only water, and no visit to the toilet.

They made one more attempt to get information, and after another eight hours they released me into the transit camp to await transport to Stalag Luft III at Sagan. My total time in the interrogation cells was ten days. A further seven days was spent awaiting the cattle-trucks to take us to Sagan.

On arrival at *Luft* III late 29/30 August, I was encased in the Centre Camp (or compound) where I was pleased to see several colleagues who had met similar misfortunes to me, but were alive and well.

Stalag Luft III was an Aircrew Officers' Camp. It comprised several lagers or compounds known as Centre, East, North, and later West camps, and a sub-camp or lager about three to four km away called *Belaria Stalag Luft* IIIA. In addition there were several German lagers housing their administration, accommodation and hospital.

By the end of 1943, Centre Camp had become predominantly USAF/USAAC so the RAF (myself included) and Allied air force personnel were moved to *Stalag Luft* IIIA at Belaria in January 1944. It is worth noting that East Camp was the compound from which the famous Wooden Horse escape took place mid- to end-September 1943.

North Camp was the compound from which the long Tom, Dick and Harry tunnels were dug, one of which was broken in the middle of 1944, and as a consequence fifty of the officers who escaped were murdered by the Gestapo.

During the period September 1943 until January 1944, I was involved in various camp activities: a bit of tunnel digging, amateur theatricals, the odd game of football and a little cricket. Sagan camp was built in a pinewood coniferous tree forest; the soil very thin and sandy. When one dug deeper than about one or two feet, it was very bright yellow. This fact caused considerable problems to tunnellers because this bright yellow sand had to be dispersed. Centre Camp tunnels were relatively short, but one can imagine the problem in North Camp, where they had three tunnels on the go (eventually only one), each of which was very, very long. After our move to Belaria, where the sub-soil was clay (it being slightly higher than Sagan), escape projects were always being progressed, but none was completely successful.

By the middle of 1944 (6 June to be precise) the 'Invasion' occurred and the Russian 'Steam Roller' had got into top gear. By the onset of the 1944 winter, refugees were passing Belaria in increasing numbers. The two local airfields which had been used for training and as staging posts, became front-line operational airfields. Shortly after the Invasion, we saw the Arado 234 Twin Jet Bomber and the Me 262 Twin Jet Fighter flying around. Just after Christmas 1944, we were marched out of Belaria and Sagan and made our way westwards ahead of the Russian advance. After ten or twelve days of marching (the first eight of which was in very very cold weather), we boarded some cattle trucks and arrived at the multi-national camp of Luchenwalde, about forty km south-west of Berlin.

In early April, an attempt was made to move us again, this time to Southern Germany. It was unsuccessful because the Germans just hadn't got the rolling stock to handle such a large contingent. Food by this time was very scarce, and rations were not enough to really keep us alive. We all lost considerable weight and were pretty weak when the Russians arrived on 22 April 1945.

After another month of hanging about, the Russians provided transport to take us to the River Elbe, where we walked across a pontoon bridge and boarded US Army trucks which took us to the airfield at Halle-Leipzig, where we waited for the weather to clear for flights to Brussels. Four days later we arrived in Brussels: one night stop, then a short one hour twenty minutes flight to UK, arriving on 28 May 1945.

Memoirs of a Squadron Medical Officer

Noel Murphy

In 1943 I was Senior House Surgeon at the Southend General Hospital. I heard that 125 (Newfoundland) Squadron was being formed and knew that the Newfoundland Government was anxious to staff the Squadron as far as possible with Newfoundlanders: I was a Newfoundlander, volunteered and was offered the position of Squadron Medical Officer .

After basic training (including foot drill!) and a spell at RAF Hospital Halton, I was sent to Abingdon, a training centre. Here new bomber crews were going out over enemy occupied territory at night to drop leaflets and to get the feel of coming under anti-aircraft fire.

My duties included daily sick parades and night duty in case of accidents or emergencies. I was surprised at the young age of the aircrews, and whilst I understood their excitement and enthusiasm, I soon became aware of their stress and anxiety as they trained and went on sorties.

On one of my first mornings I was called by the SMO (Station Medical Officer) to fly to the West Country and bring back a crew whose plane had just crashed. The pilot had been killed. Fortunately none of the remaining aircrew were injured but they were very depressed, shaken up and silent. I could do little to cheer them up.

The day after I took up my duties, SMO advised me that I was now in charge of the Decompression Unit. I had no idea what this was. A good way to begin.

The operators took me into the unit, where we put oxygen masks around our necks, but not over our faces. The idea was to simulate air pressure at varying heights. Individuals show varying signs and symptoms due to the lack of oxygen, finally resulting in loss of consciousness. I had a writing pad and a pencil. My mask was still around my neck when the altimeter showed 20,000 feet. They suggested I start writing a nursery rhyme. I began writing 'Mary had a little lamb' and was suddenly aware of a voice saying 'Well go on writing, Sir', and realised my oxygen mask was on my face and that my writing had drifted off to a few senseless scribbles. The altimeter was at 32,000 feet. They explained that I had begun to get disoriented at 23,000 feet and lost consciousness at 29,000 feet. They put on my mask and I recovered. I now knew what our aircrew would go through if they were not prepared in advance.

The staff and ground crew of the station had their normal quota of illness and accidents. The Bomber aircrews were somewhat different. They too had their quota of illness and accidents, but some were showing signs of anxiety and stress. It must not be forgotten that part of their training was genuine wartime activity over enemy territory and they were facing live anti-aircraft fire and the real possibility of being killed, wounded, or taken prisoner.

One had to be very careful to diagnose these cases. None of them were cowards. They were on active service and some were stronger than others. It was easy to say that some might not be fit for the duties they were expected to perform – but it was important to me to try to find out what they were experiencing and the effects of these pressures.

I went to the SMO and explained that I would have a much better understanding of the problem if I could go with an aircrew over enemy territory and learn for myself what they were experiencing. He felt I had a point, and would see what he could do. Next day he told me it was agreed, and I would be flying two nights later.

That evening I realised I had better make some preparations. I had to make my will and write letters to my Wife and to my Mother – just in case! As I sat there trying to put my feelings into words I began to understand what these young men were going through as they underwent their training. Next day I felt I had a somewhat different outlook on life, and the realisation sank in even more.

On the day I was to fly, the SMO sent for me – 'This signal has just come in. You have been posted to 125 Squadron at Exeter and you are to leave immediately. Goodbye and good luck.' I had two distinct feelings. First a sense of relief that I would not have to worry about the danger of a flight over enemy territory, and secondly the excitement of my posting to the Squadron.

The Squadron ground staff were already aware that I was a Newfoundlander, and they wasted no time in telling me about their problems and seeking my help. They were from various places in Newfoundland and they were upset because they had seen advertisements inviting them to join the RAF as aircrew. But after joining it was discovered that they did not have the necessary educational qualifications or ability. Mostly they had been fishermen, miners or woodsmen, and few had finished schooling, starting work at ages ranging from twelve up. Few of the aircrew were Newfoundlanders, for this was a night fighter squadron.

Next day I was on night duty. It meant that I was to sleep in Sick Quarters and be available for any emergencies. I quickly fell asleep and was awakened at about 2 a.m. by banging on the door. Somebody shouted 'Come on, Doc, we have an emergency. The ambulance is waiting'. An officer said 'We think a plane has crashed and you had better go look for it.' I asked what kind of plane and in what direction. He thought it was a Lightning and vaguely pointed towards the south-east. 'Good luck' he said, and I took off down the stairs.

After driving in the pitch dark along the country lanes we saw a fire burning in the middle of a ploughed field. The flames were lighting it up and we could see that it was mud all the way. Ammunition was exploding, machine gun bullets and cannon shells were going in all directions. We moved as close as we could to try to find the pilot. If he was alive and injured he might be somewhere close. If he was dead we might be able to see him in the wreck. We moved around in case he had parachuted, but we found nothing. Shortly afterwards the Royal Marines sent out a search team and found the pilot several hundred yards from the crash. He had jumped but there was not enough time for his chute to open before he hit the ground, and his body was about six feet into the soft earth.

Back at Sick Quarters I found that my uniform was covered in mud. It was the only one I had and my Corporal arranged to have it cleaned, meanwhile providing me with a Battle Dress. Before my uniform came back we had a visit from the Group Medical Officer. He told me in no uncertain terms that I was not allowed to wear Battle Dress, but when I explained what had happened he saw my point of view. A few days later I was advised that we would in future be allowed to wear Battle Dress on duty. Later we wore it all the time.

I felt strongly that while I was a doctor carrying out regular duties, I was also caring for a group of Newfoundlanders who were far away from their native land and I felt responsible for their well-being. I let them know that I was available to help if they ever needed me. There were inevitably times when news from home was about family deaths, or illness, or they may have got into trouble in one way or another. Not long after I was made Welfare Officer.

One night I was called to Dispersal as one of our planes appeared to be in difficulty. I found the Flight Commander talking to the pilot who was preparing to land. He said he was at 18,000 feet and was letting down his undercarriage. The Flight Commander told me that there was a real problem, and he was looking to me to help. I began to talk to the pilot. I felt it possible that he was short of oxygen and disoriented. I asked him to check his oxygen line but he said he was too busy. I told him I couldn't hear him and asked him to come down a couple of thousand feet. Grudgingly he agreed and in a minute said he was now at 16,000 feet. I said I still could not hear him and asked him to come down further. He complied but not very willingly. Again I said I couldn't hear him and asked him to come down even further. By the time he got to 12,000 feet he was getting the required amount of oxygen and recovered. I asked him again to check his line and he found that it was trapped under his seat and his oxygen had been cut off.

Early one morning one of our planes returned shot up, but still able to fly. The Observer had been hit in the leg. There was an entrance wound but no exit. It appeared that there might be a foreign body embedded and it should be X-rayed. We had no X-ray machine, so he would have to be sent to a Hospital in Exeter. He asked me to do something, as he was due to go on leave that morning and did not wish to lose any time. Before I joined the RAF I had rigged a small portable radio with a metal probe, which when it made contact with metal would indicate where it was located. I had brought it with me and this seemed a good time to use it. It worked like a charm: I located the bullet in his thigh, removed it, applied a dressing and told him to report to the nearest hospital if any problem developed.

One morning at about 9.30 a.m. two of our ground crew came to my office and complained that they had been unable to get breakfast, being told that they were too late. They had been rearming, refuelling and maintaining planes which had been very active through the previous night. They asked for my assistance. I went to the Airmen's Mess and found a group standing outside the locked door. I told them to wait and went to the Mess Officer's office. He said that they did not serve breakfast after 9 a.m. I reminded him in no uncertain terms that there was a war on. We were in the middle of it. We were on active service and all hands had worked through the night servicing the planes. They did not stop what they were doing for meals nor did the aircrews. I demanded he feed the men without any further delay. He lamely agreed and let the men in. As an apology he gave them bacon and eggs! – usually reserved for aircrew. They were delighted and so was I. I made a lot of friends that day!

The next morning the Tower advised me that a plane was approaching with wounded personnel on board. A transport plane landed and I went up to it and waited patiently beside the door. Strangely there was not a sound from inside. After several minutes I called for a ladder, opened the door and saw a plane full of people. Every seat was occupied and not one showed any sign of life. There was no sound from the cockpit. It was creepy! I moved to the nearest person and gently shook him. He gave a slight groan and moved a little. He was alive. I tried the next one and the same thing happened. Gradually the entire plane came to life. As I reached the door to the cockpit it opened and a very sleepy crew member appeared. The plane had come from North Africa with a complete load of wounded. The Southern half of Britain was enshrouded by fog and they just had to keep flying North until they found a clear landing field. There were approximately sixty wounded on board. I took over and we started to move the patients to Sick Quarters where we could sort them all out. It was now clear that they had been flying for about twelve hours, and they had been lulled into a sort of trance by the sound of the engines. They were all exhausted – even the crew. We transferred them all to the Sick Quarters.

About mid-January I developed a bad cold which turned into pneumonia. A chest X-ray suggested that I had Pulmonary Tuberculosis. It was decided that I should proceed on sick leave immediately for treatment. After about three weeks I was re-X-rayed and declared fit to return to active service. I was, however, posted to Martlesham for light duty, very disappointed that I was not allowed back to the Squadron.

THE MEDITERRANEAN

On 10 July 1943 the invasion of Italy began with landings on Sicily under cover of a huge air umbrella. As the landings became established, temporary airstrips were constructed to provide better air cover.

Italy surrendered on 3 September 1943.

The capture of major airfields such as are those around Foggia enabled the strategic air forces to relocate from their bases in North Africa. They were now better placed to carry out offensive raids on the Romanian oil fields and also to try to help the tragic uprising of partisans in Warsaw.

Invasion of Sicily

Wing Commander H. D. Costain MBE

I was a pilot with No. 154 Squadron which took part in the Allied 'TORCH' landings and the subsequent Tunisian campaign, and fought until the Axis surrender on the Cape Bon peninsula. We moved from Protville in North Africa to Takali in Malta at the end of May 1943 to prepare for the invasion of Sicily. I think that without exception, when we landed at Takali, every pilot remarked that their engines sounded rough as we crossed out on the long sea crossing. However, our battle-weary Spifires performed well and the flight to Malta and landing at Takali went without incident.

Imagine a sun-baked dusty airfield with a short concrete runway attached to one end, having an influx of five extra squadrons – approximately ninety aircraft. That was Takali, where preparations began for the forthcoming invasion of Sicily. The atmosphere was tense as there was still the ever-present danger that the Axis Air Forces still were capable of attacking a crowded airfield. In the blast bays the ground crews placed wooden supports under the wings in an endeavour to fool any reconnaissance aircraft that they were dummies. Aircraft were kept on continuous standby.

Operations prior to the invasion were sweeps over the Sicilian airfields trying to entice the German and Italian Air Forces to engage our aircraft, which they were loath to do. These fighter sweeps were extended to Catania and the Messina Straits. Interspersed with the sweeps the Squadron escorted Marauder, Mitchell, Fortress and Warhawk bombers attacking the airfields and troop concentrations. Additionally convoy patrols were carried out and these increased as the invasion force approached Sicily. The Battleships HMS Rodney and Nelson were among the RN ships escorted.

On 10 July 1943 Sicily was invaded and an extract from the Squadron Diary reads:

> 'Sicily invaded: Throughout the day we patrolled beaches of Sicily covering the ground forces. Nine aircraft are airborne at 0530 hours to patrol 'CENT' beaches. Nothing to report. Landings being made at Scalambri area and cruisers seen shelling the Gela area. All aircraft landed safely at 0700 hours. We were airborne over the (CENT) beaches, fires were observed at Gela and Comiso. Eight Me 109s attacked, of which one was destroyed by W/Cdr. Gray DSO DFC and one damaged by P/O Costain. One of our aircraft crash-landed at base having been damaged by enemy action. The pilot was uninjured. The last patrol of the day landed at 1900 hours with nothing to report. Weather was good all day. Total flying hours for the day 51 hours 55 minutes.'

In the following days air operations were continued in support of the land forces. Patrols and bomber escorts were carried out in the Gela to Scalambri area from first light to dusk. Although enemy aircraft were sighted no further engagements took place. As the invasion progressed patrols and escorts were extended to cover (ACID) Beaches and further north to Catania where heavy predicted Flak and intense low level flak was experienced.

Six days after the landings the Squadron received orders at lunch time to embark the main party of ground crew for a move to Sicily. The aircraft were to continue to operate from

Spitfires at Salerno (AHB)

Takali until the ground crews were ready to receive them in Sicily. At 1630 hrs the same day 154 Squadron moved from Takali to embark on an LST at Valetta. This operation went off without a hitch and by 2100 hrs the squadron had pulled out of the harbour and the white bastions of the fortress shimmering in the moonlight, fell back into the depths of the night. All ranks received the most cordial hospitality from their opposite numbers on the ship and the night was quite uneventful. Sicily was sighted at about 0710 hrs the following morning and the squadron disembarked at Syracuse at 1200 hrs.

There was considerable activity at the quay where a number of landing craft were in the process of disembarking. The fastest route out of the port was taken through dirty uncleaned streets. The freshness of the orange and lemon groves were welcomed and the main party pitched camp in a meadow two miles south of Priolo.

Meanwhile 154 Squadron aircraft had been in action again: 'At 0800 hrs the squadron went on patrol over Gerbini and Catania areas. Enemy aircraft were sighted on this patrol and in the ensuing engagements, one Me 109 was destroyed and two probably destroyed. One Macchi was also destroyed. One of our aircraft was damaged by enemy action, it crash landed at base, the pilot was uninjured.'

The Squadron ground crews were not to stay at Priolo for long, and the next day were ordered to move to Lentini. They were on the road by 1800 hrs. The road had been practically undamaged by the enemy except in one place where a bridge had been blown up, necessitating a not inconsiderable detour to cross the river further upstream. All along the road especially in Carlentini the local people appeared to give the convoy a genuine ovation, showing the 'V' sign and giving presents of fruit. The airmen responded with gifts of cigarettes.

The Squadron reached its destination, a newly made airstrip south of Lago di Lentini. Camp was set up on a wooded bluff about a mile from the airstrip. As the front line was only a very short distance away guards were doubled. The Squadron aircraft were expected to fly in from Malta the next day.

The aircraft arrived at Lentini at 1715 hrs and within the hour were airborne, patrolling the base area. Operations now moved to the North of Sicily and sweeps and escorts were concentrated around Milazzo and the sea areas around the volcanic islands of Stromboli and Lipari. The Germans and Italians were preparing to evacuate Sicily and retreat to mainland Italy. The escorted bombers – mainly Baltimores and Bostons – concentrated their attacks on Milazzo and the neighbouring beach, as Ju 52s were using the beach to supply and evacuate the retreating Axis armies. On 25 July, three Squadrons from the Wing intercepted the Ju 52s landing and had a field day destroying many and damaging others.

The Lentini airstrips were not the easiest to operate from. They were sited at right angles to each other. The drill if Lentini East and West were scrambled together was that East kept low after take off and West climbed – very dodgy at times! In addition we had the ever present dust problems. An oil filter was manually fitted to the intake prior to take-off, and immediately wheels were lifted and before airspeed had built up, the procedure was to throttle back and throw it off. If a pilot was not quick enough the filter stayed in place and acted as an airbrake.

At this time, to avoid the very heavy flak in the Messina Straits, the squadrons flew up the west side of Mount Etna to reach patrol areas on the northern coast.

On the night of 11 August the enemy had a final fling and launched an attack on the Lentini airfields. About thirty-three bombers attacked the airfield. Dive bombing attacks were made and a number of aircraft were destroyed and damaged on the ground. Fortunately there were no casualties among squadron personnel.

On 17 August 1943 I did my last operational sortie with 154 Squadron and was posted to the Canal Zone as an instructor at 73 OTU Abu Sueir.

A Liberator Squadron in Italy 1944

Gus Taylor

Our intake travelled overnight from Naples on the backs of open trucks loaded, it seemed to us, with boxes of ammunition. We arrived at the Squadron early in the morning in late July at the same time as the crews returning from a raid, I believe, on Ploesti in Romania. Being tired and longing to get to bed, they were not best pleased to see us wandering about amongst their tents, looking for somewhere to park our kit

It might be useful here to try to describe the 178 Squadron camp. There were a couple of permanent farm buildings which served as the Squadron Headquarters – a two up and two down affair. A large Nissen hut which served as a briefing and de-briefing facility, the Officers' Mess and the Sergeants' Mess and in addition, a semi-permanent affair, the Wing Commander's caravan.

All the accommodation for the crews and camp staff consisted of tents. Tents of all types, shapes and sizes. Most of these were well past their 'sell-by date', and nearly all of them leaked and were prone to blowing down in the fierce winds which occasionally blew across Foggia Plain. This was particularly tiresome for crews returning from a long flight early in the morning. I can remember some chaps just hauling their wet beds out of the wreckage and falling asleep in the open air.

Some entrepreneurial types built huts out of old packing cases which were weatherproof and warm. The rest of us continued to put up with dripping, flapping canvas and, when winter came, dug trenches around and through our tents to prevent flooding. Having written all this, it can be said that on the whole we made ourselves more and more comfortable as the weeks went by. Latrines were in the open air in a complex consisting of about eight oil drums, suitably modified, and set in a circle surrounded, in the officers' case, by a screen of sacking. I can remember being comfortably seated in my early days on the Squadron when the Wing Commander entered. I leapt to my feet and wished him 'Good morning!' 'Morning, Gus' (my nickname) he replied, 'please carry on'.

The Officers' Mess consisted of a converted farmhouse, with a Nissen hut attached as the eating area. It was small and could only accommodate a few at a time – but the food on the whole was adequate. But no traditional bacon and eggs on our return from a trip. Bit of a myth that, certainly in our neck of the woods.

We had a bar, which was used less than might be imagined. I remember clearly a grizzled veteran of some twenty 'ops' saying to me 'Chaps who drink too much do not survive. Keep fit, Gus, there's a good fellow'. A few days later he and his crew were lost on their way back from Warsaw and old Tommy did not drink at all. Life was a bit like that – unpredictable, no pattern.

After a week or so getting used to things, the Warsaw operation took place and lasted for a couple of weeks. For many of us it was our first operational trip. I went as second pilot to Dougie Wright and his crew. A couple of days or so later, Dougie, who had been my instructor when training in South Africa, went out again and did not return. As the days went by the losses mounted and, by the time this tragic affair finished, nearly half the squadron had been lost.

Our tour continued with raids on various parts of southern Europe and the Balkans. Mainly on enemy communications, such as railway yards and bridges. We managed to hit a few. Not laser guided bombs, you understand. We just bunged them out and hoped for the best.

The opposition consisted mainly of flak accompanied by searchlights – most off-putting as they tended to blind you and if you happened to get caught in them, you attracted the full attention of the anti-aircraft gunners. Fighters we saw from time to time and if by any chance you didn't see them, it was very often terminal. They used to come and fly next to you out of range of your guns, sometimes with a red light showing. To begin with, your mid-upper and rear gunners concentrated on the so-and-so and failed to see his mate steaming in from the other direction. Bit unsporting!

Our other role was supply dropping to partisans and other underground organisations in the Balkans, mainly Jugoslavia and later Northern Italy. Most of these sorties were in daylight. We did carry out a few daylight bombing raids, including two on places in the news recently: Sarajevo and Podgerica in Montenegro.

Over Sarajevo, we collected a couple of dozen holes, lost our starboard aileron and the oxygen supply, which made us feel unnaturally cheerful and light headed until we lost height to a more healthy level. I do not believe that our beloved, faithful old X-ray ever flew again. Some wag told me that I had bent it. Briefly on that particular subject, one distinguished pilot put his aircraft u/s due to what he described as 'slow electricity'.

We dropped leaflets asking the Germans to pack it in. I have no doubt that they used them for the same purpose as we used theirs. We dropped mines in the Danube from a very low level until one crew reported that he had observed two stout poles, one on each bank of the river, connected by a length of heavy cable.

Liberator with engine on fire. Italy 1944 (AHB)

As the winter took hold, the weather became worse and operations became more hazardous. Icing, thunderstorms and low cloud and our blind landing system consisted of a row of paraffin flares each side of a pierced steel planking runway. We shared Amendola with a couple of Groups of the US Air Force B17s – Flying Fortresses. They did the day stint in massive formations over some really horrible targets and we did the night shift.

We became tour-expired in December 1944 just as we were beginning to enjoy it, and that was why we became tour-expired.

A few days after we had finished and were awaiting our next posting, an amusing if not embarrassing incident occurred. Early one morning, a long caravan of horse-drawn carts, escorted by a couple of very ancient trucks, all puffing out dark grey smoke and backfiring explosively, came down the long track, which wound down from the mountains and arrived outside the Officers' Mess. A delegation of hill farmers climbed down from the first two carts, headed by the driver of the fire-breathing lorry. Through an interpreter (an attractive young woman) they informed us that they had come to dismantle and remove the major part of the Mess. Everyone rolled around with laughter not, however, shared by our guests. 'We own it and we have come for it and we shall take it away' the leader said and so as to emphasise his point 'We have paid for it – 30,000 lire' (about £300). 'Three of your officers sold it to us last week!' 'Who were they?' we asked. Descriptions followed, which as they emerged fitted closely three not very senior officers, who had left the Squadron for a destination a good many thousand miles away! The Wing Commander took over the problem with commendable courage and tact and arranged for the Royal Air Force to reimburse our visitors plus, I believe, a small amount as damages, so we kept our dear old Mess.

It had been a hectic six months, but as you will have detected, the memories remain vivid. It was a privilege to have taken part and above all, to have shared it with some really wonderful chaps.

Some Colourful Me 109s

Air Chief Marshal Sir Peter Le Cheminant GBE KCB DFC

Sigonella was a very large field on the plain to the west of Catania. It was littered with well over a hundred Me 109s and Fw 190s in varying states of disrepair. Most were wrecks but the *Luftwaffe* had pulled out in a hurry and my flight sergeant thought he could make at least one serviceable Me 109 out of what was lying around. He asked me if I would like him to do that and I said 'yes', thinking, if I thought at all, that it would give the men a challenge and that we would probably have moved again before they were finished anyway.

I was therefore very surprised and somewhat disconcerted when two days later he beamingly informed me that the squadron now had a serviceable Me 109G which he had had sprayed red all over for recognition purposes. It was his clear expectation, and that of his team, that I would now fly the thing. To this day I don't know whether they thought they were giving me a lovely present or whether they were secretly hoping that I would break my neck – but either way I was committed.

My officers gathered, expecting I know not what. Dual controls were very uncommon during the war, and were of course non-existent in single-seaters, so one was accustomed to taking on a new aircraft without tuition: but one normally had words of advice from someone experienced on type and, crucially, one had Pilots' Notes. In this instance I had nothing, not even an ability to read German. The ground crew had managed to install an airspeed indicator calibrated in mph, so at least I was spared having to cope with km/h.

On running through the cockpit with the aid of my Flight Sergeant most things were self-explanatory. The controls were pretty standard, the only difference that I can remember was that there was no flap selector but instead a large wheel on the port side with which one wound on flap as required. I found it preferable to our normal system as there was no sudden change in trim. At that time I had not flown a Spitfire and had only the Hurricane and Tomahawk to guide me, which was not really a lot of use.

I scared myself to death on start-up because I had the throttle a bit too far advanced and the Daimler Benz 605 engine started with a huge roar, so that the aircraft was straining on the chocks for the split second before I throttled back. After that it was relatively plain sailing, the only snags being the lack of vision when taxiing and the very narrow undercarriage. I flew it on that occasion for thirty minutes and to my great relief managed to pull off a very respectable landing. Although more powerful, it was not as nice to fly as the Hurricane, and the ailerons were distinctly heavy. I flew it again the next day and regularly until mid-September, often with Freddie Rothwell, a new flight commander, for whom the ground staff had put together a second Me 109G, this time primrose yellow. We flew in the early morning, and NOTAMS (Notices to Airmen) were issued warning that two friendly 109s painted red and yellow would be flying in the area. This didn't stop us being beaten up on one occasion by twelve US Lightning P-38s in line astern. We were not sure they had seen the NOTAMS so, to be on the safe side, as they started to dive on us we cut our speed right back, lowered our undercarriage and waggled our wings.

Two days later I flew my 109 for the last time. In the afternoon Sinclair, now promoted Air Commodore and commanding the Tactical Bomber Force, came to call. Seeing my 109, nothing would do but he had to fly it, so I briefed him on the cockpit, paying particular attention to the operation of the undercarriage, which was slightly complicated until you got used to it. He seemed to take it all in and took off in fine form. He was an exceptional pilot and after some thirty minutes getting used to the aircraft he treated us to a smooth display of the most elegant low – indeed very low – aerobatics. He then came in for a tight turn on to finals, rolled out and landed: the only snag being that his undercarriage was still up and he ended up in a somewhat dramatic cloud of dust. I went out in a Jeep to bring him back, expecting him to be full of apologies for breaking my splendid aeroplane. To my total astonishment, far from being contrite, he tore me off a tremendous strip for not having briefed him properly. How he had the barefaced gall to do it I don't know; but perversely I have always admired him for it – *l'audace, toujours l'audace*!

Me109 and Spitfire servicing. Sicily 1943 (AHB)

A Different Kind of Rescue

C. W. Meacock

I joined the Air Sea Rescue unit at Gorleston in January 1942. This consisted of three High Speed Launches (HSL), endearingly known as 'Whalebacks' because of their low, sleek appearance in the water and a superstructure shaped like a whale's back.

The crew consisted of a commissioned Skipper, two NCO Coxswains, three motor-boat crewmen, a Wireless Operator and a Wireless Mechanic, a Medical or Nursing Orderly and two Fitters Marine.

By September 1943 I was in North Africa at Mersa Matruh. Our craft this time was American, nicknamed 'Miami'. This was better suited to overseas conditions. In the UK we had lived ashore. Here we lived, prepared food and ate on board.

Following the surrender of Italy the Germans took over most of the islands in the Eastern Aegean. The British mounted an expedition to occupy the Dodecanese but by October their position was hopeless and it was decided to evacuate as many as possible.

We were directed to sail from Mersah to Alexandria where we were victualled for a long journey – our armament checked and ammunition topped up. We had twin VGOs in the two gun turrets (Vickers Gas Operated machine guns). Our initial destination was Paphos in Cyprus where we stayed for a day or so checking all of our equipment and supplies. Next we headed for Castelrosso, a very small island off Turkey which was a very convenient supply base for craft operating in the Dodecanese. It was kept supplied by Sunderland aircraft operating from Fanara on the lakes of the Suez Canal.

Two of our Miamis had been attacked by German fighter planes at the cost of one German aircraft. A deck hand on one of the launches had a go at them and one was reported to have crashed further up the coast.

We now headed for Budrum in Turkey which involved sailing close to Rhodes and other islands already occupied by the Germans. The journey had therefore to be made under cover of darkness. We could not silence our engines but the Germans mistook them for aircraft engines, and their searchlights were directed to the sky. This allowed us to get past and safely into Budrum harbour. Neutral Turkey had many RAF and Naval craft in the harbour and I suspect a few German Gunboats on the other side.

Our orders were to go to the nearby island of Kos and rescue our servicemen who would be gathered near a certain cove. It was pitch black in the early hours of the morning when our wireless operator flashed a code letter ashore and we waited. The appropriate code letter was flashed back and embarkation started. We had gone in as close as possible and I had used a hand lead line to sound out the depths. The soldiers and airmen swam out to us and those who couldn't swim were towed out by Army Long Range Desert group lads who had some canoes. We had a launch full of passengers – far more than it was designed to carry. Someone went back to tell the others that we would be back tomorrow night at the same time. Code signals were arranged before he left.

Miami – *dressed overall at Aden, VE Day (C. Meacock)*

We did this twice and there appeared to be no more left ashore. On returning to Budrum the survivors came under the control of the Navy who were loading them on to a tank landing craft. We were then instructed to sail for Leros in the early hours of the morning, to receive an Army Captain who had been operated on for peritonitis. He came with two Army medical orderlies. We took him to Budrum where he was handed over to the Navy and we stood by for further orders.

Again very late at night two Army officers came aboard and went straight into the skipper's cabin. It was start up engines and put to sea; now of course everything was secret orders. By then we had a spot of moonlight and had realised that our charts for these waters were not exactly reliable. The skipper asked me to go up to the bow and keep an eye open for sand banks or rocks. Sure enough somewhere off Samos we were heading for a nice pile of rocks. I could just see water breaking over them and we altered course to miss them. The moonlight helped on this occasion.

I estimated we were heading for a place on the coast of Turkey somewhere in the region of the Island of Khios. However we heaved to in a bay and the skipper ordered the dinghy to be launched. Our two guests appeared from the cabin and came on deck and I was asked to take them ashore.

As I neared the shore I could see figures there to greet my two passengers. It was a sandy beach, so we grounded and they hopped ashore, waved goodbye and disappeared into the darkness. The senior officer was Lt Col the Earl Jellicoe DSO MC.

I returned to the launch and the dinghy was hauled aboard. We then left and headed for a small cove to anchor, for it would soon be daylight. We covered our launch with camouflage nets. Having set watches, the crew got down to some sleep, leaving one man on deck to keep watch. The night passed well and the sea was calm. It happened that I had the watch that saw the sun rise and with it some 100 or so Turkish soldiers rose from behind bushes in the bay pointing their guns at the launch. I went below to the skipper's cabin and woke him and told him what was happening.

The guns were still pointed at us and an officer was waving. Very quickly the skipper outlined what was to be done. He told our Sergeant fitter to remove an ignition key from an engine panel as he wanted only one engine to start. I then rowed him ashore in our dinghy. Our dinghy was small and would only carry four people. I returned to the launch with the skipper, the Turkish Officer and one of his soldiers with instructions to bring back three more soldiers. This done the skipper explained in sign language that one engine was good and the other, well thumbs down. The Turkish Officer understood. It was time for a demonstration. The hatch into the engine room was quite small, however the skipper followed by the officer and two soldiers plus the all important sergeant fitter assembled in the engine room.

Previously the sergeant had switched the ignition on for the good engine, and the skipper pointing to the dud engine asked the sergeant to press the starter button. The engine only turned over but didn't fire. Now it was the turn of the 'thumbs up' engine. For those who don't know what a 650 horse power engine sounds like when it fires, be assured that in the confined space of the engine room it was little short of an explosion! The Turkish Officer followed quickly by his men flew through the hatch and into our well deck and requested to be rowed ashore.

Now it was a waiting game, but the skipper said that we should be allowed twenty-four hours under international law to make repairs before the launch could be impounded. Quite late in the day I rowed ashore to be given a piece of paper by the Officer, This was permission written in Turkish for us to carry out repairs.

We waited until dusk when both engines roared into life and we departed for Budrum. The skipper reported to the officer in charge of operations and was advised to return to base which was Paphos, Cyprus. All sailing in those waters was carried out during the hours of darkness.

However, before we departed we were asked to take five captured German pilots with us to Cyprus. Orders were not to talk to them. They were assembled in the well deck aft, overlooked by one of us armed with a Sten gun. It was a moonlit night with a calm sea. We sped past Rhodes where once again the Germans insisted on scanning the heavens for us. There was a man on the helm and one alongside keeping a weather eye open, also armed with a Sten gun. It was now that one of the Germans decided to speak and in perfect English said, 'You know we shouldn't be fighting one another.' I replied in a grunting voice 'Oh', my finger on the trigger, 'together Britain and Germany should conquer the world, with Britain ruling their old Empire and Germany the rest of the world and sharing out some of the spoils together' – a remarkable statement to hear when you are miles from home.

We called in to Kastelrosso on our way back to Paphos to refuel, and moored up alongside a pair of Royal Navy Motor Gun Boats. Talking about their experiences up in the Dodecanese Islands, they asked if we came across any 'E' Boats? 'No!'

They said 'We had one which we trained our guns on in the Samos Strait'. 'Oh yes?' On checking our log books, that 'E' Boat was us. Strangely enough I had seen these dark shadows close inshore but our instruction were only to fire if fired upon. I had my guns trained on them but they let us pass!

On arrival at Paphos the Germans were handed over to the Army Military police, but not before we became aware that all could speak very good English.

We were given a good meal at the base, loaded up with wine and brandy for the Officers' Mess and headed back to Alexandria.

A Miraculous Escape

Lloyd Lyne

(Awarded the Polish Cross of Valour and Warsaw Uprising Cross)

On 13 August 1944 I was the bomb aimer in a Liberator 'C' Charlie of 178 Squadron. We were based at Foggia but went to Brindisi for briefing for a supply drop on Warsaw.

The trip was long and tiresome, and five hours had elapsed before I saw the moon glistening on the great river Vistula. Soon I saw a dense pall of smoke from the city and the navigator warned us to be ready for the drop. We were down to 400 feet and the ground flashed by. Ahead we could see the ghost-like appearance of once beautiful Warsaw. Light flak was hose-piping skywards ahead and the captain sent me back to the beam gun position to try, together with the mid-upper and rear gunners, to silence some of the AA.

I left my parachute in its usual position at the front of the aircraft. Flak was tearing through the plane and the engines and wings were ablaze. We dropped the urgently needed supplies from the bomb bays and the pilot turned and dived.

General Bor-Komorowski at his Headquarters in the Old Town saw the blazing aircraft cross the Vistula, crash and explode in Paderewski Park. All still on board were killed.

For myself, I had lost consciousness and came to on an island without my flying helmet, flying boots and parachute harness. I imagined I was on an island in the Vistula and my first reaction was to try to swim away. I found I could not get up and lay there semi-conscious.

Eventually I heard voices and several German soldiers lifted me gently into a rowing boat. I was taken by lorry to a casualty station where the MO gave me an injection. I woke later in a bed with white sheets and pillows. I drifted in and out of consciousness for some time, and later Polish girls working in the hospital brought me hard boiled eggs and cakes. They also held a mirror for me. My hair had been cut off, my head was bandaged and I had face lacerations and burns. My hands were also heavily bandaged. My biggest worry was that my uniform and identity discs were gone.

About fourteen days later I was taken by stretcher to a hospital train filled with German soldiers coming from the Eastern Front. During the journey we were all given the same food – hot stews and very dark brown bread. Two tots of

HM The Queen returns a fragment of aircraft to Lloyd Lyne (Lloyd Lyne)

vodka or cognac were brought round daily but these had to be purchased. Not once did my companions fail to buy them for me.

After three days and nights we arrived at a town called Gira and I was taken to a civilian prison and put in a dark cell with damp walls and a metal door. There were two trestles with wooden boards and a blanket. I was given *ersatz* coffee, and black bread with a sweet spread.

Next day another train journey, which ended at a *Luftwaffe* station and yet another cell. Eventually I arrived at Frankfurt-am-Main and the interrogation centre *Dulag Luft*.

The first interrogator claimed to be a Red Cross official and demanded answers to all the questions on his form. These included identification of squadron, raid particulars, and other operations etc. I wrote my name and rank and number and was put into solitary confinement for four or five days with very sparse rations. I was then taken back to the office and the desk thumping interrogator said that without uniform or identity discs I would be handed over to the Gestapo as a spy.

Back to the cell and little food. After another four or five days a quiet interrogator. He accepted that I would only give name, rank and number, asked if my medical needs had been attended to and returned me to my cell.

At my next interrogation my questioner amazed me with his knowledge. He knew our training systems, the squadrons which had taken part in the supply drops and had pencilled my squadron's number on the form. He told me I would be sent to a permanent POW camp. This was music to my ears!

Two days later I was taken to a room full of aircrew from different countries. We were taken by train to a transit camp, Wetzlar. Here I had my first shower for six weeks. This was difficult as my bandages had not been taken off. We were given Red Cross items, clothing and a reasonable meal by the Red Cross.

Another long journey and eventually *Stalag Luft* I at Barth. Life here was boring and we were often short of food. We were eventually liberated on 1 May 1945 by Russian Cossacks. One column was headed by a female Lieutenant.

The Russians were extremely friendly and immediately offered to send us 1000 pigs. We accepted fifty gratefully as a first instalment! Meantime we were free to wander round and see the full horrors of the war in Germany. We saw a German family by the road, Father, Mother, children and a pram. All were shot through the head. A gun lay nearby. They had obviously decided that they would be better dead than exposed to the vengeance the Russians were taking on the civilian population. Dying slave workers were brought to the POW hospital.

After eleven days we were flown home by American Flying Fortress.

It was in 1986, my first visit to Poland since 1944, that I pieced the story together from accounts by Polish friends who had fought in the uprising and had witnessed the demise of 'C' Charlie. I must have been flung from the aircraft as it disintegrated in the air. My fall had been cushioned by small bushes and soft ground. Even if I had my parachute I would have been far too low to use it.

The people of Warsaw still remember the air crews who tried to bring them aid and the graves in the Military Cemetery in Krakow, where my friends lie, are strewn with fresh flowers, as are the numerous lone memorials to be found all over Poland.

Normandy landings

The D-Day landings on 6 of June 1944 were supported by overwhelming air power.

Allied aircraft totally dominated the battlefield. The lessons learned in North Africa about effective army-air co-operation were now put into effect.

Airspeed Horsa (Museum of Army Flying}

Stirlings and the Airborne Forces

Wing Commander H. E. Angell DFC

Early in 1943 I was appointed a Flight Commander in 196 Squadron of 3 Group Bomber Command equipped with Stirling 3 aircraft. The Squadron was moved to a holding base at RAF Leicester East and later to RAF Tarrant Rushton in 38 Group. Here we started working up to the task of towing Horsa Gliders and dropping supply containers. From there we moved to RAF Keevil on 17 March 1944 and were primarily engaged in learning to drop Parachute Troops with supply containers.

From here I carried out my first two operations over occupied France for the Special Operations Executive. On or about 3 June my crew, along with all the other designated crews, were called to a briefing at HQ 38 Group, then located at Netheravon, in preparation for Operation 'Tonga', the airborne element of Operation 'OVERLORD' and it was revealed that we were to be among the first to fly elements of the 6th Airborne Division to the shores of Normandy on 5 June. We were briefed by means of a scale model of the Normandy Beachhead arranged in such a way that the run in from the coast to the various Dropping Zones (DZs) could be simulated. My particular mission was to drop twenty parachute troops of the 7th Light Infantry Battalion, together with two containers of equipment, on DZ N just north of Ranville and about three miles inland from the coast, from a height of 600 feet and at an airspeed of 120 mph. We were, in fact, to be in company with about 130 other Stirlings and Halifaxes all dropping on the same DZ.

As is now well known, the planned date for the invasion was postponed by twenty-four hours and we eventually took off at about 2330 hrs on 5 June.

The point of rendezvous and departure from the English coast was designated as Bognor Regis. The weather across the channel was reasonably good with intermittent moonlight, but on approach to the Normandy coast we noticed low cloud forming at just about our planned run-in and dropping height. Our briefed landfall was made just to the east of the mouth of the river Orne and we were to follow the line of the Orne river and Caen canal to the DZ. A Pathfinder force of Albermarles carrying troops of the 22nd Independent Parachute Company had arrived about half an hour ahead of us with the task of setting up visual and radar beacons to guide the main force in. However, poor visibility over the DZ caused the Pathfinder troops to be scattered, with the inevitable result that several of the beacons were not activated. Consequently our drop and many others were made at the end of a timed run from the coast assisted by accurate map reading by our bomb aimers. Having met with little opposition from the ground, our drop was made at the planned time of 0050 hrs on D-Day, 6 June. However, sadly, two following Stirlings with all their passengers and crews were lost to flak. After dropping our load we made a climbing turn to port and returned to Keevil above the cloud without incident.

Short Stirlings (AHB)

Between the Normandy invasion and Arnhem I was engaged in operations for the Special Operations Executive (SOE) and the Special Air Service (SAS) These were two quite separate organisations, working with a common aim of inflicting as much confusion and damage as possible by sabotage within France and other occupied countries of Europe. The men and women comprising these two agencies were dependent upon reception parties on the ground, and all operations were arranged by coded signals between these agencies in the field and London. The final clearance on the night to say that the operations were on was given by a pre-arranged message over the BBC after the News Bulletin.

Such information was usually made available to 38 Group stations during the night prior to the drop and was subsequently passed to aircrews at briefing during the afternoon. Almost invariably it was required to have a moonlight night with reasonably clear weather – particularly at the Dropping Zone, as most flights were carried out at low level, with drops being made at heights around 500 feet above ground level. DZs were identified by a code letter in Morse. The ground reception party was supposed to be on site and ready for the arrival of the aircraft at a given time, and aircrews were briefed to drop only if they could identify the DZ and only if they were given the correct code. For fear of detection by the enemy, the DZ was not usually illuminated in any way until zero hour, and then only for a minimum time. It is worth noting that sometimes it happened that the reception party was compromised, resulting in their being either captured or shot before the arrival of the aircraft. In that tragic event, either there was no reception or there might be a false identification letter. Hence our pre-flight orders were not to drop until and unless the DZ was correctly identified. So far as I know, the DZs were chosen primarily in areas least likely to be detected by enemy forces but, of course, where the Free French and the SAS were active. Many of the people who were transported for the SOE had probably had very little or no training in parachuting and were therefore simply using dropping as a means of transport back to their home country. On the other hand members of the SAS were fully trained professionals.

Our aircraft operated singly and, as previously mentioned, were usually routed at low level to fly under radar and fighter cover and to avoid as far as possible known enemy defended areas. Whilst it is true that GEE was available, it was unreliable at low level. Therefore the crews resorted to basic Dead Reckoning navigation, with the highly experienced Bomb Aimer giving frequent visual pinpoint-checks to the navigator, who then calculated course corrections if required to maintain the pre-planned track. Timing was of the utmost importance and the track was planned to bring the aircraft to an easily identifiable landmark such as a river, a small lake, a railway junction etc., at a given time. This pinpoint would be only a short distance, say ten miles, from the DZ. Based on the wind speed and direction calculated during the transit flight, the navigator calculated a course to steer and a time to fly from the landmark to the DZ. The run-in was flown at dropping speed and height, and using a stop watch for timing. Hopefully, at the end of the timed run the DZ lights would appear with the expected identification letter and the drop would be made – no lights and identity, no drop.

It must be remembered how meticulous the map reading had to be as the early SOE flights, going back to 1941, took place at a time when Bomber Command did well to know what country, let alone what county they were flying over, whereas aircraft on special duties had to find not only the county but particular fields within them.

As has been said before, GEE was available but was unreliable because of low height. Additionally, all aircraft were fitted with Rebecca/Eureka but few if any of the DZs had this sophisticated navigation aid mainly for fear of compromising the frequencies should it fall into enemy hands. Consequently this equipment was used mainly on major operations.

I flew some ten of these operations prior to joining 295 Squadron at Harwell just before Operation MARKET GARDEN (the airborne assault at Arnhem). My Glider load for the first sortie of this operation consisted of Lieutenant General Browning together with part of his Corps Headquarters staff. I well remember him arriving immaculately dressed with his highly polished Sam Brown and requesting that he be given a seat in the glider between the two pilots. His need was satisfied by providing him with an upturned beer crate from the NAAFI!

We released him on 17 September 1944 over the DZ near Nimegen, returning to base after four and a half hours flying to prepare for a re-supply trip the next day and another two days after that. On both these subsequent sorties we released twenty-four containers and four panniers on our pre-planned dropping zones – not knowing, of course, that they had been overrun by the Germans. Consequently we were, in fact, delivering our supplies into enemy hands.

I carried out two further supply drops for the SOE before attempting to help feed the Dutch by dropping food to them at Grevenbroig and at Udem, followed by a supply drop to the Norwegians on the 20 February 1945.

On 24 March I towed a Horsa Glider on what was to be the last European major operation, Operation VARSITY (The Rhine Crossing), and this was followed by further supply missions over Holland and Denmark, with my last operational sortie being to Denmark for the SOE on the night of 22 April 1945.

The Normandy Landings

Iris Bower MBE ARRC

It was June 1944 and Mollie and I were preparing to board a Landing Craft bound for Normandy.

Everything was moving at a tremendous pace. We found ourselves approaching the LCT (Landing Craft Tank)which seemed enormous to me. It was one of the bigger invasion vessels, with an enclosed tank deck reached through doors and a lowering ramp. Lighter vehicles were carried by lift from the tank deck. In addition to all the tanks and vehicles, hundreds of troops were also carried. The next thing I knew, I was embarking. It was an incredible feeling. I seemed to go through all the motions automatically. I didn't utter a word, neither did anyone milling around me. Tanks, vehicles and men poured on to the craft at tremendous speed and in no time at all this laden LCT proceeded to take its place in a vast, Normandy bound, convoy. It was 11 June.

Casting one's mind back, some things are as vivid as when they first happened. I remember, so clearly, standing with one of the Medical Officers, surrounded by troops gazing in silence out to sea. There was a never-ending convoy of ships and escorting naval vessels. A couple of men started counting aloud, they reached two hundred. It was an incredible sight. The ships seemed to be packed so tightly, one wondered how they could move with safety. I felt strangely elated at the impressiveness of the scene. We stood there silently and then there was a roar of aircraft overhead: twenty fighter aircraft were patrolling the skies. The reassuring noise remained with us for all the hours of daylight.

I don't know how long it was, but the moment came when we could see the Normandy beaches in the distance. The convoy came to a halt and we had to wait for a suitable tide. During this time we were a sitting target, but mercifully, with the protection of the naval vessels and fighter aircraft patrolling the skies, we were not hit.

After what seemed to be an eternity, we were told that the tide was suitable for landing. It had been arranged for Mollie and me to have an escort. We had been assured that the RAF beach party would conduct us off the beach and guide us to the Assembly Area. Well it didn't work out like that!

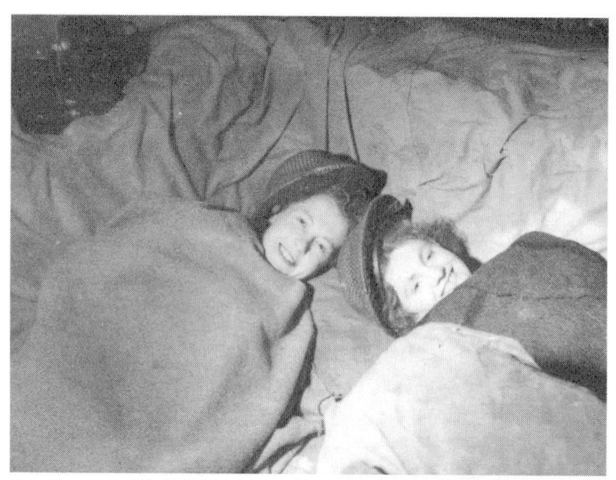

Iris Bower 'Fluffy' (right) and Mollie in a Normandy slit trench, June 1944 (Iris Bower)

Orders were given to disembark. The ramp doors were lowered and vehicles were started. When the first waterproofed lorry had descended, preparatory to driving ashore, an untoward incident occurred. I watched the lorry leaving the ramp then it tilted alarmingly, all but overturning, and it was obvious that there was a large hole in the shingle, blown by a mine. It was therefore necessary to wait, until the tide receded sufficiently for this hole to be filled and then wait for the next tide to re-beach.

Unfortunately by this time it was dark. At some stage we became aware that disembarkation had commenced again. We were guided down to the lower deck. I remember standing next to Mollie in the dark, on the left side of the lower deck of the LCT facing the ramp. The inside was towering above us. I felt as though I was inside a monstrous whale, listening to the noises of the vehicles edging their way down the steep ramp to the shore. Lifts brought the lorries down from the upper deck. I couldn't see what was happening in the darkness, but I was very aware of vehicles noisily moving and personnel dashing about. It had a strange effect on me. I felt no emotion, nothing at all, just standing there with my pack on my back. Suddenly we were told to go. We scrambled down the ramp and the next thing I remember was feeling sand under my feet. I had landed on Juno/Red Beach near Courseulles-sur-Mer, in the pitch darkness on 12 June 1944.

It was dark and noisy. We were urged to move on by some ghostly figures of the Military Police. We waited, with other personnel of our unit, for the RAF beach party to conduct us off the beach. A search was made without success. Mollie and I were instructed to go with our escort, find our way to the Assembly Area and wait there for our unit. We found ourselves following shadowy figures until we came to a bit of a slope.

The three of us stuck together like glue. I suddenly heard a loud voice, almost in my ear, shouting 'Where are you off to?' I stopped dead in my tracks. It was one of the beach-masters. I found my voice and said we were with No. 50 Mobile Field Hospital RAF, making our way to the Assembly Area. He came right up to me, looked into my face and said 'Good God'. By this time we were completely separated from any other members of our unit. There was so much movement and the gunfire was getting more frequent, it was ill-advised to hang about.

'Follow me' said the beach-master, 'I'll take you down here and arrange for a jeep to take you'. We had no idea what he meant by down here, but, after walking a few yards, we found ourselves standing by some concrete steps leading to what appeared to be an underground shelter. We quickly descended and suddenly heard voices of troops. We were given a tremendous welcome. The beach-master disappeared and said he would be back shortly.

We stayed with these wonderful young men for about twenty minutes. When the time came for us to follow the beach-master out of the shelter, I think they were really sorry to see us go. We reached the top of the concrete steps to find the whole sky lit up, and the noise of firing was deafening. I didn't know at that time whether it was from the naval vessels off shore or from the Germans. We hurriedly climbed into the jeep and off we went, but we hadn't gone many yards when the driver stopped. 'Get out' he said, 'and take cover'. We had one further go in the jeep but it was no good. The driver said 'You will be better on foot'.

I found myself crouching by a bush, it wasn't a very big one, I felt very lonely at that moment. I could see what appeared to me some red balls of fire in the sky. They seemed to be coming straight at me. I was told afterwards that they were often called 'flaming onions' and apparently were not all that close. This knowledge didn't help me at the time, neither did the knowledge that troops had penetrated to a depth inland and the actual fighting was a few kilometres away. I was convinced I was going to be killed before attending to one casualty.

Suddenly there was a lull and Mollie and the escort appeared from somewhere, equally shaken. We walked as fast as we could towards the road again and mercifully got a lift from some lorries going in the direction of the Assembly Area.

Owing to the congestion, the dark night and action from 'Jerry', we didn't reach our destination until 4 a.m. In the meantime, the other officers of our unit had no success in locating the beach party to conduct them off, so the unit formed up and drove off the beach. It turned out that they arrived at the Assembly Area before us. All concerned were glad to see us in one piece.

It had been decided that all personnel would sleep in their lorries until morning. The Flight Lieutenant in charge of this particular Assembly Area gave up his tent to the two unexpected females. We were guided to it and to us it was like reaching a five star hotel. Inside were two slit trenches and this was our first experience of such accommodation. We were excited but pretty tired. We were soon to discover that slit trenches were very essential, particularly at night.

The Germans, throughout the period of the bridgehead fighting, usually sent a few planes over, dropping anti-personnel bombs, and they could hardly fail to hit something. The area was packed tight with troops, vehicles, ammunition dumps and anti-aircraft guns. The trenches looked very inviting. Mollie and I took our packs off and descended to a trench each. I put my tin hat over my face and fell fast asleep. About 6 a.m. we were called. We washed our faces, combed our hair, put on a bit of lipstick and found our colleagues. We made ourselves some tea with our 'Compo' Rations and had some army biscuits. The noises had subsided greatly from the sound of deafening gunfire we had experienced in the night, although I don't think any of us trusted the lull.

The convoy once again formed up and we set off for our allocated site. The movement of vehicles and tanks made our progress slow, although, strangely enough, some parts of the countryside, immediately behind the coast, looked fairly peaceful, but as the 2nd Army only held a strip of coastline, about twenty-two miles long and five to ten miles deep, most of the inland places were within easy range of German guns and mortars. I remembered passing German notice boards in the odd place, with the black skull and cross bones and the words '*Achtung Minen*'. However our journey was without incident and the moment came when we reached our destination.

Contact was made with our advanced medical team and we learnt, with great sadness, how Squadron Leader Grant was killed. We understood he was blown up, with others, while landing on the beach. However, everyone was now busy making initial arrangements for the early evacuation of casualties, by air, from a nearby strip.

Our months of training now came to the fore. Large and small tents, ridge tents and some marquees were erected in well regimented lines. Slit trenches were dug inside the tents, providing our sleeping accommodation. A forty foot blood-red cross, on a white canvas background, lay spread out on the grass, forming a fitting centrepiece. This was comforting and we hoped it would be clearly visible from the air. The cook house had been sited and was soon functioning.

We soon settled down to the strange life in the bridgehead, with a tremendous sense of solidarity and comradeship. I was glad I was there.

It was an emotional moment for us all as a team when the first casualties arrived. The worst, very serious ones indeed, were from the neighbouring Army Casualty Clearing Station. We were to look after them in readiness for their embarkation by sea, on an LCT back to England the next day. Some were a very sorry sight. The Medical Officers, Mollie and I, Medical Orderlies and other personnel worked non-stop. We were seeing to field dressings, Intra-Venous Infusions, giving injections – Morphine and Penicillin mostly. It was a tremendous blessing that we were already using Penicillin in the Services. It was vital to keep infection at bay.

I must have given gallons of hot tea and fed those who could eat, and got down to the important task of giving urinals and bedpans. We spent as much time as possible talking to them and lighting the odd 'fag' for those who were dying for a smoke. It was a wonderful feeling to be with them. My reward was to see smiles on their faces and in their eyes. I know they appreciated any little thing we could do for them. Next morning, the ambulance arrived to take the serious casualties away, to start their journey back to the UK. We saw to their comfort on the stretchers and made certain the correct up-to-date information was on their Medical Cards. We wished them well as they left for the beachhead. Little had they realised, when they landed, that they would be revisiting the beaches so soon. On their journey they were being looked after by a Naval Medical Team. Our thoughts were with them and wondering if they would have a safe passage. Enemy gunfire could be heard, as well as gunfire from our naval vessels off shore.

After a few hours, air evacuation of casualties was getting under way. Our unit was to assist in this task, the work demanding surgical intervention in our operating theatre tent: the other tents retaining casualties prior to their evacuation. I have always remembered the efficiency of the Sergeant in charge of the theatre equipment and sterilisation. Mollie and I were to take it in turns to accompany the casualties to the improvised air strip, flattened by the Royal Engineers, and covered with wire meshing.

Ambulances arrived in a long convoy. There were just over two hundred surgical cases to be evacuated and many in poor shape. Some had to remain for immediate surgery. It took quite a time to sort out their needs.

Tempests into Action

Wing Commander R. P. Beamont CBE DSO DFC

Following a period of Special Duties List attachment to the Hawker Company, I was summoned in February 1944 to HQ No. 11 Group to report to the AOC, 'Dingbat' Saunders, on the status of the new Tempest fighters which were beginning to emerge from the Hawker factory at Langley at that time.

Dingbat listened with great interest, prompted me with some searching questions. and then said he wanted the Tempests as soon as possible, and when did I think squadrons could be made operational. I said that, depending on how quickly they could be processed through the Maintenance Units, it might be possible to get two squadrons trained and fit by April.

Fine, he said, but he wanted a three-squadron wing to be made ready for Operation OVERLORD (the invasion of Continent-Europe), and that because of the Tempest's hoped-for high performance they were also to be prepared to spearhead the air defence against the imminent 'special weapon' attack (V1 flying bombs) on London, which had to be expected in the very near future.

I told the AOC that the Tempest (a much improved Typhoon) should prove excellent in ground attack and superior in air combat at low and medium altitude, and that its speed and steady gun-platform characteristics would probably give us an edge over the V1s if intelligence estimates of their performance proved right. 'Good' he said, 'now go away and form the first Tempest Wing!'

The new Wing, No. 150, was formed in No. 11 Group 2nd TAF in March 1944, with 486 (NZ) Squadron completing re-equipment at Castle Camps and 3 Squadron at Bradwell Bay, and was soon into formation, training day and night.

Then, after a successful armament camp at Aire in April which showed encouraging 20 mm cannon scores, the Wing moved down to RAF Newchurch on Romney Marsh, still with only two squadrons due to a hold-up in flow from the factory.

The pilots, mostly Typhoon experienced, took quickly to the similar, but livelier and faster Tempest, and 150 Wing was declared operational on 7 May.

A busy month followed with a wide variety of operations across the Channel into France and Belgium, which included many strikes at rail, road and canal communications and airfields, with some particular successes. On 21 May a midget submarine and trailer was set on fire near Brussels; three Ju 188 bombers destroyed on 28 May and – most effective of all – over forty trains attacked on 22 May as part of the combined fighter forces 'softening up' attacks on the enemy transport prior to 'D-Day'.

All these actions were completed without loss to the Tempests, and when dawn broke on the morning of 6 of June, 'D-Day', the new Tempests had been proved capable and effective, and the squadrons were fully ready for the expected battles ahead – but the Tempests had not yet experienced air combat.

We patrolled the shipping lanes on 'D-Day' without excitement, and then were surprised to be scrambled at last light in bad weather with 'all available aircraft' to intercept hostile activity over the British sector.

This was going to be a full night, bad weather formation sortie, and I queried with 11 Group Ops if they really meant it – they did!

A stream take off down the flare-patch in pairs in the rain, and then a 'snake' climb into the base of a warm front at 500 ft. Most of the Tempests re-formed on top of the cloud sheet in the now clear moon and starlit darkness, and headed for the Seine Bay, and a few that did not landed back at various bases in the rain and darkness (no approach aids in those days) and none were lost. The cloud sheet below broke at mid Channel and soon the gunfire flashes ahead showed clearly the beachhead battle area. Blackgang RDF (radar) then recalled the Wing, as enemy activity had died down, and they gave a diversion to Ford as the Newchurch base was weathered out. After an interesting integration with returning Spitfire Wings which were already milling round Ford in the darkness, the Tempests all landed safely after midnight, and returned to Newchurch early the next day.

An uneventful Wing sweep to Le Havre–Lisieux took place on 7 June, and then in a classic long range radar control operation on 8 June Blackgang RDF (Isle of Wight) directed 3 and 486 squadrons into an up-sun, with height advantage intercept of a loose formation of BF 109Gs over Rouen. Leaving 486 to cover (to their subsequently clearly expressed disgruntlement) I attacked with 3 Squadron. At least three 109s were destroyed (two seen to burn) in this combat, which began with far superior overtaking speed and was continued with clearly superior manoeuvrability – and this was a clear sign for the future.

Then, after a few more sweeps of the left flank approaches to the invasion area, on the look-out for any possible attempts at penetration by the *Luftwaffe*, the Tempest wing was brought to Readiness with all available aircraft on 15 June for day and night defence against the VI flying bombs. The attack on London had begun.

This began a two month period of intense activity sustained by the grit, skills and determination of all the Wing's ground personnel, and by the high quality and professionalism of the pilots, which enabled standing patrols of Tempests to be kept up continuously in pairs from dawn to dusk: frequently by single aircraft at night, in almost all weather conditions and often despite the unwelcome and dangerous attentions of 'friendly' anti-aircraft fire.

There was a steep learning curve in this critical operation to save London – for it was no less than that. The flying bombs were coming in waves at around 400 mph in the height band of 1500–3000 ft in any weather: so that Ops planners, radar controllers and pilots were stretched to their limits to evolve timing and tactics to achieve intercepts and destruction of these small, fast targets early enough to prevent them reaching the prime target area, Greater London.

This all put the Tempest under the closest scrutiny and the outstanding qualities of this fighter were clearly proved when, after six weeks from the arrival of the first flying bomb the Newchurch Tempests had destroyed over 600. This was by far the highest score of any of the fighter wings and more than one third of the overall total destroyed by all the hundreds of other fighters involved.

Wing Commander R.P. Beamont's Tempest 'RB'. 150 Wing Newchurch and 122 Wing, 1944 (R.P. Beamont)

By mid-August the re-concentration of the anti-aircraft guns, by now equipped with American radar directors and with 'proximity fixed' shells, produced dramatically improved results and the fighters began to be released back to their offensive roles.

The Tempests had scored over 700 V1s when the main battle for London had been ended in September by the capture of the V1 launch bases in France and Belgium by the British and Canadian armies, and this total had been achieved in part with additional input in August by Tempests from the Manston specialist night fighter squadron, 501.

The Newchurch Tempests returned to wide-ranging ground attacks in Belgium and Holland in September, and escorted daylight heavy bombing attacks as far afield as Emden and Geilenkirchenj; and then the Wing rejoined 2nd TAF under AVM Harry Broadhurst, where they celebrated their arrival by destroying three Fw190s on the day they arrived.

The Wing moved forward to what was to become their main base for the battle for Germany, Vokel in Holland, less than five miles from the nearest enemy 88 mm battery which used to open fire on the airfield with Teutonic regularity at 11 a.m. each day.

The Tempests were soon in action over the Reichwald front area and beyond the Rhine over Germany with further successes against 190s and 109s, still without losses in air combat although casualties were mounting in ground attack. This was the beginning of the second, final and operationally most aggressive period of Tempest operations.

The Volkel Wing, now a five squadron Wing, spear-headed the 2nd TAF onslaught across the Rhine in the harsh fighting winter of 1944/45, in air superiority sweeps (air combat) and in wide-ranging attacks on transport and military installations. It proved to be one of the most effective multi-role Wings in air superiority (CAP), tactical strike and reconnaissance, and special operations.

An example of the latter began in early October when Bob Cole of 3 Squadron sighted a Messerschmitt 262 twin jet fighter bomber travelling very fast near the Reichwald and, diving his Tempest at well over 500 mph in a long chase, caught the jet and shot it down near Grave.

This was the first 262 to be shot down by fighters, and although this formidable type was being misemployed at Hitler's direct order as a fighter bomber (Volkel had been attacked by one of them with anti-personnel bombs, causing some casualties on the previous day) its real potential as a bomber-interceptor had been regarded as a serious menace and a problem.

It was thought that no Allied fighter would have sufficient performance to counter a full-throttle 262: Spitfire IXs, P47s, P51s and Meteors which had not yet reached a suitable stage of development certainly could not, and only the Griffon Spitfire XIV and Tempest V seemed likely to be able to intercept in favourable circumstances. It was now seen that the 550 mph operational dive of the Tempest could give it a good chance.

Thus began a regular additional task for the Volkel Tempests and the Spitfire XIVs from Grave from October 1944 onwards, which was to establish patrols over the forward operating base of the 262s at Achmer near Hanover, with the object of attacking them on climb-out after take off, or during their descent to base on landing approach. Naturally the enemy took every possible precaution, endeavouring to launch 262 sorties only when Allied fighters were not present, and mounting a formidable concentration of light flak all round the Achmer base.

This became a hazardous and difficult operation in which the Spitfires had some successes, but the Tempests proved the most effective with at least thirteen 262s destroyed by them in the winter of 1944/45, and many probably destroyed and damaged.

A major success occurred in November 1944 when a Volkel Tempest shot down the Achmer 262's base commander, leading fighter 'Expert' Major Walthur Novotny.

From January 1945 through to VE Day, as the Allies advanced and the German forces retreated into ever-decreasing remaining home territory, they continued to fight fiercely in the air and on the ground. This resulted in a multiplicity of targets and in two new circumstances of significance. The many ground targets became protected by denser and more deadly light flak defences, and the now desperate *Luftwaffe* fighter arm, which had lost the great majority of its experienced leaders, was now operating with pilots mostly just out of training school. These factors resulted in a heavy increase in ground attack loss-rate, and in a dramatic increase in air combat successes.

The air fighting into the German heartland was as fierce as at any time in the war, and the Tempests were in the thick of it to the end.

Following the capitulation in May, a 2nd TAF Intelligence Summary recorded that 122 (Tempest) Wing had not only achieved the highest Wing score of enemy aircraft destroyed – equal with a Spitfire Wing, but that 122 were also the highest scoring Wing of all against transport targets.

The Tempest had well and truly proved itself.

Spitfires over Normandy

Air Vice-Marshal J. E. Johnson CB CBE DSO DFC

On D-Day, 6 June 1944, we flew over the beaches in Wing strength of three squadrons – thirty-six Spitfires. We had flown in this fashion since the splendid Tangmere Wing of 1941, but once in Normandy, where we had to take off at short notice, we found a Wing, except for special occasions, too big and too time-consuming and we began to fly in squadron strength of twelve Spitfires in three finger-fours. The enemy, too, flew in smaller formations than before and we soon found that the close and swift skirmishes over Normandy made it impossible for a leader to handle more than a dozen fighters.

Although we lacked a long-range fighter we had – almost

Spitfire fighter/bomber (AHB)

by accident – produced a first-class fighter-bomber and the Typhoon, designed as a day fighter, proved a formidable weapon in Normandy. Flown by courageous pilots and directed by 'Cab Rank' Broadhurst, the Typhoons struck at German armour once they left the cover of the Normandy bocage. On the morning of 7 August 1944 the Typhoons came into their own when a German counter-attack penetrated several miles against the 30th (US) Division near Mortain. Typhoon pilots of 121 Wing, led by a splendid Rhodesian, Charles Green, found the German armour and attacked with rockets and bombs. Before dusk fell the Typhoons had flown nearly 300 sorties, destroyed many Tiger tanks and defeated the German attack. The Typhoon squadrons were unleashed and when they arrived over that small triangle of Normandy bounded by Falaise, Trun and Chambois, they trapped the desperate enemy on the narrow lanes by sealing off the front and rear of a column by a few accurate bombs and then working over the enemy armour with rockets, bombs and cannon. Immediately the Typhoons withdrew, our Spitfires attacked the soft-skinned transports with cannon. There was no sign of enemy fighters so that Broadhurst, ever the opportunist, instructed that his fighters should, to save time, operate in pairs over the battle-field.

On 19 August thousands of German transporters were destroyed or damaged. Thick smoke from the burning vehicles covered most of the battlefield, and the stench of decaying bodies even penetrated through the cockpit canopies of the Spitfires. Thanks to the fighter-bombers Falaise was one of the greatest killing grounds of World War II. So ended the Battle of Normandy. An outstanding triumph for air power, especially tactical air power, and more especially the accurate, timely and deadly fighter-bombers. Tactical air power kept an unrelenting pressure on the Germans when Montgomery's break-out was delayed and all our previous disasters at the hands of the Germans – Norway, Dunkirk, Greece and Crete, and set-backs in the Desert were, at long last, avenged.

During the late summer of 1944, when we were trekking from Normandy to the Rhine we began to hear ominous reports of the first appearances of fast German jet fighters. Occasionally we saw sleek, twin-engined Messerschmitt 262s over our beleaguered First Airborne Division at Arnhem, but we could not engage them because of their remarkable speed and climb. Suddenly, our piston-engined fighters were outmoded, and our first jet fighters, Meteor 3s of 616 Squadron, based near Brussels, were no match for the German jets.

Broadhurst, realising that his Spitfires, Tempests and Mustangs could not tackle the jets once they were in the air, ordered frequent strafing attacks to smash them on the ground; but these were costly, because the thick and accurate flak brought down many of our fighters, so he kept standing patrols near their airfields to hit them taking off or approaching to land. Thus, the handful of the revolutionary German jet fighters were contained until their airfields were captured by our advancing armies, but I have often pondered about the outcome of the Normandy landings had the Germans possessed a thousand Me 262s.

The Flying Nightingales

Anne Mettam

In Spring 1944 I was a Nursing Orderly in the sick quarters at RAF Filey, and whilst reading Daily Routine Orders (DRO's) my attention became riveted on a paragraph calling for volunteers from suitably qualified Medical personnel to undertake specialised training for air ambulance nursing duties.

The winter at Filey had been severe, with temperatures frequently below freezing. Personnel arriving from the warm climates of Jamaica for their basic training soon found the severe winter conditions almost unbearable. The resulting sick parades proved arduous for the medical staff, with many reporting sick.

After a short period of reflection, I decided that this opportunity to enhance my medical knowledge, together with the mobility of air ambulance travel, was just the challenge I required. I registered my request with the Orderly Room, and went on with my routine sick quarter duties, wondering if I had any chance of selection.

It was only a few weeks before I was posted to RAF Hendon, for my four weeks' intensive medical training, which would enable me to cope with injuries not normally encountered in Station Sick Quarters. In addition to broken bones and missing limb cases, I was required to recognise – and care for – head injuries, burns, colostomies, and many other very serious injuries. These would require special care and attention during transit, including the possible use of oxygen and morphine if required.

Sandwiched into the course were several hours of flying experience. On one occasion I was detailed to join a Dakota crew on night flying and glider-towing exercises. These were carried out with the aircraft cargo door removed. I remember sitting on my parachute with my back hard against the cockpit bulkhead, staring at the open door, too terrified to move in case I slid out of the door – especially during take off and when the glider was released, which caused a considerable jolt in the Dakota. The presence of my parachute did nothing to allay my fears during these early training flights.

I successfully completed my training and was posted to 46 Group, RAF Transport Command. This consisted of three airfields: RAF Down Ampney, near Cirencester (my base), RAF Broadwell, near Burford, and RAF Blakehill Farm, near Cricklade. There were two squadrons, each with eighteen Dakotas at each base: a total of 108 Dakotas in all. The six Squadrons had a three-fold role:

a. delivery of airborne troops and supplies
b. transport runs to the continent
c. retrieval of wounded casualties (casevac).

Each station had its own RAF Casualty Air Evacuation Centre (CAEC), capable of handling approximately two hundred casualties a day.

Although we did not know it at the time, women were prohibited from flying in operational aircraft. All outbound aircraft to the continent carried stores to supply the troops and were classified as 'operational flights', and therefore could not carry the 'Red Cross Insignia'. The homebound flights, with casualties aboard, were classified as 'Air Ambulances'.

Problem – how to get the Nursing Orderlies to the casualty pick-up points on the continent? The Air Ministry eventually agreed to some proving flights with the WAAF Nursing Orderlies classified as aircrew. On these flights, we had to wear a parachute. However, on the homeward flight with our casualties, the parachutes were locked away. Whatever the regulations said, it was impractical to attend to the eighteen stretcher cases and six sitting patients while wearing a parachute.

These difficulties were only revealed when the surviving twenty-two Air Ambulance Nursing Orderlies gathered at the Royal Air Force Club, Piccadilly, London, on 15 July 1999. We were there to receive framed Air Ambulance insignia from Air Commodore Bob Williams, Chief of the Tri-Service Medical Services.

The plaque was inscribed: 'Presented in recognition of your services as an Air Ambulance Nursing Orderly in the Royal Air Force.'

My Wings at last! The first three WAAF Nursing Orderlies to go on operational duty flew with 233 Squadron on Friday 13 June 1944 (D-Day + 7). The first evacuation of casualties, from France by air was successfully completed.

The flights to the continent, with WAAF Nursing Orderlies as part of the crew, were then authorised by the Air Ministry. On Saturday 14 June 1944, the national newspapers published a photograph of the three WAAF Nursing Orderlies, in flying kit, beside a Dakota, and gave an account of their duties. This was under a large print heading – 'Flying Nightingales' – a title that has remained with us to this day.

I arrived at RAF Down Ampney during August 1944. Numbers 48 and 271 Squadrons were engaged in training exercises, towing gliders with airborne troops and practising drops on Salisbury Plain. We realised from the intensity of the daily schedule that something big was brewing, but had no idea what it could be.

On 17 September 1944, 48 and 271 Squadrons took off to participate in the initial assault on Arnhem, code-named Operation 'Market Garden'. Each aircraft carried airborne troops, and towed a Horsa Glider which was flown by specially trained army NCOs and also loaded with fully equipped troops ready for the assault, following the landing at their designated landing zone (DLZ).

Five days after the initial assault on Arnhem, on 23 September 1944, combined supply and casevac flights recommenced. Destination – the nearest landing strips to the Field Hospitals supporting the Arnhem conflict. Stores carried could be anything from food, clothing, tents, and medical supplies to mail, etc. Aircraft take-off time was usually at dawn. I was responsible for a large hamper of Medical Supplies, and a hamper containing refreshments (tea, coffee, chocolate, etc.), and my parachute.

Anne Mettam receives wings from Air Cdr Bob Williams 15/7/1999 (Anne Mettam)

One morning, in the rush to get loaded in time, I was a bit too enthusiastic, throwing my parachute into the aircraft, somehow catching the rip cord, resulting in mountains of silk canopy everywhere. The crew was not happy, but gathered and stowed the parachute away, and we got airborne on time. As I was not allowed a parachute on the return home flight, I insisted we got on with the task. The parachute section subsequently fined me two shillings and sixpence!

Immediately we had parked on the landing strips, the ground crews quickly unloaded the stores. While this was proceeding I had to liaise with the Field Hospital nurse in charge of the casualties for details relating to their injuries. Those requiring special care or treatment I loaded last, which gave me quicker access to attend to their requirements during the flight back to Down Ampney. This also meant that they were first into CAEC when we landed.

During the flight home, those that could drink wanted tea, tea and more tea; whilst some others just wanted a reassuring smile and a female voice to show they were in good hands. Many fell asleep, lulled by the constant drone of the Dakota engines: a few required assurance, having not flown before.

When the aircraft arrived back at Down Ampney, I supervised the unloading of the casualties, escorting them into the CAEC, with a hand-over of case notes, and details of any treatment I may have given during the flight. The stretchers were placed on concrete blocks, which positioned the casualty at a suitable height for the Medical Officer's examination and any further treatment, if required.

They were then redirected to the appropriate specialist hospital. Burn cases went to Odstock, Salisbury, head injuries to St Dunstan's at Radcliffe, spinal injuries and skin grafting to Stoke Mandeville. Canadian casualties were flown on to Farnborough and into the Canadian Hospital at Aldershot.

While this reassessment was going on, I checked the operations board to find my aircraft, crew, and take-off time for the next day. I would try to grab something to eat, with a bit of luck, and then find out which hospital I had to escort casualties to. After I had handed over the casualties and documents to the hospital it became a mad scramble to get back to Down Ampney and hopefully manage some sleep before the early call to collect my hampers for the next day's detail.

On one occasion two Dakotas took off loaded with stores for an airstrip laid in the Black Forest. On landing, the stores were unloaded in a flash, and the weather closed in just as quickly. The soldiers who unloaded the aircraft asked what they could do for us. We asked for a cup of tea. It came back so thick a spoon could have stood up in it. This was my first, and last, experience of tea made from 'compo' rations. We asked where we could sleep for the night. Being the only two women in a camp full of soldiers brought some amusing suggestions, none of them acceptable. I decided that we would both sleep in one of the Dakotas!

The next day was well advanced before we could take off for Eindhoven. The casualties were not assembled, so both aircraft were fully loaded with refugees, which we took to Airstrip B56 (Brussels Evere). Again, we were not able to take off due to the weather closing in. This time I thought we were in luck, being informed that there was WAAF accommodation in the main square. On arrival, we were directed to the bedding store, and then to the top floor. The other Nursing Orderly and myself staggered up to the fourth floor, with all of our bedding, to find a filthy room, just as the German Troops had left it. Not a great improvement!

Next morning, after breakfast, we handed our bedding into the store. Our crew advised us that we were still grounded. A local lady took us to have our hair shampooed and set. This was a marvellous, unexpected treat.

In the afternoon we were able to return to Eindhoven and load our casualties, who on this occasion were all heavily bandaged burns cases.

It was inevitable that things did not always go smoothly. On one occasion, I had issued several urine bottles, and I was at the rear of the cabin. The lad on the top forward stretcher had completed his task, and was holding his bottle over the central passageway. By the time the other lads had got my attention his arm had dropped sufficiently for the contents to be dribbling out. I had to straddle the stretchers along the central passageway to reach him, only to find that the contents had been descending onto the face of the lad on the floor stretcher, who could not move his head out of the way. I cleaned him up, all the while trying to assure him that it would do wonders for his complexion. The unpredictable schedule and stopovers, due to weather conditions and load diversions, together with the pervasive smell of burnt flesh made this flight an experience I shall never forget.

On one flight to Nijmegen, the cabin was full of jerrycans full of petrol, secured to the floor by passing canvas straps through all the handles. We reloaded with German Officers. The language difficulties and rather pompous attitudes were not conducive to the friendliest of atmospheres. They had some really horrible injuries, and I did my best to communicate and assure them that they would be well looked after. While transferring them to CAEC reception at Down Ampney, I went to collect an officer's private belongings, which had become dislodged from his stretcher. He lashed out at me, probably thinking that I was trying to take away his copy of Mein Kampf. I felt very upset for him, he was very young and had lost both legs. He must have thought that I was going to keep, what to him, was his Bible. As a result of that encounter, I had a beautiful black eye to explain away.

The air ambulance Nursing Orderlies had become unofficially known as 'The Flying Nightingales', but did not have the same status, privileges or rations that the aircrews enjoyed: however I did receive eight pence a day whilst on flying duties.

The Flying Nightingales have little mention in history, which I find incredible, considering that over 100,000 casualties were transported, by air, safely back to the UK. Some of the Nursing Orderlies were decorated for their service and dedication during this time. We did have two casualties of our own: Nursing Orderlies M Walsh and M Campbell were posted missing on 21 February 1945, presumed killed whilst on nursing duties.

I was proud to join the twenty-two surviving WAAF Air Ambulance Nursing Orderlies, from 46 Group Transport Command, who were honoured to be invited to a Royal

Garden Party at Buckingham Palace by Her Majesty, The Queen, on 15 July 1999. Princess Alexandra spoke to each of us, showing considerable interest in our World War II nursing duties.

Every year at Down Ampney a reunion and memorial service is held in the Church in September, followed by a short service on the remains of the airfield. This includes a fly-past by an RAF Hercules aircraft of Transport Command in honour of Flight Lieutenant David Lord VC DFC – the only VC awarded to Transport Command.

It is probably unique that many Squadron and CAEC personnel of the three stations elect to have their ashes interred in the RAF Garden of Remembrance situated beneath the Memorial window in the Church.

ASR Beacons in the Channel

Tom Jackson and Cliff Burkett

HSL 2655 of 43 ASRMCU in the English Channel 1/6/1944 on trials before D Day (Cliff Burkett fifth from left) (Cliff Burkett))

On the afternoon of the 5 June 1944, four High Speed Launches of No. 43 Air Sea Rescue Base, Mount Batten, slipped their moorings from opposite the 'Hoe' and made their way out of Plymouth Sound through an American Battle Fleet and into the English Channel to begin their role in the combined operation known as D-Day. It was an operation from which the crews were not expected to return, for the launches were to be used as beacons for the initial airborne assault.

The rescue crews involved had known about their intended role through a briefing which had been given days earlier by the Air Officer Commanding and held in a locked hangar, guarded by armed sentries. Sealed orders had been handed to the skippers and the Wireless Operators were given the codes to be used on the operation.

The crews had already been given an early warning of their participation when some days earlier they had been given instructions to paint a white five pointed star on the foredeck of the launches. The painting had to be done behind a canvas screen which hid the activity and prevented observation from the Hoe. On the afternoon of our departure on the 5th we were somewhat bemused to see some Royal Navy matelots busy painting white stars on their ships in the Sound.

The launches left the safe haven of the Sound, turned to port and travelled towards Start Point in Devon, where they were joined by a Royal Navy Motor Gun Boat. From there the launches proceeded towards France and to what were to be the invasion beaches.

The sixty-seven ft long laminated plywood rescue craft were driven by 100 octane petrol engines and armed with a single 20 mm Oerlikon cannon, together with two .5 in machine guns mounted either side of the beam, plus any other .303 in hardware which could be accommodated on a crowded deck space.

Eventually land ahead was sighted. My old colleague Cliff Burkett, a Wireless Operator Mechanic on one of the other launches, has managed to retain his log after all these years and confirms that we were 'on station' off the beaches from 11.30 p.m. on the night of the 5th until 5.30 a.m. the following morning.

The MGB departed as soon as we arrived off the beaches. Throughout the long night the engines were shut down and the launch, being wind-borne, wallowed in the sea, with the only break in monotony coming at twenty-minute intervals for the engines to be started up to bring the craft back on to station in what we, an experienced crew, thought was a moderate sea. Nevertheless it was a draining and tiring experience to be bounced around for hours at a time with no respite, and this tested the resolve of the crew. The explosive noise of the engines being restarted must have been heard all along the Normandy shore line but we remained unchallenged.

Round about midnight we were in a grandstand position to watch the fleet of bombers pounding away at the defences at the back of the beaches. At one time it looked as if the whole shore line was aflame and dancing with the explosions. Although much later it was established that only twenty-five per cent of the defences had been put out of action.

Between the hours of 1 and 2 a.m. formations of gliders appeared overhead with navigation lights on, as if on a flying display. By then the launches below also had their navigation lights on, lit up like Christmas trees, but still nothing was thrown in our direction.

As dawn broke the invasion fleet appeared over the horizon with landing craft going into the attack, and the noise of battle took over on what was to be an eventful and historical day. Somewhat later at around midday we received a call of an aircraft down off the coast of Guernsey.

A Ju 88 which had just taken off from Guernsey airport flew directly over the launch but did not attack us. We concluded that the pilot had not seen us, or mistook us for an E Boat.

Much later, on the early evening of the 6th, we were

instructed to return to base at Mount Batten for refuelling etc. On our return to Plymouth the Hoe was packed with thousands of people and we were directed to refuel at the Barbican, to be bombarded with questions from the public asking us 'How was it going?' That was the most emotional time of all, because we recalled where we had been and what we had achieved without suffering a single casualty.

The E boats remained in their pens in Cherbourg harbour because the German High Command had decreed that the sea was too rough for a sea-borne invasion. When the enemy finally realised that the Invasion was for real, the E boats came out of Cherbourg on the night of the 6th of June and sank forty-four units of the Invasion fleet including a Royal Navy frigate, HMS *Blackwood*. The survivors were picked up by an RAF Air Sea Rescue launch which was operating off the beachhead.

We crews of the four RAF launches involved in the combined operation on the night of the 5th of June, now realised that on the night in question luck was very much on our side and that the good Lord had smiled down on us.

North West Europe

The Allied air forces now had two main tasks:

Defence of London against Hitler's V Weapons by destroying flying bombs in the air and by attacking launching sites.

Support of the Allied advance across Europe towards the Rhine.

Per Ardua ad Astra ad Coningsby

John Chatterton DFC

I remember a night in early 1944, when over the New Year we did three trips to Berlin in five nights in our Lancaster KM–Y-Yorker. The second one involved spending all New Year's Day preparing for a take-off that was put back to midnight, resulting in our landing back at 8 a.m. on 2 January amid a flurry of snow. It was snowing so determinedly by the time we got to bed at 9 a.m. that we were blissfully sure that we wouldn't be flying again that evening. How wrong can one be?

The batman in our hut shook me urgently awake in the afternoon 'Wake up Sir. You're on again tonight'. Having only been a Pilot Officer for a matter of weeks I politely told him to 'go away', which was reiterated by the two Aussies next door in less inhibited terms. He returned with cups of tea – 'We can't be flying' I said, 'The runway's covered in snow'. ''Fraid not Sir, they've been clearing it all day – even the Groupie himself has got a shovel!' 'This should be worth seeing' I thought, so I stumbled out of bed, dressed with minimal ablutions and staggered out to the Flights. Here indeed was a hive of activity, but alas, the great man himself after setting a leader's example had been called away to more managerial duties.

My crew had assembled and the two Scots (Wireless Operator and Rear Gunner) were reflecting on the ancestry of Butch Harris, our grudgingly respected Chief, and deciding that he could not have any Scottish blood in his veins, since anyone with an ounce of common decency knew that the period following Hogmanay was a time for quiet reflection and relaxation, over a bottle of malt.

That would have to wait a bit now, but we were all feeling rather weary both in mind and body as we took off again at 11 p.m. on another murky night. It was our eighth trip as a crew and our fifth to the 'Big City', and although still with a lot to learn we were beginning to think of ourselves as a competent fighting unit.

The start was not auspicious. As we left the English coast in cloud, a shot from 'friendly forces' (could it be the Navy again?) shattered the Perspex above my head, nicked my helmet and put me in a daze for the next hour or so as we ploughed through the layers of cloud to the target. Berlin was cloud-blanketed but lively with flak and fighters. Once again we were lucky and having bombed passed through unscathed, although there was one heart-stopping moment when the great radial engine of a roaming Fw 190 swept head-on a few feet over the cockpit.

The jagged hole in the canopy was beginning to cause a few problems as we turned for home. More Perspex vibrated free, and the topographical maps 'borrowed' from the Bomb Aimer to bridge the gap had been sucked out into the night, souvenirs for some German boy. It did nothing for the cabin heating and I was glad I had put on all three pairs of gloves for a change. The draught tugged at the Nav's blackout curtain, letting out streaks of light which interfered with our night vision in the cockpit, and he was struggling to keep his charts on the table and searching for missing 'flimsies' in a whirl of strips of 'Window' and loose 'Nickels'. The latter were propaganda leaflets which were meant to persuade their German readers of the folly of war, but which were more probably received gleefully to help solve the paper shortage in a more earthy fashion.

Running for home we re-entered the cloud barrier. Cloud was heaped upon cloud, up to 28,000 feet according to the

Lancaster (AHB)

Met. man at briefing. He had said nothing about thunderstorms but mentioned 'a bit of static'. I had forgotten this, and was suddenly startled as the cockpit was bathed in blue light. It was St Elmo's Fire, causing whirling blue circles round the propellers and streaking across the Perspex of astrodome and gun turrets. Eerie but harmless, this was just the element's curtain raiser. The next act was a sudden and nasty bout of icing, which stiffened the controls, made the engines cough, and sent bits of ice from the props rattling on the fuselage. Ken, the Flight Engineer, cleared the engines by selecting 'Hot Air', and I put the nose down to get into warmer air.

Alarmingly, the airspeed did not increase – the pitot head was frozen, so I had to watch the climb and descent needle to avoid getting out of control. Then, to cap it all, we were hurled over sideways by a lightning strike, and instead of being surrounded by a comforting array of luminous dials, the instrument panel registered instant chaos. The gyros of the Artificial Horizon and Direction Indicator lay toppled and useless, the DR Compass was dead, never to return, and the stand-by P4 compass by my left knee wallowed aimlessly. I was frozen with panic, and the aircraft was plunging headlong to destruction, when by some miracle, out of the depths of my brain I heard the nasal twang of my old bush pilot instructor in Arizona – 'Now boy! we've toppled all the newfangled instruments and we'll have to rely on the basics – what are they?' Needle, ball and airspeed! With an effort I pulled myself together and using the turn and bank indicator, climb and descent needle and the thawed-out altimeter finally got Y-Yorker straightened out again. In the warmer air, the air-speed indicator revived, showing over 300 m.p.h. and I was thankful that my farm-boy's muscles (fortified by long hours of muck spreading) were able to ease her out of the dive.

Surprised to have no comments from the crew, I tried the intercom. It was dead, so I looked around for Ken who had been pinned to the floor by 'G' forces whilst checking his fuel gauges. He lifted the earpiece on my helmet and shouted 'All the electrics are off, I'll go and sort it out'. I applauded his confidence and set myself to fly straight and level in the unfriendly dark hoping the compass would settle down. Eureka! – there was a faint lightening in the gloom ahead and suddenly we burst out of the cloud into glorious starlight. What a marvellous relief: the real, tangible world again. Well, we seem to be right way up – but where are we heading?

I looked round for Polaris and found him behind us instead of on our right where he ought to have been. I used him to zero the now settled directional gyro and was able to steer west for home while Jack the Navigator used his sextant for an astro fix. He worked swiftly and managed to get a couple of these before we plunged into cloud again. They showed us to be well south of track, heading for the Atlantic Ocean. I altered course on the dubious P4 compass, while Ken and the Wireless Operator, with the help of bits of wire, got some of the electrics and the intercom working again, but the WT set and the gee box were burnt out beyond repair. The lost gee box meant that Jack would not be able to get any radar fixes as we neared home, and the wrecked WT meant that the Wireless Operator could not receive the half hourly broadcasts with vital information about barometric pressure, weather at home and possible diversions.

After a long, cold, weary time on instruments I was dog tired and not very confident when Jack said we had reached the Dutch coast, but a few desultory bursts of flak confirmed this and sharpened me up for a bit. Safely out to sea, I let down to just below the cloud base with the altimeter reading 1000 ft and still in inky blackness. Jack was saying in the confident way that navigators do, even when they've been on Dead Reckoning for the last two hours 'ETA Norfolk Coast in five minutes'.

'Can you see anything down there Scotty?' The Bomb Aimer's reply was an anguished yell 'Pull up Johnny!', as out of the darkness ahead a single searchlight sprang up, illuminating the cloud base and showing the sea menacingly just a few feet below us. Wide awake, I yanked Y-Yorker up to the cloud base again until I recovered my wits once more. Surely the crew deserved a pilot less careless than this! – but if only the WOP had received those vital broadcasts, the adjusted altimeter would have indicated how dangerously low we were.

Using a recognised homing procedure the coastal searchlight now lay horizontally pointing to an unknown airfield, so I used the distress call 'Darky' to find that it was 'Little Snoring' (just the place for a sleepy pilot) and they gave me a course for Dunholme Lodge, our base near Lincoln – omitting to tell us it was closed.

I thankfully extricated myself from the mesh of weaving navigation lights of other diverted aircraft while Jack drew a reciprocal on his chart to find out where we had been, and wished longingly for the local maps lost through the roof. The visibility got worse as we crossed the Wash but Scotty picked out the practice target at Wainfleet a few hundred feet below. Lincolnshire at last! So I tried to call Dunholme on the RT and at the third attempt heard faintly 'Hello Y-Yorker – regret base is closed, land at Spilsby'. No problem, I had been to school at Spilsby! So I turned right, and with permission to land was groping around the circle of Drem lights trying to find the funnel leading to the runway when Ken reminded me we hadn't put the wheels down. Heaven forgive me – forgotten the landing drills! Down came the wheels but a red light showed one was not securely locked. Ken pulled the 'Emergency Air' lever but with no result. Let's hope it's only a micro-switch fault.

While all this was happening Spilsby also closed down and sent us to Coningsby, where we finally landed after giving way to another aircraft from our squadron – on three engines. The red light still gleamed reproachfully as we held our breath and touched down, but thankfully the undercarriage held firm. As we switched off the Nav said for all of us 'Well, that was a trip full of interesting incidents, and not one of them due to Hitler!' The WOP, extremely frustrated without his wireless, burst out 'It was a bloody German thunderstorm that wrecked my set!' Jack replied 'They told you when you joined, it would be *Per ardua ad astra*'. I said 'Thanks to the navigator it's been *Per astra ad* Coningsby'.

As the crew gathered their gear and stumbled down the fuselage to the rear door, I unplugged my intercom and eased the helmet off my sore head and Merlin-numbed ears. I opened the side window to the Lincolnshire dawn. It was blessedly still, the only sounds the tinkling noise of cooling engines and somewhere below the muted murmur of Ken telling the ground sergeant about the undercart. The fresh air was cool on my cheek and tasted good. I was very glad to be home.

Hitler's Terror Weapons

Jack Batchelor DFC

In June 1944 I was posted to 1 Squadron which was flying Spitfire IX Bs. After only a few days we moved to RAF Detling, a small grass aerodrome overlooking Maidstone from the Weald of Kent. We did not require any briefing as to why we were there in our specially tuned Spitfires – we were on the direct route for the V1 (Doodlebugs) from Pas-de-Calais to London. The squadron flew a great number of sorties from 21 June to 11 August, destroying a useful number of V1s.

One day at Lympne a pilot was scrambled to intercept a Doodlebug. As his undercarriage was retracting on take off, the V1 crossed in front of him. He pulled his aircraft round in a steep climbing turn, fired a terrific deflection shot with his cannon shells and exploded the Flying Bomb in a massive fireball. He was airborne for only two minutes!

Pin-point bombing of German Headquarters, The Hague 30 March, 1945 (Crown copyright)

Later on 15 September we attacked a large storage area east of the Hague. There was a tremendous explosion. This was the first destruction of a V2 rocket site by a fighter squadron.

I was now posted to 249 Squadron at Coltishall. During the next few days the Squadron number was changed from 249 to 603 (City of Edinburgh Squadron).

On 15 of January we started flying our clipped-winged Mark XVI Spitfires across the North Sea to attack V2 Rocket launching sites. Our aircraft carried a 250 lb bomb under each wing, a thirty gallon slipper jettison tank under the fuselage to increase our flying time by twenty to thirty minutes, a pair of wing-mounted 20 mm belt-fed cannon and a pair of wing mounted 50 calibre machine guns.

The use of continual flights of four aircraft over Holland, briefed to attack specific targets, allowed fighter operations to divert flights already airborne to attack sites where Operations Control had received information, via Intelligence, that a V2 was being erected for firing. Such knowledge was not normally known more than forty-five minutes before the V2 being fired. Obviously such instructions were acted upon immediately but weather conditions at that time of year often frustrated effective attack.

Our next operation across the North Sea with twenty-four Spitfire XVIs was to bomb flak positions and attack anti-aircraft with cannon fire, to permit thirty-six Beaufighters to attack German destroyers and shipping off Den Helder. The flak was intense but the Beaufighters pressed home the attack with torpedoes, sinking one German destroyer which blew up: a second destroyer and tugs were damaged. The flak at deck level was even more intense, causing six Beaufighters to be lost. All the Spitfires returned safely to base.

Tribute must be paid to the ground crews who prepared and serviced the aircraft in the appalling weather conditions each day. Throughout the night they had to keep running the engines up to keep them warm, which meant refuelling each Spitfire with the small amount of fuel used. They had to de-ice the wings and control surfaces and ensure that aircraft were available for action at any time. All work was carried out in the open, and during the night in the light of hand torches or mobile lanterns. In bitter arctic winds it was certainly no picnic.

From early February efforts were made to increase attacks on the V2 sites in Holland.. We now were able to fly with one 500 lb bomb under the fuselage as well as the 250 lb bomb under each wing, in effect double the bomb load on each sortie. This was possible by flying from Coltishall, dive bombing sites in Holland, then landing at a forward airstrip at Ursel in Northern Belgium, refuelling and rearming before carrying out another bombing mission on the return flight to Coltishall.

Our first flight each day was scheduled for take off at first light but we endeavoured actually to be airborne whilst still dark although the weather controlled this. It was quite an experience for a close formation of four Spitfires to open the throttles to take off, and see the long blue intense flames emitted from the exhausts and stretching, just below cockpit level, toward the tail planes down each side of the fuselages. The exhaust stubs along the engines were white hot and had the appearance of tubular neon lighting. The flames were there during take off in daylight but could not be seen and I do not know of anyone who put his hand out of the cockpit to find out.

Looking eastward as we approached the Dutch Coast we could see the corkscrew vapour trails form at 30,000 feet as the V2 rockets accelerated through the atmosphere to a height of fifty miles then fell in a parabolic curve at 4000 miles per hour to a position approximately 200 miles from the launch area. We made our early take off in an endeavour to be over the Rocket sites before firing, but even then we were frustrated by layers of low cloud or fog and we would actually see the V2s slowly appear through the low cloud to continue accelerating vertically towards the stratosphere. On such occasions we would search for alternative sites or targets of opportunity such as railway junctions, bridges or anti-aircraft sites.

On the last flights of each day we would arrange to carry a variety of bombs, including delayed action bombs which would explode later during the night and disrupt the activity on the launching sites. We were instructed only to fire our cannon and machine guns when absolutely necessary in order that our aircraft could be refuelled and bombs fitted for a rapid turn round after landing. In endeavours to press home attack notwithstanding the weather or the low cloud, we commenced our dive bombing attacks as low as 5000 feet, sometimes clearing the target at less than 500 feet. This was a little hazardous as we were within the range of light flak.

Our normal bombing practice was to approach the target at 8000–10,000 feet, taking up echelon formation, rolling over to an almost inverted position and dive as steeply as possible up to 80° at a speed of around 370 mph. Although higher speeds had been used up to 475 mph this was discouraged as this resulted in corrugated ripple forming in the metal wing panels due to the excessive 'G' forces exerted on the wings during the recovery from the dive, and consequently made the aircraft unfit for further service without extensive repairs – including fitting of new wings. If the formation was split up after bombing and taking evasive action from the flak, we would rendezvous off the coast at 8000 feet at a pre-arranged point.

Particular care had to be taken to avoid unnecessary damage to Dutch property or civilians. These instructions were given by the Prime Minister Winston Churchill himself. Consequent upon this a planned attack on a production plant producing liquid oxygen rocket fuel in a tramway depot at Loosduinen was cancelled because of the possibility of Dutch casualties.

Although we continued our attacks across the North Sea, additional training was made for us to dive bomb a building as an attacking force of twelve aircraft with pin point accuracy. At this time our sister Squadron (602 City of Glasgow) had made two low level attacks on a building in the Hague, just skimming the house tops on the approach to the target. Damage to the target was minimal because of the necessity of avoiding Dutch casualties.

However we at 603 Squadron were briefed on 30 of March to attack the target with twelve Spitfires carrying one 500 lb and two 250 lb bombs each. The target was the concrete office block of the Bataafsche Petrol Company built in the Hague prior to 1939. It was a reinforced concrete building now being used as Headquarters and barracks for German Intelligence affecting the V2 programme. We studied the photo reconnaissance snaps of the building and immediate area. As I was to lead the attack I decided to attack over an area of garden or scrubland to the rear of the building. It was vital to avoid Dutch houses adjacent to, and a large church opposite the front of the building.

We were airborne from Ludham on time forming three vics of four aircraft about fifty yards apart, crossing over Great Yarmouth at 250 feet to fly across the wind-swept North Sea below low cloud. On approaching the Dutch coast we changed formation into three flights of four in line astern, closing up into a tight box of twelve aircraft to climb through the low cloud. We broke through into brilliant sunshine at 4000 feet and found that the cloud cleared immediately inland from the Dutch coast.

We were able to see large areas of glass greenhouses glinting in the sun. We climbed to 8000 feet, positioning ourselves into echelon starboard as we approached the target. I pulled my aircraft up and over in a roll to port, and from an inverted position pulled into a near vertical dive with the target clearly in view. I released my bombs late in my dive, pulling out at 1000 feet and roaring into a climbing turn to observe the accuracy of the bombing. It was a great thrill to see the direct hits and to note that none of the salvoes fell more than thirty-five yards from the target. We reformed at 10,000 feet, setting course for Ursel in Belgium to refuel and take on another load of 500 lb and 250 lb bombs. We repeated our attack on the same target on our return flight to Ludham. Further direct hits were registered, with all bombs falling in the target area. Particularly gratifying was that photographs taken by PRU aircraft between the two attacks showed the direct hits on the target building and no direct damage to the Church or adjacent Dutch buildings. All the squadron pilots and ground staff were elated by the success of the operation.

The advance of the army into Germany and Holland virtually finished supplies to the German V2 launch pads and we were transferred to escorting Lancasters on daylight raids over Germany.

At the end of April the Squadron returned to its home base at Turnhouse, Edinburgh.

The Ultimate Pathfinders

Ron Curtis DSO DFC

'Oboe' was a ground-controlled blind bombing device which enabled aircraft to release bombs on a target from 30,000 ft with an average operational error of 300 yards. At lower heights the error was even less. It was the brainchild of A. H. Reeves, a scientist at TRE (Telecommunication Research Establishment) at Malvern, but the development did not commence until it came under the aegis of Professor R. V. Jones.

The system required two ground stations situated on the English coast about 100 miles apart. One station, called the 'Cat', sent signals to the pilot which enabled him to maintain a constant track over the target, and a second, called the 'Mouse', sent position signals to the Navigator followed by the release signal.

In the aircraft there was a receiver and a transmitter. Thus signals could be received, and transmitted back to the ground stations, thereby allowing the exact position to be calculated. When the aircraft was exactly on the arc of the circle with its centre at the Cat station, the pilot heard a steady note in his headphones. If nearer the Cat station, dots were received and, if outside the range, dashes were received. The width of the beam (steady note) did not vary with the distance from the Cat. The navigator received As (in Morse code) at ten minutes' flying time from time-on-target, Bs at eight minutes, Cs at six minutes and Ds at three minutes. At approximately two minutes after Ds the release signal was sent. This was five high-speed (half second) dots followed by a two and a half second dash, then silence. At this point the navigator pressed the bomb release button and switched off the transmitter. Thus the exact time of release was recorded and the next aircraft could be called.

I was a navigator with 109 squadron which had carried out all the original experimental work with TRE and was the first squadron to use this equipment operationally. There was one other Oboe-equipped squadron. This was 105, like 109, flying Mosquitos.

Unlike heavy bomber operations, we climbed to operational height before leaving the English Coast. We wore our oxygen masks from take-off to avoid any possibility of blacking out. Our flight plan was based on the Met forecast of wind speed and direction given at briefing. To the time calculated to reach Point A, ten per cent was added as a safety factor against any adverse conditions which might be encountered. Being at operational height on leaving the English Coast, the navigator could obtain the actual wind speed and direction and revise the ETA (Estimated Time of Arrival) at Point A. Invariably it was necessary to lose part of the extra ten per cent. A rate 1 orbit would lose three minutes and a 60° dogleg one minute. Timing was of paramount importance to avoid 400 or 500 main force bombers being in the target area waiting for the target markers. The receiver was switched on well before arrival at Point A.

Each crew had its own call sign. Ours was TR. This was sent to us when it was our turn to be called in. On receipt of this, the navigator switched on the transmitter so that the ground stations could see our exact position and send the control signals. To obtain the accuracy of release and timing, each aircraft required ten minutes to settle on the run.

Flt Lt John Burt and Flt Lt Ronald Curtis of No. 109 Squadron at Little Staughton stand in front of their Mosquito B.IX ML907 with their ground crew after completing the aircraft's 100th operational sortie late in 1944 (Ron Curtis)

As more ground stations became operational, more aircraft could be controlled at the same time. One also had to fly dead straight and level and at a constant speed so that the Mouse could calculate the groundspeed and send the release signal. It was also necessary to fly at a height which was equivalent to a tangent to the earth's surface at the ground station. Above this was OK but below it the signals were obstructed by the earth itself. Thus to cover targets in the Ruhr at a distance of approximately 300 miles, we had to fly at 28–32,000 feet. Targets nearer England could be reached at correspondingly lower levels. The only aircraft which could fit these requirements was the DH Mosquito.

Following numerous experimental and calibration nights, once the accuracy was established Oboe was first used to mark a target for a major bombing attack on 5 March 1943 (my twenty-first birthday). This was on Essen against the Krupps steel plant. That night Herr Krupp telephoned Hitler directly, saying that the British had found a new method of bombing. From then on many attacks were carried out on the Ruhr where it was very difficult to find any target by ordinary visual means.

As the war developed and an invasion of Europe was imminent we were switched to attacks on marshalling yards, transport centres, airfields, etc., in Holland, Belgium and France. These raids generally consisted of smaller numbers, but as we were bombing occupied territory an even greater degree of accuracy was required.

Initially TIs (Markers) were dropped in salvo, i.e. four simultaneously, but this resulted in a certain sideways spread. Experiments with dropping a 'stick' proved to give better results, so we then always dropped our target indicators with a quarter second delay between each. Quite often a Master Bomber was used to control the raid. He would assess which TI was the most accurate and call in the main force to bomb that one.

On the night of 5 June 1944 Oboe had ten targets to mark along the Normandy coastline. These were gun sites. I was over the beachhead at 0300 hrs on 6 June. We had a good run, it was very dark and no armada was visible in the Channel. I did not know that the invasion had started until I heard the midday news on the BBC. During the following weeks we were very busy indeed, mainly attacking supply and communication centres leading to the battle zone.

Our first attack on a buzz bomb site was on 23 June. Although our primary task was marking targets for main force bombers, we also led formations of other Mosquitos on strategic targets and, on one occasion, a formation of Halifaxes. When leading formations from March 1944 onwards, we often carried a 4000 pounder. On the release of this the following formation dropped its load.

Oboe was also used in the bombing of the Dykes, causing flooding and impeding the retreating Germans.

As the Allied armies became well established on the Continent, mobile ground stations were set up, which enabled targets at greater range to be attacked. Berlin was eventually covered. Oboe also dropped target markers for aircraft carrying food to the Dutch, during Operation MANNA.

My pilot John Burt and I did 104 sorties using the Oboe technique.

I would like to conclude by quoting from the book *Bomber Offensive* by our boss, Air Chief Marshal Sir Arthur Harris:

> 'At long last we were ready and equipped. Bomber Command's main offensive began at a precise moment,the moment of the first major attack on an objective in Germany by means of Oboe. This was on the night of March 5/6th 1943, when I was at last able to undertake with hope of success the task which had been given to me when I first took over the command a little more than a year before: the task of destroying the main cities of the Ruhr.'

The Sinking of Tirpitz

Squadron Leader Tony Iveson DFC AE

We were playing football on the RAF airfield at Woodhall Spa, Lincolnshire, in late August 1944, when one of the players was asked to leave the field to take a telephone call. The 'we' were the aircrew of 617 Squadron, a special duties bomber squadron known as 'The Dambusters' because of the epic attack on the great dams of Western Germany in 1943. The player who departed the game was the Commanding Officer, Wing Commander J. B. Tait DSO DFC.

That telephone call initiated nearly three months dedication to a particular target, although what it was to be was not revealed for some time.There followed a period of intense activity. Night flying gaggle practice over the North Sea – thankfully soon abandoned. Long cross-country flights at different all-up weights, altitudes and power settings with newly fitted flow meters to check fuel consumption and the best air miles per gallon. Lots of dinghy drill – in the event of a sea landing. Many hours of high level bombing practice. From all this we conjectured the target was a long way from our base and that the route was mostly over water. Also, it wasn't a low level job!

Eventually, at briefing, we learned what our target was. The 56,000 ton German battleship *Tirpitz*, the most powerful warship in the Western Hemisphere at that time, which had spent its war virtually in hiding in the Norwegian fjords. Yet it was regarded with fear and trepidation by Winston Churchill and the Royal Navy. Its potential for disaster, so far as the Allies were concerned, was enormous. Its threat to Allied troop, fuel and food convoys in the Atlantic, to the weapons and war materials convoys to Russia, and to the Royal and United States Navies, was real. Nearly 300 yards long and 40 yards in the beam, with its eight 15 in guns with a range of over twenty miles, its powerful secondary armament, torpedo capability and anti-aircraft defences, its heavily armoured decks, long distance radar, endurance of over 8000 miles and speed of over 30 knots, made her indeed a floating fortress. The Navy remembered it had taken a fleet of battleships, cruisers, destroyers, submarines and aircraft carriers to finally destroy her sister ship *Bismarck* in 1941!

Between January 1942, when *Tirpitz* slipped out of Wilhelmshaven for Trondheim in Norway, and the autumn of 1944 when she lay deep in Alten Fjord near North Cape, she was attacked by RAF Halifaxes, Hampdens, Wellingtons and Whitleys, Soviet bombers, dive bombers and fighters of the Fleet Air Arm and midget submarines. She withstood bombs, mines, torpedoes, rockets and cannons, and although damaged on occasions she was never seriously disabled.

By the late summer of 1944 the Admiralty was seriously troubled by her continuing presence in Arctic waters. She was almost a 'fleet in being', and as such kept several battleships swinging on their anchors in Scapa Flow in case she emerged into the Atlantic or the North Sea. These ships were needed in the Pacific theatre to engage in the war with Japan so, in desperation, they approached Air Chief Marshal Sir Arthur Harris, Commander-in Chief, Bomber Command. He agreed to intervene in what he called 'this war of the dinosaurs' and said Bomber Command would sink her 'in

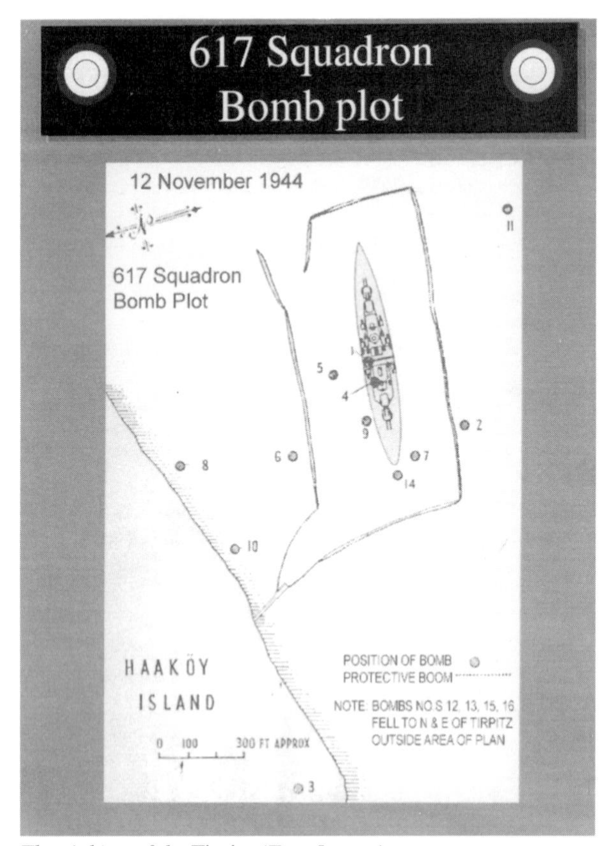

The sinking of the Tirpitz *(Tony Iveson)*

our spare time'.

He gave the task to 617 Squadron – perhaps because he heard we had nothing to do but play football – supported by 9 Squadron, whose long and distinguished history stretched back to 1915.

In September 1944 *Tirpitz* lay in Alten Fjord – 70° N, 23° E – well out of range of our Lancasters even from the north of Scotland. So, on 11 September (my birthday), we flew from Woodhall Spa to an advanced base in northern Russia, not far from Archangel – an airfield called Yagodnik on the river Dvina. There were adventures during the twelve and a half hour flight because of the weather and the lack of contact with the Russians through language problems. Someone had forgotten that our own and the Russian alphabets were not compatible, and the call signs we were given proved useless! The force was scattered and six Lancasters were eventually abandoned there.

On arrival we discovered we were famous. We were received with musical honours, and 'Welcome to the glorious flyers of the Royal Air Force', read the banner over the gangplank of the ferry-boat which was to be our home for a few days. Other things gave us a welcome too. The boat was ancient and the home of millions of red bugs, and a lot of scratching resulted. The only one to escape was our CO, Wing Commander Tait. As one of our gunners remarked 'So even communist bugs have a respect for rank!'

After waiting a few days whilst Mosquito reconnaissance aircraft checked the weather, twenty-seven Lancasters took off for Alten Fjord on 15 September. Although I saw *Tirpitz* quite clearly on the approach, I also saw the cunningly placed smoke generators start up and fill the fjord and cover the target by the time we reached our bombing position. We held on to our bombing run and dropped the 12,000 lb Tallboy in the faint hope of a strike. One bomb, however, from the leader James Tait, did hit the battleship on the bow, although we only learned about this much later. The rest fell all around and no other damage was done.

Next day we flew back to England, losing one aircraft in the Norwegian mountains. To this day, no one has discovered why.

Soon afterwards the Russians launched a land attack across north Norway and *Tirpitz* was moved some 200 miles to the west to Tromso fjord, bringing her within range from the northern Scottish airfields. Our Lancasters were fitted with more powerful Rolls-Royce T24 Merlin engines with paddle blade propellers. The mid-upper turrets and all armour plating were stripped out and with a reserve 250 gallon petrol tank packed into the fuselage, we were ready for the second round.

The first attempt from the Scottish airfields of Lossiemouth, Kinloss and Milltown on 29 October was unsuccessful. Layers of thick cloud over the fjord had us circling and descending but we had only brief glimpses of the ship and though most aircraft did bomb, the conditions prevented any direct strike.

We knew we weren't done with her. Our Group Commander, Sir Ralph Cochrane, made it very plain we would go back again and again until we sank her! But time was running out. By 21 November the sun would not be seen over the horizon in Tromso and to find *Tirpitz* in the dark, at that range – 1200 miles away – and in the Arctic weather, would be impossible.

On 11 November we set off again for Scotland from Lincolnshire, carrying our 'giant bombs' – the 12,000 lb 'Tallboys' invented by Barnes Wallis of the 'bouncing bombs' which destroyed the Dams. These weapons passed through the speed of sound on their way down and could penetrate 100 feet into the ground before exploding!

At 2 a.m., in freezing conditions, we clambered into our Lancasters, and after the wings had been defrosted, took off again for northern Norway with an all-up weight of 68,000 lb! We flew past the Orkneys and the Shetlands and on to 65° North, 7° East – our turning point for the Norwegian coast. On over the mountains into Sweden to Lake Akkajaure, our rendezvous point, then taking up positions behind Wing Commander Tait as he turned northwards towards Tromso fjord.

The day developed bright and clear and we could see for miles and miles across the snow-covered mountains and the blue sea as we climbed to our bombing altitudes of between 13,000 and 15,000 feet. The thought occurred to most of the crews that this was it, this was our big chance: for conditions were perfect for our high level bombing expertise with 617's special stabilising Automatic Bomb Sight (SABS). With bomb doors open, this required a steady five-minute bombing run to allow the speed and flight path to settle down whilst the computer in the sight correlated height, speed, barometric pressure, wind-speed and drift. The bomb-aimer conveyed any required changes through an extra indicator on the pilot's panel, and these were made by gentle banked turns until the target moved inexorably down the line on the sight's graticule and the computer automatically released the bomb at the correct instant.

One worry was nagging away during that climb. Where was the *Luftwaffe*? We knew a fighter squadron had been moved to Bardufoss, an airfield some fifty miles south of Tromso. Their Messerschmitt 109s were at least 100 mph faster than our Lancasters and were armed with 20 mm cannon, against our single turret with its four .303 in machine-guns. It would have been rather a one-sided contest!

For some reason or other – and I've heard many – they missed us. Thank God. It's good to know, and that was much later, that the so-called super-efficient Germans could also cock things up. Later, too, we learned that the Squadron Commander and others were court-martialled and severely dealt with.

The attack, in the perfect conditions, was routine. Some flak but no smoke screen this time, so down went the Tallboys. All eighteen 617 aircraft bombed within four minutes and of the first nine bombs which rained down on Hitler's last battleship within one and a half minutes, two were direct hits and three near misses! The ship started to list within seconds of the first strike by Wing Commander Tait's Tallboy, and after eleven minutes the 56,000 ton floating fortress had capsized to an angle of 135°. Her masts and upper works struck the seabed and prevented her sinking completely. Nine hundred and seventy-one German sailors, including the captain and most senior officers, were killed. eleven of 617 Squadron's aircrew were lost.

The analysis of the attack on 12 November confirms the claim that it was the supreme high level precision bombing operation in the World War II. Two direct hits and three near misses (within twenty-five yards) in the first nine bombs, within one and a half minutes, on a target the size of a matchstick from the average bombing height of 14,000 feet, was surely unbeatable!

A final comment: Sir Arthur Harris told the Admiralty that Bomber Command would sink the *Tirpitz* 'in our spare time', as our main business was with Germany. Well, I believe in a normal world, nine o'clock on a Sunday morning is universally accepted as 'spare time'!

Belsen

Iris Bower MBE ARRC

The order came for us to proceed to Celle, about twenty miles north of Hanover, and our journey took us through areas badly bombed, but nothing could wipe the memory of Caen out of my mind. This move was very significant: it was to be near Belsen, the concentration camp.

It had been liberated by British troops four days previously. Our officers were aware that the medical arrangements for dealing with the victims were in the hands of the RAMC, but as soon as they possibly could, they visited Belsen to offer any assistance. It had been considered that myself and another would accompany them on this first visit, but it was decided at the last moment that we should not go.

When they entered the camp, although it was four days since the liberation, what they saw was horrendous. The dead were still being buried and hundreds of emaciated victims were near death. Dirt and excreta everywhere, although every effort was being made to make some improvement in the situation. The stench was overpowering, they were shocked and stunned, and although experienced in witnessing disturbing scenes, they admitted being physically sick. When they returned to the unit, we could see that they had been deeply affected. They told us what they had seen and we found it unbelievable. A colleague mentioned one particular thing that has always stuck in my mind. He said he was walking past what he thought was a pile of old clothing when he saw movement. There were indeed more victims still alive.

It was decided to fly a few of the victims, who were in a better physical condition and able to make the journey, to a hospital in Belgium. I was asked the following day to assist in their care, during the period of transferring them from their stretchers on to a Dakota.

The ambulances would bring them from the Concentration Camp to the nearby airstrip. I remember, while I was waiting, the dreadful smell in the atmosphere. Some of the pilots told us afterwards that when planes flew at a certain height over Belsen the stench would sometimes penetrate into the planes. The ambulances arrived and I was apprehensive as the first stretchers were unloaded and placed on the grass near the Dakota. I went up to the first victim and was stunned. As more were unloaded, I looked around and they all had the same look. Most of them appeared like old men, but, when I read the medical cards pinned on their clothing, I discovered they were mostly young. The extraordinary thing was, looking back, I don't think I smiled at any of them. I find that unbelievable and very sad now. I don't know whether I was too shocked or couldn't bring myself to smile, and yet I had smiled a great deal at some of the troops who had become serious casualties.

I felt so very inadequate. Their eyes, I think, were the most haunting, staring and almost lifeless: there was no emotion. I don't know whether they realised what was going on. I did give them the odd drink and saw to their comfort on the stretchers. When the last was loaded on to the plane, we stood there until it had taken off. Our contact with them was so brief, it was over in no time, but we were deeply affected. I felt so very humble. Some episodes of that journey through Europe more than fifty years ago have completely vanished from my mind, but those moments with the Belsen victims, on that patch of grass near the Dakota, will stay in my memory all my life.

The Flying Fortress
Flight Lieutenant Gordon Carter

My experience as a Flight Engineer began after six months of intensive training with the emphasis on engines and airframes, at RAF St Athan in South Wales. I graduated in September 1943 as a Sergeant and this was followed by selection for the aircraft type in which you were destined to fly.

This process was very much a hit and miss affair. All the graduates were assembled in a hangar and the numbers required for each aircraft type were read out. There were only a few vacancies for Coastal Command, but as this was considered to be a safer option, there was no shortage of volunteers to step forward. People were nearly killed in the crush. To this day I am convinced that all coastal command engineers made either good rugby players or bouncers.

The next stage was a heavy conversion unit, in my case to Stirlings at a Conversion Unit in Suffolk. Crewing up was akin to a 'slave market'. The pilot, navigator, bomb aimer, wireless operator and gunners were already a crew from a Wellington OCU. Once again the hangar was used. The engineers stood in a group waiting for something to happen. Suddenly a pilot stood in front of you and asked if you would like to join his crew (no documentation – he must have just liked the look of you), and then the serious business of conversion training began.

There was very little ground instruction – no simulators, no mock-up aircraft, but straight down to sorting out the gauges and levers as the aircraft lumbered into the sky. The screen engineer occasionally slapped your hand and encouraged you if he was so minded. The heavy conversion unit standard of maintenance was very poor compared to the high quality experienced later on operational squadrons.

In under three months as a crew, we had an undercarriage malfunction, narrowly escaping a collapse on one side. On another occasion, complete brake failure on landing resulted in an over-run into a field beyond the aerodrome. Oil pressure failure on an inner engine, with a loss of auxiliary systems, nearly wrote off the air traffic tower due to a swing on take-off caused by a hydraulic throttle control leaking. Worst of all, a fractured elevator hinged arm on an aircraft signed up as serviceable: if I hadn't noticed it on a pre-flight check we would have crashed for sure.

The fuel system on the Stirling relied on gravity feed, and tanks being used in sequence, the cocks for fuel tanks not required were turned off to prevent inter-tank feeding. On my first cross-country trip a well kept fuel log was essential, gauges being far from accurate. However, late in the trip when the fuel state was critical, condensation dripping from my oxygen mask due to the lack of heating covered the paper of my log, ruining all my readings. Without upsetting the crew I turned on all the cocks, balance as well, and prayed for continued aileron control and a safe return.

The Stirling experience ceased when we were posted to Sculthorpe in Norfolk, to join 100 Group Bomber Support and Radio Counter Measures (RCM) operations. There we were introduced to American Flying Fortress crew members, who had arrived with some tatty war-weary aircraft.

Conversion to these Flying Fortresses was carried out on an entirely friendly basis, and some firm friendships were established. The local Norfolk farmers were less impressed, as during our solo conversion training we regularly 'beat them up' as they stood on their haystacks. The aircraft still had American markings and any complaints would have been made to a puzzled American 8th Airforce Headquarters.

The engineer on a USAAF Fortress was also the top gunner, and two pilots were always carried to make up the crew. We already had a mid-upper gunner who became our top gunner, and as the policy of the RAF was to have only one pilot, the engineer occupied the co-pilot's position.

Although we were not qualified to be pilots we were compelled to spend hours in the old Link Trainer to practise let down and flying on to the final approach, and we had to be able to relieve the pilot whilst in flight. Some 'brave souls' achieved reasonable but unofficial touch downs on real flights. My pilot actually fainted at altitude on a training flight, but when I brought the aircraft down to a lower level, he recovered in time to land: a worrying event that turned out alright. In the event of a pilot 'snuffing it' we had been advised by the Flight Commander to attempt to 'belly flop' at one of the three special airfields Manston, Woodbridge or Carnaby.

The engineer's task on the Fortress was the usual requirements of fuel handling, engine setting and monitoring temperatures and pressures.

The early Fortresses had hydraulic waste gate controls for the Turbo-Superchargers. Sometimes at altitude the oil would congeal, and then suddenly one or more of the engines would start to roar as the turbine over-sped, swinging the aircraft off course. The engineer would then fight to bring back control by devious manipulation of the cockpit levers. The later Fortress Gs (Mark 3) had electronic control: one simply dialled a number to set all four engines.

One drawback with the Fortress was that its optimum cruising speed was about ten knots slower than the Lancasters and Halifaxes, so in order to keep up higher power than desirable had to be used. This considerably reduced our endurance. The engineer's part in this was the management of a manual mixture lever labelled 'auto lean &

Boeing Fortress III (BU-W) of 214 Sqn (RAF Museum Hendon)

auto rich'. The power settings were a combination of manifold pressure (boost) and rpm – i.e. above a certain figure 'auto rich' was required to keep the cylinder and oil temperatures within limits. A chart kept by the engineer recorded the consumption for all engine settings. This figure had to be continuously divided into the remaining fuel to establish the endurance figure. The compilation of the engineer's log was therefore quite important. The clerical work in compiling the log was far from easy, the paperwork was on a small board, the control column was in the way, only a little red light could be used (otherwise the pilot's night vision was impaired), and too much light was hardly wise over enemy territory. Added to this, heating appeared non-existent so cold hands didn't help.

One trip in mid-1944 was to Konigsburg, East Prussia, flying over Sweden at a height of 9000 feet and a nine hour forty minute duration. The aircraft's endurance was stretched to the limit. For such trips the aircraft relied on the use of so-called long-range or Tokyo Tanks: these tanks had no gauges, but relied on cocks being operated around the bomb bay area to turn them on. The fuel from the Tokyo Tanks gravity-fed into the main tanks. There was no indication of fuel flow: all one had to go on was that the main tanks appeared to be reducing their usage. All the aircraft on this trip experienced very low tank readings on our return over the North Sea. One engineer kept a small hacksaw in his toolkit and panicked to the degree that he sawed through the hydraulic pipes of the Tokyo operating cocks, as we had been led to believe that pressure held them shut.

One other thing for the engineer to do was keep a good look out: with a hundred or more aircraft with no navigation lights on, all eyes were important.

In conclusion, the Fortress was a much more docile aircraft than the Stirling, more like a four engined Anson from a handling point of view. The low powered, but very reliable, 9-cylinder Wright Cyclones were no match for the twelve-cylinder Merlins or the fourteen-cylinder Hercules of British aircraft. However the turbo blowers enhanced the performance at altitude.

Our task in RCM operations was to neutralise German defences as much as possible and thus help to cut down our night bomber losses.

We carried devices to jam German Air Interception radar and Ground/Air communications. These had strange code names such as 'Jostle' and 'Airborne Cigar'. We carried German-speaking Wireless Operators as extra signallers. We dropped 'Window' to blanket German radar. We carried out spoof raids in which an aircraft would head towards a target and hopefully draw the attention of German defending forces from a genuine raid. We would then drop 'Window' and withdraw under its cover. We might repeat this manoeuvre several times during one night.

Stirlings of our Group would similarly orbit in wide circles over the North Sea in a manoeuvre known as 'Mandril Circle' – also designed to neutralise German radar detection. Bombers would then emerge from behind its cover, hopefully on a course German defences had not anticipated.

During our tour on the Fortress, we were damaged by flak, attacked several times by fighters, and had a minor mid-air collision with an out-going (friendly?) aircraft which damaged our tailplane. The pilot received the DFC after thirty-nine operations; the Rear Gunner the DFM for shooting down an enemy plane.

We were safer in the Fortress at night because we had four Air Gunners with 0.5 in ammunition. However, our RCM role with 'spoof' raids on German cities became more hazardous in early 1945, as the enemy started getting wise to our tactics and aircraft were shot down in the circuit of our final base at Oulton.

Despite these early experiences I went on to 'engineer' in many four-engined RAF aircraft until the early 1970s. By then I had just about got the hang of it!

Introduction of the Meteor

Wing Commander R. P. Beamont CBE DSO DFCC

In the summer of 1944 11 Group Intelligence Summaries began to record sightings and interception of high flying Mosquitos and PR Spitfires by twin-engined jets over Holland and the Rhine.

These interceptions showed greatly superior speed over the Allied aircraft and the attacks were only evaded, when sighted in time, by the greater manoeuvrability of our aircraft. But this was seen to be a potentially serious problem in view of the mounting daylight bomber attacks on Germany at that time. Two or three *Gruppen* of Me 262s in the fighter role would be likely to seriously alter the shape of the air war in the prelude to the imminent invasion of occupied Europe in the coming months.

Meantime the only squadrons of our fastest fighters, Tempests Vs, P51 Mustang IIIs, and Spitfire XIVs had had to be diverted from Operation Overlord (the Normandy landings) to defend London against the massive attack by V1 flying bombs which had begun in mid-June. Mosquitos were also committed to cover the hours of darkness, with some of the day fighters giving night cover when serviceability permitted. This was a massive operation which could not be reinforced as the larger numbers of Spitfire Vs, IXs and P47s had all proved too slow and had to be withdrawn from the V1 battle.

It was soon realised that with only eight squadrons of our fastest fighters available and none of them with long-range capability, a major increase of Me 262 activity could very soon affect air superiority over the Low Countries and Germany, more especially as the 430 mph approx. maximum of our fighters could not match the 500 plus of the 262s. But the latter did not appear in large numbers due to development delays; and also due to the direct order by Hitler that the whole production of 262s should be committed to the *Kampfgeschwader* for low level bombing operations, and a limited number for reconnaissance.

Meteor 1 of 616 Squadron Manston, August 1944 (Imperial War Museum)

Towards the end of July '44 I learnt at 150 Wing Newchurch in an ADGB (Air Defence of Great Britain) Press Release that an experimental squadron of Gloster Meteor 1s was being deployed to Manston 'to counter the flying bomb threat'. This sounded interesting and improbable, so I called the CO, Andrew McDowell – an old friend, and he said 'Come over and fly one!' It was as easy as that and reflected the informal and non-bureaucratic front-line activities of those times!

Parking my Tempest as far as possible from the end of an impressively formal line-up of Meteors on the East side tarmac at Manston, I queried with MacDowell the high risk, as I saw it, of such a close line-up of these very secret jets where they were approximately only eight minutes away from the bases of the strafing attack Fw190s and Me 109Gs, which happened all the time at Manston; and he said 'I did mention it, but ADGB insisted on it for an AM photocall!'

At close quarters the Meteor was not impressive. The short barrel-shaped engine nacelles suggested high drag, and the high semi-Tee-tail seemed likely to be affected by downwash from the wing at high angles of attack. But the real surprise to a practising fighter pilot was the lack of good vision from the cockpit resulting from its excessive iron-to-glass ratio, and virtually nil rear view. This was only surprising in the sense that all British fighters that had arrived in service in the past ten years had suffered from inadequate 'combat' vision, especially the Typhoon (the Me 109 had been no better), and it had been left to Focke Wulfe to solve this problem in 1942 with their 190.

This set a new, and for the first time acceptable standard, and the British followed in 1943 with the Tempest 'clear view' cockpit; but now in 1944 our new generation jet fighter had arrived with cockpit vision as restricted as the first series Typhoons!

Once in the cockpit the nose-down attitude conferred by the tricycle undercarriage provided a significant improvement in the view for taxiing, and the cockpit layout was simpler but conventionally British in its array of add-on brackets and 'Jubilee' clips. Industry and the procurement agency still had a long way to go at that time to provide good ergonomics and practical 'furnishing' design for fighter cockpits.

Briefing by one of 616 Squadron's flight commanders was straightforward, with emphasis on care to avoid compressor surge in engine handling (identified by rumbling vibration and sharply rising jet-pipe temperatures (JPT). Slowdowns to stalling were covered, then acceleration to max speed – about 485 mph IAS at 2000 ft – 'at that point you'll only have just enough fuel to get home!!'

Then a detailed brief on the tricycle undercarriage (new to most of us). 'At Vr smooth back-stick for rotation to airborne (no flaps). Hold climb angle at 180 mph until undercarriage retracted. Accelerate at full power to climb-speed 350, or accelerate to 485 mph IAS. Power back to cruise, and return to Base.'

'Roll rate poor throughout; Rudder tendency to snaking in turbulence; smooth but heavy in pitch – she's all yours!'

In taxiing out I found that near full power was needed to get going – it was not over-powered on the ground! Control on the ground was excellent with nose-wheel steering, and that was the first 'good point' noted, together with the very quiet smoothness of the jets, accompanied all the time by the smell of paraffin.

Lined up on Manston's vast westerly runway. Wind up quite slowly to max power. Release the brakes, and then no vast surge of acceleration but more a gentle trundle down the centre-line to rotation (a new word!) at 120 mph and then smooth climb away while retracting the undercarriage.

Handling on the climb smoothly conventional but heavy and unimpressive. View outside claustrophobic!

Maximum speed at 20,000 ft unimpressive and not much more than a Tempest. Diving to low level at full power gave an impressive rate of speed increase and showed that the Meteor had been thrust-limited rather than drag-limited in level flight.

Levelling at 2000 ft and heading back to Manston with the dwindling fuel state. At 484 mphp at that level there was little more to come (415 on a Tempest in these conditions), and control in pitch was smooth and heavy: in roll lighter but still heavy for a fighter, and in yaw imprecise with a continuous 'snaking' oscillation.

The fuel gauge was now demanding urgent attention as I steered this heavy, half-blind and imprecise aircraft back into the Manston circuit. Here it all became easy, except for the extreme difficulty of keeping a safe lookout for other traffic – there were blind spots everywhere.

Downwind the u/c and flap operations produced no serious trim changes and then it was just a matter of trimming to smoothly reducing power until the main wheels touched nose-high. Then throttles closed, stick gently forward to nose wheel contact, then roll-out straight down the centre-line with this splendid tricycle u/c!

This and the smooth, quiet turbine power were the only aspects enjoyable in this new-era aviation development, but it was a long way short of being a practical fighter aircraft at that stage.

Andrew McDowell's engineers, ground crews and pilots made a strenuous and courageous effort that summer to establish credibility for the Meteor 1, but the official record shows that, despite all the Air Ministry propaganda at the time, 616 Meteors destroyed only nine V1 flying bombs in August 1944, and this at a time when the neighbouring Tempests at Newchurch destroyed 638. There was an order of magnitude difference in capability, and as I flew my Tempest back home I reflected that at its proved and frequently used VNe (maximum speed, never exceed) of 545 mph IAS the Tempest was still sharply controllable on all axes, whereas this Meteor was almost 'solid' at 500.

The Meteor was of course improved in development up to the Meteor 8 which, with the 'E28 tail' and fully revised windscreen and rear-view canopy was being described as 'much improved' by the squadrons in 1947.

In specially prepared form, Meteor 4s established RAF world speed records in 1945 (605 mph) and 1946 (616 mph); and in the trials for the latter, Glosters encountered 'compressibility' pitch-down at 200 feet over the Avon river near Bristol. The Meteor was never going faster than that and the Company set a 'never exceed' safety figure of 616 mph IAS for the RAF's record attempt. In the event, Teddy Donaldson set up that precise figure in his two-way runs on one load of fuel – a very admirable performance.

Meteors gave good, though limited, service in ground attack, but had no successes in air-air operations in 1945 in Germany. Later in Korea they were used in courageous low attack operations by the RAAF, but they had to be kept well out of the way of Mig 15s! (*See account by John Price – Korea 1950*. Ed.)

And this saga all ended in 1948 after George Welsh's successful dives through Mach 1 in the first splendid XP86 Sabre, when CFE/West Raynham sent out their famous Christmas card: 'Please give us swept-wings for Christmas!'

The Meteor provided the RAF with a valuable introduction to the jet-turbine era, but it was never a class-act fighter.

The Aegean

After the surrender of Italy, both Churchill and Hitler turned their attention to the Balkans and Aegean. The Aegean sea is almost completely landlocked – bounded on the west by Greece and on the east by Turkey. Its southern approaches are guarded by mountainous Crete and Rhodes, its waters studded with hundreds of small islands.

The Germans were strongly entrenched in Greece where they had between six and seven divisions. They also had four divisions dispersed over the islands of the western Aegean, including Crete. The only weak point lay to the east in the Dodecanese, a group of islands adjoining the coast of Turkey.

These had been garrisoned by Italian forces. From Churchill's point of view, possession of the Dodecanese, hopefully with Italian co-operation following their surrender, offered glittering prospects. The Turks might be impressed enough to abandon their benevolent neutrality and actually join the Allies. Turkey would bring forty-six divisions and well placed air bases to the Allied cause. This would threaten the whole of Germany's flank in south-east Europe. Control of the Dardanelles and Bosphorus would open an easier southern supply route to Russia than the dangerous and costly Arctic convoys.

Churchill failed, however, to convince the Americans, who feared that such a venture might slow the advance in Italy and even siphon-off forces destined for the invasion of north west Europe.

The British were therefore left to go it alone, with woefully inadequate forces, over extended, vulnerable supply lines, and insufficient fighter cover. Hitler, on the other hand, had no-one to restrain him. Months before Italy fell, he had declared that the Italian peninsula could be sealed off but that the Balkans were of vital importance. On 28 July 1943, he had approved a contingency plan code named AXIS against possible Italian defection. This decreed that if Italy fell, all Italian forces would be disarmed, and all Italian warships, aircraft, military installations and equipment would be taken over by the Germans.

Anti-shipping strike by Beaufighters (AHB)

British Forces occupied most of the Dodecanese islands by mid-September, including Cos and Leros.

The outcome had always been inevitable. The Germans inexorably closed in on the small Allied enclave. Cos fell on 4 October, Simi on the 12th. Leros held out until 16 November and Samos until the 22nd. Only ten weeks after the invasion started, all Allied forces had been driven out of the Aegean.

No fewer than ten German divisions were however compelled to remain in Greece and the Aegean, to repel any further Allied invasion. Field Marshal Alexander later commented: 'Even so, they were unable to keep their communications open all the time.'

The principal instrument for the disruption of German communications and supply routes was the Allied Air Force in North Africa.

The Aegean Campaign 1944

Wing Commander A. E. Ross DFC

In his book *Royal Air Force At War* Air Chief Marshal Sir Christopher Foxley-Norris GCB DSO OBE wrote of the Aegean Campaign 'It was a serious and often hazardous campaign, with a major objective which was eventually attained. But it had a highly individualistic flavour, was never dull, routine or monotonous. If all campaigns were the same, war might become dangerously and deplorably attractive and entertaining.'

In more serious vein, however, he pointed out that the heavy casualties in anti-shipping squadrons resulted from a defect in armament. The aircraft had to point directly at, and usually over-fly, a heavily defended target at low level. At the end of 1942 Air Ministry had calculated that the chance of surviving one anti-shipping tour was just over twenty-five per cent. The chance of surviving two tours dropped to six per cent.

Number 603 Squadron, equipped with Beaufighters, was based in Libya at Gambut III, perched on the edge of a shallow escarpment some ten miles inland from the Mediterranean. To the east, south and west stretched hundreds of miles of sandy desolation littered with the debris of recent war – burnt out tanks, lorries, aircraft and abandoned guns. Over 200 miles to the north lay Crete and the Aegean over which the Squadron was operating.

The ground was uneven and the engineers had created Gambut by levelling part of the desert with bulldozers. They then laid a thin layer of tarmac to form a single runway. Although the bulldozers had produced a reasonably flat airstrip, they had broken up the compacted surface skin and exposed the loose sand underneath. Anything more than a slight breeze raised clouds of dust which hovered sullenly over the camp whilst the surrounding desert lay clear and unruffled. This provided a useful, although hardly welcoming landmark for returning aircraft.

The main aim of the Allied Air Force in North Africa was to weaken German garrisons in the Aegean islands by attacking their supply lines. These included formal, well defended convoys; large single supply vessels; landing craft, lighters, inconspicuous wooden caiques and Ju 52 transport planes. Other targets were heavily defended ground installations, airfields and radar stations. Additional tasks included armed reconnaissance, escorting convoys and seeking out and destroying U-boats in the Mediterranean. No two operations were the same! They ranged from set piece attacks by up to seventy aircraft on large convoys to single aircraft intruding over enemy airfields at night.

As a theatre of operations, the Aegean was unique. It possessed some of the most beautiful scenery in the world. If the weather was fine, we could enjoy the blue sea, studded with countless small islands with white-painted villages, churches and windmills. Most operations were not rigidly planned. We roved around seeking out supply vessels which might be on the open sea or hiding in sheltered inlets. We might encounter Ju 52s. If at the end of a patrol nothing had been sighted, we would make a surprise attack on ground installations, airfields or radar stations, rather than take our rockets back home!!

To offset these attractions, the tactical problems were formidable. To reach the Aegean, it was necessary to cross 240 miles of open, often stormy sea. Directly across the path lay Crete – 160 miles long with mountains rising up to 7000 feet. To the east of Crete were the almost equally mountainous islands of Scarpanto and Rhodes. To the north-west was the heavily defended mainland of Greece. There were numerous airstrips in the Aegean, many housing the Beaufighter's most formidable opposition – the Me 109s. Enemy radar cover was adequate, and fighters could quickly be summoned to intercept raids.

To counter radar, operations were carried out below the level of the radar screen – i.e. well under 100 feet. Rather than fly over Crete, patrols would enter and leave the Aegean via the narrow straits at either end of the island. It was essential for aircraft to fly at the correct height. If they were too high, they would be detected by radar. If they were too low, their slipstream might leave a wake on the water easily seen by high flying fighters. If the water was very smooth, it was difficult to judge the altitude precisely and aircraft could, and did, fly into the sea.

Countering the menace of the Me 109 was more difficult. The Squadron was operating beyond the range of single engined fighter cover, even of Spitfires with long range tanks. The Me 109 had a speed advantage of about sixty mph over the Beaufighter. It carried one 20 mm cannon and two machine guns. Correctly handled, a Beaufighter formation's manoeuvrability and fire power could make combat less one-sided.

The Beaufighter was immensely strong and had formidable armament – four 20 mm cannon plus a free firing rear machine gun. It also had eight rocket projectiles (RP). These could be fitted with either 60 lb explosive heads or 25 lb armour-piercing heads. They were fired manually in four pairs, or a by device nicknamed 'Mickey Mouse' which fired a timed salvo, giving a spread across the target. For an attack on a large vessel, both 25 lb and 60 lb heads were loaded on to the same aircraft. The armour piercing heads were aimed just short of the vessel, thus hitting the hull below water line. The 60 lb heads were fired immediately after and aimed above the waterline at the superstructure and guns. This was not an easy task. With cannon, the pilot could observe the fall of shot and make necessary corrections. With rockets, he had no such opportunity. The last pair was in the air before the first had struck. No one in the Eastern Mediterranean had any experience of rockets and their accurate use was a matter of trial and error .

On 27 January 1944, 603 scored one of its biggest successes. Four aircraft took off on an offensive sweep over the islands of Syros and Mykonos. We encountered three Ju 52 transport planes escorted by four Arado 196 fighters. Two Ju 52s were quickly shot down in flames and the third ditched. Despite spirited resistance, the four Arados were also destroyed.

This incident had a surprising sequel. Almost exactly 10 years later, the British Resident in Herford, West Germany, was visited by a local architect Herr Hermann Cremer. Herr Cremer explained that he had been the pilot of a Ju 52 shot down in the Aegean, and that as a token of reconciliation he wished to present a silver cigarette box to the Squadron concerned. Herr Cremer explained that he was leading the formation of Ju 52s, each of which contained twenty-one German soldiers. After the first aircraft was shot down, he took evasive action but was hit and had to ditch. Eleven survivors scrambled into dinghies with the burning wreckage of the formation scattered all round them. The Beaufighters swept low over them and *Oberfeldwebel* Cremer waited for them to open fire. There were no witnesses: the other machines had been destroyed with all their occupants. Instead the Beaufighters flew off and the survivors were, he said, filled with new hope and gratitude. They reached a neighbouring island and were eventually picked up by a naval cutter.

Whilst the air crews could relax, there was no respite for the ground crews. All servicing had to be carried out in the open, often in sand or dust storms. There were no well-equipped workshops at hand. Men stood on upturned oil drums to reach engines and control surfaces. Each rigger and fitter was intensely proud of his aircraft. If an aircraft was unserviceable the day before a planned operation, the men would work through the night rather than let their crew fly a spare aircraft. Far from the eyes of higher command, there were huddled discussions between ground and air crews about unauthorised modifications which might improve performance. The Direction Finding loops were of little use in the Mediterranean and their plastic housing resulted in unnecessary drag. They were promptly removed! Surfaces were rubbed down and polished. The armoured doors in the fuselage were heavy and many felt that if the aircraft was hit, it might need careful nursing back to base. A lighter aircraft might be that much easier and certainly faster, so the doors were removed. Modifications were made to the belts feeding the rear mounted Browning which was gradually replacing the drum fed Vickers gas operated machine gun.

By 8 March, the weather had improved enough for the Squadron to try night intruding. The Beaufighter's ASV radar (Air to Surface Vessel) was not accurate enough for attacks in complete darkness. Some moonlight was necessary to give a good chance of success. The plan was for an aircraft to fly along the north coast of Crete to Heraklion and lie in wait until a Ju 52 came in to land. Once the landing lights were switched on, it should be an easy target.

We set out on our long, lonely journey towards the eastern end of Crete. Accurate dead reckoning navigation was essential to reach the narrow entrance straits: there were no radio or radar aids. At length, the rocky promontory of Crete loomed up in the darkness and we turned along the coast, flying as low as the night visibility permitted. The moon was rising and casting a long silver path across the quiet dark waters. The island of Dia could just be seen on the right when the radar showed traces of something on the water. We banked away in a wide arc down moon so that whatever was in the water would show up in the moon path whilst the aircraft itself would be in the darker part of the sky. The radar relocated its target and the cautious stalking began. Suddenly there were dark shapes ahead: two large

Beaufighters of 603 Squadron low-level bombing of shipping at Missolonghi, 19 August, 1943 (A. E. Ross)

vessels in line astern steaming towards the harbour. Once more we swung away, this time to make a carefully planned attack. The correct height was reached and the dive began. The range closed. The 'Mickey Mouse' was set for a salvo at 800 yards. The glowing rocket exhausts streaked ahead and a bright yellow light suddenly appeared on the leading vessel. We pulled sharply away to starboard to avoid silhouetting ourselves against the moon. As we resumed our attack position, flames were leaping high into the air from the doomed vessel. Another attack was made on the second ship, this time with cannon since all the rockets were gone. Some hits were observed, but in the darkness the damage could not be assessed. Intelligence sources later confirmed that a destroyer, the *Francesco Crispi*, (taken over by the Germans after the Italian surrender), had been sunk.

The high degree of co-operation between the diverse squadrons in Libya was graphically illustrated in a major operation on 1 June 1944. The constant attacks on shipping and transport aircraft had left the German garrisons very short of supplies. A large convoy was therefore assembled at Athens and loaded with essential items for Crete. It consisted of four merchant ships, all flying barrage balloons to discourage attack by low-flying aircraft. The escort was formidable: four destroyers, three torpedo boats and four E-boats. All available Ju 88s and Arado 196s were assembled to provide air cover. The convoy was shadowed throughout the day by Baltimores. It was known to be heading for Candia Harbour on the north of Crete. Allied Forces were briefed for a massive attack. Seventeen Baltimores of 454 and 15 SAAF Sqns, and twelve Marauders of 24 SAAF Sqn were to carry out a medium level bombing attack, flying directly over Crete. Fighter cover was provided by twenty Spitfires and Mustangs of 94 and 213 Sqns. The Beaufighter force would meantime enter the Aegean at low level through the straits between Crete and Scarpanto. They would then fly west along the coast and strike the convoy just after the bombing attack, when there would be maximum confusion. Four Beaufighter Squadrons were involved – 252, 227,16 SAAF and 603. The rocket attack on the merchant vessels was to be carried out by eight aircraft of 252 Squadron. To give them as clear a run as possible, eight aircraft of 603 would go in first to destroy anti-aircraft defences on the starboard side. Six Beaufighters of 16 SAAF Sqn would similarly attack on the port side. Four Beaufighters of 227 Sqn would act as close escort to drive away any attacking fighters.

The attack was a complete success. The *Sabine* and *Gertrude* were left stationary in the water. The *Tanais* was blazing and her crew abandoned her. Several of the escorts were damaged. One Me 109 and two Arado 196s were destroyed. Next day two reconnaissance Mustangs found *Gertrude* in harbour blazing. There was no sign of *Sabine*. Four Beaufighters were shot down.

The Far East

Supreme Headquarters South East Asia was established in autumn 1943 under Admiral Mountbatten. Air Marshal Sir Richard Peirse commanded Allied Air Forces with the US General Stratemeyer as his deputy.

Towards the end of 1943 Mountbatten launched a four pronged offensive. Each operation was totally dependent on air support.

Air operations continued despite appalling weather conditions. By mid-1944 Allied air strength was supreme. The Japanese army was in disarray. It faced crushing attacks from tactical air forces on the battlefield. Air Chief Marshal Sir Keith Park of Battle of Britain and Malta fame now took over as Commander of the Allied Air Forces.

The Chindits destroyed Japanese lines of communication. Allied strategic air forces hit railways, dumps, bridges and even mined the rivers. The RAF Regiment played an invaluable role.

General Slim's army swept through to victory in May 1945.

There remained the task of rescuing and repatriating thousands of prisoners of war and, as Sir David Lee describes, this proved a difficult and dangerous task.

The War at Sea

Group Captain the Rt Hon. the Earl of Selkirk KT GCMG GBE AFC AE

I found the anti-submarine war in the Indian Ocean very different in character from that in Europe. Flying boats were the main weapon at the RAF's disposal and we had three squadrons of Catalinas and one of Sunderlands.

At the end of 1943 there were two Japanese and one German submarine operating in the Indian Ocean. In November the Japanese sank three merchant ships and made an unsuccessful attack on another. One of the Japanese submarines was an I-boat which carried an aircraft in a hangar forward of the conning tower. This aircraft enabled the Japanese to carry out regular reconnaissance of Allied bases.

A British warship in Mombasa reported an aircraft flying at less than 1000 feet. It was a long wing monoplane with a radial engine and twin floats. It dropped foil strips to confuse the radar stations. The same aircraft made an appearance over the Seychelles before its parent submarine headed back to its base at Penang in Malaya, sinking the Norwegian tanker *Scotia* on the way.

Swings from violent and sustained action to the monotony of weeks of routine flying with no sightings were typical of Indian Ocean operations. Any respite gave opportunities for naval/air exercises in submarine recognition – a subject unfamiliar to many newly arrived aircrews. Anti-locust flights could also be carried out.

In March 1944 the Japanese aircraft again tormented the RAF. It flew over Diego Suarez on the north of Madagascar in bright moonlight. A little later it explored Mombasa, gliding in from the sea from 1500 down to 500 feet. Curiously it displayed a white light but this was extinguished when three anti-aircraft batteries opened up. It flew away south and was tracked by radar for thirty miles. Two naval Swordfish were scrambled but failed to intercept.

The Catalinas sometimes ran into trouble on their long flights over this immense ocean.

On 21 February 1944 a Catalina of 209 Squadron had to force land by a small atoll eighteen miles north of Assumption Island. It radioed for help and with the assistance of HMS *Sondra*, Pinnace 94 and flying boats of East Africa command, a new engine was fitted while the Catalina lay in the water. It took off safely from the lagoon and returned to its base.

Next month there was another rescue. A Catalina from Mahe had been escorting a convoy. On returning from patrol it failed to find its base, and having run out of fuel landed safely on a calm sea some forty miles south of the Seychelles. Another Catalina located her and homed HM Trawler *Mastiff* on to the stranded flying boat. The trawler towed it safely back to base.

A classic example of naval/air co-operation occurred in August 1944. On 5 August the SS *Empire City* signalled the presence of enemy units in the Mozambique Channel. She was then torpedoed and sunk by *U-198*. On 7 August the SS *Empire Day* was sunk in a position a little further north. On 8 August *U-198* signalled its base that conditions were favouring its operations and two other U-boats in the area were therefore sent north to leave the field clear.

The Navy and Air Force now began a combined hunt for the German submarine.

As reports came in from both Navy and RAF sources the area of operation of the U-boat was more closely defined. Aircraft shadowed the U-boat for seven days. Although not able to attack they slowed it down so much that a Naval Carrier Force managed to arrive in the area to take part in the hunt.

Early in 1944 the Combined Chiefs of Staff had decided that carrier forces should maintain pressure on enemy submarines in the South East Asia Command area to force their dispersion. They were used mainly to escort convoys. In June Admiral Somerville began to employ Force 66 as an anti-submarine unit, initially without success. This Force, consisting of the escort carriers HMS *Begum* and HMS *Shah* and the four frigates HMS *Taff*, *Findhorn*, *Nadder* and *Parret* now joined the combined operation. Catalinas of 246 Wing continued the search from three bases.

The submarine was sighted from the air on 10 August and HMS *Shah* attacked without success. The submarine dived and contact was lost. The hunt was now three-pronged. In addition to the naval vessels there were carrier aircraft and land-based flying boats searching relentlessly for the U-boat. On 12 August a Catalina of 259 Squadron made contact which showed the submarine moving eastwards. The Naval Task Force Commander believed that *U-198* might be running short of fuel and attempting to return to Penang. That same day an aircraft from HMS *Shah* saw the submarine on the surface and attacked. The enemy dived, then resurfaced and fired on the aircraft. It circled for about twenty minutes with its steering gear possibly damaged. It then dived again and contact was once more lost.

Other ships had by now arrived and HMS *Godavari* made contact, which she held for nearly an hour until two other frigates *Findhorn* and *Parret* arrived. After the first attack underwater explosions were heard and oil patches and wreckage rose to the surface.

Unfortunately whilst this successful hunt was going on, two other U-boats rounded the Cape from the South Atlantic and sank five merchant ships in the extreme south of the area. One of these was the SS *Hadbury*. There was no time to send an SOS signal, and the ship was reported overdue from 20 August. Her fate did not become known until two months later when a Catalina found survivors on a lonely island where they had lived out a strange existence under the courageous leadership of the Chinese Chief Engineer. Massive efforts were made to locate the attackers without success. Every known pattern of patrol was exploited but the area of possibility was too vast and the density of air cover insufficient.

The U-boats were far from defenceless against these attacks. On 20 August 1944 a Catalina of 265 Squadron was shot down by U-boat gunners. An SOS was sent and ships and aircraft searched the area for four days. No trace was discovered.

So this remote war continued, with successes swinging sometimes one way, sometimes the other. Tragic though the shipping losses were, the efforts of East Africa and Aden Commands helped keep them as low as possible. During one month some 2,000,000 tons of shipping passed through the area and less than 1% was lost.

Minelaying

Air Vice-Marshal J. N. Stacey CBE DSO DFC

After six months in Cape Town and another six running a small flying boat conversion unit in Mombasa, I returned to Ceylon, via Socotra, an island off the north east tip of Africa where they still punished thieves by hand amputation! After another intriguing detachment to Mauritius where we helped the Navy to sink a German ship intended to refuel their submarines, I was sent as a Flight Commander to No. 160 Liberator Squadron based at Sigiriya, about the middle of Ceylon. It was now March 1944 but the return to landplanes after four years on flying boats posed no problems. In October '44 I was promoted and given command of the squadron, and our role was changed to minelaying.

Loading mines into a Liberator (AHB)

We moved to Minneriya, about ten miles from Sigiriya and again in the centre of the island, because it had the longest runway which we needed as we were now operating at 64,000 lb, against the designed 56,000 lb.

The object of mining was to sink ships, or at least to disrupt shipping supplies by compelling sweeping of port channels before they could be used again. Aircraft could not carry the WW I mines which were anchored to the seabed with the mine sitting on the surface. Our mines sat on the seabed and were dropped by parachute to avoid structural damage: it was important to ensure the mines were laid where ships would go but not in a depth greater than that in which the mine would be effective. We also had fun with the characteristics of our mines. We had electronically and acoustically triggered mines, and either could be set for various 'ship counts'. In plain words, the mine could go off when the first ship passed, or any number up to twelve – and this of course greatly lengthened the sweeping process for the Japanese.

The targets were sea ports in Thailand, Malaya and Sumatra. Losses were likely to be prohibitive in daytime, so we operated at night when the moon was enough to identify geographical features. We dropped visually from 200 feet for accuracy, which would have been hazardous but for the Lib being fitted with a radio altimeter giving precise height above the sea. To avoid abandoning the sortie if bad weather prohibited visual dropping after the long sea crossing, we developed an alternative technique for dropping by radar.

Early in 1945 our masters in Colombo were seeking a means of extending the offensive spirit more deeply into Japanese occupied territory. We were pressed to drop mines in the entrances to Singapore but it was a long way, over 1500 nautical miles, i.e. a round trip of 3400 statute miles, and this was well beyond our range. We eventually solved the problem in various ways. The weight of the Liberator was reduced to the minimum. I can't remember all the details, but we reduced by some 2000 lb: for example, all guns were removed, except two rear ones which had only about 200 rounds each, and all oxygen equipment was removed. But we still could not make it.

We always stayed low level – about 250 feet – to avoid alerting defences and to reduce losses. The approach and withdrawal for Singapore would therefore normally involve a fair dogleg north of Sumatra and through the Straits of Malacca. We could save much fuel, however, if we went in this way but came back the direct route over Sumatra at some 10,000 ft to clear mountains: our fuel consumption would also be far less at this height. By fitting Catalina overload tanks of 150 gal capacity over the bomb bay of each Lib, we then had just enough reserve to justify the attack.

Nine aircraft took off at minute intervals about noon on 23 March; our take-off weight was 68,000 lb. We met no opposition and all dropped their mines as and where planned. The return trip was very uncomfortable as we had to fly along the inter-tropical front most of the way: the turbulence, lightning and rain were constant and most unenjoyable. All aircraft landed back safely late morning on the 24th. The average flight time was 21½ hours and fuel left in the tanks was enough in theory for about one and a half hours !

Number 160 Sqn had the usual mixture of people from the UK, Canada, Australia, New Zealand, South Africa, the United States and others; and every crew had two or more nationalities. But, as elsewhere in the Royal Air Force, there was no suggestion that a 'national' crew should be created: mutual trust quickly grew in every crew and this overrode all else, including national feelings. It is a pity it takes a war to break down barriers which at other times seem insuperable!

Air Supply in Burma

Group Captain D. W. Groocock AFC

In February 1944, 194 Dakota Sqn was moved to Assam, and immediately became involved in supplying our ground troops who were now beginning to take on the Japanese forces on their own terms. It soon became clear that in a country like Burma, practically devoid of roads, railways, and navigable waterways, air supply was essential if the troops were to succeed.

Successful air supply operations rely on two main elements – an efficient base organisation and air superiority. Supplies were delivered to the ground forces either by air landing, or air dropping.

Air landing, wherever possible, was on existing airfields, but it could involve landing on airstrips constructed by the ground forces themselves. These strips were behind enemy lines and usually only about 1000 yards long. Landings were mostly made at night and were particularly hazardous when the strip was surrounded by hills.

Air Dropping could either be 'free fall' or utilising parachute containers. Free fall was used when the items to be dropped – e.g. rice – were not liable to damage on impact. It could be particularly hazardous to those on the ground! On locating the Dropping Zone, which in Burma was usually very small, the aircraft would need to make eight to ten circuits to get rid of its load. The hilly conditions would often involve the aircraft in tight, steeply banked circuits and this made life very difficult for crew members.

The monsoon comes to Burma in May and lasts until October. Prior to 1944 it had been considered that active campaigning during this period was not feasible. However, this all changed in 1944. The army were trained to fight in the jungle in monsoon conditions and the same air supply effort was therefore required throughout the year.

The art of monsoon flying was to keep below cloud as much as possible: only flying into cloud (usually a giant cumulo-nimbus) when it was impossible to avoid doing so. This involved much flying down small valleys, with high mountains vanishing into the clouds on either side. The effort was so intensive that within a very short time we knew the landscape of northern Burma like the back of our hands, and knew just which valleys we could fly down without coming to a blind end.

With practically nothing in the way of navigation aids and not terribly good maps, finding the Dropping Zones posed a major problem and required great skill on the part of the navigator. Fortunately, at night, the recognition signals used by the troops on the ground could be seen from a fair distance.

194 Squadron SEAC Dakota FD 835 loading bullock, 24 March, 1944 (RAF Museum Hendon)

All these operations would have been quite impossible without an aircraft like the Dakota. It was robust and reliable and had an extremely high serviceability record.

Dropping supplies on small bases in narrow valleys could be exciting, but even more exacting were the landings made behind Japanese lines. My crew and I flew into 'Broadway' the night after the gliders landed, and over the next two months landed twenty-one times at night on various air strips. We actually got away with one landing staggering up a tiny valley at about 75 knots.

Not only did we carry troops into Burma, but also mules in large numbers and some oxen. The latter were known as 'food on the hoof'. It could be very tricky loading mules: often one would make a break for liberty and it was amusing to see four or five soldiers trying hard to restrain one when they couldn't get a grip on the monsoon-sodden ground.

Our relations with the army were superb: they were very grateful for the food, ammunition and mail we provided. We were full of admiration for their spirit and cheerfulness whilst operating under fearsome conditions. At least we got back to base fairly often and were able to enjoy comparative civilisation.

On one occasion we were one of twelve aircraft briefed to make a drop on a Dropping Zone north of Kohima. We were loaded (and badly overloaded) with bags of rice for free-fall dropping. We were on our way north when we found ourselves flying above 8/8s layer of cloud and could see nothing of the ground. However we pressed on, hoping that in the vicinity of the Dropping Zone we would find a break in the cloud which would enable us to make a visual let down. We were flying at 8500 ft, which gave us a clearance of 1500 ft above the mountains which rose to 7000 ft. When we got to where we thought the Dropping Zone should be, I told the wireless operators to prepare the loads for dropping. This entailed opening the rear door and piling up bags of rice ready for pushing out.

A few minutes later, to my great consternation, the aircraft's airspeed, normally about 135 mph, started to drop off for no apparent reason. I put on more power to no avail – the speed just dropped off faster. The nose reared up and the aircraft flicked over into a right hand spin with a rate of descent of over 2000 ft per minute. This gave us about forty-five seconds before we hit the mountain. We were now in the cloud and could see nothing. I took the normal spin recovery action – power off, full opposite rudder and stick forward – and thought this was the end. I saw the altimeter go down to 6000 ft, 5550 ft, 5000 ft and still we hadn't hit. The next second we came out below cloud at 4500 ft, under control and in a valley with great peaks vanishing into the cloud on either side.

Trembling like a leaf, I flew down the valley and considered what had happened. Fortunately all the crew were still with me. They had not been wearing parachutes and were still trying to struggle into them when we broke cloud. We realised that the aircraft must have been very badly loaded and removing some of the load near the door ready for ejection must have put the centre of gravity right outside the limits, causing the aircraft to become uncontrollable. Once in the spin, the sacks near the door fell forward, putting the centre of gravity back within limits and enabling us to recover.

Suddenly ahead we saw a column of smoke coming up from the ground and flew towards it. To our amazement it was the Dropping Zone, displaying the correct recognition letters. We flew round and round it, waving like mad to the chaps on the ground and pushing out the rice which had so nearly been our downfall. We now realised that there was no way of flying out of that particular valley at low level, and that we would have to climb out of it through the cloud. Selecting the widest part we could find, I put the aircraft into a steep climbing turn into the cloud and prayed that we would not drift into the ridges on either side of us. After what seemed an age but was actually about five minutes, we emerged out of the clouds into bright sunshine and headed back home.

Out of the twelve aircraft which set out we were, of course, the only one which had dropped. The others, finding no way of getting down through the cloud had wisely brought their loads back.

The next day we received a signal from Rear Brigade headquarters. 'Congratulations to the pilot who dropped at QK 21.'

Little did that Column Commander know how the drop had been accomplished!

Special Operations in the Far East

Terence O'Brien

After a few months' staff duty in Calcutta in 1942, I was posted to Bombay, an acting squadron-leader, to command:

1. RAF station Juhu – the only operating one on the west coast.
2. A new one, being constructed, at Santa Cruz.
3. The OTU at nearby Andheri, and
4. The RAF Naval Liaison Depot in Bombay city.

Low flying SEAC Liberator (AHB)

In this quadruple command my responsibility for air defence of India covered some eight hundred miles of the west coast. I had six aircraft for that – four Ansons and two biplane Dominies.

With a house on Juhu beach, a seaside flat in Bombay – and two enchanting Anglo-Indian secretaries – the job was widely envied, but not exactly what I had in mind when rushing off from the Solomon Islands to join the war. So when a signal came in April 1943, inviting volunteers for what was described as a dangerous mission, I grabbed for the escape – and finished up in the jungle with the Gurkhas training for a behind-the-lines stunt in Burma.

An eccentric Brigadier called Wingate had been inside for two months, was now pulling out, and our brigade would take over. But Churchill had noticed Wingate's operation and called him to England. Then he was taken to Quebec, where Roosevelt too was beguiled – he was an impressive zealot, Wingate.

Promoted to Major-General he now took over our brigade as part of his Chindit force – which was fantastically endowed with aircraft. This was Colonel Cochrane's US Air Commando: 100 Li LS light aircraft, thirty-five Dakotas, fifty Mustang fighters, thirty Mitchell bombers, ten helicopters, 100 gliders. All for us.

And we were less than divisional strength.

Most of GHQ staff in Delhi were critical of this favouritism for Wingate – but our Air Commando did, in one action, have significant effect on the whole Burma war. This was in March '44 when the Japanese, preparing for operation 'U-Go' – the invasion of India, deployed the bulk of their regional air force forward to Burma. A Cochrane recce spotted the accumulation, and in the next three days – the RAF joined in the kill – ninety Japanese aircraft were destroyed on the ground. That finished effective air opposition in Burma for the rest of the war.

The Chindits were to be landed on three separate jungle clearings, two major groups on the near side of the Irrawaddy, our small group far beyond it. Gliders would land an advance party with a bulldozer, make a strip ... and then aircraft would bring in the brigades.

But now comes the weird bit. Wingate, with a bizarre sense of security, forbade his aircraft to go anywhere near the clearings. They had some old photographs – they were good enough. (The RAF had much better ones – PRU Mosquitos were overflying the areas twice every week.)

Luckily for us, on D-Day itself Cochrane decided this was madness too far, and he ordered photographs, without permission. The pictures arrived at the strip that evening, when the advance parties of the two major groups were about to embark in their gliders. Wingate and the assembled brass, Slim among them, were shocked at the sight. They showed one clearing was blocked murderously with logs. Did the Japanese know something?

The second site looked fairly clear – but had it, also, been compromised ?

Faced with that critical decision, with all the gliders lined up on the strip, Brigadier Calvert – he had been a column commander in the first expedition, and was a close friend of Wingate – declared himself ready to take in the advance party of his Brigade to that second clearing.

It was a close-run thing. Less than half the sixty gliders landed safely. A hundred men were killed or seriously wounded. But they did finally manage to start work with the bulldozer, and on the following night the strip was completed and had begun taking in planeloads of men and mules and equipment.

The night after that, our small group, with eight gliders, went off to the far site, beyond the Irrawaddy. Among our losses was the bulldozer – with all its crew. So, that left me to take on the strip-building that night with a platoon of Gurkhas, five spades, and our kukries, cutting through the elephant grass and smoothing down the ridges as best we could. But by dawn – when we had to pull back into the jungle – we had cleared some four hundred yards. It was enough for a glider with bulldozer to land safely next night, and four hours after that the Dakotas were streaming in to our jungle clearing.

For the next three months our column toiled away northwards through that mountainous terrain along the Chinese border, setting up road blocks, withdrawing after action, searching for water – we had one hundred and fifty mules, remember – and taking supply drops.

The standard of marksmanship for these, from both RAF and US, varied. Rarely did a pilot start with a single parachute and then adjust after its fall. But the overall air support was truly astonishing. For a 12,000-man armed force to be landed in enemy-occupied territory and then be supplied entirely by air for three fighting months, was a remarkable feat for the time. Any time, perhaps. Just think of taking on the Falklands campaign – without using ships.

Wingate had reckoned three months was the limit of human endurance in our conditions, but when he was killed the Chindits came under control of the appalling General Stilwell, who refused to release us. Chindit commanders were close to revolt when Slim finally sent a regular division to take over. Most Chindit survivors were lifted out from Myitkyena area, some from Lake Indawgi by Sunderland flying boats, we from our strip across the Irrawaddy – 104 of us out of the 1350 originally landed.

I turned up at Air HQ presently to redeem the Air Marshal's promise – a choice of postings. My choice was command of a Dakota flight, to be established in a Special Duty squadron.

There were dozens of new squadrons by Autumn 1944. But clandestine activity was still sluggish – only eighteen sorties in the two full years up to January 1944. A few were by Catalinas, but most by Hudsons from a parachute training school – just occasional one-offs.

But that autumn clandestine operations ended in Europe, and matériel and expertise were suddenly available for India. The change for us was dramatic. By December '44 a new Liberator squadron had joined us at Jessore: our own Liberator flight was up to sixteen aircraft; our sixteen Dakotas were fully operational; we had a Lysander flight in preparation; and we had a new CO fresh from England, with a wealth of experience in clandestine work.

The clandestines took quick advantage of the bonanza. As against those eighteen operations in the two years up to December '43, there were seventy-one in the month of December 1944.The majority were for SOE and, to a lesser extent, MI6 – but we also served MI9, MI19, D Division, Psychological Warfare, the American OSS and others, with more than two hundred sorties each moon period by the summer of 1944.

And the value of it all? Well, there was dross, certainly. But there was also one real nugget: Operation CHARACTER – worth the whole RAF investment in clandestine operations, according to the Head of SOE.

'Character' was composed of several British-Karen groups – set up purely for intelligence gathering – in the hills east of Toungoo. They were important for the XIVth Army, because Toungoo was the last obstacle on the road to Rangoon, so it had to be closely monitored.

The deadline for its capture had been set at 25 April, the traditional start of the rains – otherwise the army could be bogged down at the end of a monsoon-flooded support line of some six hundred miles. It had seemed an easy target at first, held by just one brigade, but then two full Japanese divisions – pulled out from Mandalay – set off down through the hill road: a motorable road bypassing Meiktila, which we had captured.

Once the Japanese divisions arrived the town was going to be a formidable obstacle, and Mountbatten flew down to reassure the army commander. He wrote: 'I told him I would personally take responsibility for his getting anything up to 3000 men killed to capture the town.'

Slim had not entirely given up hope of reaching the town first. He said afterwards that it seemed the Japanese would beat us to the town, but that he 'had one last shot' in his locker. He fired it on 14 April – sent a signal to 'Character', urging that they switch from passive spying to direct action. He asked that they do everything in their power to hold up the enemy divisions, so that his forces – fighting their way down the main road – might get there first.

That was just twelve days before the monsoon deadline of 25 April, with the enemy divisions then closing fast on the town. Both squadrons at Jessore were immediately involved in this critical race for Toungoo – for we were the only supply line to the guerrillas.

And the outcome? This is from Slim's book:

> 'The Japanese, driving hard through the night down the jungle roads towards Toungoo, ran into ambush after ambush. They had to fight each inch of the way, slower and slower... until about fifty miles east of the town and there they were, held up for four vital days by demolitions and ambuscades. We entered the town on the 22nd of April – the Jap divisions had lost the race for Toungoo.'

That cleared the way to Rangoon – it fell a week later.

As against the three thousand lives Mountbatten was prepared to pay for the town, it cost the Army ... just seven. The SOE guerrillas ... five. The RAF ... eleven – in the three aircraft lost in the monsoon storms.

Such a concentrated effort on one particular clandestine operation was unusual. But it did happen again just after the fall of Rangoon, when the Lysander flight became totally committed to the guerrillas fighting the Japanese groups trying to escape through the hills; and also on Operation ZIPPER, when the Liberators, some flying out of the Cocos Islands, were dropping SOE teams to prepare for the sea-borne assault on Malaya – the atomic bomb saved us from that.

Among the minor clandestines D Division provided the most diverting sorties. Their objective was to deceive the Japanese – their mistake was to assume Japanese Intelligence was as sharp as the Germans' – for example ... one of their stunts was a copy of The Man Who Never Was, but whereas the European corpse did possibly affect enemy decision, ours was completely ignored. So too was a Brigadier's cap and map case with phoney information that we dropped in another ploy of theirs.

Behind-the-lines work has always had great dramatic appeal – and some years ago I listed thirty-one books by, and about, the agents out there. But I couldn't discover one about the aircrews who had serviced them. Yet it wasn't down in the exciting, dramatic, jungle that the greatest danger lay. Aircrew at Jessore suffered forty times greater loss of life than the men we dropped – only five of them were subsequently killed in action in Burma, none at all in Siam nor Malaya.

But it was a gratifying experience working with the clandestines, and now, when I think back to those moonlight flights over the hills of South East Asia, it is nostalgia I always feel. Not like memories of the nights on bombers. With the clandestines, your arrival on target, and the loads you dropped, were always welcomed by those down below.

Fighter Bomber Operations in Burma

Wing Commander Jack Rose CMG MBE DFC

Towards the end of 1944, after a tour of duty flying rocket-firing Hurricane IVs and Typhoons from bases in England and France, I boarded a Sunderland flying boat at Poole early in October bound for Air Command South East Asia (ACSEA).

In mid-October I reached AHQ at Kandy in the hilly country of central Ceylon.

Within a few days I was off again to Imphal in India's Manipur State to join 221 Group. By the beginning of November I had taken over command of No. 113 Squadron, based at Palel and equipped with Hurricane IIcs. The single airstrip was about twenty miles south of Imphal. The floor of the Imphal valley, some 2–3000 feet above sea level, is surrounded by hills rising in ridge after ridge up to 9–10,000 feet. There can be few more striking views than those offered by the Manipuri hills at sunset in fine weather. But when storm clouds sat on the surrounding hills, soaring to 4000 feet or higher, negotiating a path back to the valley floor in a single-engined fighter aircraft could present problems.

My arrival at Palel coincided with the beginning of the final phase of the war against the Japanese. After the humiliation of the fall of Singapore in February 1942, the long retreat back to India and the hard-won lifting of the sieges of Kohima and Imphal, the XIVth Army under General Slim, supported by the aircraft of 221 Group, had begun its great drive down through central Burma.

After flying over the surrounding country for an hour or so to familiarise myself with local landmarks, I began to lead the Squadron's attacks on Japanese positions pinpointed for us, usually by forward troops of the XIVth Army. These targets might be defensive bunkers, troop concentrations, bridges or stores dumps.

Air superiority had already been established but it was comforting at times to be given cover by No.17 Sqn's Spitfire VIIIs under Squadron Leader J. H. (Ginger) Lacey while we were concentrating on aiming our bombs and shooting our 20 mm cannon at ground targets. Meanwhile squadrons of Republic Thunderbolts at nearby Wangjing were carrying out longer range attacks on airfields and escorting Dakotas on supply missions. Although at this stage we were relatively free from the threat of enemy fighter opposition, the hazards associated with low level attacks on defended targets in broken country were ever present. One aspect of the air fighting over Burma which contrasted with operations over occupied Europe was the likely fate of a pilot unlucky enough to be taken prisoner. In general the Germans tended to treat captured aircrew with a reasonable degree of correctness, but the stories of the inhuman treatment of their captives by the Japanese were legion. Their reputation was even further debased by Intelligence photographs which circulated at the time, showing a row of captured aircrew, kneeling and blindfolded, in the act of being beheaded by a Japanese soldier while a group of his grinning fellows looked on.

A typical day would begin with the Army Liaison Officer gathering target information and photographs well before dawn from Army Intelligence sources. We would then brief the Squadron pilots. At first the targets were mainly in the Chindwin valley, and involved round flights averaging about an hour and a half: much of the time flying over the mountainous country surrounding our base or negotiating the valleys dividing the mountain ranges. A normal day would find each available pilot flying two or three sorties spread over the daylight hours, but later on, as our bases were advanced into the central plain where the heat became so intense that it was impossible to touch the aircraft with a naked hand, flights were restricted whenever this could be managed to early morning and evening.

When the targets, particularly the Japanese bunkers, were close to our forward troops, they were usually pinpointed for us by orange smoke shells. The Allied troops, in readiness about 200 yards from the targets, launched their assaults as swiftly as possible after the air attacks had ended. Where the country was thickly wooded and very broken, as in the Chindwin River valley where it was crossed north of Kalewa, it took our troops so long to cover the 200 yards or so from their unmarked safe bomb line to the bunkers that the enemy had time to recover from the air bombardment and offer tough resistance from their strong positions. The answer was to reduce the distance between the bomb line and the target. This was achieved by the forward troops holding up orange golf umbrellas which were shielded by the intervening trees from the enemy view but were clearly visible to us from above. The distance to be covered by the troops to reach the bunkers could thus be reduced to as little as fifty yards, and the time gap greatly shortened. Reports that filtered back to us were highly appreciative.

From Palel we moved to Yazagio in the Kabaw Valley ('Death Valley' as it was known, owing to the very high incidence of malaria and other parasitic diseases.) On one of his tours of the forward areas, Lord Mountbatten, the Supreme Allied Commander, visited us at Yazagio. He produced a large map of Burma which was colour-graded in accordance with a scale indicating the prevalence of diseases which could, if unchecked, seriously undermine the effectiveness of the forces. On this map the Kabaw Valley was coloured purple, showing it to be the unhealthiest area in the country. As the allied forces were well supplied with prophylactic medicines, in contrast to the enemy's reported shortages, Lord Mountbatten explained that he had chosen the timing of the fighting in the Kabaw Valley to place the Japanese at the maximum disadvantage. Here, as the trees were too thinly scattered to give reasonable shade, we rigged camouflaged supply drop parachutes between the trees to keep some of the sun's intense heat at bay. From here we advanced behind the ground forces to Onbauk and Ondaw in the central plain, where the heat was even more intense and the absence of shade more marked.

On arriving at a new airstrip the first task of all concerned, before our tents were erected, was to dig rectangular holes about two feet deep to take our camp beds. There were two reasons: protection from blast injury during a possible night bombing raid and as a precaution against attack from a small enemy force under the command of a Japanese officer known as the 'Mad Major'. He was described in Intelligence reports as a suicidal fanatic who had remained behind when the main Japanese forces retreated, in order to harry the Allied forces. One memorable night on Onbauk we were all thankful for the relative comfort and safety of our bolt holes. For what seemed an age, but was only fifteen or twenty minutes, thousands of rounds of machine gun and rifle fire from all directions kept our heads well down. When quiet was restored we learned that we had not, as we had thought, survived an attack by the Mad Major, but had been subjected to a barrage from the Indian troops defending our airfield who had let fly with all their weapons in response to a single revolver round fired into the air by an idiot pilot.

In central Burma we flew many sorties daily, and occasionally at night, mainly in support of 19 (Indian) Division commanded by Major-General Rees. He was charged with the task of taking Mandalay by forcing a crossing of the Irrawaddy River north of the former capital. General Rees became increasingly conscious of the value of air support, and thought up a variety of tasks for us in addition to our customary role as a highly mobile artillery. These included low level standing patrols to cover the noise of tanks moving up, and (at night) of barges ferrying the tanks across the Irrawaddy.

After Mandalay had fallen, General Rees arranged for me to accompany one of his units into the city, primarily to inspect the damage we had inflicted on Fort Dufferin and elsewhere. The enterprising Burmese, a day or two after the Japanese had been evicted, were busy counterfeiting Japanese battle flags to be sold to souvenir hunters. As the Japanese were driven steadily south we were sometimes directed on to pockets of resistance in some of the pagodas which dotted the vast central plain. These targets were readily pinpointed, but it was always with a feeling of sadness that we did what we were required to do. We were never called upon to attack a target on Mount Popa, a striking landmark several miles west of Meiktila. Perhaps this was because the conical mountain, rising abruptly from the plain, was reputedly the haunt of innumerable hamadryads, the deadly poisonous giant king cobras. This mountain was also noted as the source of Mount Popa stones which, when polished, resemble star sapphires but with the star substituted by a gleaming tiered pagoda shape.

As the conflict in Burma came to an end, apart from some mopping-up in the Pegu Yoma, an area of rugged country north of Rangoon between the Irrawaddy and Sittang Rivers, I spent a few weeks in 221 Group Headquarters in Rangoon. Here one day an Army major called to enquire if I could arrange for a 'small cargo' to be flown to Shwebo in central Burma. The 'small cargo' turned out to be two lengths of hanging rope. As the Allied forces had moved down through Burma, a large administrative vacuum had remained. Bands of dacoits, well-armed with abandoned Japanese weapons, were looting, raping and generally terrorising the villagers. When caught, they were given the briefest of trials by the Allied military administration, who were understandably thin on the ground at the time, lined up and shot. One of the convicted dacoits, the equivalent of a barrack room lawyer, had demanded his right as a civilian to be hanged instead of being shot. As always the Army, assisted by the Royal Air Force, went to some trouble to oblige.

Mule Transport
Squadron Leader C. R. Turner AFC

My World War II career in the Far East started enigmatically in South Africa. As an operational pilot I had been seconded to 29 SAAF Squadron in February 1944 to convert to Lockheed PV 3s prior to moving to the Middle East. Then, out of the blue, the SAAF hierarchy decided they no longer wanted 'Blue Jobs' in the SAAF and I found myself with three others posted to Far East Air Command.

We found ourselves on a 1500-ton mule (plus other domestic beasts) ship sailing solo to Karachi at a maximum speed of fifteen knots! The manifest was interesting in that it listed in detail all the animals to be transported and, as a concluding item: 'Four RAF officers'.

It needs little imagination to appreciate the all-pervading, polluted atmosphere. Needless to say we spent most of the time at the pointed end of the ship. To add to our constant miseries, our cabin for four measured some eight feet by six feet. Getting up by numbers was the order of the day.

The monotony was broken when, about four days out from Karachi, as dusk fell we saw a submarine about a mile off our starboard bow. There was the inevitable panic – ship changing course, throttles full open and the four of us alongside the bridge with revolvers drawn trying to keep the native crew at bay as they tried to take over the lifeboats. Fortunately the submarine made no attempt to attack and it had disappeared by daybreak.

It was later confirmed as a Japanese submarine, possibly surfaced to carry out damage repairs after a 'pack' had attacked a convoy .

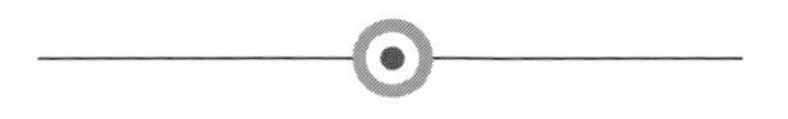

Mosquitos in India and Burma
Squadron Leader C. R. Turner AFC

Number 110 Squadron arrived at an airfield near Bangalore on 13 October 1944 to convert to Mosquitos. We were delighted, until an 82 Squadron Mosquito on a shallow practice dive-bombing run lost half its starboard wing, which crumbled and disintegrated. An immediate inspection of a number of Mosquitos revealed that heat, exposure, and humidity caused the glue in the main spar laminations to crack and powder. Investigations revealed that aircraft in which formaldehyde glue had been used were clear of the problem. All others were scrapped.

It had been decided that the Squadron should revert to Vengeance dive bombers, when I was called before the CO who told me that I was grounded. Needless to say I was flabbergasted, until after a pause he went on to say that the Adjutant had checked Officers' records and found that I was an experienced accountant. The truth came out. The CO, or his predecessor, had overlooked – or more probably not bothered – to submit statutory accounts of the Squadron's non-public funds. I was given a trunkful of receipts and other paraphernalia and ordered to get them out of this mess. The result, I must modestly admit, was a 'cookery book' masterpiece. The accounts were accepted and the CO was off the hook.

To my utter relief, just around the time I completed the accounts, cleared Mosquitos were filtering back to squadrons. These were Mosquitos Mark VI, powered by Rolls-Royce Merlin 21s. They had a 2000 lb bomb load (four x 500 lb). Two bombs were carried when the aircraft was fitted with a long-range wing or belly tanks. The aircraft had four cannons and four machine guns, quite a formidable strike power.

We carried out long-range 'rhubarbs' (reconnaissance patrols of around four hours' duration), along roads, canals, rivers etc. We were briefed to attack virtually anything that moved, shooting up railway trucks, sampans, any obvious installations – even bullock carts, to deny the Japanese any means of supply.

Initially no bombs were available, so all attacks were made with cannon and machine gun. Bridges, which would deny Japanese escape routes, were a priority target, but these proved most difficult to neutralise, some being in very difficult flying terrain, deep gullies etc.

All flying was carried out at very low level, below treetop height, and the navigator had always to be on the alert to warn the pilot of tripwires, a favourite and successful Japanese trick!

DH 98 Mosquito FB VI of 110 Squadron during strike against Indonesian rebels (RAF Museum Hendon)

All this activity around the Irrawaddy Delta came to a climax on 1 May with the launch of operation DRACULA – a sea-borne attack on Rangoon. A preliminary and successful assault was launched by paratroops to take Elephant Point – a vital strategic target. Mosquito's and Beaufighters carried out 'cab rank' details, awaiting calls from ground observation posts to attack specific Japanese targets – e.g. pillboxes – with bombs and guns.

I should record here the fact that it was the RAF represented by 110 Squadron who actually captured Rangoon!! Our CO, Wing Commander Saunders, had heard that another Squadron had seen a slogan on the roof of the prison in Rangoon saying 'Japs gone – ex digitate'. He carried out a close reconnaissance of Rangoon and its environs, and seeing no movement and no flak, decided to land at the adjacent airfield. He was met by three characters waving a white flag. They turned out to be members of the Indian National Army, mainly Sikhs, a Japanese fostered organisation.

They confirmed that the Japanese had gone. So Saunders and his navigator set off for Rangoon, called in on the jail, and then commandeered a sampan, and with two INA and two sepoys set sail down river to meet the invasion force moving cautiously upstream. Although fired on, they boarded a minelayer, reported the situation and Saunders was quickly transferred to report to General Chambers, Commanding 26 Division!

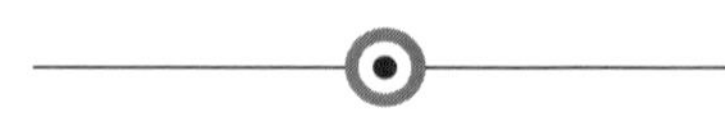

Special Duties
Air Vice-Marshal J. N. Stacey CBE DSO DFC

In May 1945 I left 160 Squadron and went to the RAF Headquarters in Colombo as the staff officer responsible for Special Duty Operations, and 160 changed to this role at that time. These operations were carried out by Catalinas and Liberators and consisted of dropping agents and supplies into Thailand and Malaya; the Catalinas occasionally landed near enemy coast on moonlight nights to pick up agents for the return journey.

The main task was to supply potential guerrilla forces in Malaya with arms, leaders and instructors to support the impending invasion by sea. In the event, this invasion never took place because the Japanese there surrendered after the two nuclear bombs were dropped on their homeland.

Ironically, most of the guerrillas were communist, and the arms we supplied provided them with the means to generate the emergency there after the war, which lasted until the early sixties.

There were other more devious activities, the most intriguing of which was Deception. For example, if an agent with his radio was captured, the Japanese would not disclose the fact but pretend to be the agent and continue to operate the radio in the hope that some vital information might be disclosed. We would then learn of the agent's capture, but would conceal this to provide authenticity to false information sent ostensibly to the captured agent, but meant to mislead the Japanese. The Japanese would then become aware of this position and would exploit this by ... And so it went on. The people who handled these situations were quite remarkable – the type who could play a dozen games of chess at the same time – and win most!

VJ day, 15 August 1945, was one of the busiest days for me. While others were preparing for the great jamboree the occasion deserved, I left Colombo at dawn for a meeting at South East Asia Command (SEAC) Headquarters in Kandy which lasted until after dark – to plan how best to help our prisoners of war (POWs) after the surrender: we were responsible for those in Malaya and Sumatra and my involvement was because the aircraft operations I had controlled to support clandestine activities provided the quickest means of aid for those POWs. We knew casualties had been severe and survivors would be in desperate need of medical care and food. We therefore planned to drop medical officers, medical supplies, food, radio sets and operators and so on, by air, starting the next day.

Much preliminary work was necessary to pinpoint all POW camps and to assess the needs and priorities of each. Doctors and others with parachute training had to be found, as did the required medical supplies, food, radio sets, clothing, etc. The air plan was then devised, i.e. allocating specific aircraft to specific POW camps, and arrangements made to get the right personnel and stores moved to the right airfields and loaded on the correct aircraft. All this for dispatch of the first aircraft within forty-eight hours!

We all worked hard that day. As I remember, we had no meals but worked continuously from about 0830 to 2000 hrs, sustained only by lime juice and the odd bite while working. But for me, and I'm sure for many others, it was the best day's work of the war. For most of the previous six years our efforts had been orientated towards destruction of one sort or another. This day, however, was devoted solely to humanitarian activities: helping our colleagues who had suffered greatly, most for many years, including witnessing the death of many of their friends. To me, there could not have been a more dramatic illustration of the change from war to peace and I shall always be grateful I was in a position to contribute in a small way to it.

Java

Air Chief Marshal Sir David Lee GBE CB

In June 1945 I took command of 904 Wing which was re-forming at Ulunderpet in southern India. It was to incorporate four P 47 Thunderbolt squadrons which were being withdrawn from Burma in readiness for the offensive, first into Malaya and thence to Singapore. The withdrawal from Burma had been chaotic and I was given three months to get the Wing fully operational for the expected assault in September.

The unexpected capitulation of Japan on 14 August threw all our plans into confusion.

Command in the East had hitherto been divided between General McArthur in the south-west Pacific and Lord Louis Mountbatten who controlled India, Ceylon, Burma, Siam, Malaya and Sumatra. To Lord Louis' command were now added Borneo, the Celebes and part of Indo-China. This vast area contained around 128 million people, including 750,000 Japanese, of whom 630,000 were armed forces. More importantly, there were some 123,000 Allied prisoners of war and internees scattered in camps throughout the theatre. There were no civil police forces and, apart from Siam, no civil governments in any of the newly surrendered territories. No plans existed for the immediate occupation and control of these hitherto enemy territories.

The first and most vital task was to rescue our POWs and allied internees. Because Japan had never complied with the Geneva Convention we had only a vague idea where many of the prison camps were located. A new organisation was therefore set up – RAPWI – Repatriation of Allied Prisoners of War and Internees.

To support this, my Wing was to be reconstituted and sent to Java. All I knew was that this was a large island beyond Singapore. My four Thunderbolt squadrons would not be suitable for the liberation of thousands of allied prisoners. I was to retain two, and acquire a very large Dakota squadron. In addition I was to be given two squadrons of the RAF Regiment and various administrative elements.

Number 904 was a mobile Wing, self-supporting in every respect. It had refuellers, fire tenders, tents, medical facilities, clothing, food and ammunition stores, communications and maintenance equipment etc. We would eventually total 2600 men and some 100 vehicles.

In September we learnt that RAPWI had parachuted intelligence officers into Java. The situation there was not good. The Japanese had earlier recognised that their position was hopeless and had armed the Indonesians in order to hamper the return of the Dutch, who had been the pre-war colonial power. Chaos reigned and it was difficult to identify all the areas and camps in Java where POWs were held.

I embarked with the Ground Party and all its equipment at Madras in a fleet of three ships. We had strict instructions to maintain wireless silence, since there might be Japanese submarines which had not received the 'cease fire' order. Our destination was Batavia on the north-west corner of Java. We had no idea whether we would be expected to make a ceremonial entry or attempt an opposed landing on the beaches!

The liner had Landing Craft (Assault) which also doubled as lifeboats. We therefore stopped for an hour or two *en route* to give the Regiment practice in manning the craft for possible beach landings. At the same time white belts and jungle green battle dress were cleaned in case a formal parade was necessary.

We approached Batavia with great caution in the heat haze. A long, low grey shape emerged and a signal lamp started winking. It was a British warship which gave us details of a swept approach through a minefield.

The harbour was a scene of utter devastation. There was no sign of life. The cranes were mostly demolished and the quays were littered with the rubble. We cautiously berthed alongside what seemed to be the largest and least cluttered quay. There was no help in docking and the few natives who came in sight took no notice of us. It was now four o'clock in the afternoon.

We assumed that there must be some Allied force in the town to account for the presence of the destroyer and the newly swept channel. Armed guards were posted and we awaited the morning.

Next day we decided to land two jeeps and reconnoitre the city with a Regiment escort. Just then a figure hurried up the gangway. It was Group Captain Sorel-Cameron. He confirmed that there was absolute chaos. An Indonesian Government had been set up under Dr Sukarno, but it controlled only Batavia and its immediate surrounds. It was reasonably friendly towards the British, realising that we had come to disarm the 26,000 Japanese and extricate POWs and internees. The general population were however very suspicious and feared they would be handed back to the Dutch.

There was a small Allied Force in the city under General Christison and an Air Headquarters was being set up. We were to take over the airport at Kemajoran on the edge of the city. This was also a shambles and the Japanese Air Force were still in occupation.

We drove on to the tarmac littered with dozens of Japanese aircraft, all wrecked and lying at drunken angles. The runways were cracked, the parking areas grass, which would be unusable after heavy rain, and the buildings were desolate. It was a sight which filled me with foreboding.

General Christison briefed me on his plans. He had elements of 5 Indian Division approaching by sea. He planned to land them first at Surabaya on the north-east of the Island and then at Semarang in the middle of the north coast. With Batavia he would then have three bridgeheads from which to penetrate inland to the prison camps.

The first landing was planned for 25 October, only five days away, and as yet I had no aircraft on the island. The furthest bridgehead, Surabaya, was 415 miles from our base at Kemajoran, and the landing could be covered by Thunderbolts with long-range tanks but without bombs. Some quick planning resulted in thirty-five Thunderbolts landing safely on 23 October, followed next day by the Dakotas.

Brigadier Mallaby's 49 Brigade landed on 25 October but had to fight its way into the centre of Surabaya. Mallaby himself was murdered next day whilst attempting to negotiate with the fanatical Indonesian opposition. The Brigade then called for an air strike on Indonesian positions on the outskirts of the town and this was successfully carried out by twelve Thunderbolts.

Attention now turned to the original Batavia bridgehead. Bandoeng, some fifty miles away, contained a large number of prisoners who were being starved by their captors. General Christison sent a heavily escorted train loaded with medical supplies and food. This was ambushed and many of the Gurkha guards killed. Bandoeng itself was relatively quiet but there was considerable guerrilla activity in the surrounding countryside. Bandoeng had a single runway airfield which looked to be in good condition. Sufficient troops were established to protect landing and unloading and the Dakotas began regular flights taking supplies in and bringing released POWs and internees out. Attempts to supplement these flights by road convoys with fighter cover sooner or later ran into trouble and members of the Wing's Air Control team were killed.

The regular heavy use now began to take its toll on the runway at Kemajoran. We put the Japanese to work sweeping it daily but it was clear that repairs would be necessary. The runway could not be closed. Our humanitarian and fighter missions must be maintained. The solution came in the form of a highly experienced senior works engineer from Singapore, Mr Atkinson.

We talked of Pierced Steel Planking which was made of interlocking metal mesh. Mr Atkinson explained that as Dakotas landed they would push a wave of metal several inches high in front of them. A few days and the metal would be completely out of shape. Eventually he came up with the ideal answer – 'Bit-Hess'. This consisted of sheets of jute hessian soaked in tar and laid several thicknesses deep. It took a day or two to dry. Low barrels were placed down the centre of the runway below wing level. One side of the runway was treated whilst flying continued as usual on the other. When one side was dry the other was repaired. Within three weeks we had a brand new runway. It was like landing on a mattress!

A few pieces of Bit-Hess lifted during landing but we stationed Japanese with tar buckets and brushes to replace them. The runway served our needs faithfully during the ten months we were there. In wet weather the Dakotas landed like destroyers at speed – sending vast wakes of water from their wheels. They needed very little braking.

In the meantime, the fanatics turned on the prison camps and perpetrated many atrocities before the inmates could be rescued. In one instance fourteen prisoners, some women, were locked in a house and burned to death.

The midway bridge at Semarang had been occupied without opposition and this gave us another useful airfield. By mid-November 1945 Soerabaya and its airfield had been captured and we were able to provide local operational air

Republic Thunderbolt 47 D (AHB)

support to our troops.

It was clear that despite the formal ending of all hostilities three months earlier, the Wing was involved in another war. Although we were beginning to get prisoners out of the more accessible camps, there were thousands more in the interior and they might well be massacred before they could be reached. Even around our main base at Batavia there were dangers. A young Regiment airman was killed by a sniper and his funeral service next day also came under fire.

Every attempt to extend the three bridgeheads met fanatical resistance and army casualties mounted alarmingly. It was said that 23 Division had more casualties in four months in Java then during a year's hard fighting in Burma. Intense and accurate anti-aircraft fire was encountered: so good that we suspected that Japanese might be firing the weapons. Two Thunderbolts and a Mosquito were shot down and the crews killed.

Camps at Ambarawe were eventually reached and 10,000 internees released. Unhappily the Indonesians had killed and mutilated a number of men, women and children before the troops arrived.

One of our Dakotas was taking twenty fully-armed Indian soldiers from Batavia to Semarang when it had engine failure. It forced landed in a field only four miles from our main base. When the plane was eventually reached by a rescue party it found that the crew of four and all the soldiers had been killed and their mutilated remains buried in a river bank. General Christison ordered the entire village to be razed to the ground. Numerous weapons were seized and many young fanatics arrested.

By January 1946 the Army had imposed a degree of order and Batavia at least was returning to normal. The locals began to realise that we had no intention of ousting their new government and they became more helpful.

The lull was short lived. With the advent of drier weather in March, the rebels became active once more, disrupting road communications between Batavia and Bandoeng, virtually the twin capitals of Java. We gave every road convoy an Air Contact Team which could call for support in event of attack. Thunderbolts fully loaded with rockets and ammunition were kept at readiness and could reach a convoy in about ten minutes. Targets were attacked as close as fiftty feet from the convoy, and this spoke volumes for the accuracy and steadiness of the Thunderbolt pilots.

Hostilities gradually died down but it was impossible for our forces to advance into the interior where many prisoners were still held. Everything depended on politics and negotiation and the success of the new government in gaining control over the rebels.

On 25 April Lord Louis Mountbatten visited Java. He said that talks with the Prime Minister had gone well and he expected a strong line to be taken against those rebels who are were still attacking road convoys. He believed we had rescued at least two-thirds of the POWs and internees and was confident that negotiations to fly out those still in the interior would soon be successful. He hoped that we would be able to leave Java within six months.

At last an arrangement was reached which called for a good deal of trust on our side. Two Dakotas a day could fly to an airfield near Soerakarta. The Indonesians would bring truckloads of prisoners to the airfield daily in whatever numbers we could handle. No weapons were to be carried and there were to be no escorting fighters. I had lost six aircraft in the last few months, but the risk had to be taken.

The first Dakota brought back thirty passengers, two on stretchers. I was shocked by their frailty. They had to be helped down the steps and were desperately thin, with swollen bellies and legs, the sure sign of beriberi and malnutrition. There had been nothing for them to eat or drink at the airfield where they had waited since dawn. The mid-day temperature was 90° and there was little shade or shelter. It was obviously vital that we take everyone waiting, to avoid prisoners being sent back to the prison camps at night.

The airfield was just about adequate for the Dakotas but it was surrounded by sullen, unco-operative Indonesians lying in the long grass with machine-guns and rifles. We would have to exercise every restraint to avoid an unfortunate incident.

The airlift continued every day for the next two months with only the occasional hiccup. The RAPWI staff estimated that all POWs and internees would have been evacuated from known camps by early July. They were fairly certain that no unidentified camps existed. Those released could be accommodated in Batavia to await suitable transport.

It was now twelve months since Japan had officially surrendered, and there is no doubt, so far as we were concerned, that the Japanese in Java had managed to prolong the war throughout this period. It had been a vicious and costly campaign, but the great humanitarian task of releasing tens of thousands of Allied prisoners of war and internees from the terrible conditions in which they had existed for years was complete.

1946–2002
THE BERLIN AIRLIFT

By the end of the World War II it was clear that there were major differences between the Western Allies and the Soviet Union both in terms of geographical interest and political approach to problems. One major difference was the economic rehabilitation of continental Europe and in particular Germany.

Sunderland in Havel Sea, West Berlin (Shorts)

At the end of the war, Germany had been divided for control purposes between the Western Allies and Russia. Berlin, located in the Eastern Zone, was treated separately and was split geographically between the four main interested parties: USA, Britain, France and the USSR. The Western Powers had access to Berlin across the intervening Eastern Zone both by land and by air. Air rights were covered by written agreements but right of land access was much less clear.

When it became obvious that potential differences were hampering development, the Western Allies pressed ahead with building up a Western German administration. Stalin objected to this and began to apply pressure through his control of the territory surrounding Berlin.

On 24 June 1948 the Soviet authorities in Eastern Germany cut all road, rail and canal routes from the Western Zones of Occupation into West Berlin. The Allies had foreseen the possibility of trouble and had drawn up contingency plans.

Within four days of the start of the blockade the first airlifts started.

The Early Days of the Berlin Airlift
Wing Commander J. F. Manning AFC

In the spring of 1948 I was Flight Commander Training on 30 Squadron stationed at RAF Oakington in Cambridgeshire. At that time 46 Group had eight Medium Range Transport Support Squadrons all equipped with Dakotas Mk IV.

Although we flew regular scheduled services to destinations in Europe and North Africa, and special flights moving personnel and equipment between RAF stations, our main task was in support of the Army. To this end we were trained in supply and troop dropping by day and night, and in towing the Horsa glider.

At that time, 30 Squadron was commanded by Squadron Leader A. McC. Johnstone, a wonderful man for whom I developed the highest admiration, trust and affection.

On 29 April he led us in formation out to Schleswigland in Germany. There we carried out a transport support practice camp in conjunction with 27 Squadron, also from Oakington and 47 Squadron with their Halifaxes from 38 Group.

It was a successful camp. We got on well with the other two squadrons, played them at soccer and cricket, and between us provided most of the players for Schleswigland's station teams. It was a period which saw the opening of Sylt as a leave centre. Sylt had a tiny airfield which had been a *Luftwaffe* fighter station, and for the opening weekend I flew a Dakota-load of service personnel there so that they could enjoy the amenities of the leave centre, especially the good beach. The airfield was not active, but was opened temporarily just for our benefit, with emergency services provided by the local fire brigade. A very officious German civilian was marshalling me towards the unloading dispersal along the narrow taxiway which barely accommodated the wide undercarriage of the Dakota, when I had to stop because of an obstruction which the marshaller could not see as it was behind him. After some signalling from my open window, he turned and spotted the offending cow which was blissfully ruminating close to the taxiway. His reaction was prompt and effective. A hefty kick on the rump moved the cow and we were able to move safely past!

Towards the end of June we were aware that something was going on throughout the western zones of Germany. The Allies called in the old *Reischsmarks* and began to issue the new *Deutschmarks*, much to the annoyance of the Soviets. It also left us short of spending money because very few of us had drawn *Reischsmarks* on our paybooks, and only those which had been so drawn could be exchanged for the new currency. The new notes were all flown out to Germany by the Dakota squadrons.

We flew back to Oakington on 25 June, and while in circuit for our stream landing, Johnnie was notified by Air Traffic Control that he was to report to the Station Commander immediately after landing. We barely had time to unload and assemble in the crew room before he was back to tell us that we all had forty-eight hours to sort ourselves out, collect fresh clothing etc., because we were going back to Germany with all the other Dakota squadrons.

On 29 June we took off again with all serviceable aircraft for Wunstorf to begin what became Operation PLAINFARE, or the Berlin Airlift.

Poor Wunstorf, it hardly knew what hit it. From being a rather cosy single fighter squadron station it was suddenly descended upon by eight Dakota squadrons complete with servicing personnel, equipment and the necessary loading and movements organisation. It was a permanent ex-*Luftwaffe* station with a fine Officers' Mess. Number 30 Squadron was the last of the eight to arrive, and by the time we got there all the beds had been taken. I slept on an armchair in the anteroom the first night, and I remember there being bodies all over the place, even on the billiard table.

The following morning, 30 June, all reported to an improvised operations room and began flying in to Gatow along the east-west corridor. We carried only basic commodities to begin with, such as flour, meat and tinned foods. I personally flew four sorties on that first day and into the night, catnapping between flights until, after twenty-two hours on duty, I was released with my crew to go to bed. On the third night, conditions were somewhat better in the mess.

There was a large attic under the steeply pitched roof, and beds were put up there. I managed to get one of these, and they were much more conducive to sleep than the armchairs in the anteroom and operations room.

We continued like this for a few more days: flying, eating between flights and catnapping until, when reporting as ready, there was not an aeroplane immediately available which was both serviceable and loaded; we were then sent off to bed. Then the weather broke and it rained and rained. The fifty-plus Dakotas were parked on the grass which became more and more muddy as our clothing became wetter and wetter. Instrument landings at both ends became commonplace, and after one such arrival at Gatow on 7 July I was informed by the controller that mine was the 1000th aircraft of the operation.

The Yorks began to arrive at Wunstorf on 3 July, and matters became more complicated. They were much faster than the Dakotas and carried a bigger load. This led to problems over air safety and loading, particularly after a York load was put on a Dakota, and the pilot concerned managed to get off using all 2000 yards of runway and muttering something about what a sluggish old cow they had given him. So much for the good nature of those wonderful machines.

At the end of July the whole Dakota force moved to Fassburg, another permanent *Luftwaffe* station which had the facility of a railway line running right into the camp. From here, we carried nothing but coal. This was bagged in sacks which could be easily handled by one person. Many of the unloaders at Gatow were women. With this coal the Berliners were able to sustain the one and only power station in the western sectors of the city. By this time we were operating a proper shift system so that we all knew when we were going to be on duty, and flying a one-way traffic scheme inwards along the north/west corridor and back along the east/west corridor. We were now flying at standard heights to cater for the problem of the varying airspeeds of the different types involved. We were also getting regular time off, but it is interesting to recall that on one day in each three day cycle we carried out four return trips to Berlin. For a while we enjoyed fine, hot summer weather which made us perspire somewhat. The inevitable coal dust stuck to our faces and bodies, so it can easily be imagined what we all looked like after four return flights.

It was at this stage that we began bringing back sick and undernourished children for succour in the West. Sometimes we had return loads of economic freight – manufactured goods – which helped to keep the economy of the city going.

Then on 20 August the C54 Skymasters of the USAF began to arrive from America and join us as coalmen. We got on very well with their aircrews, and appreciated the higher standards of messing which came with them. They too, carried only coal, and by the end of the month had built up their numbers to an extent whereby we Dakotas had to move on again.

I personally flew to Lubeck on 12 September, and there the Dakota force remained until the operation ended. By this time, we were all highly organised and a bit blasé about the whole thing. Also, as only first line or route servicing was carried out in Germany there was a small but regular flow of aircraft between Lubeck and the UK for second and third line servicing. This was very popular with leave-takers. Lubeck accepted the invasion very well, although the accounts section soon got fed up with shift workers rolling in at all hours of the day to draw money. This prompted the accountant officer to publish a notice in SROs to the effect that 'In future pay may only be drawn on Tuesday and Friday

Left to right: Signaller I. L. Barlow, Navigator F/O F. Stilwell, James Manning (James Manning)

mornings'. This prompted Johnnie to publish a notice in the ops. room to the effect that 'From this day, accountant officers will only be carried to the UK on Tuesday and Friday mornings'. It worked!

Throughout the lift we flew as crews, in squadrons. This built up a wonderful *esprit de corps* because we always knew who was in front of and behind us at the same height. It also meant that we had time off as a squadron, with the inevitable end-of-shift parties. Voices became easily recognisable on the R/T and although it was all very disciplined, quite a lot was carried on using Christian names rather than call-signs. We were bound to make position calls at various beacons, the principal one on approaching Berlin being at Frohnau. This was corrupted by the Americans to *Fraulein*, and then to 'on top of the *Fraulein*'.

When the third airfield opened at Tegel in the French sector (the 2000 yard runway and connecting taxiway were completed within three months) I flew the first aircraft to land there on a proving flight with some staff officers from 46 Group Headquarters. Tegel is now Berlin's main international airport.

Then on Christmas Day, on my second trip in the morning, I was briefed to carry out an interview with Chester Wilmot of the BBC. This was recorded on the first miniature tape recorder I had ever seen, and was broadcast on Radio Newsreel that evening. On the same day, the 50,000th aircraft of the lift was flown.

On New Year's Eve, a thick fog covering the whole area kept us in Gatow overnight, and by the time midnight came many of the crews other than the captains had disappeared to various messes to have their own personal celebrations. However, they all turned up safely in time to take off towards dawn.

And so it went on, day after day, twenty-four hours a day, in all weathers. I did not see the end of the operation with 30 Squadron. In March 1949 I logged my 2000th hour as a pilot and in May I was posted to HQ 47 Group as a training staff officer. For most of my 203 round trips to Berlin my navigator was Flying Officer Frank Stillwell, and my wireless operator was Signaller 1 Les Barlow. They were a splendid crew, and it was a privilege to have been able to get them back safely through so many arduous flights.

HMS *Amethyst* – April to July 1949

Under the treaty of Tientsin between Britain and China, British warships on friendly missions were permitted to visit all Chinese ports for provisioning and making necessary repairs.

On 20 April 1949 the Frigate HMS *Amethyst* was sailing up the Yangtze river from Shanghai to the inland port of Nanking with routine supplies for the British Embassy.

The situation in China was tense. The Nationalist government of Chiang Kai-shek was being attacked by the Communist troops of Mao Tse-tung and these had now reached the north bank of the river Yangtze. They issued an ultimatum to the Nationalists demanding an unopposed crossing of the river, failing which they would launch a full-scale offensive on 21 April. The British authorities believed that *Amethyst* had time to reach Nanking before this deadline expired.

Crew returning to Kai Tak in spare Sunderland after Amethyst *incident (Crown copyright)*

Despite this, Communist forces opened fire on the *Amethyst* at 0920 hrs on the morning of 20 April. By the time the shooting stopped twenty-three of the 183 on board were dead or dying and thirty-one were wounded. Among the dead was the *Amethyst*'s Doctor. Furthermore the ship was now trapped in the river.

Attempts to reach *Amethyst* overland failed and on the following day it was decided to send a Sunderland from Kai Tak in Hong Kong with an RAF medical officer and medical supplies.

Amethyst signalled Far East Station

> 'Sunderland landed 1720 hours and was at once near missed by Communist fire. RAF doctor only had time to transfer to waiting sampan. My gunner sent out to meet was caught in plane on take-off. Thereafter fire was directed against Amethyst and six hits were sustained including one on waterline, since repaired, one in Dynamo room and one in number seven oil fuel tank. Meantime anchorage was shifted to position in small creek. Suggest another Sunderland lands: it should do so up this creek screened from enemy fire if Amethyst remains here.'

Amethyst remained trapped until the end of July when Lieutenant Commander Kerans made a successful dash down river, braving the gauntlet of Communist guns now on both banks of the river.

The story of the RAF's participation is told by Gerry Morbey, the Sunderland's signaller.

A Mercy Mission

Gerry Morbey

In 1949, 88 Sunderland Squadron was stationed at Kai Tak, Hong Kong. We were mainly occupied with the transport of mail and freight between Japan, Singapore and Borneo. Sunderlands were particularly useful where there were no adequate airfields.

On the afternoon of 20 April we heard that HMS *Amethyst* had been fired on by Communist guns on the Yangtze. There were urgent talks between the Navy and RAF and it was decided to send an aircraft to Nanking with medical supplies. These would then be sent overland to *Amethyst*. All this changed when it was learned that *Amethyst*'s medical officer had been killed. The plan was now for a Sunderland to land on the river as close to the ship as possible so that an RAF doctor could be sent on board.

Group Captain Jefferson, the station commander, decided to come himself with the RAF medical officer Flight Lieutenant Michael Fearnley, a naval doctor, and two experienced army parachute droppers who could release supplies over the ship if landing was impossible.

We had reached the Yangtze, flying at 5000 ft when we were told by HMS London that landing under heavy fire would be too dangerous and we were ordered back to Shanghai at the mouth of the river.

After lunch we heard that *Amethyst*'s situation was even more desperate than we had thought and it was decided to try again. We took off at 1630 hrs. During the flight it was realised that there might not be time to transfer cases of medical supplies to the ship. We broke open the boxes and the doctors filled their pockets and knapsacks with plasma, anaesthetics etc.

As we got closer to *Amethyst*, Ken Letford came down very low, flying along a creek. Suddenly there was the main river and as we circled we saw the ship up close to the south bank, the crew waving to us from the deck. Ken decided to land in the lee of the *Amethyst* where we would have some protection from the Communist batteries. He came to rest less than 100 yards from the ship.

Monaghan, *Amethyst*'s commissioned gunner, had left *Amethyst* in a sampan rowed by women. He persuaded them to turn to the aircraft. We opened the door and Monaghan climbed in. At that moment the Communist opened fire and Michael Fearnley saw that the terrified women were rowing away again. He hurriedly jumped in and the sampan zig-zagged away back to *Amethyst* leaving Monaghan, the Naval doctors and the medical supplies behind in the aircraft.

Although everything was open and the anchor down, Ken shouted that he was going to take off at once. Myself and Price ran down to the bow doors and chopped the anchor away. We shut what doors we could and we climbed away, followed by fire from the Chinese guns.

As so much had been left behind we decided to make another attempt next day and this time to take a Padre to bury the dead. The Group Captain demanded, and got, a much fuller Briefing.

We tried to signal *Amethyst* with an Aldis Lamp as we approached but to no avail. On landing alongside *Amethyst*

Left to right: Sig. Jerry Morbey, Sig. Ldr. Don Gray, Eng. Paddy Doyle, Sig. Gordon Price,
Nav. Maurice Marshall, Capt. Ken Letford, 2nd Pilot Ken Dillow (Jerry Morbey)

we opened the rear door and launched a rubber dinghy, attaching it by rope. Once again several bursts of shell and other gunfire forced us to make an immediate take off. Good bye dinghy!

Next day we were airborne again from Shanghai to carry out reconnaissance in the area where *Amethyst* was. We were hit by ground fire and the port main tank was holed causing heavy leaking of petrol into the bomb bay. Also on landing we discovered the main aileron control, running along the floor between the signaller's position and the captain's position, was almost severed and two bullets were lodged in the navigator's computer which was in his navigation bag.

The bullets had entered the port side of the wardroom, continuing upwards through the control housing in the floor of the upper deck. Luckily the computer stopped the bullets travelling in line for the Group Captain who was standing between the two pilots. The .5 in bullet that entered the starboard side passed through the sleeve of Ken Dillow's uniform and did no harm. So we all reckoned that Lady Luck was on our side.

Believe it or not, while staying in the Palace Hotel we heard a Chinese lady singing 'Slow boat to China' for the first time! Quite an eventful few days away from Kai Tak.

NATIONAL SERVICE

Following conscription during World War II, compulsory call-up continued in the form of National Service until 1957.

Postwar National Service

Air Vice-Marshal George Chesworth CB OBE DFC

On 28 July 1948, in response to the contents of a brown envelope marked OHMS, I left my home in Surrey to report to No. 3 Recruit Centre, Royal Air Force Padgate. Here I met up with several hundred other conscripts or National Servicemen as we were known.

The vast majority had never been away from home and the induction process left many in a state of shock. The food, a most important matter to eighteen-year olds, left much to be desired. I recall that every day we had porridge for breakfast, corned beef with POM (reconstituted potato) and piccalilli (mustard pickle) for lunch and evening meal, all washed down with tea containing a heavy dose of bromide.

As an ex-Air Training Corps cadet I, and about fifty others, had been provisionally selected for aircrew training, and after a few days at Padgate attended the Aircrew Selection Centre (ACSC) at North Weald. None of our party were given the results of the selection at North Weald but were returned to Padgate where we started recruit training.

As ex-cadets we were all proficient at drill and therefore escaped the worst ministrations of the drill instructors on the parade ground. But the acting corporal DIs were in complete control of our lives. They saw us as about to escape their clutches and sought to make our lives a misery with extra duties, additional 'bull' nights and other restrictions. They were best described as little Hitlers.

After what seemed an eternity, but I expect was only a matter of days, the successful candidates at ACSC were posted to the Aircrew Transit Centre at Kirton-in-Lindsay. We were not sorry to leave Padgate, for it was a truly awful place and undoubtedly coloured the view of many RAF National Servicemen. At Kirton we were split into groups of twenty-four, allocated to pilot or navigator courses, and sent on our way to Initial Training at either Wittering or, for the lucky ones, to Southern Rhodesia. Now in the training machine proper we became Cadet Pilots or Navigators, and indistinguishable from direct-entry cadets who had their introduction to the Service at Cardington.

I remained a National Serviceman during my flying training until I was commissioned in May 1950.

At that time I believe only former ATC Cadets undertook aircrew training during National Service but later this was extended to 'ordinary' conscripts. Certainly when I was instructing at 2 FTS in the mid-50s there were mixed courses of direct entrants and National Servicemen who were not ex-cadets.

I enjoyed National Service; but I was lucky to be flying. Many did not for a variety of reasons. Some resented the disruption to their lives, especially the students. However, hindsight being what it is, the majority will now admit they do not regret the time spent in the Royal Air Force.

RESERVE OF AIR FORCE OFFICERS

Even as the World War I ended, Sir Hugh Trenchard was anticipating the possible need to strengthen air power in an emergency, but a long way short of general mobilisation. He adopted a practical approach. There were many ex-Royal Flying Corps and Royal Naval Air Service pilots who were not needed in a slim new Royal Air Force. They could, however, form a reserve of fully trained officers who could be quickly available if needed. He therefore established the Reserve of Air Force Officers in 1920.

After a spell with a Regular Squadron they had an annual commitment of two to three weeks training each year. They were liable to call up in case of emergency. In 1950 such an emergency arose when North Korea invaded the South.

An Unexpected Posting

Wing Commander J. R. C. Young AFC

I was enjoying life as a Captain with BOAC, when on a beautiful early May morning in 1950 a few minutes after nine the mists of summer were just clearing. I was clipping the hedge on the left front of my house; behind me the little lawn where the children picnicked and sunbathed.

Suddenly the postman, saying 'I hope it's not bad news, Guv!' delivered into my hand a telegram. It read 'At 1430 hours today report to the uniform section at RAF West Drayton with your cap, medal ribbons and personal toiletries for immediate posting overseas'. I phoned BOAC: 'Was it a joke?' No, they had a copy. Frantic activity followed. Bank Manager to arrange all domestic out-goings. Trains to get there on time. Money to buy a ticket!

I duly arrived on time, to be shown a neat pile of tropical kit, complete down to underpants and crowned by a brand-new Identity Card complete with a recent photograph. Where on earth did they get that?! Check the sizes. All correct. The shorts at suitably discreet distance below the knee. And by five to nine the next morning I was just getting into a bed at Castel Benito having been bussed to Lyneham to meet a York crew and be fully briefed on our duties for that day. Delivered a Yorkful of airmen complete with kit, tools and weapons to RAF Fayid, Egypt and repositioned our aircraft back to CB.

From then on life was full. An expedition to Shaibah – one brown C type hangar, brown runways and taxiways, brown sky full from a distant sandstorm. On take off again, with a Yorkful of airmen, an engine failure (No. 2). Divert to Habbaniya. Three heavenly days drowsing by the Mess swimming pool. Sand storms far away to the North and East. Temperature at the time 44°C, one degree below the York's temperature operating limit of 45°C (or was it 40°C, memory fails me) – so it was just as well the surrounding countryside was, as they say, rather flat. And of course it was yellow-brown not blue as described in that song 'I've got those Shaibah blues!'.

I had the same sort of trouble in 1939. Having received a letter from Kingsway that my presence back on the Active List was required on the first of June I wrote back a very nice letter pointing out that Cambridge University was still on the Julian calendar and that the May Ball of my college, which my wife wished to attend, was actually on third of June Gregorian Calendar and, with a suitable recovery time, perhaps June the sixth?

Older and more senior members of the Service will remember that in their youth there was the cry 'Give us back our eleven days'. By 1939 it had grown to seventeen, I think. I did not get a favourable reply to my request.

Life was Hell in the RAFO Class AA.

The Flight Engineer

The advent of larger aircraft in World War II required a specialist crew member to monitor fuel and engine performance. This role was initially assigned to an air gunner, but the trade of Flight Engineer was confirmed in September 1942 with the introduction of the 'E' brevet.

A Testing Start to a Long Career

Squadron Leader Michael Cawsey

I enrolled for training as an engineer at RAF St Athan in March 1950. Our Course was in three phases, each lasting six months. The first was basic, where we did all our initial service training, metal bashing, and academic work; plus aircraft recognition, sport, PE and basic aircraft systems.

We lived in 'P Lines' which were wooden huts heated by two stoves, and this was another learning curve: keeping them alight on the frugal fuel supplies.

On the second phase we concentrated on system components; whilst the final phase covered Gas Turbine Engines, Aircraft Systems, Performance and Engine Running. We also had to do four exercises in a Lincoln to learn to handle the controls. This flying experience amounted to fifteen hours of which nine were a single night flight!

It was now early 1951, and with the planned introduction of the Canberra, the demand for Flight Engineers was about to change dramatically. Our course was abridged and we passed out with a Brevet but still as Cadets. We were then posted to a holding Squadron prior to attending an Operational Conversion Unit for Type training on Sunderlands, Hastings or Lincolns. I was attached to 97 Squadron.

As a total anomaly, cadets with a Brevet, we were outcasts. Senior to the Airmen's Mess, yet not promoted to Sergeant. We lived in a Drying Room, and ate behind a partition in the Airmen's Mess. The squadrons did not really want us. We spent many days working on the Station Farm or keeping out of sight. Shortly afterwards our promotion to Sergeant came through.

On the first day at the OCU, people were expected to form themselves into complete individual crews. Everyone gathered in a large room: a mixture of ages, experience, ranks and trades. There were people on their first tours and others more experienced. Sergeants through the ranks up to Flight Lieutenants. There were Pilots, Navigators, Signallers, Engineers and Gunners. Those who had been around and knew the score quickly sorted themselves into a crew, whilst the greener ones found themselves wandering around asking 'Who still needs a navigator?' or whatever. This had been a traditional method of crewing up and had worked over the years.

The definition of a Flight Engineer's duties and responsibilities was given in an Air Ministry Order:

(i) To operate certain controls at the engineer's station and watch appropriate gauges.
(ii) To act as a pilot's assistant, to the extent of being able to fly straight and level and on a course.
(iii) To advise the captain of the aircraft as to the functioning of the engines and the fuel, oil and cooling systems both before and during flight.
(iv) To ensure effective liaison between the captain of the aircraft and the maintenance staff, by

Avro Lincoln (British Aerospace)

communicating to the latter such technical notes regarding the performance and maintenance of the aircraft in flight as may be required.

(v) To carry out practicable emergency repairs during flight.

(vi) To act as a standby gunner.

That definition provided a sound basis for what evolved. The flight engineer was the pilot's assistant, technical supporter, systems handler, limitations minder; in addition to being able to relate to the ground crew, and if necessary carry out simple repairs. He was also required to be competent to service and replenish the aircraft if it landed away from support.

Before flight the flight engineer carried out an extensive external and internal inspection. I remember at the Lincoln OCU each student had to sit in his flight seat and touch any control or switch the instructor nominated, whilst wearing black goggles. During flight a log was maintained of all power settings, the indicated and predicted fuel consumption and fuel remaining, calculating range and endurance information.

Engineers started the engines and carried out the run-ups and power checks when required, and apart from taxiing, kept check on initial take-off power application when asymmetric power was invariably needed to control the swing. All in-flight power settings (Cruise Control) and propeller synchronisation were carried out by the engineer.

We eventually graduated as a crew and were posted to 12 Squadron. The Conversion had taken four months and we had flown ninety-six hours, almost half at night, and this was going to be the pattern for future flying in Bomber Command. I spent only three months in 'Shiny' 12. In that time I flew with six different skippers, learnt about 'GeeH' Bombing systems, did an Air Test for the first time, and flew a sortie out to a Weather Ship, where we dropped a container of Mail and then ended up on three engines for four hours. High Level Bombing and Air to Sea firing were regular events. I physically flew the aircraft for about fouteen hours, and added another seventy-seven hours to my Log Book.

The Canberra was now being introduced into RAF Service. Flight Engineers, Signallers and Gunners were not needed on this new machine and we were all put up for disposal.

Posted back to 97 Squadron I was crewed up with Sgt Ken Marwood. Ken was a masterful pilot and believed he did not need any help from me. We had a number of disagreements before settling down to work well as a team. He had a stable crew which produced exceptional bombing results, and that was the yardstick of success. I remained crewed up with Ken until he went to be commissioned in early 1953. I did not believe I was being utilised to best of my abilities, and had ideas of getting a posting on to Hastings or even Washingtons, so I applied to change aircraft type.

The Squadron Commander called me in for an interview. At the end he said 'Well Cawsey, the choice is yours. As a result of The Lawrence Minot Bombing Competition, your crew has been selected to fly to the USA to participate in a Bombing Competition: you can have this application back and go with us, or I can process it and you may or may not get a posting, but you will not have this trip.' Of course I rescinded the application and went back to the crew room to spill the beans. Our aeroplane had become a very personal thing and we nurtured it and always wanted the latest and best fitted to it.

The Bombing Competition was the US Strategic Air Command Bombing and Navigation Competition. Two Lincolns and two Washingtons were going, and it was being held at Davis Monthan Air Force Base in Arizona.

Preparation got underway: the engines were replaced as necessary, new wheels fitted, the aircraft serviced in anticipation of being away for a month. In addition two 400-gallon fuel tanks were fitted in the bomb bay. The Overload Fuel tanks, which increased our capacity to 3650 gallons, were piped into the normal fuel system inboard tank. There were no tank selectors on the Lincoln: fuel feeding was by gravity into a collector tank, which fed the engines. This meant that transfer could not be started until the main inboard wing tank level had dropped enough to accept a transfer, and the outer tanks, fed by gravity, emptied first. A very primitive system, which would not meet any safety standards in this day and age. The aircraft was committed to continue the crossing on the assumption that the transfer would take place! Modern design concepts would reverse the order in which fuel was taken from the wing in order to provide a relieving load and reduce stress and upwards bending in the wing.

Our aircraft had no problems with the fuel transfer on the Atlantic crossing, but we did spend six hours out of the ten in cloud at about 500 feet. With no Anti-Icing or De-Icing fitted we had little choice but to stay low. We later discovered the atmospheric pressure at the centre of the depression was much lower than we had set on our altimeter, so we had been flying at about 500 feet above the sea in cloud. On our arrival there was no sign of the other Lincoln. Eventually it arrived but desperately short of fuel. Trouble with the fuel system transfer and the loss of nearly 400 gallons of fuel due to a leaking joint had caused them to reduce power and fly slowly in an effort to conserve what little fuel they had.

On arrival at Davis Monthan Air Base we discovered that our Lincolns did not have the range to complete the full route set for the competition, even with our overload tanks, so our results would be assessed against those of the comparable B29s, B50s, and B36s.

Our take-off time on the first day of the competition was 2130 hrs. We had to fly three sorties of over twelve hours each on alternate nights, and carried a USAF Major as Observer.

Five hours after take off we arrived at Kansas City and completed a simulated bombing run by radar; two and a half hours later we repeated this at Dallas. Our blind bombing radar was known as H2S: it had a rotating antenna in a very large cupola under the fuselage, and the presentation was on a circular scope. The radar navigator lived under a black curtain during the run-ins. Our scores were calculated by ground radar plots from the moment we called 'Bombs Gone'. Our results were consistent at 250 yards for every run in the contest and this was a superb achievement.

The next target was at Phoenix, just three hours away. This was a visual bombing attack on a drainpipe on the corner of a bank. The final task was two hours flying from Phoenix to a desert range at Tucson, to drop two 500 pounders before returning to base. We had not been able to calibrate our Bomb Sight and as a result the visual bombing scores were not up to our UK achievements. That said, our crew results were the best for the RAF, and on a comparative basis against all entrants we were fifth.

Back home once more, Bomber Command was a regular spoiler of weekends with exercises on Saturday nights. Many of these exercises were flown with a maximum command effort: all aircraft on the same route in darkness and without navigation or resin lights. When the exercise was complete each aircraft passed through a gate position and put their lights on. This was when the sky lit up and you realised how many other aircraft were around you. Above and below, ahead and astern, to the left and the right. The system of timing seemed to work, and the collision record was small, although there was, I believe, one such incident.

'Sunray' was an exercise which enabled crews to experience long-range overseas flights, a variation in operating conditions, and the opportunity to carry out some daylight bombing during the winter months when the weather in the UK was not suitable. The Base Station was RAF Shallufa in Egypt, at the southern end of the Bitter Lakes. During the exercise we carried out regular visual and radar bombing, gunnery air to ground exercises, and simulated gunnery during fighter affiliation, when the aircraft was flown fairly violently in corkscrew manoeuvres in an attempt to stop the fighter getting hits with his cine-film gun cameras.

We also had a fighter affiliation exercise called 'New Moon' with the Turkish Air Force. This involved a transit to Nicosia and back with a couple of days in Cyprus.

We had settled down on the return flight when the i/c burst into life. 'Mid upper to pilot' – 'attack, attack from the port beam'. When interrogated, the gunner said he had seen two Turkish fighters in a tight turn coming for us, white puffs were visible and he was convinced we were being shot at. It eventually turned out to be condensation or vapour coming off their wings in the tight turns. Sanity returned as they came into formation prior to a session of real fighter affiliation and evasive action.

I had now been in the RAF for three years and this had been a good start to what proved to be a long career. I could not then foresee that I would serve thirty-seven and a half years in the Royal Air Force and fly over 12,000 hours, in seven major types.

Korea 1950

Cold War tensions built up to a major confrontation and a savage war in 1950.

The peninsula of Korea had been annexed by Japan in 1910. During the Second World War the Allies pledged that when Japan was defeated Korea would again become an independent state.

After entering the war against Japan very belatedly, the USSR occupied northern Korea. United States forces then occupied the southern half. Purely in order to facilitate the surrender of Japanese troops in Korea the USA and Russia agreed on the 38th Parallel of Latitude as a temporary dividing line. Negotiations dragged on and eventually the United Nations organised elections which led to Syngman Rhee becoming President of South Korea in August 1948. One month later the Russians set up the Communist Democratic Peoples Republic of Korea in the north.

Although the USA gradually withdrew its forces from South Korea the Russians encouraged military build-up in the north. On 25 June 1950 the North Koreans launched an invasion of South Korea using eight divisions. The United Nations demanded withdrawal and, when this was ignored, the Security Council authorised the use of force to support South Korea. The Russians had boycotted the meeting and were unable to veto the resolution.

On 27 June 1950 President Truman appointed General MacArthur Commander in Chief of the United Nations Forces which included units of the Royal Navy and British troops. Because of its other commitments, only limited RAF assistance could be made available. This in no way hampered operations as the US had strong air forces in the region. The Far East Flying Boat Wing was made available for reconnaissance and transport duties. In addition two highly decorated and experienced RAF officers were seconded to the 5th United States Tactical Air Force to advise on tactical operations and, in particular, night intruder tactics.

Wing Commander P. G. Wykeham-Barnes (later Air Marshal Sir Peter Wykeham) flew on a number of sorties and saw that tighter control and co-ordination of intruder missions was essential. He produced a 'charter' under which squadrons were to be allocated specific target areas, flares used for identification of targets and air/ground communications improved. This was accepted and implemented by General Partridge and resulted in significant improvement in night intruder operations.

The initial thrust of the North Koreans' attack had carried them almost completely through South Korea and penned United Nations Forces into little more than a bridgehead around Pusan. The effectiveness of the new intruder tactics in destroying North Korean supply lines helped General MacArthur mount a counter offensive which forced the

Roads through 'Gloster' valley looking SSE, Korea 1952 (Museum of Army Flying)

North Koreans back beyond the 38th Parallel.

Air Vice-Marshal 'Sandy' Johnstone recalls that when he visited Tokyo with Aidan Crawley, Under Secretary of State for Air, General Carl Stratemeyer, C-in-C of Far East Air Forces told them that if it had not been for Wing Commander Wykeham-Barnes the United Nations would have been pushed into the sea.

Wing Commander J. E. Johnson (later Air Vice-Marshal) was also seconded to take part in, and advise on, US air operations. Other RAF pilots were attached to USAF and Australian fighter squadrons.

The war was a vicious one, characterised by the atrocious conditions and the appalling treatment of prisoners of war by the North Koreans and Chinese. When a truce was eventually signed in July 1953 approximately 350,000 men of the United Nations force had been killed or wounded. Enemy casualties were estimated at not less than 1,500,000. A terrible toll for a far from satisfactory truce.

Report on Korea – an Anecdote Illustrating the Flexibility of Air Power

Air Marshal Sir Peter Wykeham KCB DSO OBE DFC AFC

In August 1950 I was a test pilot at the RAF Experimental Establishment, Boscombe Down. We were hard at work probing the Sound Barrier with aircraft which totally refused to fly faster than Mach .95. On 6 of August my wife had given birth to our first child, a daughter, in a hospital which has since become the Lanesborough Hotel at Hyde Park Corner. I first saw her on the 6th. On the 7th I was ordered to report immediately to the USAF (United Nations) in Korea. The Commandant of the AAEE was not pleased, nor indeed was I, but I was airborne on the 8th. Such is military life.

It seemed that some RAF expertise in night ground attack was urgently needed, and only I could supply it. This was not totally surprising, for five years after the end of WW II most of my friends who had been in the night ground attack business were dispersed or otherwise unavailable. With them, towards the end of the war, I had specialised in the art of pin-point attacks on SS/Gestapo Headquarters in Occupied Countries (which I recommend as the only really enjoyable aspect of warfare) and also in the suppression of surface military movement by low-level night ground attack.

On the BOAC Argonaut which took me to Tokyo there was only one other warrior bound for the wars, an American from a great US tobacco company. 'Do you realise', he said to me in a voice of thunder, 'that there are fifty million Japanese women who don't smoke? I'm going to make them smoke'. I envied his confidence and hoped I would do half so well. We were twin soldiers of the United Nations.

In Tokyo at last I was taken to MacArthur's HQ: immense, impressive, and air-conditioned almost to refrigeration point, where I met General Carl Stratemeyer, Commander of all Far East Air Forces. Bluff and genial, as all American Generals should be, he put his arm around my shoulder and explained his problem.

'Commander, we are pinned back around Pusan port, our last foothold in Korea' he said, 'while those gooks are running about all over the country building up strength to push us into the sea. Have a cigar.'

'But Sir, besides your own aircraft you have an RAAF Meteor squadron here. You can easily stop all movement.'

'Sure as hell we can by day. But then they just run around all night. Now listen to me, Commander. You have to stop them gooks running around all night.'

'Do you think your aircrew on the spot will take any notice of a test pilot out of England?'

'They certainly will, Commander, after I've sent them this here TWX, so on your way, and good luck.'

A B17 took me to Pusan airstrip, on the tip of Southern Korea. General Partridge, commanding all air forces in Japan, met me and set out the situation. 'We are back on our heels around this port' he said. 'We are just holding them out of artillery range of the docks, and we have to keep them weak until our great counter-offensive. If you'll come with me tomorrow, Commander, I'll show you the front line.'

The General's way of showing me the line was to fly an unarmed Dakota very slowly round the perimeter at 1000 ft. I class this as the most frightening sortie of my entire life, for I could easily see the enemy soldiers, to say nothing of their AA guns. I asked General Partridge why we were not instantly blasted out of the sky. 'They durst not, Commander', he said, jerking his head upward. 'My fighter boys are above us, and one squirt from them gooks and down they come.' I thought this answer relied too heavily on the good sense of the opposition. One squirt would be enough.

General Partridge, briefings complete, sent me to his Third Bombardment Wing at Iwakuni, on the southern tip of

Honshu in Japan, the base of some thirty B26B (Douglas Invader) day ground attack aircraft. I was greeted by Col. Leland Walker, OC Wing, with the easy hospitality I had already experienced in so many USAF units in America. The Wing was half in squalid buildings and half under canvas. I was allotted a small cell and a strikingly unattractive Japanese lady to make my camp bed. Colonel Walker then fixed for half his aircrew to assemble for a lecture on night ground attack, the other half to catch the same lecture next day.

I therefore delivered two one-hour lectures, hastily improvised, on the techniques used by 2 Group's Mosquito Force to immobilise the German Army in France, before and after D-Day. I explained that the effects of night ground attack are one-tenth material damage and nine-tenths paralysis by instilling an exaggerated fear of the aeroplane overhead in the dark. Soldiers usually over-estimate the perception of the night marauder, and fear to move when he is in their area. As the lecture went on I thought I could detect a faint whiff of scepticism, which General Stratemeyer's TWX had somehow failed to disperse. I had met this attitude before in the USA. Americans do not like to be told. They like to be shown. But once they are convinced, they catch on very fast indeed.

So Colonel Walker allotted me Invader 4347, and Captain Crosby checked me out on it. This Invader had been in storage since 1945, and she showed it. I was assigned Captain Lewis as navigator, and Sgt. Gomalski as rear gunner. Both looked far from happy. 'You sure you know how to handle these birds at night, Commander?' 'Don't worry boys' I told them, 'I've done scores of these types of missions.' I hoped my exaggeration would bolster their confidence; though I knew that they knew that I could not possibly have done anything of this kind for five years at least.

With the Crew Chief, I had a good look round 4347:

'Those tyres look dangerously worn, Chief.'

'They certainly are, Commander.'

'Where's that engine nacelle panel?'

'We haven't seen that in weeks, Commander.'

'You're short of spares then?'

'We get plenty stores, Commander. If this war was fought with brushless shaving cream we'd have won a long time ago.'

But the strong old bird could fly. She had been hastily fitted with twelve .5 forward-firing guns, plus two in an after-turret, and she carried eight 250 lb fragmentation bombs. Guns, bombs, and ammunition made a formidable load, and 4347 could just about drag herself off Iwakuni strip, though once she was up she flew like a Douglas. But she was much too heavy and clumsy for the job.

Korea is a 5000 ft plateau, threaded with the valleys which hold the rivers and communications, and to get at the roads and railways it would be necessary to creep down into these valleys. Not too bad with a moon and no cloud, but with cloud cover and no moon, and with rather casual dead-reckoning navigation, highly disagreeable. When you reached the head of a valley you had to climb 5000 ft to get out. It was a bit too close for comfort.

Our first trip, to Pyongyang, five hours of low-level, produced the usual meagre quota of flying targets. Korea below was dark as the pit. Because of the total blackout it was just possible to see movement, and only the army moved. We used up our bombs and bullets, and made it back to Iwakuni. Captain Lewis looked a little more cheerful; so did Sergeant Gomalski.

I gave another talk to the aircrew, stressing the difference between the heavy B26 and the agile Mosquito, on which my tactics were based. I emphasised the importance of not being too heroic, for a B26 and crew was a poor exchange for a Korean truck.

On my third trip with my first crew we got our sights on a good-sized convoy near Taejon, dived to firing range, and let go with the front guns. Immediately, there was a blaze of flame and sparks all around the inside of the cockpit, as the rigged-up wiring of the front guns blew its insulation. I heaved her into the dark sky, the cockpit filled with smoke; Captain Lewis squirted everything with a portable fire extinguisher, I cut the main circuit breaker, and we were still flying. We limped home damp with sweat and extinguisher fluid. Colonel Walker gave me another aeroplane.

A couple of sorties later, with a new crew, PFC McHale on rear guns engaged a convoy above us on a mountain road. This was the trip on which, after four hours of crawling around the valleys, the navigator confessed he had no idea where we were. This was not disastrous, for if we steered south-east we would pick up the powerful Iwakuni homer. But our pilot-operated MF was tuned by a handle at the pilot's elbow and after a couple of turns it released itself and fell onto the cockpit floor. At that moment we seemed very far from Japan, and even further from Hyde Park Corner.

Douglas Invader A-26B-15-DL 41-39158 on loan from the USAAF, July–Nov 1944 (Philip Jarrett)

With no radio we began a nightmare search for base, feeling down through cloud for the Korean coast, marking the water's edge by the twinkling lights of countless fisherboats out over the dark sea, groping for the coast of Honshu, weaving along the beach – until with fifteen minutes of fuel left, we sighted the lights of Iwakuni.

I flew only nine sorties with the Wing. It was a trifling effort, but I found the five to six hour missions quite a strain. The fact was that even a new B26 was just not the right aeroplane, and as the other crews began to go out at night and get results my admiration for them grew and grew. They showed the same gritty determination as my other hero, the Master Sergeant Chief Cook of the aircrew tented Mess. This Chiefie never left his easy chair in the centre of his kitchen. Day and night he sat there, seldom dozing, only taking his clothes off for a shower: and the food was excellent, better than in my own Mess back in England.

Half-way through my mini-tour I took a B26 over to Pusan to see General Partridge again. A taciturn man, he gave a grunt or two signifying satisfaction at the way things were going, and went so far as to hint that he was applying for my permanent attachment to his Air Force. I thoughtfully returned to Iwakuni and flew missions with two more crews: the usual black night under the clouds, the same creeping up the valleys to find the convoys, the same stumbling home through the mountains and over the Sea of Japan. Debriefing, and then into Chiefie's Mess for an excellent omelette, and so to bed.

The crews were now going out regularly by night as well as day, and a twenty-four-hour interdiction plan was set out to cover all the routes from Pyongyang south, to close down the enemy's logistic back-up. The aircrew did not like it much; but they were almost convinced that it was working. Intelligence said so, anyway. One shadow lay across their morale: not fear of death but fear of capture. Already it was known that POW of the Koreans never reappeared: dragged off to the North, probably prisoners for life.

I had just begun once more to get a feel for the old business when the astral forces which had plucked me out of England exerted themselves once more. General Partridge called on radio, and told me to get to Tokyo and write him a report. I said goodbye to Col. Walker and the boys, guessing that this was a recall to UK. 'Watch it, Commander', they said. 'Glad to have known you.'

General Stratemeyer was generous. 'You've got our boys going, Commander, and I reckon those gooks will take a lot longer now to move their stuff to Pusan. Now they want you back in England, and I can't do a thing about it.' I told him about the B26s. 'They're all I've got right now, Commander. But write me a report.'

Five days later I was back at Boscombe Down, where my pilots were still probing the Sound Barrier with aircraft which would only fly at Mach .95. The Commandant asked me to write him a report. In deference to the Oriental nature of my detachment I followed the example of the military commander in 'The Wallet of Kai Lung' and entitled it 'A Benevolent Example of the Intelligent Arrangement by which the most Worthy Persons Outlive those who are Incapable'. But the Commandant changed it to 'Report on Korea'.

The Far East Flying Boat Wing

Group Captain Dudley Burnside DSO OBE DFC

The comparatively small but significant part played by the Royal Air Force during the Korean campaign is not generally known. Press coverage at the time was minimal and relatively little has since been written about the three squadrons of Sunderlands of the Far East Flying boat Wing which were the only aircraft to be operational throughout the three years of this vicious conflict.

Although individual officers and airmen, both aircrew and ground crew, saw much operational service in combat in and over Korea while seconded to American and Commonwealth units, this article describes the operational involvement of the RAF Sunderlands of 88, 205 and 209 Squadrons which flew continuously on long patrols throughout the Korean War.

At the beginning of 1950 there were three Sunderland squadrons in the Far East. Number 88 was based at Kai Tak, Hong Kong; 205 and 209 were at Seletar, Singapore.

First to operate over Korean waters was 88 Squadron which kept a Sunderland detachment at Iwakuni on the southern tip of Japan. From there they carried out long reconnaissance patrols off the Korean coasts in support of Royal Navy warships. This squadron not long before had done great work in flying a doctor and medical supplies to the ambushed Royal Navy Frigate HMS *Amethyst* under shell fire from Chinese batteries on the Yangtze river. They had subsequently evacuated large numbers of British civilians from Shanghai to Hong Kong.

Kai Tak (Jerry Morbey)

As the operational pressure on 88 Sqn increased, the decision was taken to form the three squadrons into a Wing. The immediate purpose of this was to keep the detachment at Iwakuni supplied with sufficient aircraft from all three squadrons to meet the ever increasing operational demands of the Korean situation.

By great good fortune I happened to be between postings in Malaya at the time and although I had never been on a flying boat training course it seemed that I was the only Wing Commander locally available to be given the privilege of command of the new Far East Flying Boat Wing. I was indeed a very lucky man, although aware that there would be many an eyebrow raised within the close knit flying boat community at the impertinent intrusion of this Bomber Command character with not a vestige of verdigris on his cap badge. But this was a war situation and there was no time to send me back to the UK on a Sunderland training course. I was to learn on the job as I went along. So learn on the job I did, and I must say there were plenty of exciting opportunities to do it. In due course my cap badge and buttons began to show a glimmer of green as I worked my way into the elusive flying boat union, much helped by the three squadron commanders and, above all, by the great spirit within their squadrons.

The Wing set up its headquarters at Seletar under the administrative control of Air Headquarters Singapore. Its rotating detachment of about six Sunderlands was based at Iwakuni some 3000 miles away. This came under direct American operational control and received its orders from the American navy flying boat depot ship USS *Curtis*, moored in Iwakuni bay. This ship also controlled a squadron of PBM Mariner flying boats whose mission was much the same as that of the Sunderlands.

Their flying was closely co-ordinated with ours and we worked together in the blockade of Korean ports. Frequent very long patrols were carried out from Iwakuni up each coast of Korea to just off Port Arthur on one side and Vladivostok on the other. Working in co-operation with the Royal Navy and United States Navy, many anti-mine and anti-submarine sorties were flown covering shipping lanes, particularly in the Tsushima Strait between the south Korean coast and southern Japan.

We also escorted invasion forces during Allied amphibious landings on the mainland of Korea such as that at Inchon in September 1950.

At first much of the operational flying from Iwakuni bay was done by day, but the emergence of MiG-15s, flown from their safe airfields in so called neutral territory on the other side of the Yalu river in Manchuria, compelled more of the sorties to be carried out under cover of darkness. The Sunderlands were no match for this modern enemy fighter.

Another enemy was the weather. Many operations had to be flown in temperatures as low as –2°C and the less than favourable weather conditions associated with this part of the Far East, particularly in winter. This, together with the mountainous terrain around the approaches to Iwakuni Bay, added to the hazards confronting tired Sunderland crews on their long patrols of often ten hours or more. Weather conditions were also of vital importance during the many long-haul flights which were necessary between Singapore and Hong Kong and from Hong Kong to Japan so that aircraft could rotate to keep up the unit strength at Iwakuni. Indeed it was on one of these long flights that the only loss of life occurred in the Wing's involvement in the Korean conflict. A Sunderland flew into a mountain on Formosa in appalling weather with the tragic loss of all on board.

Diversion bases suitable for emergency landings were few and far between and sometimes we had to make for Saigon or Okinawa if low cloud prevented us getting into Hong Kong or Iwakuni. On one such occasion I recall having to refuel in Okinawa bay from petrol lines passed to us from over the stern of an aircraft carrier. Juggling with the outboard engines in an endeavour to keep station beneath the great stern towering above us was an interesting but distinctly tricky manoeuvre.

All three squadrons had their moments of fear and apprehension and they were indeed incredibly fortunate that no Sunderland was shot down. On one occasion, however, they came very near to it. Orders were received to stand by to rescue American Marines and troops of the British Commonwealth in the area of a reservoir in the mountainous backbone of Korea. As much gear as possible was to be removed from the hull of the Sunderlands to lighten them and provide space inside to accommodate the maximum number of troops. The plan was to risk enemy ground fire and alight on the reservoir to rescue as many men as we could with rubber boats. In the event the operation had to be cancelled because the water became frozen over and as a tragic result hundreds of United Nations troops were either killed or taken prisoner.

Life was never dull at Iwakuni. Although based for operations on the flying boat depot ship USS *Curtis*, we lived ashore on the airfield where the Meteors of 77 Sqn, Australian Air Force, were heavily engaged in flying extensive sorties over Korea. Reminders of World War II were many – the Shinto shrine where Kamikaze pilots worshipped immediately before they took off – the local sports shop run by a Kamikaze pilot who was on his last leave when the Japanese war ended – and the boatman who ferried us out to our Sunderlands moored in the bay who turned out to be no less than an Admiral in the wartime Japanese navy.

As the intensity of operations increased, and as reports of the bitter ground battles reached us, I think what caused us most apprehension was the thought that at any moment an incident such as a Russian submarine being sunk by a depth charge or the bombing of the MiG airfields on the other side of the Yalu river, accidental or otherwise, would be the spark to herald the start of World War Three. In the event neither of these things happened.

At the age of eighty-one one's memory of events of forty years ago fades and details of many happenings, however exciting, become blurred. Not so, however, when it comes to recalling the squadron spirit of a first class Royal Air Force unit.

In my case I was indeed lucky to have been associated with three such squadrons, albeit for a short time, and I will never forget the unstinting support, encouragement, endurance and fearlessness of the air and ground crews of 88, 205, 209 Sunderland squadrons in the Korean conflict.

Fighter Tactics

Air Vice-Marshal J. E. Johnson CB CBE DSO DFC

Although the Royal Air Force did not send fighter squadrons to the Korean War, several fighter pilots, including the writer, were seconded to the USAF and flew operational missions.

We soon found that despite the introduction of jets, fighter bomber tactics had barely changed since World War II. Finger-four sections of F-80 Shooting Stars and F-84 Thunderjets arrived over the front line at regular intervals, having already clocked-in at the joint operations centre which directed them to one of the many tactical air control parties working with the troops who, in turn, passed them to a forward air controller either on the ground or in the air. Whenever possible the FAC marked the target with coloured smoke, and the jets peeled off, bored in and attacked with high explosive bombs, rockets, machine guns and Napalm fire bombs.

We preferred to fly jets, since having fewer moving parts than, say, the P-51 Mustang, they could withstand more flak damage, and not having a propeller they gave pilots a better view forwards and downwards; also the cockpit of an F-80 was far quieter than that of a P-51, which made the jet less fatiguing to fly.

Those splendid fighters, F-86 Sabres, did not carry sufficient fuel to assemble over their airfields in squadron strength and fly to the Yalu River. Moreover, once in the combat area a leader could not hold together sixteen Sabres at very high speeds, because everyone flew with high engine revolutions to keep the speed up and pilots did not have enough reserve power to catch up once they fell behind.

Leaders flew near the speed of sound, for if they allowed their speeds to fall off they were sitting ducks for the enemy's MiG-15s. Survival could no longer be found in tight turns, and wingmen had to keep up at all costs, for the leader was still the gun and his wingman the eye. Sabres flew, therefore, to the Yalu in finger-four sections, and staggered their take offs to arrive at five-minute intervals so that sections could support each other. Thus the number of fighters flying together diminished further.

Meteors in Korea

Air Vice-Marshal John Price CBE

When the Korean War started on 25 June 1950, 77 Sqn. RAAF was based in Japan as part of the British Commonwealth Occupation Force (BCOF), and flying the trusty and well-beloved P 51 Mustang. As the war ebbed and flowed squadrons were gradually re-equipped with jet aircraft. For 77 Squn the choice was Meteors.

On 29 July, sixteen aircraft were tasked to fly as top-cover to F86s on a fighter sweep over North Korea. The aim of these sweeps was to tempt the Soviet-operated MiG-15s into combat, to establish and maintain UN air superiority over the peninsula, so that other air operations and ground operations could proceed unhindered. The MiGs were not tempted on the 29th, but duly obliged during August, and shot down a Meteor and damaged two others without loss. The squadron was withdrawn from fighter sweeps and given the task of bomber escort. But it was painfully obvious that even in this role the Meteors were no match for MiG-15s and after losing three aircraft in one engagement on 1 December the squadron was relegated to duties where MiGs were unlikely to be encountered.

Relegation rankled and a more aggressive role was keenly sought. The answer was found in satisfying the growing need for ground attack aircraft, not only to interdict the North Korean lines of communication but also to give close support to the often hard pressed ground forces. Although this was not, nor ever was, a role in which the RAF used Meteors, the Australians decided to 'give it a go'.

It was felt that the Meteors could be shielded from marauding MiGs by co-ordinating their operations with those of F86s on fighter sweeps to the north up to the Yalu River: by and large this worked. The clinching argument for the change of role was that the Australians had the Meteors and they were not going to be exchanged. But a popular squadron song was 'All I want for Christmas are my wings swept back'.

Pilot losses on GA (Ground Attack) operations, which started on 8 January 1952, came almost entirely from ground fire, often unaimed but always heavy, from the Chinese and North Korean troops who were present in very large numbers around every target. I think one flew into the flak rather than the other way round. The loss rate was far greater than expected – four pilots in two weeks for example. After a while the RAAF faced a shortage of suitable pilots and asked for volunteers from the RAF.

Much as I was enjoying Germany and the Venom, the lure of real operational flying was much more attractive and shortly afterwards I was on my way to join 77 in Japan.

After a Meteor 7 check ride and eight solo ground gunnery/rocket sorties, an RAAF Dakota (better known as the Gooney Bird) took me to Kimpo airfield a few miles north of Seoul. We lived in tents, heated by oil-burning stoves against the –15°C cold; the Meteors were in sand-bagged revetments where much of the servicing was done, unless the work called for a move into a canvas servicing shelter. Quonset huts (USAF Nissen clones) housed the ops. int. and briefing rooms, flying clothing and, most importantly, the bar. There was no crew-room, nor was one needed, as you were either working/flying or 'at ease' in the tented area. Meals were taken at the USAF all-ranks chow-line, a bus-ride away on the other side of the base – miss the

Gloster Meteor T.7 (WA 732) being reassembled, Iwakuni Feb 1951 (RAF Museum Hendon)

bus and you went hungry: those were the days before aircrew buses!

We showered once a week when the bath-train pulled into the base. The ground was frozen in winter to a depth of about six feet, and a steady wind blew from Siberia taking away the top-soil at a fast rate and raising the chill-factor. In summer the temperature rose to around 30°C, which lengthened the Meteor's take-off run considerably and raised its laden unstick speed to somewhere around 160/170 knots.

Kimpo had one runway, but its capacity was sometimes increased by landing aircraft simultaneously in both directions: 'Everyone keep to the right' was the message from the efficient non-com USAF controllers. Standard radio communications, a GCA unit and an NDB completed the ATC *ensemble*.

The pattern of a tour on 77 consisted of twenty-eight days on operations followed by two days Rest & Relaxation (R & R) back at Iwakuni, reunited with one's kit, the pleasures of a peacetime overseas station and the chance of two night's undisturbed sleep. One tended not to know which day of the week it was during those twenty-eight days, although some reckoned they knew from the colour of the daily tablet in the chow-line – white was Sunday. Mid-way through the six-month tour one had a fourteen-day break in Japan.

We were given intensive briefings about the enemy's order of battle and capabilities – particularly about his anti-aircraft inventory – and told about rescue and survival in the event of being shot down. One or two small off-shore islands were in Allied hands, and the idea was to make for one of those: I was rather dubious about the likelihood of success as I couldn't see myself – an obvious Caucasian – passing unnoticed in the oriental crowd. The importance of making and keeping up-to-date a personal 'flak' map showing the location of all known AA sites was stressed time and again: I spent hours making and updating mine and never flew without it. It kept me away from many hot spots when going to and from targets. There was considerable emphasis on never flying on the same heading or at the same height for more than a few seconds – apart from when tracking a target, of course – so as not to give the AA gunners a steady aim. Radar-laid AA had started to appear, and as their predictors seemed to be programmed that Meteors flew about 50 knots slower than was the case, there was a powerful incentive not to lag behind your leader and get caught by the 'undershoots'.

So, on 8 January 1953, I flew my first operational sortie as No. 2 to Johnnie Rose – a combat-experienced pilot – on an area recce of the east coast designed to show me the SOP (Standard Operational Procedure) for a mission: departure, crossing into and out of North Korea (going North you armed RP (Rocket Projectiles) and guns and fired a couple of rounds; coming South one hoped to remember to put the switches to 'safe'), radio calls and IFF squawks, battle-formation positions ... and so on. Somewhere in the sortie my ASI packed up, so Johnnie decided to lead me in to Seoul's longer runway. This seemed a good idea at the time, but I changed my mind when I came under fire on finals from some keen quad 40 mm gunners whose aim, luckily, was no better than their aircraft recognition, and I landed unscathed.

Missions included combat air patrols over a designated area covering a recce sortie or a strike on a target; bomber escort missions – B 29s or 26s were the usual customers and they liked to see friendlies near at hand; road recces, which involved flying along a specified road/railway line and attacking any targets spotted (if you were very lucky you might find a train, but as these normally spent the daylight hours in a tunnel one's best chances were at first and last light); strikes with rockets and guns against targets such as supply dumps, vehicle parks, fortified positions, and very occasionally a power station – always a good firework display when the RPs went in; together with various alert states with various weapon-loads to meet urgent calls for close air support.

Nights were also broken if 'Bed Check Charlie' – a PO2 biplane with incredible slow-flying characteristics, armed with hand-grenades and hand-dropped bombs, was at work. One knew he was around when the base generators went quiet a few minutes before the sirens sounded. A secondary duty which I acquired was ARP Officer: trying to persuade Australian pilots to leave warm beds for a slit trench was one of my sternest missions in Korea!

'Charlie' set fire to the large fuel dump at Inchon and it burned for days. He flew so low that the base's AA guns could not be sufficiently depressed to be brought to bear and he flew so slowly that only a hand-held machine-gun in the rear cockpit of an AT6 (Harvard to us) finally brought him down.

Missions started with a check of the master flak map and updating one's personal map as necessary: if it was a strike or a road-recce you gave particular attention to target defences. A quick check of the general int. picture and a look at the latest rescue and survival gen. – those friendly offshore islands had a nasty habit of changing hands and it would have been embarrassing to walk ashore shouting 'I'm here', only to find a different landlord. Then, about an hour before take-off, the formal briefing started: met. (usually given by a USAF officer with an extensive non-standard vocabulary), target, int., weapon load, route in and out, other Allied activity in the area, and any changes from tactical and/or procedural SOPs, were covered. The mission leader then pulled it all together.

Our flying clothing was a very mixed collection: in winter we wore an early pattern US immersion suit, as the sea temperatures were so low that, without protection, consciousness would last only a few seconds; helmets were to personal choice – one could acquire an American Pl for a bottle of whisky – but I thought they were clumsy and vision-restricting, preferring a leather helmet in winter and a fabric one in summer so as to see better what was around, and taking a chance over a bang to my head; Mae-Wests were similarly to personal choice. Survival equipment was fairly basic: the dinghy pack plus a few items in pockets – cigarettes and a lighter, of course, any penicillin which one could 'get' (even out-of-date stuff was reputed to be the best currency to carry in the North), a shell-dressing, and I carried a hunting knife in place of a pistol, reckoning it had more uses than a gun.

The taxi-tracks were surfaced with an American version of PSP, and rattling over this sometimes shook an RP off the rails. So an Armourer followed alongside in a Jeep to re-install 'drop-offs'. On a road-recce we operated in pairs, going round the route at about 8000 ft to be above light flak and below the heavy stuff; looking for targets and attacking them as quickly as possible after sighting to reduce their chances of escape and also to get in before the flak got organised. Having made an attack you never made a re-attack. One day Bugs Burley (RAF) spotted a good-sized convoy on a mountain road and attacked the leading truck first, quickly followed by an attack on the last one. Having halted the convoy, Bugs called for reinforcements and an excellent score was achieved. Strikes by sixteen Meteors were quite impressive: if the target was at extreme range the order was given 'Drop ventrals, drop ventrals – GO' – and sixteen ventral tanks plunged to earth. I often wondered about a poor North Korean peasant tending his paddy-field when that lot arrived. If he survived, I reckoned he could start a good scrap-metal business.

After a multi-aircraft strike the formation reformed at a pre-briefed rendezvous and a radio check called to see if anyone was missing. This was then retransmitted back to control so that appropriate agencies could be alerted. I was not aware of a combat rescue organisation, but USAF or US Marine rescue helicopters were used south of the front line.

The route back to Kimpo necessitated passing through several 'gates' to ensure safe passage, as the IFF was not always reliable and sometimes we had to orbit either to be identified or to give priority to damaged aircraft or those short of fuel.

The squadron was mainly used for daylight missions, although night take-offs and night landings were quite common in order to keep maximum pressure on the enemy. In an effort to add more pressure on his supply routes some road-recces were flown at night if the weather and moon-phase were co-operative. Ground-attack at night in areas with 8000 ft mountains was certainly character-forming. We flew singly round the track with about 10 minute spacing between four aircraft, looking for lights on the ground and attacking them with rockets and guns. One night I was following two RAF pilots (Charlie Babst and Mike Whitworth-Jones – who won a DFC in Korea) around the traps, when I heard Mike's cultured and somewhat pained English tones enquire 'Charles, what have you bin doing to these people – there's flak everywhere'. But Charlie was not the culprit – Mike had left his downward ident light on, and so was providing a nice target for all the AA batteries.

Just about fifty per cent of 77's pilots were killed in the campaign. I was therefore somewhat put out nearly thirty years later when a senior RAF officer said to me 'Of course the RAF pilots only got to 77 when the war was over, and you just sat around for six months'. I thought of my friends, alive and dead, and of their achievements: I thought I must have dreamt of them, and I must certainly have dreamt of the 114 missions in my log-book.

Middle East

RAF Mounted Police

Ray Foster

I joined the RAF in November 1950 and was posted to RAF Cardington to sign on the dotted line and be kitted out. After a few days we were dispatched to RAF Bridgenorth for six weeks 'Basic Training' better known as 'Square Bashing', and then on to the RAF Police school for further trade training. This was a three month course, followed by six weeks training to be an RAFP D/H (Dog Handler). Discipline at the Police School made Square Bashing look like a holiday camp by comparison!

After completing all training, my first posting as a fully-fledged AC1, acting Corporal (unpaid), was to Bomber Command at High Wycombe where I stayed for a time before proceeding on the troopship *Empire Ken* to the Middle East. I disembarked at Port Said and then went on to RAF Devesoir and later RAF Kasfareet before being sent to RAF Habbaniya in Iraq.

Imagine my surprise when, on my very first day, an RAF Sergeant Mounted Policeman apprehended me for riding my issue bicycle the wrong way round the roundabout. After showing my credentials and explaining I was of the same breed as the Mountie, I admired his pure Arab horse and told him I had been involved in the riding world prior to joining the RAF and would be very interested to look round the Police Stables. He immediately instructed me to see the Officer i/c the RAF Police Section with a view to taking a very basic riding test and joining the Mounted Section.

After the test, which consisted of tacking up Police Horse 'George' and then a chance to show off my skills as a horseman in the outdoor school, I was told 'You are now a Mounted policeman and one of an elite band. There are only two Mounted Sections in the whole of the RAF, the other section being in Germany.'

Work started at 6 a.m. with a general patrol of the perimeter of the Camp, better known as the 'bund'. This involved examining the perimeter fence and checking the Guardroom staff at the three entrances to the camp, signing in the Guardroom incident book and keeping the Police notebook entry up to date.

As the sun got hotter it was back to the stables to give the horses a hose down with cold water. This they absolutely loved and would have stood all day with the water being played on them. They then had a roll in the sand pit before being fed and left to their well-earned rest. Meantime we wrote any reports etc. relating to the morning's work.

When the sun's heat had cooled we would return to the stables for another patrol of the camp area to check on security prior to the end of the working day. We might be required to do crowd control at a station sports event, continue with the training of the horses or just generally try and look as if we were gainfully employed by the RAF!

There were six horses on the strength of the Mounted Section, called Wolf, Chota, Wildfire, George, Rajah and Romani. Police establishment was one Sergeant and five Corporals. Three grooms or, as they were known, syces were also employed. Their duties consisted of cleaning out the stables, cleaning the tack, grooming and feeding the horses with made up feeds. There being no blacksmiths the horses' feet were trimmed with rasps by any competent individual. The Arab horses wore no shoes and their feet more or less kept themselves in trim.

Occasionally we had to do trips out to the Bombing Range, a distance of twenty miles or so, to keep the local Arabs off during bombing practice and also to stop them collecting the spent shells and spent cordite etc. This could be quite dangerous at times: the Arabs were so intent on getting to the shell cases etc. first that they would lie low and then make a dash with the Mounted Policeman in hot pursuit. This duty was not popular since no water could be carried. The only liquid available was a small amount at midday break and a drink for the horses.

Some of the more popular duties were as Escort to the late King Faisal on his visits to the Station, and as escorts to the horses and jockeys at the regular monthly race meetings held during the winter months. If it was not too hot, occasionally a patrol into the desert would be undertaken to visit a local sheikh and partake of his hospitality or we might ride up to the 'Rest and Leave Centre' some five or six miles away on the shores of Lake Habbaniya.

All in all, my two years in Iraq were most enjoyable, and many happy memories remain with me.

Mounted RAF police, Habbaniya (RAF Museum Hendon)

Security in the Canal Zone

Flight Lieutenant C. E. Seppings CPM

After serving as a CID Superintendent in the British Burma Police and in the Army with SOE during the Burma Campaign, I joined the RAF Police. In November 1952 I was posted to 3 RAF Police Wing, Ismailia in the Suez Canal Zone.

I looked forward to serving with an old friend from the Far East, Wing Commander Peter Hicks, who was Deputy Command Provost Marshal. He informed me that my temporary appointment was as Security Officer at 3 Police Wing HQ, but in view of my past with SOE the Command Provost Marshal and Army Intelligence planned to broaden the sphere of RAF Police Security/Intelligence to combine with Army Intelligence and Special Branch. He also told me that there were several Army Intelligence and Special Branch officers stationed at Ismailia and Fayid who knew me from Burma, and that I was to spend time in meeting these people.

However, the OC of 3 Police Wing said that my job was at Wing HQ. I therefore spent my time looking through past security reports, which concentrated mainly on RAF Station security and Control of Entry. Wing HQ seemed to be offering very little in the way of advice to Station Commanders, leaving station security very much in the hands of the station police assisted by RAF Police Auxiliaries of Egyptian and Palestinian origin and of questionable loyalty.

With some exceptions, these auxiliaries, both RAF and Army, stood by us during the Abrogation and the conflict which followed, but when the diplomats moved in and the tough men moved out, an uneasy truce seems to have been engineered – much to the advantage of the Egyptians. They then proceeded to do what they liked, egged on by the Egyptian army first under General Neguib and then later under Colonel Gamal Abdul Nasser. Assurances that the Egyptian army and police would not reinforce their depleted units in the Canal Zone were ignored, and men and arms were covertly introduced into the Zone: odd servicemen

Carl Seppings and Standard Vanguard Estate, Egypt 1953 (Carl Seppings)

were killed shopping in towns like Ismailia, Port Said and Suez; military camps were infiltrated by criminal gangs inspired by and under the direction of Egyptian Army Intelligence in order to steal military equipment. Those Egyptian subjects and stateless Palestinians working for the British as auxiliaries or in other civilian capacities, and who had to live in villages and towns outside service camps, were threatened and intimidated by Egyptian Police and Intelligence.

The most serious case occurred when the most senior RAF Police auxiliary, Inspector Sabry, based at Ismailia Camp but living in the town, was abducted by Egyptian Intelligence on the Canal Road in broad daylight whilst travelling in service transport to RAF Devesoir. For a long time nobody seemed to know where he was, until an informant told us that he was being held in Cairo prison for an unknown reason. Now all the other auxiliaries were worried because they felt that the British authorities had made no representations to the authorities in Cairo to secure Inspector Sabry's release, or at least to have him represented. It was difficult to explain to them that, even though he was employed by us, Sabry was an Egyptian subject and there was little we could do. This of course did not sound convincing and was no comfort to them.

The big danger was that Egyptian Intelligence could put pressure on them to assist in the break-ins of camps and also to divulge the exact location of stores containing the aircraft spares urgently required by the Egyptian Air Force. We and the station security staff therefore started a hunt to identify those who were vulnerable to pressure and might act as enforced agents for our opponents. This turned out to be a sensitive and long-drawn-out job because we had to rely on other auxiliaries who might be closer than we thought to our targets.

I was not with the Police Wing for long, because a reorganisation moved both security and criminal investigation to 205 Group where there was a RAF Provost Office.

We took two staff cars (Standard Vanguards) with us. One with RAF markings and the other painted black and bearing Egyptian number plates. This was the one which I used most often to get around to contacts in the Zone. In addition, I did not attract too much attention when in civilian clothes and accompanied by locals. The problem was that I or my RAF police driver could be stopped by the Egyptian Police for any reason. We always had firearms with us which included automatic pistols and Sten guns.

My agent set-up was well and truly under way by mid-1953, when a vehicle containing, I suspected, Egyptian intelligence officers in civilian clothes tried to run our vehicle off the road just after Nifishia village on the Canal Road. I saw that the front seat passenger of the left hand drive vehicle had a pistol in his hand. Our car was right-hand drive and I was in the front seat and nearest to this man. I told my driver to brake as the other vehicle came alongside and as it passed, I was able to give the man with the pistol a good burst from the Sten gun I had on my lap. The other vehicle veered off and rolled over into the dune which bounded the road. We did not wait to see the damage done and sped off south towards Devesoir. The Guardroom there abutted the road and as the other vehicle was a large maroon American model, we waited to see if it would pass.

I later learned from Captain Maraki, our Egyptian police liaison officer, that two Egyptian police officers had been fired on by locals in another car near Nifishia village and both were in Ismailia Hospital suffering from bullet wounds. As both my driver and I were in uniform at the time, their story did not tie us with the incident. However, according to Maraki, the police believed that there were armed locals working against them and they were very cautious when driving down the Canal Road which was flanked for many miles by British service establishments. These, they felt, might be directing these locals and playing them at their own game!

As Flight Lieutenant (Security) I inherited an RAF clerk of Anglo-Egyptian origin who spoke Egyptian Arabic fluently. I realised that I could not use him in an operational role but merely as an interpreter and reader of Arabic newspapers published from Cairo. These often contained anti-British propaganda and general information about goings-on in and out of the Zone and other areas in Egypt.

To make my job effective, I planned to recruit people to work with us. As a start I made contact with Colonel Sir Edward Malet, the Civil Affairs Officer in the Zone, and learned from him that we employed Egyptians (Muslims and Coptic Christians), Palestinians, Israelis, Greeks, Poles and White Russians in our various Army and RAF camps. These I believed could help me form an intelligence and agent network to combat the problem of break-ins at sensitive establishments.

It was through my clerk that I met a Palestinian Christian called Gabriel Zifteh, who was to become my close assistant in forming an agent network, and to become a trusted and close friend. He and his family had had a bad time in Palestine during the Mandate, and at first he was very suspicious of any attempt on my part to form a close friendship. I took my time, and as I had handled other races (Burmese, Karens, Chinese, Indians and Malays) during my time in the Burma Campaign and the Burma Police, I believed that by understanding his suspicions about British intentions and letting him air his views without too much argument or explanation, I could win his confidence. This is exactly what happened as time went by.

He was single, lived in the civilian cantonment at Kasfareet and shared a bungalow with a Coptic Christian Egyptian called Antoine. Antoine, who had relatives living in the Egyptian villages of Kasfareet and Devesoir also had Muslim Egyptian friends known since boyhood and was therefore a useful member of my prospective team.

Gabriel also had a good Israeli friend called Sapota who was working with the AMWD at RAF Devesoir, and later when Gaby got to know and trust me, he suggested that Sapota was very worth while cultivating as he had many friends, both Jewish, Eastern Europeans and Egyptians who could be useful to us.

My first consideration was of course RAF security, but I took the opportunity of contacting the head of Special Branch. I also forged a link with one of his assistants, a Frenchman who lived in Mauritius and who had contact with The Mauritian Regiment which was stationed in the Zone. I contacted other old friends from SOE in the Burma Campaign and through him met other useful people.

At weekly Intelligence briefings, I learned of the considerable losses suffered by the Army in the way of firearms, field pieces and even light tanks – but that is another story. Suffice it to say that the Egyptian Army were making a thorough nuisance of themselves by disregarding any treaty arrangements and were waging a sort of unwritten war and keeping us very much on our toes.

If the Army and RAF had had their way they would soon have stamped out this activity, but our diplomats in Cairo and the UK had taken over, so we had to adopt a 'softly softly' approach. This was very irritating, hence our undercover methods of thwarting the Egyptians. The links with the Army, Civil Affairs and Special Branch were useful by way of exchange of information and assistance where necessary but I made clear from the start that my operations were low level, mainly to combat intrusions into RAF establishments.

As time went by, my network started to pay off. The AOC was very supportive when he was made aware of my plans and saw to it that I was provided with funds to bribe and provide hashish to prospective informers. We started to capture or shoot intruders at RAF Kasfareet and RAF Devesoir. The increased number of RAF and Army police dogs at the Ammunition Depot at Abu Sultan put paid to intruders or assisted in their arrest.

On interrogating those captured, we learned that they were long-term convicts from the Egyptian Penal Settlement at El Arish on the Mediterranean coast east of Port Said. They were given parole to their villages in the Zone, provided they worked with Egyptian Intelligence in their quest to break in to sensitive establishments and steal essential equipment required by the Egyptian Air Force.

Those captured were confined in a secret detention centre run by the Army known as the 'Ice Box' at Moascar, where they were kept indefinitely and nobody, even those in my team, knew where this detention centre was. The CSM in charge only answered to me or the Head of Special Branch, and by this means we kept Egyptian Intelligence wondering where their men had got to. The word was spread in the villages that all who disappeared had been killed when they were caught in the camps.

I thought it was important to know who their controller was, and we soon learned that he was an Egyptian Intelligence officer only known to them as 'Captain Zikki', who directed them through an Egyptian policeman named Sayed stationed at Fayid police station. Zikki and Sayed, together with one of the gang who acted as foreman, met at a Greek bar on the Canal Road. One of my network knew the real identity of all three persons.

I felt that it was important to remove this controlling source and I obtained approval to capture Zikki and his pals.

I had dark hair and eyes, and the Egyptian sun had tanned me sufficiently to blend in with the colour of my team. We were kitted out in Army uniforms with Mauritian Regiment shoulder tags, and having found out in advance what sort of car Zikki drove, we entered Alex's bar late one night when Zikki and his friends were there and captured all three. We whisked them off, first to the cells at RAF Abyad Guardroom and then at the dead of night the next day to the Ice Box at Moascar.

We heard nothing from any Egyptian quarter about Zikki's disappearance until about a month later, when I met our Egyptian Police Liaison Officer Captain Maraki, who told me that the Sub-Governor (Police Chief) Ismailia, Mr Ali Riffifi, was concerned that one of his police officers had disappeared after he had been captured by some British Army soldiers on the Canal Road.

Nothing was mentioned about Alex's bar, for which I was thankful because Alex would have suffered. We also set a rumour going that Zikki and the Egyptian policeman Sayed had defected to the Army and had been given safe passage to a British establishment outside the Zone.

In fact while at the Ice Box Zikki did a lot of talking, and gave us a list of names of Egyptian Army Intelligence officers operating in the Zone, including the name of one Serougi who was instrumental in the capture of our Police Auxiliary Inspector Sabry, who was then languishing in prison in Cairo. (Sabry was later hanged). Zikki was quite happy where he was and did not want to be released because of the information he had given us. In due course, he and the other two were shipped to Aden where they were given jobs with our forces. Finally, although we did not eradicate petty thefts on RAF establishments, we seemed to have discouraged further organised attempts by Egyptian Intelligence to penetrate sensitive establishments.

However, my concern was to protect those who served in my network. Thanks to the Civil Affairs Officer in the Zone I was able to deploy my team to safe havens of their choice. Gaby and Antoine and his three relatives went to Cyprus, and I was able to leave The Canal Zone at the beginning of 1955 knowing that I had been able to keep the good name of the British intact by not letting our friends down.

Some Developments in the Air and on the Ground

The Lightning – a British Supersonic Success

Air Vice-Marshal George Black CB OBE AFC

As I recall, the briefing went something like 'At the take-off point move both throttles slowly up to 85% power setting, check the brakes are holding, make a final glance around the cockpit then move both throttles quickly to full power'.

Even to seasoned Hunter pilots the acceleration was breathtaking and the exhilaration certainly left one with the distinct impression that the aircraft was in charge of things for the first few seconds. With the airspeed increasing at what seemed an unbelievable rate it was time to ease the control column back and lift the fifteen-ton aircraft into the air. Yes, the Lightning was without doubt a large machine for a fighter, but immensely powerful and purposeful for its size.

Still recalling my brief, I had to reach quickly over to the undercarriage button to ensure the wheels were fully locked up before the limiting speed of 250 knots. This was no mean feat on the early conversion sorties as one was still just that fraction of a second behind the aircraft and slightly overwhelmed by the sheer performance. The climbing speed of 450 knots was soon registering on the airspeed indicator, which one had to anticipate by establishing a 20° angle of climb from about the 400 knot point. Failure to get into the climb would see the aircraft go quickly through the sound barrier at Mach 1.0 much to the annoyance of the local inhabitants! The rate of climb was impressive: 35,000 feet being reached in under two minutes. I can still remember looking back into the cockpit rear view mirror and seeing the north Norfolk coast disappear behind me in what seemed a 'rocket-like' fashion. Similarly, one was equally conscious of the rapidly decreasing fuel state with both engines at full power developing some 30,000 lb of thrust in the climb.

As soon as the aircraft was put into level flight it would buffet mildly and go supersonic effortlessly, and after engaging reheat on both engines the acceleration was marked by another large jump in speed. Inside three minutes the needle would register 2.0 on the machmeter, twice the speed of sound in just over five minutes from take off. Although the aircraft had three-axis auto stabilisation, the handling qualities were excellent throughout the speed range whether the auto stabilisation was engaged or not. This one important feature said volumes for the Warton design team, who clearly achieved an excellent handling performance throughout the flight envelope.

By now with less than half the total fuel remaining it was time to complete a supersonic turn and head for base, simultaneously reducing power to commence a slow descent towards the airfield. As one began lining-up with the runway the speed was reduced progressively to achieve 175 knots a few miles from the threshold, aiming to land the aircraft at the touchdown point at 165 knots. Slower speeds gave a higher nose-up attitude with the risk of striking the tail. The aircraft settled firmly on the main wheels, the nose wheel was lowered, and the tail parachute deployed to decelerate the aircraft quickly to avoid harsh braking.

George Black 111 (F) Squadron, with Lightning 1A 'A' XM184, RAF Akrotiri, Aug 1964 (George Black)

With much delight and a certain sense of relief, my first solo in a Lightning Mk 1 of 74 (Tiger) Squadron had been completed successfully. There being no Lightning dual training aircraft in the early days this sortie was typical of one undertaken during the conversion phase. Back in the crewroom the sheer performance of the aircraft left me with an indelible memory throughout my flying career. After the Hunter, RAF Fighter Command now had a fighter aircraft whose breathtaking performance and operational capability could deal effectively with any potential adversary it was likely to encounter in the world. No other fighter had the unique characteristics of an integrated weapons system combining air-to-air radar, missiles and guns: the Lightning was clearly in a class of its own at this particular time (1960–63).

So for me began an association with an aircraft I was to fly for the following fifteen years. Not surprisingly, the challenges during this period were immense; as the service continued to develop and enhance the operational capability. Having had the good fortune to command three Lightning squadrons, including being the Chief Flying Instructor/CFS Agent at 226 Operational Conversion Unit, I had the opportunity to fly most of the different marks of aircraft, including those of the Royal Saudi Air Force – arguably the best, and final, aircraft to leave the English Electric/BAC lines at Warton. My time as the CFS Examiner for the Lightning Force also allowed me the unique opportunity to fly with every single unit at home and overseas, to ensure standard operating procedures were being followed throughout the force.

In any article on the Lightning it would be remiss to suggest that it was all success from start to finish. Technically, the aircraft was very advanced for its time, so a number of engineering problems were anticipated, which did in fact arise from time to time as one might expect. In terms of engineering support and servicing access to the aircraft it certainly was not the easiest to maintain, and many long and tedious hours were spent by the ground crew in getting to the root cause of problems. Spare parts were always at a premium, but on the plus side there was outstanding co-operation between the manufacturer and the units to minimise delays in operational availability. Throughout these often difficult engineering tasks all squadron ground crew gave sterling service in maintaining the aircraft in excellent airworthy condition and it is largely as a result of their fine efforts that so many noteworthy results were achieved.

One would constantly find individuals with immense respect and undivided loyalty throughout the Lightning Force: proud of being part of such an elite force. A healthy squadron rivalry was always evident and the morale was seldom affected by the 'ups and downs' of a busy routine squadron life. Indeed, reflecting back, there was something special about the aircraft that brought out the very best in people, thereby continuing the fine traditions of the Royal Air Force and more particularly the *raison d'être* which Fighter Command had always inspired in its air and ground crews.

To mention but a few of the highlights from my own experiences is not easy when reflecting over such a long period. However, getting the aircraft cleared for Air-to-Air Refuelling to extend the range and deployment capability was clearly a major step for such a short-endurance fighter. Air-to-Air refuelling made a notable change to the *modus operandi* throughout the life of the Lightning in RAF service. My own recollections were of deploying No. 5 Squadron to RAP Tengah, Singapore, for a six week detachment with only one *en-route* stop outbound. The versatility of the aircraft to undertake long endurance flights was remarkable, to say little of the human endurance in coping with a cramped and small single-seat cockpit!

One further memorable occasion in 1965 was flying No. 111 Squadron T5 to Amman, Jordan, to fly HM King Hussein. This was a demanding deployment to undertake with only limited ground support. Since Jordan had no compatible navigation facilities; the Israeli border was in close proximity; and being unable to communicate with anyone on the ground – the Lightning only had UHF radio and all Jordanian ground units were VHF equipped – made operations interesting, to say the least. Streaking east across a featureless desert at Mach 2 with a Royal at the controls certainly had the adrenaline at high levels. However, HM King Hussein did ensure we had sufficient fuel to make one low pass over the Royal Palace before a final circuit at Amman Airport. Interestingly HM the King often recalled this flight with great affection on several occasions when we met in the years to follow. A photograph of the event has also been given pride of place in a Silver Jubilee book on the history of the Royal Jordanian Air Force.

By way of a conclusion it is perhaps worth mentioning my final flight in a Lightning at RAF Binbrook, shortly before leaving the RAF in May 1987. My younger son, Ian, had the unique distinction of being the very last RAF pilot to convert to the Lightning and then join the only remaining squadron, No. 11. Thus as a farewell gesture I was given the opportunity to fly with my son in the Lightning T 5. As it happened this particular aircraft had served on 226 OCU when I was Chief Flying Instructor. It was a wonderfully nostalgic last flight and in my view I could think of no finer way to bid fond farewell to a thoroughbred aircraft that I had spent many memorable hours flying over the years. Sadly, it was also to be the first and last truly all-British supersonic fighter ever built, and a great tribute to those design teams in the aircraft industry .

Spinning the Javelin

Air Vice-Marshal David Dick CB CBE AFC

As a test pilot at Boscombe Down my main project was the Javelin, which started its clearance trials in 1955. It was delayed because three aircraft had been lost during the firm's development programme. Two test pilots were killed: one had entered a spin and the pilot made an unsuccessful ejection; the other was lost without trace, but was also thought to have entered a spin. Thus when the Javelin finally arrived at Boscombe it was not with the happiest reputation.

In the light of its troubles, extensive wind tunnel and model dropping tests had offered some understanding of the likely behaviour in a spin. Wing Commander 'Dicky' Martin DFC AFC, who had recently been appointed Chief Test Pilot at Glosters, then successfully carried out a remarkable – and hazardous – investigative flight test programme for which he deserved the greatest credit. The programme centred around Mk. 1 aircraft XA 548, with XA 561 as a reserve.

Both were fitted with a spin-recovery parachute, and XA 548 had extensive flight test instrumentation. In the summer of 1955 Dicky Martin carried out many spins on XA 548, and demonstrated that a spin always followed a stall, and that there had been consistent behaviour. So two of us from 'A' Squadron assessed it at Boscombe Down, confirming Gloster's findings.

The behaviour was unique. Before entering a spin there was a sudden reversal of lateral and directional stability. Control had been lost: the nose would then rise up and speed fell off rapidly; the rudder would move itself fully over in one direction and the aircraft would yaw accordingly, but roll in the opposite direction. After a pause, with the IAS 'off the clock', it would then spin.

No two spins were identical, and it was seldom possible to enter a spin in any particular direction: the Javelin determined the direction of spin! The oscillatory spin was not violent: the rate of rotation was slow – about one turn in seven or ten seconds. The nose pitched up and down, often through as much as seventy degrees. As the nose rose, the rates of yaw and roll decreased and sometimes stopped altogether as the nose reached its highest point. As the nose pitched down again the rates increased sharply as the aeroplane yawed and rolled into the spin once more. Often in mid-spin, when the nose was at its high position, the Javelin would decide to reverse direction of rotation. This was heralded by the rotation ceasing momentarily, the rudder slamming fully over in the opposite direction and the aircraft rolling sharply into a spin the other way. In the spin, Dicky Martin had recommended holding the stick fully back and central, the rudder forces being extremely heavy, and it was left to do its own thing throughout the spin. It would position itself fully in the direction of rotation.

Recovery action had to be taken at the optimum moment – immediately the nose started to pitch down from its high position. With the control column right back, full aileron had to be applied in the same direction as the spin. The control column was then moved sharply right forward, still keeping on the full aileron. The rudder was still left alone. This action seldom had any immediate effect, but nevertheless these actions had to be maintained, and if the direction of rotation reversed, the control column still had to be held fully forward, but moved sharply over into the corner of the new spin direction, and held there.

When the Javelin decided to stop spinning, it would do so after the nose was at its low point in the pitching cycle. Usually the rotation would cease and the aeroplane would hang in a nose-down attitude for a second or two – but this was a trap! Centralising the controls then would lead to re-entering a spin. The control column had to be held in the fully forward corner until the aircraft did a quite unmistakable, sharp nose-down pitch – minus 2 'G' was a typical value.

Once the Javelin had shaken off the spin in this way, recovery was complete: the IAS rose rapidly, the controls could then be centralised and the aircraft eased out of the dive. Naturally there was a large loss of height and recovery by 15,000 feet was essential.

The end of a very flat spin from 42,000 ft (AVM Dick)

Thus the central problems of the Javelin were that there was much less natural warning of an impending stall than on previous night fighters: that a spin always followed a stall. The inevitable spin was highly unconventional, as were the spin recovery actions. Assuming that all Javelin spins were like those on XA 548, the A and AEE's concern was twofold: whether the behaviour at the stall-plus-spin was acceptable for pilots to be trained to do, and then to carry out regularly, including recovery on instruments. Perhaps even more important was to decide whether, in service use, the natural stall warning was adequate for fighter pilots to avoid inadvertently spinning – especially off turning flight at high altitude when both the indicated airspeeds and engine thrusts were low.

We could not reach agreement on the second point, and it was therefore decided that to get three more opinions we would convert three more 'A' Squadron test pilots to spin the Javelin, using the reserve aeroplane, XA 561. Because all the spinning had been done on XA 548, I carried out a check flight on it on 8 December 1955. I did three spins. The first two were similar to those experienced on XA 548. On entering the third spin on this flight, off a spiral turn starting at 42,000 feet at 240 knots IAS, I entered a spin which was utterly different from all the others.

It was smooth and flat. I described the whole event into the voice recorder, and took all the actions which we had rehearsed in the event of such a situation, but none had any effect. I knew it was vital to get some information back, and I passed three radio messages to Boscombe to let them know of my problem. At about 20,000 feet I streamed the spin recovery parachute, but it did not fill because there was no wind outside! When I saw the altimeter pass 15,000 feet it was time to go. After a quick 'Mayday' call, as I was near the sea, I jettisoned the useless spin recovery parachute, as I did not want to be fielded by it. I then pulled the handle which ejected first the cockpit canopy and then me. Some weeks earlier I had stood beside (later Sir) Jimmy Martin at the wind tunnel at Boscombe as this latest one-handle-operation integrated escape system with the 80 foot per second Mk 3 ejector seat was tested on a Javelin fuselage. Little did I realise that I would soon take the place of that articulated dummy.

I quite understand how Sammy Wroath had felt after such an event – rather lonely at the end of the table! In contrast to the case of the prototype Magister, there was no dispute over Gloster's flight testing with which we were fully familiar; it was agreed that the proper understanding of the problem was poor. Clearly there was a real risk of an irrecoverable spin. After the Swift, rejecting the Javelin was not practical politics. A method of preventing pilots from unwittingly reaching the stall-plus-spin was essential. Even for a fighter aircraft an artificial stall prevention or warning device was the only alternative.

An intensive programme to develop and prove a stall warning system was given high priority. The RAF's Aero Flight, the Institute of Aviation Medicine, Glosters and A and AEE were all involved. Activated by a pair of electro-mechanical vanes on each wing, an unmistakable duplicated two-stage audio warning, which could not be 'muted', was fitted to all subsequent Javelins. Pilots were cleared to pull into the buffet as far as the first stage warning.

The second stage, set further into the buffet but still leaving a safe margin from real trouble, signalled an emergency, demanding that the pilot must immediately push the stick sharply forward.

The A and AEE's programme to prove its safety, reliability and effectiveness involved hundreds of spiral dives, covering every corner of the flight envelope up to 45,000 feet and Mach 0.95, was done at all realistic loadings, by two pilots and – to ensure that the results were not particular to one aeroplane – on two fully instrumented Mk 4 Javelins. The result was successful: the Javelin saw service in many theatres and was the RAF's first fighter which it was not permitted to stall.

From Blanket Stacker to Duvet Consultant (in only 30 years)

Wing Commander Brian Mitchell

I was commissioned into the Equipment Branch in 1956, after two and a half years training at the RAF College. In all about thirteen of our entry survived the rigours of the lengthy course: only two were 'equippers', two were scribblies and the rest were pilots. It had been a fairly recent policy decision to merge GD/Pilots, Equippers and Secretarial Cadets into the college, and during our training we were indistinguishable one from the other. On the great day when we got our commissions (Field Marshal Montgomery was the reviewing officer at the passing out parade) we suddenly realised that we were different: our left breasts were bare, we had no Wings, we were the Wingless Wonders.

My first appointment was to the Equipment Section at Abingdon, where I arrived full of the bounce and self-confidence (cockiness) which only Cranwell could provide. I had no problems, I knew it all, I had been at Cranwell for two and a half years. Within twenty minutes I was cut down to size. To the amusement of the camp I had saluted three Flying Officers, and to the airmen in the Equipment Section I knew little or nothing about unit equipment procedures.

In those days the Equipment Branch revelled in paper: mountains of it in a host of different colours to help us create a mystique and to confuse our customers. The term 'user friendly' had never been invented. It would take us about two days to notify a customer that we couldn't meet his demand from stock and hence would have to refer the requirement to the depot for satisfaction. The problem in those days lay in the fact that the responsibility for getting stock onto the shelves was vested in the more junior ranks, who were responsible for determining the nature of a transaction, constructing a supply pattern, calculating a stock establishment and placing replenishment demands. In theory it was a good system, but in practice it was close to being unmanageable because the supervising staff were bogged down in paper. Not for nothing was our motto defined as 'You Want It, We Got It, You Try and Get It'. Obviously I have slightly exaggerated the situation, but today I have been granted artistic licence.

Unbeknown to me at the time there was already a move afoot to streamline equipment procedures with something called Electronic Data Processing (EDP) later to be known as Automatic Data Processing (ADP) and finally Information Technology (IT).

A team of expert suppliers with the ability to think well ahead of the (then) extant technology produced in 1957 a Systems Specification which was issued to industry as part of an Invitation to Tender. The result of the team's recommendations was the establishment of the Supply Control Centre (SCC) at RAF Hendon together with the purchase and installation of two AEI 1010 Computers. It became the foundation of the RAF Supply ADP System which more than earned the national and international acclaim which it was given.

Back to me. I have to admit that I have never been a good equipper: I did reasonably well as an Air Mover (if you ever wanted air moved etc.) but I have to admit that I found the paper empire boring. I was sent on two EDP courses in November 1961 and April 1962 respectively; I was convinced that working on a computer would be a fate worse than death and I wouldn't even be able to lie back and think of England. I improved at work (I could hardly get worse) but on 21 June 1966 I was sent to London to sit an ADP Aptitude Test which I passed, and the result of which was a posting to Hendon in January 1967. It's just as well that you can't see into the future because, but for two relatively short breaks, I was destined to remain at the SCC until I retired in September 1992. In advance I would have been horrified, but with the benefit of hindsight I should have been delighted, because I was given the unique honour of helping to translate us from a group of blanket stackers to an organisation of highly trained duvet consultants.

The 1010 was truly a dinosaur by modern standards: it had an enormous body surrounding a relatively pea-sized brain, and literally filled the very large operations room. The prime source of data capture was a keyboard accounting machine (KAM) which vaguely looked like a typewriter five feet wide, four feet high and three feet deep: a good operator was doing well if he, or she, achieved eighty transactions in an hour.

Fortunately for me the Equipment Branch insisted on effective training which helped my natural aptitude for computers. I had left mainstream work because of my horror of paper and my first task was to work with a printer which could function at 750,000 characters a minute – even modern hardware would find it difficult to match that printing speed.

Because we were so new we had to host lots of visitors, and an early task was to explain the printer which was known as 'The Xeronic'. The printing process comprised the following:

Data was converted from central storage via photo-electric cells into magnetic light energy. The light, in the form of recognisable characters, was beamed on to paper capable of accepting a magnetic charge. The paper passed under the light source at a steady speed. Having accepted the charge the paper passed through an area of dust bearing a charge opposite to that on the paper. Opposites attract and the dust adhered to the images. The paper was then shaken to remove surplus dust prior to entering an oven where the dust was baked on. The danger was the variation in the speed of the paper as it could burst into flames in the oven. Consequently we had to position an airman with a fire extinguisher alongside the printer when it was running, just in case.

Try and visualise people's expressions when I was explaining this cycle of events. To this day many believe it was a leg-pull to enliven their visit.

The 1010 was able to advise a customer of the availability of stock at the depot within a maximum of two hours for a high priority, or twenty-four hours for a low priority demand. This was an enormous improvement on the old manual or clockwork system. We were inordinately proud of our achievements but were only too aware that things could go wrong – one of our main problems was the type of data communications facility available. On one occasion an Air Officer was scheduled to visit a Supply Squadron (new title) to see the system in operation. Both we and the unit staff wanted the demo to go without a hitch, so they sent us the message the day before the visit so that we could prepare the appropriate reply. We were advised of the time of the visit and hence agreed the time we should transmit the 'reply'. No one told us that the AO had been delayed and he was quite impressed to receive the reply two minutes before his message was transmitted. More than hands were slapped.

1967 also saw the creation of the nucleus of the development team whose aim was the production of a system to replace the 1010. By the end of 1969 the team was almost fully established with in excess of 100 members. The new system, the 4-72, gradually assumed responsibility for the RAF Supply Automatic Data Processing System over about a year, and the last live run of the 1010 started at 1600 hrs on the Friday before Christmas 1975.

The 4-72 was a major breakthrough in modern technology with visual display units (VDUs) replacing the Keyboard Accounting Machines, and meeting a response time of two and a half seconds. The 4-72 was replaced by two ATLAS 10s and then by two Hitachi Data Systems EX38 machines. However the basic design structure and program language was retained, and hence we no longer had a dinosaur but rather a 'Mekon' with a super brain and a tiny body.

The Supply Automatic Data Processing System provided total on-line stock control and management information for 1.6 million items of equipment at 160 locations world-wide from Hong Kong to the Falklands, utilising 1500 VDUs and 1000 printers. The System coped with approximately 242,000 transactions per day (with 8,000 per quarter of an hour at peak periods), and achieved a response time within the range two to five seconds. To draw comparison with commerce, the Supply Automatic Data Processing System equated to 160 'Sainsburys' or twenty-five 'Marks and Spencers'. The System ensured a unit off-shelf satisfaction rate of more than 70% with a further 20% of demands being satisfied from depot stocks. Inter-unit transfers were a matter of course, with full control of stock which included inventories and dispersed locations. A distributed system was introduced, to provide units with a significant role in war or transition to war, with their own mini-computers linked on-line to the central system, and provided them with their own control of stock even without the assistance of the Central Computers at Stanbridge. And most significantly there was far less paper produced. Sophisticated printers were used and laser technology replaced the Xeronic – the end product certainly looked far more professional but without the excitement of the superseded equipment.

During the Falklands Campaign VDUs were installed in Ascension on Day One, and a satellite communications link helped provide immediate supply support for our forces. When the Falklands were liberated we were able to provide VDUs which operated successfully in a tent on Mount Pleasant, and helped dispose the myth of environmental control for sensitive hardware.

During DESERT STORM our distributed system was extended to include our bases in Saudi Arabia, and once again our forces had the full benefits of sophisticated supply support. Blanket stackers where are you now?

The Supply Automatic Data Processing System then took the lead in the provision of computerised technological facilities for the supply of weapon systems produced by national and multi-national consortia, using relational databases and fourth generation program languages. An Initial Provisioning Support System was already in place for the European Helicopter and was originally designed for the European Fighter Aircraft. Royal Air Force Supply Branch staffs continued to play a prominent and significant role in the committees which helped to produce the interfaces between the various Air Forces and the major participating contractors in the UK and on the Continent, where their technical experience and ability were recognised and appreciated.

Computers get smaller and smaller as their brains get larger and more proficient: computer staffs (designers, analysts, programmers and operators) will still be necessary as will be the need for their creature comforts. We will still need to stack our blankets even if we have to consult our duvets.

Keyboard accounting machine (Wg Cdr Mitchell)

The Far East

In the late 1920s the Malayan Communist Party was formed with the objective of establishing a communist controlled republic in Malaya.

When a Japanese invasion of Malaya seemed imminent in 1941, a network of subversive agents was needed to operate behind enemy lines when the country was occupied. Ironically, the only organisation capable of carrying out this work was the Communist Party who formed the mainspring of the resistance. After the war the Malayan Communist Party revived its aim of establishing a communist state. It fomented labour disputes and infiltrated public organisations.

By the beginning of 1948 the Communists realised that their efforts were little more than an irritant, and embarked on a programme of intimidation and demonstrations, murder and sabotage. Having openly committed themselves to armed resistance the Communists set themselves a three stage programme. Firstly to cause terror and economic chaos in rural areas. Secondly to 'liberate' selected rural areas. Thirdly to 'liberate' urban areas and declare a communist republic. They estimated that each stage would take six months. They failed, but it took the Government and Security Forces twelve years to bring the emergency to a successful conclusion.

Throughout this prolonged period the RAF had three main tasks: support of ground forces; transportation, including air supply and the positioning of airborne and parachute forces; and finally reconnaissance. By 1954 the threat of armed revolution had been broken.

During 1955 Federal elections were held to hasten transition from Colonial rule to Independence. This was achieved on 31 August 1957. The United Kingdom, Australia and New Zealand agreed to continue to provide assistance during the final phase of the emergency.

British plans to bring a greater degree of independence to the remaining British territories in South East Asia included the incorporation of British North Borneo and Singapore Island into a Greater Malaysia. This aroused fierce opposition from Indonesia which saw its dreams of total domination of Borneo slipping away.

In 1962 elements in Borneo, strongly supported by Indonesia, objected to the proposed Federation, and rebellion broke out on 8 December 1962. Although the initial revolt was crushed early in 1963 an increasing number of raids began to take place from across the Indonesian border.

On 16 September 1963 Greater Malaysia came into existence with the full support of Britain, Singapore and the North Borneo States of Sarawak and Sabah. The arrangement was approved by the United Nations. Indonesia immediately broke off diplomatic relations with Malaysia.

Guerilla incursions continued, many involving regular Indonesian forces. These were initially confined to Borneo but later there were attacks on the Malayan mainland and Indonesian paratroops were dropped north of Singapore. Since war had not been declared the armed forces were unable to pursue enemy troops or intruding aircraft across the Indonesian border. Hostilities continued until August 1966 when a peace treaty was signed between Malaya and Indonesia.

The experience the RAF had gained in Burma and Malaya stood it in good stead. Air Vice-Marshal (later Air Chief Marshal) C, N, Foxley-Norris stated: 'The Borneo campaign was a classic example of the lesson that the side which uses air power most effectively to defeat the jungle will also defeat the enemy.'

Passing of The Majestic White Birds

Cliff Hall

Being a crew member of a Sunderland flying boat was a unique experience: nothing in my subsequent career ever equalled it. A sentiment shared by every ex-boatman bar none. As well as my role as Flight Engineer, I was expected to be proficient as a refueller, gunner – and most importantly as a cook. Crew members were chosen as much for their culinary skills as for their flight-deck ability. One crew member, it is said, successfully baked a cake during a fourteen-hour patrol. Generally stews and steaks were the order of the day.

In January '52, after completing the Sunderland Mk V OCU at RAF Calshot, I flew to Singapore in a York and joined 209 Squadron at RAF Seletar, affectionately known as the 'Kipper Fleet'. This was the beginning of eight unforgettable years.

The Flying Boats' role at that time was to strafe and bomb terrorists in Malaya, support the Royal Navy by patrolling the Yellow Sea and the Tsu-Shima Straits, and carry out Search and Rescue in Hong-Kong. Unlike today, Royal Naval vessels had to stop to refuel, and were sitting ducks for enemy submarines. The flying boat's task was to search for these, and patrol and drop depth-charges if necessary.

A flying boat was well armed: it carried four nose .303s (fixed) operated by the Skipper. The nose turret had two .303s, the Waist hatch one ·5 on either side and the rear turret four .303s. The bomb racks could carry four depth-charges either side or Lindholme gear.

However in flights over the Malayan jungle it was found that dropping bombs mechanically took far too long so crews took the initiative and tossed them out by hand.

Should an aircraft crash in the jungle, crews were prepared for such an eventuality by participating in a ten-day survival course. This took place in the Malayan jungle during the Emergency. Fortified with twenty-four hours' food ration and advice on how to exist, we were taken into primary jungle. After ten days of heat, leeches and mosquitoes (no

The heyday of the Sunderland – the production line (Shorts)

terrorists fortunately), we were taken to a point several miles from base: our task was to reach base, evading patrols. Being captured meant hours of interrogation; escaping capture meant a welcome meal and release. Not a particularly enjoyable experience, but in hindsight a worthwhile one.

In March 1952 an RAF Vampire pilot ejected over the sea off Hong-Kong. He was rescued by a the crew of a cargo ship, but as he was in need of urgent medical care we were alerted. We landed near the ship and took him aboard, but unfortunately he was dead on arrival at base.

To celebrate Queen Elizabeth's coronation, Singapore pulled out all the stops. Dragons sailed across the harbour, every building was lit up, and the RAF's contribution was a fly-past of twelve flying boats over the city. The reaction of the citizens was one of sheer amazement: I don't think they could believe what they were seeing. A truly unforgettable sight.

During our six to eight weeks' detachments in Iwakuni, Japan, our task was to patrol the seas around Korea. We shared accommodation with an Australian squadron of fighters and bombers and an American squadron of flying boats. Generally we got on well, but some friction was caused by the England/Australian Test series taking place at that time. Delighted to say that was the year England won back the Ashes.

Naval terms were always used in the operation of the aircraft. For instance the Captain was known as the Skipper, the kitchen area as the galley and the lavatories as the heads.During a good will tour of Sandakan, Borneo, following Naval protocol our crew decided to pay their respects to a RN destroyer anchored in the bay by flying the RAF Ensign and having half our crew lined up on the fuselage. This gesture was greeted by astonishment and incredulity by the destroyer's crew, who were in the act of dumping their waste overboard at the very moment we sailed by. All was forgiven on the cricket field the next day.

In May 1952, due to a meteorological error, our crew flew through a typhoon instead of around it. The aircraft and crew survived due to the outstanding skill and determination of the Skipper, a New Zealander called Lou Day. An incredible feat that he was long remembered for.

In 1954 I was posted to RAF Pembroke Dock in South Wales. Here the flying boats' role was less varied: we operated long patrols and took part in exercises with the Royal Navy in Londonderry at JASS (Joint Anti-Submarine School).

We were often asked to participate in fly-pasts and during one practice a 'too close for comfort' incident occurred. Our No. 2 decided to fly over the top of us but didn't make it. He knocked two feet off our tailplane and was damaged below the waterline; fortunately both aircraft landed safely.

In June 1955 a flying boat flew to Eastbourne for an RAFA celebration. Tragically, on landing it hit a submerged cable and crashed. Several crew members were killed and many injured. A black day for an aircraft that had enjoyed such a high safety record. In 1956, to celebrate the Battle of Britain we were asked to land our Sunderland on the River Thames and taxi to the Pool of London where the public were to be invited aboard. Much to our surprise, Tower Bridge was raised for us to pass. The crew spent a week as guests of Her Majesty in the Tower of London, an unusual but interesting venue.

Due to the disbandment of flying boats in the UK, 201 and 230 Squadrons were given the choice of a tour on Shackletons or a final tour in Seletar. Needless to say the majority chose the latter, and in February 1957 I set off in a Sunderland – Singapore bound. The trip took nineteen days, longer than scheduled due to unserviceability in Malta. From Malta we flew to Tobruk; then Habbaniya, Bahrain, Korangi Creek, China Bay and Penang, and landed at Seletar on the 31 March.Although the war in Korea was at an end, 205/209 Squadron still had work to do. Carrying out anti-pirate patrols in Borneo was still a priority, as was Search and Rescue in Hong Kong. A new important task emerged. A staging post for transport aircraft was needed in the Far East and the Island of Gan (Maldives) was selected for this purpose. The plan was to restore an old wartime coral runway on a nearby island. This was needed so that land aircraft could ferry in supplies and materials to build the runway on Gan. Our task was to supply food and materials to the original workforce.

The era of the Sunderland flying boat came sadly to an end in May 1959. Number 205/209 Squadron was disbanded and the crews dispersed. The boats were left at Seletar and broken up by Chinese scrap merchants. Rumour has it that they ended up as saucepans – a tragic end for what a commentator during the Queen's coronation fly-past described as 'those large white majestic birds'.

A fitting epitaph for a truly unique aircraft.

Helicopters in the Emergency

Squadron Leader C. R. Turner AFC

On completing the RAF Staff College course at the beginning of 1955 I was hoping for a posting to Canberras. Instead I was told that I was to take over 194 Squadron at Kuala Lumpur, Malaya, flying helicopters.

I spent two and a half months on the conversion course at South Cerney flying Westland Dragonfly helicopters, and in spite of my earlier reaction this really did prove to be the beginning of a very happy relationship.

The Air Ministry had arranged for me to take my family with me, but on arrival I was ordered to report to the AOC. I was literally torn off a strip for bringing my family, since although the trouble in Malaya had been called an emergency for convenience, it was in fact a full blooded war against a ruthless and determined enemy – the Communist Terrorists (CTs).

Four operational squadrons were based at Kuala Lumpur: one equipped with Pioneers, plus one Dakota which had a loud hailer for broadcasting propaganda messages over areas where the CT's were known to be hiding. The second was a Royal Navy squadron equipped with American S 55 helicopters mainly for ground troop deployment. Number 155 Squadron had Westland Whirlwinds, also operating in a troop lifting role.

My Squadron, 194, was equipped with Bristol Sycamore and Westland Dragonfly helicopters. The latter were being phased out and replaced by Sycamores. When I took over there were ten Sycamores and four Dragonflys on strength. Most of the airman were National Service, and I have nothing but praise for their first class attitude and reaction to the pressures put upon them.

The Squadron's operational directive covered:

> Tactical movement of troops, including reinforcement of outposts.
> Tactical reconnaissance.
> Casualty evacuation.
> Search and rescue.

Although we were involved in all these roles, Casualty Evacuation (CASEVAC) was the Squadron's primary activity. We were however called upon more and more frequently to carry troops and cargo. The Sycamore was never designed for such a role, since at most it was only possible to carry two fully-equipped troops compared to the eight a Whirlwind could take. This presented problems when concentrated deployment of troops was necessary to carry out surprise operations.

On one occasion it was necessary to deploy 100 fully equipped men as a matter of urgency. Unfortunately all the Whirlwinds had been grounded that day and I was called on to undertake the task. My own serviceability was low and I had to pressurise my ground staff to produce as many serviceable aircraft as possible within twenty-four hours. They worked throughout the night, and around dawn I was able to take five Sycamores on the operation, leaving one for CASEVAC standby.

The SAS were assembled at the advanced landing zone, and we shuttled 100 fully equipped men into and out of the deep jungle where they went successfully into action against the CTs. This action was completed in less than three-and-a-half hours flying time: a record I feel for helicopters not designed for troop-carrying.

Because of the need for swift casualty evacuation, one aircraft and pilot was always standing by on immediate readiness from dawn-to-dusk and at weekends. The service was important to troops on the ground for two reasons:

Operations could continue without delay: otherwise troops might have to withdraw to escort casualties down a long and possibly difficult track out of the jungle. They would then lose contact with the enemy in what might have been a tactically advantageous operation.

Secondly, and of immense importance, a high level of morale was maintained because troops knew that if they had the misfortune to become a casualty they would always be helicoptered out of the jungle and into hospital in relatively short time. This was illustrated when a patrol of the Malayan Regiment was ambushed and suffered eight casualties. A helicopter happened to be in the area and the pilot made four sorties to lift out the casualties in around thirty-five minutes.

One of the not-so-pleasant tasks was the up-lift of bodies of dead CTs required for intelligence purposes – particularly when they had been dead for a few days. This was less gruesome than the Paras' macabre practice of decapitation and flying out the heads only!

A considerable burden was placed on the pilots. Weight limitations and the need for maximum fuel loads made carrying a navigator impossible. Navigation over the jungle

The support helicopter, operating in the forward area, has to be operated and maintained under very difficult conditions, taxing both piloting and engineering skills (Westland)

to find a hastily cut clearing was rather like flying over the sea, since primary jungle forms a canopy of unbroken green foliage with no specific landmarks to check position. Pilots had to maintain visual contact flight, and after a relatively short time they got to know the operational area very well. In addition, because of the swift deterioration in weather conditions pilots had to develop the ability to identify symptoms, particularly when flying among the so-called hills of up to 6000 ft. It would be all too easy to get trapped in a valley with the sudden blocking of both ends by swift-lowering clouds full of destructive turbulence and very heavy rain. This was often accompanied by an unpleasant thunderstorm. Other adverse ingredients were the temperatures of up to 100° F and 100% humidity. All these factors made it difficult to accomplish vertical descents and ascents into and out of tight jungle clearings hastily prepared by sometimes inexperienced ground troops who had no idea of the limitations of a helicopter.

The role of the crewman was all important. Operations were often long and refuelling necessary. The stay in the operational area might last several days, and the crewman would be required to carry out servicing in all trades, often with no supporting facilities. He provided invaluable guidance in a negotiating the descent into, and climb out of, clearings and in helping ground troops to load casualties on stretchers.

Both pilot and crewman were armed and carried survival packs. These were invaluable, as I proved when the engine of my Dragonfly lost power over primary jungle and I crashed. Although injured I eventually escaped out of the jungle, but had to spend two months in hospital.

The Bristol Sycamore HR 14 was better adapted for the CASEVAC and troop lift roles, although it had not been designed for these. The centre of gravity could be adjusted by an electrical pump, such a boon when hovering in a clearing taking on a casualty. In the Dragonfly the pilot had physically to lift and place weights on a post above the flight instrument panel. This was very hit-and-miss, and a difficult manoeuvre when hovering in a clearing.

Whilst the Dragonfly was narrow, the Sycamore was wide – easily facilitating the accommodation of a stretcher or two fully equipped soldiers. In addition, the crewman could sit next to the pilot as a lookout, instead of sitting behind him as in a Dragonfly. However the low sweep of the rotor blades and unguarded tail rotor was always a matter of concern when passengers were carried, or when there were uncleared tree stumps in a tight jungle clearing.

There were three sorts of landing zones:

Permanent bases which ground troops established and from which they carried out offensive patrols. They would normally prepare a helicopter landing pad, and some of these left much to be desired. The foundation was prepared on a slight rise with a strip bamboo mat battened down on it. This mat was not serviced and in time the bamboos became non-resilient and cracked easily. With the onset of the rains the foundation became undermined, making landing quite hazardous. In one case the wheel of a Sycamore jammed in the mat and it rolled over when the pilot tried to lift off. Where practicable I preferred to hover rather than set the helicopter down.

Eleven jungle forts were established, manned mainly by the Police Field Force and used as bases for offensive operations. Most of the Forts set up a shop and in some cases a school for the local population. These Forts offered support and protection for the locals. All had helicopter landing pads.

A third type of Landing Zone was the unprepared (emergency) clearing. When a patrol suffered a casualty deep in the jungle away from their base, they would prepare a clearing to the best of their ability and usually without any knowledge of the helicopter's limitations. Since in primary jungle trees can grow up to 200 feet, an inexperienced unit would have little idea of the number of trees to chop down to enable a helicopter to carry out a controlled approach into this 'hole in the jungle'. They might leave huge stumps at the base of the trees felled, making it impossible to put the helicopter down. They might not have cleared the area of fallen tree branches, undergrowth etc., which would tend to dissipate the essential ground cushion so essential to effect a clean lift off the ground. On a number of occasions pilots had to turn down a clearing and pass on instructions through their base as to what was needed.

Apart from my accident, and despite all the problems, this was an enjoyable and rewarding tour of duty.

Formation of the Royal Malayan Air Force

Air Vice-Marshal Sandy Johnstone CBE DFC AE

In 1956, whilst serving with the Royal Air Force at Headquarters, Malaya, I was invited by Tengku Abdul Rahman, Chief Minister of the Malayan Provisional Government, to become a member of the Armed Forces Council, whose principal role at the time was to prepare plans for the creation of an Army, Navy and Air Force to serve the country when granted its Independence the following year. The Council was chaired by the Tengku himself, and otherwise comprised a number of senior Malayan Army Officers, civil servants from the Ministry of Defence and officials from the Department of Finance. Its Terms of Reference related only to the setting up of permanent forces and was not concerned with the day-to-day running of the Emergency, as that was still the responsibility of the Commonwealth Director of Operations and his staff.

It had been agreed previously that the British Government would bear the capital cost of equipping the new Air Force, but that its upkeep, or recurring costs, would become the responsibility of the Government of Malaya after Independence.

Therefore, when the original plans were being drawn up, the limiting factor was the size of the annual budget allocated to the RMAF. At first, an estimated sum of $M 15,000,000

Twin Pioneer in Malaya (AHB)

was fixed although this later had to be reduced by a half when the bottom fell out of the Tin Market.

I was then asked to submit proposals for the creation of an Air Force.

'I want you to get started as soon as possible, Johnstone.' The Tengku was enthusiastic and eager to get matters under way.

'But where do we start, Tengku' I exclaimed. '... I have never been asked to form an Air Force before!'

The Tengku thought for a moment before inviting me to attend the next meeting of the Executive Council (Cabinet), where I was able to obtain an outline of what the Ministers wanted of their Air Force.

The principal factors to be taken into account were:

a. The aircraft should be easy to fly and simple to maintain.
b. The prosecution of the Emergency had opened up much of the country hitherto considered inaccessible, and a number of police posts had been set up in the interior to maintain control of the Aboriginal population living in the deep jungle. As these were likely to continue after Independence, it was necessary for our aircraft to be capable of operating from jungle strips.
c. Aircraft should be capable of undertaking more than one role.

After studying the various types of short take-off and landing aircraft available at the time, it was agreed that the Twin- and Single-engined Pioneers of Scottish Aviation Ltd best suited the situation, particularly as the latter were already in service with the Royal Air Force in Malaya. We envisaged the aircraft could be employed in the following roles:

a. Short Range Transports.
b. Troop Carriers.
c. VIP Transports.
d. Air Ambulance.
e. Voice Aircraft.
f. Coastal Patrolling.
g. Limited bombing capability.
h. Photographic Reconnaissance.

As an acquisition of helicopters had been ruled out on account of the relatively high operating costs, an initial order for six Twin Pioneers was placed with Scottish Aviation Ltd, and arrangements made for four single-engined Pioneers, already in Malaya, to be transferred from the RAF to the RMAF.

The three existing squadrons of the Malayan Auxiliary Air Force at Kuala Lumpur, Penang and Singapore provided a useful nucleus of trained air and ground crews (most were trained to Harvard standard), whilst others were selected for training at RAF Cranwell. The Templar School at Port Dickson would be a fruitful source of recruitment for this. At the same time a number of candidates in the ground trades were selected for training at RAF Seletar, in Singapore, thus saving precious dollars in not having to send them on courses overseas.

Thus we progressed from one Armed Forces Council meeting to the next, the Tengku always at the helm and taking a lively interest in everything that went on. I was officially appointed Deputy Chief of Staff (Air) at the Ministry of Defence and CAS (Designate) in July 1957, and submitted proposals for uniforms and aircraft national markings, both of which were approved by the Council. My design for the RMAF Standard was also approved at this time and Dato Razak took over as Minister of Defence at the end of August 1957.

The first Twin Pioneer was handed over to the Malayan High Commissioner at a ceremony at Prestwick in the early Spring of 1958, and flown to Malaya by a crew seconded from the Royal Air Force. The flight was not without its problems, however, as the Suez crisis was uppermost in everyone's minds at the time and British stock was at a low ebb in large parts of the Middle East. So, not wanting our new aeroplane to be impounded by some unfriendly state, I arranged for the RMAF markings on the fuselage and wings to be covered with canvas strips, and the plane registered as a British civil aircraft for the long flight to the Far East.

All went well until the crew ran into stormy conditions over Turkey and were forced to make an emergency landing at a remote military airfield tucked among the mountains. Alas, one of the strips of the civil markings had become detached in the storm, leaving the Captain with the difficult task of explaining to a young Turkish officer, who spoke no English, how it was that a number of Royal Air Force personnel were flying a hitherto unknown type of aircraft bearing a civil registration on one side and an equally unknown military marking on the other, from the United Kingdom, which he had heard of, to Malaya, of which he had not! Indeed the situation became so farcical that the young Turk was eventually only too pleased to have the aircraft refuelled and sent on its way before he was faced with the problem of explaining it all to his superiors.

I met the aircraft at Butterworth on a bright sunny day in April 1958 and piloted it on its last leg to Kuala Lumpur where it was given a resounding reception by an enthusiastic crowd, headed by the Minister of Defence himself. At last we were truly an Air Force, albeit with only one aeroplane! The Air Force Bill (1958) putting the final seal of approval on the Royal Malayan Air Force was passed by the Legislative Council on the 1st of May 1958.

Six years later, as Air Commander of the Commonwealth Air Forces in Borneo during the Period of Confrontation, it was a source of great pride to me to have several units of the RMAF flying operationally under my command. It was noticeable that they performed with all the aplomb of seasoned aviators and were acquitting themselves with great distinction, having clearly absorbed the best traditions of the Royal Air Force during their short time in existence. Nowadays, of course, the Royal Malayan Air Force ranks amongst the most effective Air Forces in the world.

The Indonesian Confrontation

Air Vice-Marshal 'Larry' Lamb CB CBE AFC

I was at Cranwell in early 1965, seated in the Assistant Commandant's chair, when I was alerted to my posting to Labuan as deputy to COMAIRBOR (Commander Air Borneo) – AVM 'Sandy' Johnstone. First, a visit to the Gieves shop at the College, where an understanding manager – having measured me for tropical kit – suggested I send my vital statistics to one Shaft of Seletar who would make it up for about a quarter of the price. And on 8 March a twenty-three and a half hour flight from Heathrow via Istanbul and Bombay to Singapore, where followed some ten days of briefing and visits. Finally, on 18 March I flew to Kuching, where Roy Scott, the present Deputy, and the Forward Air Commander explained how operations in West and Mid-West Brigade were conducted. They stressed the virtues of parcelling out the few available helicopters amongst the various battalions, with each chopper flying as tasked by the local army CO. I met the Brigade Commander and the taciturn Australian who commanded Kuching, both of whom went out of their way to indicate in response to my queries about the helicopter tasking that, whilst glad to meet me, they would not welcome this new broom sweeping at all, let alone clean. Even today I can recall my distinct uneasiness at this reaction as I journeyed onwards to Labuan for a final take over on 26 March 1965.

So what had I inherited? About a third of the total land mass of Borneo whose interior – virtually every square yard of it – appeared to be covered by tropical rainforest never felled by man. No railways, few roads (500 miles) but many, many miles of river which formed the main line of communication. Within this area lived the varied indigenous tribes amongst whom were deployed Commonwealth and Ghurka troops, and it was COMAIRBOR's job, despite the terrain and the weather, to transport these troops to and from their operational areas, to supply virtually their every need, to rescue them if injured, to keep the skies above them inviolate from a reasonably proficient enemy based not so very far away, and finally to patrol those areas of coastline where the threat of incursion was thought to exist.

We had two main bases at Labuan and Kuching and a host of forward operating locations, many of which needed a constant resupply of stocks of aviation fuel to support the SRT aircraft using them. The JFHQ in Labuan and the RAF element of it were small and compact, and it fell to my lot to take responsibility not only for over-seeing air operations, but for many administrative tasks. A conventional joint operations room controlled and tasked the various forces operating out of Labuan. From there Kuching seemed to be not only out of sight, but at times out of mind as well. However each day appeared to pass on well-worn tramlines. At morning prayers the top brass – Army and RAF – listened to their staffs giving potted versions of hours flown, troops and stores airlifted or dropped, problems such as the recovery of parachutes which were in short supply, the occasional aircraft accident or incident and, in closed session, cross-border operations under the code-word 'Claret'. Then came evening tasking meetings, where resources were married to commitments. The Shell bungalows and messes we occupied made the jungle appear remote. But confrontation was barely an hour's flying away from our comfortable existence.

I have already referred to some uneasiness in the early days over just who controlled who or what, but as a new boy I was reluctant to challenge the perceived wisdom of those whose experience in the theatre was greater than mine.

It was the dropping into the sea of an underslung Land-Rover from a Belvedere shortly after I took over which strengthened my resolve not to take anything for granted, not least because no one – Army or RAF – appeared to take this particular incident anything like seriously at the time.

From what I could see initially, most of the operational flying pattern certainly seemed to be highly effective, but my early visits into all the Brigade forward areas did little to dissipate the feeling that somehow we weren't using what helicopter lift we had to the best effect, though I was conscious that I had little or no helicopter experience to guide me. My log book reveals that in March, April and May of 1965 I flew in no less than sixteen differing types of RAF and Army aircraft, logging some 110 hours as I visited locations, some of whose names still roll easily off the tongue: Long Semado, Sapulot, Bario, Balai Ringin and Pasia. I made trips by longboat down the River Rajang to Nanga Ghat and flew to many LZs characterised by a letter and number (e.g. R30) rather than by a name; to describe them as postage stamps would be gross exaggeration.

The warmth of my reception everywhere was equalled

Argosies (AHB)

only by the conflicting advice – from soldiers as to how best the RAF should operate to meet their needs, and from some of the air crews with whom I flew as to the limitations placed on them by JFHQ, ATOC, FATOC, Uncle Tom Cobley and all, which inhibited (so they suggested) the successful prosecution of the campaign. Faulty memory or no, I remain convinced to this day that at the sharp end at least, the junior commanders would not have opposed some modifications to the current *modus operandi*, but whether this would make cost-effective sense was by no means clear. Let me make it clear – I inherited no Augean stable.

There was or had been ample justification for many of the methods, some of the deployments and most of the tactics I had inherited. How to achieve maximum utilisation and economy of effort, whilst satisfying the soldiers' priorities, filled our waking hours. But the situation on the border – particularly in West Brigade – was still tense, and the Army staffs at JFHQ seemed eternally anxious to maximise the degree of support we could give the front-line troops. Air defence, LRMP, photo reconnaissance, V Bomber deployments to Singapore etc. – although part of the overall air campaign designed to discourage the Indonesians from engaging in anything other than skirmishing – were of limited concern to the soldier in the jungle fox hole, largely because they were out of his sight: whereas air supply most certainly was his concern, being under his very nose. To the soldier this meant not only the Hastings, Argosys and Beverleys air-dropping fuel, heavy defence stores, corrugated sheets etc. but also the ubiquitous helicopters which took him forward, ferried him his supplies, redeployed him, occasionally rescued him and finally brought him home again. The soldiers were all too young to remember the Dunkirk cries of 'where is the RAF', but if I had any sleepless nights in Labuan, it was that I was going to be the man responsible for having that charge levelled at the RAF in 1965. Hence air transport operations were top of my priority list and the lists of many others, by a long chalk.

But there were other problems, inculcating a sense of responsibility amongst the young helicopter pilots without crushing their press-on spirit. The helicopters were so valuable we could not afford the loss of a single one – particularly if that loss was caused by stupidity. If I needed any evidence that not all was as well as it appeared on the surface, it came from an unlikely source – the Royal Navy – whose Wessex helicopters of No. 848 squadron had established themselves in some style at Nanga Ghat on the River Rajang in Mid West Bde. Here they acted, I have to say, almost as a law unto themselves. My recollection of this is supported by some extracts from the F540 of Labuan and Kuching – and I quote.

> 'Labuan: "No. 848 Sqn. were, it has to be said, unused to centralised control and JAW methods of tasking, and they resisted all attempts designed to make them conform to our pattern of operations."
>
> 'Kuching: "Numerous difficulties have been experienced in making the best use of the capabilities of No. 848 Sqn. The eventual resolution of these is vital if all services are to benefit from their presence in Borneo. Their tour of duty here should give future Air Warfare staffs enough material to teach a very valuable lesson to future commanders."'

They were highly publicity conscious – an RN PRO and photographer made a monthly visit from Singapore – and the world was flooded with pictures of RN helicopters, carrying, as it were, the main burden of 'hearts and minds' as well as operations. Their activities led indirectly to a visit from the Inspector General of the RAF, following questions in the House of Commons as to what part the RAF was actually playing in Borneo. Number 848 did of course do much good work but priorities were as perceived by its CO or by local army units, and not necessarily what the Brigade Commander in Mid West Bde wanted. Incidents and accidents were frequent but often we were left unaware of what actually went on. One incident, however, could not be covered up because of the fatalities which resulted. Entering a clearing, the tail rotor of a Wessex snagged on a rock. The young pilot, full of the press-on spirit, in the words of a witness 'smoothed out' the irregularities of the damaged rotor blade with a knife, took off with several passengers, and at 100 ft or so crashed out of control into the river killing all on board. The Board of Inquiry was a completely naval affair and I for one, never saw its findings. But again let me stress, despite this cavalier approach, they did much good work in their areas particularly for 'hearts and minds', and their contribution should not be slighted or diminished by their occasional displays of independence and 'press on' spirit.

Was my continuing unease a figment of my imagination or was there something fundamental that really needed changing? The demands for airlift, air drops and helicopter support seemed never ending. How to get the proverbial quart out of the pint pot! Was I being logical in the face of facts or merely doctrinaire? That was my dilemma.

It was a visit from an old friend, Group Captain (now Air Chief Marshal) Sir Robert Freer – then OC RAF Seletar – which helped crystallise my thinking. He had recently formed his helicopter squadrons at Seletar into a helicopter Wing under a highly experienced chopper pilot, and because the implications behind this centralisation concept appealed strongly to me, he offered to send his expert Wg Cdr John Dowling to Ibuan to talk things through.

Dowling soon put his finger on the same problem that had plagued me, and urged me to impose a tighter degree of centralised control in certain areas rather than dispersing our helicopter effort so widely in penny packets. We agreed some flexibility was necessary – and that centralised solution was more likely to be effective in West than in Central, Mid-West or East Brigades where, in any case, the threat in 1965 was less serious and distances inhibited over-centralisation at Labuan.

It may have been coincidence, but in June 1965 Edward Crew, another old friend, succeeded 'Sandy' Johnstone and I found him very receptive to a form of centralised control of the helicopters, particularly in West Brigade. Let me make it abundantly clear: 'Sandy' Johnstone had never been asked by me to change things, let alone had he declined to do so. By the time he left I had only just become convinced that what my instincts were urging me to do was in fact the right thing for the situation we faced. Equally, coincidence or no, it was about that time that the AOC asked me to move to Kuching as Forward Air Commander, and in so doing appeared to give his blessing to the ideas on centralised control I was by now expounding in public. On arrival in Kuching I had first to sell the concept to Brigadier Cheyne and his Battalion commanders. Generously, he called them all to Kuching and let me express my views to them. Opposition by individual battalion commanders to the loss of 'their helicopters', and 'their pilots' was strong, but Bill Cheyne eventually backed me all the way. The penny packets were withdrawn and concentrated at Kuching, the Battalions passed their demands to Brigade who assessed priorities, and the FATOC staffs tasked the helicopters accordingly – and it worked. Air lift went where the Army needs demanded. This change was a turning point in West Brigade – the scene of many vicious little actions bringing a VC and a DFC.

If I have concentrated on the air transport side of affairs that is because logistics and supplies occupied most of our waking hours. Our main enemies were the terrain and the climate. The Indonesian air force had, so we now know, a healthy respect for the RAF – and were not over-active. Even their ground forces dispersed from investing one of our sites after hearing the noisy Javelins fly low overhead. We were left in virtual peace from air attack, though at one stage we did see fit to deploy Bloodhounds at Kuching where a mobile GCI gave a degree of close control over the local area. Our helicopters were not 'gun-ships', but occasionally we fitted SS 11 – an air-ground wire-guided missile – to a Whirlwind with limited effects. The question of the sanctity of the border was a vexed issue, and for most of the time the air forces respected it – but there were occasions when aircraft just had to cross and these were secret 'Claret' operations. Our involvement was usually to rescue injured soldiers who were operating on the other side for a variety of reasons. This in reality involved sending helicopters into unknown – possibly high risk – areas. The RVs could often only be marked by smoke or balloons. To avoid enemy LAA meant flying at treetop height, but this inhibited navigation. How could one maximise the chances of a successful RV but at the same time minimise the risk to the precious helicopters?

One day a possible solution hit me as I was flying in the forward area, when I saw the sunlight glinting on a helicopter's rotor blades. It seemed like an illuminated golden saucer, and as it remained visible to me for twenty miles or more I realised that a 'mother' ship flying high on our side of the border could guide a chopper flying at low level on the other side to a site which was visible from on high but was invisible to the rescue aircraft. Tests proved its value and the AOC readily agreed to put it into operation. I personally controlled the first few 'Claret' rescues and this became Standard Operating Procedure. We had no casualties, and I felt much easier in my mind when requesting 'Claret' once I knew the risk from enemy LAA had been reduced.

That the local population appreciated our efforts was shown in an extract from the Kuching Gazette on 20 November 1996 – the day after one of our helicopters, piloted by a recently arrived pilot, got lost, strayed over the border and had been shot down.

> 'The tragic loss of a Whirlwind helicopter on Wednesday highlights once again the debt which Sarawak owes to the security Forces.
>
> From the first gallant defence of Limbang our own forces showed that they were prepared to make the supreme sacrifice. But we would not have been able to survive at all if it had not been for the willingness of our Commonwealth and Gurkha friends to come to our aid in our time of difficulty.
>
> The men who have been lost were not supermen or swash-buckling soldiers of fortune but ordinary men doing a skilled professional job well and efficiently.
>
> All security work is hard and dangerous. It would not be right to have a favourite service. Nevertheless for those of us who spend their time working on the ground, there is inevitably a feeling of some special awe for those who cheerfully fly the invaluable helicopters over rough and dangerous country, in fair weather and foul. We grieve that yet another has been lost.'

I think perhaps that says it all.

In due course my one-year unaccompanied tour was over. I particularly wanted to spend my last night in Borneo in the jungle, and so I flew to a forward base and stayed with my Ghurka friends who I had got to know well. It was an emotional farewell and many were the tributes they paid to the RAF. Early next day I returned to base and on 26 March – almost a year to the day I first saw Kuching – I left there for Singapore where, after a few courtesy calls, I flew back to UK, again on a Britannia.

The day after I arrived home I had an attack of gout – my first – and was greatly amused by a junior MO at RAF White Waltham saying 'Given your time of life, Sir, and given the good life of continuous wining and dining that someone of your rank undoubtedly leads nowadays, gout is almost inevitable!'

'Continuous wining and dining' indeed! My Ghurka friends would have enjoyed hearing that.

Crash Rescue and Fire Fighting

Alan Alsop

I did my training on aircraft crash rescue and fire fighting at the No. 1 school of fire fighting RAF Sutton-on-Hull, in the winter of 1952/3. The course was crammed in to six weeks, far too short. The vehicles in use at the time were slow and barely suitable for an air force that was now operating Meteors, Vampires, Venoms; and just over the horizon, Swifts, Hunters and Buccaneers – but changes were taking place. The normal set-up at a fire section in the fifties included six or seven different types of fire appliance, and something like twenty-eight to thirty-four NCOs and men.

My first posting from the fire school was to RAF Worksop in February 1953. That was a very happy camp. Being a flying training school with Meteors, Vampires and Venoms, there was no shortage of excitement – like seeing pupils turning from downwind finals on to approach with no gear down, then a bang as a red Very light flare soared up from the tower trailing smoke; engines opened up and round again.

In May 1954 I received my posting notice: the Far East was all I knew but it was exactly what I wanted. I went to Kuala Lumpur, known from then on as KL. The airfield was roughly 'B' shape, with one end having a railway embankment and the other with a range of hills with a convenient gap. There was a wide range of aircraft.

Because Malaya at that time was in a state of emergency we were considered to be 'on active service'. The fight against the communist terrorists was set to run for a year or two yet.

As the independence talks with the Malayan leaders progressed we saw a lot of VIPs coming and going.

One day the RASC had been ferrying some rubbish across the airfield to where it would be burned that evening after flying had ceased. Like us they had been instructed what to do when driving vehicles in an aircraft movement area. They could not go anywhere until they got a green from the tower, or they should stay where they were if they got a red. We on the other hand had radios, so we were in direct contact.

Later that same day we had a visit by none other than HRH The Duke of Edinburgh, with an escort of two DH Hornets. The first Hornet landed and taxied in, then the Hastings with The Duke of Edinburgh followed by the second Hornet.

There was much shaking of hands and flashing of cameras before they all went off with the police escort to KL. About an hour and a half later HRH returned. More hand-shaking and saluting and then he boarded the Hastings. The two Hornets fired up their engines and one moved off immediately to the end of the runway, did a quick run-up then away. Those Griffon engines would soon overheat in that climate.

The Hastings with HRH on board then taxied out, turned in to wind, ran his four engines up, and then he was away.

The second Hornet now taxied out, opened up and started to roll: it was at that particular moment that a three-ton army truck that had been standing patiently on the grass waiting permission to cross the runway decided he had waited long enough. We, the crash crew, had been watching the coming and going, so for one brief moment the shock of what was about to happen froze us.

De Havilland Hornet (AHB)

The Hornet, a very fast and powerful twin engine aircraft from the same stable as the Mosquito, and like the Mosquito made mainly of wood, was about one third of the way down the runway and gaining speed fast; his tail had just lifted. The three ton Bedford truck was just about in third gear and about halfway across the same runway. The pilot, seeing the inevitable, had about one and a half seconds to do something. He did the only thing he could: push the throttles through the gate and pull back on the stick. The two Griffon engines screamed as the props clawed for the air, and the aircraft actually left the ground by a couple of feet, but tail down, nose up, and still travelling horizontally. The base of the engines and nose of the aircraft hit the side of the truck and it rolled over two or three times, coming to rest on its side on the grass alongside the runway, scattering the soldiers along the ground. The aircraft smacked down on to the ground, knocked off its undercart, careered across the grass and dropped astride a large monsoon ditch, smashing both wings off just outboard of the engines. The fuselage just forward of the rudder broke off and folded forward, the top of the rudder digging in to the top of the fuselage and the whole nose of the aircraft was smashed open giving access to the pilot.

We were quick off the mark, but the thought of a fully fuelled-up aircraft – and a wooden one at that – in that climate, and trapped aircrew, was the sort of nightmare that RAF firemen have always had but never mentioned. On sliding to a halt amid a cloud of dust we found the navigator already climbing out of the top hatch, but the pilot was trapped by his legs. Why there was no fire that day I will never know. The monsoon ditch had three or four inches of fuel in it, and I was standing in it trying to free the pilot's legs. We dare not cut any wires for fear of sparks: it only needed one and that would have done for half the crash crew as well as the pilot. It took a frantic seven or eight minutes to free the pilot, pulling and tugging at cables and splintered wood and torn metal with the ever present fear of a sudden inferno. The thought of running from a burning aircraft about to explode to save your own skin, and leaving the pilot, was a nightmare we all pushed to the back of the mind. There would always be self-recrimination: what could I have done? – what should I have done? Fortunately I was spared that, and the pilot was taken off with the navigator to SSQ for a check-up: they got away with it; the driver of the truck didn't.

I knew the army lads vaguely, having seen them in the NAAFI and around camp from time to time, so when one of them came over to me and asked if I had seen his mate I thought it was an odd time to enquire about someone's whereabouts and I looked at him questioningly. Seeing my puzzlement he added, pointing towards the truck now on its side:

'He was driving it'.

Investigating the cab had shown it to be empty.

'How many of you were on the truck?' I asked.

'Four' he replied, 'there are three of us here now, but we have no idea where Jock is'. Then I wondered 'is he under the truck... or...?'

So I went back to where I was standing when trying to disentangle the pilot's legs from the aircraft. Lying down on the sloping edge of the monsoon ditch, I peered under the wing between the starboard engine and fuselage and then I spotted him, there was a slight movement and I heard a low moan. I did not attempt to move him but called over the MO who had now arrived in a second ambulance. He and two medical orderlies gently retrieved him and placed him on a stretcher: he was covered in engine oil and fuel. If that plane had caught fire he would have died without us even knowing he was there. As it was he died before he reached hospital: a terrible waste of life for a silly avoidable mistake.

Over the years I have often wondered what the consequences might have been had he tried to cross the runway when the Hastings was taking off with HRH on board.

Atomic Tests

In November 1944 the British Chiefs of Staff asked their Technical Warfare Committee to advise them on future weapons development.

A sub-committee under Sir Henry Tizard put forward the idea of nuclear deterrence and envisaged jet bombers cruising at 500 miles per hour at 40,000 ft carrying an atomic bomb.

In August 1945 the US dropped atomic bombs on Hiroshima and Nagasaki.

The new Labour government under Clement Attlee set up a committee of senior ministers to decide on atomic policy, and in January 1947 the decision was taken to develop atomic bombs. On the same day the Ministry of Supply invited tenders for suitable new bombers. These aircraft took almost ten years to come into service, the Vulcan in 1956 and the Victor in 1957. The slightly lower performance Valiant entered Bomber Command service in 1955.

By 1952 the bomb itself was ready for testing and Britain's first atomic bomb was exploded underwater in the Monte Bello islands in November 1952.

On 11 October 1956, in Operation 'Buffalo', a live Blue Danube was dropped from a Valiant at Maralinga, South Australia. Sir Geoffrey Dhenin describes flying through the cloud of this bomb.

The way was now open for more comprehensive tests in Operation 'Grapple'. These are described by Air Vice-Marshal Oulton, the Task Force Commander.

Flying Through the Cloud

(Operation 'Hot Box' – the first manned penetration of an atomic cloud)

Air Marshal Sir Geoffrey Dhenin KBE AFC GM QHP

Every advance in the short history of aviation has produced new problems for aircrew. Man is not equipped to survive at the altitudes, the temperatures, the accelerations to which aircraft subject him. He requires physiological aids to make good his shortcomings. Aviation medicine is a science which identifies problems, analyses them, and takes a substantial part in designing and testing equipment with which aircrew can safely exploit the performance of the machines.

With the advent of the atomic weapons, the RAF was confronted by new and unfamiliar problems – the effects of radiation from the long-lived fission products generated when the heavy atoms are split. The mushroom cloud contains large quantities of this material, which sends out alpha, beta and gamma radiation. The Air Staff planning the jet-age Bomber Force operations and concerned with such matters as crew/aircraft ratios, provision of ground handlers and engineering maintenance crews, wanted to know what would happen if an aircraft should fly through an atomic cloud. Would the crew become immediately non-effective from the radiation they received, not only in the cloud but also throughout the journey back to base? What facilities would be required at bases for the decontamination process? To obtain answers to some at least of these questions, it seemed best to get experimental evidence, that is to say to send an aircraft through an active atomic cloud.

The aircraft chosen was the Canberra B2. It was rugged, manoeuvrable and dependable, had a good performance, and was simple to maintain. It also had three ejection seats. Because there were likely to be rapid decisions required in flight, the captain was a Medical Officer pilot with experience of radiation, and the Observer seat was to be filled by the consultant adviser in radiology. The navigator was an experienced ex-Pathfinder.

The English Electric factory at Wharton installed a belly tank in the bomb bay for the journey out to the test site in north Australia, and gave the machine a special high gloss finish to prevent radioactive dust getting fixed on the skin. At the Royal Aircraft Factory at Farnborough, sundry ducts and filters were arranged to obtain several samples from different sectors of the cloud. This was required for the nuclear engineers concerned with the design of operational weapons.

The aircraft took off from England on 13 September 1953. The flight to Woomera, which was to be the base for the Operation, took some twenty-five flying hours. Once there, work was put in hand to prepare the aircraft. Technicians from the Atomic Weapons Research Establishment installed the radiac instruments which would measure the radiation to which the crew would be exposed, so that the pilot would know when it was reasonably safe to enter the cloud, and when it would be prudent to leave. There were total dose recorders to measure the cumulative dose received up to the time the crew left the aircraft, since there would be a continuing effect from material stuck to the skin and from the engines. There were personal dosimeters for each of the three crew seats. The starboard wing-tip fuel tank was replaced by one containing a collector for what would be the largest sample. This was to be released by explosive bolts and dropped after landing at a remote site on the airfield. It would be left there until the contents had decayed to a point where it could be handled with reasonable safety – though with great care!

The expected hazards to the flight were:

1. The flash as the weapon exploded. The aircraft would have to be far enough away and heading from the Tower or the pilot would be blinded, at least temporarily.
2. Impact damage from material (e.g. bits of the tower) sucked up from the ground.
3. Structural damage from turbulence.
4. Flame-out of one or both engines due to ingested debris from the ground.
5. Failure of the airspeed indicator if the pitot head should be choked.
6. Excessive radiation.
7. Inhalation of fission products. The cabin was pressurised by air from the engines which would be engulfing large quantities of contaminated materials. No filters were available to remove this material, so the pressurisation system was disconnected and the cabin sealed.

Decontamination of Canberra (Sir Geoffrey Dhenin)

We flew two rehearsals in liaison with the Test Control Centre. An RAAF Lincoln was provided to act as a radio relay and as a 'bird spotter' in case the Canberra had to make a forced landing in the 'bundu' or the crew had to eject.

We took off finally at dawn on 13 October 1953. We entered the aircraft in a lighted hangar. The cabin was then sealed and the machined towed out. The Lincoln was already in orbit some distance from the weapon site and communications were established between the two aircraft and Test Control. The Canberra arrived over a dried-up salt lake and went into orbit at 30,000 ft awaiting the count down.

There was no delay and no snags. When the explosion came, we were heading away and saw the flash only by the reflection from the canopy. The cloud was beginning to develop and rising. It was not a pretty sight. It appeared to be boiling and it was dark and red, much the same colour as the desert sand. We headed towards it in a descending turn and in a few minutes reached the edge. I placed one wing into the edge so that we could get instrument readings of the radiation and then turned steeply out while the Observer calculated the probable dose during a transit. I then headed for the centre.

It was very dark inside. At first the turbulence was not severe, but as we reached the middle the buffeting increased dramatically so that I thought I might lose control. However we emerged right side up and again calculated the dose rate. We made two more transits, one through the top of the cloud and one through the base, until we decided the job was done and we should quit while we were ahead. We returned to Woomera where an Australian Canberra was waiting to shepherd us in to landing in case the airspeed indicator was giving wrong indications.

After landing we taxied round to the drop zone to dump the wing-tip filter. Here comedy took over. The tank separated cleanly and landed right in the middle of the sandbags. But it bounced and the thirty knot wind got hold of it. It began to roll towards the nose wheel. Pilot's notes for the Canberra do not include instructions for putting the aircraft into reverse! Fortunately the scientist whose specialisation this was, ran forward and managed to divert it, so no damage was done.

We taxied round to the decontamination point and left the aircraft. The sortie ended with an ice cold shower and a change of clothing. Meanwhile a guard was mounted at a safe distance to prevent anyone approaching the danger area.

But the aircraft was indeed very radioactive and we were found to have exceeded the permitted radiation dose. We were therefore forbidden to sample the second Test which had been planned. We spent the next ten days directing the efforts of a decontamination squad which succeeded in removing much of the surface activity on the aircraft, but could do nothing about the engines, generators and inverters. These would have to be removed for examination and treatment in England.

Despite the flight home, much of it through bad weather, the engine bleed valves still had recognisable deposits of red Australian dust which was still active and had to be removed by vapour blasting.

Our Canberra was eventually returned to service but disappeared in the Pacific on the way to sample an American explosion.

Testing the Hydrogen Bomb

Air Vice-Marshal W. E. Oulton CB CBE DSO DFC

At the end of 1955 the Government decided to press on with the testing of a fusion bomb, many times more powerful than the earlier kiloton bombs. The test would have to be an air burst at some remote place, where a mishap such as an accidental surface burst would not cause loss of life or widespread radioactive damage. The only aircraft capable of doing the job was the Valiant, which was really not yet in service, and it was possible that the aircraft carrying the weapon might be destroyed. All this meant building a Class 1 airfield and a major supporting base, with extensive scientific facilities, at some very remote place in just twelve months. There was no suitable organisation in being, so I was ordered to set up a task force and operate it to meet very specific requirements, which, in brief, were to deliver the experimental nuclear device at a given time to a position plus or minus 300 yards and no more in any direction. The explosion was to be minutely recorded by a vast array of instrumentation, both on the ground and in the air. Samples were to be collected from the cloud and delivered to Aldermaston inside twenty-four hours.

Christmas Island in the central Pacific, 1200 miles south of Hawaii, was chosen as the base and operational site and Malden, a small rocky pimple about four miles by three, 400 miles to the south east, was the target area and instrumentation site. The whole lot was about 9000 miles west from the UK, five days by transport aircraft; a month by a fast supply ship. The Navy would supply sea transport and deliver ashore 100,000 tons of material, equipment and supplies. They would also provide an aircraft carrier, the *Warrior*, a control ship, the *Narvik*, and other operational ships. The Army would provide a Sapper regiment plus ancillary units to do all the construction, and the RASC to feed us. Atomic Weapons Research Establishment would field a large scientific team of civilian, RAF and Army personnel to do the assembling, testing, monitoring, fallout prediction and other chores of that kind. The RAF would transport the devices and, with Navy support, carry out the tests and get the results home to AWRE.

In June 1956 we got to Christmas, a pretty barren kind of place with nothing there other than a derelict World War II airstrip, largely overgrown, and periodically a very good District Officer and a gang of some migrant Gilbertese workers to gather the copra. The so-called Port London was nothing more than thirty feet of broken-down jetty with shallow water alongside, but with very deep water in the anchorage outside the lagoon, where all supply ships had to anchor; and 1000 tons a day would have to be unloaded and delivered ashore. The Army built from scratch a tented and hutted town, with all its infrastructure for 4000 people, plus a Class 1 airbase to operate seven different types of aircraft and a major scientific facility.

Meanwhile the RAF formed 160 Wing at Hornchurch with the first batch of key personnel, and drew on Commands for the Valiant squadron to drop the bomb, two Canberra squadrons for cloud sampling and high level wind finding, photography and courier service to the UK; also, later on, 58 Squadron to back them up. Two Shackleton squadrons were available for weather, sea search and photography. The Hastings Transport Service supplied four aircraft for shuttles to Honolulu and Australia, a Dakota flight for communication with Malden and other islands, helicopters, and an Auster flight for insecticide spraying, plus staging posts along the route. Naval aviation provided a vital flight of helicopters and four Avengers in the aircraft carrier. It was all ready and in place in just fifty-one weeks – which I think was a fantastic achievement by all concerned.

Meanwhile, there was the problem of how to deliver the bomb. With an unknown yield – maybe ten megatons – it was feared that the dropping aircraft's skin temperature might rise enough to unstick the Redux-bonded construction. So, step one was to paint the Valiant a special brilliant white to reflect the heat as much as possible. Step two was to put the maximum possible distance between aircraft and explosion, firstly by dropping from the maximum height at which the Valiant was a stable bombing platform – which turned out to be 45,000 feet – and secondly, Farnborough devised a so-called escape manoeuvre – a maximum rate turn at Mach .76, 60° of bank, pulling 1.7 G for 40 seconds, which then set the aircraft tail-on to the blast-over pressure wave with a few more seconds before explosion. This gave about nine miles' separation at the moment of burst. The crew would be protected against flash by window screens to exclude all light: only the bomb aimer would have a view during the run-up, and he would place his screen in position immediately after release.

To meet the existing requirements of the tests, over 2000 modifications had to be incorporated in the production aircraft, and eight Valiants were prepared to this 'Grapple' standard. All the other types of aircraft had to have extensive modifications as well – both to do their job and to fly the very long routes, much of it through American airspace where the requirements were different. As for the prototype thermo-nuclear device itself, that would be contained in the only available bomb case of suitable size, the 'Blue Danube' case. There was a real problem in that there was absolutely no meteorological organisation in the central Pacific, so we had to set up a very extensive weather reporting and forecasting organisation.

Eventually it was all ready, and on 1 February 1957, a few days less than a year after I was given the job, 160 Wing moved into Christmas: Shackletons began weather flights, soon followed by PR7s at high level and radio Sonde from ships and shore, plus reports from many Grapple island outstations. The 'met' team began to build up the necessary background knowledge of the local weather pattern. The first Valiant, piloted by Wing Commander Hubbard, arrived on 12 March, followed quickly by three others, to commence immediately a period of intensive training and co-operation with the scientists and the Naval ships. In due course the Blue Danube cases and all their guts arrived by sea, and the special components of the first device to be tested arrived in two courier Valiants. So, in the early morning of 13 May 1957, the decision was given to start the forty-eight-hour programme leading to a live drop.

It took forty-eight hours' meticulous activity to be ready for the drop which was to be on 15 May. Hubbard and Valiant 818 would do the drop, with 824 (code named 'Grandstand') following below and behind to give another crew the experience. Bear in mind that we might only get one shot, and we wanted to get as much experience as possible. On D minus one, the final assembly of the bombers completed, the two Valiants were flight-tested and 818 taxied over to the weapon assembly area where, behind security screens, the Short Granite device in its Blue Danube case was loaded into the aircraft. At Malden, all equipment other than the installed instrumentation was buried in pits, and all personnel other than the last-minute switching-on party were lifted off to *Warrior* or *Narvik*. At midnight – that was H minus nine hours – weather flights began again, then the danger area search: a line abreast sweep by four Shackletons at thirty-mile spacing right through the area, and then two more to do a more detailed meticulous search around Malden itself; and these last two also later on to do photography and, if necessary, air-sea rescue. At five thirty on the morning of the 15th the decision was confirmed and the Scientific Director and I left by Dakota for Malden where a Navy 'chopper' was waiting to take us and the three remaining ground crew out to *Narvik*, the control ship, some twenty miles to the north. There, in the control room, we checked that all units were in position. We had three search Shackletons, one away to the south, with two more in a thirty-mile radius around Malden. We had a PR7 circling overhead keeping check on the wind and the weather, and the Dakota we had come in.

Halfway to Christmas there was a radio relay Canberra, so that VHF could be carried from Malden to Christmas. There were two New Zealand frigates on station thirty miles away ready to follow gradually behind the cloud, keeping radio sound check because our 'met' flights – PR7s – only went to 54,000 ft and we needed information up to 100,000

Nuclear cloud Grapple X 1957 (John Clubb)

ft, so the radio Sonde was the answer there. *Warrior* was dead on the bomb line. Interestingly enough, the Navy had never been asked before to fix their position within 100 yards and so they kept their position by Decca and transit on two tethered balloons on Malden, which worked very well indeed. On Christmas, all personnel, except those on essential duties, were assembled at designated points ready for rapid evacuation in case of a crash on take off. All the Gilbertese natives were safely embarked in ships at the anchorage, batteries in the Blue Danube case were hooked up, and by 0850 hrs the two Valiants started engines and taxied to the runway, The danger area was reported 'all clear'. There was nothing left to do, so I ordered the Valiants to take off.

Forty seconds later 818 was airborne and climbing away, followed by 824, and then by Canberra 'Sniff Boss' – this was the codename of Air Commodore Wilson, the sampling controller. Forty minutes later, 818 joined the Malden pattern at 40,000 ft. Valiant 824 was one mile astern and 2000 ft below.

Once down the bombing run to check wind and bomb sight settings around the bottom of the race track; and then a second run down, opening the bomb doors, switching on the master switch and checking telemetry both in the aircraft and in Narvik. Round again, and at point Charlie, which was halfway up the plot on the right hand side north bound, the instruction was given to drop on the next run.

As 818 came down the bombing line, tracked by *Warrior*, we watched the displays in the control room. It was a pretty tense few minutes. The telemeter display showed the bomb doors opening, a kink in the display; then the master switch going on, another kink; then the arming switch, another kink. Then came the bomb aimer, Alan Washbrook's voice, on broadcast both on HF and VHF, which was heard throughout the task force both at Christmas and at Malden: 'Target marker inside, skipper. Steer 202. 202, one degree starboard, 203, 203. Steady, steady steady, NOW!'

Grandstand 824 immediately went into the escape manoeuvre to get out of the way, 818 held straight and level for another ten to eleven seconds as the computer counted off the distance for the over-shoot. Bomb aimer's screen into position and the crew of 818 were now in a totally enclosed metal box. At just past ten seconds, the computer triggered the bomb release and the bomb fell away, the fourth step came up on my telemeter screen, four steps now. 'Bomb gone' broadcast Hubbard, and rolled into the escape manoeuvre. Fifty-three seconds to go to explosion. All instrumentation on Malden was now switched on by telemetry from Narvik, rearward-facing cameras in 818 were also switched on, all spectators sat on ships' decks with their backs to the bang, shut eyes and covered them with their hands, crews in aircraft looked away from the ground zero, pilots shut one eye – we didn't know what the dazzle effect was going to be – the AWRE expert by my side in Narvik calling off the seconds to go – thirty seconds, twenty seconds, ten seconds, five seconds, four, three, two, one and the telemeter display went blank.

Then the count up – five seconds, ten, fifteen, 'you may turn and look now' said Bomford, and everyone who could did so to gape at the awesome sight. Some minutes later the three Canberra B6s arrived from Christmas and as soon as 'Sniff Boss' judged the cloud to be cool enough – remember it starts at some millions of degrees – at about H plus thirty-five minutes, Wing Commander Bates, in 'Sniff One', passed through the cloud without trouble at 54,000 ft and then 'Sniff Two' at a lower level, both collecting samples of gas and debris. They returned rapidly to Christmas where crews and aircraft were thoroughly decontaminated, while the cloud samples were extracted, packed into heavy lead pots and loaded into a special carrier in the bomb bay of a waiting PR7. This, accompanied by a standby Canberra, immediately took off for Honolulu and, refuelling and slipping crews at the staging posts, on to the UK, where the samples were delivered in only a few minutes over the twenty-four hours.

So that was the first test. Two more followed exactly the same pattern on 31 May and 19 June; all very successful we thought, and the whole job having been achieved as directed with the greatest economy, the whole task force – both personnel and material – was now absolutely exhausted. So this was the moment to tell us that AWRE hadn't got it quite right and would we please do it all over again as quickly as possible – that is to say, within three months.

There was no question of doing that at Malden in such a short time but with the experience now gained, we reckoned we could do it safely at the south east tip of Christmas, itself about thirty miles from the main camp and base. So there began an immense logistics exercise to replenish and set up the task force for another test – 'Grapple X'.

After some considerable drama, we were able to do the drop following a pattern very similar to that at Malden. The bombing run then came over the north eastern tip of Christmas, over the south east corner, in the same race track pattern which was now pretty well routine.

This time AWRE was satisfied, the cloud samples got back to the UK in good time with no problems, so no further drop was necessary. The task force dispersed, leaving only a care and maintenance party on Christmas.

Dropping the H-Bomb

Group Captain Ken Hubbard OBE DFC AFC

On 1 September 1956 I took up my appointment as CO 49 Squadron, equipped with Valiants, at RAF Wittering. These bombers had been selected to drop Britain's first nuclear weapons, initially at a test site at Maralinga in Australia and later in the south Pacific.

My operational task and general training programme would be laid down by Air Vice-Marshal W. Oulton, the Task Force Commander for the test in the Pacific, code-named Operation 'Grapple '.

After an intensive training programme we set out from Wittering on 2 March 1957 for Christmas Island, via the USA and Honolulu. We arrived on 12 March in perfect conditions and began practising runs for a live drop in May.

To ensure that there would be limited radioactive fallout from the live nuclear weapons being tested, they were set to detonate at 8000 feet above mean sea level when dropped from the Valiant at 45,000 feet. Furthermore, for absolute safety, it was required to aim the weapon so that the point of detonation was one and a half nm (nautical miles) from the land aiming point on the south-east tip of Malden Island, on a pre-set geographical bomb line.

Thus on the island there was a triangular aiming point with fifty feet sides painted in day-glow red. The geographical bombing line on which telemetering equipment was installed ran on a line parallel to the coast. In the bomb-release mechanism in the Valiant, a time delay system had been fitted, which could be adjusted by the bomb aimer. On the run down the bomb line, the exact groundspeed of the dropping aircraft was calculated by the navigator; thus, in order to ensure a one and a half nm delay, the appropriate time equivalent to this distance at the ground speed was set on the time delay clock in seconds. The point in space at which the weapon would reach 8000 feet was therefore known, and it was on this point that all ground cameras and telemetering equipment would be focused. An important factor was that the turn on to the bomb line was made accurately from a set intercept point. Thereafter it was necessary for the bomb aimer, having assessed drift on the bomb line, to pass heading corrections to the captain, so that the ultimate heading of the aircraft would enable a perfect aiming point to be achieved by the bomb aimer with the graticule on his Mk T4 bombsight. At this point, although the bomb aimer would press his release button as graticule coincidence was achieved, with the time delay in seconds fed in to the bombsight the weapon would not actually leave the aircraft until the time delay had elapsed. From that point the escape manoeuvre would be initiated.

The crucial factors for accuracy on this bomb run were that the height of the aircraft must be constant, the indicated airspeed maintained, and a precise heading held. From the point where the bomb aimer pressed his release button, it was all important that during those ten or eleven seconds of time delay, the aircraft heading, height and indicated airspeed did not vary in any way, otherwise large errors were immediately fed into the weapon burst point.

This then was the procedure to be practised on the bombing range at Christmas Island. The first run down the bomb line was called a navigational run, to allow the crew to clarify exact drift, calculate an accurate ground speed and feed in the appropriate time delay to achieve the one and a half nm overshoot, calculated from ground speed.

After this run was complete, a thirty degree bank turn was made to port on to a reciprocal heading on what we termed a race track pattern, the aircraft being required to report position on this leg at five set points to HMS *Narvik*, the control ship, which was recording the flight path by means of telemetering equipment in the aircraft.

At the final reporting point, known as Echo, the aircraft would turn to port in a rate one thirty degree bank turn, thus returning to the intercept point on the bomb line fifty nm from the target.

The second run was termed an 'Initial Run', which was to enable the Scientific Weapon Team on board HMS *Narvik* to test correct functioning of all telemetering recording equipment in the aircraft and the arming circuit in the weapon. This related to a strict weapon equipment drill carried out by the Air Electronic Operator (AEO) at precise points on the bomb run. Only when the weapon team was satisfied that all equipment was operating correctly could the Valiant be authorised to carry out a weapon release run.

At this stage, all personnel on the island were made aware of an elaborate personnel safety plan, devised by the staff of Task Force Headquarters. Although personnel on Christmas Island would be 400 nm from the test site at Malden Island, arrangements had to be carefully planned for the dispersal of all non-essential personnel from the airfield area in the event of Valiant XD818 crashing on take off with the live nuclear weapon in the bomb bay, or in the event of an accident on landing, should the drop be cancelled after take-off and the aircraft required to land back with the weapon aboard.

Should such an accident occur, there would be a possibility of the weapon exploding with the impact of the aircraft, which could result in a significant level of radioactive fall-out. To allow for such a possibility the plan necessitated all personnel being assembled in designated areas and every man being accounted for. Transport would be allocated to each area so that in the event of such an accident resulting in radioactive fall-out, the instructions would be passed by radio to proceed to a certain area of the island away from the fall-out pattern.

The airfield crash crews had been specially trained to handle any accident and were equipped with special protective clothing and equipment to cut the aircraft crew free if possible, and they would be augmented on the day with a qualified scientific weapon adviser.

For the crew of HMS *Warrior*, the light aircraft carrier, and HMS *Narvik*, which would be within twenty nm of the airbursts, special instructions had been issued and here again all non-essential personnel would be below decks.

Those on deck were to be issued with anti-flash clothing, and gloves and hoods to cover the head and arms. With this clothing only a small circle of the face was exposed and this was to be turned away from bomb burst point and covered by the hands. Those assembled on deck would be seated on the side facing away from the bomb with their knees drawn up to their faces. Just prior to the explosion, when the bomb aimer's voice came over the broadcast system, saying 'Bomb gone', the order 'Close eyes' would be given.

With a nuclear weapon explosion at the instant of detonation, a very bright flash of light of some seconds duration would occur, of a brilliance that would damage the retina of the eye and cause blindness if exposed to the direct flash, up to a distance of 20 nm. This brilliance produces intense heat within the resulting fireball, and would cause mild burns to bare skin, which is why everyone was protected by the special anti-flash clothing.

Those personnel in the forward area would remain in the assembled position until the blast wave had passed. This in itself – with a high airburst at a range of twenty nm – would be quite harmless to personnel and could only cause damage to light objects or structures where the surface area was large in comparison with the mass.

I then turned to the rather delicate subject of a possible weapon release malfunction, which would not permit us to land the Valiant back on Christmas Island, due to the risk of a radioactive incident should the weapon release itself and explode during the landing run. This was a most unlikely possibility but had to be faced; therefore it was important that they all understood exactly the drill I should follow. I then explained that rear crew members would bale out from 5000 feet near to HMS *Warrior*, and the co-pilot and myself fly the aircraft away from the area downwind, ejecting at a range of 50 nm, leaving the aircraft with the automatic time and distance set for 200 nm or thirty minutes, for a controlled crash into the sea. We would be pin-pointed by a Shackleton and then picked up by helicopter from HMS *Warrior*.

After the most intense preparations everything was ready, and on 15 May 1957 we lined up on the runway ready for take-off. At precisely 0900 hrs, control gave permission.

During our climb towards the rendezvous point, seventy-five nm from the target indicator, all metal anti-flash screens were securely fitted and the bomb aimer confirmed that only his sliding shutter was open. The flight deck was completely blacked out and we were flying in strict instrument conditions; it always took a few minutes to become completely acclimatised to the fully enclosed situation.

The climb proceeded smoothly, and during it we

maintained contact with joint operations control and HMS *Narvik*. We could hear the other aircraft reporting in on their assigned positions and Valiant XD824 confirmed it was one mile astern, 2000 feet below. As bombing altitude was reached the aircraft was trimmed out and power adjusted. Some fifty minutes after take off we reported that Valiant XD818 was at RV point.

The navigator, Eric Hood, would utilise the Decca navigational equipment to obtain ground speed times and distances on the bomb run, which was of considerable importance to the bomb aimer for the one and a half nm delay factor. The bomb aimer now confirmed that visibility was excellent and the one-eighth cloud cover was not sufficient to obscure the forward view.

At the intercept point of the bomb line, Control from HMS *Narvik* gave clearance for the navigational run, to enable us to assess ground speed and drift and establish a bombing heading to maintain the bomb line. With this complete, we turned on to the race track, reporting the navigational run complete. Control came back stating it was ready for the initial run, during which every switching sequence was followed and all telemetering equipment in the aircraft and on the ground checked by the Scientific Weapon Team. Only if every piece of equipment was operating correctly would final live weapon drop clearance be given by the Task Force Commander and Scientific Director.

Having flown down the race track we turned again on to intercept point, being positioned by the navigator using Decca, and commenced the Initial Run. The only words spoken on this run would be confirmation of ground speed and distance by the navigator, the weapons telemetering switching drill by the AEO seated at the weapons panel, and from the bomb aimer, passing correction of headings to me as we flew down the bomb line.

The bomb aimer quickly aligned the aircraft to the bomb line, allowing for drift, so that our final heading settled at 202° T, with few corrections. I concentrated completely on

Nuclear cloud (John Clubb)

my blind flying instruments, maintaining heading and an accurate 45,000 feet on the sensitive altimeter, with air speed at Mach 0.76 indicated. To achieve this, the major flight instrument is the artificial horizon which provides a presentation of the aircraft's attitude in flight. Flying was smooth and I felt relaxed.

When the bomb aimer called 'Now' it indicated graticule coincidence on his Mk T4 bombsight: I therefore called 'Initial Run complete'; turning on to the racetrack – this was acknowledged. I did not expect any immediate clearance to proceed with the live weapon drop, for on board HMS *Narvik* every aspect of the results of the equipment checks would have to be evaluated. In addition, the Task Force Commander would be checking that all aircraft were in position. Only when both the Scientific Director and Task Force Commander were satisfied that all was operationally ready would we be given clearance to bomb.

By the time we had reached point Charlie on the race track, the major decision had been made. The controller's voice came through to clear Valiant XD818 for a live drop. This I acknowledged, and then the controller's voice could be heard warning all aircraft that the Valiant had been cleared to bomb.

The navigator gave me a turn on to the intercept point, from which we settled on to a heading of 203° T, the bomb aimer continuing with visual corrections. I called 'Valiant now at intercept point, commencing live bombing run'.

The run up to weapon release was steady, and thanks to good initial positioning on the bomb line by the bomb aimer, I only had very minor corrections to make to aircraft heading, which contributed greatly to smooth and accurate instrument flying.

A precise altitude of 45,000 feet was maintained, with airspeed Mach 0.76 and heading steady at 203° T. The time delay and distance had been set, and I knew that from the point of bombsight graticule coincidence with the target indicator there would be eleven seconds delay before the weapon left the aircraft.

The bomb aimer's voice was giving 'Steady, steady' and the AEO called 'Weapon Master Switch ON' which meant that the arming mechanism was now switched to its batteries and therefore fully armed. Next came 'Steady, steady, NOW!', and here I knew that over the next eleven seconds I must maintain my complete instrument flying accuracy: height, airspeed and heading must not vary. The co-pilot's left hand was in position on the throttles, and when the voice of the bomb aimer came over with 'Bomb gone, shutter closed' I heaved a sigh of relief as I called 'Full throttle, rolling into escape manoeuvre'. With sixty degree bank to the left on the artificial horizon, I applied backward pressure on the control column.

I continually broadcast, giving progress thorough the turn to the point of having turned through 135°, our heading now 073° T. I called 'Rolling out, on heading of 073° T, time elapsed 40 sec.'

The commentary was continued, stating that after fifty seconds no flash effect had been experienced in the aircraft. At two and a half minutes after estimated weapon burst, I reported that the aircraft experienced shock waves, but not violent ones. After a further five minutes control gave clearance for all anti-flash screens to be removed and Valiant

XD818 could turn to observe the development of the fire ball and mushroom cloud effect.

We removed all anti-flash screens and I turned the aircraft through ninety degrees to port; as we turned, the sight which met our eyes was truly breathtaking. There, towering above us (remember we were at 45,000 ft), was a huge mushroom shaped cloud, with the stem a cauldron mass of orange as the fireball had developed and the hot gases risen into the atmosphere, progressively fanning out and forming a foaming white canopy which can only be compared with the top of a mushroom. This top must have reached an altitude of approximately 60,000 feet, with ice caps forming. It really was a sight of such majesty and grotesque beauty that it defies adequate description.

The rear crew members could only see from a porthole on either side of the fuselage, so I allowed each in turn to climb up to the flight deck, so that they could see this fantastic development.

Christmas Island

J. A. Clubb

The British 'H Bomb' Test on 8 November 1957 was one of the high points of my life when, at precisely 1747 hrs GMT, the equivalent of several million tons of high explosives went off about twenty-five miles away from where we were orbiting at 43,000 feet in a Canberra PR7 waiting to photograph the development of the nuclear fireball.

For me the story began in 1956 at RAF Wyton when No. 82 Squadron disbanded, and overnight its crews and Canberra PR 7 aircraft became No. 100 Squadron, Reconnaissance Detachment. All crews were volunteers for the Operation and the aircraft were extensively modified with navigation equipment to help us to navigate over long stretches of water. Long range high frequency voice radio equipment (HFRT) was also fitted to allow us to pass position reports and – our main role during the Tests – weather information to the forecasters. We also had a side facing camera for cloud (normal and nuclear) photography.

In those days, flights across the Atlantic by operational aircraft were rare, and few of us on the squadron had had this experience in any aircraft – let alone a jet. Consequently, it was with not a little trepidation that I donned my immersion suit (another first) on 24 April 1957 for the first leg from Wyton to Aldergrove to top up with fuel, then to Goose Bay in Labrador *en route* to Christmas Island. Incidentally, after that first leg, we never wore the immersion suits again. Too uncomfortable and we didn't have much confidence in their life-saving qualities.

Grapple X 8 Nov 1957 (John Clubb)

The radio beacon at Christmas Island was pretty weak, as was VHF radio reception, so navigation had to be accurate.

On first sight from the air I was impressed with the size of the island – around twenty-six miles long and about ten miles across at its widest. A typical tropical lagoon and white beaches galore. From the ground very much as I had expected – except no grass skirts! Hot – very hot – but not too humid. A fair number of coconut palms, but not much else seemed to grow there. The whiteness of the coral was impressive, and we soon learned that it reflected the sunlight most effectively and could cause serious sunburn to the unwary.

The most obvious animal life were the Frigate birds and the rather ugly land crabs. The latter seemed to take great pleasure in crawling into our tents and waving their claws from close range at the person sleeping just above ground on the wire and canvas safari beds. Those more sensitive souls who wanted to put a little distance between themselves and the crabs raised their beds by putting them on beer crates, but, unhappily, this destabilised the beds and the occupant often fell out – meeting the crabs at even closer quarters! People became unreasonably afraid of these creatures – which, after all, did a good cleaning-up job on the Island overnight – and never lost an opportunity of killing them by driving over them.

We slept, worked, ate and drank in tents and, despite frequent showers during the initial operation, I don't recall getting uncomfortably wet. Also, although there were occasions when the runway was unusable after a tropical downpour, it cleared quickly and we were diverted only once for that reason.

The day after we arrived we were off on a five-hour weather sortie which entailed cruise climbing to 45,000 feet and starting a twelve minute wind-finding cycle, reporting the wind, temperature and visual assessment of cloud cover to Joint Operations Centre at Christmas Island. Often we would use the few tiny islands in the area as turning points and, when visibility allowed, we took vertical photographs to prove that we'd managed to be on track at least part of the time. What a difference a satellite position indicator would have made!

Intervals between sorties were filled with the almost daily operational briefings. So frequent and so detailed that, by the time the day of the first drop came each crew had a clear idea of what the others' roles were, what time they would take off, and where they would be at any given time.

On the day of the first drop – 15 May 1957, my 28th birthday – everyone not directly connected with the operation was moved as far as possible from the airfield end of the Island, in case the Valiant carrying the bomb crashed on take off. All 3000 or so people on the Island had to be accounted for before the Valiant could start its take-off run. Once it was safely airborne we resumed our normal activities, but kept ourselves aware of events 400 miles to the south, just in case the 'chain reaction' predicted by some of the tabloid newspapers did materialise and the World did the opposite!

The progress of the operation around Malden Island was relayed to Christmas Island and broadcast over the Island PA system. That the end of the world didn't happen was just one more reason for a fairly good party that night.

The Task Force Commander established a tradition that, at week-ends or stand-downs, he and the senior officials of the three Services and the senior scientists would tour the Messes and join in the festivities. I believe this had a huge effect on morale – even though morale was generally good anyway. The opportunity to talk informally with the very top brass about this very special operation was unique for most of us, and our guests always gave a good account of themselves. I will always remember a conversation a small group of us had with Dr William (later Sir William) Cook – the Scientific Director – one Saturday evening. We were asking him how he could be sure that the explosion just off the end of Christmas Island the following week wouldn't damage the camp, or us who would be on the Island. After a complex scientific explanation of over-pressures, air density, dissipation of forces etc. he said: 'Anyway, I'll be a lot nearer the burst than you people will' – and walked away, hands behind his back, with all his fingers crossed!

After the experience of 'Grapple', the work-up to the one bomb of 'Grapple X' was more routine, although the prospect that the bomb would be dropped just off Christmas Island rather than 400 miles away certainly concentrated the mind. This also had the advantage that we all felt very much more closely involved, and the detailed running commentary over the station tannoy heightened the drama for everyone.

Finally, on 8 November 1957, we were called from our evacuation positions where we were expecting shortly to feel the heat of the flash on our backs, to take over as last-minute substitutes for 'Photo 1' – Sqn Ldr Monaghan and Flt Lt John Pomford – whose oxygen was running out much too quickly as they prepared to take up their orbit for the Valiant bomb run. We were airborne pretty quickly and just managed to climb to our operating height in time for a last minute drift and ground speed check for the Valiant bomb-aimer before taking up our orbit for post-burst photography.

The tension as the Valiant started its live bomb run was like nothing I had felt before. To prevent flash blindness we faced away from ground zero just before the bomb left the Valiant, then closed our eyes and covered them with our hands as the bomb was falling and burst time approached. Despite these precautions and the fact that my small window was fully covered by a curtain, it was impossible not to see the flash of the explosion twenty-five miles away as a brilliant white light (some people saw the bones of their hands as if X-rayed). After twenty or so more seconds the operations controller gave the order that we could open our eyes and look towards the explosion.

I must say that when I saw the red and black fireball rising above its black stalk (before the characteristic white stalk and mushroom cloud developed) my first thought was that someone must have miscalculated and we would soon be heading north to Hawaii as the Island would not be available for landing. My second thought, as I saw the dark concentric rings of blast waves coming up towards us, was that we wouldn't be flying at all after they had hit us. Then the training took over and we had to concentrate on taking the photographs as the fireball developed.

As it happened, the scientists hadn't miscalculated: Christmas Island was undamaged. The blast waves just gave us a gentle nudge and we took some very good photographs. Six days later we were on our way back home.

Thinking of this operation many years later I still feel a sense of pride in being part of such an important event which had been conducted 'on a shoe string' in such a professional manner. From the top to the bottom, everyone involved knew what he was supposed to do, did it and did it successfully.

THE SUEZ CAMPAIGN 1956

Protection of the Suez Canal had been a British responsibility since 1888. In 1954 Egypt and Britain signed an agreement which left protection of the Suez Canal to Britain but provided for the gradual withdrawal of all other British forces from the country.

A rift between Egypt and the West developed in 1955 when Egypt began buying Russian arms. Western financial assistance for the Aswan High Dam was withdrawn. Tension escalated when Nasser responded by nationalising the Suez Canal.

Britain and France felt their national security was threatened. There was at that time no North Sea oil. A very large proportion of supplies from the Middle East passed through the Suez canal. Politicians in both countries urgently examined the possible options.

The Suez Debacle

Air Chief Marshal Sir Denis Barnett GCB CBE DFC

I returned from being AOC 205 Group in Egypt in 1956 to take up my new appointment as Commandant of the RAF Staff College. I had barely settled in when the Suez crisis broke.

The Cabinet instructed the Chiefs of Staff to prepare plans as soon as possible to regain control of the Canal. Problems immediately arose. There was no base near Egypt capable of handling large ships and landing craft. Furthermore Britain's defence plans were focused either on the possibility of a major war with the USSR or, at the other extreme, on countering insurgency in a colony. The possibility of lesser conflicts which need not escalate to nuclear level had not been properly provided for.

From my time as AOC in Egypt I knew the Egyptians had at least 100 MiG fighters and thirty Ilyushin bombers. They also had 100 medium tanks and their Czech rifles were more modern than those of the British Army. An immediate assault with air borne troops was clearly not practical. The Chiefs calculated that some two months would be needed to mount an amphibious landing

Many politicians in France regarded the nationalisation of the Suez Canal as a good excuse for using force against Nasser. The British and French Governments therefore began to develop a joint military plan.

An Anglo/French task force was agreed. The Supreme Commander was General Sir Charles Keightly with a French deputy. The Commander of the Naval forces was Vice Admiral Richmond and Lieutenant General Sir Hugh Stockwell commanded the land forces. In view of my recent experience in Egypt I was appointed Air Task Force Commander with the rank of Air Marshal. Each of us in turn had French deputies.

Early in August it was decided that some reservists should be called up. Three aircraft carriers, a squadron of Canberra bombers and troops were sent to the Mediterranean in a sabre-rattling gesture.

The plan prepared in London in early August assumed that an ultimatum would be presented to Egypt, who would reject it. The Fleet would sail, aircraft would destroy the Egyptian Air Force. On arrival of the Fleet off Alexandria airborne troops would drop to the south of the City whilst Marines landed on the waterfront. Land Forces would then march on Cairo. It was hoped that Nasser would fall before the troops reached the capital and that it would not be necessary to enter the city.

The Chiefs of Staff gloomily described this operation as harder than the Normandy landings. It was code-named 'Musketeer'.

Prime Minister Eden accepted the plan on 10 August and soon after it was agreed by the French.

By 10 September the two Prime Ministers had decided that the point of assault should instead be Port Said and that the Canal Zone should be occupied. The new plan was code-named 'Musketeer Revised'. I had seen some political point to the first plan but it was difficult to detect the political aim of the second.

The initial impetus was being lost, the Cabinet, except for Eden, were unhappy. The United Nations were unsympathetic. The USA was openly hostile. Sterling came under pressure.

We now know that the Israelis and the French had been secretly discussing military plans to their mutual advantage as early as the beginning of August. But it was clear to us as Task Force Commanders that there would be a pause, as there was at that time no obvious reason to cause us to attack.

On 14 October French envoys came secretly to Eden with a devious plan. Israel would be encouraged to attack Egypt. Britain and France would then be justified in intervening to safeguard the Canal. The Foreign Secretary was sent on an equally secret mission to France to agree arrangements with France and Israel. This plan was kept secret from the Foreign Office and even from the individual Task Force Commanders. Only the C-in-C, Charles Keightly was told.

I myself found out entirely by accident. I was with the C in C when the door opened and a paper blew off his desk on the floor between my feet. On picking it up I could not help noticing two headlines: 'Israeli D-Day' and 'Our D-Day'. I told my senior colleagues I thought I was hallucinating.

I later heard, entirely unofficially, that the French had already based bombers at Tel Aviv. These were later used to bomb Egypt's Ilyushin bombers at Luxor.

Things started to go wrong. The Israelis were to attack on 29 October. The British/French ultimatum would then be issued requiring both sides to stop fighting and withdraw to positions at least ten miles from either side of the canal. This ultimatum would expire on 30 October.

Canberra B2s (AHB)

In spite of military warnings to Eden that the Army should be given enough time to sail from Malta, the main Seaborne Task Force could not move before the ultimatum's expiry or the collusion with Israel would become clear. The main burden would thus fall on me – i.e. the destruction of the Egyptian Air Force in the first forty-eight hours followed by attacks on troops and supplies, and the dropping of leaflets to sap the Egyptians' will to fight.

I had at my disposal eighteen squadrons of Canberra and Valiant bombers. The Valiants were at Malta and Tel Aviv; the Canberras divided between Malta and Cyprus. I also had seven fighter squadrons, eight paratroop transport squadrons and three photographic reconnaissance squadrons.

On the afternoon of 29 October Israeli paratroops were dropped thirty miles East of Suez. French planes dropped food and arms to them and French Mystères and Thunderstreaks flew to bases in Israel. All this was done without my official knowledge or approval.

On the evening of 31 October 1956 I launched an attack on Egyptian airfields and supply bases using Canberras of 10 and 12 Squadrons and Valiants of 148 Squadron. They used conventional 500 lb and 1000 lb HE bombs. Around 200 planes were destroyed on the ground. Casualties among the Egyptian personnel were low as the attack concentrated on the runways and parked aircraft.

Unfortunately the Land/Naval Task Force was still six days away. This made the timing of the whole operation very unwieldy.

On 5 November 750 British and French paratroops were dropped on Port Said by Hastings and Valettas from Cyprus. Next day the seaborne invasion force landed at Port Said and began to fight its way south. Attacks on Egyptian airfields continued, with successful results.

On 6 November we were told that Port Said was prepared to capitulate and Generals Stockwell and Beaufre, Admiral Dunford-Slater and myself went in a small boat to receive the surrender. We came under fire and a bullet actually passed between General Stockwell and Admiral Slater. As there was clearly no surrender at that moment, we returned to our ship.

The Americans now exerted immense pressure to stop the fighting and a cease-fire was declared from midnight on 6 November. The political mismanagement and interference continued and some of the Seaborne Forces first heard the announcement by the BBC on the ship's radio.

The Chief of the Air Staff was shocked. He felt most for the forces who had done everything asked of them but were stopped when victory was imminent. He commented that we had had the worst of all worlds. It was unwise to launch an operation if you were not prepared to complete it.

After the cease-fire we occupied Port Said and lived in HMS *Tyne* which had been our base since the beginning of the operation. We remained there until the United Nations Force arrived to take over and did not return to England until the middle of December.

It had been a depressing interlude in my Service

The Bombing of Luxor and Almaza
Captain Mike Butterworth

From the point of view of the average squadron pilot, (in my own case the most junior pilot on the squadron), the run up to the Suez Affair was unremarkable. Life went on pretty much as normal, although there existed a certain frisson of anticipation as a result of Exercise Accumulate – a series of flights, mainly at night and to Luqa, ferrying six 1000 lb bombs for undisclosed purposes. Meanwhile there was the usual round of Bombexes, working towards Combat Rating, continuation training, hockey matches, the Summer Ball etc.

I had joined 15 Squadron, Canberra B2s, at Honington, in June 1956, together with my navigator, Flt Lt Tommy Thomson. He had flown during the War, had the medals to prove it, and was a phlegmatic and totally reliable New Zealander who got me out of all kinds of trouble. At age thirty plus he seemed old enough to be my father. I needed a bomb aimer, and was 'issued' with Fg Off. Cal Wollert who had failed a pilot's course somewhere, but being able to do numbers and joined-up writing, had successfully re-mustered. He too was senior to me; thus I was the most junior member of the most recently formed crew.

None of that seemed to matter too much, and I was thoroughly enjoying life when, on about 20 October, we were suddenly lined up, jabbed with pints of vaccines via blunt needles, issued with a revolver and five (why five?) rounds, and told to stand by. Soon after this, a number of aircraft left for Nicosia. Then all went quiet again, and by the 25th we were convinced that things had gone off the boil.

At four in the morning of the 26th we were none-too-gently woken by assorted batmen and clerks and SPs, who told us to report to Ops for briefing. We were to join our mates in Cyprus. Judged by the speed with which we got away from Honington, Operation 'Alacrity' was well named. None of us had packed properly, which caused some interesting domestic effects later, but as we sat in the sunshine at 35,000 feet, heading south-east over France, I felt well satisfied and even slightly brave. It didn't last. Abeam Paris I noticed the oil pressure on the left (or Port as it was then called) engine was at zero. I hoped it might recover, but it stayed resolutely down. One of the few points made at the very curtailed departure briefing was the pointlessness of taking an aircraft into what was excitingly called the 'theatre of operations' if it had to be mended as soon as it got there; so after a quick word with Tommy and Cal, and an even quicker shut-down in case it wasn't just electrical zero, we slipped out of the stream under strict radio silence, and slunk back to Honington.

We were not welcome. The Squadron Leader in charge of the dispatch had just finished congratulating his team on a one hundred per cent success when we fluttered into the circuit and taxied in on one engine. He pointed us at the

Left: Tommy Thompson, Right: Mike Butterworth (Mike Butterworth)

situation. Tommy Thomson hoiked me inboard just in time to avoid anything worse than a nasty graze just where my bone-dome rubbed.

But I was young in those days, and next morning, recovered in all but pride, we pressed on to Nicosia where we encountered a mixture of derision and admiration as the only crew to have arrived twenty-four hours late, but to have achieved a night out *en-route*. For a while I was known as 'Day-late Dipso'.

On the face of it, things domestic in Nicosia should have been a total shambles. Half of the offensive might of the RAF (or Bomber Command as it was then called), had descended on a station whose chief role was as part of the Transport Command route to the Far East. The mess was over-flowing, and catering and cultural facilities were grossly over-stretched. We were, of course, confined to camp, so there was no escape. My own crew plus one other slept in the relative luxury of the squash court. At least it had a door, four walls and a nice floor. Others slept in aluminium huts and a collection of tents which wasn't much fun with temperatures in the nineties. And yet I remember the food as amongst the best I came across in the service, even though dinner could be in three sittings, going on till after 10 p.m., and the bar with its hastily arranged annexes never ran dry. (It was closed for a short time after some extrovert reduced his issue of revolver cartridges from five to four during an altercation with an understandably aggrieved resident staff officer, which left a bullet hole in the ceiling. The situation was resolved with masterly common sense by confiscating all the revolvers and rounds and reopening the bar.

On 29 October an exercise was mounted to try out the 'launch and recovery' of the bomber stream. Aircraft would take off, bomb, and return to overhead at one minute intervals, but could only let-down and land at three minute intervals; so on returning to overhead, depending on position in the stream, a number of minutes had to be 'wasted'. The twentieth aircraft would have some 40 minutes to waste. A further drawback was that the Canberra was designed as a high-altitude, high-speed bomber, using rapid fixing (but ground based) nav/bombing systems, Gee and Gee H – i.e. as installed in NW Europe – so that we could bomb the advancing Russians. Here everything would have to be done visually without the benefits of modern science. Apocryphally, during one of the subsequent raids, a navigator called up the airfield he would soon be bombing, asked for a QDM (course to fly to the airfield) – and got one!

At the very end of October, things took a more serious

reserve aircraft, said our bombs would be transferred to it, and we were to be airborne within the hour. Those who flew Canberras will recall that one of its few weak points was that it sat so close to the ground that it had to be jacked up by the main gear (or undercarriage as it was then known), before a bomb trolley could be positioned under the bomb bay. The crew knew that, and the armourers certainly knew that. With the best will in the world, it would be two hours before we could leave. I was unwise enough to say so, perhaps rather flippantly, to the Squadron Leader who, strangely, didn't seem to know that. He was in the middle of a quite masterly tirade (or 'bollocking', as it was then known), when our laid-back Group Captain arrived, asked what appeared to be the trouble, thought for about five seconds and told me to go as soon as was reasonably possible to night-stop Luqa, and to go on to rejoin the squadron the next day. I have had a soft spot for Group Captains ever since, and I took great care to avoid the overruled Squadron Leader for the rest of my service career .

The flight to Luqa was uneventful; the night-stop was not without incident. Inevitably, we went into Valetta, where we fell amongst friends in the shape of a Canberra crew going in the opposite direction. They recommended a bar which they claimed sold a strain of 'Hop Leaf' which tasted quite like beer. Whether it did or not, I fail to remember, but I recall sitting in one of those ubiquitous Maltese buses as we returned to the Luqa mess with my head out of the window, trying to synchronise my brain to my stomach, but otherwise incapable of thought or movement. The bus went through a tight-fitting arch in Floriana (called, I believe, the *Porte des Bombes*), and I was aware of a vertical edge of masonry sliding along the side of the bus with two inches clearance, but I was unable to correct, or even comment on the turn. A general briefing was held to acquaint us with possible targets, which seemed to include every ex-RAF airfield in Egypt. Opposition was forecast as unlikely, but mention was made of 100-odd MiG fighters which we could probably out-climb, and radar-predicted flak up to 60,000 feet which we certainly could not out-climb. We became more attentive, particularly when one of our more senior members asked if we had all made wills, and we became unusually interested in the 'corkscrew' avoiding tactics that we had heard about from WW II.

A subsidiary briefing covered rendezvous points in the desert in the event of forced landing/ejection; we were given countless magnetic buttons and buckles to sew on to our flying kit, from which we could construct marching compasses, hacksaw blades in bars of chocolate, silk handkerchiefs printed with a map of Egypt, water purification tablets and the like. Unbelievably, each aircrew received six gold sovereigns to bribe any natives we might fall among, and even more sobering, goolie-chits to convince said natives that we should be returned intact to the nearest British representative.

Nobody was yet thinking in terms of World War Three, but armed conflict seemed probable, and sure enough, on 30 October the first raids took place on airfields in the Canal Zone. Consequently the Egyptians moved their Il 28 bombers south to Luxor, and on 1 November we set off, in the dark, to bomb that airfield from 35,000 feet using visual bomb sights. I was again late on parade due to some electrical fault in the circuit which fired the cartridge which started the engine, but we pressed on, fifteen minutes late, and dropped our bombs just as the target markers went out. No opposition of any sort was experienced, but it did occur to me as we turned for home that if any brave lad had managed to claw his way up to us in his Mig, we were a bit vulnerable, all by ourselves at the back of the stream. We felt far from confident about our accuracy, and back at Nicosia, other crews expressed the same doubts. Sure enough, next night we did the same thing again, this time descending to 10,000 feet to bomb in the hope of reducing the average error. We felt better about the bombing, but the climb back to 35,000 feet, plus the time spent in the recovery 'trombone' left some of us very short of fuel. We landed with ninety gallons (as fuel was then quantified), well below the recommended minimum of 300 gallons (Pilots Notes, Canberra B2, AP 4326B, 3rd edition, June 1956).

The results of the second attempt were either acceptable, or so bad that the idea of visual night bombing was dropped. (We were never told.) Either way the next op. was in daylight on Almaza. The possibility of fighters had been discounted, but when I drew Tommy's attention to some tiny black cumulus clouds in the distance, he came forward, identified them as flak and promptly returned to the safety of his ejection seat. That was as bad as it got for us, and we made our run, as I remember at 8000 feet, without incident. The bomb camera shots, which we were allowed to see after landing, showed that two of the six fell harmlessly into scrub, two more destroyed half of a large workshop, and another cratered some hard standing. The one I still wonder about was the delayed-action bomb, number three or four in the stick. It showed up as a dimple in the sand between two buildings, so we lost interest in it, until a reconnaissance flight some twelve hours later showed the dimple obscured by a large tent.

The Almaza raid was the end of my input to Operation Musketeer. We hung about, still confined to camp, and morale, while by no means plummeting, certainly drooped as the adverse world reaction to the whole 'Suez Affair' emerged. The food seemed to worsen, and even the local Brandy Sours in the bar (at five pence a go) lost their edge.

On the night of 6 or 7 November an odd thing happened. At about 1 a.m. the air-raid siren sounded – a noise I hadn't heard since childhood days in the Blitz. Standing outside the Squash Court we heard a jet high to the north. A pair of Meteors, followed by a pair of Hunters, were scrambled but apparently got nowhere near it. In the morning, speculation was rife, but discouraged: the inference being that it was a stray reconnaissance flight – but where from? we asked.

Purely by coincidence, we were told to report for briefing for return to the UK at once. Which we did with some relief, sensing that we had outlived our usefulness in the Eastern Med. for the time being.

As there were more pilots than Canberras, and as I was Junior Joe, but also I suspect to avoid any chance of my repeating the delays of the outbound flight, I was put in charge of a party of ground crew and we positioned back in a Shackleton, slowly and uncomfortably.

Our ears had barely stopped ringing when there arose the possibility of involvement with the Hungarian uprising. This would have been a totally different kettle of fish to swanning around over the Nile Delta, and things became quite tense for a while, but sadly, or possibly not in view of the potential for serious aggro, the uprising failed and life returned to what passed as normal.

So ended my only contact with 'Active Service'. Three raids was barely enough to get a taste for things, but it was enough for us to appreciate the grinding strain of repetitive operations suffered by bomber crews in World War Two.

From the strategic point of view, Operation Musketeer was indeed a debacle (*see Air Chief Marshal Barnett's article. Ed.*) and at the end of the piece, with all the double-dealing and political interference, must have been a depressing few months for senior management, despite its purely military successes. For a twenty-one-year old Flying Officer it was an interesting fortnight, and I looked forward to further equally safe and relatively comfortable episodes, say every three months, never over Christmas, and always somewhere warm. It was not to be. Duncan Sandys, as Minister of Defence, or something equally potent, decided that the day of the manned bomber was over (tell it to today's Tornado crews), and within a year, 15 Squadron, together with many others, was disbanded.

I soldiered on for a while as Ops Officer at Binbrook, but I hadn't joined to be a soldier, so regretfully, but amicably, the Royal Air Force and I parted company, so that I could continue a flying career with BEA and subsequently British Airways for the next thirty-three years. But that's another story, equally personal, but of no relevance to the history of the Service.

KUWAIT 1961

In 1961 Iraq renewed a long standing claim to Kuwait and began to move troops towards the Kuwaiti border.

Britain was committed to defend Kuwait and responded promptly to a call for assistance.

Contingency planning had allowed four days for positioning transport aircraft to airlift troops from Cyprus and Kenya. It also provided for interdiction, reconnaissance and bombing forces to be moved into place.

However, serious complications arose. The required notice was not given and Turkey and Sudan refused to allow over-flights.

The whole transport plan was in disarray and Squadron Leader Mike Murden describes the desperate efforts needed to retrieve the position.

A Problem of Transport

Squadron Leader M. Murden

In 1960, a year before the Kuwait Emergency, No. 8 Squadron in Aden and 208 in Nairobi were re-equipped with Hunters. The Mark 9 Fighter Ground Attack aircraft carried two 230-gallon long-range fuel tanks on the inside pylons giving the type the extended range needed for their role in the Middle East.

It was just as well the change came that year, because there were many serious problems operating the new type in Aden with its dreadful climate and frequent sandstorms. Aircraft suffered unprecedented numbers of technical failures caused by the heat and corrosive sand which penetrated everywhere. To make matters worse most of the servicing had to be undertaken in the open.

Engines, hydraulics and electrical systems all failed far more frequently than in UK. Consequently there was a serious shortage of spares and manpower was inadequate. Even more worrying, from an operational point of view, utilisation was well below target so that pilots struggled to remain current.

In what was quite an achievement, Command staffs managed to bring about many improvements in the year that followed. By February 1961, new hangars had been constructed, spares were more plentiful, technical manpower had been increased and pilots were getting more of the flying needed to remain proficient.

At the same time, behind the scenes, contingency plans were being drawn up for 'Vantage'. One of the larger exercises in the spring of 1961, this involved all three Services. Carrier-based aircraft of the Royal Navy relieved 8 Squadron at Khormaksar so that we could move to Sharjah and practice for 'an emergency somewhere in the Persian Gulf'. Army involvement in the exercise included The Trucial Oman Scouts and Coldstreams at Burami Oasis.

So whilst there was still plenty of room for improvement, we were better prepared than we had been a year earlier when, on 30 June 1961, 8 and 208 Squadrons were ordered to move immediately to Bahrain, together with 30 and 84 Squadron Beverleys carrying ground crews and spares. For 8 Squadron that meant a flight of 1300 miles from Khormaksar. But 208 Squadron had to fly from Nairobi and cover almost twice the distance. On arrival at Khormaksar 208 had a sandwich lunch, still wearing flying suits, before

Hawker Hunter Kuwait 1961 (AHB)

the two squadrons departed, 'cutting the corner' over Oman, to reach their destination early that evening.

Operation Vantage included the possible need for the Hunters to fly from Bahrain to the Iraq/Kuwait border and beyond, jettisoning tanks on the return leg. So on arrival we refuelled immediately, and I sent airmen to collect more tanks and jettison-cartridges from the contingency Stockpile. In the meantime we began painting white bands around the rear fuselages of our aircraft to distinguish RAF Hunters from those belonging to two similar squadrons operated by the Iraqi Air Force alongside their MiG-15Bs.

There were 500 long-range tanks in the Stockpile, so the planners must have expected a lengthy campaign. To my dismay the men returned to tell me that there were no explosive bolts in store. A few urgent signals confirmed that none could be located anywhere in the theatre. So the plan to 'jettison' was out of the question. A decision was made to remove the long-range tanks fitted to every aircraft and replace them with the smaller 100-gallon version.

By this stage all bowsers were full, so they could not be used to empty the contents. We had no option other than to drop every tank onto the sand, roll it onto its side, and empty the contents – being careful not to get fuel on the tyres. All the empty tanks were contaminated with sand and had to be scrapped.

Most of that night was spent reconfiguring tanks, so there was no time to finish painting the fuselages. We had very little sleep before returning to the aircraft.

Early the next morning, we were ordered to proceed to Kuwait. Together with the ground crew, I was in the first Beverley to take off, soon to be followed by the Hunters led by the CO, Squadron Leader 'Laurie' Jones. Visibility was appalling and everyone on board the Beverley was wondering about the whereabouts of the Iraqi aircraft. The crew eventually located Kuwait Civil Airport and landed, but as we taxied in we were ordered to take off immediately and continue to the partly-completed Kuwait New airport. Whilst in the air we heard that the Hunters were very short of fuel, but had located the airport and should land just ahead of us.

Coming to a standstill we saw the first three Hunters on the ground with several Royal Navy helicopters of 42 Commando overhead. Within minutes of our arrival a Kuwait Government official came to me offering over 100 cars, trucks and cranes for unrestricted use by the British forces. Petrol would be issued free to any driver wearing a British uniform.

Squadron pilots quickly volunteered to drive trucks and help unload the continuous stream of Beverleys arriving and departing. The number of aircraft on the airfield increased rapidly throughout the day, as did the helicopter movements. During the morning several Centurion tanks came out of hiding and moved to the perimeter. But we soon lost sight of them because the visibility remained at about 400 yards for most of the next few days. Consequently almost every take off and landing was a very hazardous business.

There was no let-up throughout that day even though mid-day temperatures reached 125°F. As Shackletons and Twin Pioneers joined the two fighter squadrons, we noticed that Hunters were sinking into the perimeter track because the newly-laid tarmac was melting. That added to the severe congestion which was already making movement control a headache. By the end of the first day we found places to sleep on the concrete floors of the terminal building. But it was very hot inside and some pilots found it cooler to sleep on the aircraft wings.

On the second morning we began work very early while it was still cool – the only time to do an engine change. Field kitchens had been set up and were most welcome, as was the arrival of a truckload of Pepsi Cola commandeered by Flying Officer John Volkers of 8 Squadron. There were even more arrivals that day with aircraft from Cyprus, UK and the Far East, including commandeered Argonauts and Comets.

For operational reasons Britannias mostly arrived and left by night, often staying on the runway because of congestion. Engines were kept running because there was no external power. On the third night, a tired airman marshalling a taxiing aircraft, and probably blinded by blowing sand, walked into a propeller and was killed. We were all deeply upset by the accident.

It was a frustrating time for Hunter pilots because of the dreadful visibility. After the initial rush to reach Kuwait it was at times near-impossible to carry out reconnaissance. On the third morning Flying Officer 'Flick' Hennesey of 208 was killed as he flew in the forward area. While trying to maintain visual contact with the ground he probably became disorientated and spun in. Later that same day we heard that a bomb had exploded in a Beverley at Bahrein. So we had to introduce our weary airmen to even more security measures.

That first week I was the senior engineer at the airport, so I continued to be involved in most technical activities on the base. Each morning the Oil Company insisted on signatures for enormous quantities of aviation fuel. And during the week more than a hundred technical tradesmen from UK, and some from Singapore, reported for duty. They had no tools and were not acclimatised, so it was impossible to use them all on aircraft maintenance. Many had to be employed unloading stores and armaments.

Senior officers visited each day from Bahrein, and I usually attended daily meetings with SASO, OC Ops and sometimes the AOC, who always arrived in his distinctive white Canberra. Expatriates at the Oil Company, grateful for our intervention, offered over-night use of air-conditioned accommodation to some squadron pilots.

On the fourth day there was an early morning scramble by two Hunters after a reported intrusion by an unidentified aircraft. The pilots did not encounter any Iraqi aircraft but the incident proved a timely reminder of the need to remain vigilant. The Iraqi Air Force must have faced similar difficulties with visibility in the Kuwait area. By the time the weather cleared the build-up of British Forces was nearing completion. Initially limited radar coverage of up to 80 miles was provided by HMS *Bulwark* as she stood close to shore during daylight hours. But the carrier had to move off-shore each night as a precaution against attack.

After the first few days everyone began to relax a little and a few of us visited HMS *Bulwark* by then in Kuwait Harbour. On 9 July HMS *Victorious* and her escorts arrived from the Far East and provided much improved radar cover.

There were now over 5000 men and a considerable number of aircraft there.

By mid July it seemed that Iraq had abandoned its plan to invade Kuwait.

Whilst there was a need to remain alert, settled routines were being established. Despite the order to 'Minimise', signals traffic was overloaded most of the time and great ingenuity was needed to get AOG (Aircraft on ground) parts for aircraft. The health of pilots and tradesmen suffered for each extra day spent in that dreadful climate.

Numbers 8 and 208 Squadrons began to rotate, in turn, between Kuwait and Bahrein from mid-July. Even though facilities at Bahrain were far from ideal, pilots could resume training and it was possible for everyone to have the occasional day off work. But after the Kuwait Emergency life had changed for everyone involved, as had the continuing British presence in the Middle East.

CYPRUS

21 RAF Police District – Cyprus 1963–1966

Group Captain P. L. M. Hennessey MBE

The winter of 1962/63 was bleak. I was Flight Lieutenant (Security) at HO Provost and Security Services (UK), based at that time in the dismal Government Buildings, Bromyard Avenue, Acton. Apart from our busy routine work, we were much concerned with the activities of the Campaign for Nuclear Disarmament who were intent on disrupting the work of the 'V' Bomber Stations by mounting violent demonstrations almost every week-end. It came, then, as a welcome surprise when I was informed that I was posted to command a joint RMP/RAF Police detachment at Limassol, on the sun-drenched island of Cyprus.

I arrived there in the June of 1963. The Detachment was stationed in a few old stone-built huts at the south end of a disused Army barracks, Polemidhia Camp, about three miles from the Town Centre. Limassol was the dormitory town where lived most of the Service families of the personnel from the HQ of the Sovereign Base Area at Episkopi, the resident Infantry Battalion (1st York and Lancaster Regiment), and RAF Akrotiri, all about seventeen miles away.

The town itself was quite pleasant in a somewhat shabby way. There were shops, cafes, and some beautiful beaches. There was also quite a thriving night life centred on the several night clubs surrounding Heros' Square. It was here that the single soldiers and airmen would gather each night in search of music, girls and excitement, and where the married families would go for entertainment.

My unit, about 40 strong, consisted of three sections:

a. Provost – uniformed police, for discipline, traffic control and convoy escorts.
b. Special Investigations – for the prevention and detection of crime.
c. Counter Intelligence – for all matters concerning Security.

There was plenty going on to keep all three sections fully occupied.

The Provost section mounted twenty-four-hour patrols of the town, where their work varied between routine 'showing the flag' to some quite energetic keeping of the peace when it came to sorting out the occasional drunken brawl.

The Special Investigation Section dealt with everything from minor pilfering from barrack rooms, to suppressing the blatant black market in duty-free cigarettes and liquor from NAAFI sources, up to serious assault and murder.

The Counter Intelligence Section was kept specially busy, because Cyprus, at that time, was a hotbed of spies of all complexions. There was much highly classified material on the Island and it was very necessary to keep well informed about individuals, political trends and events.

And so the long hot summer of 1963 passed very pleasantly The men on the unit were kept busy and felt themselves fulfilled. Liaison with the Cyprus Police was good and there was plenty to occupy one's time when off duty. However, all was not serene below the surface. For some time we had been receiving scraps of information to indicate that there was trouble to come. Since the end of the EOKA guerrilla warfare in 1959/60, the peace on the island had been very fragile. Although each town and village had its Greek quarter and its Turkish quarter, and Greek and Turk had lived amicably together, there was a move amongst the extremist Greeks to eliminate the Turks and to make the Island wholly Greek. The unrest, this time, was not aimed at the British but at the Turkish Cypriots. Nevertheless, living so closely bound to the local communities there was a definite risk that the British families would be caught up in any forth-coming inter-communal strife. Counter Intelligence worked overtime, and contingency plans were made.

Very early one morning in November we were awoken to the sounds of furious gunfire coming from the town. Fortunately, we had prior knowledge of what was to happen, so our patrols had been busy clearing all the British from the town the night before.

The Greeks had launched a truly murderous attack on the Turkish Quarter, and the scenes that morning in Limassol were terrible to behold. It was the same story in every town on the Island. Our task was to organise and escort convoys to evacuate all the Service families to the safety of the Sovereign Base Area, and thereafter we remained in the town to protect property and to prevent looting. The Cyprus Police were not much help, because it was they who had organised the uprising and had led the attack on the Turks.

After a few days the situation calmed down to an extent, but isolated pockets of fighting went on. At one stage all the families were put on stand-by for evacuation to UK. However, the Cypriot Authorities soon found that with the British families all gone from their towns, their economy became crippled. There were no customers in the shops and cafes and business came to a standstill.

Negotiations produced an agreement whereby families were allowed to return to their homes under promise of Cyprus Police protection, but the atmosphere was tense, with sporadic fighting flaring up and murder occurred daily as old scores were settled.

Eventually, a Military delegation visited the Island under the leadership of General Sir Michael Carver. As a result, a United Nations Force was sent to restore order and to keep the peace. Meanwhile, we found that we were the only organisation which was trusted by both sides. Much of my time was spent in negotiating between Mr Chris Benjamin, the leader of the local Greeks, and Ramadan Jemil, the leader of the Turks. We had to impose 'Out of Bounds' limitations and curfews, which my policemen had to enforce.

It was very important to impress on our people that they must not take sides, but inevitably there was a general feeling of sympathy for the Turks. A restricted amount of travel was permitted throughout the Island, but one had to pass through numerous Greek Police road blocks. At one such road block, an airman and his family were stopped in the queue. An observant Police Sergeant saw the airman's wife purposely pinch her young daughter to make her cry, thinking that thus they would quickly be passed through. The Sergeant decided to search the car, and there he found a quantity of small arms and ammunition, together with documents proving that the airman was trying to smuggle the weapons to the Turks in Nicosia. This caused a very serious diplomatic incident and made life much more difficult for the British for some time thereafter.

And so life continued, always on the edge of a situation which could flare up into serious gun battles at any time. The presence of the United Nations Force managed to keep the lid on events most of the time, but by 1965 mainland Turkey had become so exasperated by the constant harassment of the Turkish Cypriots that they launched air strikes against the North of the Island. This so shocked the Greek Cypriot government that things did settle down for a bit thereafter, but the inherent Greek/Turkish problem remained unresolved. The United Nations Force is still in Cyprus today.

In July 1966 my tour of duty came to an end, and I was posted home to the RAF Record and Pay Office at Gloucester – a massive paper empire, and as far removed from the life of constant excitement and danger which I had been living for the past three years as it is possible to be.

THE COLD WAR

The Cold War – a Personal Perspective

Air Chief Marshal Sir Michael Knight KCB AFC

'Let us not be deceived: we are today in the middle of a cold war.'

Thus, Mr Bernard Baruch, distinguished financier, adviser to successive Presidents of the United States and archetypal 'elder statesman', stated in a speech before the South Carolina Legislature on 16 April 1947.

I was a mere fourteen years old at the time; and I have to admit that the words of Mr Baruch – indeed, his very existence – were to elude me for some time thereafter. But, in a very real sense, he had spoken wisely. Others have written at inordinate length of the origins of that 'Cold War'. Coming, as it did, hard on the heels of a fearfully destructive (and extremely 'hot') global conflict – the second in a mere thirty-year span of world history – there were many who saw in the developing West-East confrontation the seeds of a third. But this time, the fast-growing arsenals of nuclear weaponry would put at serious risk the very survival of mankind.

Would it ever have come to that? Who knows – for sure? At times, it looked perilously close.

The blockade of Berlin in 1948/49, the events leading up to the erection of that city's infamous Wall, and the Cuban missile crisis, were but three of the more obvious flashpoints in the forty-three-year history of the Cold War. For, throughout that period of nervous international tension, the politicians and the military on both sides of the so-called 'Iron Curtain' remained armed, prepared and exercised to think – and, indeed, act out – the unthinkable. Such was the very stuff of the strategy of deterrence. Each side had to believe – or, at the very least, to consider it an unsustainable risk to deny – that the guys in the other corner had the capability, the training and, if it came to it, the political will to carry through a nuclear exchange, at whatever cost. Not a very attractive policy, in all conscience: but one which was to balance aggression and fear, ideology and pragmatism, bluff and counter-bluff in a generally effective fashion; and, certainly compared to the alternative, producing an acceptable end-result.

And how did all this play at 'the sharp end'? How greatly did the heavy burdens of commitment and responsibility weigh upon those whose task it might be, at little or no notice, to carry through the most destructive actions ever conceived by man? I cannot speak for all; indeed, only for myself – engaged as I was, for more than thirty years, as a pilot, commander, staff officer and planner in the deadly game of deterrence. Certainly I had my doubts about the morality of it all, but that was strictly on the personal level. Those doubts were, in large measure, dispelled by my perception of 'the bigger picture'. Simplistic it may seem to some: something of a cop-out to others. But I did come to a firm belief that what we were all doing was being done to prevent a greater evil. If it was indeed a war, it was one that simply had to be won.

The winning of it undoubtedly called for the most rigorous standards of training, expertise and readiness, day in and day out; and the sum of all that was commitment of the highest order. Not all those so tasked with what was, in truth, a less than enviable life-style might have taken that element of commitment a stage further – to absolute conviction. But membership of the nuclear strike force was certainly no place for the faint-hearted. There had to be a belief that deterrence, however uncomfortable as a national policy, did indeed work to maintain an uneasy global peace. And there are one or two more recent examples where a failure of deterrence has led directly to conflict; and where – albeit at the conventional level of warfare – hundreds of thousands of mainly innocent folk have been dispossessed: 'ethnically cleansed', maimed and killed.

My own first involvement with the British development of a nuclear weapons capability was peripheral in the extreme. For some eighteen months after having converted a National Service Commission into something rather more permanent, I enjoyed a short tour in the right-hand seat of the Comet 2, with which No. 216 Squadron was then equipped at RAF Lyneham. One of the Squadron's regular commitments was in support of the atomic weapons trials being staged in 1956 and '57 at the Maralinga range in South Australia; and although we were never observers of a test detonation, the support task did serve to impart a certain sense of immediacy to one's hitherto merely academic interest in the technology.

Some four years later, as a flight commander on my second Canberra squadron (No. 249 at Akrotiri), a nuclear strike role was added to our existing tasks of target-marking and conventional bombing. We were thus to make the acquaintance of the low-altitude bombing system (LABS), which seemed to many of us as excellent sport in practice, if unlikely to offer a survivable option 'for real'. However, it was clearly the profile which gave its gallant exponents the best chance of actually releasing a weapon in a threat-rich air defence environment – whatever subsequent disasters were to befall aircraft and crew. It was considered extremely poor form to talk of 'one-way tickets'; but that was generally held to be the probability, were those countless hours of target-study, meticulous flight-planning, last-minute loadings and LABS practice sorties ever to be put to the test. And, for me, there was to be more of the same (in fact, another tour of the same) when my time on 249 was followed by command of its sister squadron, No. 32, again at Akrotiri.

In fact, during those early years of the 1960s, four of the five Canberra squadrons then based at that exceptionally action-packed Station had nuclear interdiction and strike commitments in addition to their various other roles. The Wing was committed to the support of the then reasonably active Central Treaty Organisation (CENTO), in which context it regularly exercised with the only three other

US Mk 7 Nuclear bomb (Air Cdr Phil Wilkinson)

nations of the alliance prepared to commit forces on a regular basis. However, such exercises were strictly confined to tactical flying, and the occasional release of practice weapons in the conventional context. In truth, there was any manner of things to keep us all fully occupied, above and beyond the professional camaraderie and healthy rivalry of aircrew the world over.

In any case, our commitment to CENTO was but a part of the whole. Only when we reverted to a purely national posture did we again engage in the more serious business of our deterrent role. And serious it certainly was. To set beside the occasional excitement of a night LABS sortie or a 'survival scramble', there were those endless hours of procedural training and target study. I used to reckon that I knew certain areas of a far-off land better than I knew my own home town. Thankfully, I did not have to put that hard-earned knowledge to the test.

A mercifully brief stop-over in the UK for Staff College, and an eighteen-month tour in the Ministry of Aviation, saw me overseas again – this time to Singapore as only the third (and last) OC Far East Strike Wing. Canberras (again) in strike/attack and PR roles, but with added Hunters and, later, Javelins, Lightnings, Single-Engined Pioneers, RAF Regiment and the always busy airfield at Tengah. For CENTO, read SEATO – the soon-to-become moribund South-East Asia Treaty Organisation. I seemed to be making a habit of joining alliances which were then to fold. And that might have been bad news for my next assignment – to NATO.

As luck would have it, the North Atlantic Treaty Organisation was able to survive my presence; and I was there to learn a great deal about the politico-military aspects of international diplomacy backed, as it then was, by the now-familiar edifice of deterrence. Working directly, firstly to the AOC-in-C of the recently formed Strike Command, and then to the Chairman of NATO's Military Committee in Brussels, I was given a unique insight into the workings of governments and their military commanders in the context of a remarkably successful alliance.

This was another of those periods of heightened West-East confrontation, signalled by the Soviets' invasion of Czechoslovakia in 1968. Periodic (and extremely realistic) Command Post Exercises ran through the gamut of rising international tension, conflict preparedness, pre-emptive measures, military reinforcement, deployment, escalation and, at last resort, war – up to and including nuclear exchange and post-conflict activity. All very sobering stuff; but, in a very real sense comforting, to see how carefully each successive development was analysed, discussed and acted upon in concert with national capitals and the Alliance's most senior military commanders.

Back to the world I knew best, with command of RAF Laarbruch – then home to a heady mix of aircraft, roles and tasks; and including RAF Germany's Buccaneer strike/attack force. Numbers 15 and 16 Squadrons were then operating that great aircraft with immense professionalism and skill – taking in their collective stride the pressures of a continuous QRA commitment, the demands of no-notice 'TACEVAL', the endless training thereto and a great variety of exacting roles, including a range of profiles for weapons delivery.

'Long Toss', 'Varitoss' and 'Laydown' were but the prelude to some interesting escape manoeuvres, made none the less so by the prevalence of unfriendly weather on the North German plain. For me, a background of simulated crisis management at the highest levels of NATO proved rather useful in coping with some of the more ingenious 'injects' thrown at us in the course of TACEVAL and similar exercises.

The Royal College of Defence Studies and a tour in Whitehall were to take me temporarily out of direct involvement with nuclear affairs, but that was soon corrected by a stint as SASO, Strike Command – an appointment that 'double-hatted' as DCOS Ops & Int at HQ United Kingdom Air Forces. It was there that I made my first hands-on contact with the RAF's Medium Bomber Force – by then consisting only of the mighty Vulcan with its former companion, the Victor, as the UK's sole resource for the increasingly important task of air-to-air refuelling. This was to lead to a tour as AOC No. 1 Group, charged with the introduction of the Tornado to front-line service and, as a consequence, the retirement of the Vulcan force. It was indeed ironic that that great aircraft was to see its one and only live action during my time at 1 Group – not, of course, in the nuclear strike role for which it had been designed, but for conventional operations in the South Atlantic. That, as they say, is another story.

We have now arrived in 1983, with the Cold War still a fact of life – indeed, fast approaching its fortieth anniversary. My own next appointment was to the Air Force Board in what was, by that time, the somewhat deceptively titled appointment of Air Member for Supply and Organisation. In fact, the next three years in Whitehall served to fill some important gaps in my service experience, by forcing me to face some of the very real problems that then existed in the support of the front-line. Our efforts to merge the various elements of the structure into a framework of integrated Logistics were to bear fruit some years later: indeed, things have inevitably moved on apace since then. Yet another story. Other than as a member of the Board, the professional involvement of AMSO with nuclear matters was primarily in a supporting role – important as that was. However, a measure of responsibility for the security of weapons convoys and storage served to keep my eye firmly on the nuclear ball, particularly given the activities of various protest groups around Greenham Common, Molesworth and elsewhere.

Released from Whitehall in early 1986, I returned to Brussels for a final appointment as UK Military Representative to NATO. And it was in the course of the next three years that I saw first the stirrings, then the movement for change, and finally the collapse of the threat from the East; with the fall of the Berlin Wall, the rush to democracy of nations of the old Warsaw Treaty Organisation and, later, the disappearance of the Soviet Union itself. I had been fortunate to occupy a front seat at events marking the end of that long and, at times, rather dangerous Cold War.

Looking back on it all from a distance of ten years and more, I have some distinctly mixed feelings. In the first place, my reading of immediate post-World War II history, taken together with my own later experience of 'real life', convince me that there was really no alternative to the Allied Powers taking a very sombre view of Soviet intentions (and, certainly, of their military capabilities) at almost any time up to the mid-1980s. Whether the Soviets would ever have mounted that surprise and immensely powerful all-arms attack on Western Europe is a question that may not be fully answered until some rather dusty Kremlin files are opened – if, indeed, that were ever to happen. It was certainly not worth the risk; and the subsequent and much-criticised arms race was, in consequence, an inevitability. Clearly, it was taken too far – by both sides. But that awful 'balance of terror' did serve to concentrate minds and to shape decisions by all those charged with their making. Life in those times was never comfortable; but if those nations now developing their own nuclear capabilities were to be guided by the history of the Cold War, there is a fair chance that catastrophe might again be averted. There are certainly some very pertinent lessons to be learnt from the experience of the bi-polar power blocs that faced each other across Europe in the second half of the Twentieth Century.

On a more personal level, I and no doubt others of my generation are sometimes asked whether we have a sense of frustration, having spent literally decades in the Armed Services without ever firing a shot in anger. My answer to that is simple. We were all given a serious and very worthwhile job to do – nothing less than helping to prevent a Third World War that would have been more destructive than anything that had gone before. Our satisfaction is in having played a part in sustaining however uneasy a peace in that perennial cockpit of war – Europe. Others may well see things differently. But the fact is that conflict was prevented – as, indeed, were the disasters which some had forecast by the very possession of nuclear weapons. In the final analysis, the 43-year Cold War was to end in the way that T. S. Eliot had foretold the end of the world itself:

'Not with a bang, but a whimper'.

The V-Bomber Force

Air Commodore C. B. Brown CBE AFC

This is the view from a Bomber Station, Waddington, which I was commanding.

After the massive operations against Germany, the immediate post-war period for Bomber Command had been an anti-climax – a force of 1700 aircraft had rapidly been reduced to 150!

But with the acquisition of American Super-Fortresses; the new twin jet Canberra in 1951, and the V-Force on the horizon, the Command's image greatly improved and a strong sense of purpose returned. The advent of the V-Force again gave it a primary defence role, and also an awesome responsibility.

At first sight not very much seemed to have changed. A structure of two groups was retained. Many of the main bases were pre-war permanent stations, with their clutches of box-like hangars and attractive Lutyens style messes and married quarters; and each main base had twenty-four aircraft and three flying squadrons bearing old and cherished numbers with their records of endeavour and sacrifice.

But Bomber Command was no longer quite the old firm. A nuclear armed force poised and ready to go had to be kept well in hand, so command and control were tight, tighter than had ever been experienced before: the nature of the role and custody of nuclear weapons placed a very high premium on security; and operational procedures had to be clearly defined and strictly standardised, and foolproof in the sense that there could be no misunderstandings or mistakes.

Above all, however, the Command was to face two main challenges: to preserve and demonstrate its continuing viability in the face of a developing Russian ballistic missile threat which – in a worst case situation – could reduce the warning of an attack to just four minutes; and, secondly, to be able to penetrate an increasingly effective air defence system which had dramatically demonstrated its capability at high altitude by shooting down the American pilot Gary Powers in his U-2.

Getting the force off the ground within the four minutes warning was governed by the time it took to scramble the dispersed elements, each of four aircraft, from the operational readiness platforms at the side of the runway thresholds. As soon as he received the first Valiants, the Air Officer Commanding No. 3 Group started take-off trials at Wyton. With the four engines in each aircraft having to be started in rotation the best that could be achieved was six to nine minutes. Clearly they had to be started simultaneously. Senior experts said it was technically not possible; but, as so often happens in such situations, a junior engineering officer came up with a solution – a priceless breakthrough. From then on the force could be got off the ground in about two and a half minutes.

The task then was to develop the capability of generating and dispersing it during a period of international tension and within the strategic warning of an imminent attack. A head start was given by maintaining a proportion of aircraft and crews at continuous readiness at the main bases, the Quick Reaction Alert Force. To bring the remainder quickly into the line required centralised control of all resources, flexible second line servicing procedures, and careful management and monitoring of people to ensure that minimum numbers were always available or on immediate recall. Each station had six dispersal airfields. As well as operational communications they had pre-positioned refuellers and ground servicing equipment, spares, and rations. The force dispersed to them included balanced detachments of all trades and additional pre-packed spares and other paraphernalia.

This brought the Administrative Wing fully into the operational function. Whereas in the past the flying squadrons and their first line servicing people had been regarded as the front line and all the others supporters, now everyone was directly involved. The station became truly an operational entity and there was a remarkable uplift in enthusiasm and morale generally.

Then there was security. Security consciousness was generally very good. Physical security was less good. The best protected and most secure place was the weapons compound. Unfortunately, at Waddington this was on the other side of the main Sleaford–Lincoln road. So whenever there was a major exercise, half the population of Lincolnshire watched goggle-eyed as strange and sinister-looking shapes were trundled across the road in front of them !

It had been intended to avoid the Russian air defence completely by using the American long-range air-launched missile, Skybolt. Plans were well advanced for rearming with this weapon, including flying a continuous airborne alert, when it was abandoned by the Americans. In no way could the existing short-range stand-off missile Blue Steel be regarded as an effective substitute, and there was no alternative, therefore, but to go into the targets at low level to minimise the effectiveness of the air defence radars and surface-to-air missiles. With aircraft designed and stressed to operate at high altitudes this could hardly be a TSR 2 type operation flying at a couple of hundred feet and 500 to 600 knots.

Training at these speeds would soon have consumed the fatigue lives of Victor and Vulcan, and might even have induced catastrophic failure. Fortunately it was not necessary. Of the two ingredients, getting down low and staying there despite bad weather and difficult terrain, was more important than flying at very high speed and having to go up a little when conditions became adverse. In retrospect that would probably have soon become apparent had the TSR 2 entered service!

Sensibly therefore the Command settled for 250 to 300 knots for training and a consistent low level of 250 feet. For the final phase and the approach to the target area the speed would be pushed up considerably higher. All the other factors proved to be favourable. Although much reduced in range at low level the navigation and bombing system continued to be effective, and an unforeseen bonus was that in the hands of a

Vulcan B MkII of 617 Squadron loaded with Blue Streak (Crown copyright)

good operator it could provide a profile of the terrain ahead; and in due course this was supplemented with a relatively simple terrain following indicator – 'Go up, go down'. Despite an intensive and continuous training programme along the UK low level routes, and over northern Canada from a training base at Goose Bay in Labrador, both aircraft types stood up to the low-level environment well.

The Vulcan proved to be as tough as old boots in most respects and although there was a problem with the wing root main spar of the Victor, it proved to be manageable. And the fusing systems of the weapons could be programmed for all sorts of tricks.

The primary role of nuclear deterrence was by no means the extent of the V-Bomber story. From the outset one of the squadrons had the role of strategic reconnaissance; the Valiants, in a conventional bombing role, were engaged in the Suez affair barely a year after they entered service; and, in due course, for example, the Waddington wing of Vulcan Mk ls had a secondary commitment to provide conventional support for the Middle East Air Force from a forward base in Malta. In what might be regarded as a grand finale, on 1 May 1982 a single Vulcan attacked the airfield at Port Stanley in the Falklands. The results may not have been spectacular but the flight certainly was: a round trip of 7000 nm from Ascension Island, sixteen hours in the air, and seven in-flight refuellings.

As the RAF's need for greater mobility grew, at first the Valiant and then primarily the Victor were converted to airborne tankers. Thus the V-Bomber continued to play an increasingly important and vital role long after the strategic nuclear deterrent had passed to the Polaris submarines.

The V-Force was a great experience, but for the Royal Air Force it was something of a paradox as well. In striking power it was the apogee of the main Air Staff doctrine going back to the First World War and pursued relentlessly by Bomber Command in the Second; but it was also the swan-song of the British strategic bomber. The V-Force lifted the Royal Air Force into a new era, and then faded away.

Canberra QRA

Air Commodore Phil Wilkinson CVO

First, a little bit of RAF Germany history, to explain the presence of nuclear-armed Canberras on four bases in Germany.

The basic reason was overcrowding in UK. The Bomber Command build-up to twenty-four Canberra squadrons was galloping along in the mid-'50s. At the same time there was a major programme of airfield upgrade in readiness for the full expansion of the V-Force.

The runways and taxi-tracks on many German bases met the required standard and it was decided that four Canberra squadrons should form at Ahlhorn, beginning 1 April 1954. These operated from Gütersloh under operational control of Bomber Command, until their disbandment and withdrawal in August 1956.

By then the planned deployment of 2nd TAF's own Canberra force of reconnaissance and 'intruder' aircraft had started. This force of four squadrons of Canberras remained until the early '70s when they were replaced by Buccaneers and Phantoms.

I joined 14 Squadron in November 1963, with my trusty and formidable Irish navigator, Paddy O'Shea.

The introduction to the squadron was intensive, the aim being to qualify in the strike role as quickly as possible, and to join the rest of the crews on the Quick Reaction Alert (QRA) roster. Local familiarisation and procedural checks were the pattern for the first month. Lots of simulated low altitude bombing attacks were carried out; extended low-level sorties were flown around the extensive Low Flying Areas; and finally, one of the flight commanders gave us an extended workout in the dual-control Canberra, checking our competence to be let loose in live attacks. Later that day we flew the three-hour sortie to land at RAF Idris in Libya. Over the next three days I flew thirteen sorties, and dropped forty-eight 25 lb practice bombs.

A quick digression on the theory and practice of LABS – the Low Altitude Bombing System – and also on the weapon that would be the warload.

First, the weapon: the US Mk 7 ('Project E') 1650 lb bomb. Project E was the UK-US agreement to provide RAF tactical bomber aircraft (Canberras in Germany and Valiants in UK) with the US bomb.

Security police both USAF and RAF, provided bi-national protection to weapon storage sites and live-loaded aircraft in the QRA (Quick Reaction Alert) compound. 'Alert duty officers' (ADO) of the USAF provided half of a 'dual key' system of weapon release in the event of a QRA scramble, and accompanied the pilot and/or navigator during any access to the weapon for checks or routine maintenance. The aircraft had to be jacked up in order to get the rather bulky weapon under it prior to loading; once the bomb was loaded, the lower of its three fins protruded outside the closed bomb-bay doors.

Two aircraft from each squadron were maintained at high readiness (able to be airborne in not more than fifteen minutes from receipt of the scramble order). These were housed in the QRA hangars (open ended sheds, and a far cry from the later Hardened Aircraft Shelters) with the crews and the Alert Duty Officer inside a wired-off compound.

Crews did twenty-four-hour spells on QRA: the aircraft and weapons were rotated, involving download and reload inside the open shed every two weeks. Since the sheds were, at Wildenrath at least, within clear view of the nearby road there was no shortage of interested watchers. I've no doubt that our mug-shots were readily available to potential Warsaw Pact interrogators!

The LABS attack was practised at as many ranges as possible, but the features and time checks along the attack route to Nordhorn range targets are probably etched on the

Canberra B(I)8 with 2 X 1000 lb bombs on pylons and gun pack underneath (Air Cdr Phil Wilkinson)

memories of anyone who flew in that era. I must have done hundreds of runs down that near-featureless track. The attack was pretty inflexible, and very mechanical. Release parameters were calculated before take-off for either 'normal' attacks – where the bomb was released in the climb from low level at an angle of between thirty and eighty degrees from the horizontal, or 'alternate' attacks – with release coming after the aircraft had passed the vertical, hence the other term for it of 'over the shoulder'. The navigator, prior to getting on board, set those parameters on the release computer tucked away in a hatch at the rear of the aircraft.

Passing over the Initial Point (IP) the pilot 'pickled' the bomb release trigger, then held it firmly depressed for the period of the timer run-down set on the release computer. Just when you thought the damn thing hadn't worked, a horizontal needle dropped on the LABS dial on the instrument panel. With a pleasing rearward heave on the control column, the pilot entered a 3.4 G climb. The next excitement was a release light to signify 'bomb gone', and then the mildly aerobatic roll off the top of the loop was completed, and the aircraft taken back down to low level.

Proficiency in this manoeuvre was fundamental to accuracy of weapon delivery.

Thorough knowledge of the planned target was equally important, so a seemingly inhuman amount of time was spent on target study. This was done locked away in the intelligence vault with photographs, overheads of the target (mostly airfields) and surroundings, and indications of fixed or mobile defence arrays *en route* and at the target.

The onus was on the pilot to have the details of the first few legs after take off absolutely committed to memory. For the luckless navigator had very few reliable aids to help him: the main area navigation system was Decca, designed originally for shipboard use and no doubt quite good at those speeds. That and a Doppler were all he had; and both needed a good reliable first fix or two to be synchronised and unleashed. Thus the pilot's role as a pathfinder to those essential first and second fixes.

The navigator's work station was also pretty unfriendly. Whereas I had a Mk 3 Martin-Baker to sit on, Paddy merely lay in the nose of the aircraft, doing his map-reading, and contorting his fifteen stone and six foot two inches back to a little table and bucket seat every now and again to update the navigation equipment. In the event of a terminal emergency, he had to jettison the side door of the aircraft, and squeeze his fifteen stone etc. even more tightly to pop himself out of the door, having first clipped on a WW II standard chest parachute. Given that our normal environment was at 250 feet, one can only admire the navigators for their stoic acceptance of such a small chance of survival (but successful escapes are on record).

So, life consisted of a routine of low-level sorties around Germany, or high-level transits to the UK followed by descent to low-level for more of the same in different scenery. Some time at a range would be a part of nearly every sortie, maintaining proficiency. All NATO exercises were based on variations of low-level simulated attacks. Some large scale, involving all of 2nd TAF, some combining with attack aircraft from 4 ATAF, either over continental Europe or exercising the UK air defences.

This routine was broken very regularly, for the squadrons in Germany also had a secondary, conventional attack role. The versatility of the Canberra meant that it would be asked to do more than just hold nuclear alert and prepare for that role only. There was regular reversion to a conventional weapon fit – with a four 20 mm gun pack in the bomb-bay; and any number of weapon options from the wing pylons and the bomb stations in the forward part of the bay not used up by the gun pack.

This operational versatility was proved when 59 Squadron went to Belize in 1958 to discourage Guatemalan advances, and 213 and 88 deployed to the Gulf in mid-1961 for an early version of the Kuwait crisis (and were successful as a deterrent). During 1965 all the Germany squadrons were rotating aircraft through the bases in Singapore and Malaya, boosting the Far East Air Force strength in the confrontation with Indonesia.

Since the nuclear/conventional split required familiarity with both attack modes, and worldwide deployment demanded familiarity with world-wide conditions, the air and ground crew were regularly away on training detachments. Most often, conventional weapon training was carried out in Libya. Also used were the ranges in Cyprus: Episkopi Bay targets for shallow dive bombing, and Larnaca for both bombing and gun or rocket strafe. As well as good weather factors, all these ranges and targets had the advantage of close proximity to the base airfield. I note from my log book that many times it was possible to drop four practice bombs in four attacks on Episkopi target and be back on the ground in twenty minutes from take off. Thus a good morning's work might include six sorties, with engine-running reloads of bombs.

Geographical familiarisation was by means of Southern or Extended Southern Ranger flights.

Southern Rangers would be just into the Mediterranean: Gibraltar, Malta, Libya or Cyprus. One aircraft, the pilot and navigator, and total independence for a weekend. And lots of room in the bomb bay for Libyan oranges or Cyprus sherry.

The extended routes would go beyond Cyprus and on to the Gulf – Sharjah, Bahrain, Masirah, Djibouti and via Aden to Nairobi (also, until 1965, to Salisbury). Paddy and I were in fact on our way there in November 1965. Landed in Nairobi, we were met by an insistent diplomat who told us to stay in Nairobi and return up the route when the timings of our original diplomatic over-flight clearances would allow. Next day we heard on the radio that Ian Smith had declared UDI. I suppose it was a good idea not to have an RAF bomber on the apron on such a day.

Return routes could involve staging through Tehran, or perhaps a drop down to low level over Libya, having picked up some practice bombs in Akrotiri, for a first run attack on one of the ranges, then climbing out for the long leg back to wintry Germany.

There was one final change in the pattern before I left. In mid-1966, the 1650 lb Mk. 7 weapon for LABS attacks was replaced by a 2100 lb Mk 43, for laydown attack from low level. Crews found the profile much more flexible. Once we had got used to the lack of any decent aiming cues on our fairly rudimentary visual bomb sight, the average scores for practice bombs went from the modest LABS averages of around 180 yards to laydown figures in the order of sixty to eighty feet. Transition was quickly completed, including night weaponry using the sparse assistance of the Decca navigation system, and the squadron assumed QRA with the new weapon on 4 November 1966. To prove the point, HQ RAF Germany called us out for three alert and weapon generation exercises in the next ten days. Not a bad plan, for the NATO TACEVAL team arrived on 14 November. The squadron achieved Grade 1 (the highest) scores in all categories of professional competence – the first time ever for a strike unit in RAF Germany.

Then it was time to go home – on 4 January 1967.

Thirty years later I retired, after a last tour as Defence and Air Attaché in Moscow. The Warsaw Pact was no more; the Soviet Union was dismantled; and one year later – in 1998 – the RAF's tactical nuclear weapon (the WE177) was withdrawn from service.

I would like to think that, in some small way, I and my life-long friends from that time on the Squadron contributed to such welcome changes at the end of the Twentieth Century. There was certainly no prospect of anything like that nearer the middle of the Century: I had a hot seat for my part of the Cold War.

Two Sides of Intelligence

Air Chief Marshal Sir Michael Armitage KCB CBE

All aircrew who served on operational squadrons during the Cold War became familiar with the very high quality of Intelligence that was available on the forces of the Warsaw Pact. The V-Force, for example, was provided with very detailed information on targets, ingress and egress routes, likely enemy defences and so on. In Royal Air Force Germany, where in the late 1960s I commanded No.17 Squadron in the night reconnaissance role, the available Intelligence was even more comprehensive. It dealt not only with our pre-planned East European routes and targets, but also gave us very detailed information on the extensive Warsaw Pact ground forces facing us.

There were of course very many sources from which this Intelligence was drawn. In the early days of NATO, for example, and before the Berlin Wall went up, so much information was available from refugees and defectors that a branch of the Security Service was set up in the British Headquarters at Rheindahlen to deal with this aspect of Intelligence gathering. As time went on, air- and ground-based Signals Intelligence played an increasing role in Germany, as did radar monitoring of Warsaw Pact air activity. The fact that units of the American, British and French armed forces were stationed in Berlin – a hundred miles and more beyond the inner-German border – was a considerable bonus in this field.

Another and utterly unique source of Intelligence was the 'British Commander-in-Chief's Mission to the Soviet Forces of Occupation in Germany' (BRIXMIS for short), first set up in September 1946. Members of this Mission were nothing less than legalised spies, with freedom to monitor Warsaw Pact activities across wide stretches of East Germany. The French and the Americans had similar Missions, and much Intelligence was shared between these allies. The Intelligence 'take' from this source was absolutely invaluable, resulting as it did over the years in many first sightings and excellent photographs of new Soviet equipment such as tanks, aircraft and missiles.

Another unique source was provided by a pair of Chipmunk aircraft stationed at RAF Gatow in Berlin, from where, with the tacit agreement of the Soviets, pilots were able to fly all over the Berlin air safety zone, which meant within twenty miles of the Berlin Air Safety Centre. Equipped with cameras, some with a 1000 mm lens, a great deal of the Soviet Order of Battle was exposed to the alert observers and their analysts back at base.

Another source of air reconnaissance, but this time more covert, came from the non-combat military aircraft such as transports that regularly flew up and down the air corridors to Berlin, their track taking them inevitably over Soviet airfields and other key facilities in East Germany.

When fused and analysed, all this information from such a wide variety of sources provided RAF Germany and BAOR with a comprehensive and almost seamless picture of what the other side was up to.

The Intelligence set-up in the Mediterranean, where I served as Station Commander at RAF Luqa in Malta in the early 1970s, was quite different. In the Mediterranean our main concern was the Soviet fleet, and perhaps in particular their submarine fleet. Signals Intelligence naturally played a part in our monitoring of Soviet naval activity, but at sea

Camera-equipped Chipmunk (AHB)

there are no borders to worry about, and the NATO maritime aircraft in the region, including Nimrods based at Luqa, were often able to over fly Soviet fleet units and to provide a good picture of Soviet strengths and dispositions.

Individual Soviet submarines could usually be identified when on the surface by what was known as 'dentology' – that is recognising the inevitable bumps, scratches and dents that any boat collected on its hull during its time at sea. Each boat was bound to be unique in this respect. Another invaluable circumstance was that most of the Soviet ships and boats belonged to their Black Sea Fleet, and had to pass through the Bosphorus and under the bridges there in order to reach their patrol areas in the Mediterranean. No opportunity was lost to examine the fleet units as they made their way through the narrow waterway and under the bridges on their way out. Thus in the Mediterranean as in Germany, but from quite different sources, our Intelligence on the putative opposition was of a generally very high quality.

Up until 1982, my familiarity with Intelligence had thus been confined to tactical or even local Intelligence. In that year I became Director of Service Intelligence in the Ministry of Defence, a post that dealt mainly with strategic Military Intelligence. At that time there were two other production Directorates: the Directorate of Scientific and Technical Intelligence, and the Directorate of Economic Intelligence. Together with the Directorate of Management and Support, they made up the Defence Intelligence Staff, employing several hundred Service and civilian analysts and experts in many specialist fields. Within my DSI there were branches dealing with Navy, Army and Air Intelligence, but it was, and still is, noteworthy that these branches belong together in the DIS within the Central Staffs, and are not subordinate to the three Services, as was the case up until the 1960s.

Within the MOD, the DIS reports directly to the Chiefs of Staff Committee, but it also plays a very important part in the Joint Intelligence Committee of the Cabinet Office. This is where the efforts of the Security Service (MI5), the Secret Intelligence Service (MI6), GCHQ and the DIS are brought together to produce national rather than departmental assessments.

This was the world into which I stepped for the first time just one week before the Falklands crisis of March 1982 blew up, and as it happened I had spent that first week at a conference in Brussels. When I flew back into RAF Northolt at the end of the week, I was met by a somewhat worried looking staff officer and driven to my office in MOD Main Building, where I spent the next thirty or so days and nights.

It was a very interesting introduction to the Intelligence scene. For a start, we had practically no Intelligence on Argentina. And even if the raw material had been there we had no dedicated team of experts on Argentina who could do anything about it. Successive Defence cuts had trimmed the DIS staff back to beyond any reasonable minimum, with the result, as I recall, that there were only two staff officers watching the whole of South and Central America, and their attention was focused entirely on the possible threat to Belize from Guatemala.

Although there had been warnings of certain Argentine military activity, particularly from the very alert Defence Attaché in Buenos Aires, who forecast the coming invasion with some accuracy, the alarm bells in Whitehall did not ring. There had been false alarms before, and no one really believed that Argentina would this time take action. The result was that we were taken totally by surprise, and the British forces found themselves with practically no Intelligence on which to base their response. What we did have, however, was time to do something about it as our Task Force started off on its seven-week voyage to the South Atlantic.

A surprising amount of information was available from open sources, but this was by no means enough. By liaison with allies, with other friendly countries and with various countries that had no particular liking for Argentina, we were able to fill many gaps in our knowledge of the military capabilities our forces were likely to meet. Meanwhile, something like ninety extra staff were brought into the DIS to cope with the new demands being placed on it; some of the assets of GCHQ were reassigned to help deal with the developing situation, and quite a number of people with local knowledge of the Falklands were invited into the DIS for a chat. Specific study cells were set up in the DIS. One was the Falkland Islands Study Team (FIST), which, by the end of the brief campaign had as good a grasp of Argentine military strengths and dispositions as did the Argentine commander in the Falklands.

Several problems emerged as matters developed. One was the difficulty of co-ordinating our efforts not only with those of the HQ at Northwood, but also with the distant Task Force itself. Another difficulty was one that had arisen in previous operations, and was to reappear in other crises during the succeeding years, that of building an effective interface between Intelligence and Operations. Finally, there was the fact that having started the crisis with virtually nothing, the DIS was soon overwhelmed by the sheer quantity of detailed information and by the mountains of paper that this generated.

In retrospect, many lessons had to be relearned from the Intelligence aspects of the Falklands campaign. The main one at the strategic level was the danger of 'mirror imaging', that is to say attributing one's own concepts to the opponent. In the case of Argentina, Britain had been engaged on and off for years in negotiations with Argentina about the future status of the Falklands; and because it was not the British style to go to war while negotiations still offered a peaceful solution, many people assumed that the Argentine government thought the same way. Another strategic lesson was the danger of ignoring what I can best describe as faint signals among a lot of international noise. In 1982, Britain's strategic attention, and of course that of the Intelligence agencies, was directed mainly towards the Warsaw Pact and the unstable Middle East. Little notice, if any, was being taken of distant and very minor distractions such as the long-standing problem of the future of the Falklands.

And finally, a lesson that we in Britain seem destined never to learn, and that is that we get what we pay for. If as a nation we are not prepared to invest properly in what is after all the front line in any international crisis, Intelligence, then in the future other unpleasant surprises will jump up and hit us in the face.

Deep Penetration Reconnaissance

Squadron Leader John Crampton DFC AFC

In July 1951 I was the happy boss of No. 97 (Lincoln) Squadron, when the C-in-C Bomber Command sent for me and said that I was to assume command of a Special Duty Flight in conditions of utmost secrecy. The Flight would be equipped with the North American RB-45C four-jet strategic reconnaissance aircraft, and the crews concerned would proceed almost immediately to the United States for a sixty-day detachment to begin training on the aircraft. The Flight was to comprise three aircraft, each with a crew of one pilot, a flight engineer, and a navigator.

After a series of intense and excellent conversion courses authorised by General LeMay, USAF, we returned to RAF Sculthorpe. Here we became an additional flight with the resident USAF RB-45C squadron. We still had no idea what was planned for us.

There was much speculation, mostly centred on comparative trials of the Boeing flying-boom in-flight refuelling method against the probe and drogue favoured by the RAF. It was a tense time for us and our hosts because nine RAF aircrew flying with an elite USAF squadron raised eyebrows.

Early in 1952 I was summoned to High Wycombe with my navigator Rex Sanders. This was the moment of truth and I confess to some apprehension when the charts were unrolled to show three separate tracks from Sculthorpe to the Baltic States, the Moscow area, and Central Southern Russia. The deal was for the three routes to be flown simultaneously, departing Sculthorpe in rapid succession to rendezvous with the tankers to the north of Denmark. After a maximum top-up we were to climb at maximum continuous power at a Mach No. of about 0.68 to the highest altitude the temperature of the night would allow. Our 'targets' were ICBM sites and similar strategically important areas. We were to take 35 mm photos of the aircraft's radar display when the targets were located and identified.

Timing was critical because our intelligence agencies would be listening for Soviet reaction to our deep penetration of their airspace, and had certain diversionary exercises for keeping them clear of our routes. We were of course to fly without navigation lights and maintain R/T silence although we would have an OMG (O My God) frequency for desperate emergency.

Before the date of our live sorties had been fixed, I took my crew on a gentle probe of the defences by flying over the Soviet Zone of Eastern Germany for half an hour or so, whilst our intelligence people monitored Russian radio and radar activity. Nothing was noted and so we were all set for the big one. Four aircraft (three active and one spare) had been allocated to us, and these had to be stripped of ALL USAF markings and repainted in RAF colours. Security shackles were further weakened, because, to do this job in time, two of our aircraft were flown to nearby RAF West Raynham where a hangar was cleared and several gallons of paint stripper were put to good use by a number of very mystified airmen. In the event of one of our aeroplanes falling into Russian hands, the United States would point to the paint job and disclaim all knowledge. Similarly the RAF would state that it had no RB-45Cs on inventory. How well this improbable tale, told by a six-foot six-inch old-Harrovian, would go down with the Russians was fortunately never put to the test. Our story would be that we were lost, a gross professional insult to my crew and myself, but an acceptable one if the dire need arose – and we would have false charts to back our claim.

So in the late afternoon of a fine April day in 1952 the three 'RAF' RB-45Cs departed from Sculthorpe and headed towards the Skagerrak. We picked up our tankers, took on every pound of fuel we could, broke away, doused all the lights and headed south-east into the black night. All was going well and Rex Sanders was getting good plots on his radar and feeding me with the courses to steer to the targets. We had the long haul south-east across Russia. Sergeant. Lindsay, my co-pilot, gave us confidence-inspiring reports on the aircraft's systems and told us that we were flying on the right side of the fuel consumption curve.

My most abiding memory of the route is the apparent wilderness over which we were flying. There were no lights on the ground nor any sign of human habitation – quite unlike the rest of Europe. We continued our gentle climb at a Mach No. of about 0.68 to 36,000 feet and covered our briefed route taking the target photographs as planned. It was all so quiet as to be distinctly eerie. Finally we turned for home and in due course began the let down into Sculthorpe. We landed, without incident, after ten hours and twenty minutes in the air. The two other aircraft covered all their targets – and the operation had been a success.

A few days later we flew our aircraft, still in RAF markings, to Lockbourne AFB, Ohio. On our return to England I was given 101 Squadron at Binbrook, recently rearmed with the RAF's first Canberras – a bit like landing the Spring Double!

After a few months, in October 1952, I was summoned back to Bomber Command, informed that the Special Duty Flight was to be re-formed and asked if I would take over command again? 'Yes.' A few days later we were welcomed back at Sculthorpe and got back into the old routine. There were a few crew changes.

Rex Sanders stayed with me but Sgt Lindsay had been involved in a crash and his place was taken by Flt Lt 'MacFurze', one of my flight commanders on 101. This was an inspired choice on my part because Mac rapidly became an expert on the aircraft and its systems, and would have elbowed me out of the captain's seat given half a chance. We flew hard through November and, by the beginning of December when we were trained to concert pitch, the show was suddenly cancelled and we were ordered back to our units. Among the rumours floating around was the belief that the political risk at that time was too great. If any one of us had gone down in Russia the balloon might have gone up.

My tour with 101 came to an end in July 1953 and I was posted to HQ 1 Group at Bawtry from where, after ten very indifferent months as an operations officer, I was again summoned to High Wycombe, told that the SDF was to be revived and again asked if I would take it on. I had begun to view the entire project as mine and would have been most upset if the job had been offered to anyone else. So, in March 1954, it was back to Sculthorpe. I was concerned that our cover might well have been blown because so many people knew that we were up to something – even if they were not sure what. The super-efficient flight line procedures under which the crew chiefs could call stores or any other department at Sculthorpe using walkie-talkies, to discuss our aircraft problems and movements in uncoded language was also a worry. The least competent Soviet spy or sympathiser in the locality with a small radio tuned to the Americans' frequency could have written a manual on events at Sculthorpe.

Anyway, after a month's hard work during which the four assigned aircraft were repainted in RAF colours, I went to Bomber Command accompanied by the faithful Rex Sanders to collect the flight plans, which again showed three routes: north, central and a much longer southern route which would require in-flight refuelling outbound as well as inbound. This was the one I chose.

The Intelligence people briefed us carefully: There might be some SAM (Surface to Air Missiles) but no radar-equipped night fighters, although there was a ground control radar reporting system which would enable them to track us and position a fighter within visual range. This was not thought to be likely.

The one comforting thought was that we should be too high and too fast for any anti-aircraft fire. No flak! Good news! We were to remain silent unless attacked, in which case the OMG frequency was to be used to give a 'sitrep' to the chaps back at the ranch.

Late in April 1954 everything was GO, including the spare aircraft which we never used. Once again the three RAF RB-45Cs staggered into the air and headed for North Denmark where our faithful tankers topped us up. After a smart salute to the tanker's boom operator – all lights doused – came the long slow climb into the inky blackness east-south-east. We cleared some stratus at 30,000 feet, got a good view of the stars and were greatly encouraged by Rex's confidence-inspiring report that the ground mapping radar was working like a breeze. He gave me new courses from time to time and asked for straight and level flight as we ran on to our various target sites which he said he was having no problem photographing.

When we were south-south-west of Moscow we turned for the home run, still photographing. Occasionally I saw, reflected on the cloud cover, flashes from the ground similar to lightning or an active bombing range at night. It was causing us no harm – just puzzling, that's all. Having taken nearly all our photos, we were heading south towards Kiev at 36,000 feet and Mach 0.7 when the electric storm or bombing range flashes seemed to be getting more frequent –

John Crampton in his 1932 vintage three-litre supercharged eight-cylinder Grand Prix Maserati which he bought in 1948 and turned into a sports car. After five glorious years the car was sold and is now in a motor-racing museum near Frankfurt, Germany. Photo taken at RAF Sculthorpe in 1952 with three USAF friends and his North American RB-45C, on loan from Uncle Sam! Regulation black arm band worn immediately after the death of King George VI (John Crampton)

and always directly beneath us, which was odd for a random phenomenon. Had it not been for the absolute certainty with which the briefing officers had dismissed the possibility of flak I would have been a shade suspicious, because it all closely resembled the German variety I had seen a lot of in an earlier life. No-one else was bothered: Rex, who couldn't see out anyway, was devilling away at his photography, and Mac in the back was reporting all systems normal; leaving me to ponder on this curious departure from the script.

My reverie was rudely interrupted by the sudden heart-stopping appearance of a veritable flare-path of exploding golden anti-aircraft fire. There was no doubt about it; it was very well-predicted flak – dead ahead and at the same height as we were. Clearly the Russians knew where we were, or very nearly where we were; when I was under the impression that we were undetected. Anyway we had been told back at the ranch that the risk of flak at our height and speed was minimal. You can't trust anyone!!

My reaction was instinctive – throttles wide open and haul the aeroplane round on its starboard wing tip until the gyro compass pointed west. I began a gentle 100 foot-per-minute descent because that made us seem to go a bit faster – although it didn't because we started juddering in the limiting Mach number buffet. So I eased the power off a bit but kept up the descent on the 'it seems faster' principle, and since we had been predicted I thought it best to change height as well as speed and direction, thus giving the gunners down below three new problems. Poor old Rex piped up 'Hey, what about my photos?' I replied succinctly, explained that clearly we had been tracked very accurately, told him about the flak burst and requested a course to steer to Fürstenfeldbrück, our refuelling rendezvous and declared alternative in an emergency.

We had about a thousand miles to go and I urged Mac to keep his eyes peeled for fighters which might pick us up outside the flak pattern. Much later I learned that there were fighters about with orders to ram us on sight. Maximum speed was essential. I flew the aeroplane just on the right side of the buffet: it sort of trembled affectionately. I had time to reflect that the earlier flashes we had seen below us had been ground fire, and that our stately progress as ordered by Rex had given even the dimmest battery commanders time to track us and fire. The early attempts had ALL misjudged our height – and, thank God, the Kiev defences had misjudged our speed: they had chucked everything up a few hundred yards ahead of us.

I thought for a moment of jettisoning our now empty 1,200 gallon wing-tip tanks. Their absence might have added a few more knots to our speed but, once found, their maker's name and address would have revealed that they came from America, and there would have been the devil of a row. Anyway the thought of them bouncing down the High Street of Kiev West at two o'clock in the morning disturbing the ladies and frightening the children did not appeal. We were not flying over Russia to do that. Moreover, General LeMay would not have been best pleased at my scattering expensive bits of his aeroplane over Russia. So we kept the tanks on and finally, after what seemed an eternity, met up with our tankers; but for the first time the refuelling boom refused to stay in our aeroplane. Fearing our refuelling system had been damaged over Kiev I thought it wiser to land at Fürstenfeldbrück and refuel in the conventional way. This we did, and then flew home without further incident. It was good to see the other two aircraft back at Sculthorpe and to hear that their crews had had successful incident-free flights.

And that is almost all there was to it. But the story would not be complete without a tribute to those who set up the whole exercise – in particular General LeMay, USAF, who was determined to get the best target information for his aircrews – and to the late Sir Winston Churchill who agreed to the RAF's participation. A tribute must be paid too to Mr Llewelyn, who at the time was Bomber Command's Chief Scientific Officer and played a practical 'hands on' role in improving the quality of our radar pictures – even to giving them a stereoscopic effect.

As for the aircrews – no Flight Commander has ever flown with better men.

The Taceval Years

Wing Commander J. O. Luke

One of the developments within the Service which illustrates enlightened use of human resources, and which is perhaps less widely appreciated outside the Service, has been the utilisation of support personnel both in wartime and in training for war.

Driven by the need to secure airfields against ground threats as well as from air attack, the cold war years saw the RAF develop and refine the ground defence of airfields to a state of high efficiency in which improvisation was perhaps more important than sophistication. However, contrary to popular opinion, this function was not the exclusive province of the RAF Regiment, although the Station Regiment Officer would invariably fulfil a key advisory function in station defence planning. Designated RAF stations would have an RAF Regiment Field Squadron as part of their ground defence organisation. Responsibility for Ground Defence of RAF stations in wartime was vested in the Officer Commanding Administrative Wing, and the majority of the key players in the Ground Defence organisation were drawn from the support areas of the station.

The nerve centre on all stations was the Ground Defence Operations Centre. Typically, OC Admin Wing, as Ground Defence Commander, ran two shifts drawn principally from Station Headquarters personnel to provide twenty-four-hour manning in the Main Ground Defence Operations Centre, and another officer, also usually drawn from Admin Wing, would run a skeleton shift in an Alternate Centre at another location on the station to assume control in the event of a mishap in the Main Centre. Command and control was then exercised through the various Sector HQs and thence to the troops on the ground: the clerks, technicians, stewards and MT drivers comprising the Station Guard Force.

The folly of neglecting to secure ones airfields against ground threats needs no elaboration. However as we move towards a leaner and more mobile defence posture, it is possible that some of the folklore which accompanied the heady days of the '70s and early-mid '80s may fade. Hence this short reminiscence of those halcyon days!

In the relatively early days of ground defence, before personnel became as accomplished in ground defence as they did ultimately, it was not uncommon to find OC Admin Wings apprehensive about this 'new' responsibility which, for some, represented a step into the unknown. Consequently there were moments when caution must have seemed the appropriate watchword. One Ground Defence Commander with just such an approach was micro-managing staff to the extent that no one was allowed to make a move without consulting him. A period of silence was interrupted by a knock at the door 'Don't answer that knock' ordered the Ground Defence Commander, 'it sounds suspicious'.

There are also tales of Ground Defence Commanders who became perhaps too involved. In response to a message that intruders had gained access to the Station Commander's residence, one fearless ground Defence Commander decided that such a grave situation warranted his personal intervention. Arming himself to the teeth with blank ammunition, he effected a daring SAS style entry to the house, which was in complete darkness, and bravely engaged the enemy in a furious fire-fight. Having exhausted his ammunition, he turned the lights on to find the sole occupant of the house – the Station Commander's dog, clearly somewhat puzzled and frightened – cowering under a chair in the dining room.

Latterly though, the zeal and professionalism of gifted amateurs frequently earned justified plaudits. Technicians, stewards, clerks, painters and finishers and others became highly accomplished in their role as infanteers. One luckless Wing Commander witnessed at first hand the enthusiasm of the guard force. He had been posted to a station in Germany and, visiting the station prior to taking up his appointment, he found the station in the midst of an exercise. He then spent an uncomfortable ten minutes stripped to his underpants spread-eagled over the bonnet of his car, trying to convince the guards that he was who he claimed to be, and not an intruder.

Some of these dedicated part-time soldiers did not take kindly to those who showed less commitment to training for war than they themselves. One station had problems with vehicles failing to stop at a particular vehicle checkpoint. The checkpoint did not have barriers because it was located on a wide section of the perimeter track where there were frequent aircraft movements. Recognising that the guards concerned were fighting a losing battle, an enterprising Sector Commander decided that some of the offending drivers required a salutary lesson. The next two vehicles to ignore the guards' hand signals to stop found themselves each with four flat tyres fifty yards beyond the check point, having run over the spiked Calthrop Chain which had been hastily deployed by the delighted guards.

No one who served on a front-line station during this period will forget the endless Tannoy broadcasts – usually prefixed 'This is the GDOC' which punctuated every exercise. Some of those unaccustomed to regular use of this system had difficulty putting over messages quite as they intended. A suspect vehicle was correctly described over the Tannoy as a Hawson Van – a type of vehicle used frequently by Supply Squadrons for forward delivery. This announcement prompted one WRAF Controller to observe that she hadn't been aware that the RAF was once again making use of horses.

Following the old adage that an army marches on its stomach, food played an important part in exercises. At the well-known premier Tornado base in Germany, the distribution of doughnuts used to herald that the end of the exercise was imminent. The 'Endex Doughnut' thus became an extremely welcome phenomenon until the occasion when the well-meaning Catering Squadron, acting on incorrect information, circulated the customary 2,500 doughnuts prematurely. Chaos then ensued as commanders tried to continue the exercise with approximately half of their manpower absent – the troops having decided that the endex doughnut meant ENDEX.

Less well received on these occasions were the ubiquitous 'Egg Banjoes' for breakfast. Comprising fried egg and ham or bacon, between two slices of completely health-free white bread, enjoyment of these starters to the day depended largely on the strength of one's constitution. Some weeks after an exercise, squadron personnel were inspecting the perimeter wire of their sector in an area of the station which abounded with wild life, including badgers, foxes and deer. There, alongside one particularly remote stretch of the wire, they came across a completely intact four-week old egg banjo, which had not only been too much for the guard to whom it had been delivered, but had also been studiously ignored by all the creatures of the forest.

As well as staged incidents around the station, most exercise scenarios put the command and control of the station under the microscope at some stage by removing key station personnel to evaluate how well the station coped in their absence. Things did not always go according to plan. At a crucial stage in a damage control exercise a member of the directing staff handed the Ground Defence Commander a piece of paper instructing him to fall off his chair in ten seconds with a simulated heart attack.

The Ground Defence Commander duly complied and, within seconds, his well-intentioned deputy was on the scene to administer first aid. Perhaps he thought that he could make more of a contribution by restoring his leader to health than by deputising for him. Clearly, his first aid owed more to the silver screen than the first aid manuals, as he administered a crushing blow to the 'victim's' chest, breaking three ribs and severely winding the luckless Ground Defence Controller, turning him into a real casualty.

In compiling this short contribution, despite having tapped the recollections of colleagues, I am conscious that I have hardly scratched the surface of the rich seam of stories in this particular vein. Now there's a challenge for somebody!

EVEN THE SLIGHTEST MISJUDGEMENT

The speed and complexity of air operations demand a high degree of skill and judgement – even the smallest error can be catastrophic.

A Refuelling Tragedy

Squadron Leader K. L. Handscomb

It was 24 March 1975. It was to be a routine Air to Air Refuelling exercise of three hours' duration, with my Victor refuelling two Buccaneers. After attending met briefing, I joined the crew who were planning the exercise. The rear crew of three were a regular team, but the co-pilot was on loan from 55 Squadron, as he was in need of some flying practice prior to commencing his Intermediate Co-pilots Course, which is why, as Squadron Qualified Flying Instructor, I was in the crew.

The Estimated Time of Departure was 1100Z for a Rendezvous at 1130Z. The Towline was orientated NE/SW, 170 miles North East of Newcastle. Overall control was conducted by Boulmer Radar.

The two Buccaneers duly arrived, joining the tanker on the port side, which was the Standard Operating Procedure. After we had trailed the two wing hoses, the leader was cleared astern the starboard hose. On completion of the transfer of 2000 lb of fuel he was cleared to stand-off on the starboard side of the formation, in order to observe the other aircraft. The second aircraft was then cleared to move astern the port hose. When he was stabilised behind the hose, I gave clearance for him to make his approach to the drogue for a dry contact, that is, no fuel would be passed.

The refuelling operator, one of the Nav team, always monitored the approaches to the hoses through a downward-looking periscope. The first approach was smooth, making contact, which the pilot held in position for one minute. He was then cleared to break contact and stabilise behind the hose before his next approach. This time, he was held astern while the formation commenced a turn onto a reciprocal heading. Having stabilised, he was again cleared to make an approach. Through the periscope, it was seen that his approach was too fast.

The probe caught the rim of the drogue, causing the hose to snake between the probe and the fuselage. He went out of sight of the refuelling operator and finished above the port wing of the tanker. He then started to drop back for another attempt. In so doing, his aircraft caught the eflux from the tanker's engines, causing his starboard wing to knock off the port side of the Victor's tailplane.

My first indication that something drastic had happened was a reduction in pitch control of my aircraft. Simultaneously, the pilot of the observing Buccaneer transmitted, 'I think this is going to be a Mayday'. Moments later, my control column went completely slack, indicating that all pitch control had been lost. This was because, due to the aerodynamic forces imposed, the starboard tail plane had also gone. The tanker then started to go into a 'bunt' – an outside loop, imposing considerable stress on an airframe not designed for such a manoeuvre.

In the ensuing seconds, realising that control of the aircraft had gone, I ordered the crew to abandon the aircraft. Sadly, because of the high negative 'G' imposed on the aircraft, I knew that the chances of the three rear crew being able to leave the aircraft via the entrance door were minimal. The negative gravity would hold them against the roof of the cabin while they were trying to reach the door.

The co-pilot, apart from being small in stature, was not as tightly strapped into his seat as he should have been. As a result, being slightly unseated by the negative 'G', he was unable to reach either the handle above his head or the D-ring between his legs to operate the ejector mechanism. By this time, only seconds having elapsed and with the tanker approaching the underside of the looping manoeuvre, I had to make the decision to eject myself, no more than 2000 feet or so, above the sea.

Evidence at the subsequent Board of Inquiry suggested that I might have been blown out of the aircraft. However, it may have been coincidental, but I had two very bruised fingers to show that I had pulled the D ring between my legs.

My next recollection was of hanging in my parachute. On looking down, I saw a very wild sea. Around me I could see bits and pieces floating down. The aircraft had exploded in an enormous fireball, still carrying a large amount of fuel, and this was the after effects of the explosion.

Only a few weeks previously, I had carried out a dinghy drill, part of the annual training requirement, but conditions today were worse than usual. I released my dinghy pack on its lanyard and in a minute or two it entered the sea, whereupon I released my parachute harness. Upon surfacing, I was under the collapsed canopy. Having cleared this, I inflated the dinghy and eventually managed to climb in, not realising at the time that I had sustained severe back injuries from the '90 feet gun' of the ejection seat, and a damaged shoulder that had been wrenched during the escape.

With the canopy of the dinghy up and the majority of the sea water baled out, I noticed a ship two or three miles away. At the time, there was a twenty to thirty foot swell, so it was frequently out of view. Slowly, but surely, the German vessel, SS *Hoheburgh* edged towards me from an upwind position, the idea being to afford me shelter on the leeward side of the ship. By now, I had probably been in the sea for two hours or so, feeling very cold, as the leg of my immersion suit had been torn during the ejection, allowing sea-water to enter.

A rope was lowered from the *Hoheburgh*, but it was impossible for me to grip it, as my hands were so cold. Apart from this, one moment I could almost touch the ship's rail, the next it was fifteen to twenty feet above me. In retrospect, I have to admire the crew for positioning the ship, across wind, in gale force conditions, which was perilous to say the least. Having made a few attempts to grasp the rope, it was patently obvious to the crew of the *Hoheburgh* that I was not going to get onboard without assistance.

My last recollection, going in and out of consciousness, was of one of the Ship's life rafts being lowered into the sea, followed by its First Officer, Herr Ingolf Freireichs, jumping into the sea, attached to a rope and managing to get me into the life raft.

Meanwhile, an Air Sea Rescue Whirlwind had arrived, lowering Master Pilot Jeff Todd, who struggled to get me from the life raft into the helicopter, despite having sustained severe injuries himself from the battering of the sea. His is another story of courage and devotion to duty, for which I will be eternally grateful. In the space of three months, this rescue earned him a second Queen's Commendation for Valuable Service in the Air.

With no memory of the 170 mile journey to Scarborough hospital, I recall going down the hospital corridor with someone asking me for my name. It was Jeff Todd. After a few days, I was flown to the RAF Hospital at Ely in a Puma helicopter, a much smoother ride. Four months later, I was allowed to fly Chipmunks at Marham, where I was able to provide Air Experience to ATC cadets at Summer Camp. When another two months had elapsed, I was allowed, once again, to sit on an ejection seat, flying the Victor until my retirement twelve years later.

CYPRUS

Security Intelligence in Cyprus 1974

Squadron Leader John Walton

By 1974 the RAF Police had been carrying out Security Intelligence duties in Cyprus for many years. During the main EOKA campaign against the British occupation of the island in the 1950s, the RAF Police worked with British civil police seconded to the local Special Branch.

After independence in 1960, repeated inter-communal conflicts caused dangers to the very large number of British dependants living outside the Sovereign Base Areas (SBAs). Royal Air Force Police liaised closely with the Cyprus Police to provide the Commander British Forces Near East (CBFNE) with timely warnings of likely disturbances. In 1971, the first attacks by Arab terrorists on passenger aircraft occurred in the Middle East. Travel Control Security measures were therefore tightened up at RAF Akrotiri. After 1970, there was a significant increase in inter-factional incidents, as the Greek Cypriot right wing considered the Cyprus President (Archbishop Makarios), to be more and more pro-Soviet. In the early 1970s, there were several incidents involving Hostile Intelligence Services approaching RAF personnel, MOD locally employed civilians and British dependants.

In 1974 the threat was considered to be:

(a) Espionage and Subversion from the very well-established Hostile Intelligence Services.

(b) Danger to British personnel and dependants outside the SBA's from inter-communal and inter-factional disturbances.

(c) Attacks by terrorists (mainly Arab) on the SBA's (particularly aircraft at RAF Akrotiri) and assassination of British personnel.

In 1974 the 'Colonels' Junta' was in power in Greece, and was positively encouraging the EOKA B organisation in Cyprus in its opposition to the legitimate government of Makarios.

In Turkey, there was the traditional hawkish attitude of the military towards Greek, or Greek Cypriot expansionism.

In Cyprus, there had been few changes in the attitudes of the two very distinct communities, Greek and Turkish. After the widespread and bitter inter-communal disturbances of 1963/64, the official writ of the Cypriot Government did not run in many Turkish communities. Every town on the island had an area in which Turkish Cypriots lived a quite separate life from their Greek Cypriot neighbours. From the RAF Police point of view, this situation required us to liaise with two Police Forces: one quite open and official, the other, with considerable discretion.

EOKA B was becoming ever more daring and successful in blowing up police stations and attacking other government buildings and personnel. In retaliation, Makarios had formed a special section of the Police who acted as his personal bodyguard and as an anti-terrorist force. These people at times undoubtedly used excessive force and alienated many ordinary citizens. They were known as 'Makarios Black Berets', which referred to their distinctive head-dress.

The RAF Police personnel who carried out Security Intelligence Duties in Cyprus were never perceived as a threat by the regular Cyprus Police, the Greek National Guard, EOKA B, or any of the Turkish Cypriot Authorities.

The RAF Police had attended a Counter Intelligence course, but that is all. None of us were trained to speak Greek or Turkish. All were volunteers. All were Positively Vetted and were accompanied by their families. We had no telephones in married quarters at RAF Nicosia, Limassol, Famagusta or Larnaca. The vehicles we used were hire cars, which were generally under powered and quite old.

This lack of facilities further persuaded or convinced those for or against the *status quo* on the island that the RAF

Inter-communal riots Cyprus 1974 (RAF Police Archives)

Police posed no threat to them. An example of this was the direction to keep a certain Soviet Intelligence Colonel under general surveillance. He drove a high powered new Mercedes; the RAF Police were using elderly Volkswagen 'Beetles'!

If operational facilities were poor for counter espionage duties, they were improved when, in 1973, an assassination threat was perceived against British and American politicians. The RAF Police then had use of modern vehicles and the necessary communications and weapons. The main threat was seen to be against the British High Commissioner (Mr, later Sir, Stephen Oliver); the Administrator of the British Sovereign Base Areas and Commander British Forces in the Near East (Air Marshal Sir John Aiken), and the American Ambassador (who was later assassinated). This threat was understood and appreciated by all the Cypriot authorities to be very real. The personal protection measures introduced enabled RAF Police to observe quite overtly people and places hitherto considered off limits. The situation allowed for certain liaison duties to be more freely carried out: i.e. with the Central Intelligence Agency and the Cyprus Information Service (Special Branch).

Some of the long working day of RAF Police on Security Intelligence duties was spent in the less salubrious parts of Nicosia, Limassol, Larnaca and Famagusta. Under the guise of being on anti-vice and anti-drug duties, NCOs frequented many wine bars and spoke to the staff and the prostitutes who were based in some of the bars.

Through all of these contacts (both official and positively unofficial), the comings and goings on the island became known to us. Some movements of equipment and stores were noted. An estimate of how many local men had disappeared in late 1973 and early 1974 led to the conclusion that they were either in hiding on the island, or in Greece.

It was naturally impossible to verify most of our predictions during the weeks leading up to July 1974. In essence, our conclusions were that the illegal EOKA B, elements of the Greek National Guard (based on the island), and some of Cyprus Police, would soon attempt to remove the President by force. The precise date was probably known only to the mainland Greek Junta and very few others.

The British Intelligence Community in general terms did not accept our conclusions. With hindsight, it was probably because 'they' considered it highly unlikely that RAF Police would have sources which would know about a forthcoming coup. It was literally only days before the coup took place, that we were told 'The High Commissioner in Nicosia needs to know immediately'.

On the Saturday before the coup, several 'ordinary' Cypriots in Limassol told the RAF Police Security Intelligence NCOs that 'Next week there will be fighting on the streets'. On the Sunday, in a Turkish Cypriot kebab restaurant, both elements of the police (Greek and Turkish), sadly informed the RAF Police that 'tomorrow you will see blood on the streets of Limassol'. It was noted that these police officers (both inspectors) had always been moderate in their views.

All these messages were passed straight away to the responsible authorities at HQ BFNE at Episkopi. It is not known what, if any, action was taken. Shortly after 0700 hrs on Monday 15 July 1974, the RAF Police at Nicosia reported hearing shooting around the President's Palace. This was the beginning of the coup, which overthrew the President, who eventually escaped from the island via RAF Akrotiri.

During the morning of 15 July, hundred of members of the EOKA B, the Greek National Guard and the Cyprus Police took over Government Buildings, including police stations. They set up and manned roadblocks, looking in particular for the 'black berets' of the special force units, who all remained loyal to Makarios. Many members of the Cyprus Police simply either went home or stayed there for several days. They were not devotees of Makarios, but neither did they advocate his removal by force (or any other illegal means).

All plans to evacuate the large number of British dependants from their homes in Famagusta, Larnaca and Limassol were apparently based on the premise that any National emergency would occur outside the hours of 0730 and 1330. These were the hours when most servicemen were on duty inside the SBAs at Dhekelia and Episkopi/Akrotiri. Outside these hours, SNCO wardens were appointed to raise the alarm when necessary, and direct the evacuation of all British personnel and their dependants. As the coup occurred in effect after all servicemen had left for work as usual on a Monday morning, the many thousands of dependants were left alone in the three main dormitory towns.

During the day, RAF Police patrols reported fighting between those still loyal to the President and forces intent on changing the Government. Many of the 'unaccompanied' families were close to the fighting, and some were in physical danger from stray bullets and shrapnel. Roadblocks prevented British personnel from leaving the Western SBA at cease work (1330 hrs), and they spent an anxious night away from home.

The situation was intolerable and a way had to be found

to allow personnel to return home. During the evening a long-time source of the RAF Police was contacted. He arranged for the RAF Command Provost Marshal to meet with the Colonel commanding the Greek National Guard. As a direct result of that meeting, all personnel were allowed home on the Tuesday. All roadblocks were instructed to permit free passage to vehicles carrying British personnel, and generally speaking this happened without incident.

After the initial meeting with the National Guard Commander, frequent similar meetings were held to ensure smooth relations were maintained. It was during this period that we found out the true allegiances of many Greek Cypriot sources. New sources of information were introduced and some of the true 'ranks' and appointments of sources within EOKA B were revealed.

Although by Friday 19 July the situation seemed to have quietened down, life on the island was about to change, probably forever. Nicos Sampson was a young terrorist member of the original EOKA campaign against the British 'occupation' of Cyprus. He was also alleged to have committed atrocities against the Turkish Cypriots in the 1963/64 disturbances. While Makarios was President, Sampson ran an extreme right wing newspaper, constantly criticising the Government, advocating closer ties with Greece and using adverse propaganda against the Turkish Cypriot population.

For several years, Glafcos Clerides representing the Greek Cypriots, and Rauf Denktash the Turkish Cypriots, were in negotiations about political life on the island. Both were generally seen as moderates and if Clerides had been installed as acting President, most RAF Police sources agreed that the mainland Turkish invasion of Cyprus, might not have taken place. But instead, Nicos Sampson became President.

Immediately Turkey declared it was a gross breach of the 1960 tripartite agreement between Greece, Turkey and Britain, which guaranteed the 'sovereignty, independence and territorial integrity' of Cyprus. Turkey demanded that Britain should act to ensure the safety of Turkish Cypriots and at the same time prepared to invade the island. Britain was perceived to be doing nothing and the Turkish fleet sailed on the Friday.

The evacuation of tens of thousands of British personnel and their families principally from Famagusta and Limassol began early on Saturday 20 July. RAF Police forces helped to ensure safe passage for many families who were trapped in their homes by cross fire between right wing Greek Cypriots and Turkish Cypriot police and irregulars. Some quite astonishing scenes were witnessed.

As both sides stopped firing, unarmed RAF Police patrols escorted families (one Land-Rover had eleven women and children in it) out of the area, and then firing resumed.

All over the island as the Turkish forces attacked in the north, Greek and Turkish Cypriots fought in divided towns and villages. For the time being the Greek Cypriots united against the old enemy. At first the Greek Cypriots had a fairly easy time, but eventually the old fears about the cruelty and efficiency of the Turkish forces showed clearly. Many Greek Cypriot sources begged us to 'ask your big General to take over Limassol and Larnaca'. Some moderate sources assisted the UN Commander in Limassol, the RAF Command Provost Marshal, and the Turkish Cypriot Western SBA Administrator to negotiate a cease-fire in the area. The same sources ensured reasonable treatment of the Limassol Turkish Cypriot population, which was herded into the football stadium on the Saturday evening. Eventually when these people were housed in a school in Limassol, the sources usually assisted the RAF Police in obtaining answers to enquiries about individual Turkish Cypriots.

After the British families were evacuated to the UK on 14, 15 and 16 August, Greek Cypriot sources were helpful, so that CBFNE could gauge the mood of the population (and EOKA B) towards the eventual evacuation of all Turkish Cypriots in the South and West.

When the Turks invaded, Sampson removed himself from the Presidency and he was replaced as acting President by Clerides. After the island was divided into one third Turkish and two thirds Greek, the general situation quietened down. The old, and some new, sources passed on information discovered in former Turkish Cypriot areas. They were again helpful to us in gauging the mood of the people when reports began to circulate that Makarios would return as the President.

When this happened via Akrotiri, there were many adverse comments from right wing sources, as there had been when he escaped. In general, however, the sources of all descriptions continued to be helpful, particularly where the threat of Arab terrorism was concerned.

For over twenty years before 1974, the RAF Police cultivated many sources of information from all walks of life, in both the Greek and Turkish communities in Cyprus. By 1974 we were producing high-grade information of great use to the CBFNE. Despite this, the information was not always officially assessed as being reliable. During and after the coup and invasion, these sources proved the soundness of the opinion that 'if you look after your sources in peace, they will look after you in war'.

The Falklands Campaign 1982

On 2 April 1982 Argentinian forces seized the Falklands Islands. The British response was rapid and within days the Atlantic taskforce set sail. On 1 May a Vulcan bomber bombed Port Stanley airfield.

The massive British response resulted in Argentinian surrender little more than ten weeks after the initial invasion.

The immensities of the logistical and other problems facing the Royal Air Force are described in the following accounts by key players in the conflict.

The RAF Contribution to Victory in The Falklands

Air Marshal Sir John Curtiss KCB KBE

When the crisis in the South Atlantic arose in April 1982 I was the AOC No. 18 Group with my Headquarters at Northwood alongside the HQ of Commander-in-Chief Fleet, the Senior Naval Operational Commander. At that time the forces allocated to me consisted of Nimrod Mk 2 Maritime Patrol aircraft, Canberra reconnaissance and training aircraft and a mixed force of Sea King and Wessex helicopters for Air Sea rescue.

As soon as the Government authorised the formation of a Naval Task Force to reclaim the Falklands, C-in-C Fleet, Admiral Sir John Fieldhouse formed the FLAIR Committee (Flag & Air Officers) for the overall conduct of operations against the Argentine forces. I became the Air Commander and Deputy C-in-C. A few weeks later General Moore, who would go on to command all the land forces, joined the Committee which then became the FLAIRGO (Flag, Air and General Officers Committee).

As Air Commander, a large range of front line aircraft were placed under my operational command: Harriers, Chinooks, Vulcans, Victor tankers, Hercules and Phantoms. Also in the course of the campaign numerous Staff Officers were seconded onto my staff to provide the necessary expertise in all these roles. It was also fortunate for me that during my career I had flown with every operational Command.

In remarkably short time a Fleet (TF 617) was assembled and sailed for the Falklands via the island of Ascension, a British possession, fortuitously lying almost exactly half way along the 8000 miles that separated the UK from the Falklands. Without this island's one long runway and small aircraft parking area, our capability to support the Task Force would have been minimal.

During the time it took the Task Force to reach Ascension, Nimrods of 18 Group were carrying out maritime reconnaissance sorties in support. Royal Air Force Hercules, supplemented by civilian Belfasts, had been carrying supplies to Ascension to be loaded by helicopter onto the ships of the Task Force. The haste in despatching the Fleet meant that much cross loading between ships, and additional supplies, were needed to achieve tactical loading in preparation to retaking the Islands.

The presence of the Task Group at Ascension allowed for a final planning meeting of all the Commanders. Plans for retaking the Islands were discussed in great detail although at that time negotiations were still going on and the Government had not decided on the final outcome.

When the Task Force sailed on from Ascension towards the South Atlantic the Nimrod Maritime Patrol Aircraft could only reach about 1800 miles south, leaving another 2000 miles beyond their range. But rapid strides had been made to convert them and other air assets to in-flight refuelling. Before the Nimrods were modified it had been necessary to use the Victor Tanker Force to carry out the reconnaissance of approaches to South Georgia before its recapture by the Royal Navy.

Flight Refuelling, the vital ingredient of the air war in the South Atlantic has been fully dealt with in a separate article by Air Vice-Marshal George Chesworth, my Chief of Staff at 18 Group, and an invaluable member of the Falklands team. Suffice to say that it soon brought the Falklands within range of the Nimrod, Hercules, Vulcan and Harrier.

Once the Task Force had reached the area around the Falklands, RAF aircraft were required for a variety of tasks in their support: the Nimrods to patrol the Argentine coast to keep watch for any movements by the Argentine Fleet; the Vulcans to attack Port Stanley Airfield; the Argentine radar that kept watch on our Task Force and which was responsible for helping to guide the Exocet attacks; the Hercules to carry vital supplies and mail to the Fleet; and Harriers to reinforce the RN and RAF Squadrons already embarked in the Carriers.

These many tasks exposed the limitations of the single runway and very limited parking spaces available on Ascension. As the island is, in geological terms, a relatively young volcanic island, devoid of grass and covered in volcanic dust and rubble it was only possible to park aircraft or helicopters on hard standings. The wide variety of long range tasks required the continuous presence of a large number of Tanker aircraft and it was just not possible to deploy all the aircraft needed to Ascension at one time. This imposed a severe restraint on our operations as it meant that decisions on the priority of tasks had to be made some days in advance so that the right assets were available on Ascension.

Did the immediate situation require Long Range Maritime Reconnaissance of the waters around the Falklands? An attack on the airfield at Port Stanley? Or was there a urgent requirement for spares to be dropped to the Task Force? The last option became independent of the Victors, once the Hercules modified as a tanker became available.

The priorities were decided by the Commander-in-Chief and myself with reference to the Task Force Commander in the South Atlantic. It permitted little short term flexibility to get the right aircraft to Ascension. Those with a lesser priority had to be deployed, at least temporarily, to Gibraltar or to airfields in the UK.

To make matters worse I was concerned about the security of Ascension: a vital base and an irreplaceable asset. An air or sea attack by an enterprising opponent could have had a catastrophic effect, so I added two Phantom air defence aircraft and an RAF Regiment Squadron to our defences. The RN provided a guard Frigate.

Fuel, water and accommodation on Ascension were also extremely short.

The island prior to this conflict only existed as long-range communications base and mid down range facility for the Cape Kennedy missile testing. The airfield had been leased to the USAF for some years. Co-operation with the Americans was extremely good, and by permanently stationing an oil and a water tanker off the island we were just able to sustain our air operations. Since the war it has remained an essential link with the British garrison, using flight-refuelled Hercules, and later VC 10s and TriStars, for all logistic and personnel support to the Islands.

Canberra *at South Georgia (Sir John Curtiss)*

I believe it is interesting to relate here the manner in which the Government made the decision to land our forces and retake the Falklands. On 14 May 1982 the Northwood Flag, Air and General Officers Committee was summoned to the Cabinet Office to give the Prime Minister and her War Cabinet a briefing on our plans for the assault.

The briefing was kept short and succinct, each of us giving our portion of the overall plan, which was then summed up by John Fieldhouse, our C-in-C. The first question was from the Prime Minister who wanted to know what casualties we expected.

Bear in mind here that military wisdom suggests that the invading force should be twice as big as the defending forces. In the Falklands this was reversed. We had about 5000 men as against 10,000 Argentinians. We did not have total air superiority as on D-day. We told the Cabinet a maximum of 5000. A figure plucked out of the air. There were a number of other questions but when Willie Whitelaw, the Deputy Prime Minister with an excellent war record, asked what plans we had to deal with POWs we somehow knew the decision had been made.

Once the landings had been accomplished, victory followed quickly. The Argentine troops, comprising mainly conscripts backed up by elite regular forces, were no match for our highly skilled and motivated Armed Forces of all three Services and the Merchant Navy. Although demonstrating considerable bravery and determination the Argentine Air Force lacked the weapons and the operational training of our Navy and Air Force aviators. In addition, once the Vulcans had demonstrated their capability for record-breaking long-range bombing operations, the Argentine Mirage air defence fighters were withdrawn to defend Buenos Aires from possible attack. This meant that their fighter bombers had no escort to defend them against the Sea Harriers.

Although this campaign ran counter to all our defence policies and plans it still left us with valuable lessons for the future. In the first place although the 'ad hoc' Headquarters arrangements for the direction of the campaign worked surprisingly well, there was an obvious requirement for more comprehensive contingency planning. This lesson has since been covered by the permanent establishment of a Joint Force Headquarters at Northwood.

The vital importance of having 'in flight refuelling' for all our operational aircraft was clearly established. Without it the RAF was impotent at long range.

Above all the value of realistic operational training was underlined in every aspect. All our forces demonstrated their professional superiority at every level. For the Royal Air Force the sheer flexibility and determination of our aircrew was beyond price. Harrier pilots trained and deployed in Central Europe for operations against land targets converted in just three weeks to a carrier-borne air defence role, and demonstrated the capability to deploy over four thousand miles of sea to land on an aircraft carrier in the South Atlantic. Vulcan crews, trained for overland operations in Europe, were converted in a matter of weeks to in-flight refuelled bombing operations against a small target demanding a round trip of over 8000 miles and involving up to seven airborne refuellings. Victor tanker crews flew countless sorties over vast distances with great precision. Hercules crews flew sorties extending over twenty-four hours in order to carry vital spares and mail to the task force, and Nimrod crews flew long-range reconnaissance sorties close to the Argentine coastline of over nineteen hours. Our only aircraft losses were to enemy action. Nor should we forget the remarkable efforts of the engineers, from industry to the front line, in modifying our aircraft for in-flight refuelling, and to enable them to carry new and improved weapons. All in record-breaking time.

Overall it was a fine example of close inter Service co-operation at all levels, high morale and professionalism. It sent a message to the world that Great Britain would not tolerate military dictatorships and the invasion of peaceful territories.

The Vital Importance of Air-to-Air Refuelling

Air Vice-Marshal George Chesworth CB CBE DFC

The achievements, exploits and heroism of the Marines, Paratroops and other Ground Forces and the vital role of the Royal Navy in the Falklands Campaign are well documented. The RAF's contribution to the success of the campaign is less well reported.

There was, and is, a tendency to assume that the RAF will always be available and able, in one form or another, to join the battle wherever it takes place. Indeed the light blue contribution is usually, and correctly, taken for granted. In the 1960s and '70s – even the beginning of the '80s – this, generally speaking, did not present a problem. The RAF, like the rest of the British Forces, were equipped to counter the Warsaw Pact countries as part of the overall NATO Alliance. This called for a campaign fought over short to medium range, with the air effort being mounted from a multitude of well equipped bases supported along relatively short supply lines.

The Argentinian invasion of South Georgia and the Falkland Islands changed all that for all three arms of the Services – not least the RAF. This campaign was to be a purely national effort with the area of operations some 8000 miles from the UK. The only base for land-based air operations, general logistic support and resupply was Ascension Island – just about half way between the UK and the Falklands.

The successful conduct of air operations over such long distances called for very significant use of in-flight air-to-air refuelling (AAR). Unfortunately, the RAF's capability in this field was very limited, because previous scenarios had not envisaged it would be required except to support fighter type aircraft.

We at Northwood had, therefore, to re-examine urgently the problems of air-to-air refuelling under very different circumstances, and find ways of enhancing the flexibility and improving the overall capabilities of the RAF. While this account deals only with operations from Ascension, extensive use was also made of AAR between the UK and Ascension at all stages of the campaign.

At the beginning of April 1982 the only RAF aircraft capable of carrying and dispensing significant quantities of fuel was the Victor K2 (it could also receive fuel). Aircraft equipped to receive fuel were the Phantom, Harrier, Sea Harrier and Buccaneer. The airborne refuelling system in the Vulcan had been out of use for many years and was no longer functional.

Herculean efforts were demanded from RAF and civilian engineers, both within industry and the Service, to design and produce equipment and to modify aircraft. Similarly, the creation of new procedures and the training of air and ground crews was another mammoth task which is often overlooked – even forgotten.

These problems were solved, and by the end of the month Victors had flown reconnaissance missions to South Georgia, and a Vulcan had attacked Port Stanley; by mid-May the Nimrod and Hercules were operating over the South Atlantic using AAR. In the weeks that followed, both Vulcan and Hercules were further modified to allow them also to operate as tankers. This reflected enormous credit on all concerned, including the crews who flew the aircraft and the expert, dedicated ground tradesmen who serviced them.

The first five Victors arrived at Ascension Island (ASI) on 18 April; four more came the following day and commenced operations at night. This was not, however, an AAR task but the first of a series of radar reconnaissance sorties in support of the small RN Task Group which had left the main fleet to repossess South Georgia. The Victors, at that time the only aircraft with the range, flew three fourteen-hour missions between 19 and 25 April to provide the Task Group commander with valuable intelligence about surface contacts, icebergs and pack ice in the vicinity of the island. Each sortie required four tankers outbound and the same number for the return to Ascension Island.

Approaching VC10 from Nimrod Flight Deck (Crown copyright)

The radar reconnaissance capability of the Victor was retained throughout the campaign but the advent of the air-to-air refuelling Nimrod with its superior radar allowed the Victor to be dedicated to its primary, and vital, airborne tanker role.

On behalf of the Air Commander, I now flew down to Ascension to monitor the first operations.

At 0425 hrs local time on the morning of 1 May, a Vulcan captained by Flight Lieutenant Martin Withers opened the UK's action against the Argentinians on the Falkland Islands by attacking Port Stanley airfield with a stick of twenty-one 1000 lb bombs. A large crater was made in the runway: Argentinian ears rang and morale dampened in both Stanley and Buenos Aires; and the Falkland Islanders realised that liberation had begun.

To achieve this successful attack two Vulcans and eleven Victors had taken off from Ascension some eight hours earlier. The thirteen aircraft were launched into the night at one minute intervals in radio silence, as a Soviet intelligence gathering ship was positioned some three miles off the end of the runway. One Vulcan and one Victor were airborne reserves: both were needed. One Victor could not reel out its centre hose to transfer fuel, and the cabin of the primary bombing Vulcan refused to pressurise. Flight Lieutenant Withers, in the reserve Vulcan, was therefore to bomb Port Stanley. The ten tankers and the lone bomber formed themselves into a loose formation and began the long flight south. The problems which arose on the long flight are described in following accounts.

The Vulcan and the sole remaining Victor continued south to the last refuelling point before the target, 400 miles north of Port Stanley. On its way south the force had used more fuel than expected; this, it transpired after consultation with his Vulcan counterpart, left the captain of the Victor, Squadron Leader Bob Tuxford, with a difficult decision. He did not have sufficient remaining fuel to transfer to allow the

Vulcan to complete its mission and enable him to return to Ascension. He knew that if he passed the Vulcan what it required he would not be able to explain his predicament to Ascension for several hours, that it would then be necessary to scramble a tanker, effect a rendezvous and carry out a successful refuelling – after being airborne for some fifteen hours. If anyone of the conditions was not met he would crash into the sea about 400 miles south of Ascension.

Tuxford dutifully filled the Vulcan's tanks, turned for home and crossed his fingers for another seven hours or so.

Flight Lieutenant Withers meantime continued towards his target, reducing height as he approached the Falklands to keep below the enemy radar. Shortly before reaching the Islands he climbed to 10,000 feet for the final run to the airfield at Port Stanley. After releasing his bombs he turned for the long flight back to Ascension via a point to the east of Rio de Janeiro where he was refuelled for the last time by yet another Victor. This tanker, one of four launched from Ascension, brought to fifteen the number of Victors used in this first attack on Stanley.

Withers landed in Ascension after a flight lasting just over sixteen hours. Squadron Leader Tuxford's luck held. He contacted Ascension where, by dint of a lot of hard work by the ground crew, and re-tasking a crew who had already flown, a tanker was launched and in position for him to refuel and land safely, shortly before Withers.

For their parts in this epic and pioneering operation Flight Lieutenant Withers was awarded the Distinguished Flying Cross and Squadron Leader Tuxford received the Air Force Cross.

Shortly after carrying out his attack, and long before Tuxford's problems were known, Withers signalled its completion to Ascension, where the first concerns over the high fuel consumption were beginning to sink in. Until this could be analysed it would not be possible to plan another sortie as was being called for by the Air Commander in Northwood who, once he knew of this first success, naturally wanted to repeat the treatment.

When all the crews had been debriefed and their flight records examined, it became apparent that the higher than planned for consumption was, in the main, the result of the two types of aircraft flying in formation at a compromise speed and height. This meant that neither the Vulcan nor Victor were operating at optimum conditions. Over the very long distances and flight times involved, which had never been flown before, even small errors in planning assumptions were cumulative and normal reserves became inadequate. Once this was appreciated new procedures were devised. Where dissimilar aircraft were operating together, each would transit at their optimum speed and altitude, flying together only during actual refuelling. This procedure was used on the second raid against Stanley on 4 May and for all other air-to-air refuelling operations of the campaign: no further problems of a similar nature were experienced. Any air-to-air refuelling supported operation required a very detailed plan to be drawn up, and checked and rechecked by the UK-based specialist staffs and the planners at Ascension. Generally speaking, all operations involving air-to-air refuelling since that time have used these in-flight procedures. The only variation is when the tanker is also acting as escort to the receiving aircraft.

Until the Task Force was some 2000 miles south of Ascension the Nimrod Mk 2 was able to provide surface surveillance using its sophisticated radar while flying at high level. To enable Nimrod to support the Navy beyond this range at either high or low level the aircraft needed to refuel in flight. Modifications to provide that capability were authorised on 17 April. The first modified aircraft, designated the Nimrod 2P, was delivered to Kinloss on 3 May and deployed to Ascension, together with trained crews, four days later. Nimrod started air-to-air refuelling supported operations on 9 May.

At 0430 hrs local time on 21 May, the main landings at San Carlos and Ajax Bay were started. As part of the preparations for this most critical phase of the campaign, Nimrod 2Ps made long-range patrols which penetrated the sea areas between the enemy naval bases and the Falkland Islands, to ensure that the Task Force and the nuclear submarines had the earliest possible warning of any Argentine naval units leaving the twelve mile limit. It has often been stated that the sinking of the *General Belgrano* on 3 May had effectively guaranteed the Argentine Navy's withdrawal from the campaign. This may well have been the enemy's or even some armchair commentator's perception, but no commander at Northwood or at sea was prepared to plan on such a bold assumption at the time. The Nimrod's ability, refuelled by the faithful Victor, to make those nineteen-hour searches on Argentina's doorstep was a most welcome and reassuring asset.

The RAF Harrier GR3s, operating from the carriers of the Task Force, provided close support to the land forces ashore, and lost several aircraft and had others damaged in the process. As replacements were urgently required it was decided to fly four aircraft direct from Ascension to the carriers. Two Harriers arrived on 2 June, after a remarkable nine-hour Victor-supported flight.

Nimrods provided airborne Search and Rescue (SAR) and ships along the route kept listening watch, with RFA *Engadine* acting as an emergency landing platform half-way down track. However, there was no suitable mid-way landing platform on 8 June when the other two GR3's took the same long route, with Search and Rescue cover being extended by using long range Hercules in addition to the Nimrod.

By the end of May some Vulcans had been equipped as tankers and took their place in the order of battle at Ascension. This provided some temporary respite for the Victors and their overworked air and ground crews. It also allowed some Victors to return to the UK for long-overdue servicing which could not be carried out at Ascension because of lack of space and facilities.

The AAR-capable Hercules were by now regularly dropping urgent spares, supplies and mail to the Task Force off the Falklands as a matter of routine. These flights, often of twenty-five hour duration, continued after the Argentinian surrender, with the drops made overland until the runway at Port Stanley had been cleared. When the runway was re-opened the Hercules still required tanker support, as it had to be able to return to Ascension in the event that weather prevented it landing at Falkland. On the longest trip the Hercules spent twenty-five hours in the air during the flight

Ascension–Port Stanley–Ascension.

This short account can but give a glimpse of some of the achievements made possible by the use of air-to-air refuelling. This was already a well known capability in 1982 but it had been judged unnecessary, or too expensive, for some aircraft until then. It took a war to prove it was a vital requirement for all front line aircraft and, importantly, to make all the resources available to introduce it in a quite remarkable time scale.

The final accolade must go to the air and ground crews of the Victor force who bore the brunt of the load throughout the campaign.

The Role of the Harrier

Air Chief Marshal Sir Peter Squire GCB DFC AFC

When news of the Argentinian invasion of the Falkland Islands was announced, on 2 April 1982, the crews of No. 1 (Fighter) Squadron were deeply involved in preparing for a major exercise in Canada. The first question that came to everybody's mind was the inevitable and ignorant 'Where are the Falkland Islands?' Having glanced at a map and seen the distances involved, it seemed to me that, if we were to become embroiled as a unit, being held in reserve at Rio offered the only reasonable option. As that was quite beyond the bounds of possibility, we got back to planning our Canadian deployment.

That said, and although based in the UK, No. 1 (F) Squadron was roled as an air mobile unit: it would always deploy elsewhere in times of tension. At that time it was declared to NATO as a reinforcement squadron with deployment options in both the Northern and Central Regions of Allied Command Europe (ACE). As such, the Squadron had to be capable of autonomous operations from a 'Bare Base', that is without any form of host nation assistance.

Combat support for the unit included teams of Royal Engineer 'Sappers' to build operating surfaces, together with members of Tactical Supply Wing and Tactical Communications Wing to provide fuel and communications respectively; as well as the Mobile Catering Support Unit to look after the inner man. Because of this capability for Bare Base operations, it was not, therefore, altogether surprising that the Squadron should become involved in the South Atlantic Campaign, although if anyone had told me in March of 1982, when deployed to N Norway, that within 2 months we would be fighting a war from an aircraft carrier some 8000 miles from home, I frankly would not have believed them.

A warning order issued on 8 April, however, directed the Squadron to prepare for operations from a carrier as attrition replacements for Sea Harrier battle losses. Modification of the aircraft was the first major task. A number of 'navalisation' modifications were required as a first priority: these included the fitting of shackles on to the outriggers for lashing-down, anti-corrosion treatment, and the fitting of specialist transponder equipment to assist recoveries to the carrier in bad weather. The then Royal Air Force Harrier – the GR3 – was bought as an attack aircraft with only integral guns for self-defence.

If we were to be used to replace Sea Harriers, a better air defence capability would be required, and so within a few days of receiving the initial warning order, both industry and the Service were working twenty-four hours a day in order to give the aircraft an air-to-air missile fit. Thanks to a great deal of effort and ingenuity, our aircraft were equipped for Sidewinder, and the system proved and tested within two weeks.

Further modifications which were later incorporated to increase the aircraft's capability included the installation of a flare and chaff dispenser, an active I-Band Jammer and the ability to carry and fire the SHRIKE Anti-Radiation Missiles, used for attacking enemy ground based radars.

While the modification programme was being carried out, nominated pilots went through an intensive work-up programme. This included realistic air combat training against Mirage and Etendard aircraft provided by the French Air Force, air-to-air missile firing – of which none of the pilots had previous experience, operational weapon delivery profiles, operational low flying and initiation into the Ski-Jump Club.

At the same time as we were given our warning order to prepare, work began to find a means of getting the reinforcement aircraft, which would include not only the Squadron's GR3s but also additional Sea Harriers and helicopters, south to the Total Exclusion Zone (TEZ). After a detailed inspection, it was decided that the container ship, *Atlantic Conveyor*, would provide a very good platform for this role. Work required was relatively straightforward, and the ship was ready to sail, its five car decks having been loaded with enormous quantities of stores, weapons, food and clothing, less than two weeks after the decision to use it had been made.

The helicopters were loaded in the UK but the GR3s and Sea Harriers were flown to Ascension using in-flight refuelling. The GR3s were able to accomplish this 4000-mile leg in one hop, thus creating new milestones in single seat ferry flight times of over nine hours. Once at Ascension, the aircraft were flown onto the Atlantic Conveyor and tightly parked in the aircraft 'hide', which had been built between the walls of containers. The aircraft were also bagged to give added protection against salt water.

With a total of fourteen Harriers and ten Helicopters embarked this was a very valuable target, and during the passage south one Sea Harrier was kept at a high state of readiness for air defence duties against the Argentinian 707 used for long range reconnaissance. For the first few days, tanker support was also available to give the Sea Harrier additional radius of action. The very use of a Container Ship as a carrier of aircraft, let alone the ability to mount albeit limited offensive operations from it, is a hallmark of the Harrier's enormous flexibility.

Having left Ascension on the evening of 7 May, the *Atlantic Conveyor*, in company with other ships of the Amphibious Group, made a rendezvous with the Task Force on 18 May and the Harriers were transferred to the two carriers: ten to *Hermes* and four to *Invincible*. All the GR3s went to *Hermes* and, although none of the 1 (F) Squadron pilots had operated from a ship before, after just one day of work-up training the Squadron flew its first operational sorties on 20 May.

In the two weeks between the arrival of the Task Force in the TEZ and our arrival, no Sea Harriers had been lost in air combat and so, instead of being replacements, the GR3s were used as reinforcements and rightly dedicated to the attack role. In this capacity the full gamut of offensive support missions were carried out, ranging from offensive counter-air, to close air support and armed reconnaissance.

The aims of our offensive counter air missions were twofold: firstly to deny the use of Stanley airfield and the various outlying strips; and secondly to destroy aircraft in the open. Low level laydown deliveries were flown against a number of airstrips such as Goose Green, while against the runway at Stanley a great variety of profiles was used. Laydown attacks were successful in hitting the runway but in the process the aircraft were particularly vulnerable to the Argentinian air defences, and the resulting damage not very extensive. On the other hand, while high angle and loft deliveries kept aircraft out of range from ground defences, the accuracy of weapon delivery was poor. In the event, the runway remained open to Hercules and Pucara type aircraft, but the Argentinians were not able to use the airfield as a forward operating base for fighter bomber aircraft – and that was the Task Force's main concern. At the same time, however, the Argentinians went to some lengths to deceive our reconnaissance efforts, by both making the runway appear to be more extensively cratered than it was, and by placing decoys at the edge of the runway to simulate aircraft at high readiness states.

On one occasion, these were attacked as possible Etendards, although in the event they proved to be Aermacchi aircraft, standing on metal planking, which had been laid in the shape of swept wing aircraft.

For its attack tasks, the GR3 carried and delivered a variety of weapons, including cluster bombs, 2 inch rockets, 1000 lb bombs; and towards the end of the conflict the laser-guided bomb (LGB). The cluster bomb had a marked effect against troops in defensive positions, both in creating casualties and in the lowering of morale. This was particularly true in the battle for Goose Green, where the missions flown in close support of the 2nd Parachute Battalion had a significant effect on the outcome of that engagement. It was also a highly effective weapon against storage areas, such as fuel, and against helicopters caught on the ground.

Regrettably, the full potential of the LGB could not be made use of until just one day before the cease-fire. It was not until then that the hand-held laser target markers were positioned at the right time and place. However, four bombs delivered from the loft profiles that day achieved two direct hits on pinpoint targets and served notice on the Argentinians that we now had a weapon of extreme accuracy. This may well have been one of the factors that swayed their decision to surrender so quickly.

Wing Commander Peter Squire on return from the Falklands (Sir Peter Squire)

The GR3 was also capable of carrying a reconnaissance pod equipped with a fan of five cameras, giving horizon to horizon cover. Using this capability and the organic processing facilities within *Hermes*, the GR3 was able to find concentrations of enemy defensive positions and other lucrative targets. With so few aircraft available, however, and more than enough tasks to be met, this capability was not fully utilised.

Shortly after the landings in San Carlos Water, a Harrier Forward Operating Base (FOB) was built close to one of the settlements. Refuelling facilities were available and up to four aircraft could be parked on the strip at anyone time. As a rule, two GR3s were detached on a daily basis to provide quick reaction support for ground forces, while the Sea Harriers used it extensively in order to lengthen significantly their time on combat air patrol.

It would, however, be quite wrong to suggest that we had it all our own way. Indeed the loss of one aircraft on the second day of operations was a swift reminder that we were unlikely to come through unscathed. Experience quickly showed that the greatest threat was from ground-to-air weapons, which varied from surface-to-air missiles to small arms fire. The two major SAM systems were Roland and Tiger Cat, and it was known where these were located. We therefore planned to fly outside or below their respective engagement zones and, although substantial number of both types of missile were launched at us, none was successful. The remaining SAM threat came from the shoulder-launched variety, which were in plentiful supply – both Blowpipe II and the Russian SAM 7. Again our tactics, this time of flying very low and fast, seemed to negate the threat, although it is possible that the first of our aircraft to be shot down was engaged by Blowpipe.

The Argentinians were also equipped with a large quantity of AAA Guns ranging from 20 mm to 35 mm, some of which were linked to fire control radars. Although these tended to be sited in known areas, they posed a high threat to our aircraft and, indeed, a second aircraft was lost during the attack on Goose Green.

However, what hit us most frequently were small arms rounds; and in the latter stages of the campaign, when almost every mission took us close to Stanley, of every pair of aircraft launched one would return with holes. Apart from one aircraft which had a massive fuel leak and just failed to make it back to the carrier, all the others returned safely, and this was very encouraging as it had been thought that the aircraft might be somewhat fragile to battle damage. Not only did this prove to be incorrect, but once back on board the Squadron's engineers, with assistance from naval colleagues, were able to effect some ingenious repairs, and no aircraft spent longer than forty-eight hours in the hangar before it was flying again.

As a result of our losses, which by 8 June had totalled four – the fourth being a crash landing at the FOB – replacements were flown direct from Ascension to the Task Force using in-flight refuelling: long and apprehensive flights indeed for pilots who, without diversions *en-route*, had eight hours to prepare for their first ever deck landing.

Following the cease-fire, a full site was built ashore at Port Stanley, and on 4 July the GR3 detachment, now armed with Sidewinders and in the air defence role, went ashore and, despite atrocious conditions early on, maintained a presence at RAF Stanley until May '85, when the airfield at Mount Pleasant was opened.

Raid on Port Stanley

Squadron Leader Martin Withers DFC

The Air Force Board considered the Vulcan to be too slow, vulnerable and inaccurate to be used in anything other than a low-level nuclear strike role. In this latter role, it was considered a valuable part of NATO's inventory.

In 1982, none of the Vulcan crews expected to be asked to fly to the Falklands and attempt to cripple a runway with one stick of bombs.

A low-level attack, flown at 300 feet and about 360 knots, would have made the large aircraft very vulnerable to the Argentinian radar-guided anti-aircraft guns and their Roland surface-to-air missile system (the existence of which we only learnt about after the first attack). But of greater significance, any bomb released from low-level would have done little damage to a runway surface, because the bomb has to use a drogue to retard it as it falls to ensure that it explodes behind the aircraft. Only when dropping from more than 8000 feet above the target could the bomb be allowed to 'freefall' at high velocity and penetrate the runway before detonation, to produce a deep crater up to sixty feet in diameter.

By the end of the conflict, Harriers were armed with laser-guided bombs which could possibly have been tossed at the runway to inflict more damage than a low-level release, but these were not available initially, nor did the Task Force have the means to 'mark' the target for such weapons. So the Vulcan was selected for the task.

This would involve every available Victor tanker to escort just one bomber on its 8000 mile journey to drop a stick of twenty-one bombs, spaced to land about 100 feet apart, on an attack track of thirty degrees offset to the 150 foot wide runway at Port Stanley; with the aim of placing one or two bombs at least one third of the way along it, to deny its use to Argentinian fighter aircraft. This was achieved on the first attack, 'Black Buck 1', on 1 May 1982.

A little over two weeks earlier, my crew had been selected as one of four to train in air-to-air refuelling and conventional bombing techniques, with a view to supporting the Task Force in some way, down in the South Atlantic.

We began to train hard. There was only time to teach the air-to-air refuelling to the captains on each crew, then we practised bombing at night with real 1000 lb bombs: a first for many crew-members. New skills and techniques were rapidly absorbed and the aircraft was fitted with new navigational and electronic jamming equipment. Then we were off to Ascension Island.

My crew were to be the Reserve Crew for the Port Stanley raid. Because the Vulcan pilots lacked experience in air-to-air refuelling, and the complexity of the plan to refuel us on the seven hour flight from Ascension Island, it was decided to include a Victor refuelling instructor on each Vulcan crew.

There was no time for sightseeing. The next morning it was confirmed that 'Black Buck 1' was scheduled to take off at 11 p.m. that night. We rested as much as possible in preparation for a flight of more than fifteen hours!

More than eighty aircrew were present at the briefing, which covered the details of the take-off, refuelling plan, diversion, escape and evasion over the Falklands, and communications procedures. Crews individually completed their preparations and crew briefs, then quite casually walked out to their aircraft, trying to stay as cool as possible, dressed for survival in the South Atlantic ocean complete with thermal underwear under the rubber immersion suits, in the tropical temperature of about 30° Celsius.

In total radio silence, because a Russian spy trawler was stationed just off Ascension Island and could have relayed details of our radio transmissions to the enemy, the aircraft started up and taxied out to the runway. Four Victors followed by the two Vulcans, then a further seven Victors forming the first wave, took off at one-minute intervals, circled overhead, joined up into individual formations required by the refuelling plan, and headed south.

Within the formation was a reserve tanker and a reserve bomber, the latter flown by my crew. We expected to accompany the primary Vulcan to his first refuelling rendezvous, about two hours into the flight, and then as soon as he had started to take on fuel our task would be over and we would turn back to Ascension Island and land. But we did not have to wait that long before discovering that we had taken over as the one going all the way. The Primary aircraft developed a problem just after take off, and would not pressurise. They could not continue and broke radio silence to inform us that we were to take their place.

Suddenly the prospect of a beer in the bar had stretched from four to sixteen or more hours, and we were launching off into the night for the first time in the company of a large group of other aircraft, with few lights and no radio communications. As we approached designated positions, the Victor we were following would extend his hose and we would take up position behind and just below, ready to join up and take on fuel as soon as the little green light was illuminated. Then it was important to remain connected to the tanker, keeping our tanks topped up – right up to the planned geographical position relating to the end of the refuelling 'bracket'. Separating early would mean less fuel in the tanks at the next refuelling bracket with a different tanker. Typically, at this point the red light would illuminate, the hose would retract, and the tanker would head for home, with very little spare fuel, if any, for himself.

During this high level transit which lasted approximately seven hours, the Vulcan was planned to refuel five times, to ensure that we had sufficient fuel remaining in the tanks at all times, either to return to Ascension Island, or to divert to Rio de Janeiro. At the same time, Victors were refuelling other Victors, until their number reduced to one: this tanker was planned to fill our tanks just prior to our descent to low-level, and should then have had sufficient fuel remaining to fly back to Ascension Island.

Although no problem was apparent to us in the Vulcan, the refuelling plan was flawed. Those responsible for calculating the fuel consumption for the whole formation were able to predict very accurately how much fuel would be used by the Victors, but there was no data available on the Vulcan flying at about 10,000 feet below its optimum cruise level at heights and speeds suited to the refuelling of the heavier Victors. The four Olympus engines were using a lot more fuel than was planned. Tankers returning to Ascension Island, having dutifully stuck with us to the end of their 'brackets', were landing with no reserves. The last remaining tanker, captained by Sqn Ldr Bob Tuxford (who had imaginatively taken over as receiver when another tanker, originally planned to take us to the end, had broken off the tip of the refuelling probe while attempting to take on fuel in an area of extreme turbulence), did not have sufficient fuel remaining to permit us to complete our task.

Because of the need for radio silence, no discussion was possible between tanker and receiver, and so I was completely taken by surprise when some distance before the end of our last 'bracket', and with less than full tanks, the red light came on and Bob Tuxford would not give us any more fuel. We appeared to have about 5000 lb below the planned amount required, but I decided to continue towards the target while considering the implications of this quite considerable lack of fuel.

I knew that we could save fuel by climbing to high level after the attack instead of sneaking away at low level as planned; I knew that by careful manipulation of the fuel system we did not need all of the planned reserves before the engines started to flame out, and I also had complete faith that a Victor would be there to meet us at our rendezvous on the way home. But we all knew that there was very little to spare.

What we did not know was that Bob Tuxford and crew had taken a big risk by giving us as much fuel as they did. When they turned away, they knew they would run out of fuel hundreds of miles short of Ascension Island, yet made no attempt to alert anyone to their problem, and to request another tanker to get them home, until after the time of our attack on Port Stanley, in case a radio call might have compromised our mission.

Port Stanley runway after 'Black Buck 1' on 1 May 1982 (Crown copyright)

Five periods of about twenty minutes each spent in contact with the tanker on the way down (which in fact turned into six refuellings because we needed to check whether the broken probe end was still lodged in the basket), certainly passed the time and kept the pilots' minds off the bombing attack which was to come.

This was not the case for the rest of the crew, who had little to do during the long night flight other than to look at the latitude and longitude ticking away on the Carousel inertial navigation system. This had been fitted only a week earlier, and was still not entirely trusted. They had plenty of time to ponder the attack and the dangers involving the whole mission.

The descent to low-level, the run in over the sea and the attack took about an hour. It was not necessary to fly really low, and we gradually crept down to 300 ft. The Passive Warning Receivers were picking up plenty of activity from our own fleet, including the sound of fire control radars 'locked on'. We hoped they knew who we were! Our radar was still turned off until the navigator plotter calculated that we were forty miles from the target position, because any radar transmissions from the aircraft would have given our position away to an Early Warning Radar on the Falklands. But a few quick scans confirmed that we were close to the planned track and we could pull up to 10,000 feet and commence the attack.

Everything depended on the navigator radar, Bob Wright, being able to identify his aiming points. The runway itself would not show up on radar, so instead he had to aim at a headland, the position of which had already been loaded into the archaic bombing computer as an 'offset', over a mile from the target. While homing in on this course, he would be looking for better aiming points, such as the control tower on the airfield. If these did not stand out clearly it was not worth taking a gamble on whether he was aiming at the correct ground feature, and in fact, the bombs were released still aiming on the headland, hoping that the map and the radar pictures both looked alike.

Flying the aircraft was just like being on a training run: concentrating on accurate height, heading and speed, waiting for the bomb-doors to open and then holding the aircraft steady as it shed ten tons of bombs over a period of ten seconds. Then as soon as the last one had gone, applying full power, turning hard left away from any armed response from the ground and climbing to high level again, to make the remaining fuel last until the rendezvous with the tanker off the coast of Brazil.

I had expected the Argentinians to have been alerted to our attack and for us to be fired on by their modern anti-aircraft artillery, but there was no flak. We seemed to have caught them unawares, and one fire-control radar which managed to lock on to us had his lock broken when the Air Electronics Officer, Hugh Prior, switched on the jamming pod – another new gadget bolted under the wing specifically for that purpose.

By the time we approached the rendezvous, we were about half an hour behind schedule, luckily not a problem for the Victor, who had been made aware that we were on our way but running late, because radio communications had become possible again once out of range of any Argentinian threat. But the Nimrod which was planned to act as an air traffic controller to join us up together for the refuelling in the middle of nowhere, was himself running short of fuel and had to head back towards Ascension Island. Fortunately, the quality of the radar and of the operator enabled this task to be accomplished smoothly.

It was a lovely sight to see the Victor swing in front of us trailing its hose. I had never before been airborne in a Vulcan with so little fuel in the tanks, and it is very unlikely that we could have reached Rio without running out. So when fuel started to spray all over the windscreen on first contact with the basket, due to a defective seal on the refuelling probe, I was determined to remain connected, even though the view out of the windscreen was rather like being in a car wash. Eventually we took on enough to get us 'home' without depleting the tanker's reserves.

By the time we landed back at Ascension Island, we had been airborne for fifteen and three-quarter hours; had refuelled seven times in flight; had earned a place in the record books for the longest bombing mission; and were delighted to learn the next day from aerial reconnaissance photographs that the attack had been a success.

Refuelling the Vulcan

Squadron Leader R. Tuxford AFC

The venerable Vulcan was the only aircraft capable of flying a round-trip mission of almost 8000 nautical miles, whilst being able to deliver an effective bomb load. The Air-to-Air Refuelling capability of Group's bomber force had long-since been obsolescent. Not only had refuelling probes to be found and retro-fitted to the airframes as a priority, but their pilots required formation training and receiver training for in-flight refuelling. This was virtually impossible within the short time available. Each Vulcan crew therefore would carry a Victor AAR instructor to assist during the fuel transfers. It was calculated that eleven tankers would be required on the outbound trip, with a further five supporting the inbound trip. At least, that was the plan!

There was no alternate landing airfield available to the Tanker Force operating from this remote island base.

The primary Vulcan was unable to pressurise properly and the reserve took his place. The eleven remaining aircraft climbed to their allocated flight levels. At least the weather factor at Ascension's latitude presented no problems at this stage of the mission. The skies were clear, and visibility in the starlit night sky was unlimited. Indeed, the only problem was trying to identify which set of lights represented your own section leader. It seemed as though the whole sky was awash with flashing red beacons, amidst a clutter of red,

Crew of Tanker XL511 at Wideawake immediately after landing.
Left to right: Sqn Ldr Ernie Wallis, Nav/Radar; Sqn Ldr Mike Beer, Air Electronics Officer; Sqn Ldr Bob Tuxford, Captain; Flt/Lt Glyn Rees, Co-pilot; Flt/Lt John Keeble, Nav Plotter (Sqn Ldr R. Tuxford)

white and green navigation lights.

Transfer 1 was to take place after approximately 1 hour 45 min, some 700 nm down track. The planners knew the fuel consumption of each aircraft. A complex refuelling schedule was therefore prepared under which four tankers would refuel the other aircraft at this point, leaving themselves only enough fuel to return safely to Ascension Island. In the event, the four returning aircraft were all stretched to the limit, and found themselves with very little remaining fuel on arrival at Wideawake. There was not even time for the first aircraft to backtrack the length of the runway to vacate it for the following Victor. The first three aircraft had to land in sequence, and position themselves as close to the end of the landing strip as possible. The last aircraft was faced with the prospect of completing his landing rollout with his three colleagues blocking the end of the runway. The potential for a major pile-up did not need to be spelled out! In the event, all was well.

Meanwhile, the five-ship formation continued to the next refuelling point, situated 1900 nm south of Ascension. Here the same procedure would be repeated and two more tankers would return to Ascension having transferred as much fuel as they dared to the two tankers, and the Vulcan which would continue towards Port Stanley.

Into the early hours of the morning, the physical exertion of upwards of twenty minutes in contact during the first refuelling and over three hours of concentrated formation flying, were beginning to show. At one stage, I was alerted by another tanker as a slow and potentially dangerous roll to port was beginning to develop – undetected by me or my co-pilot. Shaking off the momentary drowsiness, I regained my position, and vowed not to let my attention wander again.
Transfer 3 began without incident. Then I started to lose sight of the stars for the first time that night. The ride became very uncomfortable. We encountered severe turbulence. Considerable St Elmo's fire was present as my aircraft started to buck quite violently. We continued to pass fuel. Brilliantly illuminated by the momentary flashes of lightning, we could see that the hose was becoming increasingly unstable. With less than half the transfer completed, the other tanker's probe snapped under the intense gyrations of my hose and basket.

The whole mission was now in serious jeopardy. Firstly, the other tanker had not taken enough fuel. Secondly, there was no assurance that my refuelling basket had not been damaged. My capability to refuel the Vulcan might be made impossible if the probe tip from the other aircraft had lodged in my basket.

The logical course of action was to take back the fuel already off-loaded to enable me to continue with the Vulcan. Hoping that the Vulcan would be able to maintain visual contact with the two of us, I placed the aircraft astern the other tanker's hose. I fought for some time to achieve contact between probe and basket. Whilst tossing about like ships on a stormy sea, the fuel began to flow. My skills were being tested to the limit during what was turning out to be the most demanding refuelling I had encountered during my time in the Tanker Force. A few minutes into the transfer, the hose became unstable with characteristic whipping up and down its length, causing me to break contact. With insufficient fuel received, it took me three to four more valuable minutes in the turbulent conditions to make a further contact.

My first break came as the glorious sight of twinkling stars filled the background around the Victor's silhouette above me, and mercifully, the turbulence subsided. As all three aircraft stabilised once more, the transfer was able to proceed amongst the comparative calm. Paramount in my thoughts was the fact that the returning tanker aircraft would not be able to receive any more fuel because of his damaged probe. I therefore warned him not to go beyond that level which would permit his assured recovery to Ascension Island. This would mean that I could expect to take on less than originally intended. Furthermore, as both tankers had now proceeded well past the end of the planned refuelling point, more fuel would be needed by both aircraft to ensure a safe return. As the implications of the multi-facetted problem began to compound, refuelling signal lights informed me that I had taken as much fuel as the other tanker was able to offer.

We were left with two very significant legacies. Firstly, we still had to prove the integrity of the refuelling basket if we were to pass more fuel. Secondly, the reduced uplift left us woefully short of that needed to achieve the mission's success.

Our hose was re-trailed for the other tanker to inspect my refuelling equipment. There was no apparent damage. To be certain however, it was decided to attempt a token refuelling of the Vulcan. In the restored tranquillity, the bomber had no difficulty in quickly making contact, and a nominal transfer of 5000 lb was successfully achieved. The two ships could at least continue towards the target for the time being.

With the frequent formation changes and the additional refuelling at Transfer 3, we were well over six hours into the mission, and around 3200 nm from our departure point.

The overriding consideration facing me was the fuel situation. The choices were two-fold: I could abort the raid whilst my aircraft had more than adequate fuel to return to base; alternatively, the mission could continue with my own reserves rapidly dwindling to the point where a safe return to Ascension could not be achieved without the aid of a tanker. In order to refuel the Vulcan with the amount necessary for it to reach the target, my own aircraft would be left with insufficient fuel to reach Ascension. A diversion for a tanker to the South American mainland had not been considered, and as far as I was concerned was out of the question.

I could not break radio silence to inform Headquarters of our predicament for fear of jeopardising the yet unfulfilled mission. I was strongly predisposed to press on. Aware however that my ultimate consideration must be for the safety of my crew, I felt obliged to hear their individual opinions. They unanimously stated that, having got that far, the mission should continue. The single most difficult operational decision as aircraft Captain that I have ever had to make was thus made easier with the encouragement and support of my crew that night.

The final transfer to the Vulcan went without hitch. We calculated that we could offer him sufficient to enable him to press on with the attack. However, I had to ensure that I had enough fuel remaining in my tanks to get sufficiently close to Ascension Island to stand a reasonable chance of linking with a tanker. However, the Vulcan Captain requested the remainder of his expected transfer. Having stretched ourselves to limit, we turned away, still leaving the hose on offer. We felt sure that the experienced tanker instructor on board would be aware of our ever-worsening fuel predicament. The next instant the Vulcan turned away, leaving my aircraft on its own for the first time in seven hours.

I put the aircraft into a cruise climb to the altitude that would give us best range capability. Whichever way we looked at it, we could only get to within four or five hundred miles of our safe haven. There would still be a lot of South Atlantic left between us!

Suddenly, the Vulcan transmitted the code word 'Superfuse', signalling a successful bombing run. There was elation that we had really helped achieve the attack on Port Stanley's runway. Soon afterwards we heard BBC's World Service announce the accomplishment of the bombing mission. We were still some five hours flight time from base, with a little under four hours of fuel remaining! From our viewpoint, the announcement to the world whilst so much was still at stake seemed rather premature.

Much discussion ensued about the procedure if we did not meet up with another tanker. Because of the design of the underside of the nose bay of the Victor, the aircraft had always been considered unsuitable for ditching. The likelihood was that because of a bulkhead to the rear of the H2S radar scanner, the whole aircraft would dive under on impact. We agreed a sequence involving the bailing-out of the rear crew, followed by controlled ejection of the pilots.

We relayed our precarious predicament to Ascension. Our situation required a tanker to meet us at least one thousand miles south of the Island. We also instructed them of the reduced fuel state in the Vulcan so that revised RV arrangements might be made.

Ascension eventually confirmed that a tanker was indeed on the way. Some two hours later, after eleven hours of savouring the comforts of the Mk 3 Martin Baker ejection seat, we were all ecstatic with excitement as we searched the clear blue Atlantic sky for that famous crescent wing. My boss, on his second sortie that day, manoeuvred his aircraft directly in front of mine after a flawless rendezvous. Tiredness was no longer a factor. With hundreds of AAR contacts in the bag, this was to be the most important of my life, literally. There was silence as I took longer than normal to stabilise in the pre-contact position astern the hose. There was no point in trying to rush. Nor did I feel the usual macho need to make contact in one – a necessity when in company with one's squadron colleagues looking on!

The fuel remaining in the tanks as I moved up towards the basket would have kept the engines going for perhaps a little over one more hour. Flying the aircraft as smoothly as possible, I narrowly missed the basket. The second approach resulted in my probe clunking home centrally inside the reception coupling. After a brief uneasy moment, the tanker's Nav. Radar transmitted the sweet words 'fuel flows': that all-important corollary to the contact signifying a positive transfer of fuel. As our tanks filled to that point where recovery to Wideawake Airfield would be possible, the sighs of relief amongst my crew were clearly audible. The final hurdle had been cleared, and the remainder of the flight was to be entirely uneventful.

A total of eighteen tanker sorties were launched during the night of 30 April/1 May 1982 in support of the two Vulcan bombers. The participating Victor crews flew in excess of 105 hours, five crews each amassing flight durations of over ten hours. Some twenty-three individual air-to-air refuellings took place, with a total of around 635,000 lb of fuel transferred.

The refuelling of the Vulcan in support of Operation 'Black Buck' One had needed every bit of expertise of No. 1 Group's Tanker Force in order to achieve the longest bombing mission in the history of aerial warfare.

My Unforgettable Ascension Island

Air Vice-Marshal David Emerson CB AFC

I still jog from time to time in a disreputable Tee Shirt, bought for fifty US cents in 1982 and emblazoned with the Ascension Island logo. This says a lot for the durability of the shirt but also brings back memories of my six-week stay on that volcanic rock during Operation 'Corporate'. Travel to Ascension had been overnight on 21 April as the only passenger on a VC10 freighter, sleeping on 10,000 cans of Newcastle Brown destined for the troops in transit to the South Atlantic. Only 9998 arrived!

In 1982 I was based at RAF Kinloss on the Moray Firth,

commanding the only squadron fully equipped with the updated Nimrod Mk 2 maritime patrol aircraft. Throughout the month of April we had undertaken contingency planning for a possible deployment to a third party country in support of the Falklands campaign, and practised hard at fighter evasion. Thus it wasn't a total surprise on landing back from a sortie on 20 April to be met by the Station Commander with instructions to be ready to fly within two hours to London for a pre-deployment brief at the Northwood Headquarters.

The brief offered no specific task or role, but was based on an assumption that the Nimrod Mk 2 would replace the Nimrod Mk 1 detachment that had been despatched to Ascension some time earlier to provide surveillance ahead of the fleet as it deployed south towards the Falklands, and that a Nimrod Mk 2 squadron commander should be on hand. For the first time the possibility of an in-flight refuelling capability for the Nimrod was mentioned, as was the need for an air-to-air missile fit to neutralise the Argentinean 707 reconnaissance aircraft which was believed to be shadowing the deploying fleet. However, I didn't for a second think that just three weeks later I would be flying on the first operational in-flight refuelled Nimrod sortie.

During my time at Ascension there were between two and five aircraft and crews under my command at anyone time, and up to fifty groundcrew. Aircraft and crews were rotated at about ten day intervals as aircraft received enhancements, and to allow crews to receive training on the new equipment.

This kept crews fresh but did mean that they had only just reached the top of a steep learning curve before leaving the operational theatre. The lack of ramp space and limited facilities often dictated aircraft numbers, and when I arrived at Ascension the support infrastructure was only just starting to build.

Fortunately, the Nimrod force had acquired the only air-conditioned working accommodation on the airfield, normally used by visiting US Navy P3 aircraft.

Domestic accommodation was desperately cramped but adequate for the aircrew, and food provided by the resident Americans was excellent. Our groundcrew, however, had to make do with tents on a site three miles from the airfield. Transport was non-existent at the start, but within a day or so the groundcrew had commandeered an abandoned American lorry, and had it running but producing a cloud of black smoke from a mixture of aviation fuel and oil. We also bought two civilian cars, and to this day I await a bill from the UK accounting authorities to cover 'the Squadron Commander's Mini', acquired for my use for $400. The local population were also enormously supportive, opening their clubs to us despite finding that stocks ran out within a day or two until a resupply route was identified.

The Nimrod aircraft were employed on a number of challenging and interesting tasks, and it was tremendous to watch both aircrew and groundcrew operating to the limits in an incredibly responsible, innovative and flexible manner. Throughout the emergency a Nimrod was kept on a one hour SAR standby (and was launched on a number of occasions to assist aircraft with emergencies), and a daily surveillance sortie was flown to ensure that the Argentinians did not launch a pre-emptive strike from the sea on this critical staging and launching base, and to keep a check on the Soviet intelligence gathering vessel which lurked around the island.

Airborne SAR was also flown in support of all long range missions launched from Ascension. In the case of the Vulcan sorties the Nimrod also acted as shepherd using its Searchwater radar to guide the Vulcan returning from its bombing mission to its waiting tanker. These sorties certainly had their moments, and I remember with absolute clarity flying beside a returning Vulcan which was attempting to refuel when it broke its probe, followed by an 'Oh shit, that's us for Brazil' from its pilot. In this case we accompanied the Vulcan to about 100 miles from the Brazilian coast where we monitored the R/T exchanges with progressively more alarmed air traffic controllers until after the Vulcan had landed. However my most vivid lasting memory is listening to the R/T during the first Black Buck sortie, when the Victor tanker crews totally reorganised the complex refuelling programme as unserviceabilities and other potential disasters occurred. An incredible performance and one so complex that it would have confused any eavesdropper.

The other major task of the Nimrod was in support of the deploying fleet, checking ahead for any sign of Argentinian vessels, and in these early days these sorties were also used to drop mail and spares to ships and SSNs as they transited south. Quite soon, however the fleet were beyond the un-refuelled range of the Nimrod, and for a while the already over-stretched Victor tanker crews, with a radar not designed for sea surveillance, had to take on this task. Then from mid-May, once in-flight refuelling equipment had been fitted and crews trained, long range sorties were flown by Nimrods to off the Argentinean coast and the Falklands, carrying bomb loads of the new Stingray torpedo, 1000 lb retarded bombs and SAR equipment. A nineteen-hour sortie allowed a five or six hour on-task period to check the lines of approach to all the Argentinean ports for naval vessels and submarines. Seven support tankers were needed to provide for two refuelling points outbound and one on the return journey. As newcomers to the refuelling game, these were challenging sorties, and it could take some time in the early days for our pilots to make proper contact with the refuelling basket: provoking the occasional call from understandably alarmed tanker crews of 'Too close, back off!!' Perhaps the most interesting of these sorties was on the night prior to the landing of British troops when, to our surprise, we could still see the lights of Port Stanley blazing brightly despite the war activities. That said, any sortie within Argentinian air defence cover kept crews alert and the adrenalin flowing! The risk of interception was low, but when flying off the Argentinian coast on a sunny cloudless day it was easy to imagine how a goldfish in a bowl feels with a cat looking in.

More generally, Command and Control of operations was complicated by the lack of secure communications with the UK. The single secure telephone available from the outset was quite rapidly supplemented by another, and ASMA, a secure computer-based system, was also installed, but crews still felt somewhat isolated from the big picture. Learning to co-ordinate operations with Victor tankers and other aircraft, including devising refuelling procedures, was another

Nimrod MR2 (BAE Systems)

interesting challenge; and the meticulous and accurate debriefing of crews who had by then already been working for twenty-four hours was more difficult to achieve than was imagined. A less than well considered report of a 'possible' Argentinian warship could result in the wasted diversion of an SSN to investigate. However, at the end of the day it did all come together with, from my perspective, the heroes being the Victor tanker crews. They and their venerable aircraft flew an amazing number of sorties, took on the many new challenges thrown at them, and allowed the air war to happen.

With the passage of time, the Nimrod involvement in the Falklands campaign has tended to take on a rosy glow – the flying was challenging and no one was hurt physically. Of course there were major problems and the operational value of the end product was not always as high as we would have hoped.

The learning curve was steep for flights over unfamiliar waters with, for example, fishing fleets operating off the coast of South America complicating the surface picture until we tied down positions and fishing boat electronic emissions, which in some cases were remarkably similar to those of Argentinean warships. The closed-loop navigation equipment of the Nimrod, designed for nine hour sortie lengths, proved to be inaccurate on the longer sorties, which in turn affected the capabilities of some of the sensors.

Nevertheless, many remarkable innovations did work well and all in all it was a fascinating experience from which many lessons were learned, and one that even made some money for charity. In late April, around 100 people were persuaded to pay $1 each for a dance to be held on the *Uganda* (a hospital ship with many nurses which sat off Ascension for a couple of weeks), and had the good nature to laugh when they arrived at the jetty to be ferried to the ship, to be told that the event was a spoof.

I only spent six weeks on Ascension Island but it was an experience like no other, and certainly affected my subsequent service career and life in general.

Some seven years later I at last set foot on the Falkland Islands when escorting the by then Admiral of the Fleet, Sir John Fieldhouse. *En route* I marvelled at the modern facilities at Ascension Island, toured all those sites with names that had become so familiar to the British public in 1982, and was grateful for the hospitality and gratitude of the Falkland Islanders. My lasting memory however is of standing beside the Admiral at the Memorial in Port Stanley to those who lost their lives. For many it was a nasty, bloody and tragic war.

Defence of San Carlos

Mark Nash

I was Operations Officer on 63 Squadron RAF Regiment, a Rapier low-level air defence missile unit based at RAF Gütersloh in Germany. It was April 1982 and the news of the Argentinian invasion of the Falkland Islands was breaking. On 7 May we were instructed to join the 'QE2' at Southampton docks.

Our Rapier fire units, missiles and vehicles embarked on the *Atlantic Causeway*, sister ship of the ill-fated *Atlantic Conveyer* which was later sunk by Exocet missiles.

There was something bizarre about going to war on the greatest luxury liner in the world. Oddly the shops were still open and the gunners started to buy waterproof cameras and other 'essential' items. A small complement of the ship's civilian crew and staff in their smart uniforms asked if there was anything we needed. The whole thing was rather surreal.

Our mission remained a mystery. I recall practising to disembark, weighed down with weapons, ammunition and equipment, but was never quite sure if this was to join another ship or to go ashore and fight.

On Friday 28 May we arrived in a bleak, misty, grey South Georgia harbour. By now No. 3 Commando Brigade landings had taken place at San Carlos. In the harbour were the *Canberra* and *Norland*, as well as a host of smaller military and civilian vessels. In keeping with the general confusion, the Squadron was split into three groups – hardly the best way for a formed Unit to make final preparations for action. Already our primary fighting equipment – the Rapier Fire Units – was aboard the *Atlantic Causeway*, of which we had heard nothing since we left Southampton. Now we were to be further split to embark on the *Canberra*, *Norland* and *Stromness*. I was to provide air defences on the latter for its return to San Carlos Water – or 'Bomb Alley' as it had become known.

I found myself once more trussed up in disembarkation gear. We shuffled to an access door low down the ship's side, clambered out on to 'scramble nets', and then jumped down into a battered old Hull trawler that was being tossed about alongside the QE2.

It was dark as we approached the *Stromness*, and I could not see how we were going to get into it from our little trawler. The ship in front of us manoeuvred alongside the tall grey slab side of the *Stromness*. With a sudden screeching of metal against metal, and just as the trawler was at its highest point on the swell, a soldier leaped from the trawler's side, grabbed the external hand and footholds running up the outside of the *Stromness* and proceeded to climb rapidly towards the railings at the top. Meanwhile, the trawler fell away to its lowest point before tipping again and scraping and screeching its way back up the larger ship, chasing the soldier as he continued his somewhat frantic scramble to the top.

The weather was getting worse and before long it was my trawler's and, more to the point, my turn to 'cross-deck' as it was known. Laden with equipment, I looked down from my perch on the side of the trawler at the inky black water heaving and splashing between the two boats and wondered briefly what would happen if anyone fell in. Someone shouted 'Jump now' and I jumped. I suppose that is the essence of military training that a civilian may not comprehend: namely the willingness of a soldier to obey an instruction against his better instincts. I grabbed the handholds and my heavily laden body slammed against the side, knocking the wind out of me. The same voice then shouted 'Go!', and I started my rapid ascent. I heard the trawler crunch back again. As I neared the top of the ladder I could see the face of a Royal Marine peering downwards, arms outstretched towards me. As I got to the top I felt him grab the straps of my webbing and haul me unceremoniously over the top of the railings. 'Well done, Sir', said the Marine, 'now get out of the way for the next man'.

We sailed from South Georgia across to the Falkland Islands. At times the Antarctic scenery was breathtaking, and at times the sea conditions were beyond my experience as we steamed our way west in what was a small stores ship.

At one point we slowed almost to a stop and pulled alongside an inflatable lifeboat. It looked as if it was from the *Belgrano* and we wondered what we might find. It turned out to be empty, but I remember thinking that we were now a sitting duck for an opportunist Argentinian submarine as we wallowed in the South Atlantic. We gathered speed again and continued our voyage west.

At first light on the morning of 2 June we sailed into San Carlos Water, clambered over the side of *Stromness* and down scramble nets into the landing craft. As we drew nearer I could see packing crates piled high, tracked and other vehicles moving back and forth on the beach, tents, radio antennae, men moving about, Browning machine gun positions, palls of smoke snaking up from cooking areas and helicopters flying here and there. It looked rather chaotic, but I guessed someone somewhere was in charge.

I had no idea what I was supposed to do next. We were now completely cut off from the rest of the Squadron. I had not the faintest idea where they might be. We arrived at the beachhead and I went to find out what was happening. An Army officer thought there was a Rapier unit setting up at Port San Carlos to the north. He said that a Sea King helicopter would be making a run across in the morning and we might be able to jump on it.

Next morning a Navy Sea King helicopter appeared and the pilot agreed take us to Port San Carlos. I saw immediately where the Squadron was deploying. We were back to being a formed unit again after several weeks of separation.

The Squadron's move ashore had been messy to say the least, with the Squadron Commander trying to co-ordinate the deployment of groups of people and equipment dispersed on the *Norland*, *Canberra*, *Atlantic Causeway* and *Stromness*. He had not even been able to do a reconnaissance of the area. We found the Squadron's Rapiers dumped unceremoniously amongst the piles of other military hardware, ammunition and stores on the beach.

It emerged that our mission was to defend the Harrier Forward Operating Base (FOB) at Port San Carlos.

This was not exactly a textbook deployment of a Rapier squadron. Indeed, it was a shambles, and if the air situation in San Carlos at the beginning of June had been less favourable our contribution as an air defence unit would have been useless if not disastrous. Indeed, the events that were about to take place at Bluff Cove reinforce this view .

There the detailed planning needed to bring Rapier units into action had not been fully appreciated. Rapiers need time to be deployed, set up, tested and adjusted, particularly in the

Argentinian aircraft – Stanley Airfield June 1982 (Mark Nash)

harsh environment of the South Atlantic and the *modus operandi* of amphibious operations: it is not a piece of artillery in the same mould as a howitzer. The Rapiers of T Battery were simply not ready at Bluff Cove, and on 8 June Argentinian Sky hawks attacked the *Sir Galahad* and the *Sir Tristram* with devastating results.

San Carlos Water was still under threat of air attack, and air raid alerts were commonplace. By the afternoon of 3 June all eight of our Rapier Fire Units were fully deployed around the Harrier FOB.

We were in communication with HMS *Fearless*, from whom we received our early warning radar reports. Our task was to ensure that we always had air defence cover available. Faults that would take just one hour to fix in Europe could take up to a day to fix in the Falklands, because of the atrocious conditions and the lack of helicopters at the time.

From time to time *Fearless* would report an incoming raid. From the rudimentary Command Post in a trench we would relay information to the Rapiers who would use their own radars to search for the attackers. On one occasion I heard the familiar bang and whoosh of a missile being launched. The sky was gin-clear blue and I watched as the projectile streaked almost vertically into the sky, a long plume of flame and smoke spewing from its tail. I was curious because it was not a Rapier missile. In fact, it was a Sea Dart that had been launched from one of the warships. I could see what looked like a civilian aircraft. The missile proceeded on its course and struck the aircraft which disintegrated in a ball of red and orange flame. The Argentinians had used a Lear jet for reconnaissance.

On the same day as the Bluff Cove attack, a raid was reported incoming towards Falkland Sound. I could hear explosions in the distance and it was clear we were under attack. One or twice our Fire Units reported that they had locked on to targets, but were unable to hold their locks long enough to be able to launch missiles. From my trench I could see a warship limping into San Carlos Water. It was HMS *Plymouth* that had been hit by four 1000 lb bombs dropped by Mirage Vs in a sustained attack. Two of the five Mirages had been hit. HMS *Plymouth* survived.

One afternoon I watched a Harrier slowly approach the temporary landing strip, making the usual tremendous racket that marks a Harrier in hover mode. As it drew closer I noticed the strips of metal pinned to the soft earth of the strip begin to lift with the down draught from the aircraft. The situation snowballed rapidly and suddenly great chunks of metal started to twist and spiral up towards the engine intakes. The pilot was by now committed to land and decided to plonk the aircraft onto the ground very quickly. In doing so, the undercarriage collapsed and the Harrier slid along the landing pad towards the Rapier Fire Unit positioned at the end of it. Some gunners were in the trench next to the Rapier and could see the aircraft slithering directly towards them. They leapt smartly from the trench just as the Harrier glided to a halt precisely on top of the trench that they had just evacuated. The canopy flew back and the pilot emerged shaken but unscathed. He climbed down, strolled across to the Rapier crew, removed his helmet and said 'Terribly sorry about that chaps. Anyone got a fag?'

Our 'routine in defence' continued much like this whilst the Commando and Infantry Brigades continued their advance on Port Stanley. My abiding memory is that it was very cold and the weather absolutely atrocious, with whiteout conditions and seriously sub-zero temperatures in the high winds. We had deployed from Germany with only what clothing and personal equipment we could carry on our backs. Rations were always in short supply, albeit we were never without food of some description. We had no idea how long we were expected to remain in the South Atlantic.

On 15 June the Argentinians surrendered. We had left Germany just forty-four days earlier, but it seemed like a lifetime. We received orders to deploy forward to Port Stanley to protect the airfield there. This time we had the opportunity to do things properly. I was sent in a Chinook helicopter to reconnoitre the airfield, assisted by a computer analysis of the surrounding ground sent to us from RSRE Malvern. The conditions at Stanley airfield were grim. There was all the debris of a defeated army. There were fires burning, partially destroyed enemy aircraft, bits and pieces of military equipment, weapons and ammunition. Groups of dejected Argentinian soldiers were gathered around, guarded by two or three Marines or Paras.

By 3 July the Squadron was fully deployed around Stanley airfield. We had to be extremely careful of the minefields, and one or two individuals from other units were injured as a result of mines going off.

Still we had no news of any plans to withdraw us back to Germany. By now, virtually all of the units with which we had landed at San Carlos had returned to their home bases. The weeks wore on and we maintained our routine defence of Stanley airfield.

Our personal circumstances deteriorated. Despite the best intentions and procedures in terms of field hygiene, we began to smell less than savoury. Our clothing and equipment was getting ever more frayed at the edges, and there is a limit to just what can be done in culinary terms with composite rations. July came and went, and we rolled on into August. By now we were in pretty much the worst weather conditions in the South Atlantic.

One day it was snowing and a group of soldiers was sweeping the runway with brooms. A Harrier was winding up for take off next to me. The men moved off to one side to let the aircraft go. As its nose wheel left the ground there was an almighty roar. The Harrier's Sidewinder missiles had malfunctioned and launched. The starboard missile shot off into some containers to the side of the strip and exploded in a shower of sparks and flame. The port missile tore into the soldiers. The scene was a mess. One soldier had had his legs blown off and another had lost an arm. Others were staggering around or slumped on the ground. Fortunately, some SAS troopers had been on the scene nearby waiting for a helicopter. They moved in quickly and started to administer First Aid and morphine. Medics arrived and a helicopter began evacuating the injured to hospital.

On 11 September, some four months after we had left Germany, we handed over to our successors. By now we were pretty much exhausted. We had been living in harsh field conditions for all that time.

We returned to a splendid welcome home from our colleagues and families at RAF Gütersloh.

THE GULF WAR 1991

On 2 August 1990, Iraq invaded Kuwait. Its action was immediately condemned by the UN. Iraqi forces appeared to be ready to move into Saudi Arabia, and the United States and its allies moved protective forces into the area in an operation code-named 'Desert Shield'.

Despite intensive diplomatic efforts, Iraq refused to withdraw from Kuwait.

The build up of international forces continued and the UN gave an ultimatum to Iraq to withdraw from Kuwait by 1 January 1991. This was ignored and operation 'Desert Storm' began with allied air strikes on 17 January 1991.

By far the greatest contribution was made by the USA.

Thirty-eight days of intensive air attacks laid the foundation for the land campaign. So effective had air operations been that only 100 hours of ground fighting was needed to complete the Iraqi defeat.

Operation Desert Shield

Air Chief Marshal Sir 'Sandy' Wilson KCB AFC

When Saddam Hussein decided to invade Kuwait on 2 August 1990, he almost certainly did so in the belief that most, if not all, the West's Governments would be in recess and many of the key military staffs away on summer holiday. He was right. But by the same token he must, nevertheless, have been taken aback by the speed with which the US and UK Governments reacted. Within six days the first US forces had arrived in Saudi Arabia, swiftly followed by the UK with Tornado F3s arriving in Dhahran on 11 August. Operation 'Desert Shield', the all important build-up to 'Desert Storm', had begun, and was to become the largest overseas deployment for UK Forces since Suez.

As the UK's designated Two-Star Commander for overseas operations at the time, I was appointed Air Commander British Forces Arabian Gulf on 10 August and, following briefings at High Wycombe (the nominated 4 star HQ), self-deployed to the Gulf on 11/12 August in an HS 125 via Cyprus.

Whilst our initial forces were deploying to the region my first and most urgent task, given to me by the UK's Chiefs of Staff, was to set up an HQ, preferably alongside the US Forces who had arrived in Riyadh a few days earlier. This was a task that was much easier said than done because in Saudi Arabia nothing happens without the approval of the ruling Royal Family, and what made political sense in Whitehall needed very delicate handling in theatre.

Fortuitously, I was known to some of the Saudi hierarchy, having visited Saudi many times as part of the UK team which negotiated the initial arms deal to the Kingdom and so, with the help of our Ambassador (now Sir) Alan Munro, I was able to gain access quickly to Gen. Prince Khalid, who had just been appointed Commander of Saudi Forces, and to the Chief of the Air Staff, Gen. Beheiry.

Although the Saudis had agreed that the US Forces should be collocated within their own HQs they were very reluctant for the UK to follow suit. Nevertheless, General Beheiry gave me an office in the Saudi Air Force HQ as an interim measure, giving the UK an essential foot in the door alongside the USAF.

Initially, the US Operations Sultan were under the command of USAF Lt Gen. 'Chuck' Horner. He made me and my small staff very welcome, and without his support the Saudis would never have agreed to my single office quietly expanding to become an expeditionary air force HQ fully integrated with the US and Saudis. No such privileges were accorded to other nations, notably not to the French.

General Schwartzkopf's arrival in Riyadh on 26 August heralded a step change in the political and military scene. Knowing rather more of Arab sensibilities than his subordinates, he immediately saw the vital need for the Saudis to be seen to be in command of all the incoming forces, and so agreed to serve under Gen. Prince bin Khalid, who was appointed Joint Commander of all Forces in Saudi Arabia. From his arrival to the day I handed over command to Gen. Sir Peter de la Billiere, Gen. Swartzkopf could not have given the UK Forces in general and me in particular more help and support. He included me in his daily 'US Eyes Only' briefings with his senior Generals, and always found time to see me on important business sometimes late into the night.

The building of the UK staff to support RAF deployments was a unique challenge.

Whilst we had well-rehearsed plans for a stand alone in theatre Joint HQ, the initial emphasis on air deployments and the circumstances in Riyadh led to the need to build the staff quite literally on a daily basis. In this I had the full support of my boss Sir Patrick ('Paddy') Hine in High Wycombe, and of the Air Secretary who allowed me to call forward key personnel on an individual basis.

By the end of August the staff had risen from nothing to over thirty. All these were crammed into just a few rooms, and with the USAF already filling the rest of the HQ I took the decision literally to buy a suite of 'porta-cabins' and erect them in the car park alongside all the US intelligence and signals vans. Thanks to the great ability of my service to improvise, within days we had a working HQ with secure communications and air conditioning (essential with the temperature reaching 45–50°C every day). Whilst this was far from perfect it at least allowed us to continue our integration with Gen. Horner's staff, and to support the build up of UK forces which by September included both RN and Army.

With the initial emphasis on the need for forward air defence, the first aircraft to deploy were Tornado F3s, and these arrived at the large Saudi base at Dhahran, near Bahrain, on 11 August, immediately after the UK Chiefs of

Staff decision to join the US in defending Saudi Arabia. They were supported by two VC10 Tankers which had to be based at Seeb in the Oman. These were followed by Jaguar aircraft which were deployed even further south to Thumrait, an Omani Jaguar base close to the Indian Ocean.

Apart from setting up an HQ in Riyadh my other priority was to secure more forward deployments for the Jaguars and the VC 10s, as well as looking for bases for possible deployment of additional aircraft. From the US's critical analysis of the Iraqis' military capability it was clear that control of the Iraqi and Kuwait air space was an essential precursor to any attempt to oust Saddam's forces from Kuwait. From the middle of August I had been taken into the confidence of the US Planners, and was privileged to have a unique insight into US strategic thinking and planning. As a consequence I became intimately involved in the detailed planning of the Air Campaign under the direction of Brig. Gen. 'Buster' Glosson.

At this juncture the UK's contribution was valued more by the US for its political impact than for its military capability. But as I became more involved in the detailed campaign planning it became clear to me that the greatest military contribution the UK could make would be to provide a weapon system for helping to close some of the key Iraqi airfields, and so with Buster Glosson's support I set about making the case for the deployment of Tornado GR l aircraft equipped with JP 233, the airfield denial weapon. Getting the UK Government's approval was one thing but finding suitable basing was quite another.

My attempts to obtain Saudi agreement for a Squadron of all weather GR 1s to join the Air Defence Tornado F3s in Dhahran met with stiff resistance, as the base was heavily committed to air defence operations and was the main airhead for US deployments (I counted fourteen wide-bodied aircraft on the ground during one August visit). My attention then turned to Bahrain's Muharraq International Airport, a former RAF airfield. A covert exploratory visit led me to the view that at a push we might base both a Tornado GR 1 Squadron and the Jaguars then based in Oman – too far away for effective offensive operations in Kuwait. But with no Tornado-experienced staff in theatre and with Sir 'Paddy' Hine pressing me for a definitive view, I took the unusual step of 'hijacking' a former RAF Tornado-experienced Group Captain, who was working for British Aerospace at the time in Riyadh; putting him back in uniform and taking him in my HS 125 to Bahrain on a covert recce. Having assessed the facilities being offered we both agreed that such a deployment could be shoe-horned into the small area available, and following negotiations with the Bahraini Minister of Defence – and a call on the Emir – a detailed proposal was put to London through the Joint Force HQ at High Wycombe. The first Tornado flew into Bahrain on 28 August and the Jaguars subsequently moved forward from Thumrait on 10 October.

Although the imperative was to have a squadron's worth of Tornado GR 1s in theatre as soon as possible, it was clear to me from the beginning of the air campaign planning that we would need at least two squadrons to make a worthwhile impact on Iraqi airfields, and furthermore that basing on the eastern side of the region would make reaching some of the more important targets almost impossible without significant additional tanker resources, even if we could find bases on which to put them. I had visited Tabuk airfield in the north west of Saudi Arabia, not far from the border with Jordan, in August when I was negotiating for GR 1 use of Dhahran, but the Base Commander saw it differently and even the good Gen. Beheiry was not prepared to overrule him. However, once I had secured the use of Bahrain, I returned to Tabuk on a series of visits to build my case. With one resident Saudi Air Force Squadron and one USAF F 15 Air Defence squadron bedding-in, the Base Commander remained adamant that there was no space available. I regarded this as such an important objective that I decided that if necessary we should seek agreement to deploy there on a self-help basis, utilising unprotected spare ramp space. In parallel, 'Buster' Glosson helped me argue my case with Gen. Horner and I sought London's agreement to pursue the matter at the highest political and military level in theatre. Thus it was that with the support of Gen. Swartzkopf and Gen. Beheiry, Prince Sultan, the Saudi Defence Minister, authorised the deployment of the second Tornado GR 1 Squadron to Tabuk and the first aircraft arrived there on 9 October.

Whilst the Tornado F 3 Squadron at Dhahran was well bedded-in, the Detachments in Bahrain and in Tabuk posed very significant logistic challenges. At Tabuk we had to start virtually from scratch, contracting builders direct to provide hardstandings for equipment storage and porta-cabins for offices as well as building a semi-hardened operations facility from empty sea containers. At Muhrarraq the emphasis was on reinforcing existing buildings against possible air attack, and at both bases great emphasis was put on NCB protection. All of this was the result of first class leadership at unit level and the skills, ingenuity and flexibility instilled during the Cold War by NATO's Taceval system

I should also mention tanker basing. Based at Seeb in the Oman, the VC10 Tankers spent a great deal of unproductive time in transit supporting twenty-four hour Air Defence operations and training by the offensive forces. It was vital to find a more forward operating base for these aircraft and those earmarked for short notice deployment in the event of hostilities, and to this end I visited bases in Egypt, the UAE and in Saudi; but as we got further in our campaign planning it became crystal clear that only forward basing in Saudi Arabia would provide the necessary fuel offload capability to support very long-range airfield operations. I had to enlist the support of Gen. Horner to convince the Saudis to allow the basing of our tankers further forward at Riyadh International Airport. This proved to be a vital piece of the jigsaw.

Whilst all of this was going on, Rapier units were deployed to enhance airfield defences. In Riyadh I was responsible for setting-up a separate UK Joint HQ, leaving the RAF HQ integrated within Gen. Horner's USAF HQ. This coincided with my appointment in September as Commander British Forces Middle East, with operational control of all UK forces in the region, including the RN stop and search operations as well as Army units such as 7 Armoured Brigade, who had just arrived in Theatre. These wider responsibilities took an increasing amount of my time and eighteen-hour days became the norm. As from the start I divided my time between Riyadh and the many units spread out by now from the North West of Saudi Arabia to Oman in the South East of the Gulf. I regarded keeping in close touch with, and visiting units in the field as a very important aspect of command.

By early October it became increasingly clear that Saddam's forces would have to be ejected from Kuwait and, whilst a case was put to Washington for an early air campaign, the US Chiefs of Staff, led by Gen. Colin Powell, took the view that only a major follow-up land campaign would guarantee success. And so the political decision was taken to commit major land forces as well as additional air power to the Region; in the case of the UK this involved the deployment of a Division: a step change from the Army Brigade already in theatre. This led to the need to upgrade the role and rank of the UK Command commensurate with the level of forces being deployed by the UK, as well as the perceived need to deal with Gen. Swartzkopf at his own Four-Star level. The Prime Minister, Mrs Thatcher, therefore decided that I should be replaced by Gen. Sir Peter de la Billiere and that I should become his Deputy whilst retaining operational command of RAF forces in the Gulf.

My handover to Sir Peter on 6 October effectively marked the end of Phase 1 of the build-up to the Gulf War. Whilst much has rightly been written about the war itself, only history will put into its proper context the significance of what was achieved in those first few months. It is already clear that without the swift injection of airpower in the days immediately after his invasion of Kuwait, Saddam Hussein might well have been tempted to move south into the all important Saudi oilfields.

The lessons learned during both Operation 'Desert Shield' and 'Desert Storm' – the UK's Operation 'Granby' – have undoubtedly made a significant contribution to the reshaping of UK Forces: especially to their ability to operate in an expeditionary environment and, when required, on a coalition basis. For those involved like myself it was a remarkable experience, and I feel very privileged to have led UK Forces in such an important operation. But above all it was a team effort and I am immensely grateful to all those from all three Services who gave me such loyal support, often in very difficult circumstances; especially those who commanded the various detachments and built-up bases virtually from scratch; to those in the staffs who built the joint structures without which the eventual war could not have been fought (especially Sir 'Paddy's' Team at High Wycombe); and, last but not least, to my small personal staff, including my HS 125 crew who flew some 60,000 miles with me in my three months in the Gulf.

Having spent just under two months ensuring a smooth handover to Sir Peter and overseeing the bedding in of the additional RAF forces, I handed over my RAF duties to AVM 'Bill' Wratten: both, of course, went on to lead our forces during Operation 'Desert Storm'. I left Riyadh on 1 November, flying myself home via Cyprus to my appointment as AOC 1 Group before taking over as Commander-in-Chief of RAF Germany the following Spring.

A Tribute to the RAF

General Sir Peter de la Billiere KCB KBE DSO MC

Sir Sandy Wilson hands over to Sir Peter de la Billiere (Sir Sandy Wilson)

Phase 1 of the Allied air campaign in Kuwait Theatre of Operations had a simple objective – to achieve air superiority and significantly damage Iraqi strategic capabilities. This resulted in an operation of astonishing complexity. The whole campaign was a masterpiece of human planning and computer-controlled aggression. It was directed with a degree of precision which far surpassed that of any air attack in the past.

An Air Tasking Order (ATO) was prepared each day. This consisted of over 100 pages of orders, in the most minute detail, co-ordinating every sortie by each allied aircraft throughout the twenty-four-hour period. Such was the precision of the operation that one sortie by an aircraft with an Alarm missile designed to destroy enemy radar was aborted, because its launch would have had to be one minute too early.

The success of the air war was a tribute both to technology which enabled aircraft to be kept apart in space and time, and to the discipline and courage of the aircrews who flew each sortie with such precision.

The air campaign started just before midnight on 16 January 1991. By 27 January we had achieved complete air supremacy.

It would be invidious to single out any one element of the air operation for special praise. All played a vital role and success depended on their combined efforts.

For the courage and skill of the Tornado crews I had nothing but admiration.

Their bravery was of a quite exceptional order. They were the first to go into action and face the full fury of the sophisticated Iraqi anti-aircraft artillery (AAA) and missiles. Their aircraft had never been tested in war and most of the aircrews had never flown in action against an enemy. Now they were required to fly to the limits of survival, not once or twice, but night after night. To do this required a very special kind of courage.

When I talked to them they told hair-raising stories of how, as they approached their target, the horizon ahead would suddenly erupt in streaks, flares and whole curtains of yellow, white and red lights as AAA and surface-to-air missiles stormed up to meet them.

The Buccaneer was twenty-one years old and known affectionately as the 'flying banana' because of the slightly undulating shape of its fuselage. In spite of its antiquity its crews loved it, and swore that as a weapons platform it had no equal. It proved its worth immediately as a team mate with the Tornado GR ls. On their operational debut two Buccaneers escorted four Tornado GR ls, with a third Buccaneer as backup. The Buccaneers' radar and the Tornados' bombs achieved complete success, punching clean through an important bridge over the Euphrates.

The Jaguars achieved the destruction or neutralisation of almost all Iraqi naval units in a sustained attack lasting ten days. They also turned their deadly attention to missile sites and artillery batteries. They quickly adopted tactics completely different from those they had practised in NATO exercises.

The 3 Nimrods provided invaluable maritime surface picture information to US naval forces and to the Royal Navy's Lynx helicopters.

The RAF's tanker aircraft, although small in numbers gained a well-earned reputation for flexibility and efficiency. The elderly Victor detachment completed every one of the 300 tasks allocated to it.

The Hercules, Pumas and Chinooks of the Air Transport Force performed miracles under the most adverse conditions.

In conclusion, I have no hesitation in saying that this war was won primarily through the effective use of air power using high-technology precision-delivered weapons systems. Without this chillingly effective support, the ground war, which was in itself an essential part of victory, would have been prolonged and our army casualties would have been substantially greater.

The Logistics Build-up

Air Commodore Barry Dickens

During the first week of August 1990, I was on leave in the North of England. Like so many others, I had stayed close to the bulletins about Saddam Hussein's invasion of Kuwait, not thinking, as a staff officer at HQ 1 Group, about the impact his actions were shortly to have on my life. As I entered the front garden at home, a neighbour ran out to say that our phone had been ringing many times during the day and that it seemed somebody wanted to get in touch urgently. I immediately rang my boss who told me my AOC, AVM 'Sandy' Wilson had been nominated as Air Commander of the UK Forces' contribution towards halting Saddam, and in all likelihood he would take some of his HQ 1 Gp staff officers out to Saudi Arabia with him. My call to the colours eventually came and I spent a day receiving hurried briefings at High Wycombe before deploying to Riyadh to join the nascent Air HQ on 31 August 1990.

By this time, the Air Commander and his key operational specialists had been in theatre for close on three weeks and had a raft of logistical issues for me to deal with. The most pressing of these were progressing urgent operational modifications such as the fitment of radar absorbent material intake tiles and IFF Mk 12, and exploring opportunities for Host Nation maintenance and supply support. To do this and the myriad of other tasks coming my way, I called for experienced Tornado GR 1 and F 3 engineers, and supply and armament specialists to join me. I was given leave personally to choose these people and with one eye on their professional background and the other on their team-working and staying-power qualities, I very quickly made my nominations. In very short order my small team of four Squadron Leaders and an SNCO was in place.

Whilst my principal role was to provide the Air Cdr with specialist logistic support advice, I had also been charged by AO Eng. & Supply (AVM Mike Alcock at High Wycombe) with personally keeping him in the picture and also maintaining a close watch on weapon safety. In these days of e-mail and wide availability of secure communications equipment, it is perhaps worth recalling that in 1990 the Air HQ was limited to one secure phone and the three Air Staff Management Aid (ASMA) terminals. ASMA, although slow and cumbersome to use by modern standards, proved a boon, enabling the Air HQ staff to keep abreast of UK and Gulf detachment operational, logistics and personnel activity and make timely inputs.

I sent AVM Alcock a weekly report in which I was encouraged to be as candid as I liked. This did not always endear me to some of his staff, but individual sensitivities sometimes had to be ridden over in the interests of getting the job done.

My most immediate aim was to visit the detachments so I could assess priorities in the logistics build-up. Within a week I had been to the F 3 detachment at Dhahran and the GR1's at Muhurraq. At Dhahran one of the key issues was whether the RAF could use the very well founded and BAe-manned second line bays for Tornado support. The matter needed delicate and high level handling with the Saudis to get clearance and so enable us to reduce the numbers of turn round spares, and second line personnel needing to be deployed.

At Muhurraq the GR 1s of No. 14 Sqn had been shoehorned into a very small ramp. This and the limited facilities for airfield weapon storage and break-out posed armament safety problems. A pragmatic course of action was taken, recognising that until more facilities became available,

Tornados and Jaguars share a ramp at Muhurraq, Bahrain (Sir Sandy Wilson)

armed aircraft parking and ordnance storage and preparation peacetime rules would need adaptation if operational readiness was not to be jeopardised.

One of the main operational imperatives in those early days was to assess locations for deploying additional combat aircraft and redeploying the Jaguars from Thumrait, Oman. I accompanied the Air Cdr on a reconnaissance of Tabuk air base in the North West of Saudi Arabia. While ramp space was not a major constraint, at first sight availability of suitable technical and domestic accommodation and fuel storage capacity to support intensive sortie rates cast doubt on Tabuk's suitability. The base was already host to a USAF detachment of 850 personnel operating F-15s, and the Royal Saudi Air Force Base Cdr did not feel his infrastructure could support an additional RAF Tornado force. Subsequently the Base Cdr's reservations were overcome, and planning got underway to prepare Tabuk for an initial deployment of 12 GR 1s before the end of September. Fuel storage was inadequate to support the F-15s, GR 1s and resident RSAF F-5s operating at intensive sortie rates. The RSAF's ingenious solution to this problem was to agree to set up a continuous resupply of road fuel tankers from the refinery at Yanbu on the Red Sea coast.

With the Tabuk planning in progress it was time to turn our attention to finding a new base for the Jaguars. Along with operational colleagues, I spent a day looking at Doha airport in neighbouring Qatar. There were no overriding logistical concerns about the use of Doha, but political considerations determined that room was eventually found for the Jaguars at Bahrain.

As so often in peacetime, so in the build-up to war. My next challenge was far less absorbing but nonetheless critical to our success as an Air HQ. Having arrived after the Americans, we drew the short straw when it came to accommodation in and around the Royal Saudi Air Force HQ in Riyadh. So much so that my team of logisticians had to make do with a desk in a corridor, equipped with neither a telephone nor an ASMA terminal. The Air Commander authorised the purchase of a porta-cabin which the Saudis eventually agreed could be sited in the car park. This then became the 'Sandy House', accommodating the Deputy Air Commander and his operations, logistics and RAF Regiment staff from early October.

By now we were planning for the air transport, tanker and support helicopter forces which were to be based in Saudi Arabia in support of the forthcoming land campaign. An unused terminal at King Khalid International Airport in Riyadh was opened up for use by our transport crews, and the VC 10 tankers finally relocated to the same base. The support helicopters were based at Al Jubayl and there was much to do establishing their support infrastructure, particularly accommodation – both technical and domestic.

More and more of my time began to be taken up with requests for in-theatre visits from a raft of people in the UK involved with the logistics. These had to be examined critically. What value would visitors subsequently add having 'walked the ground'? Some were staff officers who just fancied getting some sand in their boots in a war theatre. For our part, these visits caused a considerable diversion of effort as we nearly always provided an accompanying officer, who would ensure no one picked up the wrong end of the stick on an issue, or misread Saudi sensitivities.

Which brings me to our people in theatre and those with whom I had to deal. Logistics at many of the detachments was managed by a Wing Commander, often OC Eng. and Supply Wing at the squadrons' parent base, who needed little advice or direction from me on how to get on with the job. I tried to visit Tabuk, Muhurraq, Dhahran, Seeb, Al Jubayl and the airhead at Riyadh frequently to assess the situation for myself, and so be that much better able to brief the Air Cdr and AO Eng. and Supply. I also tried to strike up a close rapport with my colleagues at the bases. Those filling command appointments, especially in war, can find them a lonely place to be. Sometimes one does not want one's boss or subordinates to be aware of hesitation over the next step on a tricky situation, and so I tried to be ready to act as a sounding board or offer a second opinion if I was asked to do so.

In the final analysis, our satisfactory level of preparedness to support air operations effectively and safely depended on the quality of our engineering and supply officers and tradesmen. While the formed unit personnel who deployed were quickly able to draw upon established working relationships and camaraderie between one another, for the non-formed unit personnel, drawn from all comers of the Service, this took a good deal longer. It did not help that the two categories of personnel often had different tour lengths in theatre. Nonetheless the common causes which all espoused, of ensuring maximum mission effectiveness and not letting one another down, quickly overcame the inevitable petty whinges and moans.

So as I recall my contribution to the logistics support build-up to the Gulf War, what are the lessons I hope that were learned and solutions later applied during the conflicts of the last decade?

Firstly, our experience in the Gulf showed that more rigour was needed in the way in which personnel were selected for detached duty in a war theatre. It was all rather ad hoc for Op. Granby: nowadays personnel earmarked for early deployment are far more aware of what initially will be expected of them.

Secondly, when time allows clear definition and satisfaction of the configuration standard of the aircraft to be deployed is essential. Subsequently a capability to embody rapidly Service Engineering Modifications and Special Trial

Fits in theatre is an absolute necessity.Thirdly, weapon re-supply and storage require a great deal of management scrutiny. Less-than-ideal weapon storage sites and conditions call for sensible interpretation of armament safety rules.

Finally, it is all too easy to work in a vacuum at deployed Forward and Main Operating Bases. Only rarely will UK Forces deploy completely alone so the importance of Host National Support and mutual supply support between allied forces cannot be overstated. Valuable air transport capacity can thus be employed for transporting people and weapons into theatre, not carrying AGE and consumables already potentially available.

My Saudi Arabian sojourn came to an end in early December when I returned to the UK. On the logistics side we had laid the support foundations which were to underpin the RAF's air campaign. As importantly, I and many of those who worked with me, had amassed invaluable experience which would prove of great worth during the nineties as the RAF's expeditionary and peacekeeping roles became ever more important.

The Jaguars in Desert Storm

Group Captain Bill Pixton DFC AFC

Thursday 17 Jan 91 – Day 1

'War has broken out. I can't believe it! Kuwaitis in the foyer of the hotel in Bahrain watching CNN at 0400 hrs local – like a football match crowd! Got to work 0415. Air Raid warning Red, NBC state Black – soon all clear. Tornados on their 2nd wave. 1st wave all returned to base safely. 2nd wave all returned to base safely – so far no RAF losses. Jaguar pilots quite excited at the prospect. We await our turn keenly. 3rd Tornado wave gets airborne – still no Jaguar tasking – holding 4 Jaguars on 30 minutes readiness for Combat Search and Rescue, 4 on 30 minutes Ground alert Close Air Support (GCAS), 4 on 60 minutes GCAS. CNN in briefing room like a Ben Hur Epic called "WAR IN THE GULF". 1st Tornado lost; looks like they got out. Mood in Squadron changed – much more subdued. Launched 4 Jaguars on Kill Zone Close Air Support mission. Formation ingressed at 20,000 feet and descended to 8000 feet in a dive attack with 1000 lb bombs. AAA reported by Nos. 3 and 4. On return just like "TOP GUN", all our troops came out to greet returning pilots – emotional! END OF DAY ONE.

Everyone O.K. TOTAL SORTIES 4.'

Friday 18 Jan 91 – Day 2

'Day 2 and my 4 ship formation given our first mission.The target was the Republican Guard outfit just to the west of Kuwait, near the Kuwait/Iraqi border. Our primary target was "out" due to bad weather, so I could, quite legitimately, have brought my formation home. However, one of those stupid things that I probably should never have done, I got in contact with the Airborne Warning and Control (AWACS) aircraft and offered our services. We were immediately told by them "we've got a fast Forward Air Controller (FAC) who needs some help from fighters with Mk 82 bombs (500 Mk high explosive bombs)". It was the word "help" that caused the problem. Very difficult to ignore. The AWACS controller put us in contact with the FAC who was flying an OA-10. Once we had checked in on his frequency he was quick to say "I've been in the target area once already and it's a bit thick with Triple A and SAMs but never mind." "Never mind" was not the phrase that I would have chosen! "I've got some targets for you. I'll run in from the west. I'm going to descend until I break cloud – how far out are you now?"'

The plan was that the FAC was going to go in to the target area from the west, fire a smoke rocket at the selected target and pull off back into cloud and head off to the west. We would come out of cloud a few seconds later from the south and bomb the marked target. To clarify our situation – we were flying in pairs trail with the wing-men in close formation, in cloud, thirty-something miles into Iraq – I started to wonder 'what on earth am I doing here?' However, I start to descend, and Pete Tholen, who is my wingy, calls on the radio and asks 'Are we going down?' I said 'I suppose we ought to – this A-10 chap is obviously working very hard and taking a lot of risks for us.'

At that moment the FAC must have broken cloud, down at about 10,000 feet, because the radio was immediately jammed out by his transmission. All we heard on the radio was an unrepeatable expletive followed by 'I'm being shot at, I'm taking fire, I'm pulling off!' Well, this didn't sound too promising and again I wondered if I really needed to get us involved in this situation. We were descending through 12,000 feet and going to break cloud at any moment. We had about thirty seconds to run to the inertial position of the target that the FAC had given us. The FAC continued to describe his current 'situation', and understandably he sounded scared stiff. I said to Pete on the radio 'we'll drop our bombs on the given inertial position even if we don't break cloud.'

Just then this football-size yellow explosion went off between us. We were flying in close formation in cloud so we couldn't have been very far apart. I looked up and to my left and saw the explosion just above and to the left of my fin. Pete was flying in echelon port at the time and he saw it go off to the right of him. As we were in cloud it was difficult to assess distances, but we estimated later that it had gone off between and above our fins. This also meant that the round's trajectory must have taken it between us before it exploded. Wibble! I looked over my shoulder at Pete and there was a pair of big wide eyes looking back at me! He immediately said 'Boss, that's a triple A!' I wondered how he knew what AAA looked like. It hadn't entered my mind that it could be someone shooting at us.

We let the bombs go on the inertial position and broke right to get away from what I now realised was hostile fire. I almost immediately lost Pete in the cloud. In my haste to get away from this rather inhospitable piece of airspace my normal consideration for my No. 2 had deserted me! I'd obviously selected full dry power, rolled into the turn and pulled like mad without any thought for my wingman! Just to increase my adrenalin flow the Radar Warning Receiver (RWR) decided to tell me that a number of threats were taking an interest in my aircraft. The result of this extra flush of adrenalin was that I pulled even harder on the stick. By now I had succeeded in pulling off just about all of my aircraft's energy. I was now lower than I wanted to be, a lot slower than I wanted to be, on my own and still some thirty-odd miles the wrong side of the border.

Another clue to my aircraft's lack of energy was the insistent warbling of the alpha or stall warner. Despite this clearly recognisable warning I was unable to reduce the back pressure that I had applied to the control column. I knew I wanted to turn right and to climb so my right hand moved the stick to the right and hard back. Due to the adrenalin, which I now know has a distinctive aroma, I found it difficult to apply anything other than full control inputs, regardless of any complaints voiced by the aircraft. So, with the stall warner going off and the RWR alarming me, I at last realised that I was in deep trouble. Forty miles ago I should have said 'Sorry, the weather's not fit – we'll come back tomorrow'. But it was the word 'help' that did it. If this American FAC was flying alone in enemy territory and he needed help from somebody with high explosive bombs, who was I to turn my back? Stupid!

As slightly clearer thinking returned I decided to get rid of the drop tanks in a vain effort to improve the aircraft's performance, I didn't need to take those home. I also considered the after burner. It would increase the infra-red signature but I was in cloud, so I used it. About this time I managed to re-educate my right hand and give the aeroplane back a bit. I eventually managed to stagger up to about 20,000 feet and head for home. I heard the other three members of my formation all crossing the border when I still had ten miles to go! They obviously had enough sense to maintain their speed and to climb gently. They had all passed me in the cloud.

We had all dropped our bombs and had probably frightened a few of the enemy, but whether we hit anything I'll never know. What I do know is that the enemy most certainly frightened the adrenalin out of me! I can still remember looking at this yellow globe and thinking 'I've never seen anything like that before'. That was until Pete pointed out that it was Triple A. I'm still amazed by how long it took to register in my tiny mind and equally surprised by the strength of reaction once realisation dawned.

END DAY 2. Everyone still O.K. TOTAL SORTIES 11.

As the campaign progressed, our experience grew and our activities widened. Amongst their many other more familiar roles, the RAF Jaguars were also tasked with Surface target Combat Air patrol, or SUCAP, and maritime Combat Search And Rescue (CSAR) missions over the Persian Gulf during the early part of the conflict. We invariably flew these missions as constituted pairs of aircraft and this involved the use of Air-to-Air Refuelling (AAR) from the RAF Victor tankers, who, I'm pleased to have the opportunity to point out, were always in the right place and at the right time. Our weapon load varied from two CRV-7 rocket pods, to four BL755 cluster bombs, to four airburst 1000 lb free-fall bombs. Both of the aircraft's 30 mm Aden cannons were always loaded with 120 rounds per gun.

Sortie durations varied immensely and were dependent on the activity at the time. Plenty of targets meant short sorties because weapons were expended quickly; no trade led to long sorties, sometimes over four hours, with multiple refuellings. Needless to say the latter type of sortie was not popular with the pilots.

The following are typical of the missions we flew:

24 January. Two by two ships tasked on SUCAP over the Gulf. First pair vectored on to two inbound Iraqi Mirage F-1s. With fifteen miles to go to the merge, the Jaguars lost communications with the controlling agency (ZW), flew through the F-ls in cloud and turned back towards their own CAP position. Meanwhile, the two F-1s had been dispatched by a Saudi Air Force F-15 who proceeded to lock his radar on to the Jaguars! Fortunately, comms were re-established

Jaguar over the desert (Crown copyright)

with ZW and the F-15 was instructed to break lock. The Jaguar formation leader informed the ZW controller, in no uncertain terms, that the Jaguars were on station to counter ground targets and that the over-wing Sidewinders were for self-defence only!

29 January. During their homebound leg after attacking targets in Kuwait, a Jaguar formation reported the position of four Fast Patrol Boats (FPB) to HMS *Gloucester*. As a result of this information the first of the day's SUCAP pairs were vectored on to these FPBs. The four FPBs turned out to be a total of sixteen and the SUCAP pair were ordered to shadow but not to engage. The second SUCAP pair were scrambled from thirty-minute ground alert to relieve the first pair. Eventually, the FPBs were declared hostile and the relief pair attacked with CRV-7 and guns. Confirmation was later received that, in conjunction with the Navy, four of the FPBs had been destroyed and the other twelve damaged. During these attacks accurate AAA fire and an Infra-Red surface-to-air missile (SAM) launch was encountered.

30 January. Day 14 of Operation Desert Storm, and ships of the Iraqi Navy made a desperate dash for the northern waters of the Persian Gulf and sanctuary in Iranian waters. Only a few of them were likely to make it through the gauntlet of Allied air-power lying in wait to attack any surface contacts. Already on fire amidships after being attacked by US Navy aircraft, a Polnocny C class landing ship fell prey to a pair of rocket and cannon-armed RAF Jaguars only a few miles from the mouth of the Shatt-al-Arab waterway in southern Iraq. After a low pass to confirm the identity of the ship the Jaguars positioned for their attack which left the Polnocny sinking, ablaze from end to end.

31 January. The first SUCAP pair were re-tasked to a Battlefield Air Interdiction (BAI) mission. Their task was to search a road just over the Kuwait border with Saudi Arabia for concentrations of armour reportedly moving south. Both aircraft attacked military vehicles on the road with BL-755 cluster bombs. The attack by the No. 2 aircraft appeared to be against an Armoured Personnel Carrier (APC) parked at the side of the road. This APC was later confirmed from the aircraft's head-up-display video tape to be, in fact, a Russian built ZSU-23/4 self-propelled, 4-barrelled anti-aircraft artillery piece! Fortunately, the attack managed to combine the parked ZSU-23/4 and a passing military truck at the moment of release.

Targets effectively dried up at the beginning of February and the 4th saw the last SUCAP/CSAR taskinq for the Jaguar Squadron. All of the Squadron's efforts were then turned against targets in Kuwait and southern Iraq.

The effectiveness of SUCAP/CSAR missions was rather down to the luck of the draw regarding the appearance, or not, of targets. However, the main lesson learnt was that in a hostile environment it is particularly difficult for the pilot to achieve exact weapon release parameters. It is, therefore, essential to have an accurate, computed, weapon aiming solution for any and all of the weapons that are planned to be delivered.

Albert of Arabia
Flight Lieutenant T. J. Burgess

The 2nd of August 1990, the beginning of the Gulf crisis. Life at Lyneham was unusually quiet. At that time, in fact, LXX Squadron were just about to start two weeks' stand-down as part of an engineering recovery period intended to enable our aircraft engineers to catch up some of the servicing backlog that had developed. This period proved to be extremely short-lived as events, both political and military, unfolded terrifying quickly. The rest, as they say, is now history.

The Lyneham Hercules Wing very soon became involved with the deployment of Tornado F3s to Dhahran in Saudi Arabia, and the mode of operation used became all too familiar throughout the rest of the war. The Akrotiri slip pattern became part of life for Lyneham's aircrew. Records were set and broken, rules were bent and goal posts moved. It was not unheard of for crews to work twenty-two-hour days with twelve hours off, sharing the floor of the Ladies' Room in the Officers' Mess with two or three other crews, only to repeat it the next day or – more usually – night. Having personally clocked up over sixty-three hours flying in the first six days it became increasingly more difficult to stay awake during the long night trips across the Saudi Arabian desert.

In October 1990, because of the increasing number of destinations in the Gulf region requiring resupply by air the air transport operation changed partly to a 'hub and spoke' system. The strategic transports, the TriStar and VC 10, flew to Riyadh to off-load freight for various Gulf destinations, and loads were then broken down and distributed by Hercules. The initial deployment to Riyadh comprised three Hercules affectionately known as 'Fat Albert' by the crews, but this was quickly increased to seven. On 12 November I flew out to start the first of two Riyadh detachments. These detachments were to provide some of the most satisfying flying of my career. Finally, we were operating the Hercules in its natural role of tactical transport, not strategic airlifter as had been the case so far. A routine quickly became established whereby we worked day on day off, and flew four or five sorties per day, each normally about an hour long – no more long hours flying through the night. Initially we were accommodated in hotels until other suitable accommodation was found in the form of a newly (nearly!) completed compound where each crew had its own apartment. As the build up of coalition forces increased in late 1990, the Riyadh Hercules detachment settled into a programme of regular shuttles and milk-run schedules between the various bases in the Gulf theatre. Crews were constituted for the duration of deployment, with each crew spending about one month in theatre. I returned to the UK in December 1990, and after a couple of days stand-down

Hercules from Lyneham Hercules Wing (Crown copyright)

resumed flying the by now all-too-familiar routes from UK to the Gulf via Akrotiri in Cyprus. Prior to August 1990 Lyneham crews had considered Lyneham–Akrotiri to be a fairly long sector with unsociable hours. We were now regularly flying Akrotiri–Marham–Akrotiri for example in a day, arriving in UK in time for breakfast. In August 1990 alone the Lyneham fleet flew nearly 8300 hours, breaking the previous record of 6800 set in May 1982 during the Falklands conflict, and by January 1991 there was still no sign of a let-up.

As the UN deadline for Iraqi withdrawal approached on 15 January, all those at Lyneham not actually airborne were glued to televisions eagerly awaiting news of the impending and increasingly inevitable war. When it came, on 17 January, I was at home in between trips to the Gulf, celebrating my recent engagement.

The phone rang that night: a flight commander on LXX Squadron was getting a crew together for a Riyadh detachment which was to last for the duration of the war. It was not an invitation that could be declined. We arrived back in Riyadh on 28 January to find the detachment back in the Marriott Hotel, and were welcomed by Saddam Hussein with a Scud attack that night which demolished a school just two blocks away from the hotel.

Life in Riyadh was certainly more tense than it had been during my last stay, but was by no means without its humorous moments: certainly the sight of Hercules crews shopping in Safeways in Riyadh, with a respirator on one hip and a 9 mm Browning pistol on the other, took some getting used to.

Lyneham personnel also very quickly acquired a reputation for doing things in style. This was typified by the anonymous person seen taking a shower at a desert airstrip. A bucket with holes in the bottom had been rigged up on a frame; into this an assistant would pour water, but not just any old water – the man was using bottled Perrier!

With the air war still in full swing, speculation increased as to when the ground invasion would start. The Riyadh detachment was involved in General Schwarzkopf's diversionary plan, moving troops and equipment from the Kuwaiti border west to the Iraqi border. We operated out of a strip at Abu Hadriyah up to Qaisumah near Hafr-Al-Batin. Albert was now well and truly in his element. The route up to Qaisumah was to be flown under visual flight rules: the conditions, however, precluded this. As the smoke from the burning oil wells blacked out the sun we would often be faced with a hundred foot overcast cloud-base which, when combined with our ground level to 500 feet slot to co-ordinate with the attack packages, meant that we were forced to fly down to 50 feet at times, following the Tapline Road to Hafr-Al-Batin. This road, which for days was nose to tail with tanks and other vehicles for hundreds of miles, was an ever-present reminder of the scale of the operation to come.

As the ground war approached the reality of our war role became more apparent. The Riyadh detachment was to provide the link for casualty evacuation between the forward field hospitals and the main base hospitals at Riyadh and Jubail. As we trained with the Aero-medical evacuation squadrons the horror of the numbers of casualties expected dawned on us. Psychiatrists flew out from the UK to lecture crews on the psychological effects of the job ahead, and to forewarn us of the problems of Post Traumatic Stress Syndrome.

As the invasion progressed at phenomenal speed – 180 miles in 100 hours – another airstrip was constructed in about twenty-four hours enabling further resupply by air to the front. By 28 February it was all over bar the mopping up. Once the cessation of hostilities had been declared the priority became the restoration of the British Ambassador, Sir Michael Weston, to office in Kuwait city. Our crew was called upon for the task. We left Riyadh in the early afternoon of 28 February and flew up towards Kuwait at medium level in clear blue skies. We began our descent about thirty-five miles south of the city and entered the thick black cloud of smoke at about 10,000 feet. From my seat I was unable to see the air-to-air refuelling probe – visibility was down to less than six feet and the blackness can only be compared to being in a flight simulator with the visuals switched off. According to our intelligence brief, Kuwait International airport had effectively been reduced to an airstrip, there was no radar, no serviceable approach aids, no lights, nor any air traffic control.

Still in complete darkness we pushed on down to about 500 feet, our only means of navigation being the Hercules' rather old, unreliable weather radar used in ground mapping mode. Fortunately it was being operated by an ex nav-radar from the Vulcan force.

As we broke through the base of the smoke the sight before us left us stunned: all around, huge columns of flame spurted from the ground – the only light was the eerie orange glow they produced, and the turbulence from them tossed us around so much that control of the aircraft became difficult. From the ground clutter on the radar the nav picked out a motorway bridge on the extended centre-line one mile from runway 33 Left, which we used to line up on. At about half a mile finals we picked out the headlights of two jeeps parked either side of the threshold. After touching down from a tactical approach we had to use maximum reverse thrust and braking as demolition teams and combat engineers had only cleared the first third of the runway of unexploded bombs: beyond that the runway was cratered and littered with burnt-out cars and baggage pods. We taxied clear of the runway and, after being nearly hit by a baggage pod blown towards us by a Chinook lifting off, parked next to the wreckage of the BA 747 destroyed on the pan. The final shock was to get off the aircraft to find it cold, raining and dark at 3 o'clock in the afternoon in Kuwait City. The British Ambassador was back in residence.

Far from winding down after the ground war finished, tasking for the Hercules detachment stepped up a gear. The Coalition forces came under pressure from all sides to return the troops home as quickly as possible. More airstrips were levelled by the Royal Engineers to speed up the withdrawal of British troops. It very quickly became apparent that whilst doing an engine-running on-load of troops the slowest part of the operation was stacking their kit and getting them seated and strapped in. The solution was simple: take the seats out. This meant that we could carry half as many soldiers again with them sitting on their own Bergens. Whilst initially this may seem to have been an obvious and trivial deviation from our standard operation, it was felt at the time to be a worthwhile victory for common sense and flexibility over our sometimes over-restrictive rules.

Before leaving Riyadh for the second time we flew the shortest and yet most memorable trip of the war. My crew was on standby on 6 March 1991 when we were called to fly to Riyadh Military to collect some passengers whom we were to fly back to Riyadh King Khalid, our home base, a round trip of some thirty miles. On arrival at the military airfield we were marshalled to a distant corner and told to wait. Before long a Red Cross jet arrived to be met by a huge reception committee including Generals de la Billiere and Schwarzkopf: it was the return of the first of the allied prisoners of war. After their official welcome the British POWs, who by now were household names, were brought to our aircraft to be flown back to a waiting VC 10 at King Khalid airport for their onward journey to Cyprus. Emotions were high on both sides, particularly as some of the aircrew POWs were personal friends or colleagues from flying training days.

Our crew left Riyadh for the last time on 25 March and travelled direct to Lyneham as passengers in the back of a Hercules, which we shared with five other crews and an Iraqi anti-aircraft artillery piece. The reception we received at Lyneham was far beyond our expectations, as loved ones and senior officers alike met us with champagne and camera crews. On reflection I feel justifiably proud to have been part of a team which I feel demonstrated the Hercules, Lyneham and the Royal Air Force at their best.

Tornado Attack

Air Commodore J. J. Witts DSO

For those of us in Saudi Arabia, the UN's long-awaited final deadline for Iraqi forces to leave Kuwait passed at 8 a.m. local on 16 January 1991. Overnight, Air HQ in Riyadh had ordered us to cease further Tornado training flying and 'load to the Frag' – the fragmentary order, or that portion of the Coalition air campaign plan which spelled out the specific tasks for my Tornado GR 1s. Clearly, offensive operations would be starting sooner rather than later. The latest update of the Frag had come in overnight and I worked through it carefully with the Intelligence team to ensure that we understood exactly what was required of us. Now, a single piece of information stood between us and combat. The timing of each and every Allied mission would depend on a co-ordinating start time, or 'H-hour'. Until that last highly classified piece of the jigsaw was issued, we had no idea whether our initial sorties would be flown in daylight or at night. We hoped it would be at night. Either way, the Frag demanded that in the first twenty-four hours we were to attack two targets, each with four aircraft loaded with JP 233 airfield denial weapons. Only ten of our eleven Tornado GR 1s were serviceable. I told the engineers to load them all.

As the day drew on, we continued with final preparations. Each of the aircrew was issued with a range of 'goodies' that had been held in readiness for this moment.

Tornado GR 1 (IDS) rendezvous with a Victor Tanker for in-flight refuelling over Saudi Arabia (BAE Systems)

Among these were twelve gold sovereigns, which might be used to bribe or pay off anyone who assisted escape in the event of being shot down. Naturally, we had to sign receipts for them! We were also given copies of a 'goolie chit' which, in three Arabic dialects, stated that the British Government solemnly promised to pay the sum of £5000 for the safe (and complete!) return of the bearer. Other items included silk maps and survival kits or 'go-packs' to supplement what was already contained in our parachute packs. Soon investigated by the ever-curious aircrew, amongst many other things, the 'go-packs' were found to contain some condoms and a tampon. Predictably, this sparked off ribald and none-too-subtle speculation about their potential uses.

The tension was palpable around the Detachment. By mid-afternoon, after checking and rechecking that everything was in order, I stood the aircrew down to try to rest and relax as much as possible. I went back to my quarters and settled in front of the TV to watch CNN. All was quiet in Baghdad, which blew away my latest theory that, as a means of saving face, Saddam Hussein would allow the deadline to pass before immediately starting to withdraw. Then the telephone rang:

'Come to work, Boss. The rest of your formation are on their way in'.

This must be it! My mind raced as I hastily gathered my kit. It would be nice to claim that I was totally calm and collected as I leapt into the car and hurried back to the airbase. However, something seemed to have gone wrong with my nervous system as my legs and feet stubbornly refused to obey my brain's commands and I repeatedly crunched the gearbox like a learner driver. Fortunately, the symptoms disappeared as I screeched to a halt at our Detachment HQ. Gp Capt. Cliff Spink, the Dhahran Detachment Commander, was waiting for me. We went to my office and he showed me a cryptic top secret signal from Air HQ stating that H-hour would be 0001 GMT on 17 January – one minute past three local time the next morning. So this indeed was it. After so many months of hard work and preparation, we were finally having to go to war. For a moment, I felt very angry. One man's stupidity had brought us to this, and now people would have to die before it was all over. Anyway, it was time to get down to business. I broke the news to the rest of my formation.

They were beginning to realise that flying the Detachment's first combat sortie was one of the more dubious perks of being in the CO's four-ship. We had always thought that we were the best. Now was the time to prove it. Our target was an airfield in south central Iraq. We would be Mission 4431 GA, 'Belfast' formation, four aircraft, each armed with two JP 233s. To make our allocated attack time, we would have to get airborne a couple of hours before 'H' hour. The navigators busily checked and rechecked their planning while we pilots kept them supplied with coffee and tea. Eventually, they decided that we needed to take off at 0130 local to make good our required time on target of 0315 local. We still had a lot of time to fill and we took advantage of this to brief ourselves as thoroughly as possible on every aspect of the forthcoming mission. Subjects like escape and evasion suddenly became hugely important, and we went over our survival equipment a dozen times. In due course, it was time to brief the sortie formally. Then, in a final, rather poignant piece of administration, the Int. boys collected all our personal belongings. After that, I felt rather like I imagined a condemned man must feel.

We climbed aboard our crew bus and were driven out to our aircraft. Although it was a very warm and humid night, we were dressed in full flying kit with cold weather jackets, just in case. We had armfuls of kit: NBC hoods and gas masks, Night Vision Goggles, flying helmets, personal weapons, maps and charts. Our groundcrew, who now realised what was about to happen, were uncharacteristically subdued but highly professional, as they scurried around the aeroplanes making last minutes checks and adjustments.

Eventually, after one last cigarette, I climbed into the cockpit and strapped in. Flight Lieutenant 'AJ' Smith, my navigator, was busy coaxing the avionics system into life as I 'cranked up' the engines and checked out the aircraft systems. I still felt tense and, although my hands were not quite shaking, it still took me three attempts to punch in correctly the coded sequence of numbers to 'enable' our secure radio.

Eventually, all was ready and, as we slowly taxied out, the accustomed bustle of Dhahran airport continuing around us unabated. Freighter after freighter landed and took off, still delivering essential materiel for the Coalition cause. But now, everything seemed to have a new relevance. Switching to tower frequency, I obtained take off clearance – although we would have gone anyway! With our four aircraft correctly lined up, we powered up the engines. A quick check that everyone was ready, then into reheat and release the brakes. Unsurprisingly, the aircraft was sluggish at first. With full internal fuel, two 2250-litre external fuel tanks, two JP 233s, two Sidewinder missiles and fully loaded cannon, I had never flown a Tornado as heavy as this. Nor, in all probability, had anyone else. As AJ called the speeds, it seemed to take forever to accelerate: '100, 120, 130, 140'. Now we were moving... '150, 160, Rotate!' I pulled back on the control column and, after a last fleeting reluctance, the aircraft 'unstuck' and we were airborne. I quickly retracted the undercarriage and started a lazy turn to allow my formation to cut the corner and take position. As soon as they were 'aboard', we switched radio frequencies and checked in with our designated AWACS. So far so good. Now AWACS knew that we were airborne and on our way 'as fragged'. They would track our IFF throughout the sortie and provide any necessary information to us. For the moment, however, we switched to our air-to-air refuelling frequency, ready to rendezvous with the pair of Bahrain-based Victor K2 tankers that had been assigned to us, leaving our second radio tuned to our secure private formation frequency. Suddenly, on this radio, No. 2 called to say that all his EW equipment had failed and he was trying to reset it. He tried everything in the book to recover the equipment without result, so I reluctantly ordered him to return to Dhahran. I was not going to let him risk the enemy defences without some form of self-protection.

By now, we were cruising at our designated altitude of about 10,000 feet. Away from the lights of the Dhahran area, the night was just thick blackness. The weather did not look very promising, with scattered clouds and quite a lot of turbulence. Hopefully, we would still be able to find our tankers easily enough. AJ spotted them on radar, and eventually they appeared out of the murk as we manoeuvred into a trail position. The refuelling was to be carried out in radio silence. With No 2. gone, I took station on the lead tanker as Nos 3 and 4 moved in on the second. When my tanker's lights indicated that he was ready to start the first refuelling, I closed in to make contact with one of the

Victor's two trailing hoses. The turbulence was now quite bad and it was more by luck than judgement that I managed to get the probe into the refuelling basket. This really was hard work, and AJ worked tirelessly to encourage me as I laboured like a one-armed paper hanger to stay in contact and keep the fuel flowing. Above us, we could see the cloud tops skimming past. Even a small increase in altitude would have brought us into smoother air. However, with so many aircraft airborne on this wave, the tanker obviously dared not stray from our assigned altitude. We would just have to tough it out. The conditions continued to deteriorate and more than once we fell out of the basket. However, we simply had to have this fuel, and visions of landing back at Dhahran in disgrace flashed through my mind as we struggled all over again to regain contact. On the rear tanker No. 4 was obviously having considerable difficulty because he had already 'spoked' the tanker's left basket. Sensibly, No. 3 moved forward to join me on the lead tanker. No. 4 was the Detachment's most junior pilot and he was doing a terrific job just to 'hang-in' in these conditions. We all were for that matter. Then No. 4 'spoked' the rear tanker's other basket (by putting his probe through the spokes of the basket and rendering it un-aerodynamic and therefore unusable). There was also a risk that fragments of the basket would be ingested by the Tornado's engines and, in peacetime, one would divert for a precautionary landing if this happened. In war, it was an acceptable risk.

I was about to call him up to the front tanker when the rear tanker sensibly decided to retract his now useless shredded wing hoses and trail his third, central hose. This was a heavy-duty hose that might be slightly more stable. Fortunately, it seemed to do the trick. We spent so much time getting fuel during the first bracket that it was soon time to start our second refuelling. Fortunately, we had now broken out into slightly clearer and less turbulent air and things started to go much more easily. Even so, by the time we were ready to leave the tankers, I was exhausted. And we hadn't really started yet.

At the appropriate point, we broke away from the tankers and started to descend towards our planned low-level entry position. During the descent, I switched on the Terrain Following Radar and locked in the auto-pilot. AJ was busy getting a last radar fix before leaving friendly territory. He was fretting slightly because of the errors that had accumulated in his navigation system, and he had begun to suspect that the Inertial Navigation (IN) system was not performing as well as it should. As we dropped towards the desert floor it became darker and darker. Cloud cover obscured what little starlight there was and it was impossible to see anything outside the cockpit, except the lights of our two formation colleagues in the distance. As we crossed the designated 'lights off' line, even these small comforting signs disappeared from view. The terrain was fairly flat with nothing showing on radar to interfere with our progress.

After a while, we flashed across the international border and into Iraq itself. AJ and I marked the moment by wishing each other luck before returning to business. Things had been fairly quiet until now but, suddenly a faint 'strobe' began to paint in the one o'clock position. As we sped towards it, the strobe became stronger and our threat warning equipment annotated it as a Fulcrum. My heart sank. The Russian-built MiG 29 Fulcrum was the one Iraqi fighter that we did not wish to meet. Iraqi pilots might be an unknown quantity but the Fulcrum was an agile high performance fighter with a 'look down-shoot down' capability. Here we were, only ten minutes inside Iraq, and it looked as though one had shown up. We changed course slightly to the left and the strobe slowly moved around the clock on our right hand side. Although there were no other threat indications and no warnings from the AWACS, the warning receiver stubbornly insisted that there was a Fulcrum transitioning for a tail shot on us. There was nothing else to do but 'think small' and wait to see what happened. Thankfully, after a tense few minutes, the strobe faded and disappeared.

By now, AJ was searching hard for our final pre-attack radar fix. This was essential to update the accuracy of our navigation and bomb aiming system before our attack run. Eventually, he found it, but needed to take a very large error out of the navigation system. Clearly, the IN was now drifting badly and feeding false errors into our navigation system. I knew that the terrain between us and our target was pretty flat, so I selected an auto-pilot mode that would maintain our height at about 200 feet by reference to the ground immediately below us. This meant that I could put the terrain-following radar to standby, reducing the radar emissions that might warn the Iraqis of our approach. We then completed pre-attack checks on the weapons system and I accelerated to about 500 knots and turned left to intercept our final target run as AJ started to 'work' the final aiming mark with his radar.

AJ made some small final corrections, and when he was satisfied I reselected the auto-pilot and the aircraft turned sharply left to take out the aiming error. I still couldn't see anything ahead – just darkness, and the slowly unwinding circle in the fluorescent green HUD symbology, indicating time to weapon release. With about five miles to go, AJ took one last look with the radar to make sure his aiming was spot on. It was. I rechecked the safety switches, which would ensure that the JP 233s dispensed automatically at the computer-calculated release point. Finally, I flipped the cover to expose the bombing commit button on top of the control column. Once this was held down, everything else would happen automatically.

This was really it then! For the first time in my life I was about to drop real weapons on a real enemy target. I was tense but there was no fear. I was more concerned that we had done everything possible to make the attack successful. After all this trouble, I did not want to have to return to base with some feeble excuse about messing up the switchery. It had to be right. AJ counted down the seconds to release. 'Thirty. Twenty. Fifteen. Ten.' I had a fleeting impression of a few lights and buildings on the ground ahead and, with about five seconds to go, I held down the commit button. AJ continued the countdown and then, right on time, the aircraft started to vibrate rapidly as our two JP 233s started to dispense their warheads. I could see a rapidly pulsing glow in my peripheral vision. I knew that the JPs could take several seconds to dispense fully but it seemed to take forever. Then, suddenly, two massive thumps came from beneath the aircraft. Simultaneously, various alarms sounded off, warning lights flashed and the aircraft snapped into a sharp climb as the autopilot safety circuits took over control. I thought we had been hit or had flown into something. However, as I struggled to get the aircraft back under control, I realised that the thumps had been the empty JP 233 canisters being jettisoned and that, somehow, this had caused the autopilot to drop out. Meanwhile, I could see all kinds of flashing lights and explosions going off outside the cockpit. AJ was yelling at me to get the height down as MA tracer arced over and around us. We very nearly hit the ground as I over-controlled the aircraft in my attempts to get down too quickly. Now I was frightened!

Afterwards, No. 3 told us about SAMs being fired off at us, but in the melee neither AJ nor I had seen them. Just as quickly as things had started, a semblance of calm returned as we hurried away into the darkness. AJ reported a warning strobe from a missile site ahead and to our left. We altered course to the right – but not too far, because the sky in that direction suddenly erupted in orange flames, quickly followed by a curtain of incandescent white lights as more and more anti-aircraft artillery barrage fired into the darkness. That too disappeared as quickly as it had started, as we rushed onwards as fast as we could away from the target. When it seemed safe to do so, I called the other two aircraft to check in on the radio and breathed a huge sigh of relief as they both answered promptly.

Carefully, we avoided the area where we had been warned that helicopters might be operating, and at last we were able to start heading back towards the Saudi border. Much later, I learned that the Apache and MH-53J Pave Low helicopters were a US Special Forces operation to neutralise a critical radar post. We were among the first to gain advantage from the hole they had made in the Iraqis' defences. Their operation was so important that they were scheduled to attack twenty-two minutes before H-hour.

Now we were concerned to make sure that we were 'squawking' the correct identification codes on our IFF so that we did not alarm our own side. The last thing we wanted was to get shot down by our own defences. After what seemed an age, we crossed back into Saudi territory and the tension dissipated rapidly. As I retarded the throttles for the first time since crossing into Iraq, it was very tempting to relax completely. We had survived. We were also pretty sure that we had done an accurate and effective job. However, as we climbed into friendly Saudi skies to rendezvous with the VC 10 tanker that should be waiting to give us enough fuel to return to Dhahran, there was no sign of the rest of my formation. Where were they? Our lights were back on and a radio cross-check of positions indicated that we ought to be in the same area. However, search as we might, we could not see them. It began to be clear that our navigation system was now so completely out to lunch that, to put it bluntly, we were lost. Tension returned with a vengeance! At least we were still in radio contact.

The others had now made visual contact with the VC 10 and were closing in to refuel. Jerry Gegg, in the back of the No. 4 jet, had a brainwave. He told us that he was about to fire off an Infra Red Decoy (IRD) flare. Incredibly bright even in daylight, these were visible for miles at night. AJ and I searched the sky in front of us but saw nothing. The tension rose another notch. I started a turn onto a reciprocal course and asked Jerry to fire another flare. Suddenly, there it was – absolutely miles away. AJ asked for another flare, just to make certain. No doubt at all this time, so I accelerated towards the flare's origin.

By now our fuel state was getting perilously low and I asked Jerry to keep firing flares periodically as we flew as fast as we could towards them. It seemed to take an age to catch up, and by now there would be no room for error getting on to the tanker. We would have to 'plug in' immediately or make an emergency diversion to whatever airfield might be available. By now, No. 4 was plugged into the VC 10's left wing hose, still firing flares, as we barrelled in from behind. Number 3 had taken a quick top-up from the starboard hose but now held clear to let us in. For once, I got it right first time and speared straight into the refuelling basket. As the fuel began to flow, AJ and I finally began to relax in earnest. With more than enough fuel to get us home, we disconnected and waited while No. 3 topped-up. We could probably have led the Team home from here but AJ was having to use a much less reliable navigation mode and it made more sense to hand over the lead to No. 3 and take seat on the wing for the ride home.

As briefed, No. 3 had passed our in-flight report to the AWACS. Now, with the dawn rising in front of us, we flew in an easy, relaxed formation towards Dhahran where, despite some early morning mist, Shifty skilfully led us in for a stream landing. Eventually, with the undercarriage down and full flap selected, it seemed very peaceful gliding in on the still morning air towards touchdown. And it was wonderful to feel terra firma beneath our wheels again as we touched down, braked and taxied back to our dispersal. A large group of our groundcrew was waiting to meet us, huge grins on their faces to match our own. We climbed out of our cockpits and there were congratulations all round but, as soon as we could, we climbed aboard the crew bus to take us back to the Squadron for a full debriefing. The Team were exhausted and emotionally drained. As we slumped into the coach's comfortable seats I pulled out my cigarettes and lit one. AJ grabbed it and started to inhale deeply.

'Hey, AJ!' I exclaimed. 'You don't smoke.' 'I know' he replied.

An RAF Lawyer in the Gulf

Air Commodore R. A. Charles

I was on leave with my family in Denmark in the summer of 1990, when I heard about the Iraqi invasion of Kuwait. At the time I was a Wing Commander on the staff of the Deputy Director of Legal Services at Headquarters RAF Germany in

Rheindahlen. I was responsible for giving legal advice in disciplinary cases and court-martial prosecutions. It was therefore with some surprise that on 27 October 1990 I found myself leaving RAF Lyneham on a Hercules bound for Riyadh in Saudi Arabia to take up my post as Legal Adviser to Commander British Forces Middle East, who was then Air Vice-Marshal Sandy Wilson. The ten-hour journey was broken by a short stop at RAF Akrotiri in Cyprus, where I was met by two colleagues from the RAF Legal Branch who had the good fortune to be serving there. I shared with them what was to be my last alcoholic beer for some time.

On my arrival at HQ BFME I was given a warm welcome, coloured by the customary banter about lawyers that the operators feel is necessary on such occasions. My Terms of Reference made me responsible for advising commanders on the Law of Armed Conflict (LOAC), the basic aim of which is to ensure that the use of armed force does not inflict unnecessary suffering and that the force used is proportionate to the military objective. The LOAC governs all aspects of military operations, and at various times I was particularly focused on the treatment of prisoners of war and the injured, and weapons usage. In addition, I was expected to advise on and interpret the Rules of Engagement handed down through the chain of command. These rules are intended to clarify the circumstances in which a military commander can authorise the use of force, and set out the amount of force that can be used in particular circumstances. The main idea is to make sure, in so far as it is possible, that a war is not started by mistake. Some of the issues were complex, but this was the inevitable consequence of being part of a multi-national coalition with each force operating under its own national ROE.

Discussions about the harmonisation of ROE took up much of my time and I came to know my US counterparts very well. I enjoyed visiting my opposite number, Lieutenant Colonel Bernie Donahue, USAF, a lawyer at CENT COM, as he seemed to have an inexhaustible supply of doughnuts! In addition to ROE, we discussed and drafted various US/UK agreements, including one dealing with the possible transfer of any Iraqi POW taken by the UK forces into the custody of the US.

The arrival of General Sir Peter de la Billiere as CBFME and Air Vice-Marshal Wratten as the Air Commander brought with it an increase in the tempo of life, as the build up continued and the shuttle diplomacy had little success. Christmas and New Year passed without event, although it was increasingly clear that the forces of Saddam Hussein would have to be kicked out of Kuwait.

The Headquarters went on to twenty-four-hour manning on 13 January 1991, and a couple of days before, Squadron Leader Alastair McGrigor had arrived to share the legal load. By this stage, in addition to the two RAF lawyers in Riyadh, four officers of the Army Legal Corps were scattered throughout Saudi Arabia providing legal advice to commanders and personnel. Back in UK RAF and Army lawyers provided round-the-clock support from the Joint Headquarters at High Wycombe.

At 3 a.m. on 17 January 1991 Alastair McGrigor rang me to say that the air offensive had started. This was not a complete surprise to me as I had been listening for a while to the roar of US KC 135 tanker aircraft getting airborne from nearby airfields. At this stage the nature of our work changed – the ROE profile for offensive operations was sufficient for the planned operations and well understood. The focus of our work shifted to advising on the Geneva Convention, in particular in relation to the treatment of prisoners of war.
This work brought us into contact with delegates from the International Committee of the Red Cross (ICRC) and on the eve of the land offensive I escorted one of these delegates to a POW camp which had been built by the Army in the desert near to the border with Kuwait. Lieutenant Colonel Charles Garraway was the legal adviser to the Camp Commandant and hosted the visit. After an inspection which ended with afternoon tea, including cucumber sandwiches on a white table cloth, we returned to Riyadh with no adverse comment of substance being made.

The brief visit to the desert reinforced my belief that I was very fortunate in my accommodation. I shared a villa with another RAF officer in a complex called Arabian Homes located on the outskirts of Riyadh. The Scud missile attacks on Riyadh were worrying to begin with, principally because of fears of what the warheads might contain. During the first attack we sat in the cupboard under the stairs in our villa dressed in Noddy suit, respirator and helmet watching American football on CNN through the open cupboard door and listening to the launches from the nearby Patriot battery. The incongruity of the picture was not lost on me and we moderated our behaviour. However, the nature of the threat and the local security situation was such that my respirator was always at hand; as was my Browning pistol when travelling away from the Headquarters.

The most satisfying legal work I did was as a member of the UK delegation at an ICRC-sponsored meeting in Riyadh on 7 March 1991 between the Coalition Forces and an Iraqi delegation, to discuss the mutual repatriation of prisoners of war and civilians taken into captivity. There had been real concerns about the fate of captured RAF aircrew and others. The memorandum of understanding drafted and signed at this meeting cleared the way for their repatriation.

When I arrived in Riyadh I was struck by the ad-hoc nature of the Headquarters, in that, with the exception of a small core, we had all been drawn from diverse areas of the UK Armed Forces and some of us had been asked to work in unfamiliar areas. However, the spirit was tremendous and strong leadership moulded us into an effective team. There were many lessons to draw from the Gulf War in relation to the integration of uniformed lawyers into operational headquarters in order to provide the advice which is now a mandatory requirement of international law.

At the time it seemed to me bizarre that RAF lawyers were not involved in RAF exercises, but were expected to participate on operations. I am pleased that the lessons have been learnt, as over the last ten years we have become more and more integrated into the operational activities of our own Service. Royal Air Force lawyers have participated in numerous exercises and deployed on operations in the Gulf and Kosovo as well as acting as UN military observers in Georgia.

On 17 March 1991 I boarded an RAF TriStar at King

Khalid International Airport outside Riyadh and returned home in considerably more comfort than the outward journey. Most of the passengers were bound for RAF Brize Norton, but four of us got off at RAF Wildenrath to find a completely deserted air terminal. I had to call out the duty armourer to take possession of our personal weapons but the lack of a reception did not diminish my pleasure at being home!

Chariots of Fire

Wing Commander Jim Hughes

It is now over ten years since the Gulf War was successfully and rapidly prosecuted. Some memories of the period are crystal clear, some hazy, some personal, many trivial – but all had a major effect on me and the light armoured squadron which I commanded. To this day, they still act as the catalyst for war stories amongst old comrades and friends. This short story is a personal recollection of what happened to No. 1 Sqn RAF Regt during that war.

Number 1 Squadron's badge is an Assyrian Chariot, to reflect the time the squadron had previously served in the Middle East, based at Habbaniya in central Iraq. This was in the 1920s as part of Trenchard's policy of using air power to dominate the vast areas of Iraq, Syria and the Trans-Jordan. It was ironic that we should return some seventy years later in similar circumstances.

When the Iraqi army invaded Kuwait in August 1990 and the Western Powers began to react very positively against it, I decided that unlike the Falklands War my squadron would be involved. Based on this feeling alone we embarked on a series of demanding exercises and a rigorous training cycle that focused upon the need to fight the squadron in the Middle East desert. I had not made my prescience known to the squadron, because I did not want them to build up to the possibility only to discover that the squadron commander had no direct line to the MOD and in the grand scheme of things could not actually affect the allocation of troops to task. So, trying to retain my air of infallibility – adopted fallaciously by all commanders – we carried on with the training whilst I nagged the chain of command, as much as it would allow me, to send us to the Middle East. No doubt my men wondered why they were being pushed so hard, but no one complained, and as in everything they were ever asked to do, they did so with consummate professionalism. When we were eventually given the order to deploy, I was confident that we were as ready as we could be.

Our involvement got off to a bad start. I was instructed to take about half of the squadron to Bahrain to relieve 58 Sqn RAF Regt tasked with the defence of the Tornado detachment at Muharraq. This was definitely not the desert war I had planned and I did not relish the prospect of having the squadron split up. On 16 January 1991 we flew via Cyprus, where we night stopped on the evening that the Air Campaign started. I recall vividly, and with great amusement, the interest the C 130 crew took in their NBC (Nuclear, Biological, Chemical) equipment! I hadn't seen that sort of keenness in training. RAFDET Muharraq had an air of quiet professionalism, with aircraft being prepared during the day for nightime operations over Iraq. Our task was to secure the base and make sure that no-one and nothing would interfere with the Tornado operation.

One event we could not prevent was the nightly SCUD rocket attack alarms: we had seven minutes from warning of attack from Fylingdales to impact. Muhharaq escaped unhurt as none landed too near, but they did provide the most wonderful spectacle as the Saudi-based US Patriot missiles were fired at them. When the attacks first started everyone was terribly conscientious and very quick to don protective clothing and respirators. Because no missiles had landed on Bahrain an air of complacency crept in as the weeks went by, and the drills slowed with those able to follow the alert on CNN news. Of course, many followed the conflict carefully on the television, creating a great deal of worry and concern as they became, unbeknown to us, as close participants to the war as we were at that time. We, of course, thought little of their feelings, not because we did not care, but because we were caught up in our own cares and concerns and did not really appreciate the access they had to our war.

On 24 January 1991, a further flight group was sent to the northern Saudi desert to support the deployed Support Helicopter Force. Shortly thereafter I visited the detachment, and in a long conversation with the SHF commander we agreed that what he really needed was a fully equipped RAF Regt Light Armoured Squadron (mine!) under command if he was to ensure the security and defence of the SHF during the coming land war.

This visit produced a couple of strong memories. The first is of the 'tap line' road, which runs up the coast of Saudi Arabia and then east to west, paralleling the Iraq/Saudi border. At this time, the allied forces were secretly repositioning to the west for the right hook. This was a massive undertaking and recreates the frightening memory of being sandwiched in our minute Land-Rover between fully loaded tank transporters hurtling westwards. We wondered if we would ever survive to see the land war start! The second is of being temporarily disoriented and asking for directions in a 'tap line' road town – not on the map – to be invited in to the town sheikh's tent where we were introduced to the 'Town Prince' and his friends, all of whom had their silver-plated Kalashnikovs and brave words against the Iraqi invader. We were given twelve Saudi Rials to use the telephone, had 'sticky' over strong coffee, and played with each other's rifles. We could probably have quietly passed the rest of the war there in some comfort had we so wished. Their hospitality was spontaneous and generous and was my first contact with Middle Eastern culture.

Having survived the rigours of the Saudi equivalent of the M25 and the temporary disorientation, the SHF Commander and I prepared a case for a Light Armoured Squadron and fired it off to Air HQ in Saudi Arabia. Within a

The Regiment in 'Desert Storm' (Crown copyright)

couple of weeks, the military system worked wonders – it is at its very best in such circumstances – and we were relieved of our task in Bahrain. Our CVR(T) were delivered by C 130 to Al Qaysumah and King Khalid Military City in northern Saudi Arabia and we regrouped as a squadron for the first time in over a month. With the use of a map drawn in coloured chalk on the side of a building, I was able to explain to the squadron the aims and conduct of the land campaign and our part in it. This was more like it and I sensed a great deal of satisfaction amongst the officers and gunners. I also sensed that they were beginning to realise that this was for real. However, there could be nothing more satisfying than the prospect of playing a part in what was about to unfold even if it was just a very small part. My Second in Command had worked wonders and managed to get men, materiel and vehicles into the same spot in the desert at the same time. For the majority of personnel, this meant moving by C 130 from Bahrain, and from there into the desert by Chinook helicopter. During this flight, we flew over much of the deployed UK Division and had a wonderful view of the military power – mostly armoured – spread across the desert in encampments. After three days we had regrouped and organised the squadron to advance with the SHF as they supported 1 UK Armoured Division. Before leaving Bahrain we had raided the US Forces theatre map store and had taken a copy of every map ever printed on Iraq, including that which covered the Habbaniya air base. You never know what might happen, and if we got anywhere near it I was determined to visit it one way or another.

We were encamped in the middle of a vast and featureless desert; no sand dunes and not a camel in sight. We were in the middle of the divisional assembly code-named Area RAY, in the midst of the largest British land deployment since 1945. Each night the artillery could be heard conducting artillery raids on the forward Iraqi positions and then withdrawing back to the relative safety of the assembly area. The rumble of artillery in the distance, and the ground vibrating below one, was the first real indication for me that this was for real and not some giant exercise. Each night we also heard the allied aircraft overhead on the way to their targets in Iraq. By this stage, we were keen to just get on with it and go home, so talk of cease-fire and last minute agreements was not terribly welcome. We did not really have any idea how long the ground war would last and many people had their hair cut very short to make care easier – most regretted it as well.

The UK Division's part of the plan was to follow the US 1 Div 'The Big Red One' through the breach in the Iraqi border defences and then to swing to the east heading for Kuwait. In so doing, it would also protect the right flank of the US forces heading north-east to engage the Republican Guard situated in Southern Iraq. The SHF was to provide casevac and logistic support for the advance. Our part was to ensure that they could do so with little effective interference from Iraqi ground forces, which might have survived the passage of the division.

The night before the attack I drove to the final assembly area where the disparate parts of the supporting elements would meet before the advance. As I did so, I came across the whole of the division's fighting element arrayed in long lines facing north ready to advance. As we drove past there were a few pale and serious faces protruding from the tank turrets. For them the difficult part was about to start and no doubt many had butterflies in their stomachs. When it came, the move forward started in the early morning and was surprisingly calm. The division had already cleared the Iraqis from the line of advance and we saw many hundreds of prisoners rounded up in temporary POW cages surrounded by lights and soldiers. The weather was absolutely foul, and we were dressed in all the layers we possessed, including our NBC kit, body armour and waterproofs.

High above us we could see the Tornado F 3s providing the Combat Air Patrol, and they circled us, no doubt taking in the ant-like shapes far below them. We could also see the tankers air-to-air refuelling the fast jets going north and north-westwards. They gave a sense of security very important to the morale component of our fighting power; they were good for our confidence.

As we advanced further east towards the Kuwait border, we came across the results of the allied attacks. The first was a BRDM (a small four-wheeled Soviet reconnaissance vehicle) which had been struck by an air-to-ground missile fired from the south, and which had not only destroyed the vehicle but had pushed it some ten metres off the road. We then came upon a number of T 55 tanks and MTLB armoured troop carriers, all of which had been destroyed, clustered around primitive trench systems. The interiors of all were utterly filthy, with foul blankets and half-consumed food. We presumed that the surviving crews were already prisoners who would be benefiting from our compo rations, water and chocolate. At this point the Adjutant decided to reveal the contents of a parcel from his mother, who, concerned that he would be unable to change his underwear often enough, had sent him many pairs more. Included in the package was a black balaclava with only eyeholes, to keep him warm. The squadron HQ team was greatly amused as he was coerced into parading in his new possessions.

Late on that day we took some Iraqi prisoners who were in very poor shape and who, once they realised they were in no further danger from us, were happy to be prisoners. The natural compassion of the British serviceman immediately came to the fore, and the gunners guarding them gave them water and chocolate. One of them, normally domiciled in the USA, had been conscripted in to the Iraqi army during a visit home. He was not a very happy chap. Another had no boots, only training shoes to complement his scraggy uniform. They were the complete opposite to us, who were fit, very well equipped and had a collective sense of purpose. We were generally a lot bigger than they were and I think that this just added to their feelings of hopelessness. I suppose we all felt a bit sorry for them. There followed an immediate reality check when we were told on the radio that the opposing Iraqi Corps Commander had requested chemical release. This added a new twist and got our immediate attention, but nothing came of it and we were able to remove our NBC suits for the final time.

On the second and last day in Iraq we approached the depression known as the Wadi Al Batin to come across the results of a blue-on-blue air-to-ground attack which had destroyed a British armoured vehicle – very sobering, and reason for all of us to recheck that the Union Jacks we were flying were as visible as possible.

Our final destination was just to the west of the Basra Road that runs north from Kuwait City to the Iraqi border. This we found littered with the devastation of the air attacks that had caught the retreating army. It was easy to imagine the horror of the events that created this carnage, but frankly most gave it no more than an interested glance. Although the war was effectively over, we had to wait for formal declarations before we could start to go home. After about a week, we were released by the SHF, and, due to a shortage of tank transporters, decided to convoy the squadron the 460 kms back to Saudi Arabia. We recovered independently to Al Jubayl on the East Coast of the Gulf where we unloaded vehicles, returned ammunition and prepared to go home. Conscious that the vast majority of the British Army would soon be trying to do the same thing, I got agreement to move the squadron from there back to Bahrain from where we would fly to Germany. The only accommodation available in Bahrain was in five-star hotels and so we had to put up with those for a long weekend. Some announcements to the squadron are easier to make than others and this was one of them. It was a terribly tough way to finish a war but someone had to do it!

We arrived home at RAF Laarbruch to find the Commander in Chief RAF Germany, our own Commandant General, a full band and – most important of all – our families waiting on the tarmac to welcome us home. This was probably the greatest shock of the whole experience and when we had recovered from it were touched by their sincere words of welcome.

As a final irony I was sent to Northern Iraq two years later to command a company of Kurdish 'Peshmarga' as part of Op. 'Warden'. Nearly all of the men under my command had served in the Iraqi army and many during the Gulf War!

Postscript: During the Gulf War the vast majority of the RAF Regt was deployed overseas on operations in different theatres and it is worth recording that here. Numbers 3, 4, 6 and 33 Wg HQs, Nos. 1, 2, 20, 26, 34, 51, 58, and 66 Sqns deployed to the Middle East. Nos 27 and 63 Sqns continued to provide the GBAD defence of the Mount Pleasant complex in the Falkland Islands, and Nos 16 and 37 that of Airport Camp in Belize. Number 3 Sqn continued its CT task in Northern Ireland.

Humanitarian Operations

The Royal Air Force has a long tradition of humanitarian assistance. There are accounts of rescue from the deserts of Iraq and Sudan in the 1920s and 30s. Sir David Lee recalls 60 Squadron flying its Wapitis to Quetta in 1935 to evacuate injured families from the earthquake. From the earliest days aircraft were converted into ambulances.

As the following accounts show, this tradition continues today, although in a much more highly organised and comprehensive form!

Operation Haven 1991

Load Master Dutch Holland MBE

Saddam Hussein's treatment of his own people had become even more intolerable. In the Northern areas of Iraq the Air Force and Army were bent on genocide and at best were pushing the Kurds further northwards to eventually expel them from the country. The United Nations quickly and boldly stepped in to create an exclusion zone to stop the atrocities being committed, but severe damage had been done to the Kurdish nation. The exclusion zone now contained a displaced population of several million people, and conditions for them had deteriorated at an alarming rate. Harrowing scenes in the newsreels showing the bitterly cold weather, the starving people, the homeless and diseased, shocked the relief system into motion.

At Royal Air Force Lyneham the Hercules fleet was just beginning to recover from nearly nine months of the most intensive flying it had endured since the Falklands in 1982. The station has long and justly prided itself on its ability for rapid response and never more was it to be demonstrated than in the mounting of Operation Haven to send relief to the Kurds. The initial 'head-up' was received at 0900 hrs on a Saturday early in April and a detachment Ops Cell was formed immediately with personnel from LXX Squadron. By midday the chance had become a probability, and by late afternoon official authority was given. At 2350 hours the first of three Hercules C Mk 1 aircraft laden with the Detachment Ops Cell, its pack-up and support personnel left RAF Lyneham for Incirlik AFB in Turkey. During that day, the 47 Sqn Air Despatchers had beavered tirelessly to build containers of relief supplies, and only four hours after the first aircraft departed, two more Hercules left, fully loaded with sixteen 1-ton containers each.

Arrival in Turkey, due to the time difference, was early afternoon, and within one hour of arrival the RAF Det. had been met by the USAF hierarchy, billeted, given transport, and briefings had begun. The USAF, who had already started dropping supplies, were running the operation, and intensive briefings followed for the rest of the day both for ground and aircrews. It was obvious that the Iraqi military was not trusted to stay out of the exclusion zone, so the Americans had coupled together an extremely effective and professional defensive package for the protection of the transport aircraft. The RAF crews were surprised but clearly delighted to be scheduled for a 1000 hrs (local) departure the following day for the first of what was to be daily deliveries of relief stores. The arrival of the last two Hercs and the remainder of the support personnel completed the RAF Detachment. Working through the night, the three aircraft were serviced, checked, refuelled and rigged finally for the drop the following day.

Night loading (Crown copyright)

The crews rose at 0600 hrs, and after breakfasting, began further detailed briefings and the intensive planning that was to become the routine for the following weeks. As each 'package' – as the USAF call a sortie – contained up to twenty-three various defensive aircraft, these briefings were not only essential but highly complex for the aircrews, and there could be no margin for error. Final briefs and checks complete, the first RAF 'package' lifted off at 1000 hrs precisely, only forty-eight hours after the heads-up at Lyneham. A remarkable feat even by RAF standards. Having set off on the one-hour transit to the drop zone, the crews were to experience the most arduous and demanding flying of their lives. Rapidly changing weather conditions, inaccurate maps, and the inability of up to 80,000 refugees to be in the valley they are supposed to be in, combined to test the skill and professionalism of the aircrews. Flying heavily-laden aircraft at slow speeds in some of the most inhospitable terrain in the world put a high demand daily on these attributes.

Having located the camps, each aircraft would complete at least four drop circuits, despatching four 1-ton containers on each pass. Careful control was held over the type of stores dropped. Relief agencies on the ground informed the authorities of the most urgent type of relief needed, and each aircraft would drop supplies according to demand. Some loads could be water and blankets, while others could well be food and shelter. Dropping successfully completed, the aircraft would return to Incirlik after an average sortie length of four and a half hours.

Meanwhile back at the base, the support personnel were working flat out preparing and building another forty-eight 1-ton containers for the next day. With the safe return of the Hercules the busiest part of the day would start. The 'front end' aircrew away for debrief and a well-earned cold drink, the Loadmasters and despatchers would load all three aircraft with the fresh containers, while the engineers completed after-flight checks and refuelled. The movement staff would meet and unload the daily charter with its cargo of supplies for the Kurds, and the Ops cell would be busy co-ordinating and smoothing the flow of the work within all these elements. With the same slot time for take off everyday, a well-oiled routine was quickly established by the detachment personnel. Late into the evening with all checks complete, task done, VIPs hosted, paperwork filled in etc. etc., everyone would meet for a richly deserved but quiet wind-down. Thoughts were aired and problems discussed and solved by the teams at this stage: bed and sleep followed very shortly after.

So the daily effort continued for nearly eight weeks without a break. No sorties were lost due to unserviceability of aircraft or lack of supplies. The system functioned perfectly, and only five days were lost when the weather stopped the crews reaching the DZ. Those who saw or flew with the Royal Air Force held them in the highest esteem, and they were the envy of those at Incirlik. The professionalism and sheer hard work of all concerned is well documented, but the humour and lack of complaint in quite adverse conditions created a memorable and hugely rewarding experience for those fortunate enough to be involved.

The Search and Rescue Helicopters
Flight Lieutenant S. A. Hodgson

It was late December in the busiest year on record for the Rescue Helicopter Flight of 202 Squadron based at Royal Air Force Lossiemouth.

We had been tasked to take our spare yellow Sea King helicopter to HMS *Gannet* for twenty-four hours. The reason, to hold Search and Rescue (SAR) standby, thus enabling the Navy SAR unit at Prestwick to attend their Christmas Party.

On arrival at Prestwick we took over responsibility for SAR in the region and wished the Navy a pleasant party, with no need to rush back to work in the morning.

Our plan for the next day was to visit our SAR counterparts in Ireland, and spend the night in the Isle of Man before returning to Lossiemouth. We settled down to an evening meal, followed by some time in front of the TV. After a final check of our plans for the following day, we then retired to bed. What followed was not the quiet night we had anticipated.

Just after 4 a.m. I was roused from a deep sleep by a colleague saying something about reports of red flares and a ship in distress. One look out of the window told me it was the sort of night to stay tucked up in bed. It was a very black night with torrential rain appearing to fall horizontally because of the strong wind. A short time later we found ourselves airborne and in the dark – in more ways than one. We were *en route* to a ship obviously in serious trouble, but had scant knowledge of the nature of her problem. The ship, it transpired, was a Russian factory ship with fifty-one crew. She had been seriously damaged by a freak wave, the impact of which had killed a couple of crew and resulted in a total loss of power. Someone aboard with a smattering of English and a small hand radio was speaking to a nearby ship, who then relayed the information to the Coast Guard.

During our transit we were told that an unknown number of crew had abandoned ship, and it was uncertain what equipment, if any, they had. The mission changed instantly from uplifting a few injured people from a ship to that of finding an unknown number of people in the water at night, knowing they had only minutes to live. Approaching the ship, we spotted four life-rafts, the fourth of which contained one cold, uninjured person. We winched our winchman to the life-raft, and he returned to the helicopter with the survivor. Unable to locate further survivors, we continued to the ship.

We found a blacked-out ship lying across the swell, rolling violently, with the people requiring to be winched located amidships. The fifty to sixty knot wind over the stricken vessel was creating vicious turbulence and this, combined with the violent rolling motion, made winching amidships impossible. Thus we gave instructions to move people to the bow where we hoped we might be able to winch.

The technique used in these situations involves lowering a length of rope to the ship. The winchman is winched down to the correct height whilst holding the top of the rope, which is then used to pull him to the ship. Thereafter, it is used to greatly reduce the time taken to transfer personnel from the ship. Our explanation obviously lost a little in translation because immediately after we lowered the rope, our winchman was plucked from the helicopter before being able to let go.

Sea King from RAF Brawdy (AHB)

After re-briefing in pidgin English, a second rope was lowered and five successful transfers then took place. These included one stretcher and eight walking casualties.

We left the scene as the sun was coming up, to take the injured to hospital in Northern Ireland, and to refuel before returning to the incident. On return, the ship was being evacuated by other aircraft, so we were tasked to search for five life-rafts and five people who were unaccounted for. We found all five life-rafts, the fifth of which contained six extremely hypothermic seamen, who were immediately taken to Irvine hospital for treatment. We returned to Prestwick and gave responsibility for SAR in the area back to the Royal Navy, along with suitable wisecracks to confirm they would be able to cope without us.

Unfortunately, our visit to Ireland was cancelled. We did, however, manage to escape much of the attention of the media by going to the Isle of Man, where we slept like babies before returning home.

In all, the rescue only took five to six hours, but those hours contained more adrenalin than many others I recall, or would wish to repeat in a hurry. They were, however, a fitting end to a very active year.

The winchman was awarded the Air Force Medal for his

part in the rescue. He either fully deserves it, or should be certified insane for going on to a ship when her crew only wants to get off. The pilot was awarded a Queen's Commendation, and the other three crew members, including a Royal Navy medical orderly, received the Air Officer Commanding in Chief's Commendations.

Mountain Rescue

Peter Kirkpatrick

How could a dead person be waving at me? My eyes must be mistaken. Tiredness and the constant peering into the mist were creating false images. It could not be true, but if it was, by hell, it was some surprise.

Those five days had started with the Leuchars Mountain Rescue Team undergoing a normal weekend training exercise in the Arrochar Alps. During every week-end, the six RAF MRTs train around their hills to maintain their fitness levels and expertise. The usual result is contented and weary outfits who return late on Sunday nights to their Units.

This Sunday, and the next few days, started to change shape around Crianlarich. Over the radio, we could hear a rescue taking part on the Buchaille in Glencoe.

Our offer to help was accepted. The incident involved a crag-fast climber high on the mountain. In good, true, MR fashion this meant the need to carry the world to the scene, with the hope of not using the multitude of equipment, but reluctant to ascend the mountain with hope alone. Happily, the climber was recovered and assisted off the mountain, alive and well, very late on Sunday night. The team went to ground in the Kingshouse Hotel on the edge of Rannoch Moor, four to a room – one snorer per room!

Monday, the rain lashed down and the windows rattled. Inside the dining room the team tucked into a civilised breakfast, girding their loins for the drive back to Leuchars – or so we thought. Telephone call – assemble the team and report to Hamish McInnes in Glencoe.

Two overdue climbers had left yesterday for a route on Stob Coirre Nam Bieth, and had not returned. The weather was causing concern. It seemed wise to combine Kinloss, Leuchars, Lochaber and Glencoe MRT members to go and find why.

That day, the teams rescued five climbers from the mountain. Three who had never been reported missing but who needed help, and the original pair who walked in uninjured, having survived an enforced bivouac. The MRT workforce had put in a considerable effort due to the gale-force winds, difficult ground and snow conditions. Another night in the Kingshouse, too tired to go home.

Tuesday – telephone call, report to Fort William Police Station and assist in the search for a missing seventeen-year old lad called Gary Smith, lost on Ben Nevis since yesterday. Quickly formulated opinions passed through the brain. As yet, not for public consumption. Yesterday's weather, his lack of experience, the statistics of the big bad Ben – this lad was a goner.

Over 120 people swamped the mountain, and helicopters scoured the visible areas. Danger spots were probed carefully and fearfully. His parents had travelled up from Manchester. This was not another lost person: it was somebody's son. There was his mother. I have a son the same age who is capable of the same misguided mountain enthusiasm. Mountains are there for pleasure and adventure. Epics are great if you survive. The trick is only having the same epic once and learning from it. Was this lad still capable of learning?

We helped to search the Five Finger Gully and expended more nervous energy than physical. So, in a last chance throw of the dice, a night search seemed appropriate. A small group went out. A lone Land-Rover remained in the Glen, hopefully awaiting a positive radio call: no such call came. The searchers returned to their sleeping bags, depressed.

Wednesday – new search areas, but no new information. Tired legs and sad hearts ascended the mountain. No stretchers were carried. Private opinions had been voiced – bodies don't need rescuing, only finding.

My team were tasked to search the slopes north of the footpath above the half-way Lochan. Difficult ground to walk on, let alone search, in the misty and sleety conditions. The area was finally reached, and the separate parties moved slowly across to their designated 500 ft of mountain and started to sweep across.

I was in the top group, and five minutes into the search I could see an arm waving from a red shape. A mixture of emotions and thoughts raced through my mind – relief, guilt, concern and professional questions on what to do next.

Satisfaction would only be allowed if we got him off this mountain alive. Barely conscious, he was soaked through and half covered in a plastic sheet torn to shreds by his crampons. He was alive – just.

For the next fifteen minutes other party members arrived, dry kit replaced wet clothing, sleeping bags, hats and gloves eventually cocooned his body. The message of 'You've been found, but it's not over yet, hang on, don't give up now', was firmly implanted – repeatedly!

Down below, the news had revitalised all the people involved in the SAR operation. A tremendous combined 'Will to Live' seemed to transmit upwards. Below, beneath the mist line, sat the Leuchars 22 Sqn. Wessex, only sixty seconds flying time away, poised, waiting for the opportunity to snatch the casualty and save him an hour of bone-jarring manhandling. Suddenly, a window of opportunity appeared in the cloud. Rapid plans were made between the ground party and the helicopter. A quick in and out, a difficult winching operation, pray for a break – let's do it!

The helicopter closed carefully, a constant eye on the swirling mist. The winchman descended into our welcoming arms. Strops were placed. Checks were made – thumbs up.

'GO, GO, GO' – gone. Gone to live another day.

Humanitarian Operations in Macedonia

Squadron Leader Phil Spragg and Flight Lieutenant Rachel J. Harrison

During the late morning of 6 April 1999 I was told that a small team of medical personnel was to be deployed to Macedonia to assist with humanitarian medical support to refugees from Kosovo. In the immortal words of the OC, I was asked 'Spraggy, do you fancy it?'

I was fortunate in being stationed at RAF Lyneham: this made kit preparation, weapon collection and the obligatory completion of pre-deployment documentation that much easier. Rachel Harrison was stationed at Leeming, and another colleague, Squadron Leader Steve Kilbey, at Cottesmore. They made similar preparations and travelled by road to Lyneham. We departed on the afternoon of 7 April and arrived in Skopje at approximately half past ten in the evening.

We were met by the Aeromedical Evacuation Liaison Officer, Squadron Leader Dave Hutton, and taken to the 'processing tent' – an area were new arrivals were recorded and given initial theatre briefings and taskings. The briefing gave us the first real snippet of definitive information – we were told that we were to be deployed to the Brazda Stankovec camp just eight kilometres south of the border with Kosovo. Following the briefings we were collected by personnel of 2 Armoured Field Ambulance for our journey to Brazda. As a passing aside, we were told to wear helmets, flak jackets and to load our weapons. Welcome to the theatre!

On our journey from Skopje to Brazda we were afforded a not-so-traditional Macedonian custom of welcoming visitors called – 'Let's stone a vehicle!' – and we duly were. Often – in fact on every opportunity the locals got. Unfortunately, this practice became progressively worse, culminating in the dropping of a dustbin full of concrete off a motorway bridge on to a 4-tonner, causing considerable injuries to the occupants.

On arriving at the Brazda Stankovec refugee camp, we were told to store our equipment in a supply tent and were then introduced to Commander Med. Following a hasty welcome, we were briefly informed of conditions at the camp, during which the extent and gravity of the situation became all too apparent.

Our first night was spent in the medical supply tent, sleeping between boxes of intravenous fluids and baby milk. Following approximately four to five hours uncomfortable sleep we washed, and the men shaved in a bowl of cold water. We were then fortunate enough to experience the Glastonbury effect of sharing two 'porta-loos' with forty other personnel.

In the light of day we were able to see the refugee camp just 400 yards away. On being taken to the medical facilities for the first of our twelve-hour shifts, we were afforded our first glimpse of the refugees: 40–45,000 of them. The area was covered by a vast expanse of tents and makeshift shelters. The Royal Engineers did a fantastic job, and worked non-stop digging toilet trenches and burning rubbish in order to clear the air of a persistent heavy pungent smell. Possibly the most abiding recollection is that of orderly queues of people waiting to be supplied with bread, water and basic food, or to use the toilet or medical facilities.

Medical facilities provided both primary and secondary care on a twenty-four-hour basis, and we worked in association with our Dutch, Norwegian, French, Italian, Israeli and British military, medical counterparts – not forgetting the locally recruited interpreters who proved to be a godsend in many ways.

On average the medical facility treated approximately 1500 people per day. The main ailments were those associated with exhaustion, dehydration or both. Many had walked hundreds of miles, over snow-covered mountains, in winter, in bare feet, dressed in the only clothes they possessed, with no drinking water, no food, no contact with other family members and living in constant fear of their lives.

And they came to Brazda and queued, and when they had finished in one queue they joined another – in an orderly manner, grateful, always courteous, never complaining – happy to be alive.

The most common conditions that required treatment at the medical facilities were: injuries following assaults by para-military, skin conditions, dental problems, stomach upsets, rat bites due to refuse in close proximity to domestic accommodation, sunburn due to exposure to the elements, inability to access medication for chronic conditions such as epilepsy and diabetes, and of course, psychological trauma.

We were employed at Brazda for a week before the Non-Governmental Organisations – such as *Médecins Sans Frontières* and the Red Cross – replaced us; and having assisted them to erect their medical facilities, the Brazda three were separated and deployed for a further five days on other taskings to support 23 Parachute Field Ambulance and to provide primary health care to the remaining personnel at Brazda.

After just thirteen days in theatre we, unlike our patients, went home.

Macedonia. Flt/Lt Rachel Harrison (centre), Sqn Ldr Phil Spragg (left), Sqn Ldr Steve Kilbey (right) (Phil Spragg)

Hurry Up and Wait

Revd (Squadron Leader) J. W. K. Taylor

I was posted to RAF Odiham at the end of March 1999 from RAF Valley, and it almost seemed as if I had joined a completely different air force. Who were all these aircrew who wore berets with their grow bags? Why were people as likely to wear green as blue? And where was everybody? I didn't realise that at any given time, about a third of the service population at Odiham would be away somewhere: be it Bosnia, Northern Ireland, the Falklands, any one of many trouble-spots in the world – or even just Salisbury Plain.

My married quarter was being refurbished when I arrived, which meant that I spent my first few months in the wonderful Officer's Mess, which has a very special atmosphere quite unlike any other I've ever stayed in, while my wife and two boys aged six and three remained behind at Valley. However, because Padres work weekends (and yes, I've heard the old joke about only working one day a week, thank you very much!) I didn't get to see wife and wains much during that period.

The news was full of stories about the worsening situation in Kosovo. Then the bombing campaign began, and the tension in and around Odiham grew tangible, because everyone knew that the Support Helicopter Force is always involved in troublesome places.

At last, my quarter was ready, and I looked forward to renewing family life. My sons were a bit apprehensive, but I told them about how close we would be to London, and the exciting things we could do there, including shopping in a certain five-storey toy shop. So, against a backdrop of increasing tension at Odiham, we finally got back together.

In addition to our professional training as clergy, we also participate fully in all the other military training that any service person has to do – apart from weapons training, as we are non-combatant by the terms of the Geneva Convention! I was deployment-ready, and looking forward to putting my training to good effect if or when the Station deployed. However, I had a phone call from my Command Chaplain to tell me that my role would be to remain behind to offer support at home to the wives, dependants and the remaining station community. This call came on a Thursday morning, and I must admit to being a little disappointed not to be joining in with the rest of the Station. On the afternoon of the following day, Friday, I heard my name mentioned over the Station tannoy... 'Padre Taylor to contact the Main Guard Room.' The message was to contact my Command Chaplain; so when I called his office at High Wycombe, he told me to get ready to leave on Op 'Agricola' as soon as possible.

'How long will I be gone for?' I asked.

'Until it's over' I was told, 'But we promise to replace you if it's more than six months'.

'Who is going to provide cover for the Station Church?' was my next question.

'Er... could you sort that out – phone round a few chaps and see if they can cover Sundays...'

CS 95, the new combat uniform which had been standard for the army since 1995 (hence 'Soldier 95') was like gold dust. So, at twenty to five on a Friday afternoon, I went to clothing stores to see if I could get hold of deployment kit – sleeping system, CS 95, Bergen, webbing ... I joined a massive queue, as about 300 of my fellows had been called forward at the same time. What I hadn't realized was that a late Friday afternoon call was par for the course for RAF Odiham to be activated to deal with some sort of crisis or another.

The suppliers worked like Trojans. The medical centre and the dental section were on red alert, ensuring that those who were out of date in jabs, or dentally unfit, were made ready to go. Many people who came back to work weren't going to Kosovo, but everyone came in to help. Engineers had already been working round the clock to make sure that the Chinooks were ready, and Odiham did what it does best – got ready to deploy at a moment's notice.

As I was in a queue of literally hundreds of people all trying to get ready at once, I arrived home rather later than my family had anticipated. My wife and boys were in the middle of their evening meal, while mine was being slowly cremated in the oven. I was given that 'You've been to happy hour without telling me you weren't coming home' look that wives reserve for husbands who come in late on a Friday evening (OK, with justification quite often!), and the boys started telling me of their plans for me to take them to Hamley's the next day. It was our first weekend as a family at Odiham, and they had taken me at my word.

'Sorry, kids' I said, as I began to explain that I would be going away for a while. This was difficult, especially as I didn't know how long it would be for. I was going to need the weekend to sort out my kit, take it back to clothing stores and see if I could get anything that fitted this time, and work out how to put my webbing together. On the Saturday afternoon, we ended up going to a pet shop to buy a hamster as a sort of dad-substitute. (The sickening thing is that it worked, and by the time I came home from Kosovo, I had been completely supplanted in my sons' affections by Harry the Hamster.)

Finally, Monday morning, and it was time to go. Adrenaline was high as we set off on the first leg of our journey – two ships heading for Prilep in Macedonia, by way of France and Italy. I had been in a Chinook once or twice before, and really enjoyed being airborne in one of these noisy, vibrating, workhorses, but one of the things I had neglected to find out was the location of the P-tube on the Chinook. As we flew over France, this started to become a problem – however, I discovered mercifully that a fully laden Chinook's fuel tank empties at the same rate as my bladder fills, and we made our first refuelling stop just in time. At our next stop the other cab went u/s. This necessitated an unintended night stop in Nice, which proved to be a very pleasant distraction. It also added a surreal quality to the journey, as on the one hand we were headed to a war-zone and on the other we were changing into civvies and going out for an evening on the town.

The following morning, we set off – crossing the Med. to a refuel stop at an Italian Air Force base just outside Rome.

Once again, disaster struck. As we were taxiing in, there was a small explosion from the auxiliary power unit. This would necessitate a further delay.

The Italians left us sitting on the pan for seven hours before they could organise transport to get us the kilometre or less to the front gate of their camp. It was late morning, and we were stuck through the blistering heat of a June day, able to almost see the camp gates but not get to them. Eventually, the Italians provided MT, and we found ourselves at a hotel. It took a couple of complete days for the aircraft to be airworthy once more. So there we were, anxious to get to the job, waiting at a hotel pool. While it sounds luxurious, it was in fact, outrageously frustrating. We were on the doorstep of historic Rome, but unable to leave the hotel in case the aircraft was repaired sooner rather than later.

At last everything was ready, and the military detachment left the hotel – another strange and anomalous way to go about warfare! It felt completely surreal as we left the hotel lobby in our combats, still keyed up and rarin' to go to Kosovo, while tourists stared at us and continued their holidays in the eternal city.

At a refuelling stop at Brindisi, we were told to make straight for Petrovec, the international airport at Skopje. A few hours later, and nearly four days after we left home, we arrived in Macedonia.

The whole SHF had moved to Skopje, a short distance from the Macedonia/Kosovo border, in anticipation of 'the Big Push'. We arrived in the midst of mayhem and confusion. Our camp was being established on the southern side of an international airport. It seemed really odd to look across at a 'real' airport, with airliners full of tourists and businessmen and women leaving and arriving.

At first, our area consisted of six Pumas, and seven Chinooks – ours being the eighth. Our delays in Nice and Rome had meant that we arrived as things were already being set up. The camp commandant was working hard to establish some semblance of order, but to my inexperienced eye, it looked deliciously chaotic. My previous experience of out of area operations had been to Gioa del Colle with the fast jet fleet, and Ancona with the Hercules. These detachments in no way prepared me for a Support Helicopter operation. For example, when I had arrived in Gioia, expecting field conditions, I was whisked to Hotel Svevo, a luxurious hotel complete with air conditioning, shower, marble floors, a bar – and Local Overseas Allowance. By contrast, my first night at Petrovec was spent in the 'Boeing Hilton' – a euphemism for a quick doze in a Chinook, as there was no tentage available. It was impossible to get any rest, as engineers had to do all sorts of technical stuff on the cab while people tried to sleep. The next few days and nights went by in a daze, with a constant round of activity, O-groups, briefings and false alarms. Everyone seemed to be working about twenty-hour days, collapsing into a sleeping bag, and waking ready to work some more. I remember the first few nights were spent in my sleeping bag under the stars, but when I woke up in the morning my face was pock-marked with mosquito bites. Despite all the detailed briefings, big picture information was hard to come by.

Then came 'The Big Push'. The intensity of the previous activity made me think that we had been in Petrovec for ages before the Big Push came, but my diary reminds me that in fact it was less than forty-eight hours. Others can give a much more military picture of what went on when men and materiel were first taken over the border into hostile Kosovo, and up the Kajanic defile. What I remember was a feeling of exhilaration and apprehension. At that stage, we had no idea whether the VJ withdrawal from Kosovo would be orderly or not, or whether or not there would be a shooting war all the way to Pristina. We didn't know if the roads and fields would be mined, or if ambushes would be set up to attack landing troops and equipment. After a false start, the Big Push was on, and troops had been massed close to the border. The Support Helicopter force was to ferry troops and underslung loads into enemy territory, and the initial lift would take place at just before dawn on 12 June. I remember crawling out of my sleeping bag (still in the middle of a field at this stage), and rather numbly stowing all my sleeping kit back into my Bergen, which was leaning against the side of the Ops tent at about 0230 hrs. All around me, people were getting up and ready, briefings were taking place, engineers were doing last checks to aircraft, and then in a short space of time, the rotors on fourteen helicopters were turning. The noise was almost deafening, and then it was time to go. It was a truly awesome sight to see so many cabs taking off at once (the deeply cynical amongst us would say it was also an awesome sight to see so many cabs serviceable in one place), and then following one another towards the border and who knows what on the other side. Support Helicopter Force people are inveterate camping gadget collectors, and one of my favourite 'must have' things is my folding chair. It is sanctuary, a place where I can sit and relax, or read, or think and pray. I remember unfolding my chair, and sitting on it as I watched the Puma and Chinook force disappear out of sight, praying that God would be with all who were there, and that peace would be established in that troubled place. I don't think my prayers have been answered yet, as ethnic conflict has spilled over into Macedonia two years later, but it was a relief to hear that the VJ withdrawal had been orderly, that the troops and hardware had been landed safely and that the job had been much more easily accomplished than might have been the case.

When the operators came back, they were ecstatic and elated. They had done what the Support Helicopter Force does best, and had supported the initial entry into Kosovo quickly, efficiently and safely. Men, women and machines had been pushed close to limits in terms of effort and hours worked. And then slowly the pace lessened, as the initial task was complete. The job changed significantly, as it proved impossible to get to Pristina within the initially planned timescale.

When people are working very intensely in a confined space, it is very easy to lose a sense of perspective. The operators – the aircrew who were actually flying – could see the result of what they were doing. It was a marvellous feeling to fly at combat heights over the ground, being waved to by the civilian population, who had felt rescued by the NATO forces, but for groundcrew who couldn't leave the camp area, it was hard to see what had been achieved. There was an enormous refugee camp on the other side of Skopje, about half an hour's drive away, which had been packed with ordinary people. These people had left houses and possessions, and sometimes family and friends behind, and ended up living in wretched conditions in tents laid out in rows. I'm told there were about 10,000 tents there. The people who were there had nothing to do, had no idea how long they would be there, and didn't know whether they would have any possessions to go home to. I was privileged to be able to take groups of RAF personnel to visit the refugee camp. Now there wasn't anything constructive we could do when we visited there, apart from the traditional military thing of handing out boiled sweets to children. But our being there gave us a sense of perspective – we certainly stopped whinging about the mud and the hard work (and, worst of all, the chemical toilets!), when we saw how the refugees were. At least we knew that we had homes to go back to when we finished our stint on Op Agricola, and our food in the MCSU field kitchens was about the best anywhere (how on earth do they produce better food under field conditions that we have in our messes at home?). I think that our presence at the refugee camp was good for their morale as well – as we were a visible sign that the rest of the world was interested in their plight, and working to get them home again. I met all sorts and conditions of people there – from a little old Albanian man wearing a traditional white fez, who had a weather-beaten face and only one tooth, and with whom I had no common language. This man was so keen to thank NATO, through me, I suppose, that he wanted to offer something in return. All he had was a battered packet of cigarettes, and although I'm not a smoker, there was something special about accepting a cigarette from this man, and standing smoking together, our verbal silence being interspersed with smiles and hand gestures. I met some teachers and a young law-student from Pristina who had come as a refugee to that camp, having lost her younger brothers and sisters when they had fled. She had subsequently found the rest of her family, and they had then gone to stay with relatives somewhere safe. But she had stayed on to work with Save the Children in the camp, helping other families being reunited. I asked her what she would do when she got home, and she told me 'This is day zero. For me my old life has gone, and a new life has begun. I will commit my life to making sure this will not happen again'.

A short time after that people began to drift home, back across the border into Kosovo, and within a few weeks, that particular refugee camp, Stankovic A, was empty, and I never saw, nor ever will see, those people again. I pray for them occasionally, but unlike the idealistic nineteen-year old student (whom I hope keeps her idealism and passion intact), I'm cynical enough to know that things like this do happen over and over again, and humanity never learns from past mistakes. After all, within a year of Odiham's involvement in Op Agricola, the Support Helicopter Force was actively involved in Sierra Leone, and it was as if Macedonia/Kosovo had never happened. I do think it is sad that peace and tranquillity has not been restored out there, but after all, since pre-history the Balkans have never been at peace, and it is naïve to expect that after our few months there, everything will be calm. Two years have elapsed since my involvement there, and many other RAF people have been there since, and 33 Sqn still have a very active detachment in Pristina. My little snapshot of the Support Helicopter Force involvement in that particular theatre is still very vivid, and in a strange sort of way, it was a pleasure to have been there.

I haven't mentioned anything about my role as Chaplain to the RAF men and women, as this piece has been about personal reflections, not about work. But it was a privilege to have served with, and hopefully to have served, the service men and women who were there – in the best traditions of the Chaplains Branch (whose motto is *Ministrare, non Ministrari* – 'To serve, not to be served'). To all who were there, as the Support Helicopter Force detachment – I enjoyed your comradeship, and I hope you enjoyed mine.

Deliverance In Mozambique

Flight Lieutenant Michelle Jurd

Standing out in the vast wasteland that the floods had created was the village where we were to deliver our aid. We could already see the beginnings of a crowd forming near our landing site. Below us the road that had been submerged for several miles re-emerged, leading up into the once prosperous village, now isolated and reliant entirely on the aid we carried. As we came in to land, the dust billowing around us, the press helicopter that was our full time companion closed in for some prime-time footage just as the villagers closed in for maize and medical supplies …

Cyclones and floods are a regular event in Mozambique: however the staggering damage and devastation caused by the latest one caught both the Government and the aid organisations off-guard. Unusually heavy rain began in early February 2000, and then, on the 22nd, Cyclone Eline hit Zimbabwe and South Africa. It burst the banks of the Limpopo River: the artery that links those two countries to the Indian Ocean, through the vast Limpopo Valley in Mozambique.

Within days, Mozambique's valley communities were drowning in the floodwaters. At the time neither the Government nor aid workers had an accurate understanding of the full scale of the death and destruction. Initial estimates put 350 dead, with a further quarter of a million in desperate need of aid. In the immediate aftermath of the floods, small squadrons of helicopters from neighbouring South Africa and Malawi bore the brunt of the relief effort, saving thousands of people from the ravaging floodwaters. These were the images so effectively captured by the world's media: scared and weary villagers being winched to safety after days spent trapped on rooftops or in trees.

It was at this time that 33 Squadron took a sudden but perhaps rather predictable change of direction. I had been a navigator on 33 Puma Helicopter Squadron for two years,

33 Squadron Pumas (Flt/Lt Michelle Jurd)

and I along with the rest of the squadron was captivated by the dramatic images of the rescues that were broadcast world-wide. At the time of the floods I had recently returned from a six-week training exercise in Norway, where the squadron had conducted extensive preparation and training for the annual NATO exercise. The squadron was due to deploy back to Norway in several days time, and as a consequence we were fully kitted-out with arctic clothing, an advance party had already deployed to the exercise area and the Puma helicopters had been prepared for flying in the arctic conditions.

However, soon after, the world was alerted to the devastation in Mozambique and it became clear that international aid was required. The Norway deployment was postponed and the squadron was put on standby for the warmer climes of Africa. Having lived in a snow-hole only weeks previously, I for one was not too upset about our participation in the NATO exercise being cancelled. From the moment the decision was made there was a real feeling of purpose on the squadron: the nightly news footage had given me a very clear understanding of the task in hand and of the importance of reaching the disaster scene in good time. So with just over forty-eight hours' warning before we were to deploy I had some urgent preparation to get on with.

Two days later we boarded a TriStar at Brize Norton carrying with us bags full of tropical clothing, mosquito nets, malaria tablets and medical supplies. The four Puma helicopters we were going to fly in Mozambique had to be re-roled from arctic to tropical fit: they were then subsequently broken down by our squadron engineers, so that they could be loaded onto an Antonov transport plane. Although initially it was hoped that this would only necessitate removing the main and tail rotor blades, unfortunately the main rotor gearbox also had to come off. The preparation had been hurried, but ultimately, through the hard work of our ground crew and administrative staff, a squadron bound for Scandinavia had been turned around in two days, ready for Southern Africa.

We flew out on 2 March, joining forces with other elements of the British relief effort. These included signallers, Tactical Supply Wing, medical staff and staff of the Permanent Joint Headquarters who were to have overall control of the British operation. Landing in South Africa, we encountered a bizarre example of bureaucracy interfering with life saving. Initially we were refused permission to land at Hoedsprite in South Africa and then, when our pilot did so anyway, we were kept waiting at the airfield for several hours before being moved to Johannesburg, the opposite direction from Mozambique, whilst the political implications were ironed out. On 4 March, politics resolved, we returned to Hoedsprite and unloaded our Pumas from the Antonov. The engineers put in an outstanding effort and by the early hours of 5 March two aircraft were ready to fly.

At dawn on 5 March the first two Puma helicopters left Hoedsprite bound for Mozambique, with the other two Puma helicopters due to follow shortly. Three days after leaving the UK we were finally bound for the country that had requested our help. The aircraft were crewed with a pilot, a navigator and two crewmen. I was fortunate enough to be one of the navigators in the first formation and as we departed from the air base and headed south a wondrous sight greeted us. Our routeing took us overhead the Kruger National Park, and as the sun rose and sent a myriad of colours drifting across the sky, we were privileged to look below us and see many different types of animals wandering through the bush or replenishing themselves at waterholes. It was a truly glorious sight to behold. In complete contrast, as the park came to an end marked by a huge game fence impenetrable to animals or poachers, we entered Mozambique. By this time the sun had risen to give promise of a very hot day to come: as we crossed the border the previously lush countryside had changed to a barren area of muted coloured scrubland. Initially the land was sparse and very dry, but as we continued to track further into Mozambique the flooding soon became apparent and gave us an indication of our task ahead.

Our initial destination was the main airport of Maputo where we were to meet the aid organisations that were controlling the distribution of food and supplies throughout the affected areas. Arriving at Maputo we were immediately struck by the feeling of co-operation and international camaraderie. Having up to this stage been frustrated by the delays, it was extremely refreshing to commence working with teams from around the world whose only aim was to help those in need of assistance. Within an hour of arrival we were back in the air and on our first aid mission, delivering food and rescuing stranded villagers. Over the course of the next two weeks the four Puma helicopters and five crews flew almost 400 hours, moved 425 tonnes of aid and 725 passengers.

The operation was in all respects a success, but in many ways challenging. Logistically it was complex, though its relatively short duration helped considerably. The destination was particularly difficult, with the flooded roads making it hard for our Tactical Supply Wing to pre-position aviation fuel in the areas where we were operating. Although the re-supply of spares did not become a serious issue, had the operation continued for much longer there is no doubt that demand would have been high. The hours we were flying and the extra strain imposed by the poor conditions were already taking their toll at the end of just two weeks. In addition to the normal wear and tear you would associate with flying eight-hour days, we had significant trouble with sand-scoring in the engines and heat cracking the windscreens. We also had trouble with our radios, which seemed unable to cope with the constant moisture, as well as becoming contaminated with flour and maize, causing us to make difficult decisions regarding flight safety. Navigation also became difficult, not just because most landmarks were now below the waterline. Our maps were out of date and poor in quality but, just as importantly; in one aircraft both the GPS and the compass quickly became unserviceable. Faults that could have been fixed within the constraints of peacetime flying, but serious issues when lives are at stake on an urgent humanitarian mission. The result was undoubtedly that some aid was not delivered where it was intended.

From a flight safety point of view, apart from the equipment concerns I have already outlined there are several points deserving mention. The first was the confusion resulting from the saturation of air traffic control and the high density of aircraft operating from a small area. Not only was Maputo in use; so also were several other small airfields in the vicinity. We were also landing in places that would not generally be considered ideal landing sites: their only recommendation being that they remained above water. We had to be particularly aware of overhead power lines and the lack of hard standing made dust a serious problem. In addition to the problem of FOD (foreign object damage) we also had the problems of locals congregating where we were coming in to land, not understanding the dangers of the aircraft that brought the aid. Another strain on safety was the long hours being worked by everyone on the detachment, in far from ideal conditions. The engineers and ground crew did outstanding work keeping the aircraft airworthy, and those of us doing the flying felt the strain of fourteen successive eight-hour flying days in stifling heat. The Press added an extra dimension of pressure, closely watching our every move in the early stages of the operation, their helicopters shadowing our every move. On one occasion we jokingly suggested to one film crew that we could place someone in a tree so that they could film us recovering them. The film crew only rejected the idea because they thought that they might get caught out! However I have no doubt that their presence was primarily constructive: the footage they shot doing much to generate international aid.

After two weeks' work our presence was no longer essential. The waters receded quickly and the civilian aid agencies were then able to move in by road to continue aid operations. The operation was a particularly satisfying one to have participated in, it being a rare chance to contribute so directly to an area where help was clearly needed. As a squadron we practised the art of flexibility to a remarkable degree and ultimately achieved our aim. The aircrew and ground crew worked hard to prepare for and carry out this operation, and the positive publicity it generated for the RAF was considerable. In Mozambique the co-operation between nations assisting in the relief effort was superb. It was a thoroughly rewarding operation to be a part of, and as we boarded our flight to return to England the irony of our clean dry clothes and full fresh lunch boxes wasn't lost on us. We had hopefully helped families who had lost everything in the floodwaters; we had provided them with emergency food and then with new blankets, pots and essential supplies: the rest was now up to them. The cycle of life and hardship in Africa goes on once again.

Aeromedical Evacuation – Sierra Leone

Flight Lieutenant Shaun Pascoe

In June 2000 I was deployed to Sierra Leone as Aeromedical Evacuation Liaison Officer in support of Operation 'Basilica' which was part of a mission to train one thousand local recruits for the democratically elected Government's army against the threat posed by the Revolutionary United Front (RUF).

Sierra Leone posed a significant health risk to the average British soldier, with its intense heat, monsoon rains and proliferation of diseases such as Malaria. It was therefore assumed I would be very busy and I was given two Flight Nurse Assistants, three search and rescue kits and a significant amount of aeromed equipment.

Commander Med. decided to base me initially at Benguema Training Camp, whilst my Flight Nursing Assistants remained at the airhead in Lungi with the RAF detachment. The first couple of weeks were rather quiet, but this was anticipated as individuals became acclimatised but the incubation period for diseases loomed.

My first priority was to establish air assets and to establish communications with all the necessary individuals who might be involved in a potential aeromed. We were fortunate to have access to three Chinooks and a Lynx from HMS *Argyll* and later used them to their full. Assets on the ground included an excellent hospital facility provided by the Indian UN element and a Regimental Aid Post at Benguema. Although we were not part of the UN contribution at the time, we had an agreement that allowed us to use this excellent facility, and the staff were more than helpful. The Regimental Aid Post provided a commendable response to the primary health care needs of our troops. Communications were seamlessly provided by 30 Signals Regiment.

Overall the mission went smoothly with the aeromed of five confirmed malaria cases and various admissions to the UN hospital, including conditions ranging from heat-stroke to gastro-enteritis.

My first impression of Sierra Leone was the overwhelming heat, which meant a daily consumption of nine litres of water. This amount of fluid intake had the unfortunate side effect of regular trips during the night and the inevitable broken sleep!

After arrival at Lungi airfield I was educated in the standard procedure of sitting on your flak jacket during the helicopter trip to Benguema, a jungle scene reminiscent of a bad Vietnam movie. As the only member of the RAF on this side of the water, the usual RAF hotel jokes followed but having never stayed in an 'RAF hotel' I quickly settled into tentage.

A daily brief kept everyone informed of rebel activity, mission developments and camp housekeeping. A visit by Kate Adie and the Deputy Prime Minister John Prescott was, I am sure, meant to instil confidence but instead served to unnerve us.

I arranged a weekly Chinook trip to the RAF detachment to review the primary health care patients the Nurses had seen. This trip was relatively busy with presentations ranging from diarrhoea and vomiting, a bot-fly maggot and the odd wound suturing. I also managed to do some teaching for the Regiment medics in the evening on trauma management and 'chilled out' with the RAF. These trips became less relaxing once information came through that the Rebels now had Anti-Aircraft Guns and Surface-to-Air Missiles!

During the second week it was decided I would be moved to the Headquarters of British Forces, as it was close to the UN hospital and someone was needed to review the in-patients daily and tend to their welfare needs. With the return home of the Commander Med. shortly after I moved in, I became Staff Officer 2 Med. by default. As a nurse in a hospital there is often three months preceptorship for new staff and a clinical supervisor. As Staff Officer Med. it was a case of 'there's the file'!

I quickly established an aeromed and casevac procedure, which was used that night as HMS *Argyll* responded to a Mayday call from a Spanish registered vessel offshore, bringing me a civilian with cholecystitis. This individual I reluctantly admitted to the less-than-equipped local hospital and reviewed him daily until his repatriation.

My role as Aeromedical Evacuation Liaison Officer was tested with five malaria patients, but using our own air assets it proved relatively straightforward.

My responsibilities as Staff Officer 2 Med. included liaison with the UN hospital; liaison with local and civilian medical agencies; liaison with the Regimental Medical Officer at Benguema on issues of British soldiers' health; a weekly MEDSITREP; statistics, and UN hospital admissions to Permanent Joint Headquarters. I had daily contact with my Nurses, I visited British UN hospital admissions and organised their welfare needs and discharge, I collaborated with the Environmental Health Officer on primary health care for the Headquarters, including the taking of appropriate anti-malarials. This allowed little free time, which meant the tour went quickly. I was able to relax for a few minutes on a nearby UN-protected beach, a surreal experience with combat 95s and a rifle.

The first positive case of falciparum malaria was casevac'd at night, which led to logistical problems as a curfew was imposed at 2200 hrs and road movement was through several UN checkpoints. Even disturbed at 0200 hrs the local police were helpful in escorting us through the checkpoints, and on arrival at the proposed helicopter-landing site, in textbook fashion I placed the two Land Rovers so as to intersect headlights. I was then duly roasted by the loadmaster as I had compromised their night vision capability – the exception the textbook neglects to mention!

After transferring the patient to the UN hospital, work commenced with all the notification of casualty and AEROMED request signals to complete. With a normal full day ahead it was exhausting.

My liaison with the local hospital was eye-opening: a sub-standard bullet-ridden building with few supplies, but an obvious enthusiasm and professionalism by the staff who welcomed the British.

One day, at his own request, I took the Commanding Officer to the local hospital and introduced him to the various personalities. Sadly one of the doctors we met died the next day from Lassa Fever he had acquired whilst working in a jungle clinic. The reassurance from HQ that Lassa Fever was relatively difficult to catch did little to pacify us, and the ten days of potential incubation were possibly the longest days of the tour: I also seemed to have less friends for a while!

My role then turned into one of counsellor, when six British soldiers came across a civilian road accident involving some twenty civilians. A particularly horrific incident, as the vehicles involved were carrying makeshift containers of caustic soda on their roofs, which inflicted serious burns. The lads responded swiftly, mobilising the wounded on any available vehicle, and made some rather difficult triage decisions. The next day I took them to the local hospital to see how the survivors were. Six had died at scene, fifteen were brought in and three more had died during the night. The trip was a positive experience as it firmly established that without the prompt intervention of he British soldiers many more would have died.

Towards the end of my tour aeromeds became more difficult, as the air assets had been withdrawn and the incoming aeromed team could come no further than Dakar.

Communications were occasionally unreliable and vehicles were limited. Acquisition of the Brigadier's Land-Rover Discovery and a last minute jump on to an unexpected C 130 managed to get my Nurse and two patients to Dakar; and after hand-over with the aeromed team, the Nurse was resourceful enough to jump on the Secretary of State's VIP Lear jet back.

Later I utilised Royal Fleet Auxiliary's Landing Craft for casualty moves, again escorted through Freetown by local police. It took two days to hand over to my replacement; a therapeutic and reflective experience. I hadn't realised quite how much I'd done until I had to hand it over. I spent one night on Royal Fleet Auxiliary's *Sir Percival* before my flight home which, with a couple of beers and a real bed, was my best night's sleep for six weeks.

What can I pass on to others about my experience?

1. Early on get to know your available assets, your team, the plan and available resources.
2. Be above all, flexible.
3. Don't work alone. Time and again the input of others made the mission and job in hand a success and my job easier.
4. If you're not sure whether to pack an item, take it anyway. You will not get one out there!

Finally, I gained a great deal from this, my first overseas tour, and arriving there with an open mind and a little enthusiasm made the time go by that much quicker.

Distinctive Units

The Queen's Flight

Air Commodore Sir Archibald Winskill KCVO CBE DFC AE

I had the honour of holding the appointment of Captain of the Queen's Flight from 1968 to 1982.

The Queen's Flight, which the Royal Air Force operated at Benson in Oxfordshire, was a unique institution, existing solely to carry the Queen, members of the Royal Family, visiting Heads of State, Ministers, Service Chiefs of Staff and selected Government officials on their business journeys.

The Flight was also unique in that, although a part of the RAF and within Strike Command, it was an institution on its own and most of its personnel were not subject to the normal operational tours of duty which obtained in other parts of the Service. For example, some of the aircrew and ground crew had been with the unit for periods of up to fourteen years or more. Once a man was selected (and no Officer, NCO or Airman was forced to join the Flight, he was invited) and provided he liked the job, he could remain there for a long time. Since every man on the Flight was aware he was serving the Queen and members of the Royal Family in a very personal way, these two facts made for a special brand of enthusiasm, loyalty and energy.

The origins of the unit can be traced back to flights in 1917 and 1918 by the Prince of Wales (later King Edward VIII), and Prince Albert who became King George VI. Prince Albert took a flying course with the RAF and received his Wings as a qualified pilot in 1919. Later the Prince of Wales bought and operated several aircraft privately, but it was not until 1936 that the King's Flight was established with public funds. It was officially formed at Hendon on the accession to the throne of King Edward VIII. At first the King's private de Havilland Rapide was used, but after the abdication this aircraft was sold and subsequently replaced by an Airspeed Envoy, which had been ordered by the Government and built to Royal specification.

Wessex of the Queen's Flight over Windsor Castle (Crown copyright)

In line with other appointments in the Royal Household (e.g. Master of the Horse) it was at the behest of the monarch that the Commander of the unit carried the title of Captain of the King's Flight. The first incumbent was Wing Commander E. H. Fielden (later Air Vice-Marshal Sir Edward Fielden GCVO CB DFC AFC). Affectionately known as 'Mouse', he remained in charge for more than a quarter of a century.

It then became tradition that when an Air Commodore was appointed Captain of the Queen's Flight he took up the post as a serving officer. After a short time, if he was found acceptable, he was quietly invited to retire from the Service and continue in the post as a civilian. This added to the unique character of the Flight because its civilian boss controlled five RAF aircraft and a staff of about 180 Service personnel. In accepting his post the Captain became a member of the Royal Household, and a proportion of his time was spent in journeys to and from Buckingham Palace for consultations there. His terms of reference were as unwritten as the British Constitution but it was generally accepted that he acted as adviser to the Queen and all members of the Royal Family on all aspects of Air Travel.

This could give rise to some odd experiences as the following brief anecdote illustrates:

> 'Letter received by Prince Philip from Mr B with invitation to fly in his latest Hydrogen Balloon and passed to me for comment. Know nothing about this type of air vehicle and borrow book on the subject. Mr B's total balloon flying experience 9 hours. Consider this insufficient for Royal Flight. Most experienced Balloonist in the country is Wing Commander T, who is also the Balloon Pilots Licence Examiner. Decide that, if flight takes place, T will be the skipper and B the navigator. B reluctantly agrees. Meeting at Farnborough with Controller of Aircraft and galaxy of experts all shaking negative heads. State that HRH unlikely to accept simple NO for an answer, unsupported by in-depth info, logic, statistics etc. etc.
>
> 'In order to renew Licence, Wing Commander T due to carry out flight in hydrogen balloon owned by government. Controller agrees I go along as passenger. Take off from Cardington near Bedford. We are six passengers in crowded basket, including a pebble-spectacled man from the Ministry who is responsible for renewal of T's Licence. He has never flown before either.

'First landing aborted to avoid High Tension cables. Second attempt crashed on barn roof and bounced over farm house, landed in a pile in a cornfield. Greeted by Mr Pile the farmer (no kidding). Whilst crawling out from under canvas collided with man from the Ministry who asked my opinion. Reply unprintable. Licence of T renewed. Advise HRH against Balloonatics Club. He reluctantly agrees.'

On the outbreak of the World War II it was considered that Hendon was both busy and vulnerable and the Flight was moved to RAF Benson, an airfield forty miles west of London. In the meantime the Envoy had been replaced by a Hudson and a deluxe version of the de Havilland Flamingo, with an Avro Tutor for liaison work.

However these aircraft were little used and in 1942 the Flight was disbanded and formed the nucleus of 161 Squadron which was engaged on special operations, often involving the landing of agents and equipment behind enemy lines in occupied Europe.

The King's Flight was reformed in May 1946 with four Vickers Viking aircraft: one for the King's use, one for the Queen, one for crew support and one fitted out as a workshop.

On the 1st of August 1952, following the Accession of The Queen, the Flight was renamed the Queen's Flight, and between 1955 and 1961 the Vikings were gradually replaced by de Havilland Herons. In 1959 two Westland Whirlwind helicopters joined the Flight, although other helicopters had previously been used on loan.

In 1964 the first of the Andovers arrived and in 1969 the Wessex replaced the Whirlwinds. April 1986 saw the official hand-over ceremony of the first British Aerospace 146; the second aircraft arrived two months later. In January 1991 the third BAe 146 was delivered to replace the last remaining Andover after 27 years' service. The Flight then operated three BAe 146 and two Wessex helicopters.

During the early 1950s the Unit flew about sixty Royal Flights each year, but from 1954 when the helicopters began to be used this total progressively increased to some 1200 flights a year, of which half were by helicopter. Most air journeys involved positioning of the aircraft or helicopter at the beginning and end of the Royal Flight, so that the Queen's Flight flew some 3200 flights a year. All were mounted to the same high standards of safety, reliability and precise timing without recourse to the preparation of spare aircraft: thus other Royal Air Force aircraft were seldom diverted from their normal tasks for Royal Flights.

Because of the limited range of the BAe 146, most very long-range flights for major Royal visits overseas were undertaken by RAF transport or civil airline aircraft under charter, but under the supervision of the Captain of the Queen's Flight. It was usual for these aircraft to be 're-roled' with a special internal fit to contend with sleeping, changing and dining requirements, together with office space and typing facilities. On these occasions a BAe 146 was often positioned overseas to fly the Queen from small airfields in the country concerned.

To assist the Captain there were two Deputies of Group Captain rank, and to fly the aircraft there were five BAe 146 crews and three helicopter crews – one of the Wessex pilots being an officer from the Royal Navy. The Duke of Edinburgh and the Prince of Wales, being qualified pilots, usually flew the aircraft themselves. When time was not critical, the 146 was well able to undertake world-wide journeys and the Duke of Edinburgh often used the aircraft in this way.

For flights in British airspace, air traffic control lanes known as Purple Airways and Royal Low Level Corridors were established, which enabled special arrangements to be made for separating Royal aircraft from other air traffic. All the aircraft were painted in a distinctive red, white and blue livery, and the helicopters were completely red for ease of recognition in the air. When on the ground, they flew the Personal Standard of the Member of the Royal Family on board, and in addition when overseas the flag of the country concerned was flown.

Technically the Flight was completely self-contained in its offices, hangar, work-shops and stores, and unlike other RAF units it enjoyed an engineering backing in depth which permitted it to carry out first, second and third line servicing – that is major overhauls of aircraft and installed equipment. But however comprehensive the facilities, it was the skill, dedication and tireless devotion of the chaps on the shop floor which were responsible for the world-wide reputation for safety and reliability which built up around the Flight over decades.

It is to them this article is dedicated.

No. 32 (The Royal) Squadron

Squadron Leader Graham Laurie MVO

The 1994 Government-commissioned 'Pocock Report' concluded that rationalisation of the communications fleet would save money and provide a better service to the customers – moving up to three BAe 125s to the Queen's Flight and civilianising a number of the functions of the Flight. Additional improvements were suggested in tasking at Group and Ministry level. The Ministry of Defence countered this, indicating yet further savings could be achieved: The Queen's Flight would move to RAF Northolt alongside No. 32 Squadron.

The net result was the disbandment of the Queen's Flight on 31 March 1995 and the formation of No. 32 (The Royal) Squadron at RAF Northolt on 1 April 1995. The three BAe 146s and two Wessex helicopters were transferred, together with the aircrew, some of the operations staff and a handful of engineers.

For many years No. 32 Squadron had led the field in contractorisation of its engineering; thus overnight this civilian company had taken on, arguably, the Royal Air Force's most prestigious unit. Some engineers from the

Queen's Flight left the RAF and moved to Northolt, but much of the expertise came from former British Aerospace workers made redundant when BAe relocated from Hatfield to Manchester.

I was one of the BAe 146 captains moved, having already served fourteen years at Benson. The early days were difficult: merging two operations, engineers familiarising with new types – not least the Wessex helicopter, which required ever more nurturing on the ground for every minute in the air! The post of Captain of the Queen's Flight also disappeared, and Air Commodore The Hon. Timothy Elworthy became Her Majesty's Senior Air Equerry and moved office to RAF Northolt; overnight he relinquished control of the aircraft and men formerly under his command. The plan had been presented to our Royal passengers on the understanding that it would be a 'seamless' transition and the service would remain the same. It is to everybody's credit that this was achieved. The analogy of elegant swans on the surface and frantic paddling underwater comes to mind, as the new Squadron evolved.

The addition of the BAe 125 to Royal Flying duties enabled the shorter trips to be more effectively tasked. The size of the cabin and lack of privacy, however, made it less suitable for longer journeys.

A further policy change in the funding arrangements for the Royal Family and thus Royal flying, saw the office of the Senior Air Equerry changed to the Royal Travel Office: the Air Commodore became 'Director of Royal Travel and Her Majesty's Senior Air Equerry'. At the same time the Wessex helicopters were retired, and the Royal family commenced operations with their own helicopter, a Sikorsky S76 operated by a newly formed civilian unit at Blackbushe known as the Queen's Helicopter Flight. Many Royal Flights were now subject to tender and thus the Squadron was pitted against civilian operators. The costs involved generally proved the Royal Air Force to be more expensive than their civilian counterparts: it was not uncommon, therefore, to see a senior member of the Royal Family undertake an official overseas tour in a Swiss-registered Boeing 757!

The Squadron regularly flies Her Majesty The Queen and other senior members of the Royal family within UK and North West Europe. Her Majesty has also carried out State visits to Thailand, India and Pakistan. His Royal Highness The Duke of Edinburgh has twice been round the world in a 146. Her Royal Highness The Princess Royal visited Nepal and Bangladesh, and HRH the Duke of York has been to the Gulf and the Caribbean. In another change of emphasis, the Prime Minister, Foreign Secretary and Defence Minister regularly travel, particularly when on European Community business.

From a personal viewpoint, one event stands above all others. The Royal Squadron was thrust into the limelight upon the tragic death of the Princess of Wales. On 31 August 1997, I was due to fly HRH the Prince of Wales, Prince William and Prince Harry from Aberdeen to RAF Lyneham in the late afternoon. Arriving at Northolt at 7.00 a.m., knowing that the early morning accident had proved fatal, nobody expected the day's events to unfold in the way they did.

It was soon clear that a trip from Aberdeen to Paris would certainly be required, but there was a possibility we might return to Northolt with HRH's body. To cover both eventualities, one 146 was prepared with a false floor in the rear hold, with the second in normal passenger fit. My crew was already arriving for the original schedule and we were quickly able to provide a second, with the majority of Squadron personnel telephoning their availability.

The 146 left for Aberdeen via Wittering at 10.30 a.m., with the question of the coffin firming up all the time. The aircraft crew were busy all day, but their efforts paled into insignificance when compared with life on the ground at Northolt.

A quiet Sunday morning became hectic, as arrangements were made for the 'formal' reception of HRH's body back on English soil. Yes, there was a plan, but this gave some days for the organisation! Station and Squadron personnel were given jobs and hosting was organised. The world's media were arriving in force.

By the time the aircraft touched down, the roads surrounding Northolt were thronged with people. At 7.00 p.m. the doors of the 146 opened and the hushed crowds watched as the Royal Air Force Regiment carried the coffin from the aircraft to the awaiting hearse. Having flown Her Royal Highness over 200 times I was proud to have flown her on her final flight.

Twenty-five minutes later we were airborne for Aberdeen with HRH the Prince of Wales.

The rest of that week will go down in British history, together with the poignant scenes the following Saturday. The transformation of the Station over ten hours that Sunday was staggering and showed No. 32 (The Royal) Squadron, RAF Northolt and the Royal Air Force, in their finest light.

The coffin of HRH Diana Princess of Wales carried by the Royal Air Force Regiment from BAe 146 (Crown copyright)

The Hercules Reserve Aircrew

Squadron Leader Roy Harper

Founded in 1925, the Royal Auxiliary Air Force flying squadrons were disbanded in 1956.

Between September 1994 and March 1996 a trial, using two previous Regular Hercules crews, was conducted to assess the viability of part-time volunteer reservist aircrew. In 1996 the Air Force Board authorised the recruitment of nine Hercules reservist crews as members of the Royal Auxiliary Air Force, to support the RAF Lyneham air transport force in times of crisis and war.

The crews were selected from retired RAF Hercules aircrew. Recruits came from Civil Aviation, civilian careers, the self-employed and retired personnel.

Number 57(R) Squadron (the Hercules training squadron), organised a fifteen-day refresher course that provided training for aircrew to a standard equivalent to Limited Combat Ready (LCR). Recruits signed a High Readiness Reserve agreement to ensure that individuals and their employers (where applicable) accepted the terms and conditions of the Reserve Forces Act 1996.

The short training programme was structured on the assumption that the aircrew's recent past experience on the RAF Hercules would ensure a high probability of success. The course consisted of ground school, simulator and local flying on 57(R) Squadron. The concept provided for additional 'burst training' of approximately three weeks, to enable aircrew to achieve the standard required for them to join squadrons when needed to meet surge requirements in times of crisis or war.

The HRA Flight was initially formed as a part of 2624 Squadron RAuxAF, based at RAF Brize Norton. Number 2624 Squadron was an Air Transport and Air-to-Air Refuelling Support organisation with a primarily RAF Regiment role. A Hercules Reservist Aircrew Co-ordinator and an admin. clerk were established to organise and manage the Flight, but they were located within the 57(R) Squadron building at RAF Lyneham.

By April 1999 all nine crews had been trained and allocated to 24 Squadron and 30 Squadron, RAF Lyneham, for continuation training and flying supervision.

On 14 November 1998, after serving almost two years as a part time Reserve Aircrew navigator on the Hercules, I took command of the Reserve Aircrew Flight. I was delighted to return to full time duty at Lyneham (over many years I had served on most of the Hercules squadrons). It meant giving up my civil service job in the RAF Lyneham Flight Simulator.

On taking up my new reservist post I immediately changed the title of the post from Hercules Reservist Aircrew Co-ordinator to Flight Commander Hercules Reserve Aircrew, and restructured the flight. I also faced up to the 'political challenge' of separating the HRA Flight from 2624 Squadron and placing it in its natural home, the Hercules Flying organisation at RAF Lyneham. Little did I know just how time-consuming that process would prove to be. However, because I had the support of the Reserve Aircrews I persevered and gained agreement from Headquarters. On 21 October 1999 the HRA Flt. was transferred from 2624 Squadron to 57 Squadron, Lyneham.

The allocation of crews to 24 and 30 Hercules Squadrons placed an unacceptable training and administrative burden on these squadrons (a degree of resentment still exists because of the heavy commitment placed on them). Although Reserve Aircrews were formally established at RAF Lyneham, the level of support for them varied across the station. In my first year the atmosphere was, in some areas, unwelcoming.

I therefore brigaded the nine crews into two groups with the aim of offering real utility to the Hercules Squadrons, and the atmosphere improved.

Brigading took the form of allocating one fully-qualified crew to each of the four Hercules squadrons. The remaining aircrew were placed in a 'Pool Flight' on 57 Squadron. The Reserve Aircrew on Pool Flight are able to maintain the minimum standard of training required in the event of a call-out. This system has been in operation for two years and, following some fine-tuning, it is broadly a success. The HRA Flight now enjoys much improved relationships on the station.

Early in 2000, the additional task of 'peacetime utility' was added to the role of Reserve Aircrew. Because I had anticipated this utility element of RA activity, fully qualified RA aircrew already designated to the main squadrons satisfied the new policy. I knew that the 'regulars' would be irritated if they saw no actual return from the training they were called upon to provide for Reserve Aircrew. My move to place RA on each squadron, who could fly on any task allocated by the squadrons, enabled reservists to demonstrate their commitment and enthusiasm.

During the last twelve months Hercules Reserve Aircrew have been involved in all areas of Hercules training and flight operations. Their involvement shows a high level of commitment from pilots, navigators, air engineers and Air Loadmasters.

In addition to squadron simulator and local flying training, Reserve Aircrew regularly fly on operational tasks within Europe, the Near and Middle East, North America, Africa and the South Atlantic. Some reservists have flown on tasks to the Far East and Australia. Most importantly, six reservists were called-out in support of Operation 'Palliser' into Sierra Leone. Hard work and personal pride has ensured that Reserve Aircrew have gained flying qualifications to the same standards as their regular counterparts. One navigator is assessed as Combat Ready (Select), the highest possible qualification! Several Reserve Aircrew of all trades have gained Combat Ready (Advanced) assessments (above average). Most are Combat Ready, but all have achieved the minimum standard of Limited Combat Ready and are available for call-out.

In every respect the HRA Cadre has achieved everything (and much more) than was asked of them. Given the initial resistance to Reserve Aircrew, the Hercules reservists' achievement is significant. I am encouraged by frequent reports from 47 Squadron, 70 Squadron, and my host – 57

Squadron – that the RA are a welcome addition to RAF Lyneham and are acknowledged and respected as competent operators with a sound pedigree on the RAF Hercules. Some squadrons and sections have advised me that the RA have enabled them to complete tasks they would otherwise have had to refuse or cancel. They provide a degree of stability and add to the quality of life for regulars who, because of heavy tasking, have had long periods of disruption and uncertainty in their lives. All aircrew potentially gain from the broader view of the aviation world brought back to the station by the reservists.

None of the Reserve Aircrew I have selected and recruited have failed to reach the same high standards as their regular counterparts. All are enthusiastically committed to the Hercules Reserve Aircrew Cadre.

Am I proud of them? You bet your life I am!

Meteorological Research

In 1913, Shaw, then Director of the Met. Office, realised the potential of aircraft as a platform for meteorological measurements and research. He suggested mounting vanes on aircraft to measure vertical air motion, an accelerometer to measure 'bumpiness', as well as 'other meteorological measurements' including atmospheric electricity. The technology, funds and resources were not available to give Shaw's proposals practical effect. Weather-dependence of aviation had created a demand for meteorological reporting and forecasting services from the beginning, and resulted in 1920 in the absorption by the Air Ministry of the Meteorological Office. Later, the rapid technical development of aircraft, forced by the operational demands of two world wars, revealed further weather-related hazards, (airframe icing; visibility of aircraft contrails to enemy aircraft, and fog) which created a requirement for applied meteorological research.

During World War II, it was apparent that the lack of observations from the Atlantic Ocean (the source of most of our weather) and the rudimentary state of forecasting, did not meet aircraft operational requirements. This led to the formation of duty meteorological reconnaissance flights at RAF stations throughout the UK. In 1942, several daily flights were made from up to forty stations to observe temperature, humidity, winds, cloud amount, base and top height to altitudes of up 20,000 ft.

Based at Boscombe Down from 1942–46, the Meteorological Research Committee (MRC) operated two Boston and one Spitfire aircraft. In time Fortress, Mosquito and Hudson aircraft were added. The Flying Fortress was the first that could routinely reach the stratosphere. However, the Mosquito was better liked. Pilot and meteorological observer sat cosily side-by-side in the aircraft cabin and co-operated very effectively.

Post-WW II, the practical and scientific success of the High Altitude Flight (HAF) led to the establishment of the Meteorological Research Flight (MRF) at the Royal Aircraft Establishment (RAE), Farnborough. It now had more scientists, two Mosquitos, two Halifaxes and RAF crews. These aircraft were replaced by Hastings, Varsity and, in 1952, by Canberras that could be coaxed to 49,000 ft. Eventually came 'Snoopy', a vastly modified Lockheed C-130 Hercules, the only one to be designated WMk 2.

Sadly, in April 2001 the Meteorological Research Flight was disbanded.

The Met. Flight

Flight Lieutenant Tony Simpson

I was pushed reluctantly into the Meteorological Research Flight (MRF) in April 1997. My unwillingness to move was not borne of a dislike for the job, for I knew nothing of it. It was, however, a pleasure to renew my acquaintance with the Hercules, not only for the superb and spacious flight-deck with its panoramic views of the world below, but also because of the surfeit of power normally available from the four Allison T56-15A turboprop engines, coupled to what was, at its inception, the most sophisticated constant speed propeller ever devised. Not only brilliant, it has proved to be an exceptionally reliable system considering the thousands of Hercules flights world-wide. For over forty years the Hercules has taken me and thousands of crews to remote, often grim and some wonderful destinations very safely.

'Snoopy', the MRF's Hercules, is a strange-looking aircraft with its 6-metre long red-and-white striped nose boom. This allows sensitive instruments to be carried ahead of the air disturbance created by the aircraft. They allow the vertical, horizontal and turbulent motion of the air to be measured.

Inside the aircraft space is at a premium with every corner filled with instrumentation. A typical crew consists of two pilots, a navigator, a flight engineer and as many as sixteen scientists.

When a UK-based sortie is to be flown, the day begins with a briefing at 0830 hrs local. Here the sortie type and location are decided on the basis of the meteorological situation provided by the forecaster. Once the most suitable area for the required research is selected, the Loadmaster and Flight Engineer and the five to sixteen scientists who operate in the rear of the aircraft depart to 'wind up' the plethora of systems, sensors, analysers and associated computers that are

Meteorological Research Flight 'Snoopy' (QinetiQ, Farnborough)

essential to all MRF data-gathering. The two pilots and navigator then plan the sortie in detail with the aircraft scientist whose project is being flown, and who is responsible for direction of the flight. He or she is usually a Doctor of a weird sub-branch of meteorological science, vaguely connected with either atmospheric chemistry, cloud physics, homogeneous stratocumulus etc. The navigator produces a computer flight-plan of the sortie, using the latest winds and temperatures to determine the precise fuel load and flight duration. (Too much fuel restricts max. altitude if required; too little reduces sortie time meaning lost data.) Where necessary a low-level booking is made if flying below 2,000 ft. over land or, if operating out in the Atlantic or North Sea, marine activities have to be checked. This is important as a typical MRF profile starts or ends at 50 ft (over the years a number of ships' captains have reported a large aircraft attempting to land on the sea!). There are two designated MRF navigators because of the complexity of planning daily four to ten hour sorties, some of them venturing into European airspace, so as one nav. flies, the other plans next day's sortie, or the next detachment.

Engines start begins twenty mins before take-off, and when all four generator/alternators are on line, the critical power changeover is co-ordinated between Flight Engineer and the Flight Leader, a boffin sitting in the 'caravan' back in the freight bay. The electrical power changeover has to be closely co-ordinated to avoid a power interrupt to the sensitive equipment used by the scientists. Once airborne, rapid transits are made at medium level to the area of operation in order to maximise time on task; it is common to loiter around the Shetland Islands, Faeroes, or 300 nm SW of Land's End for up to seven hours.

During the daily routine, the non-flying nav. is normally fully committed in his secondary role. This has a vast remit: negotiating for Diplomatic Clearance with embassy staffs, ordering flight-catering, filing ATC flight-plans, booking a low-level clearance if the sortie requires runs at 100 feet, and a plethora of tasks that have to be completed prior to an overseas detachment.

As the following examples demonstrate, MRF flights always demand very precise flying!

One part of the highly complex meteorological research programme is a sortie profile called a 'Lagrangian': literally 'chasing the parcel'. The parcel in this context being one of air. The aim is to follow the movement and behaviour of the parcel as it moves through the atmosphere. In this particular sortie a freighter crammed with tons of meteorological research gadgets sailed daily from the Spanish port of Sagres. Having located the parcel of air the ship began to launch balloons at hourly intervals. (Each balloon is over six feet in diameter and has a smaller balloon inside filled with helium. The 'parent', or larger, balloon is inflated/deflated remotely to control its altitude.) The MRF, based a thousand nautical miles away in Tenerife, knew the launch times, and so one crew got airborne at 1000 hrs local, racing North-east for 500 miles at medium level (FL 200 or 20,000 ft) to intercept the balloon. The transit altitude was limited by the take-off weight, with 55,000 lb of fuel for a nine-hour sortie, and the high temperature. High temperatures reduce engine power and also reduce performance in speed and height.

The transit took approximately one hour forty minutes. At a range of 90–100 nm from the area a 'Profile Descent' was initiated. This differs from a normal Hercules en-route descent. In the latter case throttles are set and pitch trimmed to maintain 230 K IAS (Indicated Air Speed) at 2000 feet per minute descent. Snoopy's Profile descent is more complex and is initiated by the operating pilot and marked in time on voice data recorders and in the Nav's Scientific Log.

At the precise second the Pilot announces 'Commencing profile descent from FL 200 at 180 kts, 1000 fpm, in 3-2-1-NOW'. On this executive word of command the pilot simultaneously resets the power with one hand on the throttles, while the other hand smoothly eases forward the control column to establish the Rate of Descent (RoD). Then, imperceptibly, his thumb caresses the elevator trim switches to ease the load on the control column.

It is MRF Standard Operating Procedure (SOP) at FL50 or 5000 ft to reduce the RoD (Rate of Descent) to 500 fpm, the speed remaining a constant 180 kts. All the various scientific sensors and analysers are calibrated to operate most effectively at 180 kts; this speed is the closest to what the scientists base their data calculations on world-wide – 100 metres per second (100 m/s); by pure and thorough calculation, not luck. It also happens to be the ideal speed for optimum absorption by all of the many external probes and samplers that collect atmospheric samples and pass them directly into the internal analysers through various filters.

Why reduce the RoD below 5000 ft? The reason is both simple and revealing. The highest concentrations of pollution 'particulates' and naturally the densest air occur at the surface, or at least very close to it. So to obtain optimum results it makes sense to transit down through this data-rich environment at a lower rate.

Now back to the sortie. At 25 nm I could pick up the balloon on the aircraft radar, an old but tried and tested ECKO 290, with 180° lateral sweep and range out to 175 nm. This radar was dubbed 'Cloud and Clonk' for obvious reasons. When set in the weather mode (Wx) it showed cloud, and in Contour mode it showed which cloud was the nasty one with the less healthy centre: that is to say if you were foolish enough to fly in, the odds were very much on the cloud's side, in that you'd come out of it right enough, but in smaller, wet pieces. A good operator could also pick up other aircraft, and more importantly surface vessels and even an abandoned dinghy, as once happened. This mode was used widely in Search and Rescue missions often carried out by the squadrons at Lyneham.

I selected 'Manual' to make the dish aerial transmit a pencil-beam and adjusted the gain and contrast. Then I varied the up/down tilt of the sweeping aerial a few degrees at a time to scan the area into which I had calculated the balloon would have drifted. And there it was – a small 'cigar' shape on the CRT. Finding the balloon was the easy part. Now, in the final stages of the descent to 50 ft above the sea surface the fun would really begin. The RoD was steady at 500 fpm down to 200 ft when the pilot reduced it to 200 fpm, tapering it at a height of 150 ft above sea level to 100 fpm or less; as the flight engineer started to call the radar-altimeter height every 25 ft down to an altitude of 100 ft, and thereafter at every 10 ft. Manoeuvring an aircraft with a wing span of 133 ft down to the height of a well-grown Leylandii calls for cool nerves, skill and precise timing.

Flight Engineer: '90, 80, 70, 60, 55, 50 ft. NOW!'. The instant the pilot registered this hysterical bark, his hand was already advancing the throttles smoothly but rapidly towards the 'firewall', and his other hand was pulling back the control column and easing Snoopy back up to a more sane height of 100 ft. Well of course it is more sane if you can see over the top of the waves and avoid that rather large freighter off the starboard bow.

Having found the balloon, the next four to five hours were spent flying box patterns around it at various altitudes from 100 ft to 5000 ft: the sides of the squares 15–20 nm long, depending on the altitude. It was all done on timing, so the higher the box the longer the sides, as speed increases with height.

You must bear in mind this was also being done at night. That is to say in the dark, with headlights off. Fortunately Snoopy had a galley wherein the duty loadmaster (steward) concocted all manner of things to enthuse over and eat, then regret it. No matter, there was lots of tea and coffee to drink and stay awake; also a decent toilet with a washbasin.

Apart from the odd incidents, mercifully few and far between on the Hercules, for the crew one of the most goose-pimple-raising parts of MRF flying is sweeping majestically over the waves at 100 ft for anything from a two-minute run to an incredible one hour forty mins. (From just off the Norfolk coast up to Aberdeen in 1998). It is a time of intense concentration for all on the flight deck. The operating pilot's eyes scan methodically across his instruments: the Air Speed Indicator, Altimeter (barometric), Horizontal Situation Indicator and Attitude Director Indicator; looking up out of the window as someone calls: 'Mind that ship/oilrig twelve o'clock three miles'. The pilot flies the barometric altimeter, set with the surface pressure derived from the forecast pressure and checked against the Radar Altimeter. Although the Rad Alt is more accurate, if the pilot followed it when flying over a sea running at thirty feet everyone would be fed-up and very seasick.

Among my responsibilities is starting and ending the runs, whether they are in straight lines or executing other patterns for the particular research as required by the lead scientist. This could be a Box pattern formed by timed runs, a Clover-leaf through a central point, or even 'Sawtooth', starting at a prescribed altitude and profiling down to a lower altitude; and on reaching that, reverse it all and profile back up to the start altitude, then down, and up and down, until it is time to go home. Time is recorded to the second, read from a highly accurate recording system in the 'van'. My 'Science Log' has twelve columns. These show time to the nearest second; Snoopy's course; the indicated airspeed to the nearest knot (nautical mph); true air speed; drift; ground speed; wind velocity and direction; temperature; atmospheric pressure; precise location, and the task being performed. I evolved the log over three years: it was required as a 'manual' backup in the unlikely event of failure of the sophisticated electronic recorders. The log has about eighty lines for entries, so on a seven-hour sortie in which I easily filled in sixty lines, I would have written over 1500 characters. I still wear a wrist support.

This sortie was over Northern Sweden 'doing' Cloud Physics and Cloud Chemistry research into the formation and dispersal of Lenticular Cloud, (*Altocumulus Lenticularis*) or Lee-wave cloud. They are created by strong winds 'rolling' the air mass over high ground to form the horizontally aligned 'tear-drop' cloud. We were operating from a Swedish Air Force base built atop a plateau called Frøsen – literally translatable as 'brass monkeys'.

Three detachments to Germany (Hamburg, Köln/Bonn and Munich, the latter providing a torrential downpour all weekend (so naturally several of us had to seek refuge in the Hofbrauhaus for a mere five hours). Two more detachments to Sweden, Ascension Island, Thessalonika, and a long detachment in and around Africa: my time on MRF has always been interesting, fun, and educative. The last big detachment involved a transit through Porto Santo for fuel, then on to Sal in the Cape Verde islands: 29–35° C and 97% humidity. Hot and humid? No air-conditioning in the hotel: step out of shower, towel yourself dry under the large fan, and slip on clean shirt in time for it to stick to your chest and back.

From Sal we flew a nine-hour sortie to Niamey, capital of the central African state of Niger. It was primitive to say the least, but the hotel was cool enough, the food just edible and we stayed long enough for everyone to get 'Dheli-belli' before going off to Ascension Island for two nights, before flying back into South Africa and the pleasantly European-style city of Windhoek at an altitude of 6000 ft. The air was so fresh with a daytime temperature of 24–30°C and the humidity 4%. Over the first few days we began to experience cracked and bleeding lips, nose-bleeds and dried cuticles. But it was worth it! After two weeks of dining rather well in the safari hotel we left to go back to Sal, 97% and 33°C. We did become acclimatised over the next eighteen days, but, interestingly, on the third night the sky grew black and the heavens delivered the worst rainstorm Sal had experienced in forty years – or so the barman said.

The next morning we paddled our way to breakfast through ankle-deep water to see the ground staff scooping up water in dustpans and sloshing it into – wheelbarrows. They were not used to that amount of rain, you see. Naturally we got the blame: after all, our aircraft had the logo on the fuselage, one that I hope will never be forgotten:

'THE METEOROLOGICAL RESEARCH FLIGHT'.

Different Aspects of Training

Flying operations make challenging demands at all levels – from novice to highly experienced aircrew. Training is an essential element.

First Flight

Group Captain P. J. Rodgers MBE

After an extended overseas tour in the Headquarters of Allied Air Forces Central Europe, I was repatriated to the Royal Air Force College Cranwell to be resettled and retired. Whilst there, I watched with envy as smartly-dressed young hopefuls went through the officer and aircrew selection process, and successful candidates went on to their initial officer training. They were at the beginning of their careers, and mine was almost over. It had been a happy and rewarding career, and I was finding it difficult to come to terms with the imminence of my departure. But, having confided my misgivings to an old friend and colleague, I was reminded of the Air Cadet Organisation and their continuous need for volunteer staff. After all, it was the Air Training Corps that had prepared me for the fulfilment of my ambitions, and I now had the opportunity to repay a debt of gratitude by offering my time to one of the Volunteer Gliding Schools.

There were two such units at nearby Syerston, which is also home to the Central Gliding School. My request for consideration was favourably received, and arrangements were made for me to undertake a conversion course on the Vigilant T Mk 1, which is described as a motorised glider. On the completion of my consolidated flying course I was offered an appointment with No. 644 Volunteer Gliding School, where I received a warm welcome from the instructors and staff. Some of them had Service backgrounds and some, like me, were still in the Service. But the majority were the product of the Air Cadet Organisation and the gliding school system of training. As cadets they had undertaken gliding scholarships and had remained with the gliding school as staff cadets, before going on to adult service as civilian instructors, or as officers of the 'Volunteer Reserve'. Their task was to provide flying experience to air cadets, and to provide instruction to the lucky few who had been selected for the gliding scholarships which lead to solo flights, and the award of Air Cadet Wings.

Vigilant (HQ Air Cadets)

As a newly qualified Grade 1 pilot I was cleared to fly passengers but I was not yet qualified to instruct. So most of my flying was concerned with the provision of air experience to recently recruited cadets. From time to time cadets approach these twenty-minute flights with an air of indifference, because they have flown in civil aircraft or they have already flown in high performance military aircraft. But the vast majority anticipate these flights with an infectious air of excitement, which can result in an exhilarating experience for pilots and passengers alike, and I am often mindful of the first of these occasions.

I had just flown one of the 'indifferent' variety, whose father had a friend with a Cessna something-or-other, and I remained in the cockpit whilst my next charge donned his parachute and listened to the pre-flight briefing from one of the staff cadets. His broad smile testified to the fact that he was going to enjoy himself, and he made no attempt to conceal his excitement as he clambered into the cockpit. Indeed his smile now threatened to split his face in half. 'Have you ever flown in one of these aircraft before?' I asked. 'No, Sir, I've never flown in anything before.'

Unable to resist, I gave him the checklist and responded 'Neither have I, but never mind. They've given me this instruction book. You read it out and I'll see if I can find the switches'. When I subsequently recounted this event to no lesser personage than the Commandant of the Central Flying School, I was suitably admonished. 'Poor little beggar, you could have frightened him to death.' But there was no chance of that. This 'little beggar' was ready to have the time of his life and nothing was going to frighten him.

With the engine started and checks completed, we taxied towards the runway and began to engage in conversation. In response to my passenger's questions, I told him something of the history of Syerston, and mentioned that Guy Gibson had once flown from there. 'Wait 'til I tell my granddad' he said. 'He was on 617 Squadron and he knows everything that there is to know about the Dambusters.' There was a pause, and then he asked 'Have you ever been a pilot?'

'Well I fancy I still am. That's why they're letting me sit here with you'.

'No, I meant have you ever flown a proper aeroplane? My uncle flew Buccaneers.'

No offence was intended, and none was taken, but he was doubly reassured when I mentioned Victors, despite the fact that 'granddad' had been on Vulcans.

By now we were ready for take off, and with checks completed, we rolled down the grass strip and into the air. At this point my young charge exclaimed 'Wow!' and began a commentary, which would not cease until we were back on the ground.

'What's that?'

'It's the river Trent.'

'I thought it was bigger than that.'

'What are they?'

'Cows.'

'I thought they were sheep.'

'Where's that?'

'Newton.'

'Where are the runways?'

'It hasn't got any.'

I gradually realised that I was now reliving the thrill of my own first flight through the eyes and observations of this young man, and I was beginning to share his enthusiasm. The city of Nottingham spread before us and he strained to see his house. He described the general area. He lived near a golf course, and his father had just given him a half-set of golf clubs for his thirteenth birthday. His mother had given him a guitar, but the best birthday present was being able to fly in a Vigilant. I thought I knew what he meant, but I urged him not make this comparison in the presence of his parents.

Although I was not a qualified instructor, I was clearly obliged to acknowledge this coming of age for Air Cadet flying by letting him control the aircraft. So after a brief spell of 'following-through' I talked him through a few gentle manoeuvres, which he undertook with consummate ease.

All too soon the authorisation sheets beckoned, and we had to recover to base. As we touched down he uttered yet another 'Wow', and as we taxied back to the dispersal he waved at anyone and everyone who happened to be looking in our direction. When at last the cockpit canopy was opened he alighted and ran off to his waiting friends. Doing a little jig that was somewhat reminiscent of a Morecambe-and-Wise routine, he punched the air, and shouted 'I'm a natural. He told me I'm an absolute natural. A natural born pilot!' Then, as his little group disappeared and the next passenger climbed aboard, I remembered his words as he prepared to depart the aircraft and shook me by the hand: 'Thank you, Sir, I enjoyed the trip and I'll never ever forget it'.

I reflected that I would probably remember it too, and with that I turned to the next customer: 'Now then, young lady. Have you ever flown in one these aircraft before?'

Tornado GR 1 Mission

Flight Lieutenant Ken Delve

The task arrives – Offensive Counter Air (OCA) to destroy a fighter airfield, time on target as soon as possible. The previously peaceful scene becomes chaotic. Firstly, plot the target to see where it is. From then on teams can set to work on various aspects of the sortie. Pilots study the target area map to decide on attack direction, weapons, type of delivery and such like (the all-important weapons-target matching). The aim of the mission is to destroy the fuel dump on the airfield.

Meanwhile, the navigators start work on the route out to the target and back.

There is frequent cross-checking to make sure that both ends are going to tie up! The target maps are copied while co-ordinates are calculated and the route is typed into the ground planning computer. Using the map table a route can be transferred into the computer in a manner of minutes; additional mission information can then be added and the computer asked to provide a plan of the entire mission – times, fuel and so on. When satisfied that it all looks good and should work, it's time to take copies of the data onto a cassette tape for later transfer into the aircraft computers. It is also a good idea to take a hard copy of the information just in case the tape doesn't work!

Into the briefing room for a time check and down to the nitty-gritty of the sortie. The lead nav. briefs the route, and the lead pilot the target and tactics. At the end of the briefing the four crews know everything they need to know to fly the mission and anyone can take the lead should it be required. It's a true statement that a good sortie starts from a good brief, and with the tolerances that the formation are working to it is essential that everyone is fully in the picture. The time for questions is now and not on the attack run at 500 knots, in cloud and just behind another aircraft.

A final check that no new intelligence has been received about the target or the route area, and it is time to go out to the HAS (Hardened Aircraft Shelter). Snug in its concrete house the aircraft sits waiting, armed with four 1000 lb bombs, two Sidewinders, Skyshadow and BOZ (chaff/flare dispenser), plus a full load of ammunition for the Mauser cannon.

No ALARM anti-radiation missiles on this aircraft but two of the formation are carrying ALARM as well as the rest of the fit. A follow-up mission due on target a few minutes after yours is carrying the JP 233 airfield denial system. No time to waste as check-in time is not far away. A quick exchange of banter with the ground-crew and the nav gets in to wind up the rear seat kit, while the pilot does a quick walk-round check of the aircraft. The ground crew have already warmed up part of the navigation system by aligning the Inertial Nav (IN) and so it's switch on the Main Computer and feed in the cassette tape with the route details – taking care to check through that all the details are correct.

Time to taxi and to see if the other members of the formation are ready. One, two, three – good, everyone appears to be on time. Each aircraft moves into place on the runway for the take-off as two pairs, and still no word has been spoken on the radio. Lead gives the wind-up signal and the power increases from the one and two, reheat Combat power and away down the runway. Twenty seconds later the second pair follow and soon all four are climbing away from the airfield and into the greying sky.

This is the boring bit: a fifty-minute flight to the tanker. Time to check through the route in the computer and make sure that everything is working as it should.

The VC 10 tanker is at the planned RV, and a rapid join-up is followed by the first two aircraft sliding into place behind the wing hoses, checks completed in each Tornado. Cleared to contact, the first aircraft moves slowly forward to plant its probe into the 'basket', the nav providing left-right up-down information as required. Good contact and fuel flowing: within a matter of minutes both aircraft have taken on the required amount of fuel and so disconnect and move to the other side of the tanker whilst the second pair take on their fuel. All complete, a silent goodbye to the tanker, see you again on the way back.

Time to go down, engage the TFR (Terrain Following Radar) and plunge into the layer of cloud. It's a mixed blessing as the radar emissions will give the aircraft away to anyone listening out, but it is the only way to get down to low level through the cloud. Five hundred feet and at last the cloud layer breaks up. The radar is fearless, it doesn't think about the mountains which lurk in the gloom: all it knows is the height it has been told to go to – this can prove quite heart-stopping as the aircraft comes out of cloud in a valley with sheer rock walls climbing up into the cloud on either side.

However, safely down and the TFR can go back to standby so that the aircraft can run electronically silent. Now comes the time to get down and hide behind any folds in the ground, small valleys, hills: anything at all that will make the aircraft hard to see or track. Speed up to 450 knots and keep an eye on Number Four who is in battle on the port side: scan ahead to pick up the other aircraft some distance ahead, sometimes catching a glimpse as they manoeuvre.

Approaching bandit country and 80% of the time is spent scanning the sky all around the formation, but particularly in the 6 o'clock of your mate to check that no-one is sneaking up on him. He is doing the same for you. The other 20% of the time is spent monitoring the aircraft and the navigation, weapons and Electronic Warfare systems. Time to look at a pre-planned radar fixpoint to check that the nav kit is accurate. A quick squint on the radar to decipher the green blotches of ground returns, use the hand control to move the fixing cross a bit – only a small error, so reject the fix and let the computer get on with it.

Tornado of No. 2 Squadron (Ken Delve)

The Tornado Main Computer is an amazing piece of kit and the general rule is that it knows better than you do most of the time – check it against the radar but be wary of moving its position too far. Unless it is having one of its very rare bad days (usually nav-induced) it works to within feet and the data it feeds to the pilot's Head Up Display is more than accurate enough to get the aircraft into the target area. A glance at the moving map display in the centre of the nav panel and a confirming glance at the passing countryside gives great confidence in the system.

Fix over and it's eyes back outside as the countryside flashes past.

'FELIX 3 AND 4, COUNTER PORT. BOGEY 9 O'CLOCK, CLOSING!'

In come the burners as the aircraft is wracked around in a tight turn to the left. Scan the sky then try and pick up the bogey as you strain against the sudden 'G' force and the inflation of the 'G-suit' constricting the blood flow to the legs.

'BOGEY 12 O'CLOCK, IT'S A PAIR, TWO MILES.'

'TALLY.'

The counter has nullified the attackers' attempt to sneak up, and the aircraft pass nose to nose.

Now comes the tricky bit as it looks like going into a turning fight. Get the head right round to watch what the opposition is up to, turning back in with a hard turn to starboard. As usual, it comes down to one on one, but you have to watch the whole fight to make sure that they don't both switch to you or try a sneaky shot as you pass the nose. The lead pair will have heard the calls and will have 'bustered' away from the fight as fast as they can to get to the target – the job of a bomber is to bomb the target, not get involved in a fight. This is not the best time for a Tornado to fight, and the decision has to be taken to keep the bombs or ditch them: there is no point in holding on to the bombs if you are about to get shot down!

For some reason the fighters break off the engagement and run out in the opposite direction. Reverse and truck on towards the target a little puzzled. How much time and fuel has the combat cost, can we make the target on time? Look at the route, cut a corner here, fly a bit faster on that leg and you can still get to the IP on time, great. No sign of your mate; so for now you are on your own and all of a sudden you feel very exposed now that no-one is watching your tail.

Down at 100 ft the pilot concentrates on flying the aircraft over or around natural and man-made obstructions while the nav 'manages the mission'. Timing's good for the target, everything seems to be under control. Suddenly a more urgent note sounds in the earphones: the audio part of the radar warner – a glance inside at the display screen to work out what it is and where it is. A bit of judicious switching leads to the conclusion that it is a ZSU 23-4 GUNDISH radar in the 10 o'clock. This particular one seems no threat as it cannot maintain radar lock, and will therefore be unable to lay its guns onto the aircraft. No need to use any of the ECM kit, but keep a wary eye on it in case any of the associated systems are in the area.

With its Marconi Skyshadow jamming pod and the BOZ chaff/flare pod the Tornado is able to look after itself well in the EW (Electronic Warfare) environment. The addition of the anti-radiation ALARM missile has made this capability even greater as the aircraft can now 'shut down' an enemy threat radar by launching a homing missile in his direction – even if it doesn't strike home it is sure to encourage the operator to switch off until you have gone past!

So far, so good, but in twenty miles the route goes near an area which intelligence reports suggest may be used as a build-up area for second echelon units. It is amazing how many small folds and creases there are in a seemingly flat landscape and full advantage is taken of every one – the best way to avoid getting shot down is to avoid being seen, and the best jammer in the world is a few million tons of granite! The radar warner bursts into life with a confusing array of signals, far too difficult to sort out: switch on the jammers, dump a bit of chaff and leg it away as fast and low as possible keeping your fingers crossed. Missile launch in the 4 o'clock! More chaff and manoeuvre, sink even closer to the ground as the trees flash past at 500 kts.

Back to the job in hand and time to check the accuracy of the computer again. Ten minutes to target, into the target routine. Weapons selected and appropriate settings made. Keep the radar off until the last minute. It is now that the radar comes into its own – the 'kit' will give a bomb measured in less than 100 feet. By using the radar to give a final tweek the accuracy can be measured at a fraction of that: add the laser ranger into the equation and the accuracy is second to none.

The weather is getting worse! Low cloud and mist, good Tornado weather. Fifteen miles to target, quick peek at an offset shows the kit is good. Timing is good, eight miles to go: switch to the target, not convinced so bomb on the offset mark. Five miles to go, this is close enough, light the burners, pull up and throw the bombs into the target area. The aircraft leaps as the four 1000 lb bombs go sailing off towards the airfield. Roll over, get the nose down, cut out the burners and leg it the other way as quick as possible.

Within seconds it is back to trees and granite flashing past on either side. Didn't see anyone else. No time to relax as you still have to get out of bandit country and back to base. With appreciably less fuel and no bombs the aircraft goes like a greased weasel and turns like a fighter.

An uneventful trip towards the FEBA (Forward Edge of the Battle Area), only twenty miles to go. Was that a bleep from the radar warner, maybe a fighter in the 9 o'clock, scan the area. There it is, three miles and smoking in at a great range of knots. Counter towards him to negate any missile shot. Now we can turn and the fight is on. Pull hard as he passes the nose, keep the turn going as he has started to turn back in. Wings forward to tighten the turn and radar into the air-to-air mode. He looks to be on his own, but keep looking all around for any more unwelcome visitors. This one-on-one fight is developing into the standard circle, with each aircraft trying to close the circle and get a firing solution. Play with the wing sweep and manoeuvre devices to gain a bit in the turn. Radar lock in range, Sidewinder growl as the missile acquires its prey. Commit (missile launch), and film the Phantom as it sits in the ranging circle.

No fuel left to play about, and so off to the RV with the tanker to pick up a couple of thousand kilos of fuel before going home.

Twenty minutes later and the four-ship 'breaks' into the circuit for landing. Downwind checks complete and throttles rocked outboard to pre-select the thrust reverses and lift dump. As soon as the wheels hit the deck the spoilers deploy to kill all lift on the wings and the thrust reverse buckets motor to cover the engine exhausts: jam the throttles forward and all the thrust is deflected by the thrust reverse buckets to slow the aircraft down. When a Tornado hits the ground with an intention of stopping short, it really does stop short!

It has been a good exercise. In many ways the easy part is over: now comes the analysis, bombing scores will have been passed and the fighter 'mates' will be on the phone to discuss the results of the combats. Every part of the mission is looked at: films of Head Up Display, the radar and TV/TAB are examined and then lessons hoisted aboard for next time.

By the way, the range says that the missile got you – perhaps.

THE THAW

Mikhail Gorbachev's reforms played a pivotal role in changing the political climate in the 90s and ending the cold war between East and West.

Air Commodore Wilkinson describes one interesting result!

Now It Can Be Told – Aboard the Russian Bear 1994

Air Commodore Phil Wilkinson CVO

I have already had the chance to express my delight at the irony of a last tour of duty in the former Soviet Union. ('Cold War – Canberra QRA' – Ed.) That alone would have been a delight -and most certainly it was. But there were one or two highlights that made my three and a half years in Moscow and around the old USSR quite incomparable.

During my time in Moscow there had been a measurable relaxation of some of the restrictions on travel, and the occasional chance of access to some real Russian hardware – under controlled conditions to be sure, but at least access. But nothing prepared me for the shock I got when I asked for a ride in a Bear, and they said 'Yes'!

I need to explain the system, introduced in an earlier period and definitely still in play in 1994. The Russian Ministry of Defence External Relations Directorate was very well known to generations of attachés by its Russian initials 'UVS'. When I wanted to make any kind of contact with any element of the Russian armed forces, or lay the foundations for one of the many official visits that were becoming the vogue – or indeed when the Russians wanted to make contact with me – the conduit was inescapably the offices of UVS, opposite one of the main Russian MOD buildings in central Moscow.

Each country's attachés were handled by either a small team of contact Russian officers or by a singleton, depending on the size of the attaché complement. In 1994 I had a team of seven attachés (principals and assistants) and we would be handled at such meetings by one or other of the five Russians who dealt with English-speaking NATO attachés. The theoretical function of UVS was to 'facilitate' bilateral contacts: the reality ranged from bureaucratic complication and delay to outright obstruction.

So when Paul Bowen, director of the RAF Benevolent Fund's International Air Tattoo, phoned and said he wondered if I could persuade the Russians to send a Tupolev 'Bear' or two (!) to the 1994 Show at RAF Fairford, I knew I was in for a long and complicated series of meetings. When the supplementary bid came in for Central TV to make a documentary of the whole event I knew I was in for some serious disappointments. A UK TV team on board a Bear? Unlikely was hardly the word for it.

So it was with the greatest of surprise that I heard the basic request – for the Bear (perhaps even two Bears) to fly in for the Show – got a virtually immediate answer 'Yes'. But my follow-up call on UVS to broach the idea of a TV documentary got the totally expected 'Nyet'! However, over the next few weeks I persisted, and started to sow the idea of the amazing publicity value such an exercise would create for the newly-opened Russian military machine. 'Picture the scene' I said to my Russian interlocutor: 'the British audience will see a benign and highly professional Air Force at work; the Russian audience – for of course the UK TV programme will be offered to Russian TV for showing domestically – will see the same. And both will see a reminder of the Cold War as the Royal Air Force come up to intercept the Bear on its way into UK air space.' And suddenly the game was on. But at a price.

My next call to UVS, to iron out some details, revealed the terms of Russian agreement to the deal. The Bear (or Bears) would have to be accompanied by technicians and other representatives of the Russian Navy and Air Force. They would have to travel in an accompanying 'Candid' (Ilyushin 76). The aircraft would obviously require full refuelling at UK expense; the accompanying team would need accommodation at UK expense for the week of the Show; there would sensibly have to be a little assistance with entertainment and hosting of the crews and accompanying team. That team would, with Bear and Candid crews, total seventy-one officers. Paul Bowen was not amused.

While he absorbed the impact of this astonishing bid, I thought I should capitalise on the still – to me – incredible willingness of the Russians to let the UK TV team fly with the operational aircraft and film inside it. Wouldn't it, I suggested, be sensible to have me on board to act as an airborne interpreter and to explain UK procedures as they were broadcast to the Russians? Another moment of stunned disbelief – the answer was again 'Yes'.

Things then moved very fast. The deal was done: two Bears, one Air Force Tu-95 and a Naval Aviation Tu-142, plus the accompanying Candid, and the entire set of accompanying 'delegation' members and ground crew. I still

Tornado escort moves in close! (Air Commodore Wilkinson)

have the list; and there were eight generals in the delegation, two colonels in the Navy Bear's crew, one in the Air Force's, and the ground crew were led by another Colonel. Finally on the Candid there were two Warrant Officers, but neatly matched by a couple of Lieutenant Colonels.

First event was the arrival of the Central TV team – one producer/director and the cameraman. Together we went out to Tchakalovsky, the main Russian transport base near Moscow, and climbed on board the Candid for the first leg, which took us to a Naval Aviation base in the Baltic enclave of Kaliningrad. The whole supporting delegation was on board, and I made my appropriate salutations to the two senior men. These were a couple of real stars: Lieutenant General Vasilyi Akporisov, Chief of Staff, Naval Aviation; and Lieutenant General Mikhail Soroka, Deputy Chief of the Russian Air Staff.

They made me very welcome. On arrival in Kaliningrad we made our way to the Mess and were told to get into something casual since the next event was a trip out to the beach for a picnic.

The next fifteen hours were – I suppose – quite a picnic! A convoy of the Russian equivalents of Jeeps and Transits took us out of base, through some very North German appearing agricultural land – complete with nesting storks and good-looking cattle – and dropped us off on the cliff-top overlooking a deserted beach – deserted except for the rusting hulk of a small freighter that must have run aground at least thirty years before. On the cliff edge was a long table set with lots of picnic salad things and probably more bottles of vodka than were sensible for a very hot afternoon. Beer and wine made up most of the rest of the space. Then the cooks started to put hot food on the table: the base commander had brought along his senior chef plus a helper, and for the next two hours they cooked vast amounts of meat and fish while the rest of us swam in the Baltic, explored the wreck, and scavenged along the beach for amber, pausing only to take a swig from the beer bottles that I had persuaded the Russians to keep cool (or at least cooler) in the sea. But eventually it was back to the table, and the feast began.

Several hours and a couple of dozen toasts later, the convoy wended its way back to the sparse wooden huts that made up the Mess living accommodation, and the two TV heroes, if no-one else, hoped for a quiet evening. Wrong! It was now time for the evening feast and trip to the 'banya' – the Russian sauna. It all got a little blurred here, but the day ended without serious casualties. The only real incongruity was the Russians' insistence that I put on a cloth shower cap before each plunge into the cold pool. Hygiene? Stopping the head from exploding? Some cunning ruse to implant a listening device into my scalp? Would look very funny on the photos? Probably the latter. All the photos of that day are very funny.

The next days were not funny – just amazing. As we boarded the two-star bedecked but very clapped-out bus to go to the airfield, and drove through the free-range cows around the Mess, the two senior Generals started to explain the change of plan. They now wanted the Central TV team to fly in the Candid, using the nose blister windows to give good shots of the expected interceptions by NATO fighters over the Baltic and North Sea. The TV pair were not in any real mood to argue either way; the previous day had obviously got to them. The prospect of a flight in anything was causing alarm and despondency. But my spirits went right up when the Generals said I would therefore have a seat in a Bear! Before anyone could change the collective mind, I found out which of the two parked Bears I was bound for and got on as quickly as possible.

Twelve crew made me welcome, and we settled into the lengthy pre-flight preparations. All four engines were started, and all four given lengthy run-up checks before shutting down two outboards and taxiing in turn behind the Air Force Bear; with me settled in one of the sonics operator's seats on the left-hand side, looking out along that enormous wing through the contra-rotating discs of both port engines' propellers. Take off was ponderous but not too much – a bit like a Britannia at max all-up weight. Climb was surprisingly agile and we settled at 18,000 feet for the transit of the Baltic. Unfortunately the Candid was never given the chance to catch up, and I don't think they got any airborne shots of the next phase.

Norwegian and Danish F-16s gave us close attention before we crossed out into the North Sea, and then soon after the first RAF Tornado F 3 came up alongside. When the second one arrived I was able to get some good air-to-air shots of it, and had the pleasure of presenting a copy of the best one to the pilot, (then) Air Commodore Cliff Spink. Everyone in Fighter Command/11 Group has their shot of the Russian Bear; some have shots of themselves in formation with a Bear. I don't think anyone, until then, had a photograph taken from inside the Bear.

Air traffic handling into Fairford was routine, and with the F 3 and a chase Hawk in tow, we made a very smooth arrival in time for tea. The Bears were objects of great interest, and were parked alongside a USAF B-52 and a B-l, which gave great opportunities over the next few days for exchange visits on board. There were other visitors to the Russian aircraft, too. King Hussein of Jordan had a good look round inside and met all the crew.

The nicest moment, which the crew and supporting Generals nearly missed (must have been something to do with the morning after the night before), was the visit to the aircraft of Prince Michael of Kent. Not only does HRH look astonishingly like the late Czar Nicholas II, he also speaks Russian. As the crew and a handful of the delegation assembled at the foot of the aircraft stepladder, Prince Michael was already on board with a couple of other Russian minders. The look on the faces of the bunch outside as this Nicholas look-alike came over and addressed them in Russian was a sight to behold. They almost gave up vodka – but not quite!

During the Show days the Air Force Bear gave a polished short display routine. I had the unenviable task of trying to keep the rest of the Russians from straying too far from sight, or too far from the programme schedule which kept them busy and very well entertained. The final night's aircrew party was hugely successful, with exchanges of gifts and mementoes between the senior Russians and the Benevolent Fund Chairman, Air Chief Marshal Sir Roger Palin.

The last round-up was the following morning, when it became clear that the Russians' planning had gone wrong and they had run out of vodka twelve hours too soon. So, with considerable raising of the eyebrows, the dining-room manager at the Hungerford 'Bear' Hotel found and served some ice-cold vodka for the final breakfast. I should stress that the aircrew refrained from that particular serving, and were on perfectly good form for that day's return flight.

This time I was invited to take up the sonic operator's seat again, and had a long and tear-stained monologue from one of the on-board colonels about his journeys to Cuba in such a Bear, and how he missed the sun, sand, and cigars. To cheer himself up he had a quick rummage on the floor among the chaos of the crew's shopping and found that he had got some vodka after all. While he settled himself down with that, I was called forward and took up post in the co-pilot's right-hand seat for the rest of the flight to Kaliningrad.

Once again we were the object of lots of air defence attention – Tornados again, and the Scandinavian F-16s. The handling of the mighty machine was surprisingly light, although with a tremendous amount of lag, so that the final approach and landing were definitely sporting! But the smooth and stable feel of the aircraft at cruising height and speed, and the excellent sound insulation, made the whole flight a truly pleasant experience.

Once down, we had a few final team photographs and then I joined the delegation in the Candid for the leg back to Moscow. A remarkable few days, and a unique moment in our Nations' relationship – to the best of my knowledge no-one from the UK had ever managed to fly in a Bear before. Oddly, the media totally ignored that element, except for the Russian Press, where I was interviewed for the Armed Forces 'Red Star' newspaper, plus a couple of aviation magazines.

I am delighted that this story – or at least a small percentage of it – can now be told. The two senior Russians were also let well off the usual hook, and both attended the annual Battle of Britain Reception in my Moscow residence a couple of months later, bringing their wives with them – at the time highly unusual.

As I said at the beginning, there were one or two very special highlights to my tour in Moscow. This extravaganza must rate as one of the finest.

Open Skies

Flight Lieutenant Tony Simpson

I thought I had the best job in the RAF; namely that of the navigator on the UK 'Open Skies' (OS) crew. From its consolidation in 1994, this was involved in establishing complex navigation and flight procedures required to implement the OS Treaty, including the monitoring of arms reduction in former Warsaw Pact Countries. This was done photographically, with a specially-equipped Hawker Siddeley Andover PR 1, using framing, panoramic and video cameras.

This job opened up a world hitherto denied to RAF aircrew – not only flying over previously 'hostile' territory to photograph military installations, but also staying in those countries for four nights. This enabled us to feed, not only on different culinary delights, but also on the rich culture offered in the capitals and in each nation's environment.

It was a revelation of the changing of political times when I was asked by a former strike/attack crewman to photograph one of the capital's bridges that had been one of his secondary targets during the Cold War.

The Balkans 1993

Growing revulsion throughout the world at the atrocities being committed in Yugoslavia forced the UN to act but with little idea how the situation could be stabilised by military means. It was, however, clear to the West that helicopters had played an important part in sustaining the various war efforts; that a number of light aircraft had been used from Serbia in a quasi-OAS role in eastern Bosnia, and that control of the air would be vital not only for any other operations that might be required, but also to deny the airspace to any nation wishing to support the protagonists.

Resolution 781, approved on 9 October 1992, established a ban on military flights in the airspace of Bosnia-Herzegovina; the only exceptions were for flights conducted by the UN Protection Force (UNPROFOR), in support of humanitarian assistance. This resolution directed UNPROFOR to monitor compliance with the ban. It called upon member states to take nationally, or through regional agencies or arrangements, all measures necessary to provide assistance to UNPROFOR, based on technical monitoring and other capabilities.

Operation 'SKY MONITOR' began on 16 October 1992 in support of this Resolution.

In support of Operation SKY MONITOR the Royal Air Force initially deployed two E-3D Sentry aircraft to Aviano in northern Italy in late 1992. These aircraft, together with three E-3As from Geilenkirchen operated from orbits in the Adriatic, and also from Hungary where they had the privilege of being protected by Hungarian QRA fighter aircraft.

Following protracted negotiations in the UN, the Security Council passed UN Resolution 816 on 31 March 1993. The Resolution extended the ban to cover flights by all fixed-wing and rotary-wing aircraft in the airspace of the Republic of Bosnia and Herzegovina, except those authorised by UNPROFOR. More importantly, it also authorised member states to take all necessary measures, in the event of further violations, to ensure compliance with the ban, proportionate

Hercules at Sarajevo. Operation Cheshire/Pippin 40,000 tons flown-in in Bosnian conflict (RAF Lyneham official photo)

to the specific circumstances and the nature of the flights.

The North Atlantic Council (NAC) provided the UN with its contingency planning on the enforcement of a no-fly zone over Bosnia-Herzegovina by the end of 1992. On 2 April 1993 the NAC directed the Supreme Allied Commander Europe (SACEUR) to take preparatory steps to permit implementation of UN Resolution 816, in line with the requirements of the resolution calling for close co-ordination. The NAC informed the UN Secretary General that NATO military authorities were prepared to begin the operation on Monday 12 April 1993, at noon GMT.

The operation (Operation DENY FLIGHT) began with fighters from France, the Netherlands and the United States of America. British and Turkish fighters followed during mid April. The contribution of the United Kingdom was then: Eight F-3 Tornado fighter aircraft at Gioia del Colle; two K-1 Tristar refuelling tankers at Malpensa Air Base, and three E-3D NAEW aircraft operating out of their home station at RAF Waddington and forward operating bases at Aviano and Trapani, Italy.

Additional forces were added as the campaign progressed.

Operation Deny Flight

Air Commodore A. P. N. Lambert

I have the somewhat unusual distinction of having served on 23 Squadron, albeit intermittently, for eighteen years. Returning to the Squadron in 1991, but this time as OC I faced a number of new challenges: first, I had to come to grips with commanding airmen for the first time; second, I moved to Leeming which was new for 23 Squadron and myself; and finally, I had to learn how to cope with the Tornado F 3, which was still having problems with its weapons system, particularly the radar.

I have to say that commanding the airmen I found a real joy and privilege: almost without exception they were a thoroughly well-motivated and dedicated bunch, with great senses of humour despite the vicissitudes of Service Life.

Leeming proved a superb location, and the Squadron's association with the City and people of Ripon was a great pleasure, with attendance at Mayoral Events, Open Days and the flying of the Mayor (even when she was a woman!) – just a few of the features of the relationship.

The F 3, on the other hand, was a mixed blessing: it seemed to have a computer for every problem. Some worked with you; others against! The radar was great for finding targets at long range, but once they got inside fifteen miles the system lost any idea of where they had gone! In fairness, I should say that things were improving all the time and by the end of my tour the aircraft was proving adept in its 'DENY FLIGHT' role over Bosnia.

Deployment to Bosnia, in support of Operation DENY FLIGHT came as something of a surprise. The Cold War had certainly been left far behind, but it seemed that Air Power's tasks for the future would be to participate in massive firepower operations, such as those in the Gulf War. The thought that the RAF would be used to support humanitarian operations was new; that said the role of denying airspace to a putative enemy was only what we practised daily in various scenarios.

The autumn of 1992 saw the Squadron returning from the Far East after having participated in an IADS (Integrated Air Defence System) exercise from Kuantan in Malaysia. But even there the newspapers were full of the massacres and atrocities that were taking place in Bosnia. By Easter 1993, the level of rapine and the media's interest had passed a critical point and European nations had decided to act. The No-Fly Zone was to be enforced, and NATO would assume the responsibility for implementing it. From the RAF, No. 11 Sqn (nominally the RAF's Out of Area squadron) would go first, and 23 would then deploy and pick up the pieces!

The Serb aim was to gain land and expel the inhabitants. All means of terrorising the besieged population were employed: constant bombardment, starvation, forced evacuation, torture of captives, mass rapes and even genocide of males constituted the crime known as ethnic cleansing. Much was played out in the full glare of the world's Press, and the outcry in western capitals was such that the UN felt compelled to act, but at the same time with no intelligible idea how the situation could be stabilised by military means.

SACEUR had delegated overall conduct of the operation to Commander-in-Chief Allied Forces Southern Europe (CINCSOUTH), headquartered in Naples. CINCSOUTH became responsible for the overall conduct of the operation, but with operational control of day-to-day mission tasking for fighter aircraft delegated to Commander, 5th Allied Tactical Air Force at Vicenza. Specified NATO supporting forces, including Airborne Early Warning, were placed under the control of Commander, Allied Forces Southern Europe, with headquarters in Naples.

The 5th Allied Tactical Air Force assigned responsibility for patrolling the area of Bosnia-Herzegovina to a participating nation for a period, normally of three hours' duration. For the eight Tornado F3s of 23 Squadron, equipped with a high-PRF radar and night vision goggles, tasking was primarily for night operations, with the 0003Z (GMT) slot being the most predominant.

Briefing for the crews normally began two hours before the Combat Air Patrol (CAP) time, and followed a set format which included the latest Intelligence advice, a Combat Survival update including code-word of the day, details of tanking, CAP areas etc. The crews were issued with pistols, Aircrew Guides, chocolate bars and fruit juice. Crews were also reminded to review the methods by which a rescue party would verify that a survivor was genuine. Combat jackets were also issued: they contained a holster, a coded radio to replace the PLB, a survival map and a Trimble GPS (hand-held satellite navigation system) for accurate combat survival navigation!

For a 'normal' four-ship on Combat Air Patrol (CAP), six crews walked to the aircraft. Of the additional two crews, one was a 'hot spare', capable of filling any position in the sortie, while the other was designated a 'cold' spare, to cater for any further unserviceability .

In summer the temperature on the pan at Gioia del Colle rose to 40°C by mid-afternoon, but fell to 25°C at night. The aircraft, operating from the Italian V ASF ramp, were fully armed at all times. The requirement to guarantee four serviceable aircraft on CAP was a testing one, and with high daytime temperatures (which the F3 does not like) it was always prudent to have all eight aircraft available for the mission. After engine start the hot spare maintained cockpit alert with engines running until all four aircraft had checked in with serviceable radars etc. The final arming of defensive aids could not be completed until the aircraft were over the sea, at which point the hot spare reverted to a Readiness State of thirty minutes.

Co-ordinated ingress and egress routes were, of course, very much in evidence: particularly when one recalls that the route to and from the operational area passed directly over several task groups, including two carrier battle groups.

Surprisingly, except during high summer, Gioia del Colle does not enjoy good weather. Apart from rain (and in winter even snow), fog was a major concern. To the south the ground falls quickly by over 1000 ft and with the wind in this direction, fog welled up over the ridge, particularly around dawn. The weather forecasts were, to say the least, not entirely accurate, and the forecast frequently changed from BLUE to RED in the twinkling of an eye. To cater for the unpredictable weather, crews were required to hold sufficient fuel in reserve at all times to divert to Sigonella in Sicily. They needed to tank before entering the area, at least once during the CAP, and return to the tanker at the end for an extra top-up if required. For the whole of 23 Squadron's detachment fuel was provided by Tristars of 216 Squadron based at Malpensa.

Following tanking, the Tornado F 3s routed to their respective Fighter Areas of Responsibility (FAOR) via routes specified in the Airspace Control Order (ACO). Contact was established with the Airborne Early Warning Aircraft, authentication exchanged, and the fighters began their patrol.

By night the republic of Bosnia-Herzegovina could look tranquil. Street lights were on and while cars were few and far between (and those that were visible were normally up in the hills on some nefarious mission), the whole area appeared like any other in Northern Europe. However, by late July, the flavour of the war changed and took on a new intensity. In early June, using night vision goggles (NVG), it was possible to see one or perhaps two rounds fired during a three hour CAP, but by late July it became rare not to see at least one full scale battle in progress. The scene through the NVGs was, at times, reminiscent of the pictures taken of the night sky over Baghdad during the Gulf War. An initial burst of light from a big gun showed up clearly and was followed by the sight of the shell moving slowly but surely over the ground to its impact point. By day it was more difficult to see the shells, but the smoke from the fires and the flashes from the impacts were clear evidence of a battle in progress.

Tornado escorting Sentry (AHB)

Sarajevo was the focus of much of the later fighting, and had changed much, even over the last few months.

July also coincided with the end of the House of Commons' session. As part of the restructuring of the armed forces under Options for Change it was decided that a Tornado F 3 squadron would be disbanded. The decision of the Air Force Board was that it would be 23 Squadron.

Sadly, the announcement was made whilst the Squadron was still in Gioia, with two months to do, and I cannot describe the sense of sadness at the news. It was poignant that the AOC's announcement, which overran its time slightly, had to be curtailed because the Squadron had an operational mission to fly. If anything, this did however have one benefit in that it united the Squadron in adversity, as perhaps no other pressure could have done. The Squadron gritted its teeth and got on with the business.

The principal role of the Air Defence Forces was to support UN Resolution 816, and while the view of the battles was of interest (and reported to the AWACS), it was of secondary importance to the search for aircraft and helicopters.

The terrain is mountainous with the mountain ridges generally running NW to SE, but with the occasional ridge or valley running E–W. Terrain masking was a significant factor, and even with one AEW in the north and another to the west, many of the valleys remained in shadow. Inevitably, a fixed fighter CAP would have suffered similar masking, and the fighters thus roamed across the area to search valleys in turn.

By day, fighters normally visited the most-used helicopter landing sites. Several were well known, and the number of helicopters on the pans reported to the AWACS. Most detections of airborne helicopters were made by the AEW or by the Tornado F 3s own radar. The helicopter's small radar cross-section provided late contacts, with little time to carry out an intercept. Initial radar contact was normally followed by a visual acquisition. A modification to the F 3s software had enhanced our detection capability. Crews flew to the approximate overhead of the contact and inserted a datum point into the computer, around which an expanding ring was drawn showing the maximum distance the helicopter could have flown since the point was inserted. Once identified, helicopters were ordered to land by the fighter transmitting the following message on Guard (the International Distress Frequency): 'Unidentified aircraft heading (magnetic) at position (Lat/Long), you are in the No-Fly Zone in violation of UN Resolution 816. Land or depart the area immediately or you will be engaged.'

In mid-April most of the helicopters paid heed to the warning but in later months it became clear that many, particularly the Muslims, were prepared to take the risk and continue. That said, on 2 August when the battle for Sarajevo was at its height, a Tornado F 3 detected a Serb helicopter, put out the warning and then watched the helicopter land in particularly inhospitable terrain, several miles from the fighting. The rotors were stopped immediately and the troops ran off into the hills.

The debate over whether to shoot down a transgressor was always difficult. It was clear that NATO was over Bosnia in response to the clamour to provide some protection for the Muslims and to shoot down a Muslim helicopter, therefore, would hardly be beneficial. Moreover, since most Serb helicopters might be likely to sprout Red Crosses were they attacked, the destruction of a Serb helicopter in the full glare of the world's media would be portrayed as an act of negligence at best, and as a war crime at worst. The lack of engagement authority against flagrant violators of the No-Fly zone was, to say the least, galling for the crews, particularly when the results of ethnic cleansing were so patently visible, even from the air. However, as military men, we would have been foolish to precipitate a situation that was worse than the one we found.

Destruction of one helicopter would have had little effect on the war effort, would most likely have destroyed a helicopter of the faction we were there to protect, or could even have been portrayed as a war crime. Nevertheless, what must have been clear to the belligerents was that NATO had the ability to detect most, if not all of the flights, and it reserved the right to apply the UN resolution at a time and place of NATO's choosing.

However, it was clear that our participation in DENY FLIGHT had achieved a number of other goals. The British presence underscored our commitment to NATO and its evolving role.

As a world power, with a seat on the Security Council, Britain shared in the responsibilities for world security. The deployment of British troops and aircraft demonstrated our commitment to the UN and determination to fulfil our responsibilities. DENY FLIGHT gave NATO Air Superiority over Bosnia-Herzegovina. It paved the way for any other operations that might be contemplated and, equally importantly, denied the airspace to any putative aggressor.

The Squadron finished its operational detachment in early September 1993, and then returned to Leeming for some well-earned leave. For my part, a place at Cambridge beckoned, and I had little time to hand over my Squadron to my successor, Wg Cdr Andy Walton. Unusually, in this day and age, I elected to hand over whilst on operational deployment. In view of the way the Squadron had been informed of its demise it somehow seemed fitting. The hand-over week coincided with the last week of the detachment, and I recall well, as we left Gioia del Colle, saying to Andy 'Congratulations OC 23 – Look after the Squadron'.

Jaguar Squadron Commander in Bosnia

Air Commodore A. D. Sweetman OBE

It was 16 July 1993 and, after six months waiting, No. 6 Squadron 'The Flying Can-openers' were finally off to deploy to Italy on Operation DENY FLIGHT, to support the United Nation's humanitarian relief effort in the former Yugoslavia.

The previous weeks had been a flurry of activity at RAF Coltishall as preparations were made for the deployment. The Jaguars had been modified to the 'Gulf War' standard. They also sported a new all-grey colour scheme to improve their camouflage at medium level. This had proved to be something of a double-edged sword. There was no doubt that it made the aircraft more difficult to see from the ground, but it also made it almost invisible to members of the same formation! So much so, that in the early days of flying in this new livery we had to be particularly careful to ensure safe separation between aircraft.

The C 130 Hercules transport aircraft began to arrive on 15 July, the day before the Jaguars were due to deploy, and there was a steady stream of aircraft over the next four days and nights as all our equipment was air-lifted out to Italy.

It was a surreal experience walking out to the aircraft. Sunrise was still some way off, and the line of Jaguars in their new grey finish took on an almost ghost-like appearance under the orange glow of the sodium pan lights. The media were out in force with crews from all the major terrestrial and satellite networks. Their presence only served to heighten the dreamlike qualities of the moment, as they monitored our every move for their viewers. The message came from the tanker that the weather was just suitable, and we taxied for take-off a few minutes later. It was a relief to get airborne and on with the task in hand, but I soon forgot about the scenes on the ground as I searched between the cloud layers in the dim light of dawn for the first tanker! Luckily its anti-collision lights stood out in the half-light and we were able to execute a rendezvous without too much difficulty.

The transit to Gioia went very much as planned, and on our arrival we were met once again by the media. This time however, they appeared to have licence to go pretty much wherever they wanted. This concerned me, especially as some of their questions tried to focus on the controversial aspects of the RAF's involvement in the Operation. My fears were confirmed when, the following day the Daily Telegraph ran an article entitled 'Know your enemy – the RAF accountant', which concentrated on the allegedly miserly attitude of the financial adviser to the RAF detachment at Gioia. I was furious. There we were in Italy, having successfully executed a complex and difficult deployment and with the pilots facing the very real possibility of conducting operations in a hostile environment, and yet here was one of our supposedly serious national broadsheets apparently debasing the whole business by concentrating on some trivial nonsense. Such a superficial attitude demeaned the efforts of everyone concerned, including the families back home, and I determined then to ensure that any future media exposure would be properly controlled and co-ordinated.

It is fair to say that the plan for operations over Bosnia-Herzegovina was developed as we went along. During our work-up in the UK we had rehearsed the types of profiles and techniques we might expect to use, but it was only after arriving in theatre that we were able to practice these in concert with all the other nations and agencies involved in DENY FLIGHT. It is worth remembering that NATO had been enforcing the 'No Fly Zone' over Bosnia-Herzegovina since April 1993, and the deployment of the Jaguars, along with other attack aircraft, had increased considerably the assets involved in the operation. There were approximately 200 aircraft of all types available either in theatre or on recall, of which some 150 were fighters or fighter/bombers.

With this number of aircraft potentially available, co-ordination was clearly going to be a major headache, and a couple of exercises were flown over mainland Italy to try and sort out some standard operating procedures. These exercises produced some exciting moments, with aircraft from different formations – supposedly de-conflicted – meeting over the same contact point at similar altitudes, and trying to talk to the same forward air controller on the ground at the same time and on the same frequency! I will not easily forget the sight of two French Mirages passing, co-height, between my wing-man and me as we were leaving the exercise area! Fortuitously the 'big sky – small aeroplane' rule applied, and the only consequence was a few missed heartbeats!

The unenviable responsibility for pulling this show together lay with the combined air operations director at the headquarters of the Fifth Allied Tactical Air Force in Vicenzia, Northern Italy. Major General James E. Chambers chaired debriefings after each of the exercises, and these were attended by every participating squadron or detachment commander. He had a vice-like grip on the whole Operation.

The no-fly zone had been enforced by NATO aircraft for several months and Tornado F 3s had provided the RAF's contribution to this effort. We were collocated with them at Gioia, and although there was the traditional friendly rivalry between air defenders and mud-movers, they went out of their way to make us welcome. At this stage I should also mention our Italian hosts, without whose help life would have been so much more difficult. Nothing was too much trouble for them, and I am ashamed to think that I might have been rather less hospitable if, as a base commander, I was suddenly faced with the prospect of accommodating two extra squadrons of aircraft and people for an indefinite period.

The sorties over Bosnia were, in the main, extremely routine, and after several weeks it became clear that these 'low arousal' missions were doing little to maintain the pilots' edge. This was a dangerous trend because the situation on the ground in Bosnia was highly volatile, and it was important we kept our wits about us every time we went over there. We were meticulous therefore in our pre-flight preparation and briefed every mission as if it were a 'War' sortie. In many ways it was a strange 'phoney war' atmosphere, and one often felt detached from the realities of what was actually happening barely twenty minutes flying time away across the Adriatic. Even when flying over the places that were featuring daily on CNN – Sarajevo, Mostar, Gorazde *et cetera* it was difficult to believe that a couple of miles below people were doing their damnedest to kill one another.

Occasionally, one witnessed the killing at first hand. One day in August my pair of aircraft was vectored to Mostar by the airborne command and control post, as there had been some recent reports of fires around the airport. We approached from the south at about 8000 feet, and the smoke over the city was visible from some distance away. As we drew nearer, we could see a number of houses burning fiercely. Suddenly there was a bright flash on the high ground

The Jaguar (Crown copyright)

to the west of the town followed by a puff of smoke close to the city centre. We turned left towards the source of the flash and located a large calibre artillery piece in the act of discharging another round into the city. It was a bleak moment, as we sat in our grandstand seats high overhead, able only to watch as the gunners continued their deadly work.

Many of the sorties were similarly frustrating, although for different reasons. Some days one could spend the whole time in the area practising with a forward air controller, trying to find his designated target, yet still return home 'mission unsuccessful'. On other trips one would acquire the target almost immediately and complete a simulated attack against it without difficulty. There is no doubt that finding a target with the naked eye was a serious challenge, although electronic acquisition aids, such as laser target markers, simplified the problem considerably.

On the other hand, the reconnaissance missions we flew could be highly satisfying and the product from these sorties was soon in great demand. One of the difficulties, however, was obtaining detailed pictures. Low-level reconnaissance was not permitted because of the risk from small-arms fire, so our normal camera pod, which was designed for use at low level, was fine for panoramic pictures but not particularly good for high resolution work. Eventually we were given a camera pod with a long-range lens, but at the sort of heights we were flying it was very tricky to aim accurately; indeed, it was rather like looking at the world through a long drinking straw. Initially our results were disappointing: however, one of my flight commanders developed a simple method using a portable Global Positioning Satellite unit in the cockpit. This put the aircraft in the correct position in the sky so that the camera in the pod was pointing at the intended target. We soon got the hang of this and our success rate improved dramatically: so much so that missions would return regularly with 100 per cent coverage of the dozen or so targets they had been tasked to photograph. This kind of initiative exemplified the approach that everyone – groundcrew and pilots alike – took to their work. The RAF's fine reputation for professionalism has long been built on the quality of its people, and it was a source of great pride to see the Jaguar detachment at Gioia del Colle continue that distinguished tradition.

I have said already that many of the sorties were routine, but there were the odd moments of tension when it looked as if the events on the ground were going to deteriorate to the point where air strikes would be called in. At the end of July 1993 the refusal by the Serbs to vacate Mount Ignan to the south-west of Sarajevo was one such occasion, and we had aircraft loaded with live ordnance in case the delicate diplomatic negotiations failed to resolve the situation.

Fortunately that crisis was defused, but on a later occasion, in February 1994, the squadron was again involved as tensions increased. General Sir Michael Rose, the UN commander in Bosnia, had given the belligerents an ultimatum to withdraw all heavy weapons from around Sarajevo by 21 of February or face punitive air strikes. As luck (sic) would have it, 6 Squadron were holding the DENY FLIGHT commitment once more, and as the deadline drew nearer it looked as if this time the warring factions would call the UN's bluff. These were anxious days as again we geared up for bombing operations.

Predictably, the heavy media presence was repeated, but we had learned our lesson from the previous July and they were well chaperoned by our own specialists. Nevertheless, I was coming under increasing pressure from our own public relations machine to allow pilots to be interviewed for television. I have to say that this was a distraction I could have done without. I had discussed the question of interviews together with all the pilots, and the unanimous view was that we wished to remain anonymous. This was also the firm line from our conduct-after-capture experts. The TV pictures were being transmitted world-wide, including to the former Yugoslavia, and we thought it would be imprudent to go on television one day when a few days later we could be engaged in bombing missions over the heads of some of the people who might have been watching earlier.

There was ample evidence to suggest we should have little confidence in any of the sides in the Bosnian conflict having any respect for the Geneva Convention and its rules on the treatment of prisoners. I made our position perfectly clear but it was difficult to persuade people to take 'no' for an answer.

On 20th February, the day before the ultimatum was due to expire, we received a visit from the Chief of the Defence Staff, Marshal of The Royal Air Force Sir Peter Harding. As I explained our involvement in the operations, I took the opportunity to emphasise again the Jaguar's lack of an autonomous precision-guided weapon capability, and the improvements in effectiveness and flexibility that such a facility would offer. Our imminent involvement in offensive operations undoubtedly added weight to my argument, and the Chief of the Defence Staff promised to look into the matter on his return to London. The following morning, the deadline passed with each side complying with the terms of the ultimatum. Shortly thereafter the RAF detachment commander at Gioia took a call from Headquarters Strike Command asking what on earth I had said to the Chief of Defence Staff the previous evening. Apparently, Sir Peter had been as good as his word, and possible enhancements to the Jaguar's capability were now under active consideration. To be fair, such suggestions had been raised previously in post-detachment reports, but it was illuminating to see how quickly minds became focused on the problem when the Chief of Defence Staff himself expressed an interest! Within a matter of a few weeks, an Urgent Operational Requirement to fit a thermal imaging and laser designation pod to the Jaguar had been approved, and the whole of the Jaguar Force rejoiced at the opportunity to exploit this new capability. It gives me some satisfaction to think, rightly or wrongly, that my own discussions with the Chief of the Defence Staff on that February evening in Italy contributed to this achievement.

My final sortie over the former Yugoslavia occurred in early July 1994 and I handed over the reins of the squadron later the same month. Events before and since have sometimes called into question the role of NATO air power in the Bosnian crisis, and whether or not its presence has improved or aggravated the situation on the ground. For my own part, I have no doubt that it has made a positive contribution.

Airborne Early Warning over Kosovo

Flight Lieutenant J. K. Wynn

The typical Sentry (E-3D) Airborne Early Warning aircraft has a crew of seventeen. They can be neatly divided into three separate teams: the flight-deck, the mission crew and the communications operator and airborne technicians.

On the flight-deck there is a captain, a co-pilot, a navigator and a flight engineer. Their task is to fly the aircraft safely. Furthermore, when danger approaches, they either manoeuvre the aircraft appropriately or run away bravely as directed by the Tactical Director (TD). That danger may be in the form of a large thunderstorm – so prevalent in the Balkans – or a nasty and irate Serbian pilot in his MiG-29.

Next the mission crew, headed by a TD who is principally responsible for offering tactical direction to the whole crew. He must ensure that mission objectives are being met and, when necessary, arbitrate over which tasks should be given the highest priority. Otherwise, there is a great danger that when the workload becomes unmanageable, a crew attempting to do too much are in jeopardy of actually achieving little.

The TD has two teams to achieve these tasks – surveillance and weapons.

The surveillance team is headed by a Surveillance Controller (SC) who works closely with the Radar Technician (RT) to configure the radars for the best probability of detection. The simplest way of understanding the E-3D's capability is to imagine it as a great big sponge in the sky. Its computers absorb masses of data from aircraft flying within the radars' vast volumes of coverage and display that data in a usable format. Trained operators must make sense of the information and, most importantly, get the information to the commanders on the ground for them to make the necessary battle management decisions. To achieve this complex task, the Surveillance Controller has two Surveillance Operators (SO) to track all the aircraft within the nominated volume of airspace known as an Air Surveillance Area (ASA), thus compiling a Recognised Air Picture (RAP). The SC also has an Electronic Warfare Support Measure (ESM) operator to manage the aircraft's Yellowgate system which sniffs out the transmissions from all airborne and ground-based radars, and finally, a data-links manager (LM) who ensures that all the data absorbed and created by the 'great sponge in the sky' is digitally transferred to any NATO unit which requires our RAP – and that is most people! This may sound frightfully complex but, in essence, they are attempting to distinguish between the 'good guys', the 'bad guys' and any commercial air traffic which would fly within, or close to, the ASA.

Surveillance is important, but to us 'weaponeers' it is all frightfully dull. We prefer to talk to the demigods who race around the ether in their mighty chariots of fire! These days, most modern fighters are very capable and no longer require the close control necessary in the days of Lightnings or Phantoms. They just require 'big picture' information and they sort out the rest. Every so often however, there will be a desperate call from a fighter who is either running low on fuel and urgently needs to rendezvous with a compatible air-to-air-refuelling (AAR) tanker, or from one who needs help to reach his target.

While most fast-jet crews are happy to operate with a great deal of autonomy, this is not so of the more vulnerable aircraft which have to operate fairly close to the enemy. Large aircraft such as AAR tankers are relatively slow, unarmed and therefore very vulnerable to attack – all these types are given a generic title of High Value Airborne Assets (HVAA). One of our most critical tasks is to control these HVAA to ensure their safety from all manner of threats, and to ensure that the AAR tankers are always available for use by the fast-jets. Without the sterling efforts of these giant, mobile refuelling stations, the fast-jets would not be able to do their very important tasks.

Most of the mission crew are fighter controllers of one ilk or another. I, however, am a navigator, and we are rapidly becoming an endangered species. Jokes aside, the fighter controllers have benefited enormously since their excavation

Sentry (E-3D) (Crown copyright)

from their 'front-line' concrete bunkers along the east coast of the UK in WW II. They have always proven their worth, and remain the backbone of the Component.

My own title is Fighter Allocator (FA) and I am responsible to the TD for the conduct of the air battle and any air assets under our control. Normally I have just two Weapons Controllers (WC). Ideally each crew would have an FA and five WCs: however, the practicalities of life prevent us from matching the manning levels which the USAF deem essential for their AWACS operations. Furthermore, a major limitation with the E-3D is that there are only nine mission consoles as opposed to fourteen on the USAF E-3Cs.

During our planning phase, the Communications Operator together with the TD and myself, ensure that our Comms Plan is accurate and configured correctly to meet all tasks. In addition to the Communications Operator, there are three Airborne Technicians: a comms technician (CT); a radar technician(RT) and a display technician (DT). The Communications Operator and Airborne Technicians' *raisons d'être* are to configure all the mission equipment so that the mission crew can perform their many tasks – and then continue to monitor the equipment and carry out their equivalent of first-aid whenever necessary.

Missions commence with briefing and planning phases. There is a great deal of information to be absorbed before the crew can devise a workable plan. The Intelligence Officer has prepared a comprehensive brief of what has happened during the previous twenty-four hours since we last flew. Next, the mission details. These have been planned, produced and electronically distributed by the staff at the Combined Air Operations Centre (CAOC) at Vicenza. The main document is the Air Tasking Order (ATO), a massive message which specifies all the details of every single aircraft which will be employed that day.

Unlike most other flying units, who will only be interested in their own specific tasking, we require the details of every single formation that will be either flying or on alert during our on-station period. We need this reformatted so we can use it relatively easily. The task is too enormous to do manually, so there is an impressive computerised system called the Mission Support System (MSS) to help with this. This automatically strips the data from reams of pages into more usable formats, which we aircrew can readily read and use during the heat and intensity of battle.

These stripped formats list the entire flying programme – colloquially known as the FRAG – in order, by certain pre-defined categories: by time, alphabetically, by IFF Mode 3 etc. Even with this level of automation, the briefers are often faced with the frustration of the computer not understanding all the data – often, the data they receive is either corrupt or not in the correct format. The briefers have to work very hard and often against the clock to ensure that they can present all the relevant information to the crews on time.

Briefing begins with the usual domestic details: our call-signs; where we have to orbit; our on-station period; who will we be replacing and, very importantly, who will relieve us; what other E-3s or E-2Cs will be flying; and will any of the USAF mobile, ground-based, radar sites be unserviceable. This is followed by a quick resume of all the other flying activity from the FRAG.

We have been bombarded by masses of information and now split up into our specialisations to discuss the details, highlight any likely problem areas and devise a workable plan. Eventually, the mission crew and flight-deck crew reconvene for a final brief.

Now, I have to ensure my weapons team understand what we are about to do. I state who is responsible for which tasks, which radios they will have, what limitations they have to abide by and what information I expect from them. We all then quiz each other on the extant Rules of Engagement (ROEs), and emphasise that no one can authorise an engagement without receiving the necessary authority from the TD via myself. The last thing we want is a dreaded 'blue-on-blue' engagement, whereby we have mistakenly authorised the shoot-down of a NATO aircraft.

The level of tasking, as stated in the ATO, is usually far beyond what we can physically achieve. One controller will be detailed to control a Check-In frequency on which all the aircraft in the northern Adriatic will call up as they transit to and from their bases throughout northern Italy. The second WC will control Combat Air Patrols (CAPs) and an Air-to-Air Refuelling Towline over Bosnia Herzegovina (BH), while the third controller will control all the USAF strike packages and their associated support aircraft against targets around Belgrade. This, alone, is a great deal of work, especially as we will have spoken to between 100 and 200 aircraft before the mission is over. Furthermore, there are no air traffic control agencies to sequence the aircraft within the vast tactical area of operations (TAOO). Every single formation will check-in with one of the E-3s as they leave the Italian Flight Information Region and cross into the TAOO.

While the general rule of the air is 'see and be seen' (each crew are responsible for their own navigation and separation from each other) this is not always practicable. Although generally fine for the fast-jets, because they have their own radar and a very good view out of their cockpit, this is not so for the larger aircraft, who are more accustomed to an air traffic controller telling them what to do and when to do it. Add to this the further complication that it will be dark, with many aircraft not having their anti-collision lights on, and you can be assured that my WCs and I will be keeping a wary eye open to prevent any mid-air collisions. It would be very embarrassing if our brave warriors successfully avoid the Serbian air defences and hit their targets, but then have the misfortune to hit another NATO aircraft by accident.

We now have approximately one hour before our ETD. We have been briefed about the mission, formed a plan to meet all the tasks and now need to re-brief the whole crew on how we will deal with the anticipated high work load.

The SC explains how they will allocate their surveillance tasks, I cover all the salient points about what we expect to control, and the captain gives a quick resume of the weather. Finally, the TD gives his 'state of the nation' speech, thus ensuring all the various sections will act as one team. With everyone appearing to be relatively happy with the plan, we head out to our aircraft for the night.

Once happy that everything is ship-shape, the Captain signs the aircraft log-book. He is now responsible for the aircraft's safety – about £170 million of aircraft – not to mention eighteen other souls.

Our training has covered most of the areas we will soon encounter, but the sheer scale of the Operation is something new to us all and a challenge we will have to overcome. However, there is one area which no amount of training can ever reproduce: the fear of someone actually trying to shoot you down. We have been briefed that a rogue Serbian MiG-29 pilot might go for glory and attempt an attack against an E-3. Our Orbit will be only seven minutes' flying time away from a Serbian Air Force forward operating base, and we will have to keep a very close eye on the area. It will be most embarrassing if we allow ourselves to become so distracted as to not notice our own imminent doom until it is too late to react. I certainly have a few butterflies roaring around my stomach but, as I look around, all I see is a bunch of very professional aircrew getting on with their tasks, quietly but proficiently.

Forty minutes after leaving Aviano far behind, our sensors and computers are all functioning well. Our TD declares that we are serviceable for the mission and will now progress eastwards to the Orbit area over north-west Bosnia and Croatia. We have been listening to all the radio channels, building up our situational awareness – as well as speaking to our 'lords and masters' at the CAOC via a secure satellite communications net (SATCOM), and the E-3A crew from GK who we will soon replace. All is going well.

Stealth Rescue – a Night to Remember

Flight Lieutenant J. K. Wynn

On Saturday 21 March 1999 we were on station over NW Bosnia and Croatia. There was a high level of tasking and I had been given an additional Weapons Controller. We also had Captain 'Flash' Gordon USAF, an experienced Fighter Allocator, who was interested to see how we operated.

Our radar was detecting the numerous aircraft which were flying within the Tactical Area of Operations, as well as the many civilian airliners flying around its boundary. We could use our IFF system to interrogate the aircraft to work out who was who – each aircraft had been allocated a unique IFF code. By manually comparing what we saw on our mission displays with the Air Tasking Order strips we could identify one formation from another. Fortunately for us, the E-3A at present on station had already done this and we were automatically receiving all his track symbology via the secure digital data-links, courtesy of our Links Manager. Although the radar display was very busy it was relatively easy to interpret. My problems would arise from the comms, simply because there were so many channels to monitor.

Each mission crew member had a comms panel which gave access to four radios plus a UHF Guard radio. Additionally, for our internal chat amongst the crew, we had a further three secure mission nets and an insecure maintenance net. Faced with the potential of being bombarded with nine different sources of information, the management of one's comms was essential to a successful mission. The knack of monitoring the comms successfully was the ability to sort out the essential from the desirable, and not to allow oneself to become distracted by relative trivia.

The Tactical Directors of the two E-3s had negotiated a time for an official hand-over of all duties, when both crews would perform the necessary computer switch actions for us to take control. The Tactical Director commenced a final roll-call amongst the crew to confirm all systems had remained serviceable to go on-station. Any last minute hang ups and there was still time to delay the hand-over.

No, everything was fine, and the Communications Operator commenced a countdown. At the agreed time, we went out on all the radios and confirmed that we now had control – and then they were gone. Their silence spoke volumes. They had had a very busy mission and were glad to be going home.

We rapidly took over the tasks while continuing to develop our situational awareness. Nevertheless, we saw almost exactly what had been briefed three hours previously. The Adriatic and Bosnia swarming with aircraft, and the F-117As heading to their tankers with all their support and escorts – one thing you can definitely say about the USAF, they do not do things by half. I knew that all my three Weapons Controllers would have to work up to, and often beyond, their capacity. Inevitably, when working under such extreme pressures, mistakes would be made, but another of my important tasks would be to monitor my WCs and offer advice, guidance or the occasional bollocking when and as required. To err is human, and I too was certainly not immune from making mistakes. Hopefully, whenever this occurred, someone in the crew would notice and have the confidence to say so. Then, it was up to me to have the integrity to recognise the error, correct it, and try not to repeat it again. Everyone was showing a high degree of professionalism and good airmanship.

We were not the only E-3 on-station. Way to the south was another who was as busy as ourselves. She was controlling all the NATO assets going into Kosovo, as well as numerous AAR towlines which resembled bees' nests as the fighters scuttled back and forward to their tankers to suck many tonnes of fuel. I spoke to their Fighter Allocator, established a game-plan for the evening, and left him to his busy tasks.

We had only been on station about thirty minutes but it was already very busy and would get busier still once the F-117As, supported by their various escorts, headed south-east from their tankers in Hungary towards their targets around Belgrade. There was no sign of any Mig activity but the secure comms net was alive with details of the Belgrade SAM defences as they began radiating in preparation to defend themselves against the incoming Stealth Fighters.

All was going well when at 1944Z the 'smoke-detector' sounded: 'MAYDAY, MAYDAY, MAYDAY – This is VEGA 31, I have been hit by ****, stand by'. I immediately responded to his MAYDAY call on the Guard Frequency and awaited any subsequent call, while simultaneously alerting the crew and asking the TD to relay the call to the Combined Air Operations Centre (CAOC).

At 1945Z, VEGA 31 called again and said in his very calm American drawl 'MAGIC, this is VEGA 31, I am abandoning my aircraft'. No sooner had he finished his transmission than we heard his emergency locator beacon sound on the Guard Frequency, confirming he had indeed ejected and was now tumbling through the dark night air to an uncertain fate. What had promised to be a very busy night had just gone into hyper-drive, and we were right in the middle of it!

Our calls over the SATCOM net to CAOC were also monitored by various agencies in the USA, as well as tens of other units within the Tactical Area of Operations. It was only human nature that people wanted to help, but there was a great danger that too much chat on the circuit would prevent the correct units from talking to each other. A simple request from our TD to the CAOC for a 'ziplip' was replied to by CHARIOT in CAOC. God had spoken and the noise level was immediately reduced to a workable level.

My next task was to ensure this was a genuine emergency call. It sounded good, but UHF Guard is an open channel and an American accent is easy to imitate. If this had been an exercise and we had received what seemed to be a real MAYDAY, we would have made a call on the Guard frequency to terminate the exercise and all the aircraft would immediately have gone home. This would have allowed us to resolve the problem without too many distractions. Unfortunately, we did not have that luxury because we had to deal with the emergency while continuing with the live Operation. The last thing we wanted was for the Serbians to spoof us into becoming distracted from all the events going on around us.

The call-sign was definitely VEGA 31. I had not previously heard this particular call-sign but this was hardly surprising. Firstly, it was physically impossible for me to monitor all my controllers' frequencies; and secondly, I had been more involved with the bigger picture issues, leaving my WCs to deal with the specific details. Not wanting to become distracted, I gave everything to 'Flash', who spent the next five or ten minutes going through his mass of paperwork. We soon established just who VEGA 31 was – a Stealth Fighter! My immediate thought was: just where is he? Not only was he stealthy to the Serbians but to us too. Not a great start to the evening.

This process may appear to have been fairly elongated, but it was not. Only about thirty seconds or a minute had elapsed since his ejection. Whilst I was dealing with this problem the TD and Captain had already liaised with each other and our aircraft was about to break Orbit and head east to get better comms and radar coverage of the Belgrade area. Our movement would also put us closer to a Serbian air base and its inherent dangers, but at this stage the crew executives had to make a military judgement, balancing risk against the new task. We made the right move.

The power output from small emergency radios is very low, and the range is therefore probably limited to fifty miles. We were way beyond this, and even with our repositioning to the east we never again spoke to VEGA 31. However, his escorts were much closer and they eventually established comms with him.

The race was now on to locate him before the Serbs could, and hopefully mount a rescue mission if practicable. It would be wrong if I have given you the false impression that only our E-3D was doing anything. People far and wide were reacting to the situation. Meantime, all the remaining F-117As were off target and heading back to Aviano. We did a quick head count with all the USAF aircraft to ensure their

Sentry(Crown copyright)

safety. Everyone except for VEGA 31 checked in: we knew he was the only missing aircraft. My next problem was that the Air-to-Air Refuelling plan devised in the Air Tasking Order was now virtually redundant: in concert with the CAOC, we would have to dynamically manage these vital assets.

Unlike the large, multi-engine aircraft, most fast-jets have a limited endurance, especially when they are operating in a combat environment so far away from their bases. Subsequent to the shoot-down, these escort aircraft had been re-tasked to cover the crash area – once it had been discovered – and hence would need significantly more fuel than originally planned. Meanwhile, large strategic assets were on station way to the south, covering the raids into Kosovo. The CAOC rapidly re-tasked them to transit north into our area over Bosnia, to help locate the downed pilot and ultimately control a rescue. Approximately one hour after the shoot-down, we were finally given an accurate location.

The good news was he was reasonably close to the border with Serbia. The bad news was he was inside a fairly dense SAM belt. In the meantime, our request for additional AAR support to keep all the fighters aloft had been answered. Suddenly, the skies became awash with aviation fuel as the numerous tankers which had been on ground alert arrived. There was one further potential complication with the tankers. The US Marine Corps EA6Bs use a probe and drogue system, similar to the RAF. The remaining USAF aircraft required a boom tanker. It would have been very embarrassing if we sent an aircraft who was desperate for fuel to an incompatible tanker. It had been done before, but this was neither the time nor place for any such oversights.

The situation was now reasonably stable. We knew the location of the downed pilot, we had fighters, bombers and Suppression of Enemy Air Defences (SEAD) aircraft nearby, and they had sufficient refuelling support for the next few hours. The CAOC would now be devising a plan to rescue VEGA 31.

He, meanwhile, would hopefully have survived the ejection and gone to ground, to follow his pre-briefed escape and evasion plan. The Americans had been developing a concept called Combat Search and Rescue (CSAR) for such an event as this. Dedicated forces had trained to rescue downed aircrew from behind enemy lines, and they were now readying themselves to go into action. Someone, somewhere, had decided that there was a good chance of being able to rescue the pilot and that there were sufficient hours of darkness left to assemble a CSAR force and execute the plan. The specifics of a CSAR mission are quite sensitive – so much so that even we were unaware of any of the details. However, what can be divulged are the real heroes of the piece. Certain USAF A-10 pilots are trained to act as the local tactical commander, responsible for leading a CSAR package to the survivor's location, securing the area from any enemy action, and covering the rescue helicopter as it extracts the survivor. Our tasks on the E-3D were extremely demanding but there were many of us to share the burden. These A-10 pilots had to fly their aircraft, avoid any hostile fire and listen to and talk on various radios to co-ordinate the details in the immediate vicinity .

It was now after 0001Z. The CSAR package, the support package to the north and the Combat Air Patrols in Bosnia were all getting themselves ready, but the plan was not working too well because each group was coming off their tankers at different times and would not all have enough fuel to 'push' (the act of leaving a pre-defined holding point, normally within friendly airspace) across the border into the Serbian SAM belt in concert. The most critical element was the CSAR helicopter. He could not refuel and had approximately one hour's fuel left before he had to either proceed into Serbia or abort the mission. At this stage it was obvious that the A-10 pilots needed some assistance and we suggested a 'push time' for all assets to be in their respective positions. He agreed to our plan, and we then told everybody to go back to their tankers to be ready to 'push' at 0100Z. There had been a definite chance that the CSAR train would come off the rails, but that problem had now hopefully gone away.

During this last hour we detected a probable helicopter heading from Belgrade to the crash area. We assumed that it was some Serbian forces trying to get there before us. They had probably been trying to locate the pilot of VEGA 31 by triangulating his occasional transmissions. We sought and were given permission to engage the helicopter. The WC relayed the engagement authority to the F15Cs as instructed. One could imagine the horns appearing out of the F15 pilots' heads as a pair turned in to engage the helicopter: naturally, they were more than keen to protect their compatriot. Whether the Serbs heard our engagement authority to the Eagle drivers is hard to say, but no sooner had the F15's turned inbound than the helicopter appeared to turn around, fade from our radar, and was never seen again. We cancelled the engagement authority and the F15s returned to their patrol.

At 0100Z the forces were full of fuel and assembled for the rescue operation. Again the MiGs stayed on the ground – any attempt by them to influence the rescue would have been given short shrift by the Eagle drivers. However, the Serb SAM commanders were not so obliging. The EA6Bs and the F16CJs were kept very busy as they suppressed the enemy's air defences with their jamming-pods and HARMs, thus allowing the A-10 and helicopter to thread their way to the area.

It was now about 0130Z and we got the call over SATCOM: the pilot had been recovered and they were all heading west. A lot of people had worked very hard to achieve this successful outcome and had been willing to put their lives in immediate danger to save this one pilot. However, these very same people were still in enemy territory and it was very important for us not to let down our guard before the show was truly over. At 0145Z the CSAR package was back across the border and inbound to a friendly airfield. Now we could allow ourselves a small pat on the back.

We now had about thirty minutes' worth of fuel before we too had to return to base. We had remained on station by some judicious decision making by the flight-deck. Waiting in the wings for the past forty-five minutes was our replacement, a French E-3F. We had agreed in advance it would be better for us to continue with the CSAR task during such a critical phase, rather than attempt a very busy and complex hand-over. They had, however, in the meantime taken over some of our tasks and that had certainly lightened our load during a critical phase.

We eventually went through the hand-over procedure and headed back home. Much had happened so quickly in the nine hours thirty minutes we had been airborne that it is impossible to recall all the specifics. However, my overriding impression was of a difficult and often confusing job well done. Aviano was buzzing when we returned. Naturally, everyone wanted to know all the details. We discovered that a USAF Brigadier had called in to express President Clinton's personal thanks for our efforts. All very nice, but we were just pleased that a fellow airman was safe and that his family would not have to endure the pain of seeing their loved one paraded on Serbian TV.

It is not possible to say whether the Serbians had managed to overcome their SAM targeting problems against Stealth aircraft, or had been fortunate to hit the F-117A by chance. After all, if you throw enough missiles and shells into the air you will eventually hit something. Nevertheless, what had promised to be a very busy mission had gone wrong very quickly but, fortunately, NATO had reacted well to the situation, and its subsequent actions regained the initiative from the Serbians. We, as a crew, were certainly quite proud to have played a small but important part in the rescue of VEGA 31. Certainly, my memories of these events will stay with me forever.

Without doubt, it had been quite 'A Night to Remember'.

Highly Organised Chaos

Squadron Leader Stuart Mitchell DFC

At the beginning of April 1999 the skies over Albania and Macedonia were full of voices!!

'Magic, Blade 23 is for a tanker.' 'Blade 23, your tanker call sign Peso 21, 190 for 52, base plus 11.' 'Blade 23, roger.' 'Magic, Magic, Euro 23 checking in as fragged, base plus 18.' 'Magic searching.' 'Panther 11, indicating full.' 'Panther 11, disconnect.' 'He's dropping back. disconnect, red on, 3200 kg.' 'Cent 33, Magic, you're clear RTB, push Magic on 228 alpha, thanks for the work.' 'Panther 11, go echelon left, you've had 3200 kg.' 'Cent 33 RTB, thanks, so long.' 'Panther 11.' 'Panther 11 clear to leave, push Magic on 231 alpha, safe trip, *auf Wiedersehen*.' Peso 21, *vielen dank*, see you tomorrow.' 'Dodge check.' 'Dodge 23.' 'Euro 23, Magic, you're identified modes and codes sweet.' 'Spitfire 01, clear astern.' 'Magic, Dodge checking in as fragged minus one.' 'Spitfire 01.' 'Dodge, say posit.' 'He's dropping back ... across ... astern.' 'Spitfire 01, clear contact.' 'Red out ... closing up ...' 'Dodge is bulls-eye 270 for 81.' '... contact ... ...green on, fuel flows.' 'Magic searching.' 'Magic, BI-23, vectors for the tanker.' 'Blade 23, say again.' 'Blade 23, request vectors to Peso 21.' 'Standby.' 'Magic, Panther 11 off the Tanker, base plus twelve, requesting base plus sixteen.' 'All stations, all stations, Euro 23 inbound Sonoco track, 2 minutes, base plus 18.' 'Tally Euro. I reckon he's in our 4 for 40.' 'Who, Blade?' 'Yeah.' 'Panther, standby. Blade 23, your tanker 210 for 39.'

On board 'Magic', an E-3 Sentry command aeroplane, NATO fighter controllers had, quite appropriately, nicknamed the air-to-air refuelling (AAR) frequency the 'Comedy Channel' because of the volume of traffic and the number of misunderstandings. Aircraft were shoehorned into tiny blocks of airspace, or refuelling tracks, where one overworked fighter controller would attempt to join perhaps thirty to forty fast jet receivers with up to twelve tankers and then, post-refuelling, separate the whole lot.

Widespread poor weather coupled with each nation's interpretation of the English language made things interesting and every so often, just to keep people on their toes, it was all done in the dark. The result was an organised form of chaos in which our greatest fear was not enemy action, but a 'blue-on-blue' mid-air collision.

Flying a tanker is not difficult, but it certainly had its moments during the Kosovo campaign. My abiding memories are of the huge numbers of aircraft in the sky and the continual 'noise' on the radios. Trying to keep a mental picture of the air environment during a seven-hour sortie, whilst listening to transmissions on two UHF radios, two VHF radios and our own flight deck conversation became fatiguing and very frustrating.

We tanker crews have never had the kudos enjoyed by our fast jet brethren. This is quite understandable – after all, it is they who go 'sausage side' to the target whilst the tanker usually flies a racetrack pattern well out of harm's way. This traditional view was certainly challenged during the Spring of 1999, as crews from No. 216 Squadron flew Air-to-Air Refuelling tracks very close to the Kosovo border, coming under threat on a number of occasions. Of the seven refuelling tracks used by NATO aircraft, five were over the Adriatic Sea close to the Croatian coast, whilst in the early days of the campaign, we flew most of our sorties in two tracks over Albania and Macedonia.

Flying the Lockheed L 1011 TriStar, we used the 'probe and drogue' method of refuelling, whilst the biggest players, the Americans, employed the 'boom' system on their KC 135 and KC 10 tankers. The two refuelling systems were not compatible, which proved to be an important limitation. They could not refuel European aircraft whilst we could not refuel the USAF attack aircraft, for example their F15s or F16s. Mission planners at the HO in Vicenza would try to ensure that there were both 'boom' and 'drogue' tankers available on each refuelling track at any one time, thus adding to the numbers of aircraft in the already busy sky. However, in the 'fog of war' this did not always work out, and it was not uncommon for post-strike formations to arrive in the refuelling track, short of fuel, to find five or six tankers, of which none could refuel them. Not being able to help out was extremely frustrating.

With four TriStars based at Ancona on the Adriatic coast, No. 216 Squadron was able to handle a significant proportion of the fast jet probe and drogue AAR requirement. Taking off

TriStar refuelling Tornados (Crown copyright)

with 120,000 kg of fuel on board, the TriStar could fly a seven-hour sortie and still give away 50,000 kg to other aircraft. Cut the sortie length down to three hours, then the available offload went up to 83,000 kg.

This impressive give-away was enhanced during the night sorties of March and April by tankers flying in 'cell', a formation in which the number two flies 500 ft above and half a mile behind the leader.

In peacetime, TriStar aircraft were invariably given Air Transport sorties, leaving Air-to-Air Refuelling training to take second place. Consequently, less than half the Squadron's crews were AAR qualified in 1999 and they had certainly not practised night cell procedures prior to Allied Force. However, once mastered, cell offered a number of advantages.

Firstly, as one speaking unit, it cut down the radio chatter on the control frequency. Secondly, as a formation, we could offer nearly 170,000 kg of fuel on a three-hour sortie. In peacetime, most fast jet aircraft would take between 2000 kg and 3000 kg each time they came to the tanker. However, once the campaign started it was clear that these guys were spending increasingly longer periods over the target area, many of them arriving back at the tanker with very little fuel in their own tanks. Having two tankers in formation eased the situation, as there would be an extra hose available for any desperate receivers, of which there were many.

To help with this situation, VC 10 tankers of 101 Squadron were deployed to Ancona for the last few weeks of the conflict. Up until then, the VC 10s had been providing essential AAR support for the Tornado bombing missions launched from RAF Bruggen in Germany. Unlike the TriStar, which was single hose, the VC 10 could refuel two receivers simultaneously, thereby reducing the time taken to refuel a formation. However the VC 10's fuel capacity was much lower than the TriStar requiring more VC10s to do the same job.

Finally, the third advantage of flying cell was that a formation of two TriStars is pretty easy to see, even on a dark night, making the join-up simpler for the receivers.

Conversely, the first disadvantage of cell was that a formation of two TriStars is pretty easy to see, even on a dark night, making life simpler for any enemy aircraft that 'slipped through the net'. Along with the E 3 Sentry, we were considered as high value assets which, having no self-defence aids, would be easy targets for enemy air or ground units. Not a comfortable feeling. The second disadvantage of cell is that it is difficult to operate in poor weather. Unfortunately, there was plenty of poor weather over Kosovo, leading to formations of fast jets and tankers regularly losing sight of each other, thus adding to the effect on the Comedy Channel frequency.

The Squadron had been operating in the Balkans theatre since 1992: based firstly in Milan, followed by a number of years at Palermo in Sicily and, finally, the detachment to Ancona. During eight years in Italy, the Squadron had developed a good working relationship with the other nations' aircrew, as we all attempted to agree a single interpretation of the 'Standard Operating Procedure' used within the multi-national force.

During the war our main 'customers' were American EA6Bs, F14s and F18s (in contrast to the USAF, USN and USMC aircraft use the probe and drogue refuelling system); German and Italian Tornados; Canadian and Spanish F 18s; French Jaguars and Mirages and, very occasionally, RAF or RN Harriers. Perhaps surprisingly, only about 2% of our work was with other UK aircraft.

Number 216 Squadron was tasked to fly 202 sorties during Operation 'Allied Force'. Of these we successfully flew 202 sorties, a record which owes a lot to the dedication of our ground crew, a marvellous team of characters who worked long, long hours servicing the jets on the ramp at Ancona.

Until 1999, Ancona airfield was a quiet little backwater with only one international flight, two or three internal flights, and a few helicopter flights each day. Very laid back, very Italian. However, by early 1999 the atmosphere completely changed as more aircraft arrived to play their part in Operation 'Allied Force'. Air movements intensified with arrivals and departures of transport aircraft, tankers and helicopters day and night. The airport manager was delighted with this increase in business, although local residents, who lived close to the airport or under the approach path, were a little less enthusiastic.

Life on the ground in Italy carried on as if nothing was happening a few miles across the Adriatic Sea in Serbia. Restaurants, shops and the City Pub all maintained normal opening hours and CNN would be showing the results of NATO's efforts before the tanker crews got back to their hotels after a mission. It was the same strange feeling that I encountered during The Gulf War, where we led perfectly normal lives during our time on the ground, only to sense the reality when we were airborne: a feeling experienced by some who were based in Kent or Lincolnshire over sixty years ago.

Activation of Pristina Airfield

Group Captain Graham Stacey MBE

In May 1999 I was commanding No. 1 Royal Air Force Tactical Survive-to-Operate HQ based at RAF Laarbruch in Germany. A TacSTO HQ is a small, mobile and flexible HQ tailored to provide force protection command and control for deployed bases. I had been in command for a very busy and successful fifteen months. In addition to the normal round of exercises and recce trips we had led the force protection and chemical and biological defence elements in the activation of Ali al Salem in Kuwait.

In December 1998 we returned to Kuwait just in time for Op 'DESERT FOX', departing in April 1999 for a well-earned rest and to commence preparation for relocation to RAF Wittering upon the closure of Laarbruch. The news that we were on standby for deployment to Kosovo was met with mixed feelings. The anticipation and lure of a further operation was tempered by concern about the relocation both of the unit and the families. Personally I knew that the HQ was the ideal unit for the task, and having previously spent ten months on the staff of the High Representative for Bosnia and Herzegovina, knew I had valuable experience of the Balkans to add to our Survive-to-Operate (STO) experience.

At first and as usual details were scarce. The task was the activation of an airfield on the outskirts of Pristina. Initially the airfield was to be a military Air Point of Disembarkation (APOD) for the movement of troops and materiel, but in time it was expected to be used for humanitarian and then civil use. The airfield was both a Serbian military base and the local civil airport, and was a target for the NATO air campaign. It was expected that we would be repairing our own damage in addition to anything that the withdrawing Serbs did to the facilities. The risk of unexploded ordnance as well as deliberate booby traps was expected to be high.

On 2 June 1999 I joined a 3 UK Division and 5 Airborne Brigade recce party which deployed to HQ KFOR in Macedonia. At HQ KFOR it was obvious that things were progressing quickly, and even as General Jackson and his staff were giving us a full brief, plans were changing. It was also obvious that General Jackson placed a great deal of importance to the reactivation of Pristina APOD. As well as giving him flexibility when supply routes through Greece were suffering from local opposition to the whole NATO operation, it was considered to be a symbol of normality and political significance for Kosovo to have a working airfield. The commander's intent was quite clear – an operational airfield within a week of KFOR moving north. Equally obvious was that the lower formations did not see the airfield in the same light. A large area of concrete that was difficult to mine, or conceal improvised explosive devices on, was an ideal location for an HQ or vehicle refuelling and replenishment point.

By the time we departed Macedonia two days later, the decision had been made to deploy 5 Airborne Brigade, who were to use speed and mobility to secure the bridges and tunnels on the single route north into Kosovo before Serb sabotage could occur. Headquarters 3 UK Division was also to deploy in a co-ordinating role for UK assets.

After a weekend back in Germany briefing the rest of my HQ and setting mobilisation into action I met up with other elements of the APOD activation team at HQ Strike Command. The team was to be led by Group Captain John Morley from HQ 38 Gp, with me acting as his deputy and Chief of Staff, as well as OC STO/Force Protection. The UK had undertaken to activate Pristina on behalf of KFOR and, although there was talk of assistance from other nations, initially we were on our own.

Plans were made accordingly and units warned, and air and sea movement preparation began. Gp Capt. Morley led a small group of us back to Macedonia at the end of that week. Within days KFOR were making final preparations for the move north into Kosovo. The UK's 4 Armoured Brigade was to secure an area including the airfield but understandably, given the threat and uncertainty of the situation, the activation of the airfield was low down the agenda. It was agreed that I would travel forward with the Brigade on D-day and attempt to look after the long-term interests of the APOD and prevent the runway being turned into a car park.

On the eve of the move north I joined a KRH Battle Group in its final stages of preparation. I knew that the RAF sent me to the Army Staff College for a reason, and when the KRH Squadron Commander turned out to be a fellow student

In the KRH Battle Group (Gp Capt Stacey)

all became clear. He – jokingly I trust – offered me a seat in the bowels of his tank, but the comfort and protection of an EOD Mamba vehicle was a far better offer. The next twenty-four hours was a roller-coaster of events and emotions. That night we moved to a final assembly area on the border. Local Serb sympathisers ensured an eventful journey by stoning the convoys and dropping large concrete slabs off bridges. I was grateful I was not in a Land-Rover! After a few hours sleep alongside the vehicles, we crossed into Kosovo the next morning with a continuous line of RAF Puma and Chinook helicopters overhead, ferrying 5 Airborne Brigade forward. I knew what an armoured brigade was on paper but to be in the middle of one moving forward was an awe-inspiring experience. Unlike the night before, we were showered with flowers and good luck signs as we passed the refugee camps on the border.

Once the traffic sorted itself out the first few hours were relatively uneventful, but by mid-morning it became clear that all was not well at the APOD. A convoy of vehicles from the Russian contingent of SFOR in Bosnia was *en route* to the airfield. The involvement of the Russians, closely aligned with and sympathetic to the Serbs, would raise political as well as practical problems. The Commanding Officer of 5 Airborne Brigade was reported to be in a race to get to the airfield first, but to do what was not clear – a fire-fight with the Russians was not an option.

As evening, and the inevitable downpour, arrived, the Russians halted the Battlegroup on the outskirts of the airfield. My vehicle stopped next to a burning Albanian house, torched by a Serb family whose orderly departure was sent into panic, hysteria and chaos by our arrival. Our plans were rapidly changed and overnight accommodation taken in a local cement factory. The next morning we learnt that CO 5 Airborne Brigade and a small HQ group were on the airfield with the Russians. No vehicles were allowed on but I was granted permission to walk on to join them, but it was clear that the Russians were there to stay and that the future way ahead would have to be decided at a much higher level.

Later that day the HQ group pulled out of the airfield to seek a permanent location and concentrate on commanding the Brigade and securing the town of Pristina. The Serb military and special police were withdrawing, but as arrogantly and defiantly as possible. Equipped with heavy machine guns, armoured vehicles and anti-aircraft systems they were an impressive sight as they drove past – four fingered Serb salutes thrust at us. The potential for trouble was very real.

The political ramifications of the Russian move became clearer over the following days. The Russians may have had the airfield but British Forces surrounded them and a *status quo* was established. The focus of effort moved to HQ NATO and Helsinki, where agreement was sought over the airfield and the wider issue of Russian involvement in KFOR. Gp Capt. Morley, a driver and a translator were allowed onto the airfield to act as the UK POC and local negotiator. They endured an uncomfortable couple of weeks living in basic field conditions in the main terminal car park. A good rapport was established with the Russian Air Force, who seemed genuinely interested in establishing a joint operation at the airfield: but the Russian Army who had a far wider and more complicated agenda was making the real decisions.

In the meantime I returned, courtesy of a sympathetic Chinook pilot, to Macedonia where the remainder of my HQ and the advance party of the airfield activation team had arrived. A muddy site on the airfield at Skopje was to be home for thirty-five of us for the next two weeks. Communications with Gp Capt. Morley were poor, but we did learn vital information about the airfield and manage to keep him generally in touch with the outside world. Planning for a new joint KFOR/Russian operation began in earnest but not without problems. For example, negotiators in Helsinki asked us for details of the numbers of personnel and vehicles needed for specific tasks. Reaction was very positive, and it was only after we commenced detailed planning that they informed us those were the tasks the Russians would be given!

The UK role was to be air traffic and operations, air movements and local security. After initial agreement each side was to be allowed three aircraft into the airfield, which would then be shut for eight days whilst a detailed agreement on running the APOD was completed and essential repairs undertaken. Pristina was then to be open for business.

Waiting for agreement in Helsinki became a frustrating and morale-sapping period, although the thought of Gp Capt. Morley and his group camped outside the terminal in Pristina quelled most complaints. The intention was that we moved quickly once 'R' day was agreed. To facilitate this, French and UK C 130 aircraft were on standby at our disposal. I pondered on how many occasions I had wanted air transport and none was available. I now had two aircraft 'on command' and nowhere to go! Time was well spent fine-tuning plans for both the activation of the APOD and the inload of personnel and materiel. The lull also allowed us to gain a greater understanding of the overall operation, and consider aspects such as media handling, ethnic tensions, and mine and UXO awareness training. The real luxury was the fact that the air operations, communications and air traffic, Royal Engineer, MoD Fire service and force protection elements lived, planned and learnt from each other for almost two weeks. R day finally arrived, and once the Russians had secured diplomatic clearance to fly from Moscow, a French C 130 took myself and the first elements forward, with the remainder of the activation team following quickly by air and road. Exactly to plan, a NATO and Russian aircraft arrived at Pristina together. The first stage of the PR battle was won.

To those used to NATO airfields, Pristina was a strange and unusual location. A single runway running north-south was surrounded on three sides by flat open land. On the eastern side was high ground rising quickly to a height of 1000 m.

Taxiways ran from either end of the runway straight into the hillside, inside which were the military aircraft storage and maintenance facilities. Locals advised that the normal SOP was for fighters to take off directly from inside the hill along the taxiway. Some even claimed that landing was conducted in the same manner! The Russian army occupied the hillside storage and buildings nearby. Entry was strictly forbidden – a fact that fuelled rumours of a cover-up of Serb atrocities, or the hiding of sensitive technology or weapons.

The Russian Air Force detachment, along with Gp Capt.

Morley, was based near the civil air terminal. Although most operating surfaces were intact, damage throughout the airfield was extensive. As well as being generally run down, NATO bombing had been effective, and what damage the Serbs had failed to achieve the Russian conscripts had completed. Typical was the terminal building. Bombed by NATO, all removable equipment had been stripped out, and the flooded basement used as an open toilet. The local area was a microcosm of operations in Kosovo. An ethnic mix of Serbs and Albanians, a variety of terrain, a major road route to control and the ubiquitous Balkan minefields.

Once the activation team were in place at Pristina it became obvious that there were three main tasks. Commence detailed negotiation with the Russians, start work on the airfield and establish the UK encampment.

In building the encampment we were conscious of a short-term requirement, but also acknowledged the Kosovo winter that was only months away. In all matters the relationship with the Russians was both key and difficult. We had all underestimated the pride and prestige that the Russians took in the Kosovo operation and the total lack of resources that they could bring to the venture. In simple terms they wanted control and recognition without having the infrastructure to back it up. This led to some interesting decisions and conflicts.

The location of the UK encampment, a vehicle in the wrong parking place, or a visitor from KFOR without 'permission' led to immediate meetings and threats of expulsion. I was very glad that Gp Capt. Morley dealt with this aspect of the relationship and left me to get on with the airfield tasks. As usual the UK Service personnel responded with humour above all else, aided by the ability of the RAF caterers to produce excellent meals in the most demanding and basic circumstances.

The detailed agreement with the Russians regarding the operation of the airfield was eventually secured. Tortuous negotiation was prolonged by the fact that the Russians were operating with pen and paper and even had to request that we faxed their copy to Moscow for clearance. I will never take my laptop for granted again.

In the meantime, work commenced recreating an airfield. The terminal was cleaned and repaired, NAVAIDS and ATC were installed, fuel storage was built and full crash and fire cover created. At all times an eye was kept to the future and the aim of bringing normality to Kosovo. Where possible local workers were employed – Serb or Albanian, especially if they were connected to the airport in the past. Total neutrality in this approach caused its own problems. EOD clearance of the site was undertaken as part of the overall KFOR operation but dealing with incidents still caused many delays.

Despite some unpleasant and difficult working conditions the activation was completed in an impressive time. The main ingredient in the success of the undertaking was teamwork and a willingness to get stuck in. The technical expertise of Tac Comms Wing; the skill, organisation and work ethos of the Royal Engineers; the cohesion and command and control brought by my HQ: all played a part, but in the end the contribution of each individual played the most important role. In a short time confidence was established with the Russians. It became obvious that their approach to area security involved setting up a couple of roadblocks. Agreement was reached for II Sqn RAF Regiment and the RAF Police to take over the task and set up an AOR within the UK Brigade area.

The first aircraft to use the fully activated APOD was a UN humanitarian flight. As expected the event attracted much media interest and was as much a statement of capability and political intent as an operational requirement. In time the APOD use became more routine.

Shortly after full activation TacSTO HQ withdrew from Pristina. The STO requirement was based on a ground threat and was met by the RAF Regt Squadron/RAF Police operation. The UK element of the airfield was predominantly based on ATC, movements and air operations, and was more appropriately led by Flight Ops personnel. A key lesson from the operation was the preparation of RAF augmentees for this type of campaign. Specialist units such as the RAF Regt, Tac Comms Wg, Mobile Catering Support Unit, Tac Provost Support Wing are well-prepared and used to such demands. The arrival of poorly briefed and equipped individuals to a bare field site, in an operational environment where they were required to erect accommodation and showers before they could use them, caught many out. The story of the individual arriving with a bright yellow Samsonite suitcase and no sleeping bag is now legendary. This has led to a major review of the RAF training system.

The HQ and myself enjoyed another demanding but immensely satisfying operational deployment. It reinforced my opinion that flexibility, the ability to think on your feet and, of course, a sense of humour are key to such operations. No scenario I considered involved moving forward with an armoured battlegroup on D day, or leading detailed negotiations with Russians over the joint running of an APOD. Above all we were blessed with an activation party of immense quality and enthusiasm, capable of delivering an APOD against all odds.

Murder Squad in Pristina

Flight Lieutenant Tony Quinn

In June 1999, having been giving only three days' notice, I was sent to Kosovo as the 2 I/C to 92 Section, Special Investigations Branch, Royal Military Police.

The position was unique, not least because an RAF Provost Officer was given an SIB appointment in the RMP. The unit consisted of eighteen personnel: twelve RMP and six RAF Police. Later a further two RMP SNCOs would be added to its strength. All personnel were Special Investigations trained – in other words we were detectives: I had done my CID course with Lancashire Police in 1998 and

Scene of crime investigation – Kosovo (Crown copyright)

had been employed on P&SS (Provost & Security Services) duties for two years. We all had different backgrounds and had followed normal single service careers.

Upon entering Kosovo one of the main roles of the NATO led forces was to return the country to some sort of civilised normality: not an easy task when a large percentage of the population had been subject to some form of ethnic cleansing. The Serbs, who had controlled everything, had left, leaving behind a country on the verge of anarchy. There was an enormous vacuum in terms of civilian infrastructure.

NATO had to fill that vacuum – and fast, if it was to retain control and eventually hand the country over to the UN. As such, the restoration of law and order was given a high priority.

Our role was the investigation of the those capital crimes which would normally be undertaken by a CID type formation – in essence we became a murder squad dealing with murder, attempted murder, rape and the occasional kidnap. We only handled what we called 'Smoking gun crime' – that is current crime that had occurred within the last twelve to twenty-four hours.

Our office/accommodation was the central Police Station in Pristina City, where we were collocated with a company of Paras and a RMP general duties unit. It is all right being an independent specialist unit, but you need to bolt on to larger formations if you are to survive and function in what was, at that time, a very hostile and dangerous environment. The murder rate was phenomenal: within the first four weeks we had over 100 murders. The majority of the victims were Serbs who had not left the country. Returning Albanians had sought revenge.

Our concept of operations revolved around two-man crews, who were rostered to give maximum coverage over a twenty-four-hour period: on one particular day we had six crews deployed at the same time on separate scenes/investigations. During the hours of darkness two crews were always deployed to provide mutual support to each other. On a number of occasions, depending on the particular circumstances, the OC, the RSM or myself would also deploy.

Each scene was a crime scene and was treated accordingly. A number of the investigators were qualified Scenes of Crime Officers (SOCOs) and would, therefore, try where possible to recover as much evidential material as was practicable. We would also carry out enquiries with any potential witnesses. However, unlike in the UK where there is large infrastructure in terms of forensic support, we were somewhat limited. The sheer volume of crime meant that we could only spend a limited amount of time on each investigation. If we thought that suspects could be identified and apprehended, then we would set about the chase, otherwise we would collate as much evidence as possible with a view to passing the file on to the UN Police once they were established. Whilst this was a realistic and pragmatic way in which to do business, it was also very frustrating.

One scene that I often recall is that of a Serb couple who were murdered. They had lived in a small village on the outskirts of Pristina. In a former life the man had been part of the Serb security forces, probably in the paramilitary police known as the MuP: we had found his uniform in the bedroom. I say 'former life' because this couple were in their late 70s/early 80s. They were the only Serb couple left in the village: all the others had left or had also been murdered. The village itself was patrolled on a regular basis by soldiers from 1 PARA. The Paras knew about the Serb couple and had made a point of always checking to see if they were all right.

On this particular evening the patrol went through the village as usual and stopped to speak to the couple. The murderers had lain in wait, and shortly after the patrol passed two men entered the house. They had sat the couple together and then shot the woman through the head. They then turned to the old man and shot him through the face. We can only assume that they were disturbed because they left in a hurry. On leaving through the front door they came face to face with the Para patrol who, on realising something was wrong, gave chase. The men escaped into nearby houses where they were spirited away. The old man survived for about an hour, during which time he was able, through an interpreter, to give an account of what had happened, including a vague description of his assailants.

On arriving at the scene the Paras had detained an Albanian man who they thought was connected with the murder. In total five of us had turned out: three RAF and two RMP. The Paras were keen for us to take charge of their suspect. Unfortunately the evidence was flimsy – he was an Albanian male who roughly fitted the description, and he knew the Serb couple because he lived locally.

In order to establish if this Albanian was involved, I detailed two Investigators to search him, and then in company with some of the Paras, take him back to his home and carry out a thorough search, looking in particular for a potential murder weapon. Then with the two other investigators I went into the house. The scene, as with most murder scenes, was not particularly pleasant: the old woman was lying dead on the floor with a large pool of blood next to her head, and a large amount of blood splattered on the wall. There was also a blood trail leading from the sitting room out to the back door, to which the old man had managed to crawl. At least two empty shell casings were visible: from their size it looked like the murder weapon had been a pistol. Prior to our arrival the old man had been medi-vaced out. The woman was pronounced dead by an Army doctor.

One of the SOCOs set about photographing the scene, using both normal and digital cameras. Word came through that a pistol had been found at the suspect's house. To see if the weapon was linked I asked for one of the shell casings to be recovered and then, on my own, I made my way the 600 yards or so to the suspect's house. By now it was pitch black and the street lighting was somewhat poor. Walking along that street was an eerie experience, especially when going to confront a potential murderer.

One of the Investigators met me at the entrance to the house. It turned out that our man had a right little arsenal in his cellar, including a hand-held anti-tank weapon. I checked the spent case against the recovered pistol. Whilst the calibre was the same, it was obvious that the pistol had not been fired in a long time. There was no way on earth we could get a ballistics analysis carried out, so it was down to me to make the call: do we lock him up on suspicion of murder, knowing that the case would be thrown out at the first hearing, or release him. There was always a third alternative – he was arrested for possession of firearms: self-protection was one thing ... but a rocket launcher!

By the time I got back to the old couple's house the body of the woman had been bagged and loaded onto the vehicle. Then word came through that another possible suspect had been spotted in a nearby cafe. One of the Paras had seen one of the assailants when they disturbed them at the house, but only briefly. We made our way to the cafe. By now word had got round, and the local hoods were playing to the crowds. I got my interpreter to tell all the young men in the cafe to come outside so the Para could see if he could identify the murderer. The situation was tense: there were five of us and about a dozen of them. We had the advantage in that our guns were ready to use: my hand never left the handle of my pistol, the holster catch was already unfastened although you wouldn't know at a glance.

One of my Investigators, in company with one of the Paras, stood a couple of yards back; both had rifles with magazines fitted. If there was going to be a drama we were ready. Unfortunately, despite giving each one of them a thorough looking-over the Para could not identify any of them as the assailant. We drove off into the night to cries of 'NAATO, NAATO' and 'UCK, UCK' (Albanian for KLA).

As we drove back through the City Centre I saw a man in a wheelchair trying to cross the road. I stopped the vehicle, got out and helped him across: at least I felt as if I'd helped somebody that evening.

The worst scene I went to was on the night of 23 July 1999, when fourteen Serb men and boys were massacred as they returned from the fields. Six of us turned out and were assisted by soldiers from the local Battle Group. I remember turning over the body of a young boy who was roughly about the age of one of my daughters and thinking 'why?' Whilst I am convinced that I know who was responsible for this horrific crime, we could never get enough evidence.

During my time in Pristina – a city with a population of around a quarter of a million people, we investigated over 160 murders; twenty-two attempted murders; six rapes; one kidnapping; three bombings and three fatal traffic accidents – and we were only there three months!

A New Century

Tales from the Doc Side

Air Commodore T. M. Gibson QHS

It is only when you write down your reminiscences that you realise what a dull and sheltered life you have led compared to your predecessors. In this account, I shall pick out the fruit from the pudding of my last thirty-three years. When I was at medical school, I was appalled at the prospect of spending my entire professional career in one place doing one job. The Armed Forces offered the incentives of training, travel and turbulence, and payment for my last three years at medical school. I joined the RAF in particular because sea time in the Navy was limited and because the Army medical included a rectal examination whilst the medical at Biggin Hill did not.

I was fortunate to start my career at the Central Flying School, RAF Little Rissington. There were three aircraft types on base – Jet Provost, Varsity and Chipmunk, with the Gnat squadron and the Red Arrows detached at Kemble. I had a happy time playing rugby and tennis, running the CFS Pipe Band, trying to get the SMO to let me fly as often as possible and working hard. I spent many hours playing the pipes, and received two gems of advice from my first 'Staish', Gp Capt. 'Bill' Adams. 'Keep it simple', he said. 'They don't want any fancy stuff they can't tap their feet to.' And 'Always leave them wanting more Doc, not less.'

I left Rissie in the autumn of 1972: shortly afterwards it transferred to the Army as Imjin Barracks, later becoming an American Army 'turn-key' hospital; and the station is now a housing estate.

I then spent the next ten years at the RAF Institute of Aviation Medicine (IAM) at Farnborough. At that stage 'The Lab' had an international reputation initially gained during World War II and consolidated over the next twenty years. The IAM led the world on aspects of acceleration, sleep research, vestibular physiology and integration of aircrew equipment.

My initial work was on aircrew Nuclear, Biological, Chemical Headgear. By 1976, after work on several prototypes, we were stumped, so much so that an American exchange officer suggested the only way forward was to teach aircrew to fly with their eyes closed and holding their breath. The idea for the respirator that eventually went into service as the Aircrew Respirator (Nuclear Biological Chemical No. 5) came from the Engineering Physics Department of the Royal Aircraft Establishment. I made the

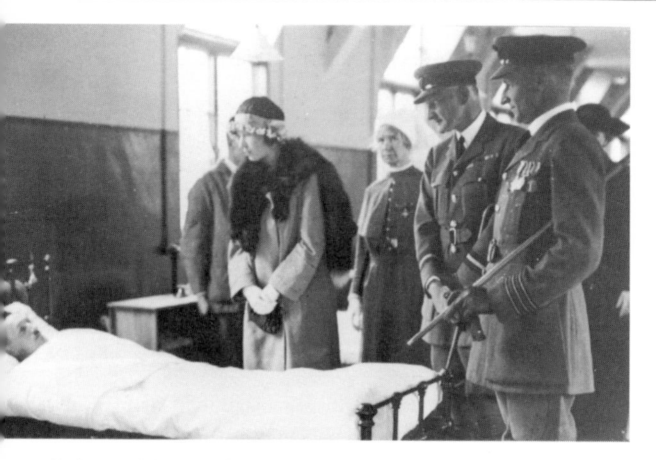

Princess Mary at Cranwell Hospital 24 April 1925. The Nursing Service – then (Nursing Service Archives)

Flight Lieutenant Lamb. The Nursing Service – now (Crown copyright)

first flight of the new respirator (in the Devon!) sitting alongside our Medical Officer (Pilot) as we flew to Thorney Island and back. I was also the subject for its test rapid decompression. I was lying down on an examination couch in the high performance chamber pedalling away on a bicycle ergometer to simulate aircrew workload. As the countdown hit zero, there was the usual hiss and instant mist from the condensation of water vapour in the air. More alarming was the way I was lifted into the air as the air in the examination couch expanded, to subside slowly with a loud groaning noise as the air escaped through two tiny relief valves in its side.

I later moved on to doing research on heat in the cockpit. We confirmed what many other researchers had found before: that when you put personnel inside extra layers of protective and impermeable clothing to work, they get hot and sweaty. What was interesting was the extent to which this could affect mental performance. This was anticipated for aircrew, but no-one appeared to have thought of the flight safety aspects of heat-degraded groundcrew.

This time at Farnborough was before the advent of ethics committees. As a result many of the experiments would not be authorised today. It was a case of 'I'll be a subject in your nasty experiment if you'll be a subject in mine'. This matched J. B. S. Haldane's statement that 'You cannot be a good human physiologist unless you regard your body, and that of your colleagues, as something to be used and, if necessary, used up'. Thus I participated in experiments to determine times of useful consciousness at high altitude after rapid decompression; to define G tolerance with different equipment and in different seat configurations; to study the effects on the brain of sudden impact and so on.

Whilst doing a pilot study on how well a radio pill could follow deep body temperature during alternating exposures to hot and cold baths at 41°C and 10°C, I measured my own blood pressure at 300+/200+ (compared to a normal of 120/70). The ten years at Farnborough was an exciting and stimulating time.

Towards the end of my time at IAM, I became involved with a colleague in writing the history of the RAF Institute of Aviation Medicine. This was an opportunity to speak to the old and bold and to hear their war stories. What became most apparent was the pace of change. During World War II, an aircraft could be introduced into service and become obsolete in a little more than a year. The Flight Medical Officers in the field used to come to regular meetings at IAM to tell the research staff what was going on and what was needed. On the other hand, we were working in an environment where it took fifteen years from concept to clearance into service of an aircraft type. This drove a change in the balance of relationships between the research staff and the field. During the '70s we told the FMOs what was new and what was going on.

I left IAM in 1982 to return to general medical duties. Ten years later, the unit ceased to exist as an RAF facility, being transformed into a civilian-led defence agency. As the Defence Evaluation and Research Agency Centre for Human Sciences, with a business orientation, it publishes little and has no RAF personnel on its staff.

I spent the ensuing two years organising aeromedical evacuation at HQ 38 Group and HQ 1 Group. This was in the immediate aftermath of the Falklands campaign and we set up the routine aeromed from RAF Stanley.

This was a weekly flight by Hercules to Ascension Island and thence by VC 10 back to Brize Norton. I only did three Hercules flights there, whereas some of the aeromed nurses did over twenty-five. However, on one occasion, when ten psychiatric patients requiring restraint had accumulated on the islands and the Group Air Staff Orders specified that only one was allowed per flight, I got permission to assess the patients and persuade the captain that we could view the orders flexibly. We eventually brought all ten back together.

The aircrew, as always, were superb.

My time at 38 Gp was also my first exposure to 'jointery'. I used to plan with an Army colleague in HQ 5 Airborne Brigade to aeromed back those parachutists whom he used to break on exercise. We have continued to work together over the years, particularly since he is now Commander Medical HQ LAND Command. In aeromed, we averaged 2000 patients a year brought back from all over the world from all three Services as well as some civilians. Despite the reduction in the size of the Armed Forces, this number is still about the same. This reflects the reduction in our overseas hospitals as well as the more expeditionary nature of the operations we undertake. I left Upavon to go to Germany. Aeromed is now run from High Wycombe and Upavon has reverted, once more, to the Army.

I then spent two years at the RAF Hospital Wegberg as OC Medical Wing (the 'Registrar' in old money) and two years as Senior Medical Officer at RAF Laarbruch. Both are now no more.

One of the best bits about being in the RAF is the opportunity to go flying, particularly in fast jets. One of the worst bits is that flying is very hard to come by if you are not aircrew. The highlight at Laarbruch (apart from being awarded the Pik Botha award by 16 Sqn. in their alternative New Year's Honours List, for being a hard line President of the Mess Committee) was the Tornado sortie. Two thirds of the way through the sortie, when trying to help with bombing on the range, I did score one direct hit – into the sick bag. What did surprise me was how little time I had to look out for any bounce aircraft, since so much time was spent operating the kit in the rear cockpit.

I then spent my first tour in the Ministry – followed in turn by two idyllic years commanding the jewel of the RAF Medical Branch, the Defence Services Medical Rehabilitation Unit at RAF Headley Court. During the Gulf War, we expanded Headley Court up to 200 beds, and gained permission and assistance from the US Army to open up their 'turn-key' hospital at RAF Chessington again as a satellite rehabilitation unit. Fortunately, the extra capacity was not needed. I am saddened that the rehabilitation unit at Headley Court, which was donated to the RAF on a peppercorn lease in memory of the deeds of RAF aircrew during World War II, has passed from the control of the RAF and is now commanded by a brigadier on behalf of the Defence Secondary Care Agency. But at least the unit is still open and very much doing the superb job it has always done.

I went from Headley to a post on the staff of the USAF Surgeon General. Travel, they say, broadens the mind. Tours in the United States broaden much more. The highlights of my time there were 14 hours of F-16 flying (to become the only RAF officer qualified as a 'fighter surgeon' in the Air National Guard); two weeks on a study delegation to the Peoples' Republic of China, and two weeks in Mogadishu conducting an investigation into perceived shortcomings (there were none) in the USAF aeromedical evacuation of casualties from Operation Provide Comfort.

I was fortunate to spend two years out of the country while Options for Change, Prospect and the Defence Cost Studies were in progress. I left a Defence Medical Services Directorate in London with a 3-star Surgeon General over two 2-star Director Generals, and with no specific single Service medical directorates; and returned just as it reverted to one 3-star over three 2-stars who were being rusticated to sit with their parent Services.

I also arrived back as we were to implement Defence Cost Study 15, which resulted in the closure of all the Service hospitals except Haslar, and a reduction in manpower of 40%. Hospital provision was to be provided by Ministry of Defence Hospital Units (MDHU) at Peterborough, Frimley Park and Derriford, under the control of the new Defence Secondary Care Agency.

Two good things came out of DCS 15. First, the medical services were focused for the first time on the support of operations. And second, the creation of the Medical Supplies Agency put the subject of medical supply firmly on a professional basis for the first time. However, morale took a beating and many good people left.

In this tour at the Ministry, I made the arrangements to move our directorate (Medical Operations and Logistics) first to Lacon House (now closed) from First Avenue House, and then to HMS *Warrior* at Northwood where we were to set up the medical cell in the new Permanent Joint Headquarters (PJHQ). Until then, I had thought that only orthopaedic surgeons did joint operations.

This was an exciting time, with ongoing major operations in Montserrat, Africa, the Gulf region, and Bosnia, as well as many smaller ones elsewhere. As a result of the validating exercise for PJHQ, we convinced the Assistant Chief of Defence Staff (Logistics) that the medical services could not adequately support all anticipated operations. He persuaded the Chiefs of Staff to conduct an operational audit and then set up a study team to propose the way forward. The team reported just after the 1997 General Election, and I was press-ganged back from Innsworth to lead the implementation.

This return to MOD Main Building coincided with the setting up of the Strategic Defence Review, and we succeeded in obtaining immediate cash relief for our problems. At the same time, it was apparent that the Royal Naval Hospital Haslar was not sustainable, in that training accreditation could not be maintained. A new way forward was required, and Commodore Tim Laurence (husband of the Princess Royal) was brought in to conduct a strategic study and I was deputed to assist. One of the most significant recommendations was the change in Haslar's status from independent hospital to MDHU and the setting-up of a Centre for Defence Medicine in conjunction with the University Hospital of Birmingham NHS Trust and the University. This was opened on 2 April 2001 by the Princess Royal, and already looks to be an exciting development.

In the RAF, when the Institute at Farnborough closed a small unit remained to carry out aviation medicine teaching (the School of Aviation Medicine). Recently this has moved, to collocate with the Aviation Medicine Training Centre, the RAF Institute of Health and the Central Medical Boards, to RAF Henlow, as part of a new Centre for Aviation Medicine. This is an exciting and vibrant new unit. The new edition of the Textbook of Aviation Medicine has received critical acclaim.

The aeromedical team recently brought back a case of

suspected Lassa fever from Sierra Leone in the patient isolator, proving the theoretical standard operating procedures in the process.

Whilst the overseas postings have gone, there are many opportunities for overseas exercises and operations albeit at the cost of significant overstretch.

So is the RAF Medical Branch dead and buried? The answer is, no, not yet. Although equipment can be bought off the shelf, personnel cannot. Much work still needs to be done to entice recruits into the Medical Branch and to retain the experienced personnel we still have. But there is a lot to be excited about and a lot to do. That is why I am still serving.

Policing a New Millennium
Air Commodore Clive Morgan

'I never saw any of them again – except the cops. No way has yet been invented to say "goodbye" to them.'

(Raymond Chandler in 'The Long Goodbye'.)

It is axiomatic that people are generally uncomfortable with change, and that they also tend to regard policemen as a regrettable but unavoidable part of modern life. The RAF is undergoing a tremendous change at the beginning of the 21st century, and change can be a demanding experience for any organisation. The old Cold War certainties are fast-fading memories, as we concentrate on joint expeditionary operations and the challenges of an increasingly volatile world order.

The start of the new century sees the RAF Police undergoing a process of change far greater than many other parts of the Service, as we plan to separate many of our responsibilities for manned guarding to a new and distinct Guard Service. However, it occurs to me that whilst the Service changes to meet the new global realities and adopt a truly expeditionary capability, we are in fact returning to our roots. This is particularly true for the RAF Police who, over the years, have undertaken a myriad of tasks as their contribution to the delivery of Air Power, but whose essential role remains what is was in 1918. We still help protect the RAF, we give specialist advice to commanders (even if it is at times unpalatable), and we help to enforce Service regulations and discipline. At best we are probably still viewed as being a regrettable but unavoidable necessity of the modern RAF.

The first RAF Police started to patrol RAF Halton in 1918, after being trained by the Royal Military Police (RMP) at that Station. By 1922 we were supporting the RAF's air policing effort over Iraq. In 1929 we became involved in our first major counter-intelligence investigation, focused on communist attempts to infiltrate and subvert our armed forces. In the 1930s the RAF Police were involved in the investigation into German attempts to obtain information about RAF airfields.

In September 1939 a fifty-strong RAF Police unit deployed to France with the Advanced Air Striking Force. The unit undertook a range of duties, including investigations, patrols and guiding RAF convoys from airfield to airfield. We again undertook this role in North Africa as aircraft moved from strip to strip in support of the ebb and flow of the ground campaign. In 1944 RAF Police supported 2 Tactical Air Force in Normandy, their first task being to establish traffic control on the beachheads on the morning of D-Day. At around the same time Sqn Ldr Kettle and No. 44 RAF Police Flight were in Athens, literally caught up in the cross-fire of the civil war between communist and government forces, as they tried and eventually succeeded in helping the local police re-establish authority.

Probably the most significant single contribution we made during WW II was the investigation into the murder of fifty RAF aircrew by the Gestapo following the mass breakout from *Stalag Luft III* in Silesia, the 'Great Escape'. A small team of RAF Police investigators led by Wg Cdr Bowes and Sqn Ldr McKenna tracked down and brought to trial those responsible for the murders. Of the seventy-two individuals implicated in the murder of the aircrew, eighteen were executed, eleven were imprisoned and eleven committed suicide.

Waffen SS General Helmut Willich arrested by Warrant Officer D. Higgins, RAF Police, in 1949 for his suspected involvement in the murder of 50 RAF officers who escaped from Stalag Luft III *(RAF Police)*

The post-war years initially saw the RAF Police on operations in support of the RAF and local police as the withdrawal from Empire began. It was during these years that the RAF Police became acquainted with the shocking realities of terrorism and inter-communal conflict in places such as Malaya, Cyprus and Palestine. These years also saw us working more closely with our sister Service police organisations on joint operations and in joint units. We also began to work more closely with the RAF Regiment as we protected Service personnel, their families and operational assets, from terrorism and sabotage; although the lack of common radios often complicated Command Control and Communications arrangements between us.

When I joined the RAF in 1969 our fighting withdrawal from our overseas possessions had been substantially completed. The Cold War was the focus of most of our efforts, and I certainly never expected the rigidity and formalisation of that doctrine to be so substantially replaced during my career. Our RAF Police were rejoicing over the passage of Thor sites, requiring static guarding in the most unpleasant and remote locations, and looking forward to a new mobile and responsive concept of security to sustain the V Force. The RAF Police provided security for the RAF's nuclear weapons from 1958 until 1995, when these duties were handed over to the RAF Regiment. The need for effective counter-intelligence within the Service was again underlined when a joint investigation by the Security Service and RAF Provost & Security Services (P&SS) identified Chief Technician Douglas Britten to be a KGB spy. Britten had been recruited by the KGB in 1962 and had passed over to them sensitive signals intelligence in exchange for money: he was sentenced to twenty-one years' imprisonment.

In 1972 we were again working closely with the Royal Military Police supporting them in policing the streets of Belfast. In 1974 we were heavily involved with the evacuation of 13,000 civilians and Service dependants from Cyprus following the Turkish invasion. The RAF was again reminded that the Service remains a terrorist target when the terrorists attacked RAF Akrotiri in 1986.

A more insidious threat to the Service also began to emerge in the 1980s with the increasing use of illicit drugs by younger personnel. However, it was the PIRA terrorist campaign during that decade, culminating, for the RAF, in the murders of RAF Regiment personnel in the Netherlands in 1988, and an RAF Corporal and his baby daughter near RAF Wildenrath in 1989, that became the focus of much of our effort during that decade.

The beginning of the end of the Cold War in 1990 saw us back in the Gulf with the Coalition Forces. RAF Policemen were employed on counter-intelligence duties, the close protection of Air Marshal Sandy Wilson and then General de la Billiere with their RMP colleagues, and the normal range of RAF Police duties within the RAF's deployed operating bases. A number of dog handlers were also used to help manage the Iraqi prisoners of war captured by the advancing British ground forces. Swift and aggressive action by these dog teams often managed to restore order amongst unruly and threatening crowds without other guards having to resort to the use of firearms in self-defence. A few Iraqis did become acquainted with the sharp end of our German Shepherd Dogs.

The RAF P&SS investigated the theft of a laptop computer, containing operationally sensitive data, from one of Air Chief Marshal Sir Paddy Hine's staff officers, and numerous sensitive inquiries and operations were mounted with sister organisations by the P&SS Central Security Cell in support of the coalition effort.

The 1990s also saw the massive increase in the use and significance of information systems within the RAF. This was paralleled by a growing acceptance that this new technology was potentially more vulnerable to attack and misuse than what went before. We invested heavily in computer security training and this significantly improved our ability to investigate computer crime, and particularly our ability to retrieve information from computers.

In 1999 the RAF Police were deployed to Kosovo in support of the RAF effort in Pristina and to assist our RMP colleagues in policing. Whilst some RAF Police were accompanying Army and RAF Regt foot patrols, others were helping to get the airport operational again. A small team was working with RMP SIB investigating multiple murders and another team of P&SS computer forensics experts were used to extract information from Serbian Special Police computers that had been left behind during their hurried evacuation. However, although the technology had changed, the young RAF Provost officers and NCOs involved in this operation were only repeating what their predecessors had done: protecting the interests of the RAF, helping to restore order amidst inter-communal violence and investigating war crimes.

As the RAF Police enter the new millennium we are again going through a change in our emphasis, shedding most of our guarding responsibilities and relearning how to deploy into the field to guide and control convoys. We are examining joint training with the RMP (at Halton, where it all started in 1918), and our relationship with our sister Service police organisations is likely to grow much closer. Our positive relationship with the RAF Regiment continues, having survived a number of attempts over the years to force us both into a single organisation. However, the complementary tasks of both remain and we work together closely in Northern Ireland and the Gulf; and we are, at last, now starting to equip with common communications.

Although the Soviet Communist threat has disappeared, Russia remains wary of NATO, and the KGB's successor, the SVR, along with the GRU, remains as capable as ever. The potential for new and deadly forms of terrorism also exists, and we may face new adversaries in the future, including some capable of conducting 'cyber-attacks' against our information systems. The Real IRA still reminds us that the peace process in Northern Ireland is still fraught with difficulty.

As Provost Marshal I hold a military appointment whose origins date back to the 15th Century, and whose role was clearly articulated in the 17th Century as being 'to see that soldiers do not outrage nor scathe about the country' and 'discover the lurking subtleties of spies'.

At the start of the new millennium, priorities, organisation and operational environments have changed and we have had a revolution in military affairs, but it appears to me that the fundamentals have not altered since the RAF was formed. As a Service we are still required to deploy and operate wherever HMG chooses to send us. Aircraft and those who operate them still remain fragile instruments of war when they are on the ground. Unfortunately, personnel still, from time to time, threaten the effectiveness and reputation of the Service with their criminal or undisciplined behaviour. Whilst the RAF, as a fighting Service, remains distinct from civil society, and whilst potential adversaries may seek to undermine our combat effectiveness through espionage, sabotage and terror, the RAF Police will continue to provide the support the RAF needs, even if we are a regrettable necessity.

Plus ça change, plus c'est la même chose.

Air Power and the Media

Air Commodore D. A. Walker OBE MVO

Being appointed as Director of Corporate Communications came as something of a surprise, as all previous incumbents had been pilots. Moreover, I had thought I was off for a year of pleasant self-improvement at the Royal College of Defence Studies.

Having taken over the post, it was clear to me that in a number of communication areas the Service needed to raise its game. Over the next year I helped the RAF develop its Corporate Communication Strategy.

This embraces a more systematic, organic approach to communication – both internal and external. A crucial element of this is how we should prepare ourselves to assist the media with its work during operations. This is now part of Strike Command's role as the deliverer of RAF Force elements at readiness. We now have a cadre of trained and equipped regular servicemen and women, mainly from the Training Specialisation, who, in operations, will be transferred from their 'day jobs' to take on the Media Ops role. They are supplemented by 7644 Sqn RAuxAF, which is comprised of around twenty volunteers with media or PR backgrounds. We are now much better prepared and this role is exercised as part of our major exercise programme.

Fifteen years ago it was very unlikely that I would have been asked to write about airpower and the media. It was a relationship we didn't have to worry about. Since the Wright Brothers, the media – and the public – had had a love affair with aviation. Through many wars and crises air power enjoyed overwhelming public support. Indeed, air warfare still captures the imagination of the media. But in the last few years there has been much greater questioning and scrutiny. So what has changed? What is the acceptable face of air warfare today? And how has the media influenced this view?

During World War I, images of pilots in chivalrous aerial duels did much to foster the general fascination with aviation. This relationship between aviation and the public continued during the inter-war years.

During World War II, when Dresden was burned to the ground by incendiary bombs there was no public or media outcry. Set against the backdrop of a war which claimed millions of lives, and for Britons who had endured the Blitz, few questioned whether this was right or wrong. When a world is at war; when it really is 'them or us', and when loved ones are being killed, we are prepared to leave the questions and doubts until later.

The acceptable face of air power changes with circumstances. The Vietnam War produced some of the most frighteningly enduring images of the effects of air power. Who could forget the little Vietnamese girl fleeing from a napalm attack, her clothes burned away to reveal her badly blistered skin?

From a British perspective little changed in the way air power was perceived and reported between World War II and the Gulf War. Media coverage of the Falklands Conflict was carefully controlled by the Government, just as bombing raids had been forty years earlier.

A decade after the Falklands Conflict, technological advances – in both weapons and communications – meant the Gulf War was reported as no other war had been before. Satellites and mobile communications enabled live coverage to be beamed anywhere in the world, and we saw the emergence of the so-called 'CNN Effect'.

For the first time, Military Commanders had to accept the probing questions of the Press, and the ever-present eye of the cameras. The 'Star Wars'-like images of precision-guided munitions captured the attention of journalists during the Gulf War.

Professor Philip Taylor wrote:

> 'For the first time, audiences could see for themselves how 'smart' weapons homed in on military targets with uncanny accuracy, prior to the screen going blank. Such footage not only gave the impression that the coalition could hit precisely what it was aiming at, but it could discriminate between military and civilian targets. This fitted well with the line pursued by coalition leaders that this was a war fought not against the Iraqi people, but against the regime of Saddam Hussein and those forces which supported him.
>
> The problem was that of all the bombs deployed during the Gulf War, the 'smart' ones formed only about 8% of the total. The remainder, old-fashioned 'dumb' weapons of indiscriminate destruction, were not seen on television screens.'

The legacy of the Gulf War media coverage endures today with over-optimistic public expectation of what air power can achieve. When NATO began its air campaign in the Balkans, the media and the public expected that air warfare would be unleashed against Milosevic's military might, whilst causing little or no civilian casualties.

There is no doubt that this was the aim of all those involved in the planning and execution of the air campaign, but the reality was, of course, different, and the media wanted to know why.

During the early days of the air campaign, RAF Harriers launched a number of sorties only to be thwarted by poor weather over the target. Journalists wrote that it seemed incredible that the RAF could be foiled by nothing more than a bit of fog and rain! – yet that is exactly what had happened in the skies over Kosovo. In fact, in a week of raids, the Harriers only carried out two successful missions.

The Ministry of Defence pointed out that these missions were intended to precisely pick off military targets while causing a minimum amount of collateral damage. But even in an age of high technology a pilot must still be able to see the target in order to guide the bomb home. Pilots would not risk dropping a bomb which might land in a non-military site, causing civilian casualties.

When things go wrong, the full resources of the media can be directed against you, as when a NATO pilot bombed a Kosovar refugee convoy after mistaking their vehicles for

Media interview, Dharan, during Gulf War (Tim Lewis)

Serb military units. This put the air campaign under the media spotlight more than ever before, and tested NATO chiefs and spokesmen to the limit. From that point forward, every bombing attack went under the microscope.

Perhaps more than any single event of recent years, coverage of the leaked report into the RAF's bombing accuracy during the Balkans campaign damaged its reputation.

Headlines proclaimed that just 2% of unguided bombs had 'hit' their targets, but failed to acknowledge that the true figure was probably much higher. Ministers and senior RAF officers worked quickly, but largely unsuccessfully, explaining that as bombs had often been dropped through cloud, pilots had not seen them impact their wide-area targets and could not claim direct hits. One good effect of these reports was to give the public a more realistic picture of our capabilities and limitations.

At the heart of these changing relationships are, of course, the human dynamics. The main stakeholders can be loosely defined as Government, Military, Media and Audience. All have undergone considerable metamorphosis. Discretionary warfare, where the nation state is no longer at risk, will inevitably be politicised. The Government will be challenged on the rectitude and conduct of the war.

This has led to much closer involvement of Ministers in detailed operational planning, often down to the clearance of individual targets. Ministers have become increasingly aware of the need to explain personally actions and decisions taken during a campaign, including facing daily press conferences. This process also has to be harmonised with allies and NATO.

In the Kosovo campaign some of the information provided proved incorrect, leading to impassioned allegations by the media of spin, propaganda and lies. As these briefings were, at least in part, delivered by uniformed officers, our general standing with media suffered by association.

On the other hand, many in the military have a deep-seated mistrust of the media. A sense that the media does not understand or respect the military's complexity or culture. That the story has often been written in advance and the journalistic quest is merely for quotes or sources to claim. There is the fear in some minds that being seen in News broadcasts compromises personal security and might result in a worse fate in the event of capture. Equally, there is the concern about 'what if I get this wrong, or what I say is distorted?' All these are very powerful incentives for avoiding the media.

Furthermore the media itself has changed beyond recognition – beyond national allegiance, often lacking comprehension of military activity, but seeing wars as good for business. Technically advanced, but often thinly resourced, they are no longer just reporters of war but actual participants in the process. The coverage, as in Somalia, can produce dramatic and asymmetric shifts in political and military decision making.

Finally the audience itself has changed. No longer, for the most part, directly threatened by conflict, and often lacking military experience other than that generated by Hollywood. Some, perhaps, even unable to discriminate fully between techno-wars and entertainment. Certainly, in the main, uncomprehending of the strategic significance of regional conflicts.

So does all this represent an irreconcilable breakdown in relationships that we have for so long taken for granted? So much for granted that recent editions of RAF Air Power Doctrine do not even mention media co-operation.

We cannot, of course, afford such a breakdown. In the words of General Eisenhower, fundamentally public opinion wins wars. And the media is the primary instrument through which this opinion is shaped. Indeed, I would argue that maintenance of public support should be elevated to the level of a principle of war, because surely a war cannot be maintained without it.

In a recent address on Kosovo, Air Marshal Sir John Day stated:

> 'An intense media spotlight was focused on all NATO's activities before and during the campaign, and it has been ever since. At times it was very intrusive, and it was certainly difficult to achieve strategic surprise or, at times, even tactical surprise. However, the media is a fact of life, and politicians and the military need to develop their media strategy rather than complaining about the unfairness of the press. The media coverage must be viewed as an integral part of the overall campaign and, at times, it will need as much attention and effort as the planning and conduct of the pure military aspects of the campaign. Losing the media battle could force you unnecessarily to lose the military battle, you cannot take the media campaign for granted.'

In sum, I would suggest that if the media are no longer airpower's unquestioning friends, we certainly cannot afford to turn them into the foe. They are part of the environment, and to fulfil our role of playing a crucial part in resolving conflict co-operation with the media is essential. We must prepare the ground in peacetime, building relationships and trust with the media and seeking to raise awareness of the purpose, strengths and weaknesses of airpower. In conflict this becomes not just important, but crucial, to our potential success. We certainly cannot afford the attitude, still prevalent in parts of the front line, that dealing with the media is someone else's responsibility, and that they should be allowed to get on with their job. It is their job. Media operations must be a distinct element of the overall campaign plan, understood and adeptly prosecuted by commanders and personnel at all levels. We don't have to like the media but we certainly have to work with them.

I will let USAF General 'Chuck' Horner, who led the coalition air forces during the Gulf War, have the final words:

> 'We in the West are stuck with a free Press. It is not always easy for us in the military to deal with our Press, yet the Press is our ultimate blessing and our lasting glory. When we are wrong, we will (sooner rather than later) be shown as wrong. When we are right, and our actions are good, that will also come out. Sure, we can try to manipulate the Press, and the Press attempt to manipulate the truth, but in the end there is enough integrity in both the military and the media to make sure that most of the truth gets out to the world.
>
> 'The CNN Effect means that God is looking over your shoulder all the time, and I think it is a blessing. It is not pleasant, and you take hits, but in the end it brings out the best in mankind when he is out doing his worst, waging war.'

Life as a Station Commander

Wing Commander Stephanie Johnston MBE

'How would you feel about going to Digby for a few months as OC Admin Wing, and then taking over as Station Commander?' – the question posed by my Desk Officer just a few weeks before I was due to announce my decision to leave the RAF and start a new career in Scotland. Digby I knew little of, only that I had been taken there in 1979 at the dead of night as a Student Officer at Cranwell, to collect a signal on behalf of the Orderly Officer. In those days, Digby was never acknowledged, or spoken about, except by those in the Comms world and it certainly didn't publicise its existence. Nowadays, it has two red military road signs off the A15 (Sleaford to Lincoln road) and No. 591 Signals Unit and the Arial Erector School talk freely about their work. The Joint Service Signal Unit undertakes research and development in the communications and communications security and electronics fields.

The decision about extending my service in the RAF was an easy one. Indeed, when I joined the RAF as an Admin (Sec) officer from University, I only signed for six years. Actually, in those non-PC days, the WRAF were only offered Short Service Commissions. Of course I loved the work and the challenges so much that I kept extending my contract, and it was helped by the fact that my husband and I were collocated for the fair majority of our time. To match the Digby profile, he was offered No. 8 Sqn. at Waddington, and so we began our joint tour as the Wg Cdrs Johnston in RAF Lincolnshire.

In the autumn of 2000, I started at RAF Digby, under the tutelage of the then Station Commander, a Group Captain Engineer. I had hoped for an easy apprenticeship, but within a week of arriving, he had been selected for Royal College of Defence Studies and so our time together was limited. In between his visits to Bosnia, Kosovo, and the USA, I tried to pick his brains on how the Station functioned.

I too was drawn away by briefing courses on Equal Opportunities, Budgets, Civilian Appraisals, an Annual Conference and two Future Commander Study Periods. I even managed to escape moving house, leaving a set of floor plans and instructions with my family and a local removal firm.

Digby is quite unique in that all three Services work alongside all three Arms of the US Forces, and 15% of the workforce is civilian. The Station is actually older than the RAF itself by three days, and heroes from the days when Mosquitos and Spitfires flew from Digby's grass airfield fill the roll of honour in the foyer of Station Headquarters. D'Albiac, Harris, Tedder, and Murlis-Green were some of the Station Commanders through the ages, and adventurous souls such as Guy Gibson and Douglas Bader trained here when Digby was utilised as an extension of the College at Cranwell. In all, there are around 1000 people working at Digby, now a fully operational base working 24/7 and 365 days a year.

I command the Support Unit, which has only about 200 personnel and is predominately light blue and civilian, but I can never forget that the base is totally purple and Jointery is the way ahead. Each of the services brings to the Station its own particular cultures, traditions and requirements, and often it is a balancing act to accommodate their needs. Today, we are in the business of a Customer Agreement Panel; there are Local Service Agreements with the agencies that provide services to the customers – e.g. the Joint Service Signals Unit, the Aerial Erector School, No. 591 Signals Unit or the HQ Air Training Corps Wing. Terminology such as the Balance Business Scorecard and the European Foundation for Quality Management are high on the agenda when we look at our output and how we perform our duties, and we are constantly on the lookout to strive to improve the services to our customers.

There have been lady Station Commanders in the past, so

AOC's inspection 6 June 2001 shows the different services on parade together outside Station Headquarters (Crown copyright)

my appointment is not a novelty, but it is new to Lincolnshire – very much a flying county – to have a lady in command. It is strange how the public perceives that there might be a difference in how a Station is run. My previous tours and training have given me the essential key skills required to undertake the challenge, but my staff are frequently asked what it is like to work for a woman. Today, the RAF has a female workforce of around 10%, with an increasing number of those in managerial appointments, and females working in all the different branches and trade-groups of the service. The only area where they have not yet been offered the chance to work is with the RAF Regiment, although the Royal Auxiliary Air Force does have females in the Regiment. Equality came in 1984 and I swapped my stick for a rifle. In the late 1980s, maternity leave was introduced, and I took advantage of the change in regulations and spent a year at home with my new daughter in 1993.

There seems to be no pattern to life at Digby. In the last year, the Unit received over 400 different visits, many of them at 1-star level and above, which give our groundsmen something of a headache. The helipad doubles up as a car park, but rarely gets used as such, and the road sweeper was on permanent patrol in the autumn to keep the pad and the Station environs clear of leaves.

The range of duties associated with the post of Station Commander is immense and extremely varied. I spend a lot of time around the parish, not on inspection but seeing people in their workplace and chairing meetings – anywhere else but the Conference Room, where I could live if I didn't have an alternative escape plan. Liaising with the local community is important: the 'Chain Gang' as they are affectionately known, are very dedicated people who work hard in the community and have a lot in common with the services. The Chamber of Commerce has much to do with service personnel resettling into the local area, and at Digby a huge proportion of our personnel live in surrounding villages because their line of work ensures that they will secure future postings to the unit.

Along with the parades, church and ceremonial services that the Council invites the Station to, there are more fun events such as Race Nights and Wine Tastings, which raise monies for local charities. One could fill the diary quite easily with invitations from these quarters alone. Neighbouring RAF stations also have events that need supporting, and it is a good way of downloading and sharing best practice with like-minded folk. Of course, one needs to keep a wary eye on the level of socialising, for the additional eating and drinking can play havoc unless some caution is applied: a long working day does not always offer the opportunity to escape to the gym as frequently as is required. My month consists of a variety of meetings such as Health & Safety, Fitness and Lifestyle, Welfare Committees, and the Customer Advisory Panel – which negotiates with the Support Unit what services are needed to run our business. Some 99% of the children attending the local primary school, located inside the wire, are service kids and so there is always a keen interest in their activities.

Amongst the varied duties in any week, I can be called upon to check on weapons, special drugs, cash holdings, CCTV tapes, or to visit the Community Centre, Crèche, Nursery, or any of the many clubs or society buildings. I can have coffee with the medical staffs, the Americans, the Navy, the wives' group or the trainees as I go walkabout around the base. In the evenings, I can attend formal functions in Mess kit or informal gatherings, visit the Amenities centre to watch the Beavers, the Brownies or the Youth Club. Red Nose Day is fun and we allow the personnel to 'dress down' for the day and contribute money to charity through a variety of sponsorship schemes. The Rainbows have a 100 metre dash in Wellingtons, the Cubs throw custard pies at the Execs, the grown-ups do a miscellany of silly things and everyone has a bit of fun, whilst raising a considerable amount for charity.

Sport plays a very big part in daily life at Digby, and we are blessed with a huge hangar, which boasts the largest gym floor at any UK base: this is ideal for national basketball and volleyball competitions. There is a twenty-four-hour fitness suite, with sauna for tired limbs; and externally we have the usual array of rugby and football pitches, tennis courts, plus outdoor basketball and baseball courts. Each month we have the Commander's Cup competition, fought fiercely over by each of the units at Digby. For eleven months, they vie for first place, and the final event, the Log Race, is a gruelling one and a half-mile run, with four people grappling with a swinging log as their team supporters cheer and chant them through the pain barrier. Weekly I hear the chants of the Squadrons as they set off for a five-mile run off camp, with a fifty-five pound Bergen pack on their backs. The singing is never so loud on the return leg, but the team effort and spirit are always apparent.

It is still early days in my tour and I am sure the variety of events that I am involved in will continue to grow. Over the next year and a half there are two big projects on the horizon which will keep my staff busy: first there are improvements to single living accommodation for the Sergeants and the junior staff and, secondly, we are having a Childcare/Community Centre built, which is a hugely exciting project. I will continue to keep my digital camera close to hand for those funny shots that lighten my day.

The job can get demanding at times, but it is always the people who help put the whole thing into perspective. Every day presents a new challenge and although it can be daunting because the buck stops with me, I know that with the support of my staff, and my family, I can tackle each one.

Halton Today

Flight Lieutenant Sarah Rea

Recruit Training today is no doubt very different from what it was in years gone by. For a start, it is now based at Royal Air Force Halton, former home of the Apprentices, rather than Royal Air Force Swinderby, of which many current serving airmen will have fond (perhaps) memories. In fact, during the seventeen months I spent as a flight commander on Recruit Training Squadron, several of my colleagues made observations regarding the differences between modern day training and their own experiences. What none of us were qualified to say, though, was what it was like to be a member of staff during those bygone days.

I am certain, however, that it must be very different now. Society changes rapidly, whether we like it or not and, as a result, the 'raw material' we had to work with as training staff had also changed. This was noticeable in many ways. Levels of physical fitness, as well as physical courage and determination, were considerably lower than we all like to think they were 'in our day'. Attitudes are also very different:

Recruitment at Halton (Crown copyright)

the modern recruit wants to know 'why?', and demonstrates less of the blind acceptance of orders than in previous eras. Perhaps I am being unfair, however: I witnessed many examples of recruits carrying on during physical training lessons despite being clearly exhausted or injured, and usually once they had been told 'why', they were more than happy to do as they were told. We should not blame them for being products of the society we have created for them.

Life as an instructor could be frantic, or it could be calm and serene, dependent, naturally, on the recruits. A good bunch could make your life as a flight commander extremely easy, while a more challenging flight would keep you fully occupied and leave you very little breathing space.

The course would begin quietly with the attestation of the new recruits, which is now performed personally by the Flight Commander at Halton rather than at the recruiting office. Invariably we were faced by a roomful of terrified youngsters, and some not so young: some physically shaking and undoubtedly wondering what they had let themselves in for; some in their attempts to appear 'cool' coming across as disinterested. What they probably did not realise was that occasionally the staff were just as nervous. A new flight commander, perhaps not very experienced in addressing a group of people, would be grateful for the fact that the attestation ceremony was mostly scripted to ensure accuracy and parity of treatment. During one notable ceremony, the two corporals assisting me had a total of four days' experience between them!

For a flight commander, though certainly not the remainder of the staff, the initial days of a course would, more often than not, be fairly quiet. Of course there was a mountain of paperwork to be done to ensure that the rest of the course went as smoothly as possible, but usually there was little that was unexpected. Invariably there would be one or two recruits who declared themselves too homesick to continue, but on the whole we refused to entertain their requests to go home for a least the first five days (which saw them through the first weekend), by which time most were embarrassed to admit that they had ever had second thoughts. Every flight commander has had to deal with some recruits who are genuinely not suited to the military way of life and need to get home as quickly as possible, for their own and others' benefit. The trick is to tell the merely homesick from the genuinely unsuited, and that, naturally, only comes with experience.

By the same token, every recent flight commander will be able to tell of their 'success stories': those recruits who swore after a matter of hours that they absolutely had to go home now, or they would be scarred for life and never forgive you. If you could persuade them to give it a few days and see what they thought of it when they had made a few friends, sometimes they changed their minds. Occasionally, as in my own experience, a recruit with doubts would go on to be one of the best recruits on the course and reach graduation swearing never to forget you (though I bet she already has!).

Being a flight commander is, in many ways, a reactive job. If you are lucky enough to have a very good course, who misbehave only occasionally and are considerate enough to pass all their exams (thereby saving you the trouble of administering re-sits or re-flighting them), then the workload could be very light, leaving you plenty of time to join in with their training. This was when the job became whatever you made of it. You could sit in the office twiddling your thumbs, or, as was more often the case, get out there and take part in the lessons. In fact, staff often participated in the physical education lessons, or showed off their prowess on the firing range. Some of the sadists among us would even demonstrate our bravery by taking off our respirators in the respirator testing facility (not a gas chamber, these days!), though usually I, for one, regretted it. Nevertheless, situations like this often produced humour: I remember, for example, being asked by one young recruit if officers were immune to CS gas! Alas, if only ...

On a more serious note, the responsibilities of being a flight commander are vast, and some of those responsibilities require more emphasis than in previous eras. Of course, staff have always been concerned for the welfare of their charges, particularly those under the age of eighteen years. Nowadays no recruit is allowed to drink alcohol until he or she has passed the first kit inspection on Day 17, and only then if he or she is over eighteen years old. We still aim to turn out thoughtful, tolerant, respectful and largely self-sufficient men and women who can be a credit to the modern Royal Air Force. However, the modern responsibilities go much deeper: in a society more litigious than ever before, the importance of equal opportunities training takes on a whole new meaning, both for your own attitudes and monitoring those of your charges. I must at this point stop myself from again being unfair to the vast majority of recruits: most have been taught the bounds of acceptable behaviour; but as with any large group of young people, there are a few who are more aware of their rights than their responsibilities and who find it difficult to accept that discipline is not necessary bullying. But I do not wish to paint a picture of staff constantly looking over their shoulders in fear of complaints: this was not the case.

One of the results of these changes, however, is the approach to punishment. The days of random and individual punishments dished out by vengeful staff are long gone – thankfully. Nowadays, more use is made of paperwork, which granted is not always effective, but for the genuinely remorseful recruit whose mischief was a one-off incident, the thought of having reports on file which, if there are enough of them, can lead to a re-flight, is often sufficient. And for those for whom this does not work, the full range of Air Force Law is available, and used. However, it is no longer acceptable to physically punish a recruit, or indeed to give an individual extra duties in response to a misdemeanour, unless the latter is part of a legal punishment awarded by a subordinate commander in an orderly room, and rightly so.

Being a flight commander could be an immense challenge and without doubt carried some heavy responsibilities, but it was also tremendously enjoyable and most of the staff had great fun. Without being corny, it really was a job where what you got out of it was directly related to what you put into it, and I can still remember how I felt on parade with my first flight during their graduation. If they were half as proud as I was, they will have been immensely satisfied.

Women in the Royal Air Force 1993–2002

Air Commodore Cynthia Fowler

I had joined the Royal Air Force in the ranks in December 1964, and by the time 1994 came round I had seen many changes. Some had been for the good; some for the not so good, and some would take many years to define themselves. In 1994 I was Group Captain and had just finished commanding RAF Uxbridge – the first woman to do so, and one of very few women who had had command at that rank at any time in the history of women in the Armed Services. It was a most challenging tour and also the most fulfilling. There was no doubt that women were playing a full part in the RAF.

A few years before, the Air Force Board had decided to employ women as pilots and navigators and many young women were ready to rise to the challenge. It's a fallacy to think that this was a 'first' for women had served valiantly in the cockpits of World War II aircraft in the Air Transport Auxiliary. There had been arguments for and against, not least of all the fears brought on by the Gulf War of 1990. How would women cope with combat, what would the public think if women were to be captured? These deep thoughts were resolved quite quickly – by public apathy. (Indeed an American woman was captured and badly treated, she did receive considerable public sympathy and few, if any, expressed doubts about the situation.)

Training pilots takes three years plus, navigators under two, so there were unlikely to be any large numbers of female aircrew for some time. Nevertheless in the succeeding decade women aircrew serve with distinction in trouble spots wherever Her Majesty's Government chooses to send the Royal Air Force.

For all of my service there had been a steady acceptance that women were as good as men in most of the jobs in which we were employed. Not only that, but women worked with the same dedication and capacity, and had been found capable of almost every job that did not require excessive strength or unusual aptitude. I think particularly of the trade of Aerial Erector. Three hundred feet up an aerial mast in a high wind is not every woman's forte – nor every man's for that matter. The only other employment that was restricted to men was the RAF Regiment, who clung to the strictures of the British Army. Whilst in all probability there will be some girls who could be riggers or gunners, there will be few who would want to be so. Curiously the Auxiliary RAF Regiment employ women, only because they cannot recruit enough men. Since time immemorial that fact alone has allowed women to show just how useful they are to Society. There are numerous examples that I will not list here, but every time there is trouble or conflict the girls step forward with alacrity.

The bane of the last decade, without doubt, is what has become known as 'political correctness'. This pall has overlaid the modern workplace and led some to believe that they are entitled to have an equal share regardless of effort or capability. Far from improving the working woman's lot it is more likely to destroy working relationships. Opportunity must be equal to all, but individuals must be equal to the opportunity.

The modern work ethic and desire to keep moving employment are all changing the personal commitment to the RAF. Changes in Employment Laws largely brought about by European Legislation have had an upside and a downside. Here I have to admit to being wrong about Statutory Maternity Rights which, I thought originally, would make women unemployable in the Services. In fact quite the opposite occurred, in that women who were committed to the RAF but naturally enough wanted to raise a family, could do so and return to duty. Many, who chose to do this, went on to be promoted in due course, often attending Staff College along the way, giving very good service to the Royal Air Force.

Since the collapse of communism and as a 'Peace Dividend', successive governments have steadily civilianised or privatised as a means of reducing the cost of Defence. As a consequence the numbers in the Armed Services has decreased.

Continuing calls for savings have been quite debilitating. Set this alongside more and more national and global commitments without full manning or relief, and this creates difficulties in retention and is a common problem for all the Armed Forces.

In the last decade there have been changes that have affected women in the Royal Air Force, but many of these changes have affected men too. Men and Women will never be equal, for nature never intended it to be so, but whatever the gender, the best will always bubble to the top. One thing I am sure about is that the Royal Air Force has some of the best people this country can offer. I know: I recruited many of them in the last four years of my service as Director of Recruiting and Selection.

Flt/Lt Mirch Tomkins, 100 Squadron Hawks (Crown copyright)

Logistic Support of the Royal Air Force – Where Next?

Air Chief Marshal Sir Michael Alcock KBE CB

First, what do I mean by Logistics Support? My definition is the Engineering, Maintenance and Spares support needed to allow the instruments of Air Power to be exercised and controlled. Summed up neatly in the motto of my former and, sadly, now defunct Logistics Command as '*Sustentamus ut Bellent*' which translates as 'We Sustain that they may Fight'.

The Air Force of today is vastly different from the early days, but I want to sketch out the evolution of support and demonstrate that a lot less has changed than you might think. The Royal Flying Corps was formed on 13 May 1912. It was intended to be employed in direct support of Naval and Army forces. Not only was the organisation tailored for deployed operations alongside the Expeditionary Force, but the Flight and Squadron system was specifically chosen for flexibility and ease of handling in the field. Each squadron – comprising three flights of four aeroplanes and an HQ flight – was intended to be a homogenous unit, with its own field repair, stores and transport services, and self supporting arrangements with its own cooks and so on. The individual flights were also self-contained and could be detached for short periods. Each squadron also had its own Motor Transport.

It was recognised that squadrons could not support themselves for more than a limited time in the field, and thus a facility was required capable of undertaking a greater depth of repair, and holding a wider range of spares and equipment. These needs were met by a workshop known as the Flying Depot, later the Aircraft Park.

By early 1918 the main elements of the logistic system were in place, the flying squadrons and the Air Parks comprised the mobile elements, while the Depots were static. This system had grown to support over 1800 aircraft – double the front strength of the RFC in 1916.

Sadly, there is no record of any logistics lessons to guide us. Had there been such an exercise it might have looked like this:

Air Power was an expensive weapon.
Maintaining aircraft away from the home base demanded considerable resources.
Attrition was immense.
Effective support demanded the ready availability of spares.
Rail and motor transport were critical to the supply system.
Manpower was the 'essential lubricant'.

To my mind the important message was that arrangements for Logistic Support had clearly been tested in intense operations. The fledgling Royal Air Force, when it formed on 1 April 1918 began with a sound structure.

The squadrons were self-contained: First Line in today's language.

Air Parks collectively looked after a group of squadrons: now we have Stations that collectively look after Second Line for their Squadron's Depots-fed spares and repairs to the Air Parks: Third Line Depots are still with us.

After World War I we virtually disbanded the Air Force, with dire consequences for our fledgling aircraft industry. By 1920 the logistic support organisation had shrunk to just six home depots and three overseas. But perhaps more importantly, there was no place in the peacetime air force for a technical organisation, and thus none of the 5000 technical officers serving with the RAF at war's end were retained. In future their duties were to be undertaken by General Duties officers and it would be twenty years before that decision was to change.

Having survived the traumas of war and of its formation as an independent Air Force, it seems that virtually no effort was made to incorporate any logistic lessons into practice in peacetime. It was still the practice for aircraft servicing to be delegated to individual Commanding Officers, with little or no direction from the Air Ministry. COs depended on advice from senior NCOs. In 1923 it was laid down that officers were responsible for their aircraft's daily, weekly and other inspections and other checks at calendar intervals. However they were not told how. It was not until 1929 that the Air Ministry issued a standard servicing schedule.

So there is plenty of evidence that the fledgling Royal Air Force neglected logistic planning in the inter-war years for a variety of reasons: not least the necessity to live off war surplus until well after 1924, thanks in part to stringent fiscal restraint.

By any yardstick, the build up to World War II was an impressive production effort in which the whole country played a part and I recently came across some interesting evidence on the relative production efforts of UK and Germany that will provide food for thought. This compares the aircraft production output between 1932 and 1945. It shows very clearly that Britain took the war seriously and put everything behind the production effort, whilst Germany did just enough to produce a formidable façade but was then caught on the run when its enemies survived the first shocks of combat.

On 1 July 1938 Maintenance Command was formed, charged with the storage and distribution of serviceable stocks of equipment and supplies and the conservation of war stocks, as well as salvage and repair activities that complemented those of industry.

Each group had a range of subordinate depots and storage units to cope with an immense inventory of kit, and innumerable committees of experts advised on the optimum organisation for aircraft support. The plan was that at outbreak of war front-line squadrons would be responsible for minor and major inspections and some modifications, with the responsibility for heavier work being transferred to the specialist repair organisations of Maintenance Command. When war began most units were in the process of reorganisation, and all their efforts were severely hampered by a general shortage of skilled tradesmen and technical officers.

All of these plans were shortly to be put to the test when the RAF again found themselves in France in September 1939 as part of the British Expeditionary Force.

The squadrons had barely set themselves up when the German attack began on 10 May 1940: that led in turn to disaster and withdrawal from the beaches of Dunkirk. From a purely logistics perspective, the defeat in France confirmed to the RAF that mobility of its squadrons was vital. Inevitably, the losses were great; including nearly 1000 aircraft from all causes in the period from 10 May until the evacuation was completed in June. Recovery would take time.

In no time at all the by-now rapidly expanding Air Force was thrown into the thick of fighting the *Luftwaffe* in the Battle of Britain. And again from a logistic view their plans were severely tested. Fighter Command started with serviceability rates of some 80% of their aircraft, which fell by a couple of percentage points as air activity intensified; but interestingly they achieved 80% of their fighters serviceable during the peak of the Battle of Britain in September 1940. The RAF was achieving better kill ratios in combat than the *Luftwaffe*, yet German fighter production declined and the British out-produced their opponents by two-to-one. And behind this production output from Industry there was a rapidly expanding storage and repair organisation with reserves of complete aircraft. At no time in the Battle of Britain was this reserve ever exhausted, nor was there any difficulty or delay in meeting the demands from the front line.

Whilst it was undoubtedly the heroism of the 'Few' which led to the defeat of the *Luftwaffe* in the Battle of Britain, it is also quite clear that our superior logistic strategy was hugely influential to the outcome. Arguably, wars are won by superior economic and logistic strategy as much as by heroism.

Victory in the Battle of Britain gave us a secure base from which to launch into the offensive. Much fell initially on the long-range aircraft of Bomber Command, as the Bomber Offensive got underway. But pretty soon war shifted to overseas theatres as new Squadrons formed and prepared for action in far-off places. The pattern was repeated with innumerable airfields and Depots – Maintenance Units – being set up to cope with a huge variety of flying operations: some having more success than others. The culmination of years of hardship, struggle and loss of life came with the liberation of western Europe that began with Operation Overlord, the 'D' day landings.

Overlord was an allied operation of quite unprecedented scale, and a logistic undertaking of epic proportions. The RAF contribution followed the well-tried principles with one interesting variation introduced to cope with the extreme mobility needed. That variation was the use of Servicing Commandos – who were mobile 'Wing'-sized servicing units, equipped with fourteen days of spares and tasked with stocking the new landing grounds and backing up Squadrons as they arrived in theatre. I was interested to discover that one of their main difficulties, unexpected in a western theatre of war, was the presence of abrasive silica dust, a by-product of the many temporary airfields. Their solution included pumping oil or seawater on to landing and taxiing surfaces, as well as using hessian strips to cover the operating surfaces. Meanwhile to arrest the huge failure rate of the Typhoon's engine all the aircraft were progressively returned to UK to be fitted with dust deflectors. And all this took place between 'D' day on 6 June, and 28 June when all nine wings of No. 83 Group were fully operational on the continent at ten airfields. Their Typhoons were credited with numerous critical successes in their ground attack role.

I wish I had known about that affair some forty-six years later when I was serving at HQ Strike Command during the Gulf War as the Deputy Chief of Staff for Logistics at the Joint HQ. Because one of our biggest logistic challenges again involved fine silica dust, not exactly unexpected in the deserts of Saudi Arabia. Our Tornados, operating at very low level during the work-up phase before combat, began suffering unusually high rejection rates on their RB 199 engines. The problem was caused by ingesting airborne dust that clogged up the cooling holes in their turbine blades, a problem that had apparently never been seen before by Rolls-Royce in that theatre. Our early experience in theatre called for a large modification and husbandry programme to ensure that our helicopters did not suffer similar fates – this time with complete success.

Sadly, time precludes anything more than the briefest glimpses of what this massive undertaking achieved in World War II but, in all of my researches on the subject it is clear that the problems of scale, technical complexity and range were enormous. The linked issues of flexibility and mobility are pervasive and it is obvious that many lessons of the first war were relearned in double quick time.

Immediately post war the scene must have been very reminiscent of the situation after the first War, with massive reductions and widespread demobilisation, punctuated only by the Korean War. And that period was followed by the long-drawn-out and uncertain times of the Cold War, which for the first time brought about a dramatic change for the RAF in the shape of nuclear deterrence with the advent of the 'V' force. The deterrent force was based at static bases throughout UK, defended by Lightning fighters and Bloodhound Surface-to-Air Missiles, all operating from static bases. So mobility declined, and we also entered a new era of sophistication of technology, particularly of weapons: both Air-to-Air missiles and our first air launched ballistic missile, Blue Steel. Thankfully, sanity prevailed and the ultimate weapon was never used in anger.

We retained an Out-of-Area capability, initially with Phantoms, then Jaguars, and Harriers, to retain much-needed mobility in our offensive posture. The fixed-wing forces were complemented by the highly mobile Support Helicopter force. However, the Strike/Attack forces – Buccaneers, and later Tornados – operated from fixed forward bases in Germany: an issue that was to pose problems for us in the Gulf War, where Tornado GR was a crucial offensive aircraft that was deployed into theatre in strength.

From a logistic view I believe that the most important post-war lesson was the necessity to continue to study and understand the dynamics of supporting a complex system such as we had become. An agenda that must have had its origins in Maintenance Command's earlier mission to study and adopt best business practice. It was manifested in the Central Servicing Development Unit, whose task was to study all manner of issues that underpinned our logistic arrangements. Reliability, maintainability, testability, repair, spares provision and breakdown, spares stockholding and warehousing policies ... and so on. Issues that are readily recognisable today as the meat of managing the Supply Chain and of understanding Life Cycle costs. We collected vast amounts of data, much of it unintelligible until we acquired more sophisticated computers capable of digesting the stuff. We used the best available mathematical modelling tools to optimise our logistics policies. And on the personnel front we studied the interaction between skills and knowledge and the technology of the day, to better understand productivity of our support personnel and the best training and employment policies.

In short, we learned our business, we began to understand the cost drivers, and became more professional and more confident in articulating the results of our studies. But it was a long struggle and I recall well the first Air Force Board paper on 'Reliability', which hit the streets in around 1981, to be greeted by derision amongst the acquisition community who felt that we were barking up the wrong tree, and one that was also impossible to scale. Today it is almost taken for granted that even complex products should perform as specified, with high reliability, ease of maintenance and with minimum life cycle cost – but it was not always so!

This whole post-war period has also been notable for the ever increasing complexity of all our equipment, often at the very cutting edge of science and technology, a factor that has undoubtedly influenced the rising cost of defence and of Air Forces in particular. Fortunately our improving understanding of system performance has allowed us to achieve considerable improvements in cost-effectiveness and, hopefully, keep half a step ahead of the Treasury's pressure on cost cutting. The squeeze is ever present though.

Let me 'fast forward' now to the big logistic changes that have taken place in recent years. In my time we set up Logistics Command on 1 April 1994, which was the culmination of a long-felt need to collocate all the staffs involved in support of the front line and so create a world class centre of excellence. The structure looked like this:

Strike Command controlled all the operational forces that could be drawn upon to form combat units, under either single or joint service command.
Personnel & Training recruited, trained and administered the whole, and
Logistics Command took on the overall responsibility for supporting and sustaining the front line.

A three-legged structure that mirrored the way air bases are organised.

Logistics Command itself had three distinct functions; Maintenance, CIS and the Support Management Group. We organised the Support Management staffs into so called 'Multi-Disciplinary Groups' which sought to break up our former 'vertical smokestack' structure, and forced specialists to work in teams given delegated budgetary responsibility for managing specific weapons systems. It was radical thinking at the time, though happily now widely adopted and indeed adopted by the 'Integrated Project Teams' that are a central feature of both the 'Defence Procurement Agency' as well as the 'Defence Logistics Organisation'. But the big difference today is that for the first time Logistic Support is no longer a single service responsibility.

When Logistics Command disbanded in October 1999 the top level structure changed to look like this:

Strike Command as before, and
Personnel & Training Command largely as before.

A structure with only two legs instead of three: a design that if used as a stool would not pass muster in any self-respecting engineering design office! The responsibility for logistic support of the RAF passed to the Chief of Defence Logistics and his many subordinate organisations and Agencies under a joint service banner. To my mind the decision to break the direct link between operational forces and their associated logistic support is at best a brave, untested experiment, and at worst a recipe for disaster that can only end in tears. Only time and operational failure will prove or disprove my contention.

But with the ink only just dry on setting up this joint service focus for logistics we are now embarked on yet another fundamental change. And I refer here to some of the more extreme 'outsourcing' proposals that are taking place as a result of continued squeeze on the Support budgets of all three services, referred to collectively as 'Smart Procurement'.

I have no difficulty with sensible outsourcing. My concern now is with the extent of outsourcing and effective privatisation of an element of operational capability that is implicit in, for example, the 'Future Strategic Tanker Aircraft' requirement to replace our VC 10 and TriStar tankers. It is a requirement for a service provision. It places the risk on industry to own, operate and provide a complete service for 'hoses in the sky' that will be integrated with both training and operations of Air Defence, Attack, Maritime Patrol and AWACS missions. That puts an entirely different set of risks and tasks on industry as well as introducing an unprecedented degree of dependency on operators to work hand in glove with their contractors. If the tanker fails to turn up the mission aborts!

It is quite true that there are many successful models in the civil airline market that do give cause for confidence. But is industry fully braced for that concept to be broadened into discharging an operation itself? I do know one thing though, and that is that flexibility of thinking will feature heavily in the contractor lucky enough to be entrusted with the delivery of such a service. Let us hope that the good work and reputation of our industry is not damaged in the outcome.

So I conclude that it was indeed a considerable organisational tribute to our forebears that the organisation for logistic support survived the test of two great wars; and after that the Cold War, the Falklands, the Gulf, the Balkans today – and is still completely recognisable. We were slow to learn in the early years, but the experience of World War II and the Cold war reinforced the importance of a sound understanding of Logistic Support. For over eighty years the Royal Air Force was responsible for its own support decisions and was not found wanting.

The Strategic Defence Review has changed those responsibilities, and has introduced two entirely untested flavours: Joint Service management and direct Industry involvement in operational output. I submit that both of these changes are more far-reaching than anything that has gone before. It will be some time before we know if the choices were wise. I certainly hope that Industry will rise to the challenges as they always have in the past. The RAF is alive and well in the 21st century, Let us hope that the men and women who tackle these new support initiatives will be inspired by the example set for us all by our predecessors.

INDEX

Page numbers in *italics* refer to illustrations.